Reading Process and Practice

Reading Process and Practice

From Socio-Psycholinguistics to Whole Language

SECOND EDITION

Constance Weaver

Western Michigan University

with chapters by
Yvonne Freeman and David Freeman
Ruth Beall Heinig

and contributions by
Marie Dionisio
Linda Erdmann
Cora Lee Five
Kathryn Mitchell Pierce
Suki Stone

HEINEMANN
Portsmouth, NH

HEINEMANN
A division of Reed Elsevier Inc.
361 Hanover Street   Portsmouth, NH   03801–3912
Offices and agents throughout the world

Every effort has been made to contact the copyright holders for permission to reprint borrowed material where necessary. We regret any oversights that may have occurred and would be happy to rectify them in future printings of this work.

Acknowledgments begin on page xix.

Library of Congress Cataloging-in-Publication Data

Weaver, Constance.
   Reading process and practice : from socio-psycholinguistics to whole language / Constance Weaver : with chapters by Yvonne Freeman and David Freeman, Ruth Beall Heinig : and major sections by Katheryn Mitchell Pierce . . . [et al.]. — 2nd ed.
     p.   cm.
   Includes bibliographical references and index.
   ISBN 0-435-08799-1
   1. Reading.   2. Psycholinguistics.   3. Language awareness in children.   I. Title.
LB1050.22.W44   1994
428.4—dc20   93-19844
                                                       CIP

Design by George H. McLean
Cover design by Mary C. Cronin
Cover photo by Hal Millgard

Printed in the United States of America on acid free paper
98 97 96 95 94 HP 7 6 5 4 3 2 1

For John, as always
and in memory of my mother,
Ruth F. Waltz

Contents

13 Whole Language Learning and Teaching for Second Language Learners
Yvonne Freeman and David Freeman   *558*

Preface

And reading itself, as a psycho-physiological process, is almost as good as a miracle.

—Edmund Huey

And psycholinguistics can help to assert the right of children to learn to read with the aid of people rather than procedures.

—Frank Smith

Whole-language educators and their predecessors believe that learners ultimately are in control of what they learn regardless of what is being taught.

—Yetta M. Goodman

This is a book about reading as a socio-psycholinguistic process in which the mind (*psyche*) transacts with the language (*linguistics,* the study of language) of a text, in a particular context and influenced by various social factors (the *socio* part of the term). But it is also much more than a book on reading and the teaching of reading.

The book has grown in scope as well as size since its origins in my *Psycholinguistics and Reading: From Process to Practice* (1980) and even since the first edition of this book, *Reading Process and Practice: From Socio-Psycholinguistics to Whole Language* (1988). As my understanding of reading as an active process has evolved into an understanding of learning itself as an active, constructive process, so the book has evolved into a discussion not only of reading theory and practice, but more broadly of whole language theory and practice, within which reading is a significant part.

Those familiar with the first edition will find several changes in format and in the organizing principles. First, the format. The text still includes, within the earlier chapters, many activities designed to help readers understand important aspects of the reading process through their own experience. Despite some concern that the end-of-chapter activities make the book seem like a textbook rather than a professional book, I have retained these sections, mainly because they implicitly extend the discussion within the chapters. Instead of annotated bibliographies at the ends of chapters, I have included unannotated bibliographies as figures within chapters, because this allows for inclusion of more references and locates them where they will be noticed. These features are designed to enhance the book's usefulness as a professional reference.

As to organization, one immediately noticeable change from the first edition is that the chapter on context and constructing meaning now precedes the chapter on phonics, thus preserving the "meaning first" ordering that begins with Chapter 2. In general, theory and practice are more thoroughly integrated in this edition. Instead of dealing with some topics (such as phonics, or patterns of miscues) across several chapters, I have concentrated them in fewer chapters, to make it easier to deal with various aspects of a topic all at once. At the same time, there is greater redundancy across chapters. While the chapters dealing with the reading process itself might best be read in order (Chapters 1, 2, 4, 5, and 6), this is not strictly necessary, and the redundancy and generous cross-referencing should make it possible for readers to begin with any of the other chapters without feeling lost. In dealing with the development of literacy, Chapter 3 relates the model of reading from Chapter 2 to whole language learning and teaching, which is emphasized from Chapter 8 onward. Chapter 7 likewise serves as something of a bridge, by describing the research that demonstrates the values of teaching reading according to the principles articulated in Chapter 3 and further generalized in Chapter 8, where broad whole language principles are explained in greater detail. Clearly there is more than one logical order in which to read the chapters.

I regret the loss, from the 1988 edition, of the wonderful chapter on whole language that was written by Dorothy Watson and Paul Crowley, as well as the impressive chapter on reading in the content areas, by Marilyn Wilson. However, we all felt that these chapters needed some updating, but (not surprisingly) these authors were too busy with other projects to undertake such revision. (Dorothy was helping Kathryn Mitchell Pierce and Carol Gilles with a book on talk in classrooms, (*Cycles of Meaning*, Heinemann, 1993) while Marilyn is co-authoring a book on reading in the content areas with Lois Rosen and Read Dornan, to be published by Boynton/Cook). As a result, we decided to omit these chapters, thus making room for my own chapters on whole language (Chapters 8 and 9) and also for chapters on new topics (Chapters 10 and 13, particularly).

I am especially grateful to those who have written new chapters. Ruth Beall Heinig, my longtime friend and colleague at Western Michigan University, having just finished another book herself (*Improvisation with Favorite Tales*, Heinemann, 1992), graciously agreed to write a chapter on integrating the oral and dramatic language arts with reading, literature, and thematic studies (Chapter 10). And Yvonne and David Freeman of Fresno Pacific College, also having recently finished a book (*Whole Language for Second Language Learners*, Heinemann, 1992), readily agreed to write a chapter on whole language learning and teaching for second language learners (Chapter 13). These chapters wonderfully enhance the book—and besides, we all had fun working together, trying to make connections among chapters and sometimes clarifying our own thinking in the process.

Chapter 12 is another that has benefitted from the contributions of others. For this chapter on the effectiveness of whole language principles and practices with special learners, I knew I needed material from current practitioners. So the chapter includes marvelous sections by Linda Erdmann, Marie Dionisio, and Cora Lee Five. In addition, there is a short section by Suki Stone of the University of Texas in Brownsville. I am particularly grateful also to Irene Fountas, a whole language teacher and teacher educator involved with the Reading Recovery program at Lesley College in Cambridge.

Thanks to Irene, Chapter 12, I believe, describes the Reading Recovery program more clearly than some articles I've read by its leading practitioners.

And then there is the work of Kathryn Mitchell Pierce. In critiquing the manuscript for the previous edition, Karthryn suggested that the book needed to deal more deeply with reading as a social transaction. At the time, I didn't see how, or where. But as this new edition was shaping up, I realized that a brief section on that topic could appropriately be added to Chapter 2, provided Kathryn would do it. She agreed. She also agreed to add a section to Chapter 9 on conducting literature discussion groups, using the story "Petronella," by Jay Williams, as her extended example. ("Petronella" is reprinted as an appendix to this book and is referred to in several chapters.) What emerged from her efforts has, I think, surprised us both. It's a truly superb demonstration of effective and empowering teaching—on the part of both Kathryn and Jean Dickinson, the classroom teacher. And again, Kathryn often served as my teacher in critiquing chapters of the manuscript. I greatly appreciate her contributions, both as author and as critic (though of course any remaining faults and weaknesses are my own reponsibility).

Among the many others who have contributed to my thinking and this edition of the book, the person who stands out most is Ruth Perino, a fifth-grade teacher at the Kalamazoo Academy in Kalamazoo. She, too, is a superb model as a teacher, and from her I learned a great deal while working with Ruth and her students. Some of what I learned from and with Scott Peterson, a fourth-grade teacher in the Mattawan, Michigan public schools, has found its way into this book, as well as the *Theme Exploration* book we co-authored with Joel Chaston (Weaver, Chaston, & Peterson, 1993). Another teacher who has made a substantive contribution to this book is Tracy Cobb, a first-grade teacher in Mattawan. Together, we had fun working with and learning from her students.

Again, I want to thank Philippa Stratton, who until recently has been the Editor-in-Chief of Heinemann, for her unfailing support. Along with her humor and wisdom and patience, what I particularly appreciate about Philippa is that in her dealings with authors, she *lives* the whole language philosophy we write about. I also appreciate the guiding hand of Joanne Tranchemontagne, the production editor for this book; she kept us all sane during the later stages of production. The incredibly thoughtful and thorough editing of Donna Bouvier has saved this book from many an error, and to her I am especially grateful. Melissa Ingles from Heinemann contributed significantly by dealing with permissions. My colleague Nickola Nelson critiqued a chapter, which is now much stronger for her suggestions and queries. Thanks also goes to Sue Myland and her son Jake, for the cover photo—and also to Hal Millgard, the photographer. The preparation of this book has indeed been a team effort.

Since I've especially acknowledged and thanked my mother, my son, my partner, and my mentor in previous books, what remains is simply to thank more generally the many students, colleagues, and friends across the country and around the globe who keep contributing to my growth as a professional. You've made more of a difference than you can ever know.

Acknowledgments

We are grateful to the publishers and individuals below for granting permission to reprint material from previously published works.

PREFACE

Page xv: From *Psycholinguistics and Reading* by Frank Smith. Copyright © 1985 by Frank Smith. Reprinted by permission of the author.

CHAPTER 1

Page 1: From "Understanding the Hypothesis, It's the Teacher that Makes the Difference" by Jerome C. Harste, in *Reading Horizons* (1977), quarterly journal, College of Education, Western Michigan University, Kalamazoo, Michigan.

Page 4: From *Psychology of Language* by David S. Palermo. Copyright © 1978 by Scott, Foresman and Company. Reprinted by permission.

Pages 6-9: From *A Camel in the Sea* by Lee Garrett Goetz. Copyright © 1966 by McGraw-Hill Book Company. Reprinted by permission.

Pages 12-14: Appendix from "Validating the Construct to Theoretical Orientation in Reading Instruction" by Diane DeFord in *Reading Research Quarterly,* Spring 1985. Reprinted with permission of Diane DeFord and the International Reading Association.

CHAPTER 2

Figure 2.5: Reproduced by Special Permission of *Playboy* magazine: Copyright © 1975 by *Playboy.*

Page 28: Bloome, David, and Green, Judith. "Looking at Reading Instruction: Sociolinguistic and Ethnographic Approaches." In *Contexts of Reading,* edited by Carolyn N. Hedley and Anthony N. Baratta. Norwood, NJ: ABLEX, 1985, pp. 167–184.

Pages 46-47: Excerpt from "Cultural Schemata and Reading Comprehension" by Ralph E. Reynolds, Marsha A. Taylor, Margaret S. Steffensen, Larry L. Shirey, and Richard C Anderson, in *Reading Research Quarterly,* Vol. 17, No. 3. Reprinted with permission of Ralph E. Reynolds and the International Reading Association.

CHAPTER 3

Page 49:   From *Learning with Zachary* copyright © 1991 by Lester Laminack. All rights reserved. Used by permission of Scholastic Canada Ltd., 123 Newkirk Road, Richmond Hill, Ontario, Canada L4C 3G5.

Page 56:   Reprinted with permission of Scribner Educational Publishers, a Division of Macmillan, Inc. from Book A of *Lippincott Basic Reading* by Charles C. Walcutt and Glenn McCracken. Copyright © 1975 by Macmillan, Inc.

Figure 3.7:   From *The Craft of Children's Writing* copyright © 1984 by Judith Newman. All rights reserved. Used by permission of Scholastic Canada Ltd., 123 Newkirk Road, Richmond Hill, Ontario, Canada L4C 3G5.

Figure 3.9:   From "Beginning Reading and Writing Through Singing: A Natural Approach" by Sheila Fitzgerald in *Highway One* 7, ii (Spring 1984). Reprinted by permission of the author and the Canadian Council of Teachers of English.

Figure 3.11:   From *Reading, Writing, and Caring* (Cochrane, Cochrane, Scalena, & Buchanan, 1984). Reprinted by permission.

Figures 3.13, 3.14:   From "Literacy: Reading, Writing, and Other Essentials" by Diane E. DeFord in *Language Arts* 58 (September 1981). Reprinted by permission of the National Council of Teachers of English.

Page 106:   From *Children's Writing and Language Growth* by Ronald L. Cramer. Copyright © 1978 by Merrill Publishing Company, Columbus, Ohio. Reprinted by permission of the publisher.

Figures A3.1, A3.2, A3.3 (top two), A3.6, A3.7:   Charles Temple, Ruth Nathan, Francis Temple, and Nancy Burris, *The Beginnings of Writing, Third Edition* (Boston: Allyn & Bacon, 1993). Reprinted by permission.

Figure A3.3 (third from top):   From "Emergent Writers in a Grade One Classroom" by Lee N. Dobson in *Reading-Canada-Lecture* 4 (Fall 1986). Reprinted by permission.

Figures A3.3 (bottom), A3.5, A3.6:   From "Emergent Writers in a Grade One Classroom" by Lee N. Dobson. Paper presented at the Fourth International Conference on the Teaching of English, Ottawa, Ontario, May 15, 1986. Reprinted by permission.

Figure A3.4:   From "Invented Spelling in the Open Classroom" by Carol Chomsky in *Word* 27 (1971). Reprinted by permission.

CHAPTER 4

Page 120:   From "The Law and Reading Instruction" by Robert J. Harper and Gary Kilarr in *Language Arts* 54 (November/December 1977). Copyright © 1977 by the National Council of Teachers of English. Reprinted by permission.

Page 121:   From "Literacy in the Classroom" by John R. Bormuth in *Help for the Reading Teacher: New Directions in Research,* ed. William D. Page. Copyright © 1975 by the National Council of Teachers of English. Reprinted with permission.

Pages 124–25:   From "Poison" in *Someone Like You* by Roald Dahl. Copyright © 1950 by Roald Dahl. Reprinted by permission of Alfred A. Knopf, Inc.

Pages 136–37:   From *The Glorious Conspiracy* by Joanne Williamson. Copyright © 1961 by Alfred A. Knopf, Inc. Reprinted by permission.

Pages 138–39:   "Jimmy Hayes and Muriel" from *The Complete Works of O. Henry.* Copyright © 1937 by Garden City Publishing Company Inc. Used by permission of the publisher.

Page 141:   From The Macmillan Reading Program. Albert J. Harris and Mae Knight Clark, Senior Authors: *A Magic Box* and *Opening Doors.* Copyright © 1965 by Macmillan Publishing Company. Reprinted by permission.

Pages 144–45:   Reprinted by permission of Dodd, Mead & Company, Inc., from *Morris Has a Cold* by Bernard Wiseman. Copyright © 1978 by Bernard Wiseman.

Page 145:   From *The New York Times,* May 5, 1970. Copyright © 1970 by The New York Times Company. Reprinted by permission.

Page 146:   From *The Power and the Glory* by Graham Greene. Copyright © 1940 by Graham Greene. Copyright © renewed 1968 by Graham Greene. All rights reserved. Reprinted by permission of Viking Penguin, Inc.

Page 147:   From *Bristle Face* by Zachary Ball. Copyright © 1962 by Kelly R. Masters. Reprinted by permission of Holiday House.

Page 148:   From *Manchild in the Promised Land* by Claude Brown, New York: Macmillan Publishing Co., Inc. Copyright © Claude Brown 1965. Reprinted by permission.

Pages 148–49:   From "Dialect Barriers to Reading Comprehension Revisited," Kenneth S. Goodman and Catherine Buck, *The Reading Teacher,* October 1973. Reprinted with permission of the International Reading Association.

Page 150:   From *English in Black and White* by Robbins Burling. Copyright © 1973 by Holt, Rinehart and Winston, Inc. Reprinted by permission.

Pages 151–52:   From *What's the Matter with Carruthers?* by James Marshall. Copyright © 1972. Reprinted by permission of Houghton Mifflin Company. All rights reserved.

Page 158:   From *Teaching Reading Comprehension* by P. David Pearson and Dale D. Johnson. Copyright © 1978 by Holt, Rinehart and Winston. Reprinted by permission.

Pages 163–64:   From "Theoretically Bases Studies of Patterns of Miscues in Oral Reading Performance" by Kenneth S. Goodman. Wayne State University, 1973. Reprinted by permission of the author.

Page 165:   From *Dandelion Wine* by Ray Bradbury. Reprinted by permission of Don Congdon Associates, Inc. Copyright © 1953 by Gourmet Inc.; renewed 1981 by Ray Bradbury.

CHAPTER 5

Page 172:   From *Understanding Reading: A Psycholinguistic Analysis of Reading and Learning to Read* by Frank Smith. Copyright © 1985 by Frank Smith. Reprinted by permission of the author.

Figure 5.4:   Excerpt from "The Utility of Phonic Generalizations in the Primary Grades" by Theodore Clymer in *The Reading Teacher,* January 1963. Reprinted with permission of Theodore Clymer and The International Reading Association.

CHAPTER 6

Page 216:   From "Testing in Reading: A General Critique" by Kenneth S. Goodman in *Accountability and Reading Instruction,* ed. Robert B. Ruddell. Copyright © 1973 by the National Council of Teachers of English. Reprinted by permission.

Page 226:   Excerpt from *Little Circus Dog* by Jene Barr. Copyright © 1949 by Albert Whitman & Company. Reprinted by permission.

Page 227:   From "An Analysis of Published Informal Reading Inventories" by Larry A. Harris and Jerome A. Niles in *Reading Horizons* 22 (Spring 1982). Reprinted by permission.

Pages 249-52:   From *Reading Miscue Inventory: Alternative Procedures* by Y. Goodman, D. Watson, and C. Burke. Katonah, New York: Richard C. Owen Publishers, Inc. Reprinted by permission.

Page 251:   Reprinted by permission of Dodd, Mead & Company, Inc. from *Morris Has a Cold* by Bernard Wiseman. Copyright © 1978 by Bernard Wiseman.

Pages 259-61:   "Jimmy Hayes and Muriel" from *The Complete Works of O. Henry.* Copyright © 1937 by Garden City Publishing Company, Inc. Used by permission of the publisher.

Pages 263-64, 277-84:   From *A Camel in the Sea* by Lee Garrett Goetz. Copyright © 1966 by McGraw-Hill Book Company. Reprinted by permission.

Pages 269-72:   From *Roll of Thunder, Hear My Cry* by Mildred D. Taylor. Copyright © 1976 by Mildred D. Taylor. Used by permission of Dial Books for Young Readers, a division of Penguin Books USA Inc.

Page 292:   From "Case Study of Jimmy" by Marie Carbo from her 1986 Reading Styles Seminar. Copyright © Marie Carbo, 1981. Reprinted by permission of Marie Carbo, Director of Research & Staff Development, Learning Research Associates, Roslyn, NY.

Figure A6.1:   M. Carbo / R. Dunn / K. Dunn, *Teaching Students to Read Through Their Individual Learning Styles,* 1986, pp. 61–62. Reprinted by permission of Prentice-Hall, Inc., Englewood Cliffs, New Jersey.

Figures A6.2, A6.3, A6.4, A6.5:   Charts on identifying modality strengths by Marie Carbo. Copyright © 1986 by Marie Carbo. From *Teaching Students to Read Through Their Individual Learning Styles* by M. Carbo, R. Dunn, and K. Dunn. Prentice-Hall, 1986. Reprinted by permission of Marie Carbo, Director of Research & Staff Development, Learning Research Associates, Roslyn, NY.

CHAPTER 7

Page 305:   From *Learning to Read: The Great Debate* by Jeanne Chall. Copyright © 1967, 1983 by McGraw-Hill. Reprinted by permission.

Pages 327–28:   From *Becoming a Nation of Readers,* prepared by Richard C. Anderson et al., 1985. Published by the U.S. Department of Education.

Pages 328–30:   Appendix from "Validating the Construct to Theoretical Orientation in Reading Instruction" by Diane DeFord in *Reading Research Quarterly,* Spring 1985. Reprinted with permission of Diane DeFord and The International Reading Association.

CHAPTER 8

FIgure 8.4:   From "Helping Children Become More Responsible for Their Own Writing" by Mary Ellen Giacobbe in *LiveWire* first issue (1984). Reprinted by permission of National Council of Teachers of English.

CHAPTER 12

Figure 12.2:   Remedial Reading Reference Chart. From "The Remedial Reader" by Rhondda Brill. In *Teaching Reading: A Language Experience,* edited by Gordon Winch and Valerie Hoogstad. Reprinted by permission of Macmillan Education Australia Pty Ltd, publisher.

Page 528:   From "After Decoding: What?" by Carol Chomsky in *Language Arts* 53 (March 1976). Copyright © 1976 by the National Council of Teachers of English. Reprinted by permission of the publisher.

Pages 535–37:   From *Whole Language Principles and Practices in Reading Development with Special Emphasis on Reading Recovery* by David Doake. Viewing guide accompanying videotape filmed at the 1985 Reading for the Love of It conference in Toronto. Used by permission of Scholastic-TAB.

Page 543:   "John" from Gilles, Carol; Bixby, Mary; Crowley, Paul; Crenshaw, Shirley; Heinrichs, Margaret; Reynolds, Frances; and Pyle, Donelle. *Whole Language Strategies for Secondary Students*. Katonah, New York: Richard C. Owen Publishers, Inc. 1987. Reprinted by permission of the publisher.

APPENDIX

Pages 627–33:   "Petronella" from *The Practical Princess* by Jay Williams. Copyright © 1978 by Jay Williams. Reprinted by permission of Scholastic Inc.

1 | Definitions of Reading: They Make a Difference

*Our findings suggest that both teachers and learners hold particular
and identifiable theoretical orientations about reading which in
turn significantly affect expectations, goals, behavior, and outcomes at
all levels.*

— Jerome Harste

THE IMPORTANCE OF A DEFINITION

What is reading, anyway? Here are some answers from children (Harste, 1978, p. 92):

"It's filling out workbooks."
"Pronouncing the letters."
"It's when you put sounds together."
"Reading is learning hard words."
"Reading is like think . . . you know, it's understanding the story."
"It's when you find out things."

There is considerable variation in these definitions. One emphasizes a medium of instruction, the workbook; others emphasize words or parts of words; and still others emphasize meaning. Of course, children do not often stop to define reading. Nevertheless, their approach to reading itself is guided by what they think reading is.

Responses to the interview questions in Figure 1.1 clarify two children's understanding of reading. Interestingly, it is the first grader who has the better grasp of reading as a meaning-making process, judging by her independence in dealing with problem words, including her apparent use of meaning in the process. The third grader conceptualizes reading mainly as a matter of getting the words.

Where do children get such definitions of reading? Mainly from literacy experiences (or the lack of them) in the home, and from what is emphasized (or not emphasized) in school.

Not surprisingly, there is a significant correlation between the kind of reading approach and children's understanding of what reading is and what it involves. Underlying some approaches is the implicit notion that first and foremost, reading means identifying words. These approaches tend to emphasize phonics (letter/sound relationships for identifying words) and/or to emphasize the recognition of words as wholes. Underlying other

1

Jenny, Grade 3

I: What do you think reading is?

J: Something that um, helps you learn words.

I: What do people do when they read?

J: They just read the words that are in the book.

I: They read the words in the book? Anything else? No? Okay, when you're reading something and you come to a word that you don't know, what do you usually do?

J: Sound it out.

I: Sound it out? Do you ever do anything else? No? Okay. Who is a good reader that you know?

J: Shaun.

I: Who is Shaun?

J: My sister, her friend um, her brother, he keeps on reading and he tries to do jump rope when he's reading a book.

I: What do you think makes Shaun a good reader?

J: He went to speech where um, they um, teach him how to read and stuff real good.

I: Do you think Shaun ever comes to a word or something in a story that he doesn't know?

J: Sometimes.

I: Sometimes? What do you think Shaun would do if he came to a word he didn't know?

J: Sound it out.

I: You think he'd sound it out too.

I: If you knew someone who was having trouble reading, what do you think you would do to help them?

J: Ask and see if they would sound it out and maybe that would help.

I: Sound it out? Is there anything else you might do to help them? What if they couldn't sound it out?

J: I would tell them the word.

I: Oh, you'd tell them the word.

Barbara, Grade 1

I: What do you think reading is?

B: When you read, it's um, kind of like you're just looking at a book but you're just saying the words because you think they're easy, but they're really not so easy. And, like, stuff like that.

I: That's a good answer of what you think reading is. When you're reading and you come to a word that you don't know, what do you do?

B: Kind of like I sound it out. It's kind of like you come to a word and you think, "Well, should I sound it out, or should I just ask somebody?" Then you see that all the people you want to ask are busy and you kind of sound it out.

I: Do you ever do anything else when you come to a word you don't know?

B: Um, most of the time I skip it.

I: After you skip a word, do you find it easier?

B: Yeah. Like when you skip a word and then go to the end, you can go back to it and read it.

I: Does this help more than sounding it out?

B: Yeah.

FIGURE **1.1** *Two children's reading interviews (Weaver, 1990a)*

approaches is the implicit notion that first and foremost, reading means constructing meaning, and using everything you know to do so. These approaches generally emphasize reading simple rhymes, poems, songs, and stories with and to children before dealing with words and letter/sound patterns within the context of literature. Writing is often approached in similar ways. That is, some programs and teachers first emphasize small units like letters, along with skills like printing and spelling and punctuation, "real" writing for the child's own purposes is often postponed until children have spent two or three years practicing such basics. Other classrooms reverse this emphasis, encouraging children to write as best they can from the very first day of school, and helping children master letter formation, spelling patterns, and punctuation in the context of writing as a means of coming to know, of self-expresion, and of communication. Children's concepts of both reading and writing often reflect the kind of instruction they have received (e.g., Rasinski & DeFord, 1988; Freppon, 1991).

Thus, if the teacher spends a lot of time teaching correspondences between letters and sounds, at least some children will conclude that reading means pronouncing letters or sounding out words. If the teacher spends a lot of time teaching children to recognize words as wholes, at least some children will conclude that reading means identifying words or knowing a lot of words. Whatever the instructional approach, it is likely to affect at least some children's implicit definitions of reading and hence their strategies for dealing with the written text. And ironically, those children who are least successful at reading may be the very ones who try hardest to do just what the teacher emphasizes. They concentrate on just these one or two strategies rather than on the several strategies that must be integrated in order to read successfully.

Studies investigating children's definitions of reading have found, too, that poorer and younger readers tend to conceptualize reading as a matter of decoding and getting words, whereas older and more proficient readers generally conceptualize reading as more a matter of understanding the text (e.g., Baker & Brown, 1984; Johns, 1986).

If children infer their definitions from the instructional program and approach, as frequently seems to be the case, the instructional approach is obviously crucial in helping children develop a productive definition of reading and effective reading strategies.

To summarize: children's success at reading reflects their reading strategies; their reading strategies typically reflect their implicit definitions of reading; their definitions often reflect the instructional approach; and the instructional approach reflects a definition of reading, whether implicit or explicit. In fact, the instructional approach may reflect a definition quite different from that consciously espoused by the teacher (Levande, 1989).

The vital question, then, is *what* approach, and *whose* definition? If the teacher has only a vague notion of how people read and learn to read, he or she may in effect adopt the definition implicit in a given reading program, perhaps a basal reading series. In that case, the guiding definition may reflect more the publisher's knowledge of what will sell than researchers' and educators' knowledge of how people read and learn to read.

Fortunately, teachers can have far more influence on the instructional approach than they often realize. Armed with a viable definition of reading and an understanding of some of the instructional implications of this definition, teachers can use almost *any* reading materials to help children develop productive reading strategies. Knowledgeable teachers are the key.

One of the primary purposes of this book, then, is to help teachers become knowledgeable enough to foster good reading strategies in children, perhaps despite the approach of the reading materials provided by the schools.

CHARACTERIZING READING AND READING INSTRUCTION

As people become increasingly knowledgeable about the reading process, they typically modify their definitions of reading. But it is helpful to become aware of where you stand at the outset. The remainder of this chapter consists mainly of three activities intended to help you determine your own views of reading and reading instruction.

Activity 1

First, please read the following paragraph from David Palermo's excellent *Psychology of Language* (1978, p. 38):

> At least four theoretical variants of the interpretive semantic theory have appeared in the literature since Chomsky first grappled with the problem of semantics. In the late 1960s, alternatives were offered by Lakoff (1968), McCawley (1968), and Ross (1967). Their arguments centered around the idea that it is not possible to separate the semantic and syntactic components of the grammar. According to these linguists, there is no single base phrase marker but, rather, sentence generation begins with the semantic component and subsequent interaction between lexical insertion and transformational rules leads eventually to the surface structure and the application of the phonological component. Thus, the focus of linguistic inquiry should give at least equal billing to the semantic component rather than merely relegating semantics to a role of interpreting the syntactic component. The generative semanticists, as these linguists have come to be called, have argued that the underlying structures in standard theory are too concrete. Once the presuppositions and implications of sentences are analyzed in more detail, it becomes necessary to postulate more abstract underlying structures which make the deep structures of sentences deeper and more complex. Ross (1974), for example, shows how a simple causative sentence such as "Dr. Grusel is sharpening the spurs" involves more than seven underlying sentence forms or propositions encompassed within its meaning including, for example, the presuppositions that Dr. Grusel and the spurs exist.

Were you able to read the paragraph, as requested? What difficulties did you have, if any? It should be interesting to discuss your response with others who have tried to read this same paragraph.

Activity 2

Probably the most effective way of determining how a person goes about the task of reading is to examine his or her reading miscues. In order for you to do this more readily, it should help to have some terms defined. Kenneth Goodman coined the term "miscue" in the 1960s to describe any departure the reader makes from the actual words of the text (e.g., K. S. Goodman, 1965). For example, if a reader substitutes one word for another, adds or omits a word, or reorganizes a sequence of words, he or she has made a miscue. Goodman's purpose in coining this term "miscue" was twofold. First, he wanted to get away from the notion that every departure from the words of the text is necessarily bad, something to be considered an error. Second, he wanted to emphasize how such departures from the text indicate which language cue systems the reader is using and not using, at least at that particular moment; the pattern of miscues thus suggests the reader's strengths as well as weaknesses, as we shall see in more detail later.

There are three major cue systems within the language of a text:

- *Syntactic cues*—that is, grammatical cues like word order, function words,[1] and word endings.
- *Semantic cues*—that is, meaning cues from each sentence and from the evolving whole, as one progresses through the entire text.
- *Grapho/phonemic cues*—that is, letter/sound cues: the correspondences between letters (graphemes) and sounds (phonemes), and larger letter/sound patterns.

Rarely does a miscue show attention to only one of these language cue systems. The following are some of the "purest" examples I have found, and even in most of these cases, the reader has paid attention to more than one kind of language cue:

truck "The little monkey had it."	Attention to syntactic cues. The reader may also have attended to a picture cue.
. . . to see if there was any afraid danger. He heard the . . .	Attention to semantic cues, with some attention to grapho/phonemic cues.
expert Every day except Friday, . . .	Attention to grapho/phonemic cues, but also attention to preceding grammar.

Given these definitions and examples, compare David's miscues with Tony's, in the following two transcripts of a selection they each read aloud. In each case, do the miscues suggest that the child is using implicit knowledge of *syntactic cues* (grammar) to predict words that are grammatically acceptable in context? Do the miscues suggest that the child is using *semantic cues* (meaning) to predict words that are meaningful in context? Do the miscues suggest that the child is using *grapho/phonemic cues* (letter/

sound relationships) to pronounce or sound out words? Which child would you say better integrates the language cues into effective reading strategies? What do you think each child's implicit definition of reading is? Again, discuss this activity with others, if possible.

The following key indicates how to interpret the major markings in the transcripts below:

Substitution   They did̸ not have books. . . . *(may above did)*
    (A word written over another word indicates a substitution.)

Omission   . . . they dove into ⟨the⟩ waves.
    (A circle around a word or group of words indicates an omission.)

Insertion   . . . splashing and spraying the water. . . . *(high inserted with carat)*
    (A carat points to whatever is inserted.)

Correction   . . . in the shade of a tall|palm tree. *(© above palm)*
    (The © indicates that the miscue was corrected, and the underlining indicates what portion of the text was repeated as the reader made the correction.)

Multiple attempt   How lucky he was to live in a Somali village. . . *(2 Sammon / 1 Sam- above Somali)*
    (Multiple attempts at a word are numbered consecutively.)

Partial word   Mohamed loved to go swimming in the sea. *(Mo- above Mohamed)*
    (One or more letters followed by a hyphen indicate that the reader uttered what he or she apparently considered only part of a word, judging by the reader's intonation.)

The reading selection is adapted from *A Camel in the Sea* (Goetz, 1966), pp. 11–14. The adaptation is from *Fiesta,* one of the Houghton Mifflin readers (1971). The line divisions differ in the two transcripts because the story was typed differently for each child.

David's Miscues

Mohamed (mo-hah′ med) loved to go swim-

ming in the sea. How lucky he was to live in a

Somali (so-mah′ lee)|village right on the Indian *(① Sami ; ② © willage on the right hand or above village)*

Ocean! The sandy shore rang with the happy

shouts (and cries) of the village boys and girls.

They liked to race one another into the surf,

splashing and spraying the water into (a) white

dancing foam before they dove into (the) waves.

younger
Mohamed and his young sister, Asha (ie' shuh),

spent all the time they could in the cool, clean

Swimming   in the water
(sea), swimming and playing water games. They

                                        s
were good swimmers because their mother had taught them.

Every day except Friday, Mohamed went to

school with the other village boys. The class

was outdoors, and the children sat on little

benches in front of the teacher in the shade of

        twee   may
a tall |palm tree. They did not have books, so

the boys repeated everything the teacher said,

        again
over and over until they knew their lessons by

heart. The girls of the village did not go to school,

for the people thought that school was not as

important for girls as it was for boys.

Tony's Miscues

①
MO—
Mohamed (mo-hah′ med) loved to go swimming in the sea.

② 2 Sammon   ③
  1 Sam-
How lucky he was to live in a Somali (so-mah′ lee) (village)

④ ran
right on the Indian Ocean! The sandy shore rang with the happy

⑤   ⑥
souts
shouts and cries of the (village) boys and girls. They liked

⑦ high
to race one another into the surf, splashing and spraying
                                                    ∧

⑧ drase
the water into a white dancing foam before they dove into the

⑨ Mola   ⑩ yūng   ⑪ Asla
waves. Mohamed and his young sister, Asha (ie′ shuh),

⑫
(spent all the time they could in the cool, clean) sea,

swimming and playing water games. They were good swimmers

because their mother had taught them.

⑬ expert   ⑭ Molda
Every day except Friday, Mohamed went to school with the

⑮   ⑯
nother viner
other village boys. The class was outdoors, and the children

⑰ beaches   ⑱ frose   ⑲ shape
sat on little benches in front of the teacher in the shade

of a tall palm tree. They did not have books, so the boys

⑳
ramped
repeated everything the teacher said, over and over, until

㉑   ㉒
other classrooms hurt   vengil
they knew their lessons by heart. The girls of the village

did not go to school, for the people thought that school was

(23)
imprentice   (24)
                          to

not as important for girls as it was for boys.

Activity 3

Having tried to read a paragraph for which you may not have had much background, and having compared the miscues of two children, you should be able to select or formulate a definition of reading that accords with your beliefs at the present time. Below are some definitions and characterizations of reading and the reading process, arranged more or less from simple to complex. Quite possibly none of these will be entirely satisfactory. In that case, you might draw upon two or several of them to formulate your own definition or characterization.

a. Reading means getting meaning from certain combinations of letters. Teach the child what each letter stands for and he can read. . . . Johnny must learn, once and for all, that words are written by putting down letters from left to right, and that they are read in the same direction. (Flesch, 1955, pp. 10, 31)

b. Reading is a precise process. It involves exact, detailed, sequential perception and identification of letters, words, spelling patterns and larger language units. (View denounced in K. S. Goodman, 1967, p. 126)

c. The [structural] linguist's concept of reading is not the concept commonly held by the classroom teacher and the reading specialist—that reading is getting meaning from the print on a page. The [structural] linguist conceives the reading act as that of turning the stimulus of the graphic shapes on a surface back into speech. The shapes represent speech; meaning is not found in the marks but in the speech which the marks represent. . . . In order to comprehend what he reads, the reader turns the visual stimulus of written language back into speech—overtly if he is inexperienced and immature, subliminally if he is a rapid, experienced reader. (R. G. Strickland, 1964, pp. 10, 13–14)

d. Printing is a visual means of representing the sounds which are language. Meaning is in these sounds. We want to equip the child to turn the written word into a spoken word (whether he actually utters it or not) so he will hear what it says, that is, get its meaning. . . . We have never found anybody who did not think that the purpose of reading was to get the meaning. The only possible defense of skipping sound and going directly from print to meaning would be that printed words are directly meaningful—that the printed word *green* means the color, but this is not so. It is the spoken word *green* that designates the color, while the printed word designates the sound of the spoken word. Various [structural] linguistics specialists have recently been stressing this fact. (Walcutt & McCracken in *Lippincott Basic Reading*, 1975, Teacher's Edition for Book E, p. xiv)

e. Reading is a psycholinguistic guessing game. It involves interaction between thought and language. Efficient reading does not result from precise perception and identification of all elements, but from skill in selecting the fewest, most productive cues necessary to produce guesses which are right the first time. The ability to anticipate that which has not been seen, of course, is vital in reading, just as the ability to anticipate what has not yet been heard is vital in listening. (K. S. Goodman, 1967, p. 127)

f. Reading is the active process of reconstructing meaning from language represented by graphic symbols (letters), just as listening is the active process of reconstructing meaning from the sound symbols (phonemes) of oral language. (E. B. Smith, Goodman, & Meredith, 1970, p. 247)

g. When the light rays from the printed page hit the retinal cells of the eyes, signals are sent along the optic nerve to the visual centers of the brain. This is not yet reading. The mind must function in the process, the signals must be interpreted, and the reader must give significance to what he reads. He must bring *meaning* to the graphic symbol. (Dechant, 1970, p.12)

h. The reader brings to the text his past experience and present personality. Under the magnetism of the ordered symbols of the text, he marshals his resources and crystallizes out from the stuff of memory, thought, and feeling a new order, a new experience, which he sees as the poem [not necessarily what we think of as a poem, but *any* literary work created by a reader in the process of reading a text]. This becomes part of the ongoing stream of his life experience, to be reflected on from any angle important to him as a human being. (Rosenblatt, 1978, p. 12)

i. If the words remain words and sit quietly on the page; if they remain nouns, and verbs and adjectives, then we are truly blind. But if the words seem to disappear and our innermost self begins to laugh and cry, to sing and dance, and finally to fly—if we are transported in all that we are, to a brand new world, then—only then—can we say that we can READ! (Wayman, 1980, title page)

FOR FURTHER REFLECTION AND EXPLORATION

1. Compare the following four sketches of children in first-grade classrooms (D. R. King & Watson, 1983, p. 70). Try to decide which of the above definitions of reading might underlie each of the approaches implicitly illustrated. Which of the children do you think will become the better reader(s)? Why? Discuss.

    • Jamie sits looking at a list of words: fat, pat, bat, sat, cat, hat. . . . Later she sees, "The fat cat sat on the bat. Pat the fat cat."

    • Josie is waiting her turn in a group whose members are reading aloud a story in which the words "green," "table," and "wood" appear ten times each. Later she will do skill exercises in her workbook.

    • Harold looks at a page with spʊn, baul, riŋ, ∫out, t∫ɜr, and tæks on it. Later he will write a story using the symbols he has learned in school.

    • Hildy sits on the floor and reads along with her friends and teacher a story the class has just written. Later she will write a letter to a friend about the book she has just finished reading.

2. Interview some children and/or teachers about their views of reading. (If you don't have ready access to either children or teachers, perhaps you can interview students planning to become teachers.) Ask questions similar to those below, modifying the language of the question as appropriate for the individual. Ask follow-up questions when the opportunity arises. (The following questions are adapted from Harste, 1978, and from Burke, 1980, as reported in Y. M. Goodman, Watson, & Burke, 1987):

   a. What do you think reading is? What do people do when they read something?
   b. When you are reading and come to something you don't know, what do you do? (After receiving a response, you might ask a follow-up question: Do you ever do anything else?)
   c. Who is a good reader you know?
   d. What makes _____ a good reader?
   e. Do you think _____ ever comes to something he/she doesn't know? (After receiving a response, ask: Suppose _____ does come to something he/she doesn't know. What do you think _____ would do?)
   f. If you knew someone was having trouble reading, how would you help that person?
   g. What would a/your teacher do to help that person?
   h. How did you learn to read?
   i. What would you like to do better as a reader?
   j. Do you think you are a good reader? Why?

   In addition to questions like some of these, you might reframe as questions some of the statements in activity 5—depending, of course, on whom you are interviewing.

3. If possible, observe several teachers during reading instruction. What kinds of direct instruction do they give? How do they respond to children's miscues? How do the activities in which children are involved differ from one classroom to another? Why? Try to decide what each teacher's implicit definition of reading must be. Later, ask each teacher how he or she would define reading and how reading should be taught. Compare these interview results with what you observed and what you inferred from the observation. In each case, does the teacher's definition of reading seem consistent with his or her teaching practices? Discuss.

   If in carrying out this activity you discover teachers with widely differing instructional approaches and/or definitions of reading, it might be particularly interesting to try a further project with some students from the most diverse teachers. With the teachers' permission, interview some of the poorest and some of the best readers from each class. If possible, tape-record the interviews for later study. Ask the kinds of questions suggested in activity 2 above, and/or some of the questions in activity 5 below, rephrased as appropriate for the children.

4. In an article reviewing thirty years of inquiry into students' perceptions of reading, Johns (1986) mentions, among others, a study of 1,655 students from grades 1 to 8. The students were asked three questions: (1) "What is reading?" (2) "What do you do when you read?" and (3) "If someone didn't know how to read, what would you tell him or her that he or she would need to learn?" Johns points out that students

often know more than they reveal in such brief interviews. In fact, many of the students' responses had to be classified as "meaningless"—no response, "I don't know," or a vague, circular, or irrelevant response. In many instances, such responses may have indicated that the student did not understand what the question might mean. In any case, in responding to the question "What is reading?" fewer than 20 percent of the students made any reference to getting meaning through reading (the percentage was higher with the older students, and lower with the younger ones). Most of the students described reading as decoding (e.g., sounding words out), or as an activity involving a textbook and occurring in a classroom or school environment (Johns & Ellis, 1976, as reported in Johns, 1986, p. 36). What do you think accounts for this low percentage of children who define reading as having to do with the getting of meaning? What do you think of the apparently high percentage of children who describe reading only as something occurring in school? Is this a matter for concern? Why or why not? Discuss.

5. To explore further your own views of reading and reading instruction, respond to the following questionnaire; you might also use it during the interviews suggested above. For each question, circle the one best answer that reflects the strength of your agreement or disagreement (SA means "strongly agree"; SD means "strongly disagree"). This questionnaire is the DeFord Theoretical Orientation to Reading Profile (TORP), included and discussed in DeFord, 1985:[2]

1. A child needs to be able to verbalize the rules of phonics in order to assure proficiency in processing new words.

   1   2   3   4   5
   SA   SD

2. An increase in reading errors is usually related to a decrease in comprehension.

   1   2   3   4   5
   SA   SD

3. Dividing words into syllables according to rules is a helpful instructional practice for reading new words.

   1   2   3   4   5
   SA   SD

4. Fluency and expression are necessary components of reading that indicate good comprehension.

   1   2   3   4   5
   SA   SD

5. Materials for early reading should be written in natural language without concern for short, simple words and sentences.

   1   2   3   4   5
   SA   SD

6. When children do not know a word, they should be instructed to sound out its parts.

   1   2   3   4   5
   SA   SD

7. It is a good practice to allow children to edit what is written into their own dialect when learning to read.

   1   2   3   4   5
   SA   SD

8. The use of a glossary or dictionary is necessary in determining the meaning and pronunciation of new words.

   1   2   3   4   5
   SA   SD

9. Reversals (e.g., saying "saw" for "was") are significant problems in the teaching of reading.

   1   2   3   4   5
   SA   SD

10. It is a good practice to correct a child as soon as an oral reading mistake is made.

    1   2   3   4   5
    SA   SD

11. It is important for a word to be repeated a number of times after it has been introduced to insure that it will become a part of sight vocabulary.

    1   2   3   4   5
    SA   SD

12. Paying close attention to punctuation marks is necessary to understanding story content.

    1   2   3   4   5
    SA   SD

13. It is a sign of an ineffective reader when words and phrases are repeated.

    1   2   3   4   5
    SA   SD

14. Being able to label words according to grammatical function (nouns, etc.) is useful in proficient reading.

    1   2   3   4   5
    SA   SD

15. When coming to a word that's unknown, the reader should be encouraged to guess upon meaning and go on.

    1   2   3   4   5
    SA   SD

16. Young readers need to be introduced to the root form of words (run, long) before they are asked to read inflected forms (running, longest).

    1   2   3   4   5
    SA   SD

17. It is not necessary for a child to know the letters of the alphabet in order to learn to read.

    1   2   3   4   5
    SA   SD

18. Flash-card drills with sight words is an unnecessary form of practice in reading instruction.

    1   2   3   4   5
    SA   SD

19. Ability to use accent patterns in multisyllable words (pho'-to-graph, pho-to'-gra-phy, and pho-to-gra'-phic) should be developed as part of reading instruction.

    1   2   3   4   5
    SA   SD

20. Controlling text through consistent spelling patterns ("The fat cat ran back. The fat cat sat on a hat") is a means by which children can best learn to read.

    1   2   3   4   5
    SA   SD

21. Formal instruction in reading is necessary to insure the adequate development of all the skills used in reading.

    1   2   3   4   5
    SA   SD

22. Phonic analysis is the most important form of analysis used when meeting new words.

    1   2   3   4   5
    SA   SD

23. Children's initial encounters with print should focus on meaning, not upon exact graphic representation.

1 2 3 4 5
SA   SD

24. Word shapes (word configuration) should be taught in reading to aid in word recognition.

1 2 3 4 5
SA   SD

25. It is important to teach skills in relation to other skills.

1 2 3 4 5
SA   SD

26. If a child says "house" for the written word "home," the response should be left uncorrected.

1 2 3 4 5
SA   SD

27. It is not necessary to introduce new words before they appear in the reading text.

1 2 3 4 5
SA   SD

28. Some problems in reading are caused by readers dropping the inflectional endings from words (e.g., jumps, jumped).

1 2 3 4 5
SA   SD

2 | How Language Means: With Implications for a Model of Reading

Normal reading seems to begin, proceed, and end in meaning, and the source of meaningfulness must be the prior knowledge in the reader's head. Nothing is comprehended if it does not reflect or elaborate on what the reader already knows.

— Frank Smith

COMPREHENDING AND LEARNING TO READ

You may never have given much thought to *how* words, sentences, and texts mean. In your daily life, you understand much of what you hear and read, while other things you doubtless don't understand. However, you may seldom have reflected upon the how or why of comprehension; you may never have constructed from your own experience a theory about how language means. It is important for teachers of reading to have such a theory, however, in order to approach the teaching of reading in a manner that accords with what is known about how language means.

Of course everyone agrees that the ultimate purpose of reading is to arrive at meaning, but there are differing views about what is involved in learning to read. Most reading instruction is based, implicitly if not explicitly, on one of the three following views:

View 1. Learning to read means learning to pronounce words.
View 2. Learning to read means learning to identify words and understand their meaning.
View 3. Learning to read means learning to bring meaning to a text in order to get meaning from, or understand, a text.

The first view reflects the assumption that once words are pronounced, meaning will take care of itself. The second assumes that once the meaning of individual words is determined, the meaning of the whole (paragraph, text) will take care of itself. In sharp contrast, the third view assumes that meaning results not necessarily from the precise identification of every word in a sentence, but from the constant interplay between the mind of the reader and the language of the text. This is *a psycholinguistic* view of reading, as will be explained below.

Many people would find the first definition unsatisfactory, incomplete: it is not enough to pronounce the words. If readers cannot also get meaning, they are not really reading. This, indeed, may have been your response to the paragraph on generative semantics (activity 1 in "Characterizing Reading and Reading Instruction" in Chapter 1). You may have been able to pronounce most of the words, yet felt that such word identification did not really constitute reading.

While rejecting as inadequate the view that learning to read means learning to pronounce words, many people unthinkingly adopt the second view, because they assume that reading means identifying words and getting their meaning. The implication, of course, is that the meaning of the whole sentence and text will automatically follow from the meaningful identification of words. Since this view seems implicitly to underlie much of our reading instruction in the United States, it is important to examine the assumption that meaning is built up from smaller parts to increasingly larger wholes.

THE MEANING OF WORDS AND SENTENCES: A FIRST LOOK

Since the mid-twentieth century, many psychologists and linguists have turned to the investigation of how people learn their native language and how they produce and comprehend sentences. There arose a hybrid discipline called *psycholinguistics* (from *psyche*, meaning 'mind,' and *linguistics*, meaning 'the study of language'). Since the early 1970s, when a psycholinguistic view of reading was first popularized through the books of Frank Smith *(Understanding Reading,* 1988 [1979]; *Psycholinguistics and Reading,* 1973) and the miscue research of Kenneth Goodman and his colleagues (K. S. Goodman, *Theoretically Based Studies . . .,* 1973), scholars in related disciplines have come to essentially the same conclusions about how language means.

Such scholarly research by socio-psycholinguists, schema theorists, semioticians, literary theorists, and reading educators simply confirms what we ourselves might conclude from thoughtful observation of how we and others comprehend. So—let us work inductively, together building a theory of comprehension.

To begin, please take a moment to write five to ten sentences using the word *run.* Try to create sentences in which *run* has different meanings.

The following are some of my sentences:

1. Can you run the store for an hour?
2. Can you run the word processor?
3. Can you run the 500-yard dash?
4. Can you run in the next election?
5. Can you run next year's marathon?
6. I helped Samuel with his milk run.
7. They'll print 5,000 copies in the first run.
8. Sherry has a run in her hose.
9. There was a run on snow shovels yesterday morning.
10. It was a long run.

Doubtless you have thought of several additional meanings of *run.*

Now the question is, in these and other sentences, how does the reader (or listener) know what *run* means? One of my small dictionaries lists nearly forty meanings for the word *run;* one of my desk dictionaries lists over eighty. Can readers arbitrarily take any one of the meanings of *run* from their mental dictionaries and apply it to the word *run* in these sentences? Clearly the answer is no. More often than not, meaningless sentences would result.

From even this simple example, then, it should be obvious that we do not simply add together the meanings of individual words to get the meaning of a sentence. To determine the meanings of the words, we use context of various sorts:

1. *Grammatical context within the sentence.* In the first five sentences above, *run* occurs in a context that signals its use as a verb. The grammatical context partially delimits the meaning of *run.*

2. *Semantic context within the sentence.* In "run the store" we know that *run* means something like 'manage'; in "run the word processor," we know that *run* means something like 'operate'; in "his milk run," we know that *run* means something like 'route,' and so forth. Interestingly, in the sentences where *run is* a verb, the precise meaning is determined by a noun that comes after it, rather than before.

3. *Situational, pragmatic context.* A sentence like "It was a long run" has several possible meanings, depending on the context in which it is uttered or written. In the context of stockings, *run* would refer to a tear (notice that the meaning and pronunciation of *tear* depends on its context, too). In the context of a dog kennel, *run* would mean an enclosure. In the context of fishing, *run* would mean migrating fish. In the context of skiing, *run* would mean a downhill path or route. In the context of theater, "It was a long run" would mean that the play was performed for a long period of time. And so forth. Situational context can be either verbal or nonverbal or both, as you can readily imagine from the preceding examples.

4. *Schematic context.* This refers to knowledge in our heads: a mental *schema* is simply an organized chunk of knowledge or experience. If we did not have mental schemas, we could not make practical use of the other kinds of context mentioned. For example, if we did not have an intuitive sense of grammar, we could not use grammatical context to limit a word's possible meanings to those that are appropriate for the verb function of the word (as in examples 1 through 5) or to limit the word's possible meanings to those that are appropriate for the noun function (as in examples 6 through 10). This process of grammatically delimiting a word's possible meanings is so automatic that we are not often aware of it, but it nevertheless occurs—and is made possible by our grammatical schemas.

Since our schemas develop as we interact with the external world, we may often lack appropriate schemas for understanding what we hear or read. For example, if you take your dog to be boarded at a kennel while you're on vacation, then return home and reassuringly tell your young children, "Gretchen's okay, she's got a long run," this sentence may make no sense to them. They may not be able to make use of the *verbal* situational context unless they have experienced the *nonverbal*—that is, unless they have actually seen the enclosure called a "dog run" at a kennel. Thus the children's schemas may be inadequate for making sense of what you've said.

From the examples and discussion so far, we can make several preliminary observations about how words and sentences mean:

1. Clearly, we do not just add together the meanings of the individual words in a sentence to get the meaning of the whole. We cannot know what a word means until we see it in context. Oddly enough, the supposedly simplest words like *in, on, at,* and *by* typically have at least fifteen to thirty meanings listed in a desk dictionary. In isolation, words have only *potential* meanings, a range of meanings that a dictionary attempts to characterize (e.g., Halliday, 1975). It is only when used in context (of various sorts) that one or more of these meanings is actualized.

2. Without knowledge in our heads, our schemas, we could not make use of the information provided by other kinds of context: grammatical, semantic, situational.

3. The observations above strongly suggest that meaning does not arise from part to whole but in some much more complex way. Bizarre as it sounds, we are able to grasp the meanings of individual words only when we see how they interrelate with each other. Thus, meaning arises from whole to part more than from part to whole.

Thus, as a first approximation of how sentences mean, we may say that *the meaning of a sentence arises or develops by means of transactions among words whose meanings are not identifiable except in context, where context includes grammar, semantics, and situation. It is the readers' and listeners' schemas—their individual contexts—that enable them to make use of these other kinds of context to comprehend language.* The truth of this observation should become clearer as the chapter progresses, as we focus on schemas and transactions, deep structure and surface structure, and contrasting views of language processing and reading. The use of context in identifying words will be discussed further in Chapter 4.

SCHEMAS: WHAT ARE THEY?

In recent years, those interested in how the mind operates have postulated the existence of cognitive schemas. As stated earlier, a *schema is* simply an organized chunk of knowledge or experience, often accompanied by feelings (e.g., Anderson, Spiro, & Anderson, 1977; Adams & Collins, 1979; Rumelhart, 1980; Iran-Nejad, 1980; and Iran-Nejad & Ortony, 1984).

To get some idea of what a schema is and how it operates in our daily lives, let us explore for a moment our schemas for restaurants (as suggested by Pearson & Johnson, 1978). What are some of the different kinds of restaurants you can think of—not specific restaurants or even restaurant chains, but categories into which these might be organized? A preliminary list might include truck stops and greasy spoons, fast food restaurants, cafeterias, ethnic restaurants, family restaurants, and fancy/expensive/gourmet restaurants. In addition, I have a concept for what might be called a cocktail restaurant. It's something between a family restaurant and a fancy restaurant: a place where you may go for drinks, a nice but not too expensive meal, and maybe entertainment on Friday or Saturday night—without the kids. Figure 2.1 shows these categories in a hierarchic, branching-tree diagram. You might add the additional categories you have thought of.

Notice that it is difficult to say exactly how big or little a schema is. We may have an ethnic restaurant schema that is part of a general restaurant schema, but the ethnic restaurant schema can be further subdivided into schemas for Italian restaurants, Mexican restaurants, Chinese restaurants, and so forth (Figure 2.2). Your own schemas for ethnic restaurants will depend a lot upon where you live and what cities and countries you have visited. Then, too, our original category, restaurants, is itself part of a larger schema, places to eat. Other places to eat might be at home, at Grandma's, in the park, in the school cafeteria, or even in bed; Figure 2.3 charts only a few of the possibilities. Obviously our schemas for these various places to eat will also differ from one another.

Most if not all of these categories are what Arthur Koestler (1969) called *holons:* each is simultaneously a whole, with its own subparts, and yet a part of something else. For example, the category "ethnic restaurants" has its own subcategories yet is itself a subcategory of "restaurants."

How are categories related to schemas? A schema is the organized knowledge we have about a category. Let's compare, for instance, our schema for fast food restaurants with our schema for fancy/expensive restaurants. Some of the obvious differences are given in Figure 2.3, but doubtless you can add others.

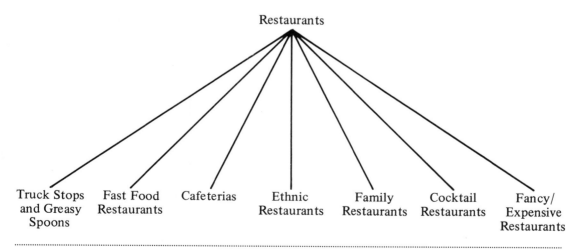

FIGURE 2.1   Schema for types of restaurants

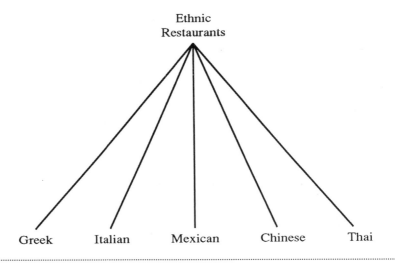

Figure 2.2   Schema for ethnic restaurants

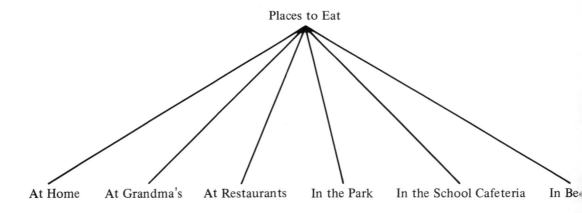

Figure 2.3   Schema for places to eat

Schema for Fast Food Restaurants	*Schema for Fancy/Expensive Restaurants*
limited menu, often consisting of hamburgers plus a few other items	generally a wide selection of foods, often including European cuisine
order food across a counter	order food from waitress or waiter (often the latter)
pay before receiving your food	pay after eating
eat quickly	eat slowly, with food served in several courses
use paper napkins and plastic utensils	use cloth napkins and silverware

Notice that cutting across the *category schemas* for types of restaurants are various *operational schemas* for selecting food, ordering, paying, and eating (see Figure 2.4). From these operational schemas, we can select elements that together will uniquely characterize each type of restaurant.

The distinctions within these operational schemas can be amazingly subtle. For example, take the schema of paying for the food. In a fast food restaurant, you usually pay for the food before receiving it. In a cafeteria, you pay for the food after receiving it, but before taking it to a table to eat. In drugstore counter restaurants (not included in the previous list), you receive the check as soon as you are served, and may be asked to pay for the food then. In family restaurants, you often receive the check as soon as you are served, but you pay as you leave. In cocktail restaurants, you usually do not receive the check until after you have finished eating and have had an after-dinner drink or cup of coffee—or at least have been invited to do so. Your waitress or waiter may take the check to the cashier for you, or you may pay on the way out. In a fancy restaurant, of course, the waitress or waiter (traditionally a waiter) will present the check on a platter or in a menu-like booklet and take the check to the cashier for you.

A moment's reflection will reveal the importance of schemas in our daily lives. Suppose someone has a well-developed schema for fast food restaurants and for family restaurants, but has never been to a fancy restaurant before. If a child, this person will surely be unprepared to endure the lengthy wait for one course after another, or the interminable adult discussions, or being repeatedly admonished to sit still and keep quiet. Where is the playground outside the restaurant? The video games? Even as an

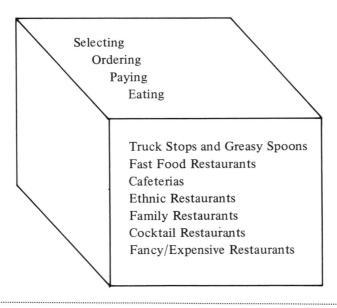

Figure 2.4 *Category and operational schemas*

adult, a person may not know what to do with the "extra" silverware and may not realize that the reason the check is served on a tray or platter is so that the diners can put their money on it for the waitress or waiter to take. As for wine tasting—what's that? One of my students related her father's first experience in a fancy restaurant. The waiter opened a bottle of wine and handed her father the cork to sniff. Not knowing what was expected, he looked at the cork and said, "Yup, that's a cork all right." Another student admitted that when first confronted with a finger bowl at a gourmet restaurant, she drank the water. Obviously their schemas for fancy restaurants did not include what to do in situations like these.

Can you think of examples when your own cognitive schemas were obviously not adequate to the situation? Can you remember times when you tried to understand an explanation or a lecture, a textbook or a library book, and found your schemas inadequate? What are some of the implications for teaching?

SCHEMAS IN READING

To explore the importance of schemas in the reading process, read one or the other of the following paragraphs once, without rereading. Then write a brief summary of what you have read.

Cost or Other Basis (on the topic of capital gains and losses)
In general, the cost or other basis is the cost of the property plus purchase commissions, improvements, and minus depreciation, amortization, and depletion. If you inherited the property or got it as a gift, in a tax-free exchange, involuntary conversion, or "wash sale" of stock, you may not be able to use the actual cash cost as the basis. If you do not use cash cost, attach an explanation of your basis.
—Internal Revenue Service, booklet on *1040 Federal Income Tax Forms and Instructions* (1985)

Dissipative Structures (based on Prigogine & Stengers, 1984)
Ilya Prigogine has demonstrated that when an "open system," one which exchanges matter and/or energy with its environment, has reached a state of maximum entropy, its molecules are in a state of equilibrium. Spontaneously, small fluctuations can increase in amplitude, bringing the system into a "far-from-equilibrium" state. Perhaps it is the instability of subatomic "particles" (events) on the microscopic level that causes fluctuations on the so-called macroscopic level of molecules. At any rate, strongly fluctuating molecules in a far-from-equilibrium state are highly unstable. Responding to internal and/or external influences, they may either degenerate into chaos or reorganize at a higher level of complexity.
—Constance Weaver, "Parallels Between New Paradigms in Science and in Reading and Literary Theories" (1985)

Now check your summary with the original. Did you leave out any important ideas? Distort any ideas? Or can't you even tell? Many of us simply do not have schemas adequate for this task. Because we do not already know something about capital gains and losses or about dissipative structures, we cannot understand much of what we are reading, and therefore we find it difficult to summarize the passage or even to evaluate our summary afterwards. We simply have no cognitive schemas for these topics.

Now let's take a slightly different situation. Again, read the following passage and then summarize it in writing without looking back. Check your summary with the original.

> The procedure is actually quite simple. First you arrange things into different groups. Of course one pile may be sufficient depending on how much there is to do. If you have to go somewhere else due to lack of facilities that is the next step, otherwise you are pretty well set. It is important not to overdo things. That is, it is better to do too few things at once than too many. In the short run this may not seem important but complications can easily arise. A mistake can be expensive as well. At first the whole procedure will seem complicated. Soon however, it will become just another facet of life. It is difficult to foresee any end to the necessity for this task in the immediate future, but then one never can tell. After the procedure is completed one arranges the materials into different groups again. Then they can be put into their appropriate places. Eventually they will be used once more and the whole cycle will then have to be repeated. However, that is a part of life.
> —John D. Bransford and Nancy S. McCarrell, "A Sketch of a Cognitive Approach to Comprehension" (1974)

Many people find that their summaries of the above passage are inadequate not because they can't understand the passage, but because they can't place the operations described within a context that makes sense to them. They understand the passage as they read, but they recall relatively little.

Now ask someone else to read and summarize this passage, but tell the person beforehand that the passage is about washing clothes. Compare the two summaries. Is the other person's summary more complete? Did this person include anything about washing clothes that was not explicitly stated in the passage? Often people will mention sorting the clothes into light colors and dark, or going to a laundromat if a washing machine isn't available at home. Clearly these ideas can be inferred from the passage, but only if you know or think that the passage is about washing clothes—and if you know something about that process. Only when we have cognitive schemas adequate to what we are reading and only when these schemas are somehow activated will we have much understanding and recall of what we hear or read.

This issue of activating one's schemas is crucial, as the terms *metalinguistic awareness, metacognition,* and *metacomprehension* suggest. Basically these terms refer to being aware that you have such strategies, and being able to use them consciously. For instance, having metalinguistic awareness means you are aware that you have linguistic knowledge (schemas) that you can use in listening and reading, as for example in predicting that a noun will come soon after the word *the.* Being aware that you have such knowledge, you can use it consciously when necessary. Here, in contrast, is an example of a college student who seemed unaware that she had cognitive strategies to monitor her own comprehension; at any rate, she had apparently not learned to use those strategies effectively in reading her textbooks. This student had just flunked her last introductory psychology exam (Santa, 1981, p. 168; italics mine):

> She had the proper "good student facade"; she underlined essential points in her text and had an adequate set of lecture notes. She also claimed to spend a considerable amount of time studying. After having her [the student] reread a short selection from her psychology text, I was somewhat amazed that she could not even answer the simplest question. Thinking she might have a poor memory, I asked her several other questions allowing her to look back in her text for the appropriate answer. Still, she had no success. *What is interesting is that she was very surprised that she had comprehended so little.* She had assumed she had understood without ever testing her assumption and *appeared totally oblivious to strategies which might help her monitor her own comprehension.*

Thus we might say that not only was this student neglecting to activate whatever schemas she might have had relevant to the understanding of psychology, she was even unaware of having strategies or schemas that might enable her to determine whether or not she was comprehending. Obviously readers need to mobilize such self-monitoring strategies as well as schemas relevant to the content of what they are reading.

SCHEMAS AND TRANSACTIONS

This discussion of schemas leads naturally into discussion of the concept of *transaction*. To gain experientially an understanding of this concept, read the following poem as many times as you wish. Then write down what you think the poem says.

To Pat

On the day you died
my lover caught a fish
a big-mouthed bass
nineteen inches long
four and a half pounds strong
they measured it.

They measured it,
stretching the tape to match
    its length,
piercing its mouth to heft
    its bulk.
They measured, examined,
    praised it.

"Fish, dear fish," he said,
"you are too beautiful to eat.
I will put you back."

But it was too late.
Like you, the fish could not

be revived.
He died in the kitchen sink.

And now I have eaten
of his sweet flesh,
the communion denied me
by the church of your people.
It is finished.

Typically, people will give different responses to the poem. One student suggested that the author—or at least the "I" of the poem—had been in love with Pat, but that the church had kept them from marrying. Another student, in a similar vein, suggested that the writer couldn't have Pat because he was a priest. Some people have interpreted "On the day you died" metaphorically: on the day you died to me, the day our friendship or romance ended. Others have taken the line literally, as describing the physical death of the person addressed. Some students take the line about communion as referring to sexual communion. Others interpret the line as referring to the taking of the sacraments in church; for some of these students, this interpretation seems to be fostered by the knowledge that certain churches forbid nonmembers to take communion ("the communion denied me / by the church of your people"). Still other students have taken that line as signaling both meanings, sexual and religious communion. Some students have seen religious elements in various parts of the poem after reading the last line. Others, not knowing that Christ's last words on the cross were "It is finished," have seen no religious elements at all. Often, of course, students have modified their opinion of what the poem says during the social give-and-take of classroom discussion, as described in a later section.

Clearly each reader has brought to bear his or her own schemas in grappling with the poem—including a schema for interpreting poetry, which often goes something like this: "There must be a deep meaning here that I don't immediately get. It probably has to do with sex and/or religion." An interesting commentary on the experience students have had with reading poetry in school, is it not? Notice, too, that although I have asked students to tell just what the poem said, not what they thought it meant, most students have not separated the two. This is common: after a very brief interval, readers typically cannot distinguish between what they've actually read and what is a logical inference from what they have read. You may have observed this with people who summarized the "washing clothes" passage knowing what it's supposed to be about. As readers internalize what they have read, recall and inference and interpretation become inseparable. (Again, you might consider the implications for teaching and learning.)

Each person's experience of the poem above, and of everything else we read, is influenced by the person's own schemas—the person's knowledge and experience and feelings. Recognition of this fact is, however, a sharp departure from an earlier (and, in some quarters, a still popular) concept of comprehension. For a long time after the introduction of Shannon's revolutionary concepts of information theory (C. Shannon, 1948), it was thought that a message would travel pure and unchanged from sender to receiver, provided the channel—the medium through which the message was transmitted—did not contain "noise"—that is, something that would distort the message. Shannon's basic concept can be represented as follows:

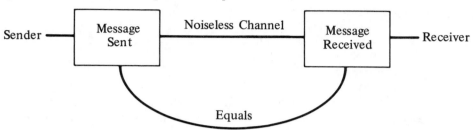

Now we understand, however, that in human communication the message received is *never* identical to the message sent, whether the communication is oral or written. This is true not because there is necessarily any noise in the channel, though there may be. Rather, the message received is inevitably different from the message sent because the receiver—the reader or listener—brings to bear his or her schemas in interpreting the message. The speaker or writer tries to encode a message in language, but because no two people's experiences, thoughts, and feelings are ever identical, the message received is never quite identical to the message sent. This view can be represented as follows:

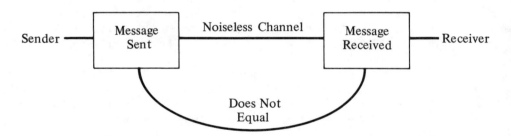

From the listener's or reader's point of view, then, meaning is not in the spoken or written word, the text itself. Rather, meaning arises during a transaction between the words and the listener or reader.

The person who has stimulated widespread understanding of this concept and term is Louise Rosenblatt (e.g., 1938, 1964, 1978), who borrowed and popularized the concept of *transaction* introduced by Dewey and Bentley (1949). To clarify the concept of transaction, Rosenblatt (1978) defines some key terms:

- *The Reader is* the person seeking to make meaning by transacting with (actively reading) a text, of whatever kind.
- *The Text is* the collection of word symbols and patterns on the page, the physical object you hold in your hand as you read.
- *The Poem is* the literary work created as the reader transacts with the text. ("Poem" refers metaphorically to *any* literary work—not just a poem in the usual sense, but a short story, novel, play.)

The crucial point is that meaning is not in the text itself, whether the text be literary or otherwise. Rather, meaning arises during the transaction between reader and text. Thus reading is a process, a transaction between reader and text in a given situational context, an event during which meaning evolves. (Implications for classroom engagement with literature are discussed in Chapter 9.)

To elaborate: the writer has, let us say, a novel in his or her head (though, of course, much of the novel typically develops as one writes). The writer chooses word symbols and patterns to represent that novel, usually knowing full well that from the text thus created, the reader will create his or her own novel. No two novels, so created, will ever be alike. The novel I created from Anya Seton's *Katherine* at age fifteen is not the same novel I created upon re-transacting with the text at thirty-five, and certainly the novel you create will never be the same as either of mine. We bring different life experiences, different schemas, to the word symbols and patterns of the text.

These schemas depend in part on a variety of social factors: our cultural, ethnic, and socioeconomic background; our age and educational attainment; our interests and values; and so forth, as succinctly illustrated in the cartoon in Figure 2.5. In addition, the activation of schemas is influenced by our interpretation of the social context in the here and now, the situational context. For example: A child may read to identify words correctly in school, because he or she has learned that correct word identification is

"But it's only a word!"

FIGURE 2.5 *More contrasting schemas*

what's expected. When reading for pleasure, however, the child may read for meaning. In taking multiple-choice "reading comprehension" tests, the child may read merely to locate the phrase in the paragraph(s) that corresponds with the phrase in one of the answers. Elsewhere, the child may again read for meaning. A personal example comes readily to mind. When my son was in fourth grade, he had vocabulary tests of the matching type: match the word to the definition. One of the words to be tested was *assumption,* defined as "an assuming." I tried to find a more suitable definition in our dictionaries at home, but with little luck; finally, I concluded that the best way to help my son understand the word was with examples from his own life. John's reply, however, was typical of the student who has learned to play the academic game. "Oh, don't worry," he said. "On the test, I'll just match *ass*'s" (the first three letters of *assumption* and *assuming).* Obviously the situational context of the classroom did not demand genuine understanding.

An example of how social and situational factors intersect may help to illuminate both. Seeking to determine why inner-city children typically score lower on reading achievement tests than children from affluent suburbs, various researchers have discovered, not surprisingly, that one difference is that inner-city children less frequently have schemas that would facilitate comprehension of the passages in such tests. The passages are often based on experiences, knowledge, and/or vocabulary that they do not have. More interesting, though, is that many children from nonmainstream cultures (e.g., black inner-city youth) apparently bring a different mind-set to the testing task itself. Though many children have learned that in responding to questions on a so-called comprehension test you're not supposed to draw upon prior knowledge but only to use information in the passage at hand, many inner-city youth do not operate upon this principle; rather, they answer test questions by using what they know (Nix & Schwarz, 1979).

Bloome and Green (1985) provide an interesting example, with an even more interesting commentary. The passage and question below are taken from a reading workbook, *Reading House Series* (1980, p. 71). The question, of course, is multiple-choice:

> Bill Benson looked only once at his homework assignment. Immediately, he started moaning to his seatmate, Candy Caries, about its length. As he shuffled out of the room after the bell, he couldn't help but remark to his teacher that the room was too stuffy to work in. The teacher only smiled and shook her head at Bill's complaints.

> Faced with the possibility of running an errand for his parents, Bill is likely to say:
> A. "Do I have to go? Why don't you ask Uncle Joe this time?"
> B. "Sure I'll go! Should I walk or take the bus?"
> C. "Okay, Dad. I'll go right after I finish my homework."
> D. "I'm way ahead of you, Pop! I took care of it already."

According to Bloome and Green (1985), one ninth grader explained why he chose option C (a "wrong" answer) instead of A (the "right" answer) by pointing out that Bill Benson had no intention of doing his homework or of going to the store, but that confronting his father—which is the situation in option A—would probably result in punishment. Thus, the student chose C, which superficially indicates compliance, but which may allow Bill to procrastinate indefinitely. Bloome and Green comment (1985, p.180):

> In answering the question, the student used his own background knowledge as a frame for interpreting the story and the question. However, when high-achieving students from the same grade, school, and background were given the same passage and questions, they gave the answer designated correct by the teacher's guide. In brief, one of the strategies some students may need to learn is to suppress their own background knowledge and assume the interpretive frame of the school.

Bloome and Green thus explain the problem as one of an "interpretive frame," adding that "Differences in interpretive frames may be the result of cultural differences, economic differences, personal experience differences, and so on" (p. 179). Thus, *social context* (the background of the student) may intersect with *situational context* (the testing situation) in such a way as to result in apparent failure to comprehend. Ironically, however, students like the one described above are doing precisely what readers must do in order to read real texts effectively: they are bringing their prior experience and knowledge to the task of making sense of what they read.

Reading, then, is not merely a psycholinguistic process, involving a transaction between the mind of the reader and the language of the text. Rather, reading is a socio-psycholinguistic process, because the reader-text transaction occurs within a social and situational context (see, for example, the longitudinal Bristol study documented in Wells, 1986). More accurately, there are a variety of social and situational factors, a variety of contexts, that affect the activation of one's schemas and the outcomes of the reader-text transaction. That is, a variety of social and situational factors influence how the person reads and what the reader understands (see, for example, Carey, Harste, & Smith, 1981; Bloome, 1985). Figure 2.6 is an attempt to capture the complexity of these relationships. In fact, reading is a socio-psycholinguistic process of incredible complexity.

READING AS A SOCIAL TRANSACTION
KATHRYN MITCHELL PIERCE

It has always been easy for me to understand how reading is a social process or transaction when readers are reading in the company of others. In classrooms, we often choose reading experiences that highlight or exploit the social nature of the reading and learning process.

For example, the Shared Book Experience (described in Chapter 3 and elsewhere) provides opportunities for learners to experience a text in the company of others. They discuss and share reading strategies, meanings they are constucting as they transact with the text, and their personal responses to the text. Many other classroom engagements have been created to support readers socially in their reading, such as literature

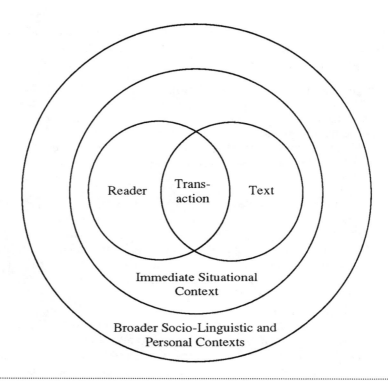

Figure 2.6 *Reading as a socio-psycholinguistic process*

discussion groups (Short & Pierce, 1990; Pierce & Gilles, 1993), Say Something (Harste & Short with Burke, 1988), and partner reading (two learners reading together from a shared text). In addition, readers may join readers' clubs, where members meet regularly to share the books they have been reading and sometimes to discuss a book they have all read. In some classrooms the students, or students and teachers together, maintain dialogue journals about their reading experiences.

In all of these situations, the reader is clearly reading in a social context. The readers are sharing the reading act with other readers, thereby providing opportunities for all participants to learn more about reading, about learning, about one another, and about their worlds. In such social contexts, readers provide demonstrations to one another of the strategies they use during the reading process, the stance or personal perspective they choose in reading, and ways in which others respond to and connect with texts. In addition, these shared experiences provide opportunities for readers to create and confirm shared meanings of the text as they work with one another to clarify what they have read and understood.

The Solitary Reader

It has been much more difficult for me to understand the social nature of the reading process for a solitary reader. I have repeatedly questioned how such an individual act is still social, and what the significance might be of recognizing and highlighting the social nature of a solitary act. The following insights and experiences have been useful for me as I have worked through this paradox.

First, reading is seldom a truly solitary act. Often, readers who are reading by themselves are doing so in a classroom context, a home, a library, or someplace where other people are, or could be. This means that even for the solitary reader, the potential exists for sharing the reading with others, regardless of whether the reader exercises this option. The fact that my friend is sitting next to me as I read influences the way I approach the text. I am more likely to think about, search for, or highlight those aspects of the text with which I feel my friend might find some connection. Children do this often in classrooms. As Jeffrey and Blake are silently reading books at a table during Free Reading, Blake turns to Jeffrey and says, "Here, Jeffrey, look at this! You could use this in your dinosaur book!" Blake and Jeffrey are friends, and Blake knows that Jeffrey is working on a dinosaur book. When Blake finds illustrations in his reptile book that compare contemporary reptiles to prehistoric dinosaurs, he thinks about Jeffrey.

Even in a home situation when one is home alone, the potential may exist for sharing the reading experience later on when other members of the home return. My mother often leaves particular pieces of mail in a more prominent location to signal to my father her desire to discuss the pieces with him as soon as he has had an opportunity to read them. Even when one is reading independently, the social context in which the reading occurs affects the meanings created during the experience (Carey, Harste, & Smith, 1981). The potential for future sharing of the reading experience may create an awareness of the social context for reading, and thus may influence the reading experience.

For example, I recently read a draft of an article on democratic assessment written by two colleagues in order to offer my responses to them. Obviously, my impending discussion with them influenced my reading of the text. At the same time, however, I was preparing for a trip to Columbia, Missouri, to discuss a current project with Carol Gilles. I found myself making stars in the margins of the democratic assessment piece I wanted to discuss with Carol, should the opportunity arise during my visit. I didn't *plan* to read the article for ideas to discuss with Carol, but the opportunity to discuss the article influenced my reading—I took special note of ideas I thought she might either take issue with or find useful.

Carolyn Burke uses a reading strategy in her graduate courses that encourages students to read with other students in mind. The strategy, which she calls "Save the Last Word for Me," requires that the reader select particular quotes or passages for one of several reasons. When using this strategy, I have readers select passages for the following reasons: I disagree with this; I don't understand this; I really like the way this is worded; I thought _____ might find this interesting; I'd really like to discuss this with _____ . The reader then puts the passage on one side of an index card, and the reason for its selection on the other side. During the next class session, the students form small groups to share their cards. The first student reads the quote or passage from the front of the card, without making comments. Others in the group discuss and respond to the quote.

When the first student has heard enough discussion, he or she shares the reason for selecting the quote and/or shares a personal response to it. Occasionally, the reader changes his or her response to the quote after having heard the discussion of colleagues. The strategy is an effective way to encourage students to read with other students in mind, and to prepare for discussion with those students by sorting out the topics, questions, and issues they most want to discuss with these particular classmates. In addition, having the opportunity to hear others discuss the quote prior to making a statement provides a support net for readers who might be reluctant to put their own ideas on the table for response.

Even when a reader has no plans for sharing the reading in the future, the reader's past social encounters may influence the reading act. Who recommended this book? How did this person describe the book and the reasons for the recommendation? How did this person connect the book with me and my experiences and interests? Our past conversations with others also influence our reading.

Shirley Crenshaw recently loaned me Mary Crow Dog's autobiography, *Lakota Woman* (1990), commenting that I would particularly enjoy it. The novel addresses such issues as the persecution of American Indians, women's rights, and the power of family culture and traditions to influence the actions of an individual. Shirley and I had both worked with teachers on the Navajo Reservation at Chinle, Arizona. Our shared history led her to recommend the book to me. As I read the book, I realized that I was not being critical of the ways in which American Indians were portrayed. Knowing Shirley's extensive work with American Indian groups, I trusted her to recommend only books that are free from stereotypes and misunderstandings. Of course, the fact that the book was itself written by an American Indian was also a factor in my stance toward the book.

In contrast, a few months earlier I had picked up *Baseball in April* (Soto, 1991), a collection of short stories about Hispanic-American teenagers. I recognized the title, but hadn't spoken with anyone who had read the book. As I read, I was looking for stereotypic images and misconceptions. Knowing very little about Hispanic-American culture, I made mental lists of the people with whom I wanted to discuss the book, if given an opportunity. The context that led to my reading *Lakota Woman* (a personal recommendation) encouraged me to take one stance in reading, while the different context that led me to pick up *Baseball in April* (title recognition only) led to a different stance.

Readers are also influenced by other readers who have provided demonstrations of the reading act. All readers have been influenced by the demonstrations provided by others of the ways one reads in this culture. Until a few years ago, I always underlined and wrote responses to books in the margins as I read (requiring that I own all the books that I read). Then I observed Shirley Crenshaw preparing for a speech she was to make. She put Post-It notes on specific pages of a book and wrote her comments directly on the notes. The notes not only provide a way to make marginal comments without damaging the book, but they can also be placed strategically on the page or left sticking out to make it easier to find particular passages. My favorite professional books are now filled with so many Post-It notes from multiple readings that I can hardly read the books!

The range of acceptable places to read can also be expanded by the demonstrations of others. I discovered the joys of so-called solitary reading in a frenzied shopping mall by observing a reader deeply engrossed in a book while shoppers bustled all around.

Other readers also demonstrate the purposes for reading in our culture. As the mother of two preschoolers, I am often struck by the demonstrations of reading that my husband and I provide the children. One day, while putting together a "some assembly required" toy, I muttered, "I wonder how we're going to figure *this* out!" Jennifer, age three and a half, responded, "We can look it up in the phone book. Dad says *everything's* in the phone book." As parents, we had provided Jennifer with numerous demonstrations of the ways we use reading to solve problems. Evidently, she had picked up on the right actions, though perhaps the wrong text for this situation.

Thus, readers are influenced by the social context in three ways. Clearly, they are influenced by the *present* social context, particularly in such interactive experiences as literature discussion groups or other classroom situations and strategies that encourage interaction among participants. Readers are affected by their *past*, by previous social experiences that may influence reading in the present. And in addition to the past and present, readers are influenced by the potential for social interaction in the *future*.

But what of the larger social context in which all readers operate?

The Reader in Society

To be readers, individuals must be members of a literate community. This community, with its socio-political culture and particular language traits, defines the potential for a given text in a given period of time. That is, the meanings a reader brings to and evokes during the reading of a text reflect the language and culture of the social groups of which the reader is a member, as well as the values, issues, and concerns of a given time and place.

For example, some years ago Jerry Harste invited a group of graduate students to identify a book that had been a childhood favorite, and then to revisit that book as an adult. I chose *Black Beauty* because, as a horse lover, I had found this book quite important to my middle school years. Upon rereading it, I was dismayed to find my treasured book to be sexist and preachy. I hadn't remembered it that way. My own adult awareness of the social issues surrounding the rights of women and minorities, reflecting a heightened sensitivity to these issues on the part of the community of which I was a member, helped create the potential for this book to evoke such a response. This response would have been unlikely prior to the Civil Rights and renewed Women's Movements of the 1960s.

Just as readers are influenced by social context, the writers of texts are also part of a social context and are influenced by the socio-political issues of a time and place and culture. In this way, the reader and the author may be perceived as engaging in a particular dialogue: a social transaction that transcends both time and place.

A part of this dialogue is carried out between the reader and the characters in the text. As the characters become believable, as the reader enters fully into the world of the text, the readers and characters engage in a social transaction. The characters, then, assume almost the same potential for influencing the reader as the real people with whom a reader might share a reading experience. Karen Smith (1990) expands on this notion of entering into the world of the text by describing ways of encouraging readers to "entertain a text" as one would entertain a welcome guest in one's home. In this way, literature assumes the potential for affecting readers.

Literature has the power to help us come to know ourselves and others in more complex ways, to understand our world and its potential, and to create new worlds, both real and imagined. Meaningful engagement with literature is therefore a socio-political transaction, since such engagements have the potential to affect action in the future.

TRANSACTIONS WITHIN THE LANGUAGE OF THE TEXT: GRAMMATICAL SIGNALS

The reader-text transaction that takes place within an immediate situational context and broader personal and social context is by no means the only transaction taking place during the reading process. In particular, there are also numerous transactions, on various levels, within the language of the text itself.

Some of these transactions are signaled by grammatical cues: word endings, function words, and/or word order. Take, for example, word endings. The ending -ed indicates past action, as in "She *chaired* the meeting." The ending -er indicates one who does something, as in "Cindy is a top-notch *runner.*" The ending -en denotes an action, as in "Bleach will *whiten* your clothes." And -ly indicates the manner in which an action is carried out, as in "She examined it *closely.*" What, however, do these same endings indicate in the following sentences?

1. The *exhausted* doctor slept all day.
2. I can't run any *faster.*
3. The tomato is *rotten.*
4. Her cocker spaniel is very *friendly.*

Here, the -ed indicates a condition or state, the -er indicates the manner of an action, the -en indicates a condition or quality, and the -ly indicates a quality or characteristic. Our knowledge of words and the endings they can take, plus our recognition of how the italicized words are functioning in the above sentences, tells us that this time the endings are functioning differently than before. Both the meaning and the part of speech are different, as readers intuitively know.

Thus, although word endings do help to signal the meanings of words and the kinds of semantic and syntactic transactions into which they can enter, nevertheless we often do not know the meaning of an ending until we see it in the word to which it is attached—and, in some cases, not until we see how that word is used in the sentence. For example, in addition to its use as an adjective, *exhausted* can be a verb, as in "The recent demand for computers *exhausted* all our supply." Thus, in isolation, *exhausted* has the potential to be either an adjective or a verb.

Function words are another major grammatical signal, for they glue together the content words—the nouns and pronouns, verbs, adjectives, and adverbs that carry most of the meaning of a sentence. Thus, the major function words or signal words are noun determiners (ND), including the articles *a, an,* and *the*; verb auxiliaries (VA); prepositions (P); and conjunctions (C). Note the examples of function words below.

After it *had* rained *for an* hour, *the* young people gave up *their* idea
　C　　VA　　　　P ND　　ND　　　　　　　　　　ND

of camping out. Instead they rented *a* room *at a* motel where they
P　　　　　　　　　　　　　　　　　　ND　　　P ND

could swim *in a* pool *and* eat *by the* poolside.
VA　　　　P ND　　C　　　P ND

Like word endings, such function words serve as useful but not infallible signals of what is coming next in a sentence. The word *this,* for example, usually works as a noun determiner, to signal that a noun is coming up in a sentence, as in *"This* problem is difficult."* However, the word *this* can also work as a pronoun taking the place of a noun, as in "I can't understand *this."* Somewhat similarly, the words *will* and *can* commonly work as verb auxiliaries, to signal that a verb is coming up, as in "Terry *will* do it" and "Maryellen *can* come." However, both words sometimes function as nouns, as in "She has an iron *will"* and "He couldn't open the *can."* Thus, although function words help to signal the relations among words, we don't always know whether something is even a function word or not until we see how it fits with the other words in a sentence.

Even when we know something is a function word, we cannot tell its precise meaning in isolation. Take, for example, the preposition *by* in the following sentences. In each case what does it mean, and *how do you know?*

1. That was prescribed *by* Dr. Lucy.
2. Charlie sat down *by* Dr. Lucy.
3. Woodstock went *by* plane.
4. *By* the way, how old do you think Snoopy is?
5. *By* Snoopy's calculations, it ought to work.

The fact that *by is* a preposition tells us little about how it relates to the other words in a sentence. It is actually the other words that give *by* a specific meaning, rather than the other way around. *By* acquires meaning by transacting with the other words in the sentence.

In fact, the meaning of the function words and often the precise function words themselves can be predicted from the content words. Try again to read the sentence about giving up camping, as reproduced below. You will probably find that you can supply most of the missing words, getting at least the gist if not the actual word of the original:

_____ it ____ rained ____ __ hour, ____ young people gave up _____ idea ___ camping out. Instead they rented _ room __ _ motel where they _____ swim __ _ pool ____ eat __ ____ poolside.

If indeed you could read the passage with little trouble and supply most if not all of the missing words, what might this suggest about the importance of function words in signaling grammar and thus meaning? Clearly, function words are useful in signaling the relations among words, but they may not be nearly so vital as is commonly supposed. (For a similar activity from which this conclusion may likewise be drawn, see the Kent State passage in Chapter 4, p. 145.)

Word order is more reliable than either word endings or function words in signaling the relationships among words. Compare, for instance, the following pairs of sentences:

1. Snoopy kissed Lucy.
   Lucy kissed Snoopy.
2. Dog bites man.
   Man bites dog.
3. Wendy loves Greg.
   Greg loves Wendy.
4. Cook the roast.
   Roast the cook.

In each case, our knowledge of English word order tells us that the first word indicates the doer of the action, while the third indicates the recipient of the action. The two sentences in each pair contain the same words, but the differing word order signals different relations, different transactions among the words. Note that the sentence "Roast the cook" may sound either cannibalistic or nonsensical to some readers, while other readers may have a schema that allows for an interpretation like the following: "Have a ceremony in which we honor the cook by seeming to dishonor him or her."

So far, then, it should be clear that word endings, function words, and word order all help us determine the meanings of words and the relations among the words in a sentence. But we have also seen that word endings are not infallible clues to word function or meaning. Function words are also limited in their usefulness. What appears to be a function word may not always be working as one; the meanings of some function words (particularly the prepositions) can by no means be determined out of context; and, in any case, many function words are often dispensable in a given context, being themselves predictable from the nouns, verbs, adjectives, and adverbs. These limitations leave us with word order as the best clue to word relationships. However, we shall see in the next section that even word order is often not adequate to signal the basic relations among the words of a sentence.

SURFACE VERSUS DEEP STRUCTURE

The grammatical clues of word endings, function words, and word order are surface structure clues—that is, clues that are visible in written language or audible in speech. As adults who know the language, we perceive many kinds of relationships that are not signaled, or not signaled adequately, by grammatical aspects of surface structure. These cues are part of the *deep structure,* a term coined by Noam Chomsky in the early 1960s to denote those relationships among words that are intuitively clear to a native speaker of the language, but that are not overtly signaled in the flow of language itself (see, for example, N. Chomsky, 1965).

Chomsky emphasized deep, underlying relationships that he considered grammatical. Take, for example, the following pair of sentences:

> The operation was performed by a new surgeon.
> The operation was performed by a new technique.

The two sentences have the same grammatical surface structure, but they mean in different ways. On the surface, "operation" is the subject, "was performed" is the verb phrase, and "by a new surgeon" and "by a new technique" are both prepositional phrases; the surface grammar is essentially the same. However, we know that in the first sentence it is the surgeon who performed the operation. "Surgeon" is the agent or doer of the action and hence the "deep" subject, as we can demonstrate by turning the sentence around and making it active: "A new surgeon performed the operation." We also know that the parallel word in the second sentence, "technique," is *not* the doer of the action or the deep subject: it would not make sense to say "A new technique performed the operation." The deep subject is, in fact, unspecified. For all we know, the operation may have been performed by a butcher. Or the operation may be of a totally different kind, having nothing to do with surgery.

Structurally ambiguous sentences provide further evidence that surface structure, including word order, is not always adequate to signal deep structure, the underlying relationships among words. Take, for example, the following sentences. What do they mean?

> Visiting relatives can be a nuisance.
> They asked the police to stop drinking.

The surface grammar of the first sentence gives us no clue to the deep grammar, to *who* is doing the visiting. Does the sentence mean that relatives who visit can be a nuisance? Or does it mean that the act of going to visit relatives can be a nuisance? In the second sentence above, the surface grammar similarly gives no clue as to the deep subject of *drinking:* are the police to stop other people from drinking, or are they themselves to cease drinking? The surface grammar, including word order, is insufficient to make the meaning or the deep grammar clear.

In context, however, such sentences are usually understood. In fact, we understand the deep grammar precisely because we understand the meaning of the sentences, given a particular situational context. Thus Chomsky's insistence on the importance of the deep structure *grammar* (as opposed to meaning) no longer seems as important as it once did. Historically, however, Chomsky's distinction between surface and deep grammar was of tremendous significance, paving the way for the widespread recognition that meaning does not lie in language itself but rather arises during the transaction between reader and text.

Modernizing Chomsky's definitions of surface and deep structure, then, we can say that *surface structure is* the visible or audible text, the squiggles and vibrations that are interpreted as words and word patterns—including the grammatical signals of word endings, function words, and word order. The *deep structure is* the underlying relationships that are perceived by, or rather constructed by, the reader or listener, on the basis of his or her prior knowledge and experience—schemas, in other words. Surface structure is what you see or hear. Deep structure is what you don't see or hear, but nevertheless understand.

Figure 2.7 summarizes these aspects of language and language processing in a surface-deep structure continuum. As the previous discussion suggests, however, we do not simply go from surface to deep structure in interpreting sentences. For example, if you have ever listened to someone speak a language that you do not know, you may have found that you could not even tell when one word ended and another began; the spoken words may have been little more than noises to you. For someone who has no acquaintance with written language, written words probably look like little more than scribbles or hieroglyphics; such, in fact, is our own experience when first encountering a radically different writing system. What enables us to make sense of language is our schemas, including our schemas about the structure of the language in question and, for written language, our schemas about the nature of print in that language. Thus, language processing goes as much or more from deep to surface structure as the other way around.

To solidify our understanding of how sentences mean, let us work through one more set of examples, considering how syntactic and semantic context, situational context, and schemas all play a role. First, quickly define the words *chair, white, run, close,* and *love,* in your head or on paper. Now see if your definitions are appropriate for these contexts:

1. Get Shirley to *chair* the meeting.
2. Separate the *white* from the yolk.
3. Angie can *run* the outfit.
4. That was a *close* call.
5. I *love* you.

SURFACE STRUCTURE Visible—Supplied by the Text			DEEP STRUCTURE Invisible—Supplied by the Reader		
Vibrations in the air or squiggles on the page	Words on the page	Surface grammar (word endings, function words, word order)	Possible word meanings	Relational meanings among words in sentences	Listener's or reader's schemas

Figure 2.7   Surface-deep structure continuum. Language processing occurs in both directions, surface to deep and deep to surface, and is even more complex than is reflected here.

In the first sentence, surface grammar is enough to signal the meaning. That is, *chair* coming immediately after *to* must be a verb, and for most of us that verb has only one possible meaning: to take charge of, to preside over. In the second sentence, *the* indicates that *white is* a noun, but we don't know much about that noun *white* until we see it in context with *yolk;* here, we must have recourse to semantic cues within the sentence. In the third sentence, *can* clearly signals that *run is* a verb, but what does that verb mean? And what does the noun *outfit* mean—clothing? A business operation? The two words can be understood only in transaction with each other.

In the fourth sentence, grammatical context indicates that *close is* an adjective rather than a verb and *call is* a noun rather than a verb, but what about the meaning of the phrase "a close call"? We need to know more about the situational context in which the sentence occurs. Is the speaker/writer describing a baseball game, a near-accident, or what?

On the surface, the word *love* in "I love you" appears clear enough: it is a verb, with *I* as subject and *you* as object. The transaction among the words is clear, but what does it mean to the person who hears or reads it? To one who does not know English, the sentence will mean nothing at all, unless the nonverbal context makes it clear. To those who know the language, it will still have different meanings under different circumstances and for different individuals. Under some circumstances, one may interpret the words "I love you" to be merely a verbal enticement to sexual gratification, while under other circumstances one may interpret the same words as an expression of lifelong devotion. It all depends upon the situation and the schemas, the deepest of deep structures that the individual brings to bear.

These examples again illustrate what we have already seen: that comprehension is not a one-way process from surface structure to deep structure. Indeed, as we interpret what we hear or read, we in effect impose deep structure on surface structure. Our prior knowledge and experience determine our understanding of the relations among the words in a sentence—or our inability to understand what a sentence means. Perhaps more surprising, however, is the fact that our entire system of knowledge and belief can affect even our perception of individual words and parts of words. While reading a story to my son, I once made the following miscue:

older
The other seals knew better.

In the context of the story, the other seals were in fact older. However, my students have insisted that this miscue was caused not so much by the preceding context of the story as by my unwarranted assumption that to be older is to be wiser. Probably they are right.

CONTRASTING MODELS OF READING

We began this chapter by discussing contrasting views of learning to read, views that seem related to contrasting views of reading itself and, still more generally, to contrasting views of how language means. Let us consider one more example of how language means before turning to models of reading and then, in Chapter 3, to different understandings of how children learn or should be taught to read.

Developing a Model of Our Own

It will help you develop your own model or theory of language comprehension and reading if, once again, you participate wholeheartedly in the activity suggested. Read the following paragraph silently, not worrying about how the words are pronounced. Just see if you can get some sense of what the passage is about, rereading the passage as necessary. Incidentally, the seeming nonsense words are actually antiquated, "lost words" (Sperling, 1977) that have been revived for the occasion:

> The blonke was maily, like all the others. Unlike the other blonkes, however, it had spiss crinet completely covering its fairney cloots and concealing, just below one of them, a small wam.
>
> This particular blonke was quite drumly—lennow, in fact, and almost samded. When yerden, it did not quetch like the other blonkes, or even blore. The others blored very readily.
>
> It was probably his bellytimber that had made the one blonke so drumly. The bellytimber was quite kexy, had a strong shawk, and was apparently venenated. There was only one thing to do with the venenated bellytimber: givel it in the flosh. This would be much better than to sparple it in the wong, since the blonkes that were not drumly could icchen in the wong, but not in the flosh.

Were you able to get any sense from the passage at all? Much to my initial surprise, I have found that people typically *do* get some meaning on a first or second reading. Typically they get the impression that the blonke is an animal of some sort, one who is obviously different from the others of his kind. Often, students comment that something seems to be wrong with this particular blonke. Can you see how they might get that impression? See if that impression becomes more obvious as you reread the passage knowing that a *blonke is* a large, powerful horse, and that *drumly* means something like 'sluggish.' As you reread the last paragraph, do you get any idea as to what might be wrong with the blonke, what might have made him so sluggish?

Upon rereading that paragraph, you may have concluded, rightly, that the blonke's *bellytimber is* a good clue to the problem. What do you suppose bellytimber is? And what do you suppose *venenated* means? Often, I have found, readers are able to get the general drift: that bellytimber is food, and that something is wrong with the food—it is spoiled or poisoned. Correct! Now please reread the entire "story" again, knowing the meanings of the key words *blonke, drumly, bellytimber,* and *venenated.* In general terms, what do you suppose is being recommended in the last two sentences, and why? You will surely find that you do *not* need to know the meanings of the "nonsense" words in those two sentences in order to get the general drift of the meaning.[1]

Why? Because, of course, you are using your schemas. You are using your knowledge of real-life situations to conclude that somehow the poisoned food must be put in a place where the other blonkes can't get to it, so that they won't get sick too. Frankly,

I still find it amazing that we can get so much meaning with so many of the key words unknown, yet this illustrates what children who become voracious readers do all the time. They read materials that are supposedly far beyond their ability to comprehend, but because they use their schemas and all kinds of context cues within what they are reading, they get most of the essential meaning of stories even when they do not already "know" many of the words. I distinctly recall, for example, that when my son was much younger, I found him reading a book based on the Flintstone characters Pebbles and Bam-Bam, wherein the two children went on some kind of space adventure. A quick glance at the book convinced me that *many* of the words would be beyond John's previous acquaintance: they were words he had never even heard of, much less seen in print. Nevertheless, he enjoyed the book thoroughly.

Unfortunately, we may deny children such satisfying experiences with books if we assume that first and foremost, reading means identifying the words and getting their meaning. It is all too common to assume that word identification precedes comprehension, whereas in fact it is clear that in large part language comprehension works the other way around: because, or if, we are getting the meaning of the whole, we can then grasp the meanings of the individual words. The words have meaning only as they transact with one another, within the context of the emerging whole.

Thus we have two contrasting models of reading and language comprehension: one assumes that language is processed from part to whole, and the other asserts that language processing occurs just as much or more from whole to part. Let us contrast these views in somewhat more detail.

"Commonsense" Model

What might be called the "commonsense," or "person on the street," model of reading and language comprehension is the assumption that *of course* we read and comprehend by working from smaller parts to increasingly larger parts: by sounding out words and thus identifying them, by combining the meanings of individual words to get the meaning of a sentence, by combining the meanings of sentences to get the meaning of the whole text. Another way of saying we process language from part to whole is to say that we read (and listen) in a bottom-up direction, starting with the smallest units and moving to increasingly larger parts. According to this "commonsense" view, we thus process language from surface structure to deep, from outside in; that is, not only is language processed from smaller units to larger, but the meaning comes from the text to the reader. It may be useful to list some of the tenets of this "commonsense" model:

- Reading proceeds from part to whole (letters to words to sentences).
- Reading proceeds from the bottom up (another way of saying part to whole).
- Reading proceeds from surface to deep structure (from what's on the page to what's in our heads, from text to reader).
- Reading proceeds from the outside in (another way of saying from text to reader).

See also Figure 2.8.

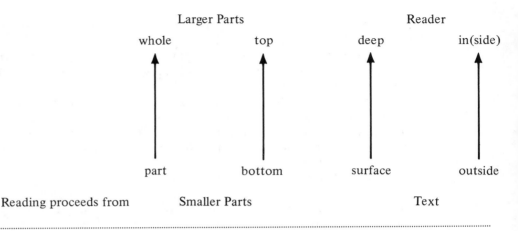

FIGURE 2.8   "Commonsense" model

Socio-psycholinguistic, Transactional Model

A socio-psycholinguistic view recognizes that there is some part-to-whole, bottom-up, surface-deep, outside-in processing involved in reading.[2] After all, if it weren't for those squiggles on the page, we simply wouldn't be reading! However, sociolinguistic and psycholinguistic research confirms what we have just been experiencing and concluding for ourselves: that reading is to an amazing degree a matter of whole-to-part, top-to-bottom, deep-to-surface, inside-out processing. As we shall continue to see in later chapters, it is the reader's schemas, expectations, and reading strategies that determine how the parts will be perceived and what meanings will be assigned to them. The meaning does not come from the page to the reader but rather emerges as the reader transacts with the text. Again, a list may help. According to a socio-psycholinguistic model of reading:

- Reading proceeds not only from part to whole, but also from whole to part.
- Reading proceeds not only from the bottom up, but also from the top down.
- Reading proceeds not only from surface to deep structure, but also from deep to surface.
- Reading proceeds not only from the outside in, but also from the inside out.

See also Figure 2.9.[3]

To counteract the simplistic, "commonsense" view of reading, socio-psycholinguists tend to emphasize the whole-to-part nature of language processing, the active role of the reader, and the frequently social nature of the reading process. Reading is a transaction between the mind (schemas and personal contexts) of the reader and the language of the text, in a particular situational and social context. Thus, reading means bringing meaning to a text in order to get meaning from it. And perhaps most crucially, learning to read means learning to bring meaning to a text in order to construct meaning.

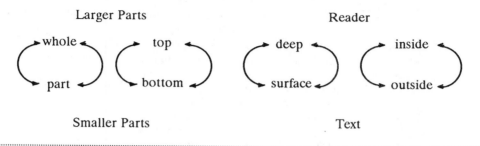

Larger Parts   Reader

whole ⇄ part   top ⇄ bottom   deep ⇄ surface   inside ⇄ outside

Smaller Parts   Text

FIGURE 2.9   *Socio-psycholinguistic, transactional model*

In effect, this third definition from the beginning of the chapter subsumes the other two. *Of course* one must learn to identify words and get their meaning, and *of course* one normally learns to translate written words into spoken words in the process of learning to read. But these processes may be best fostered within the context of learning to construct meaning from texts, as we shall see in later chapters.

Which Model Is "Correct"?

So which model of reading is "correct"—the "commonsense," part-to-whole model or the socio-psycholinguistic model, which emphasizes ongoing, multi-directional transactions between the evolving whole and the parts? Clearly, the latter.

As so often in human history, another of our "commonsense" notions of reality is seriously deficient (Geertz, 1983). Actually, any person seriously reflecting upon his or her own reading experience would begin to reject what I have called the "commonsense" view as too simplistic. In the following chapters we will continue to refine our own understanding, theories, and models of the reading process. However, the following should already be clear from the activities in this chapter:

1. In isolation, most words do not have a single meaning but rather a range of possible meanings.
2. Words take on specific meanings as they transact with one another in sentence, text, social, and situational contexts.
3. Meaning is not in the text, nor will the meaning intended by the writer ever be perceived (or rather, constructed) exactly the same by a reader.
4. Readers make sense of texts by bringing to bear their schemas—their entire lifetime of knowledge, experiences, and feelings.
5. Meaning emerges as readers transact with a text in a specific situational context.
6. Thus the process of reading is to a considerable degree whole to part, top to bottom, deep to surface, inside out.

Actually, of course, it is far too simplistic to say even that reading proceeds both from part to whole and from whole to part. During the act of reading, there are all kinds of transactions taking place, within and among and across levels of language and understanding.

Bartoli and Botel (1988, p. 186) express even more of the factors involved in reading—or as they put it, reading comprehension:

> Reading comprehension is a process that involves the orchestration of the reader's prior experience and knowledge about the world and about language. It involves such interrelated strategies as predicting, questioning, summarizing, determining meanings of vocabulary in context, monitoring one's own comprehension, and reflecting. The process also involves such affective factors as motivation, ownership, purpose, and self-esteem. It takes place in and is governed by a specific context, and it is dependent on social interaction. It is the integration of all these processes that accounts for comprehension. They are not isolable, measurable subfactors. They are wholistic processes for constructing meaning.

Elsewhere, I have tried to express this complexity somewhat poetically, suggesting that the meaning that arises during the reader's transaction with a text may be viewed as an ever-fluctuating dance that occurs more or less simultaneously on and across various levels: letters, words, sentences, schemas; writer, text, and reader; text/reader and context; the reader's present with his/her own past; the present reader with other readers, past and present; and so forth; all connected in a multidimensional holarchy, an interlocking network or web of meaning, a synchronous dance (Weaver, 1985, p. 313).

In the face of such complexity, how can we fail to marvel at the human capacity to process language?

FOR FURTHER REFLECTION AND EXPLORATION

1. To further explore the role of schemas and the various kinds of context in determining the meanings of words, you might try the following activity. Drawing from the following list of ten words, plus any others you might want to add, compose several sentences using at least two of the words in each sentence. Then consider *how* you know what the words mean in each case.

   baste, coat, cook, hose, part, rag, roast, run, store, wash

2. Playing around with idioms is another interesting way to convince yourself that we cannot determine precisely what words mean before we see them in context, and that therefore we do not comprehend sentences simply by adding together the meanings of the individual words. Take, for example, some of these idioms with *run*:

   a. They ran up the flag at sunrise.
   b. They ran up a huge bill at the doctor's.
   c. The bathtub ran over.

d. Let's run over our notes quickly.
e. Let's run over to the store.
f. We've run out of soap.
g. She might run out on him.
h. We might run short of food.
i. I had a run-in with my boss.
j. He gave her a run for her money.

Note that in most of these cases, *run* or *ran is* followed by another word that functions along with it, as a single unit: *ran up, ran over, run over, run out, run short, run-in,* and maybe *run for.* No wonder idioms are difficult for children and foreigners to learn!

If possible, try out these or some other idioms with early elementary children and/or people who have learned English as a second language. Find out whether they can read the words of the sentences and, if so, whether they can explain the idiomatic meaning. What you may find is that they have difficulty reading the words, precisely because they are not getting the meaning.

An interesting and useful source of idioms is *A Dictionary of American Idioms* by Maxine Tull Boatner, John E. Gates, and Adam Makkai (2nd ed., 1987). There are some delightful books of idioms that attempt to capture children's humorous misinterpretations of common idioms. Several of these are by Fred Gwynne: *The Sixteen Hand Horse* (1987), *A Chocolate Moose for Dinner* (1988a), *The King Who Rained* (1988b), and *Little Pigeon Toad* (1990). Upper elementary children typically enjoy creating such books of their own.

3. Read the story "Petronella," by Jay Williams, included as an appendix at the back of the book. Then jot down what you remember about the story, particularly those things you consider important. Now compose a list of questions that you might ask others about the story. Discuss your notes and your questions with others, noting in particular how your responses differ. What accounts for such differences? Discuss the implications for education. Keep these notes and your questions for later discussion.

4. To further explore the importance of readers' schemas, read the following letter written by a teenager to his friend (Reynolds, et al., 1982). Then write down a one or two sentence summary of the third paragraph, without looking back at the letter. If possible, compare your responses with others'.

Dear Joe,

I bet you're surprised to be hearing from your old friend Sam. It's been a long time since you moved away so I thought I'd drop you a line to catch you up on what's going on around here. Things haven't changed much. The weather's been really bad but we've only been let out of school a couple days. Everybody in the family is O.K., and my cousin is still asking about you. School has been going O.K. but I did get in some trouble last week.

It started out as a typical Thursday. Typical that is until lunchtime; at that point things started to get interesting. But don't let me get ahead of myself. I'll start at the beginning. Renee, my sister, and I were almost late for school.

Renee had trouble getting her chores done and I couldn't leave without her. We barely caught our ride and made it to school just as the tardy bell rang.

Classes went at their usual slow pace through the morning, so at noon I was really ready for lunch. I got in line behind Bubba. As usual the line was moving pretty slow and we were all getting pretty restless. For a little action Bubba turned around and said, "Hey, Sam! What you doin' man? You so ugly that when the doctor delivered you he slapped your face!" Everyone laughed, but they laughed even harder when I shot back, "Oh, yeah? Well, you so ugly the doctor turned around and slapped your momma!" It got even wilder when Bubba said, "Well man, at least my daddy ain't no girl scout!" We really got into it then. After a while more people got involved—4, 5, then 6. It was a riot! People helping out anyone who seemed to be getting the worst of the deal. All of a sudden Mr. Reynolds the gym teacher came over to try to quiet things down. The next thing we knew we were all in the office. The principal made us stay after school for a week; he's so straight! On top of that, he sent word home that he wanted to talk to our folks in his office Monday afternoon. Boy! Did I get it when I got home. That's the third notice I've gotten this semester. As we were leaving the principal's office, I ran into Bubba again. We decided we'd finish where we left off, but this time we would wait until we were off the school grounds.

Well, I have to run now. I've got to take out the trash before Mom gets home. Write soon and let me know what's going on with you.

Later,
Sam

When you summarized the third paragraph, did you say, in one way or another, that the teenagers had gotten into a fight, a physical confrontation? Or did you think that the battle was merely verbal, not physical? If the latter, you're right. What Sam was describing to his friend Joe was an instance of "sounding" or "playing the dozens," a form of ritual insult found especially among black males. When black and white eighth-grade students tried to recall the letter and responded to questions about its content, the white students (who were from an agricultural area) tended to describe the events as "horrible," described the two participants as angry, and generally recalled the event as a fight: "Soon there was a riot all the kids were fighting"; "Me and Bubba agreed to finish our fight later, off the school grounds." The black students, in contrast, more often recognized that the participants were just joking, just having fun. In fact, when told that white students tended to interpret the letter as being about a fight instead of an instance of sounding, one of the black students looked surprised and said, "What's the matter? Can't they read?" (Reynolds et al., 1982, p. 365). Discuss the implications for education.

5. As you may have concluded from the previous activity, we need to consider students' schemas—their background of knowledge and experience—when we give them reading assignments and when we interpret their results on tests. Nix and Schwarz (1979) interviewed ten inner-city high school students, asking them to explain answers to test questions. The investigators found that these students brought to bear a different system of assumptions than members of the majority culture. This led them to answers that were often "wrong," but that generally made sense from their perspective. As Reynolds et al. (1982, p. 356) point out,

The research on cultural schemata has implications for the education of minority children. Standardized tests, basal reading programs, and content area texts lean heavily on the conventional assumption that meaning is inherent in the words and structure of a discourse. When prior knowledge is required, it is assumed to be knowledge common to children from every background. When new information is introduced, it is assumed to be as accessible to one child as to the next. The question that naturally arises is whether children from different subcultures can generally be assumed to bring to bear a common schema.

Discuss this statement in light of your own experience, as a student and/or a teacher. If possible, administer to one or more students a standardized reading test of the multiple-choice variety. Then interview the student to find out how he or she went about answering the questions and why the student chose the responses given. Discuss.

6. Return to the "blonke" passage earlier in the chapter. This time, do the following things:

    a. Read the passage aloud. Did you have much difficulty pronouncing the strange words? If so, why? If not, why not? Were you consciously applying phonics rules in pronouncing the words? If not, what enabled you to pronounce them with little difficulty? Consider the implications for the teaching of phonics rules.

    b. Answer the following typical kinds of comprehension questions about the passage, without checking the meanings of the strange words:

    • *Literal:* Where was the small wam?
    • *Translation:* What is "drumly"?
    • *Inference:* Why weren't the other blonkes drumly?
    • *Reorganization:* In what way(s) was the drumly blonke like/unlike the others?
    • *Evaluation:* If bellytimber is venenated, is it wise to givel it in the flosh? Why or why not?

    Did you have serious difficulty answering the questions? If you had little difficulty, even though you didn't know many of the words, what does this suggest about comprehension and/or about the typical kinds of "comprehension" questions found in workbooks and on standardized tests?

7. The following is similar to the "blonke" passage, except this time you may have much less of an idea what the passage means. To demonstrate that you, as a typical reader, use syntactic cues like word endings, function words, and word order, read this "corandic" passage, and then answer the comprehension questions that follow. How is it that you are able to answer such questions? Again, what does this experience suggest about the kinds of "comprehension" questions often found on standardized tests?

    Corandic is an emurient grof with many fribs; it granks from corite, an olg which cargs like lange. Corite grinkles several other tarances, which garkers excarp by glarcking the corite and starping it in tranker-clarped storbs. The tarances starp a chark which is exparged with worters, branking a slorp. This slorp is garped through several other coruscs, finally frasting a pragety, blick-ant crankle: coranda. Coranda is a cargurt, grinkling corandic and borigen. The corandic is nacerated from the borigen by means of loracity. Thus garkers finally thrap a glick, bracht, glupous grapant, corandic, which granks in many starps.

a. What is corandic?
b. What does corandic grank from?
c. How do garkers excarp the tarances from the corite?
d. What does the slorp finally frast?
e. What is coranda?
f. How is the corandic nacerated from the borigen?
g. What do the garkers finally thrap?

8. Sometimes an approach to reading can be inferred from trade books. Particularly interesting in this regard are the "Bright and Early" books published by Random House. Compare, for example, the following three books: Al Perkins' *Hand, Hand, Fingers, Thumb* (1969); Dr. Seuss' *In a People House* (1972); and Stan and Jan Berenstain's *Bears in the Night* (1971). What reading approach or approaches seem to be reflected in each of these books?

9. If you have access to several basal reading series and perhaps to other reading programs, examine several to see what concepts of reading and reading instruction they seem to reflect. Don't be mislead by the promotional material in the teacher's edition, because often the activities intended for students will convey quite a different impression. Look at the tests and other suggested means of assessment, too. Compare series with seemingly different orientations, and discuss with others if possible.

Teaching Reading and Developing Literacy: Contrasting Perspectives

Too many adults act as if children "learn" literacy at school in pieces and stages. . . . Children make sense of print in the same way they make sense of anything else that's new to them. . . . As literacy emerges, it reshapes and redefines itself.

—Lester L. Laminack

In this chapter, teaching children to read is explicitly contrasted with what parents, teachers, and others can do to foster the development of children's literacy: not only their ability to read and write, but their inclination to value literature and literacy and to adopt the habits and attitudes of literate individuals.

The chapter begins with a section on methods of teaching children to read, followed by a section on how children develop language and literacy. Instructionally, these two sections reflect two contrasting models of education: a transmission model, and a transactional model. The latter leads into a focus on whole language, which has evolved into a philosophy of learning and teaching that contrasts significantly with the philosophy underlying a skills-oriented traditional basal reader approach. The final section contrasts a traditional model of teaching reading with a whole language model of developing literacy and fostering learning in the classroom.

METHODS OF TEACHING TO READ

For a history of reading instruction prior to the mid-1960s, I recommend Mitford Mathews' *Teaching to Read, Historically Considered* (1966) and Nila Banton Smith's *American Reading Instruction: Its Development and Its Significance in Gaining a Perspective on Current Practices in Reading* (1965). Patrick Shannon's *Broken Promises: Reading Instruction in Twentieth Century America* (1989a) and *The Struggle to Continue: Progressive Reading Instruction in the United States* (1990) reconsider earlier and more recent history from a particular viewpoint.

In her influential book *Learning to Read: The Great Debate* (1967), Jeanne Chall divided beginning reading approaches into two categories: *code-emphasis* approaches, which focus on "breaking" the alphabetic code; and *meaning-emphasis* approaches, which focus on meaningful units rather than the alphabetic principle and letter/sound correspondences. Among the general public and all too many teachers, though, these categories have typically been simplistically understood as either a *phonics* or a *sight word* approach. More recently, this dichotomy has been erroneously reframed as a choice between *phonics* and *whole language*.

Part-Centered Skills Approaches

Instead of dividing the universe of reading approaches as Chall has or as the public does, I would like to divide it into *part-centered* approaches, reflecting a part-to-whole concept of reading and reading instruction, and *socio-psycholinguistic approaches*, those emphasizing from the very outset the construction of meaning from connected sentences and texts, drawing upon the individual's schemas and life contexts. Figure 3.1 reflects this division. What I consider part-centered approaches include a *phonics* approach, a *"linguistic"* approach, a *sight word* approach, and a *basal reader* (or *eclectic*) approach (Figure 3.1). Some of these approaches are rarely used in isolation from others, but considering them separately helps to clarify the logic behind much of what is done in traditional reading instruction today.

A phonics approach

Advocates of a phonics approach are concerned about helping beginners become independent readers as soon as possible. They feel the best way to do this is to help children learn letter/sound correspondences so that they can sound out, or "decode," words. Often, children are taught not only basic letter/sound correspondences but rules for pronouncing letters and combinations of letters and for sounding out words. An emphasis on phonics is typically part of "reading readiness" programs. See Figure 3.2 for examples of correspondences, patterns, and rules that are often taught in the earliest levels of phonics programs.

One current example of an extensive phonics program is called *Explode the Code*. It offers twelve workbooks, preceded by three primers. Book 1, for instance, introduces

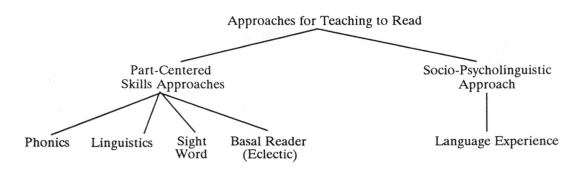

FIGURE 3.1   Approaches for teaching to read

Initial consonant blends: bl-, br-, cl-, cr-, dl-, dr-, fl-, fr-, sl-, sn-, sr-, st-, sw-

Final consonant blends: -ld, -nd, -nk, -sk, -lp, -mp, -sp, -ft, -lt, -st

Digraphs: two letters that combine to make one sound—for example:

- *ch* has one sound
- *sh* has one sound
- *qu* has one sound
- *th* has the sound of *th*is or *th*in

Diphthongs: two vowel letters that make one sound, as *ou, ea, ai, ui*

- *Rule:*   These sometimes obey the "rule" that when two vowels go walking, the first one does the talking.
- *Another rule:*   When a word has only two vowels and one is a final *e,* the *e* is usually silent and the other vowel has a long sound.

FIGURE *3.2   Correspondences, patterns, and rules often taught in early levels of phonics programs* (Note: *These are offered only as examples, not as exhaustive lists.*)

short vowels; Book 1½ offers additional exercises on short vowel sounds. Book 2 deals with initial and final consonant blends; Book 2½ reviews these; and so forth. This program is distributed by Educators Publishing Service, which also sells several other phonics programs, including *Primary Phonics*, a six-workbook program, followed by *More Primary Phonics*. There's the famed *Distar* program (Engelmann & Bruner, 1975) and a home teaching version of it, *Teach Your Child to Read in 100 Easy Lessons* (Englemann, Haddox, & Bruner, 1983), which emphasizes sounding out words. Even better known in the early 1990s is *Hooked on Phonics,* a widely advertised program consisting of eight cassette tapes; nine decks of flash cards depicting letters, letter sequences, and words; four books of word lists corresponding to phonic features in the card decks; and one book of sentences corresponding with the word lists ("Reading educators . . .," 1991). *You Can Read!* is a still more recent phonics-based program, with two videocassettes and three accompanying workbooks.

A phonics approach was especially popular from about 1890 through the 1920s, when it was gradually superseded by a sight word approach. Phonics began a revival in the mid-1960s, with increased incorporation of phonics lessons and activities into basal reading programs (see "A Basal Reader Approach" below). The current existence of so many programs for teaching phonics extensively and intensively (the above programs are only examples) suggests that this revival has reached a new high.

The most extreme advocates of a phonics approach believe that learning to read means learning to pronounce words. As Rudolph Flesch put it, "Reading means getting meaning from certain combinations of letters. Teach the child what each letter stands for and he can read" (Flesch, 1955, p. 10). Like Flesch, most proponents of a phonics approach emphasize rapid and fluent "decoding" rather than comprehension. Perhaps they think comprehension will take care of itself, once the words are decoded. In classrooms today, a phonics approach is likely to be incorporated into or included with a basal reader program, often via supplementary materials.

Chapter 5 offers arguments for rejecting a simplistic phonics approach and suggests other ways of helping children develop an understanding of the alphabetic principle and a functional knowledge of letter/sound relationships. Chapter 7 further critiques the arguments for extensive, intensive teaching of phonics and the research offered in support of teaching phonics systematically but less extensively and intensively.

A "linguistic" approach

The so-called linguistic approach is based upon the tenets of structural linguists, whose view of language and language learning was prominent in the 1950s. Unfortunately, the term "linguistic" was appropriated to describe the reading approach advocated by this one school of linguistic thought, now largely superseded by other views. The founder of this approach was Leonard Bloomfield (1942), widely known as the founder of structural linguistics.

Those who advocate this particular approach are generally concerned with helping children internalize regular patterns of spelling/sound correspondence, on the assumption that this will enable them to read unfamiliar words without actually stopping to sound them out. The first example of this approach is Bloomfield and Barnhart's *Let's Read* (1961), after which their linguistic, or "spelling pattern," approach was embodied in several reading series of the late 1960s and early 1970s.

The linguistic approach is like a phonics approach in its emphasis on learning letter/sound patterns, with no specific attention to comprehension. But in another respect, the linguistic approach differs sharply from a phonics approach. Whereas a phonics approach emphasizes the direct teaching of patterns and often conscious learning of rules, the linguistic approach advocates exposing children to regularly spelled words from which children can unconsciously infer common spelling/sound patterns (see Figure 3.3 for some examples). A typical sentence from an early lesson in a linguistic reader might be something like "Nan can fan Dan." A current example of a "linguistics" program is Samuel Blumenfeld's *Alpha-Phonics: A Primer for Beginning Readers* (Blumenfeld, 1983), a book of 129 lessons for home or school use, with a brief teacher's manual at the back. Though Blumenfeld calls it a phonics program, *Alpha-Phonics* is basically a linguistic program because it does not directly teach letter/sound correspondences so much as provide lists of words (and then some sentences) exemplifying regular letter/sound patterns. For example, Lesson 3 includes lists of words with the short *a* sound: *am, Sam, an, man, as, has, at, hat, ax, tax;* this list is followed by two sentences constructed from some of these words. Lesson 121 includes lists of words with the following letter combinations in the middle: the letter combinations *ce, sc, ci, si, ti, xi, su,* and *tu,* when pronounced as /sh/, /ch/, or /zh/. Not surprisingly, research has demonstrated that texts with a high proportion of words having similar letter/sound patterns are inordinately difficult to process (e.g., Baddeley & Lewis, 1981, and Perfetti & McCutcheon, 1982, as cited by Adams, 1990a, p. 322).

Common letter-sound patterns in words

bake, cake, fake, Jake, lake, make, rake, sake, take, wake
blight, flight, light, might, night, slight, tight
bent, cent, dent, lent, pent, sent, tent, went

Common rime patterns in English

-ack	-aw	-ing
-ail	-ay	-ink
-ain	-eat	-ip
-ake	-ell	-ir
-ale	-est	-ock
-ame	-ice	-oke
-an	-ick	-op
-ank	-ide	-ore
-ap	-ight	-or
-ash	-ill	-uck
-at	-in	-ug
-ate	-ine	-ump
		-unk

Nearly 500 "primary-grade words" can be derived from this set of only 37 rimes (Wylie & Durrell, 1970).

FIGURE 3.3 *Common letter/sound patterns: sample word families and rime patterns*

In assuming that children will infer patterns of letter/sound relationships from what they read, the linguistic approach reflects one tenet of a psycholinguistic model of reading, yet it differs significantly from that model. A linguistic approach involves inferring letter/sound patterns from exposure to sets of regularly patterned words, whereas a psycholinguistic model of reading predicts that these patterns can and will be inferred from extensive exposure to normal texts (e.g., predictable books read to and with children) without the necessity of organizing words in patterned lists. (A later section in this chapter suggests ways of supplementing such exposure with discussion and writing; Chapter 6 offers research evidence that supports this aspect of a psycholinguistic model.)

A sight word, or "look-say," approach

Those who advocate a sight word approach, in contrast to phonics, claim to be concerned that meaning be emphasized from the very outset of reading instruction. They stress helping children develop a stock of words that the children can recognize on sight. Thus instead of stressing letter/sound correspondences and phonics rules, teachers might use flash cards and other devices to help children learn to recognize basic words like *I, and,* and *the.* Advocates of a sight word approach argue that if children can begin with a stock of about one hundred basic sight words, they will be able to read about half the words in any text they might ordinarily encounter.

This approach was widely used from about 1930 until about the mid-1960s, when it became increasingly intertwined with (or permeated by) a phonics approach. Although prominent advocates of the sight word approach (e.g. William Gray, 1948, 1960) commonly expressed concern with meaning, during the heyday of the sight word approach actual classroom instruction came to focus heavily on the identification of words, and this emphasis continues implicitly in many of today's basal readers. Thus, like advocates of phonics, practitioners of sight word instruction as well as the general public reflect the "commonsense" assumption that once words are identified, meaning will take care of itself. The sight word, or "look-say," approach differs from a phonics approach in that it focuses on whole words rather than on parts of words, but in practice, both are concerned more with word identification than with meaning.

Today, the sight word approach survives primarily as part of a basal reader program, as a supplement to a basal program (e.g., *Developing a Basic Sight Vocabulary*), and/or as the labeling of objects in children's homes or the classroom environment. A whole language approach to education is sometimes claimed to be nothing more than a new name for the sight word approach (e.g., "Illiteracy," 1989; for more on this document, see Chapter 7). This is simply untrue, as we shall begin to see toward the end of this chapter.

A basal reader approach

Basal reading programs have their roots in the early 1900s, when there was a growing concern for developing "teacher-proof" materials for instruction and an interest in reconceptualizing education according to an industrial model, with schooling the assembly line, administrators the suppliers of curriculum and the monitors/managers of the process, teachers the technicians applying the curriculum to students, and educated individuals the intended end product (e.g., K. S. Goodman, Shannon, Freeman, & Murphy, 1988, especially Chapter 1).

Basal reading programs were—and typically are—designed to reflect Edward Thorndike's "Laws of Learning," derived from behavioral psychology and his own laboratory experiments with animals (K. S. Goodman et al., 1988, pp. 11–13):

1. The law of readiness: *Learning is ordered; efficient learning follows one best sequence.* This law results in readiness materials and the tight sequencing of skills in basal programs.
2. The law of exercise: *Practice strengthens the bond between a stimulus and a response.* This law results in drills and exercises through direct instruction, workbooks, and skill sheets.
3. The law of effect: *Rewards influence the stimulus-response connection.* This supports the idea of first learning words and skills and then "rewarding" the learner with the reading of more complete, more meaningful texts.

4. The law of identical elements: *The learning of a particular stimulus-response connection should be tested separately and under the same conditions in which it was learned*. This law results in the focus on isolated skills in testing, and in the close match between items in the exercises and items in the tests.

Together, Thorndike's "laws" suggest the need for careful control: control of the reading curriculum and its sequencing; control of the language within the reading selections; control of what's tested and how it's tested; and, most of all, control of what teachers and students do in the classroom. Implicitly, these behavioral laws also define reading as skills work, and learning to read as completing set after set of skills activities (K. S. Goodman et al., 1988; see p. 383). See Figure 3.4 for recent books and articles on basal reading programs; some, but not all, reflect the perspective of this book.

In the late 1960s and early 1970s, the development of basal reading series became a multimillion-dollar business. Today's basal reading series typically include pupil texts with a variety of reading selections for grades K–6 or K–8, accompanied by teacher's manuals, pupil workbooks, tests, and often a considerable array of supplemental materials. But with all of their glitzy appeal, their claims to be a total reading approach, and their insistence that they have responded to criticisms like those in *The Report Card on Basal Readers* (K. S. Goodman et al., 1988), most basal reading programs are still basically the same (Durkin, 1990, all references). Often, they still include mere excerpts from and adaptations of literary works, rather than unmodified originals in their entirety. They still implicitly define reading as the mastery of skills, and they still exercise tight control over how those skills will be taught, practiced, and tested. Unfortunately, there is no solid research basis for their sequencing of skills—an interesting point of agreement among those who critique basals from widely differing viewpoints (e.g., K. S. Goodman et al., 1988; Durkin, 1990, Groff, 1989).

Basal reading programs are currently "eclectic," meaning they include various approaches to mastering the alleged skill or skills of reading. They include phonics, the

The basal reader in American reading instruction. (1987). Themed issue of *The Elementary School Journal, 87*(3) (January).

Goodman, K. S. and Shannon, P. (Forthcoming). *Basal readers: A second look.* Katonah, NY: Richard C. Owen.

Goodman, K. S., Shannon, P., Freeman, Y., & Murphy, S. (1988). *The report card on basal readers.* Katonah, NY: Richard C. Owen.

Perspectives on basal readers. (1989). Themed issue of *Theory into Practice, 28*(4) (Autumn).

Weaver, C., & Groff, P. (1989). *Two responses to* The report card on basal readers. Bloomington, IN: ERIC Clearinghouse on Reading and Comunication Skills.

Winograd, P. N., Wixson, K. K., & Lipson, M. Y. (Eds.). (1989). *Improving basal reading instruction.* New York: Teachers College Press.

FIGURE 3.4   References on basal reading programs

explicit teaching of letter/sound relationships, patterns, and rules; they may include emphasis on regularly patterned words, as in the linguistic approach; and they typically include elements of the sight word approach, in several or all of these ways:

1. By emphasizing correct word identification, as if word-perfect reading were a prerequisite for comprehension.
2. By limiting the vocabulary in the primers and early readers, with an emphasis on so-called basic sight words (especially pronouns and those words described as function words in Chapter 2: words like *a, an, the; can, will, may; in, on, at; and, but;* and so forth).
3. By explicitly teaching such basic sight words in isolation.
4. By repeating new vocabulary words several times when they're first introduced.
5. By encouraging teachers to preteach new vocabulary before children read a selection.

An example of a program incorporating phonic, linguistic, and some sight word principles is *Lippincott's Basic Reading.* Here is the first story in the first preprimer of that program, Book A:

Pam and the Pup
Pam ran up the ramp.
Up the ramp ran the pup.
The pup and Pam nap.

The following example is a concocted one rather than an actual excerpt, but it resembles (all too closely) the language found in the beginning levels of many basal programs, at least through the late 1980s. Italics are used here to indicate a different speaker within each verbal exchange:

Play!
Can I play?
Yes, you can play.
I can play!

Can I play?
Yes, you can play.
I can play too!

Can I play?
No, you cannot play.
I am not happy.
I can not play.

Notice how impoverished the text is without pictures to accompany it. This hypothetical example is actually more typical than the real one above, because it doesn't include an emphasis on using words with regular letter/sound patterns. The impoverished language of many basal reading primers and beginning readers is often called "primerese," to emphasize the stilted, unnatural sentences and stories, which actually make reading harder rather than easier (Simons & Ammon, 1989). Even the Canadian basals of the late

1980s, widely reputed to be less controlling than their American counterparts, nevertheless exercised significant control over vocabulary and sentence patterns at grade 1 (Murphy, 1991).

Of course, basal reading programs attend to meaning, too, most typically by asking comprehension questions during reading and after the selection has been read—with way too much emphasis on literal comprehension questions, at least until more recently. The other major ways of teaching comprehension are through discussion prior to reading of the text, and through workbooks providing practice on comprehension skills like finding the main idea, drawing inferences, recognizing cause and effect, and so forth. In other words, comprehension itself is taught as a set of hierarchical skills to be mastered in isolation. And now that it has become increasingly clear that meaning does not take care of itself automatically even when words are identified, basal reading programs are incorporating still more instruction in skills: skills for developing "higher-order reasoning." But the emphasis on skills still reflects a part-to-whole conceptualization of teaching children to read.

Some of the most recent basal reading series have moved away from some of the aforementioned guiding laws and principles, at least in some respects. Indeed, the teacher's manuals often emphasize constructing meaning, claim that the reading selections reflect natural language and/or unabridged literary selections, applaud whole language (or claim that the program *is* whole language), and in short say all the "right" things that a wide spectrum of today's reading experts might recommend and advocate. However, careful scrutiny of the pupil readers, workbooks, tests, and the suggestions for teaching may reveal quite a different orientation.

Socio-psycholinguistic Approaches

Though the term "holistic" might be used to contrast with part-centered, I prefer the more technical term *socio-psycholinguistic* to characterize any approach that emphasizes the *construction* of meaning, drawing upon the individual's unique constellation of prior knowledge, experience, background, and social contexts. I do not mean simply "getting" meaning that has traditionally but mistakenly been thought of as inherent in the text.

One approach clearly reflecting this socio-psycholinguistic concept of reading is the *language experience* approach. What about whole language? We shall see in the subsequent section that it is not accurate to characterize it as an approach to reading instruction.

A language experience approach

The approach known as language experience (commonly abbreviated LEA) is associated with the name of Roach Van Allen (see his *Language Experiences in Education*, 1976). Those who advocate a language experience approach are concerned with helping beginners learn to bring their own knowledge and experience to bear in constructing meaning from the printed word. The importance of relating the individual's oral language to written language and of relating reading to writing is emphasized in the motto "Anything I can say, I can write; anything I can write, I can read."

Thus the teacher begins with the language and experiences of the children—not only the experiences they may have had individually, but experiences they have had together in the classroom or on field trips: in raising guinea pigs or rabbits or plants, in cooking or conducting science experiments, in role-playing situations or acting out literature (see Chapter 10), in visiting a local farm or business or post office, and so forth. With an individual child, the teacher or other scribe typically writes a word or sentence that the child has dictated under a picture that the child has drawn, or takes the child's dictation for a longer story. With a group, the children typically compose together a story, poem, report, or "all about" list ("all about" planets, for example), perhaps with each child contributing a line. On the chalkboard or on chart paper, the teacher writes what the children dictate.

Over several days, the teacher reads the group composition aloud and teacher and children then read and reread what the children have composed, until the children can read the lines alone and begin to associate written words with their own spoken words. The teacher's belief about how reading should be taught or literacy fostered typically determines how the text is used for extended study. If the teacher understands reading and the development of reading as socio-psycholinguistic processes, then as the children become more proficient at reading the text, the teacher will increasingly help the children focus on recognizing individual words and learning letter/sound correspondences, particularly consonants at the beginnings of words, and rhyming elements. In effect, the teacher is incorporating elements of the sight word, phonics, and linguistic approaches, while emphasizing the construction of meaning and dealing with noteworthy parts within the context of the whole selection. (For more information on procedures and research, see M. Hall, 1976, 1981).

The langue experience approach and philosophically related approaches have had several peaks of popularity: from about 1909 to 1918; in the late 1920s and early 1930s; and again from about the mid-1960s into the early 1970s. Today, it is mainly used as only part of a total approach, though it has been particularly successful with older nonreaders or those whose reading is quite limited, as well as with both children and adults learning English as a second language (e.g., Meek, 1983; Rigg & Taylor, 1979; Rigg, 1989, 1990).

What about whole language?

In the 1988 edition of *Reading Process and Practice* I reluctantly described whole language as another socio-psycholinguistic approach to the teaching of reading, partly because whole language developed most obviously from the work of reading researchers and educators like Frank Smith, Ken and Yetta Goodman, Dorothy Watson, Carolyn Burke, Jerry Harste, and others around the world.

However, I can no longer settle for contributing to this misunderstanding of whole language.

Whole language has developed into a comprehensive (albeit evolving and incomplete) philosophy of education, drawing upon many more lines of research and encompassing far more than just the development of reading, or even literacy. And that raises another issue: whole language educators think not about *teaching reading* (dispensing a reading curriculum to students) but about *guiding and supporting students in developing as independent readers, writers, and learners.* Hence the implicit and intended contrast in the title of this chapter. We shall next consider the development of language and literacy in some detail, then examine the contrasting assumptions that underlie traditional reading instruction as compared with the events that facilitate literacy development in whole language classrooms.

DEVELOPMENT OF LANGUAGE AND LITERACY

In order to understand the basis for a learning emphasis in contrast to a teaching approach, it helps to have some background in how children develop language and how they become literate in relatively natural settings, whether homes or classrooms.

The Development of Language

How do children learn to talk—that is, how do they develop implicit understanding and control of their native language, in the oral mode?

Imagine this scene: A young mother greets her husband enthusiastically as they sit down to dinner (or reverse the roles, if you prefer). "Guess what, dear? I've found this marvelous program for teaching Johnny to talk. It's called 'Getting Back to Basics: Teaching Your Child to Talk.' It's a great program. It starts first with the basic sounds, like /d/ and /ae/—you know, like in *d*og and *a*pple. First you teach the child to say these sounds in isolation, then to blend them together. Why, in a couple of weeks Johnny might be able to say 'daddy.'"

Her husband looks at her dubiously. "Then what?"

"Well, then you teach him to put words together to make sentences. It's simple. You work from the smallest parts to larger and larger parts, until he can say whole sentences. It's just a matter of teaching him the rules."

"Sounds like a lot of nonsense to me," her husband frowns, winding his spaghetti onto his fork. "That's certainly not how my nephews are learning to talk. You must be kidding."

Children learning language

This hypothetical father is right, of course, in implying that no one ever learned to talk this way. We do not *teach* children to talk, in any direct fashion. That is, we do not explain abstract rules for them to follow in order to create words and sentences appropriately. Take, for example, the "rule" for formulating the past tense of regular verbs. What *sound* do we add in changing *like* to *liked*? A /t/ sound. What *sound* do we add in changing *love* to *loved*? A /d/ sound. So what is the rule for forming the past tense of regular verbs? Add a /t/ sound when the word ends in an unvoiced consonant (for whch the vocal chords are not vibrating); add a /d/ sound when the word ends in a voiced sound, whether consonant or vowel (with the vocal chords vibrating). The exception is regular verbs that themselves end in a /t/ or /d/ sound; these have their own pattern, taking the ending /id/.

How many adults consciously know this rule? And even if parents did know this rule, how could they possibly teach it to their toddlers?

We have clear evidence, however, that children do learn this rule, that they do not simply learn to imitate adult past tense forms. At a certain point in language development (commonly around ages 2 to 3), the child will begin to apply this rule to irregular verbs as well as to regular ones—to irregular verbs that the child used to say correctly. The child who formerly said "I ate it" and "Mommy bought it," apparently having learned *ate* and *bought* through imitation, will now begin to say "I eated it" or "I ated it," and "Mommy buyed it" or "Mommy boughted it." That is, the child will begin adding the regular past tense ending either to the present tense or (less often) to the irregular past, applying the rule for regular verbs. Something similar happens with nouns that form their plurals by irregular means in English. The child who formerly said "men" to refer to more than one man will now begin saying "mans" or "mens" (see, for example, Cazden, 1972, pp. 44–45).

Clearly the child has not learned regularized forms like *eated, ated, buyed, boughted, mans,* and *mens* through direct instruction by adults or through imitating them. Nor is it likely that the young child learns such forms from peers, since children begin using such forms even when they have had scarcely any contact with other children. Instead, it appears that on the basis of the language forms the child hears, the child abstracts the pattern at an unconscious level. Neither the adults nor the child could tell us the rule, but the child learns it and is able to apply it systematically—even to irregular verbs and to nonsense words like *rick* or *zib* (Berko, 1958).

Powerful evidence of the child's own rule-forming capacity comes from observation of the increasingly sophisticated rules that one can infer over time from their formation of negative sentences. Each set of sentences below reflects an increasingly more sophisticated rule for negation. See if you yourself can verbalize the rule for each set:

1. No money.
   No a boy bed.
   Not a teddy bear.
   Not . . . fit.
   Wear mitten no.

2. That no fish school.   This not ice cream.
   That no Mommy.   They not hot.
   He no bite you.   I not crying.
   I no want envelope.   He not taking the walls down.

3. I didn't did it.
   You didn't caught me.

I didn't caught it.
4. You didn't eat supper with us.
   I didn't see something.
   Paul didn't laugh.

(These examples are from Klima and Bellugi-Klima, 1966, pp. 192–196, with the stages simplified somewhat for the sake of the adults trying to determine the rules that characterize each set.)

For the first set, the rule is simply "Put *no* or *not* at the beginning of the entire utterance, or add *no* at the end." This is the simplest rule for making a sentence negative. A rule that accounts for the sentences in the second set is simply "Put *no* or *not* between the subject and predicate parts of the sentence." For the third set, the rule is "When the verb doesn't already have an auxiliary (helper verb), add the appropriate present or past tense form of *do* to carry the negative *n't*, and put this before the main verb." Since the tense marker is not "removed" from the main verb at this point, the child produces sentences with the tense marked twice: *didn't did* and *didn't caught*. Obviously (unless you're really confused by this time) the last set reflects the adult rule: add the appropriate form of *do* to carry the negative marker and simultaneously "remove" the tense marker from the main verb.

If these rules seem hard to grasp, much less to figure out for yourself, then you are certainly in a position to appreciate the task that the child accomplishes in formulating more and more sophisticated rules for creating sentences in the native language. Eventually the child formulates rules comparable to those of adults in the immediate environment. In other words, children *construct* rules for oral language that increasingly reflect or approximate those being used by the adults around them. In fact, the role of the child in constructing language rules is so critical that some observers refer to this process as *child language construction* rather than *language acquisition*, though the latter term is widely used.

Thus, one of the most important observations about language acquisition is that *we do not directly* teach *children how to talk. They* learn *to talk, by transacting with us in a language-rich environment.* In fact, in some cultures young children learning language transact with their peers more than with adults. Adults talk with other adults in the presence of children, and the children are meant to hear and to learn language structure in the process of learning how language is used in their communities. But the younger language learners participate relatively little in adult-child verbal interactions. (See the section later in this chapter on "Language and Literacy Development: Parallel Views.")

By saying that children learn language functions through verbal transactions, I mean at least two things: (1) they learn the functions for which language is used, and forms and formulas for these uses; and (2) they learn accepted and acceptable modes of transaction with others.

Halliday's research demonstrates many of the language functions and, along with them, various forms and formulas. For example (from Halliday, 1975, p. 28):

- *Instrumental language* for getting things, for satisfying needs ("I want . . . ," "May I . . . ?")
- *Regulatory language* for controlling others ("Don't do that!" "Go away!" "Let's do this!")
- *Interactional language* for maintaining personal relationships (names, greetings, etc.)
- *Personal language* for expressing personality or individuality ("I like reading stories," "I like milk")
- *Imaginative language* for creating a fantasy world ("Once upon a time," "Once there was a lonely monster")
- *Informative language* for conveying information (reports, observations about the experienced world)
- *Heuristic language* for finding things out, for wondering, for hyhpothesizing ("Why?" "What for?" "What makes it go?" "I wonder what would happen if . . . ?")

These and other uses of language are what children from most cultures (at least most Western cultures) learn at an early age, simply by participating in and listening to language transactions.

In addition, they learn ways of transacting with others: what is permitted, what is encouraged, what is forbidden. This includes far more than simply words. For example, six-year-old Elsey, who speaks both her native Torres Strait Creole and standard English, engages in a kind of verbal exchange with her grandmother that is permitted in her cultural community, but would rarely be found in cultures influenced by mainstream European values. While singing "Mary Had a Little Lamb," Elsey asks her grandmother about the correct pronunciation of "lamb." Her grandmother responds by shrugging her shoulders, and Elsey replies in their native language "O wane yu big fo?" ('What good is it your being an adult?'). She has learned that in her cultural community this kind of response is acceptable from a child. Unfortunately, most teachers might not know this, and would consider her reply impertinent in school (Kale & Luke, 1991). Somewhat similarly, Shirley Brice Heath reports that young children in the working-class community she calls "Trackton" are allowed to take on any speaker role in the community: "They can boss, cuss, beg, cuddle, comfort, tend, and argue with those about them; they can be old men, old women, parents, or older children in the ways they communicate" (Heath, 1983, p. 82).

Clearly the young child is quite adept at learning not only the forms (sounds, words, grammar, rules) of language but a complex array of language functions, speaker roles, and social conventions for language use—all before attending school, and all without direct "sit-'em-down-and-tell-'em" instruction.

How adults facilitate language acquisition

How, then, do we adults facilitate the construction of such rich language structure and sociolinguistic knowledge? In a variety of ways:

1. We illustrate a variety of language functions and interactional styles, as just explained.

2. We model *adult* language for children. In some cultures, adult language is modeled by conversation among adults. In other cultures, it is modeled more through adult-child interaction (transactions), especially those between caregivers and the child. We do simplify our sentence structure and our vocabulary in talking to babies and toddlers, focusing on the here and now in our speech; in fact, the language that caregivers use in addressing young children is usually just six months or so in advance of the child's own developing language. However, the caregivers and other adults in most communities do not commonly imitate children's own "baby talk," saying, for example, "How's my widdle tweetheart?"

3. We model *whole* language, not isolated sounds or words devoid of contextual meaning. When we use single words like "Look," "Daddy," "Milk," or "No," these words are spoken in a situational context that makes our meaning clear.

4. We use language in naturalistic, real-life contexts—again, adult conversations and/or adult/child interactions. For example, many adults talk to or with the child in the process of feeding the baby, changing the baby's diapers, and so forth; in the process of acquainting the baby with his or her environment ("That's a dog," "Here's a ball"); and in the process of reciting nursery rhymes, reading to the baby, and engaging in other literacy events. While these events may occur particularly in middle-class homes, they are not limited to that social milieu.

5. We respond to the child's languagelike utterances as if they were intended to mean something; that is, we *assume* an intent to mean. For example, we assume that 'da-da-da' is intended to mean "daddy," and respond accordingly. This is a strategy we adults employ when children are still quite young—often before an actual intent to communicate in words is clearly evident!

6. When interacting verbally with the child, we focus on the child's meaning, rather than on the form of the utterance. Until children approach school age, at the earliest, they are not usually corrected for immature grammar ("That no fish school") or for immature phonology ("Dass gweat" for "That's great"). Young children are typically corrected only for inappropriate meaning (calling a horse a dog) or for social inappropriateness (depending upon the culture, this might include using so-called four-letter words at Grandma's house, or sassing adults) (Slobin, 1971, pp. 58–59). For the most part, we accept the child's utterances without correction. That is, we attend to the deep structure, the meaning, assuming that the surface structure will gradually come to resemble that of adults in the language community.

7. We provide feedback to the child in his or her attempts to communicate. When the child's meaning is not clear, we may be unable to respond appropriately, thus indirectly encouraging the child to expand his or her utterances in the direction of the adult forms. When we do understand the child, we ourselves may expand the utterance, modeling a fuller adult form. Thus, when the child says, "Mommy home," her father may reply, "Yes, Mommy's coming home." Simply responding to the child's meaning seems to be even more effective in stimulating the child's language growth. Thus the father might respond by saying, "Yes, now we can all go out for supper."

8. We collaborate with children in constructing meanings and oral texts. In the following mother/child exchange from Gordon Wells' *The Meaning Makers* (1986), young

Mark's utterances consist mostly of one word or simple two-word "sentences." However, his mother carries on a conversation with him by checking her understanding of his utterance, offering the conventional word for what he is trying to describe, and offering information in the form of a question, to which Mark responds affirmatively, repeating her observation (pp. 24, 47).

MARK: A man's fire, Mummy.
MOTHER: Mm?
MARK: A man's fire.
MOTHER: Mummy's flower?
MARK: No.
MOTHER: What?
MARK (*emphasizing each word*):   Mummy, the man . fire.
MOTHER: Man's fire?
MARK: Yeh.
MOTHER: Oh, yes, the bonfire.
MARK (*imitating*): Bonfire.
MOTHER: Mm.
MARK: Bonfire. Oh, bonfire. Bonfire. Bon—a fire bo—bonfire. Oh, hot, Mummy. Oh, hot. It hot. It hot.
MOTHER: Mm. It will burn, won't it?
MARK: Yeh. Burn. It burn.

Together, mother and child construct meanings and texts that are significantly beyond what the child alone can create—texts from which the child can simultaneously learn language forms, functions, and real-world meanings. In such exchanges, parents are said to provide *scaffolding* for the child's language and cognitive development (e.g., Ninio & Bruner, 1978; Bruner, 1983a, 1983b, 1986; Cazden, 1983).

9. We expect success. We assume that children will eventually learn to talk like adults, and we rarely try to push them into more sophisticated development (at least until they start school, when they're sometimes sent to a speech therapist for immature phonology). We do not expect failure, nor do we penalize children for not being on schedule.

In some respects, the last of these ways of encouraging language development may be the most important: matter-of-factly expecting success, and responding to children accordingly.

Child and adult roles: A brief summary

Briefly summarized, then, here are some of the most important observations about how children acquire their native language and, in the process, learn to talk:

1. Adults do not, indeed cannot, teach the rules of language structure directly.
2. Rather, children internalize rules for themselves, by transacting with others in a language-rich environment: an environment in which *whole* language is used for *authentic* purposes.

3. Children's focus of attention moves from the whole (the idea they are trying to communicate) to the parts, the forms. Gradually they are able to articulate more and more parts to convey that whole—by using more content words, more grammatical markers (inflectional endings and function words), and more and more complex sentence structures. They develop control of the parts in the context of the whole communicative situation.
4. We expect that the child will eventually succeed in learning the rules of language exemplified by adults in his or her language community, without direct instruction.
5. Accepting the fact that the acquisition of language is a process that will take several years (and, in the fullest sense, a lifetime), we do not usually correct the form of young children's utterances. In fact, we welcome new kinds of errors—such as *eated* and *buyed*—as evidence that children are making progress in acquiring language. We do not expect surface structure perfection for years—if ever.

Two particularly good discussions of child language acquisition are found in Lindfors (1987) and Genishi and Dyson (1984).

The Constructive Nature of Learning

A key principle in this discussion of language acquisition is that the child is necessarily in charge of his or her own learning: the child constructs increasingly sophisticated rules of language, unconsciously, abstracting rules from the language used in the child's language environment.

In discussing how people develop facility in a second (or subsequent) language, Stephen Krashen (1981, 1982, 1985b, 1985c) has contrasted *language learning* with *language acquisition.* "Learning" a language is what many of us did in school. We memorized vocabulary, studied grammar, translated passages, perhaps rehearsed conversational phrases (all depending upon the instructional approach); in short, we studied the language, but we may never have achieved much facility in listening to or speaking the language, or in reading or writing it for any authentic purposes outside of class. Such language learning involves "knowing about" a language, but it doesn't *necessarily* lead to knowing the language in the same sense as if it were truly acquired. I prefer to think of this as *learning about* or studying a language, while reserving *learning* by itself to mean something akin to acquiring language. Thus, learning (i.e., truly acquiring) an additional language may or may not occur in schools.

In contrast to *learning about* a language, then, *language acquisition* is a subconscious process that leads to functional command of the rules of language, but not necessarily to conscious knowledge about that language or its rules. What children do in the home is *acquire* their native language. A key ingredient is *comphensible input* provided by adults and others, from which the child can abstract the patterns and rules of the language (Krashen, 1981, 1982, 1985b, 1985c). While learning about the world through language, the child simultaneously learns language and learns about language (Halliday, 1975, 1984). However, the language must be rich enough to provide raw data for the abstraction of patterns and the construction of rules; an adult's imitation of baby talk will not do, nor will primerese. On the other hand, the language input must be sufficiently comprehensible for the language learner to connect meaning with form.

We have spent so much attention on the acquisition of language because it is an examplar of how humans construct knowledge (e.g., F. Smith, 1975, 1990). This constructive view of knowledge and learning underlies current efforts to reform content-area instruction in virtually every major discipline, including math, science, English and the language arts, and social studies. (See, for instance, my fuller treatment of this trend in Weaver, 1990a.)

Before turning to the development of literacy, we will consider two models of learning and literacy development that have significantly influenced whole language educators.

Holdaway's natural learning model

Drawing upon natural learning in a variety of everyday living situations, Don Holdaway has developed a model of learning—of how we construct knowledge, if by "knowledge" we include not only conscious learning but what we learn to do semiconsciously or unconsciously, like learn a language. Holdaway (1986) sees such natural learning as involving four major phases:

1. Observation of demonstrations.
2. Guided participation.
3. Unsupervised role-playing practice.
4. Performance: sharing and celebration of accomplishment.

Holdaway gives an extended example of a toddler learning to make a sandwich, but my own favorite example is learning to ride a bicycle. First, the child observes the bike-riding demonstrations of other children and possibly adults. When the child feels ready, he or she is guided in learning: often an adult or older child will take the handlebars and push the bike to give a running start. The situation is not radically different if the bike has training wheels, which provide more support for a longer time. After a while, the learner can keep the bike upright well enough to wobble down the road or sidewalk a few feet or yards; this is the beginning of unsupervised practice. When the child becomes sufficiently skilled, the child will usually want to perform for others: "Look, Mom, I can ride a bike!" Together, they share and celebrate the child's accomplishment.

Today, even driver's training is not significantly different—at least, not where we live. Over the years, children and youth have observed many adult demonstrations of how to drive. On the very first day of driver's training, the learner is given guided and supported practice in actually driving on the streets (the instructor is the guide, while the dual controls offer support similar to training wheels on a bike). This guided practice continues until the learner receives a license to drive alone and can then engage in unsupervised practice. Finally the learner may volunteer to perform: "Hey, Mom, how about letting me show you how well I can drive now?" or "Could I drive us on the trip to Florida?"

Though neither analogy is perfect, both illustrate key features of Holdaway's model. First, the learner observes others engaging naturally in the desired activity; this natural engagement provides *demonstrations* from which the process can be partially understood. Next, others usually help the learner in initial attempts to replicate the activity. After these initial attempts, the learner usually prefers to practice alone, in order to acquire greater proficiency, control, speed, self-confidence, and so forth. Finally, the learner is eager to share with others how well he or she can now perform, and together they celebrate the learner's accomplishment.

Like learning a language, most of what a person learns outside of school is not learned—and cannot be learned—by studying or following a sequence of rules. Natural learning occurs through active participation: by actually trying to *do* something, and mastering the various aspects or parts of that activity in the process of attempting the whole. We don't spend days or weeks learning how to hold the handlebars of a bike, or how to pedal it, nor do we separately practice how to maintain balance; we learn both in actually trying to ride. There is no "readiness" period during which children practice different aspects of bike riding in isolation.

As we shall see in a later section, Holdaway offers this model derived from natural out-of-school learning as a framework for early literacy instruction in the schools.

Cambourne's model of learning

Also drawing upon what is known about natural learning in everyday contexts, Brian Cambourne (1988) has developed a similar but more expanded model of learning. Figure 3.5 shows Cambourne's model as it applies to literacy learning. He suggests that immersion in texts of all kinds and natural demonstrations of how texts are constructed and used (e.g., others actually writing and reading in the child's presence) can lead to the child's willing engagement in learning to read. However, this engagement will occur only if the child sees him- or herself as a potential writer and reader, if the child is convinced that writing and reading will further his or her own purposes in the here and now, and if the child has no reason to fear criticism or punishment when attempts to write and read are not fully correct. It should be noted that the term "engagement" implies mental and emotional commitment, not just perfunctory action.

Cambourne further explains that engagement is fostered by adults' expectation that "of course" children will learn to write and read; by the opportunity to take responsibility and ownership for when, how, and what they will learn from literacy events (whether they are conscious of taking this responsibility or not); by plenty of opportunities to practice and use what they are trying to learn, in authentic and nonpunitive situations; by acceptance of their rough but increasingly sophisticated approximations of adult control of writing and reading; and by appropriate and supportive feedback and response from more knowledgeable others. All of these principles stem from observations of natural learning in various contexts, including contexts in which children have learned to write and read relatively naturally. (For a list of references on the acquisition of literacy, see Figure 3.6.)

The Development of Literacy

As the Holdaway and Cambourne models imply, acquisition of literacy can proceed in much the same fashion as the acquisition of language, in settings where children receive

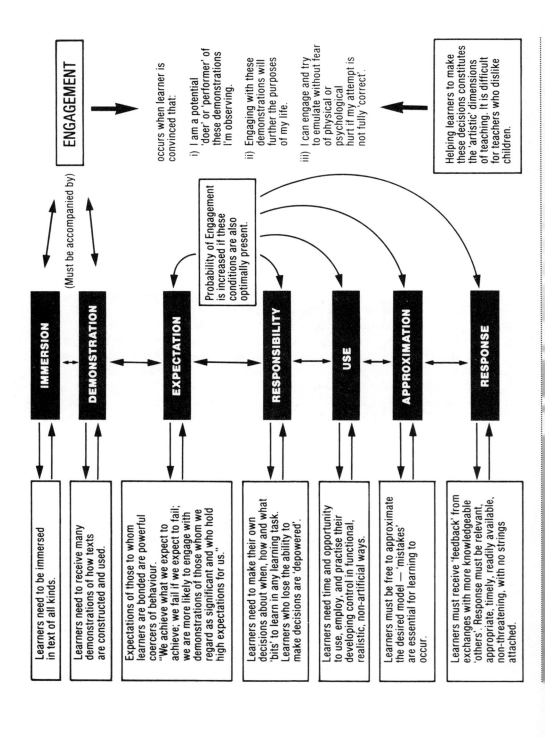

ENGAGEMENT

occurs when learner is convinced that:

i) I am a potential 'doer' or 'performer' of these demonstrations I'm observing.

ii) Engaging with these demonstrations will further the purposes of my life.

iii) I can engage and try to emulate without fear of physical or psychological hurt if my attempt is not fully 'correct'.

Helping learners to make these decisions constitutes the 'artistic' dimensions of teaching. It is difficult for teachers who dislike children.

(Must be accompanied by)

Probability of Engagement is increased if these conditions are also optimally present.

IMMERSION

DEMONSTRATION

EXPECTATION

RESPONSIBILITY

USE

APPROXIMATION

RESPONSE

Learners need to be immersed in text of all kinds.

Learners need to receive many demonstrations of how texts are constructed and used.

Expectations of those to whom learners are bonded are powerful coercers of behaviour. "We achieve what we expect to achieve; we fail if we expect to fail; we are more likely to engage with demonstrations of those whom we regard as significant and who hold high expectations for us."

Learners need to make their own decisions about when, how and what 'bits' to learn in any learning task. Learners who lose the ability to make decisions are 'depowered'.

Learners need time and opportunity to use, employ, and practise their developing control in functional, realistic, non-artificial ways.

Learners must be free to approximate the desired model — 'mistakes' are essential for learning to occur.

Learners must receive 'feedback' from exchanges with more knowledgeable 'others'. Response must be relevant, appropriate, timely, readily available, non-threatening, with no strings attached.

Articles

Fields, M. V. (1988). Talking and writing: Explaining the whole language approach to parents. *The Reading Teacher, 41,* 898–903.

Goodman, K. S. & Goodman, Y. M. (1979). Learning to read is natural. In L. B. Resnick & P. A. Weaver (Eds.), *Theory and practice of early reading,* Vol. 1 (pp. 137–154). Hillsdale, NJ: Erlbaum.

Holdaway, D. (1986). The structure of natural learning as a basis for literacy instruction. In M. R. Sampson (Ed.), *The pursuit of literacy: Early reading and writing* (pp. 56–72). Dubuque, IA: Kendall Hunt.

King, M. L. (1975). Language: Insights from acquisition. *Theory into Practice, 14,* 293–298.

Newman, J. M. (1985). Insights from recent reading and writing research and their implications for developing whole language curriculum. In J. Newman (Ed.), *Whole langue: Theory in use* (pp. 7–36). Portsmouth, NH: Heinemann.

Teale, W. H. (1982). Toward a theory of how children learn to read and write naturally. *Language Arts, 59,* 550–570.

Books

Clay, M. M. (1987). *Writing begins at home.* Portsmouth, NH: Heinemann.

Clay, M. M. (1991). *Becoming literate: The construction of inner control.* Portsmouth, NH: Heinemann.

Doake, D. (1988). *Reading begins at birth.* Richmond Hill, Ontario: Scholastic.

Hall, N. (1987). *The emergence of literacy.* Portsmouth, NH: Heinemann.

Harste, J. C., Woodward, V. A., & Burke, C. L. (1984). *Language stories and literacy lessons.* Portsmouth, NH: Heinemann.

Hill, M. W. (1989). *Home: Where reading and writing begin.* Portsmouth, NH: Heinemann.

Laminack, L. L. (1991). *Learning with Zachary.* Richmond Hill, Ontario: Scholastic.

Newman, J. M. (1984). *The craft of children's writing.* Richmond Hill, Ontario: Scholastic. (Available in the U. S. from Heinemann.)

Sampson, M. R. (Ed.). (1986). *The pursuit of literacy: Early reading and writing.* Dubuque, IA: Kendall Hunt.

Taylor, D., & Dorsey-Gaines, C. (1988). *Growing up literate: Learning from inner-city families.* Portsmouth, NH: Heinemann.

Figure 3.6   References on the acquisition of literacy

similar kinds of encouragement, support, and response, with similar expectations for gradual progress and eventual success.

Like learning to talk, both learning to read and learning to write involve the child in constructing increasingly sophisticated strategies or rules. We can see how children construct such strategies and rules in their development of written language by limiting our focus to very early writing and reading development. It is important to consider both together; not only because early writing promotes reading and vice versa, but also because they reflect similar developmental processes that have significant implications for teaching.

The constructive nature of writing development

In many homes, even where books do not abound, children are surrounded with print and frequently see adults and older siblings reading and writing for many purposes. They see literacy demonstrated and may try to imitate what more sophisticated language users do. This occurs in many low-income inner-city families as well as in more affluent suburban families (D. Taylor & Dorsey-Gaines, 1988).

A child's earliest attempts at writing may be what has been termed "scribble writing." Usually, it looks significantly different from what the child claims is a drawing; in fact, there is often some resemblance to adults' cursive writing. Figure 3.7 presents part of a ghost story written by Jane (age 3½) one day while she was visiting researcher Judith Newman. To entertain the child, Newman handed her some paper and crayons for drawing. But Jane wanted to "'make a book'" instead. She took Newman's pencil and proceeded to write the story herself, composing aloud. While Jane wrote, Newman transcribed the story word for word. To her surprise, Jane "read" the text almost verbatim, and even two weeks later still approximated the text very closely when again reading her ghost book to Newman.

Newman's comments are insightful and instructive. She observes that as Jane wrote, she moved from left to right, top to bottom. She distinguished between drawing (the two ghosts on the left) and writing: the drawings are circular, the writing linear. Furthermore, Jane had some sense of what a sentence is—each complete idea in her story was represented by a continuous mark. The story also shows Jane's sophisticated grasp of story structure: It opens with an introduction to the characters, who are placed in a setting; it proceeds with a series of events involving an antagonist, the ghost; and it ends with a resolution, in which the ghost finally leaves—and, of course, the girls live happily ever after (Newman, 1984, p. 14).

Clearly, Jane has already learned some important concepts about the functions of language (to tell a story), story structure, and the conventions of print. Her mastery of the written forms of language is much less sophisticated, but even so she differentiates drawing from writing. With the kind of encouragement and response she has already received, Jane will deepen her understanding of the functions of language and concepts of print, while gaining increasing control over the forms of language.

One of these forms is spelling. A significant body of research enables us to demonstrate some of the patterns that increasingly sophisticated control of spelling might take. (Children's writing samples with increasingly sophisticated spellings are provided in the appendix to this chapter.) However, neither Jane nor any other child will necessarily follow these patterns of development or go through these "stages" in constructing spellings and implicit rules for spelling. (Figure 3.8 suggests some valuable references on the

Mary Kate and Jane were playing outside.
Then they went inside to watch TV.
Then when they were watching TV
they saw a scary thing—a ghost.
So they hided under their covers.
Then the ghost couldn't see them.
The ghost felt sad
and he wrecked up the place.
Then the ghost finally leaved.
Then the girls lived happily ever after.

FIGURE 3.7   *Part of a ghost story by Jane, age 3½ (Newman, 1984, p. 13)*

development of spelling and strategies for spelling; see also the case studies listed in Figure 3.12, especially Bissex.)

If we remember that the following "stages" refer to increasingly sophisticated *spellings* rather than necessarily describing stages of development in any one child, we might hypothesize rules that would account for these stages in their purest (but seldom-occurring) forms:

1. *Prephonemic*: To spell a word, just put down some letters; the longer a word is, the more letters you should write. Example: TDOI, wherein the letters do not represent sounds (Temple, Nathan, Temple, & Burris, 1993). Writers operating upon this kind of rule will often write or lay out a sequence of letters (e.g., with magnetic

Emphasis on facilitating spelling development

Buchanan, E. (1989). *Spelling for whole language classrooms.* Katonah, NY: Richard C. Owen.

Gentry, J. R. (1987). *Spel . . . is a four-letter word.* Portsmouth, NH: Heinemann.

Temple, C., Nathan, R., Temple, F., & Burris, N. (1993). *The beginnings of writing* (3rd ed.). Boston: Allyn & Bacon.

Wilde, S. (1992). *You kan red this! Spelling and punctuation for whole language classrooms: K–6.* Portsmouth, NH: Heinemann.

Emphasis on understanding spelling development

Bissex, G. (1980). *Gnys at wrk: A child learns to write and read.* Cambridge: Harvard University Press.

Ferreiro, E., & Teberosky, A. (1982). *Literacy before schooling.* (K. G. Castro, Trans.). Portsmouth, NH: Heinemann.

Gentry, J. R. (1982). An analysis of developmental spelling in *Gnys at wrk. The Reading Teacher, 36,* 192–200.

Henderson, E. H. & Beers, J. W. (Eds.). (1980). *Developmental and cognitive aspects of learning to spell.* Newark, DE: International Reading Association.

Hughes, M., & Searle, D. (1991). A longitudinal study of the growth of spelling abilities within the context of the development of literacy. In J. Zutell, S. McCormick, L. L. A. Caton, & P. O'Keefe (Eds.), *Learner factors/teacher factors: Issues in literacy research and instruction* (pp. 159–168). Chicago: National Reading Conference.

Read, C. (1986). *Children's creative spelling.* New York: Routledge.

Treiman, R. (1993). *Beginning to spell: A study of first-grade children.* New York: Oxford University Press.

Villiers, U. (1989). *Luk mume dade I kan rite.* New York: Scholastic. (Spanish version also available.)

Emphasis on the effect of invented spelling

Clarke, L. K. (1988). Invented versus traditional spelling in first graders' writings: Effects on learning to spell and read. *Research in the Teaching of English, 22,* 281–309.

Gunderson, L., & Shapiro, J. (1987). Some findings on whole language instruction. *Reading–Canada–Lecture, 5,* 22–26.

Gunderson, L., & Shapiro, J. (1988). Whole language instruction: Writing in 1st grade. *The Reading Teacher, 41,* 430–437.

Figure 3.8   References on spelling and facilitating the development of spelling

letters) and ask, "What does this say?" or "What did I write?" (Clay, 1975, 1991a). They know that letters together can "say" something, but they haven't learned that there is a relationship between letters and sounds.

2. *Early phonemic*: To spell a word, use letters to represent the first sound of a word, and maybe the last sound. Example: RCRBKD for "Our car broke down," or

MBEWWMLNT for "My baby was with me last night" (Temple et al., 1993). Notice in the second example that the child has used a letter for the beginning of each *syllable* she heard in "baby." This sometimes occurs as spellings become more sophisticated. As more of the sounds are represented, early phonemic spellings shade into what are more obviously "letter-name" spellings.

3. *Letter-name*: To spell a word, write letters for at least three of the sounds in the word (if there are three or more), and represent vowels as well as consonants. Use letters whose *name* sounds like the sound you're trying to represent. (This principle is operant in early phonemic spellings also, but it's not as obvious because children are representing only one or two sounds per word.) Example: YUTZ A LADE YET FEH EG AD HE KOT FLEPR for "Once a lady went fishing and she caught flipper" (C. Chomsky, 1971, p. 509). Notice, for instance, that the "wuh" sound in "once" is represented by the letter Y, whose name starts with that sound. Similarly, the E for the vowel in "Flipper" has a name that starts with the short /i/ sound in "Flipper." (To reason your way through some of the other letter-name spellings, it may help to consult the appendix to this chapter, which explains consonant and vowel spellings reflecting the letter-name strategy.

4. *Transitional:* To spell a word, use what you remember from seeing the word in print. If you don't remember how a word is spelled, try using the rules for spelling that you've observed in print (e.g., final *e* to make a preceding vowel long, two vowel letters to represent a long vowel sound). Otherwise, continue to use letter-name spellings and anything else you know. Example: "He had a blue clth. It trd in to a brd" for *He had a blue cloth. It turned into a bird*. Another example: "At my house i have some dayseses they are flowers they growe in the spreing." And still another: "I have a ducke. I can drike wottre" for *I have a duck. It can drink water* (Temple et al., 1993). Notice the overgeneralization of the final *e* in "ducke" and "drike." Such overgeneralization of rules is common when typical patterns of spelling are being learned.

These, then, are some of the rules that we might hypothesize to account for the increasingly more sophisticated spellings between scribble writing and more conventional spelling. Any one writing sample may reflect at least two or three of these different rules, or patterns. For example, a child may spell some high-frequency words correctly, demonstrate transitional spelling on some words, and use letter-name spellings on some of the other words. As children grow in their range of spelling strategies, we rarely find pure examples of one kind of spelling strategy. Indeed, growth in spelling may consist, in large part, of growth in the range of spelling strategies that the speller can use successfully (e.g., Wilde, 1992).

Keeping this in mind, we can nevertheless better understand spelling growth partly by understanding some increasingly sophisticated spelling strategies and becoming familiar with the kinds of spellings they produce. Examples of such increasingly sophisticated spellings of the same words, but from different children, are nicely summarized in a chart from Temple, Nathan, Temple, & Burris (1993, p. 101). (For slightly different treatment of spelling stages, see Bissex, 1980; Henderson & Beers, 1980; Ferreiro & Teberosky, 1982; Hughes & Searle, 1991.)

Prephonemic	Early phonemic	Letter-name	Transitional	Standard
MPRMRHM	J	GAGIN	DRAGUN	DRAGON
BDRNMPH	P	PRD	PURD	PURRED
Brian,	Angela,	Chris,	Joyce,	Lorraine,
Kindergarten	Kindergarten	1st Grade	Ist Grade	2nd Grade

While these examples are from different children, they could have been from the same child in different phases of development. Cramer gives one such example of a child whose spontaneous spellings changed over the course of her first-grade year, as a result of transactions with a print-rich environment (Cramer, 1978, p. 107):

- October: lfnt
- December: elfnt
- February: elphnt
- June: elephant

Though a child will not always produce increasingly sophisticated spellings of the same words over time, the general tendency to do so parallels the tendency to produce increasingly sophisticated spoken utterances. Furthermore, both the spellings of individual words and the construction of spoken sentences can be seen to reflect increasingly sophisticated rules, even though children are rarely if ever conscious of them.

To determine and document such growth in spelling, teachers have sometimes asked a child to write a memorized song or rhyme several months after first writing it, or asked the child to write again something the child wrote earlier, while the teacher dictates it. (See Figure 3.9.) In this way, children's spelling and writing growth can be easily captured and documented.

We need to remember that even with the natural encouragement of spelling development, no one child will necessarily adopt the rules hypothesized above, or go through the stages of spelling that these rules seem to imply. These are simply offered as evidence that, with appropriate opportunity and encouragement, children can construct increasingly sophisticated spellings and hypotheses about spelling for themselves in the process of becoming a competent adult speller.

There are many potential advantages to encouraging constructive spelling in early writing (and later, in rough or early drafts). One advantage is that children who construct their own spellings are not limited, in their writing, to words they can spell correctly or to words they have seen in basal reading materials (Gunderson and Shapiro, 1987). Another advantage is that they are encouraged to take risks in their writing, and encouraged to construct knowledge for themselves. Still another advantage is that constructive spellers more readily learn and apply phonics knowledge (letter-sound relationships). Finally, there is even evidence suggesting that constructive spellers may do better on standardized tests of spelling and reading (Clarke, 1988); this evidence can be used with administrators in describing the advantages of encouraging children in constructive spelling. (An outstanding resource on spelling development is Sandra Wilde's

In late September, Sandra produced this rendition of "Humpty Dumpty":

HBⓈDDSAMAⓄWL LHBDⓇFAGRF

In late February, she produced this rendition:

Jandy humDy DumDy sat on a wol
humDy DumDy haD a GRayT fol
oL the cinGs horsig and the
cinGs min cyDint put humDy DumDy
Back To GEsr a Gen

FIGURE 3.9   A first grader's renditions of "Humpty Dumpty" (Fitzgerald, 1984)

You Kan Red This! Spelling and Punctuation for Whole Language Classrooms, 1992. Wilde not only describes children's development in spelling and punctuation but gives specific suggestions for what aspects of spelling should be taught, along with examples of mini-lesssons for the elementary grades.)

Clay, M. M. (1975) *What did I write?* Portsmouth, NH: Heinemann.

Clay, M. M. (1987). *Writing begins at home.* Portsmouth, NH: Heinemann.

Clay, M. M. (1991). *Becoming literate: The construction of inner control.* Portsmouth, NH: Heinemann.

Newkirk, T. (1989). *More than stories: The range of children's writing.* Portsmouth, NH: Heinemann.

Newman, J. M. (1984). *The craft of children's writing.* Richmond Hill, Ontario: Scholastic. (Available in the U. S. from Heinemann.)

Robinson, A., Crawford, L., & Hall, N. (1990). *Some day you will no all about me: Young children's explorations in the world of letters.* Portsmouth, NH: Heinemann.

Temple, C., Nathan, R., Temple, F., & Burris, N. (1993). *The beginnings of writing* (3rd ed.). Boston: Allyn & Bacon.

FIGURE 3.10   References on the development of writing

Children's constructed spellings are often called *invented* spellings, *functional* spell-ings, or even *temporary* spellings. I prefer to call them *constructive* spellings (Laminack, 1992), to emphasize the fact that the child is operating upon self-constructed rules and strategies for spelling. The term *constructive spellings* appropriately reflects the child's mind at work in the process of constructing knowledge. Again, this is parallel to what we have observed about language acquisition: it is a *constructive* process.

The purpose of this section was not to present a complete explication of writing development, or even of spelling development, but merely to indicate that learning to write, like learning to talk, is a gradual, constructive process. For those interested in studying writing development in more detail, the references in Figure 3.10 offer some good starting points.

The constructive nature of reading development

Learning to read begins long before children are first exposed to formal instruction in school. It begins when children listen to stories read (perhaps while yet in the womb) and when they first begin to notice print in their environment: the print on packages, signs, T-shirts, and so forth.

Before they know exactly what words on signs and packages mean, children often know the gist of the meaning. While they may correctly read STOP on the octagonal red sign at the end of the street as *stop*, they may say that the red COLGATE on the white tube in the bathroom says *toothpaste,* or that CHICKEN NOODLE on the red-and-white can says *soup.* Like children engaging in prephonemic writing, they know that letters put together make words, even though they may not yet have grasped the fact that there is a relation-ship between letters and sounds.

Children do not necessarily proceed through set stages in reading development, any more than they proceed through set stages in oral language or writing development. But there is substantial evidence for the following recurring patterns, or emphases, particu-larly when children's early reading experiences include the reading of predictable and enjoyable picture books:

1. *Schema emphasis*. The child turns the pages of the book, telling the story essentially from memory and from the pictures. At this point, the child may be said to be con-ceiving of him- or herself as a reader. That is, the child is engaging in readinglike behavior, even though not yet matching written words to spoken words. Rather, the child is relying essentially upon prior knowledge of the story, upon his or her sche-mas, with pictures as a cue triggering the schemas.
2. *Early semantic/syntactic emphasis*. As the child begins to match his or her oral ren-dition with the language of the text, the child learns to pick out some individual words and letters, still using picture cues to supplement the print. Words read in one con-text may not be read in another; that is, the child's reading of words may depend on the situational context and/or on the semantic and syntactic cues in the text.
3. *Later semantic/syntactic emphasis*. As the child's oral reading becomes increasingly tied to the print on the page, the child may nevertheless make many miscues that fit the context semantically and syntactically, but do not visually resemble the word on

the page. Reading "bird" for *canary* would be one example. Such miscues are typical of older proficient readers, too, but they are more frequent among emergent readers. Furthermore, at this point in his or her development as a reader, the child may not yet be *able* to correlate semantic/syntactic cues with grapho/phonemic cues very effectively, as the proficient reader can.

4. *Grapho/phonemic emphasis.* Gradually, the child evidences more and more concern for reading exactly what is on the page. The child who was formerly satisfied to read *canary* as "bird" may now struggle to sound the word out, perhaps even producing a nonword like "cainery" in the attempt. An important point to remember, though, is that the child growing through and beyond the other patterns will typically be getting the *meaning* of bird, while struggling to say the text word *canary*. This seeming overreliance upon the grapho/phonemic cueing system simply reflects the child's attempt to master that cueing system *in addition* to the others.

5. *Simultaneous use.* Eventually the child is able to use all three cueing systems simultaneously, using semantic and syntactic cues to predict what is coming next, sampling grapho/phonemic cues to confirm or correct that prediction and to make further predictions, and so forth. The child has become an independent reader.

These patterns in reading development closely parallel the patterns of spelling development outlined previously.

Such abstraction of patterns from reality helps us understand how children gradually construct their own understanding of reading and writing (even though, for illustration, we've focused narrowly on the spelling aspect of writing). However, the day-to-day, child-by-child reality of literacy development is much messier and less clear-cut. Figure 3.11 gives some sense of this, as it derives from observations of children's early literacy development. However, it too is organized into "stages" that, in reality, are far from separate or discrete. Still, the greater wealth of detail should give some sense of the potential variability among children.

Language and Literacy Development: Parallel Views

Such variability is both cultural and individual. The foregoing descriptions of language and literacy development are based primarily on research that has focused on middle-class children from mainstream cultures. While many of the patterns that emerge from such research may be universal, or nearly so, there are nevertheless differences from culture to culture—differences that are relevant for teachers working with these children. Drawn mainly from Shirley Brice Heath's *Ways with Words* (1983), the following discussion only begins to suggest the differences of which teachers need to be aware. A more thorough summary of Heath's study can be found in Luke, Baty, & Stehbens (1989).

Acquisition of language.   Heath (1983) focused her ethnographic research into language and literacy development on two working-class communities of mill worker families, one a white community and the other black. The former she called Roadville, the latter Trackton.

Pre-independent Reading Stages

1. Magical Stage

Displays an interest in handling books.

Sees the construction of meaning as magical or exterior to the print and imposed by others.

Listens to print read to him or her for extended periods of time.

Will play with letters or words.

Begins to notice print in environmental context (signs, labels).

Letters may appear in his or her drawings.

May mishandle books—observe them upside down or damage them due to misunderstanding the purpose of books.

Likes to name the pictures found in book.

2. Self-Concepting Stage

Self-concepts him- or herself as a reader, i.e., engages in readinglike activities.

Tries to magically impose meaning on new print.

"Reads" or reconstructs content of familiar storybooks.

Recognizes his or her name and some other words in high environmental context (signs, labels).

His or her other writing may display phonetic influence (e.g., wtbo = Wally, hr = her).

Can construct story meaning from pictorial clues.

Can not pick words out of print consistently.

Orally fills in many correct responses in oral cloze reading. [Completes sentences from which words have been selectively omitted.]

Rhymes words.

Increasing control over nonvisual cueing systems.

Gives words orally that begin similarly.

Displays increasing degree of book-handling knowledge.

Is able to recall *key words.*

Begins to internalize story grammar, knows how stories go together ("Once upon a time," "They lived happily ever after").

3. Bridging Stage

Can write and read back his or her own writing.

Can pick out individual words and letters.

Can read familiar books or poems that could not be totally repeated without the print.

Uses picture clues to supplement the print.

Words read in one context may not be read in another.

Increasing control over visual cueing system.

Enjoys chants and poems chorally read.

Can match or pick out words of poems or chants that have been internalized.

Figure 3.11   Observations for a reading development continuum (Cochrane, Cochrane, Scalena, & Buchanan, 1984) [adapted from original]

Independent Reading Stages

1. *Take-off Stage*
   Excitement about reading.
   Wants to read to you often.
   Realizes that print is the base for constructing meaning.
   Can process (read) words in new (alternate) print situations.
   Aware of and reads aloud much environmental print (signs, labels, etc.).
   Can conserve print from one contextual environment to another.
   May exhibit temporary tunnel vision (concentrates on words and letters).
   Oral reading may be word-centered rather than meaning-centered.
   Increasing control over the reading process.

2. *Independent Reading*
   Characterized by comprehension of author's message by reader.
   Reader's construction of meaning relies heavily on author's print or implied cues
       (schema).
   Desire to read books to him- or herself for pleasure.
   Brings own experiences (schemata) to the print.
   Reads orally with meaning and expression.
   Reads in word meaning clusters.
   May see print as literal truth: what the print says is right (legalized).
   Uses visual and nonvisual cueing systems simultaneously (cyclically).
   Has internalized several different print grammars (fairy tales, general problem-
       centered stories, simple expository).

3. *Skilled Reader*
   Processes material further and further removed from own experience.
   Reading content and vocabulary become a part of his or her experience.
   Can use a variety of print forms for pleasure.
   Can discuss several aspects of a story.
   Can read at varying and appropriate rates.
   Can make inferences from print.
   Challenges the validity of print content.
   Can focus on or utilize the appropriate grammar or structuring of varying forms of
       print (e.g., stories, science experiments, menus, diagrams, histories).

FIGURE 3.11   Continued

What differs most noticeably is parent expectations about how children will acquire
language and literacy, patterns of adult-child interaction, and forms of oral and written
discourse.

In Roadville, parents feel they bear primary responsibility for teaching children
what they need to learn before school, including how to talk, how to behave (and to talk
"right"), how to view their world, and how to interact with books. As the primary

caregiver, the mother talks extensively to the baby, frequently using baby talk. Other adults address the baby in baby talk also:

Wha's a matter, Bobby, yo' widdle tum-tum all empty?

Don't fuss, don't fuss, we're home now. We put Bobby, go all-night-night. Mommy get his bottle.

The use of childish pronunciations and vocabulary, not to mention the grammatical simplification (omission of *will* from *Mommy* [will] *get his bottle*) all signal that these adults are addressing the child in baby talk.

When Roadville children begin to make sounds that adults can link to items in the environment, adults and older children often try to teach the baby the words for these objects. They may be more directive than typical middle-class parents in trying to guide their child's language development, telling the child and correcting the child instead of simply modeling adult language use in conversation with the child. In any case, their child-rearing practices differ sharply from those of Trackton.

As Heath puts it, "Any baby born into Trackton is born not to a family, but to the community" (1983, p. 146). Whereas the young child in Roadville spends much of the time amusing him- or herself in the crib or playing alone, the young child in Trackton is passed from lap to lap among adults and older children. Older children also carry the baby around, often on their hip, and introduce the infant to their games and other social interactions. The baby is surrounded by language, but during the first six months to a year of their lives, babies are seldom addressed directly by adults. Adults in Trackton expect their children to learn language by listening to others in their environment, not by having their utterances expanded and scaffolded by a caretaking adult. Of course, community members facilitate this learning by including the baby in all activities, many of which take place outdoors on the porches or in the plaza, where everyone interacts. The child is not isolated or left to play alone.

By about twelve to fourteen months, boys are encouraged to perform verbally. They are often teased and taunted, and expected to learn to respond by outwitting, outtalking, or outacting their antagonists. They are expected to learn that different words and language routines may elicit different responses at different times, from the same person as well as from different people. In short, they are socialized to understand that language use is flexible and changing, and to adapt to the various verbal and nonverbal cues and responses in their environment. Girls have far fewer opportunities to interact verbally with adults in the community. However, all children are expected to learn language and language use through observation and participation, not by being explicitly taught.

Which procedure works better, the teaching approach of Roadville parents or the learning approach of Trackton parents? By the time they go to school, children in both communities have learned the language functions, participant roles and interaction patterns, and discourse forms of their communities. And children from each community have learned "the sounds, words, and grammatical systems of the language spoken around them" (Heath, 1983, p. 145).

Oral and literate traditions in Trackton.   While the forms of oral and written discourse in Roadville may not be radically different from those of mainstream cultures, the same cannot be said for Trackton. Some differences of particular significance for education are the following:

1. Storytelling is valued in Trackton. If the story is based upon an actual event, story-tellers embellish or fictionalize the details—and the outcome may not even resemble what actually happened. Children—boys in particular—learn early to capture an audience's attention or win favors by telling such stories, often with exaggeration and humor.
2. An adult's accusation serves as an invitation for a child to tell a good story, presumably to avoid punishment. In such instances also, the story must be "highly exaggerated, skillful in language play, and full of satisfactory comparisons to redirect the adult's attention from the infraction provoking the accusation" (Heath, 1983, p. 167).
3. In Trackton, reading is typically a social event. When adults receive notices of meetings or forms to fill out, for example, their meaning and the advisability of action is typically discussed among friends. To read alone is frowned upon; those who read magazines or books alone are accused of being antisocial.
4. In this community, adults do not read books to children, nor do children have their own books to read. Furthermore, adults do not create reading and writing tasks for children. They are left to find or create their own reading and writing tasks: "distinguishing one television channel from another, knowing the name brands of cars, motorcycles and bicycles, choosing one or another can of soup or cereal, reading price tags at Mr. Dorgan's store to be sure they do not pay more than they would at the supermarket," and reading the names and addresses of mail brought by the post-man, who then may let the children deliver the mail to the appropriate person (Heath, 1983, p. 190).
5. Jointly or in groups, the children *read to learn* before they go to school to *learn to read*. Youngsters are sent to the store along with older children "almost as soon as they can walk," and they quickly learn to use context—location, color and shape of packaging, shape of logos, and so forth—to help them read critical information like product and brand names. From an early age they learn to read prices, in order to make sure they are not paying too much. Also, reading becomes a community event among the children when they work together to modify old toys and when they read directions. "Reading is almost always set within a context of immediate action" (Heath, 1983, pp. 191, 192).

When we consider how to build upon children's strengths in the classroom, it is important to recognize the different strengths brought by children from differing cultural communities. Language and literacy development are not encouraged the same way everywhere.

Emergent Literacy: The Messiness of Literacy Development

We can best appreciate the "messiness" of each child's literacy development by considering some examples from individual children. Children's individual development reflects what is encouraged in their own home and school communities.

Zachary: From a parent's journal

Zachary comes readily to mind—doubtless because I have met and talked with him, as well as read *Learning with Zachary*, written by his father, Lester Laminack (1991). In his book, Laminack claims to have learned the principles of literacy development abstractly from my *Psycholinguistics and Reading* (1980), but it was learning them firsthand from Zachary that made a critical difference in his understanding.

Zachary's parents, Lester and Glenda, are atypical, in that Lester read fairy tales to Zachary for months before his birth, in addition to reading to him daily after his birth; they did more than most parents to assist him in processing written language in the environment; they responded positively to approximations of written words, when other parents might have corrected him instead; and, obviously, Lester spent a lot of time documenting Zachary's development of literacy. Zachary, while clearly very bright, was *not* necessarily atypical. Rather, his dramatic literacy growth illustrates what most children are probably capable of, if they are given the same kind of support for literacy development that we usually provide for children's initial language development.

To illustrate selected features of Zachary's literacy development through his transactions with environmental print, I'll excerpt a few of Lester's journal entries from *Learning with Zachary,* with comments.

December 24, 1985: Age 1 year, 3 months

Today Zachary was playing with the buttons and knobs on his grandparents' dishwasher when I saw him rubbing the words Sears Best. I walked over to him, trailed his finger across the letters and said, "Dishwasher. This is Maw-Maw's dishwasher." Just a few minutes later he had shifted his attention to the raised letters spelling Kenmore on the refrigerator. At that time I repeated my actions, saying, "Refrigerator. This is Maw-Maw's refrigerator." Each time he passed either appliance after that he would rub the letters and name the appliance. All of us were very pleased and thought this was quite cute.

Later Glenda, Zachary and I were unpacking when Zachary looked up at me and announced, "Daddy's suitcase." He was standing next to my suitcase with one hand on the handle and the other stroking the etched lettering: Samsonite. I was amazed! I walked him over to Glenda's suitcase and traced his index finger over the same etched logo. I asked, "Zachary, what does this say?" Without a pause he answered, "Mommy's suitcase!" He looked at me and grinned. I picked him up and gave him a big hug. "That's right, buddy, that's right."

Lester comments that he will never view literacy in quite the same way after that evening. I, in turn, will never view literacy development in quite the same way, having seen how Lester encouraged his young son's literacy development by teaching him that printed signs and logos have meaning that is signaled by the environment in which they occur. Lester was not merely accepting Zachary's approximations; he was actually demonstrating and encouraging them! He was showing Zachary how to use his schemas, his knowledge of the world, to make sense of environmental print.

December 26, 1985: Age 1 year, 3 months

Coming home today we stopped at McDonald's for lunch. After the Kenmore and Samsonite episodes I wondered what Zachary would do with the

McDonald's logo, which is more familiar to him. As usual, he wanted "chicken nuggets, fries and orange drink." When we were seated with our food, I pointed to the logo on Zachary's cup and asked him what it said. "Orange," he responded. Glenda and I looked at each other and smiled. "Very good. You did a good job with that," I praised. I presented the same logo on both the french fries package and the Chicken McNuggets box and asked the same question, "What does this one say?" In both instances his response was to name the item in the packaging: "fries" and "chicken nuggets."

Clearly Zachary was applying the insight he had gained two days before: that labels on things tell what they are. He had developed a strategy for reading this kind of environmental print, and was not troubled by the fact (or did not notice) that the same visual information (Samsonite, McDonald's) seemed to "say" something different in different contexts. Zachary did not, of course, remain in this same early stage of understanding. He gradually came to know specific words and to use letter/sound knowledge along with schemas to name words in his environment.

June 1986: Age 1 year, 9 months

During a trip home to see my parents we stopped at the McDonald's in Murphy, NC, our usual first pit stop. While there I showed Zachary the McDonald's logo on my coffee cup and asked him to read it for me. "McDonald's. It says McDonald's."

His voice was confident, and he proved himself by pointing out every McDonald's logo in sight and announcing that it too said McDonald's. This print symbol has become a reliable representation for the word, one he has ownership over.

Our next pit stop was in Ellajay, GA, where there was both a Hardee's and a new McDonald's that had been built since our last trip. We had lunch at Hardee's and again I decided to take advantage of the opportunity. I pointed to the Hardee's logo on my coffee cup and asked Zachary to read it for me. "Hot coffee" was his response. When I pointed to the same logo on the french fries packet, he read "Fries." And his response was "Cheeseburger" when I asked about the logo on the sandwich wrapper. I praised all his efforts, telling him what a good reader he was and how proud I was.

Though Zachary had established "McDonald's" as a word he could identify in various contexts, he resorted to his tried-and-true strategy of using schemas and environmental context when confronted with the unfamiliar word "Hardee's." Interestingly, at age 3 years exactly, he gave his first evidence of trying to use a grapho/phonemic strategy: he asked if the written word *hairdresser* said "Hardee's," a similarly beginning word with which he was now familiar. He was beginning to use grapho/phonemic cues.

It is important, too, that as Zachary's strategies for making sense of print changed, so too did Lester's responses, as the following example illustrates.

May 10, 1989: Age 4 years, 8 months

Zachary has become very interested in environmental lettering beyond logos. "What does p-u-s-h say?" he asked today. "What do you think it says?" I asked. His response was, "Come in, right?" I supported his attempt with, "That's a good idea because that's the door you go in, but it says 'push' so you know how to open the door." Pleased with the explanation, he replied, "Oh, I get it. You push the door if you want to come in." "Exactly right. Let's go in."

At the time of this journal entry, Zachary is now three years older than he was when Lester first encouraged him to "read" *Kenmore* as "Maw-Maw's refrigerator," or supported his reading of *Samsonite* as "Daddy's suitcase." Zachary has some knowledge now of letters and their sounds; he can also spell a few familiar words. Lester intuitively knows that it is no longer appropriate to agree that "p-u-s-h" spells "Come in"; he needs to support Zachary's growing use of grapho/phonemic knowledge along with context.

I have given such extensive examples of Zachary's literacy development because they indicate not only the naturalness of that growth in appropriately supportive environments, but also how the nature of that support must change with the child's changing strategies or "rules"—just as the nature of caregiver language remains in advance of children's oral language construction. *Learning with Zachary* also documents Zachary's growth as a writer, and how his reading and writing development were interrelated and intertwined. Other instructive case studies are listed in Figure 3.12. Together, such case studies clarify some typical commonalities in literacy development—the kinds of commonalities captured in the summaries of language acquisition on pp. 62–65; in the models of natural learning and literacy development articulated by Holdaway and by Cambourne (pp. 66–68); and in the trends in spelling and reading development on pp. 70–77. Separately, these case studies indicate each child's "messy" and unique development.

Rob: From a teacher's literacy biography

For me, this uniqueness is also strongly emphasized in the periodic literacy biographies that teachers in a New Hampshire literacy assessment project wrote to describe their students (D. Taylor, 1989, 1990). Here is the October summary Kathy Matthews wrote for third grader Rob (D. Taylor, 1989, p. 189):

October

Rob's enthusiasm for our focus on prehistoric life has prompted him to create a new story titled "The Cave," a chapter book about the adventures and escapades which he and his peer-characters heroically survive. Much of the story occurs in the dialogue, which moves the characters and the action across time and space. ("When?" said Rob. "How about tomorrow?" said Adam. "Okay," said Rob. "Where?" "How about Hawaii?") Rob spends most of each writing period drawing and redrawing the illustrations or consulting with friends. He often reads his story to classmates, describes what he might do next, and then actively role-plays the parts with his peers. Rob tends to subvocalize as he composes, particularly when sketching action scenes. He uses enlarged print for sound effects and for emphasis.

Rob wrote brief, often unfinished entries in both his reading journal and his daybook this month. His first entry in his new learning log reflected some of the new information he had acquired ("I never knew the knee was one of the fragilest spots") and included an illustration of a human skull with its parts appro-

Baghban, M. (1984). *Our daughter learns to read and write: A case study from birth to three.* Newark, DE: International Reading Association.

Bissex, G. (1980). Gnys at wrk: *A child learns to write and read.* Cambridge, MA: Harvard University Press.

Doake, D. B. (1988). *Reading begins at birth.* Richmond Hill, Ontario: Scholastic.

Halliday, M. A. K. (1975). *Learning how to mean: Explorations in the development of language.* London: Edward Arnold.

Harste, J. C., Woodward, V. A., & Burke, C. L. (1984). *Language stories and literacy lessons.* Portsmouth, NH: Heinemann.

Laminack, L. L. (1991). *Learning with Zachary.* Richmond Hill, Ontario: Scholastic.

Taylor, D. (1991). *Learning denied.* Portsmouth, NH: Heinemann.

FIGURE *3.12   References on case studies of literacy and/or language development*

priately labeled. Another time he speculated about being an archaeologist and still another time wistfully wrote, "I wish I knew more about rocks." Rob used written language to compose riddles, jokes, and letters which he sent to friends; to write notes to me requesting assistance or asking for specific information; to collect, organize, and describe data from a field experience (an archaeological dig); and to share his personal feelings with a classmate.

For most of this month, Rob has been reading *Chester Cricket's Pigeon Ride*, which in his reading journal he describes as being "good in one way and good in another way." The reading journal entries that he wrote were one- or two-sentence descriptions of the main idea behind what he read.

When we read such biographies from different children, it becomes clear that any generalizations we might draw about patterns of literacy development are bound to be wrong in the particulars, if we try to apply them to individual children. Individual children do not progress neatly or obligingly through our abstracted "stages" of growth. They do not completely abandon the patterns of one stage when reaching toward another. They do not show steady progression, without plateaus and without what at least appear to be regressions. They just read and write in their own way, as they construct their knowledge about literacy over time.

The Development of Literacy: A Brief Summary

From observations of emergent literacy and the parallels between that and child language acquisition, we can draw such generalizations as these:

1. Children develop literacy most readily when they have daily opportunities to observe how others read and write, and when they can engage in guided participation in reading and writing or unsupervised practice (as appropriate) and then share and celebrate their accomplishments (Holdaway's natural learning model).

2. Children readily immerse themselves in literacy demonstrations and engage in reading and writing in whatever ways they can, but they are likely to do so only when the psychological conditions are favorable—for instance, when they see reading and writing as something they can do and something that furthers the purposes of their own lives in the here and now, and when they have confidence that they will not receive negative feedback from others for their attempts and approximations (Cambourne's model of learning).

3. In such favorable contexts and under such favorable conditions, children construct for themselves a sense of what it means to read and write, and how one goes about it. This sense may be viewed as a series of increasingly sophisticated hypotheses.

4. Adults cannot actually teach children how to read or write, though they can demonstrate or model reading and writing for them, collaborate with them, demonstrate and discuss reading and writing strategies with them, and guide them in reading and writing. In all of these ways, adults facilitate children's developing ability to read and to write. But they cannot effectively teach children to read and write, any more than they can effectively teach babies and toddlers the rules for putting sounds together to make words, and words together to make sentences. All of these are processes that children must develop for themselves, with (or in spite of) the help of those who are already proficient.

5. One of the most important ways adults can foster literacy development is simply by responding positively to children's attempts at reading and writing. We facilitate literacy growth when we treat children as already readers and writers, when we accept approximations and errors as necessary to growth, and when we convey the feeling that "of course" they will become proficient at reading and writing.

6. Children's focus of attention typically moves from the whole (getting and conveying meaning) to the parts (getting the actual words, writing more and more of the letters in a word). They develop understanding and control of the parts in the context of the whole literacy event.

In the next section, we shall see how these observations about emergent literacy lead to some nontraditional notions of how best to foster literacy in the classroom.

DIFFERENCES BETWEEN TEACHING READING AND DEVELOPING LITERACY

Teaching children to read and write is what we've traditionally tried to do in the schools. At least *we* have *taught,* regardless of what or how the children have learned. Still, the increasing numbers of children sent to resource rooms for help with reading, the small percentage of students able to read critically by their senior year in high school (Applebee, Langer, & Mullis, 1988b), and the allegedly illiterate and aliterate millions of adults in our country should make us question whether we have taught with or against the grain of children's natural learning strategies.

The assumptions underlying efforts to *teach* children to read differ from those in whole language classrooms, where teachers try to help children *develop* reading, writing, and literacy more naturally and easily. Some of these differences are signaled by differences in terminology; other differences derive from how the terms are used. What these differences typically add up to is a *transmission* concept of education, in contrast to a *transactional* concept: these extremes that might more appropriately be conceptualized as different points on a continuum. Figure 8.3 in Chapter 8 lists several key differences between the two concepts or models of education. Here, some of these will be briefly described, as an introduction to the contrast between "teaching reading" and "developing literacy."

Transmission versus Transactional Models

In the *transmission model of education,* students are viewed as empty vessels into which knowledge is to be poured. This leads to curricula that require them to practice skills, memorize facts, and accumulate information, typically in isolation from the uses to which the skills and information might be put. Students do worksheets and workbooks on reading and writing skills, but spend little time reading or writing for enjoyment or other real-world purposes. Underlying this model are principles from behavioral psychology: principles such as Thorndike's laws of learning, outlined earlier in this chapter, which have specifically guided the development of basal reading programs. Errors are to be avoided and are therefore penalized, to discourage the formation of inappropriate habits. Learning is expected to be uniform; that is, students are treated and tested as if they are all expected to learn the same things at the same time. Furthermore, almost instant perfection is expected: what is taught today and practiced tomorrow will be tested for complete and accurate learning the next day. Therefore, many students will necessarily "fail," though in varying degrees. Many are labeled as needing remedial help.

In a *transactional model*, students are viewed as already having rich prior knowledge and background, with ample experience in using their schemas along with an innate ability and an inclination to construct their own knowledge (regardless of how they are taught). This view stems from what cognitive psychologists and psycholinguists have discovered about human learning, including the acquisition of language. Teachers operating out of this *constructivist* view of learning try to create rich environmental contexts and situations from which students can learn. Such teachers understand that taking risks, developing and refining hypotheses (often unconscious ones), and making errors are all necessary aspects of growth (I have yet to meet anyone who learned to ride a bicycle without falling a few times in the process). They know that the mastery of processes like speaking a language, reading, writing, spelling—to mention only the ones most obviously of concern here—takes years, and will never reach perfection. The learning (or acquisition) of such processes is expected to be individual and idiosyncratic.

Transmission versus Transactional Models with Respect to Reading

The following table lists some differences between those who emphasize teaching to read, compared with those who emphasize helping children develop literacy:

Transmission Model (teaching to read)	Transactional Model (developing literacy)
Significant time spent teaching, practicing, and testing skills	Significant time spent actually reading and writing, and discussing literature
Reading is taught as a subject, separate from writing and other subjects	Reading and writing strategies and skills are discussed and explained in the context of reading and writing for real-life purposes, such as enjoyment and learning across the curriculum
Emphasis on stages of development across individuals	Emphasis on individual and idiosyncratic growth
Concern for developing "reading readiness" prior to reading instruction	No division between readiness for reading and learning to read; emergent reading (writing, literacy) seen as continuous process, without division into stages
The term "development" typically signals commitment to stage theory	The term "development" typically signals commitment to concept of emergent literacy

Those who adopt a transmission model of education typically talk about stages of develoment in reading. For example, Jeanne Chall (1983) has developed a stage theory of reading, in which all the stages except the first look suspiciously like the way instructional programs are organized over the years. The first stage, *Prereading: Birth to Age 6*, is significantly called Stage 0, rather than Stage 1; after all, it occurs prior to formal instruction. Chall is obviously conversant with the professional literature on emergent reading, but she characterizes this stage as one of "reading readiness"—preparation for "beginning reading," by which she really means beginning reading *instruction*. Marilyn Adams, in *Beginning to Read: Thinking and Learning About Print* (1990a), recognizes the developmental nature of emergent reading and writing, but only until first grade, whereupon her recommendations reflect the typical transmission concept of reading instruction.

Thus, there is a vast difference between those who advocate traditional instruction in reading skills and those who advocate teaching designed to further children's emergent literacy, regardless of where they are in their reading development or what their grade placement might be. Those who adopt the emergent literacy perspective frequently think of themselves as whole language educators.

Getting Ready to Read versus Reading

In preschools and kindergartens that reflect a transmission concept of learning, children are typically kept busy getting *ready* to read and to write: practicing letter shapes and forms, learning letter/sound correspondences, learning to distinguish one letter sound from another, and so forth. In whole language preschools and kindergartens, children are typically involved in actual reading and writing.

Kasten and Clarke (1989) have compared the effects of these two differing kinds of classrooms upon children's literacy development (see Chapter 7). The typical differences in procedures may be illustrated by observational notes from two classrooms in that research study.

Typical of a transmission concept of reading instruction, this first observation is from a private, well-funded, highly regarded preschool with an experienced, capable, highly regarded teacher (Kasten & Clarke, 1989, pp. 74–75):

> Ms. R. cheerfully welcomes her students and introduces us to them, reminding them of our names. Children gather in the carpeted area of the room around their teacher who is seated in a chair next to an easel. After some social conversation with the group, Ms. R. introduces the "special guest," who is a puppet named "Goofy Ghost." She announces they will talk about the letter G this day. The teacher elaborates that Goofy wears glasses and plays a guitar. She develops a story orally, preparing them to participate on a given signal with repeating phrases including "/g/ – /g/ – /g/ – /goo/," and "Goofy, good grief!" On the easel is paper with pockets which hold teacher prepared cards.
>
> As the story is completed, the teacher reviews "G" words with the children, and praises them at the end. She asks the children to give themselves a pat on the back, reviews the "G" words again, and they say "/g/ – /g/ – /g/ – /g/" a few more times. At the end, all children stand up to stretch, and are directed to pretend they are watering cans, and to make /g/ sound like water gushing from the watering cans with "/g/ – /g/ – /g/" noises.
>
> Next, the teacher initiates a guessing game with questions to "fill in the blank" orally, such as "Something Mommy puts on your mashed potatoes is . . . ," and "You like to chew a stick of. . . ."

The preschoolers are then asked to do some "writing": to copy the design Ms. R. shows them on a flash card (circle, vertical line, etc.). She reminds them to do their own work and not look at anybody else's paper.

Teaching and learning are very different in whole language preschools and kindergartens. In the following anecdote from a preschool class, the paraprofessional teacher and all eight students are members of minority groups from very low socioeconomic neighborhoods (Kasten & Clarke, pp. 67–68):

> The teacher presents a DLM book [a Big Book from the DLM publishing company] and, before she can ask the title, children call out "Three Dogs at the Door." Together the children count aloud the dogs on the cover, discuss the author, Roach Van Allen (1986), and discuss what an "illustrator" means. The children curl at the teacher's feet in an organized formation. The teacher uses a pointer as the class reads chorally. The teacher points out that the word "mad" looks different from the word "disgusted." The teacher asks individuals to act out how they might look if they felt "disgusted." All eight children say "disgusted," making appropriate facial expressions as they do.

The children are extremely attentive, with all eyes on the book. They act out the next interesting word which is "upset," the same way they did with the word "disgusted." The teacher discusses with them how they can use these words when they have those feelings, labeling them for the children as "emotion words." They continue reading and come to the word "irritated." They discuss differences between "irritated," "mad," "upset," and "disgusted."

Teacher and children continue discussing the emotion words. The teacher then

flips back through the text to each emotion word and asks which, of the ones they discussed, this one is. Each time some children guess correctly, and seem to be using initial letters to assist in their guesses of "disgusted," "furious," etc.

Since the children are not yet tired of shared reading, they go on to read *I'm the King of the Mountain* (Cowley, 1984b) together, with the children chiming in and singing the repeated refrain, "I'm the king of the mountain; I'm the king of the mountain." Finally, the children have the opportunity to choose books to read by themselves, in pairs, or to the teacher.

It is worth remembering that both of these were preschool classrooms, yet in the whole language classroom children were actually involved in reading and discussing a book, not simply in getting ready to read. They were engaging in a Shared Book Experience (which will be described in greater detail below). Though in this particular example the children's attention was focused on words, with other selections the teacher and children might focus instead on letter/sound relationships or other aspect of print.

Getting Ready to Write versus Writing

With respect to writing, the situation is similar: in traditional classrooms, young children's attention is often directed toward getting ready to write, or toward rehearsing words with regular letter/sound patterns or basic sight words. Much of the latter may occur without direct instruction, as children simply imitate the language to which they are exposed in their workbooks and their basal reading program.

Examples from a study by Diane DeFord (1981) are particularly instructive. DeFord compared the writings of children from three different classrooms: a phonics classroom, where the reading materials apparently emphasized basic letter/sound correspondences (the "Nan can fan Dan" sort of fare); a skills classroom, where beginning reading instruction focused on the development of sight vocabulary using flash cards and simple stories made up of these words; and a whole language classroom, where the children read and wrote various kinds of real material, such as stories, songs, poems, and informational text.

According to DeFord (1981), about a third of the children in the phonics classroom and about three-fourths of those in the skills ("look-say") classroom produced the limited kinds of writing illustrated for each group in Figure 3.13. DeFord implies that the majority of children in the whole language classroom produced writing more like Jason's in Figure 3.14, with variety and individuality used in a genuine communication

Reed: Phonics Room

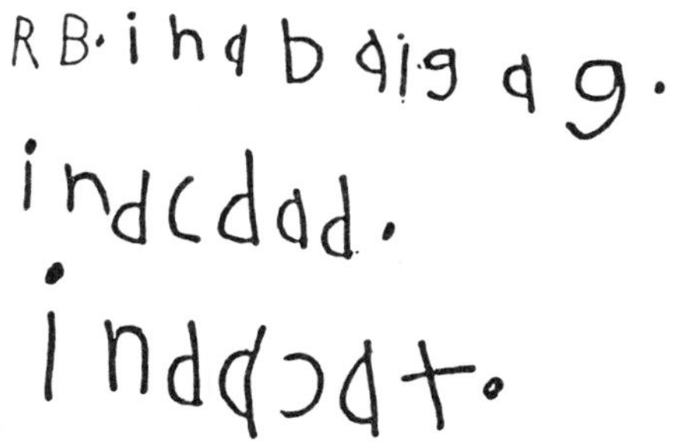

R.B. i h d b d i g d g.   I had a gag.

i n d c d d d.   I had a dad.

i n d d c d t.   I had a cat.

Jeffrey and Amy: Skills Room

Jeffrey H)

Bill can run.
Jill can run.
Jeff can run.
I can run.

Amy
Jill Bill I am Lad
Bill I am Jill
Lad I am Bill
I am Jill Bill
I am Lad Bill
Jill I am Bill Jill
I k RO
i B l k . I T

FIGURE *3.13* *Typical writing of children in classrooms emphasizing phonics (top) and sight word recognition (bottom) (DeFord, 1981)*

Jason: Whole-Language Room

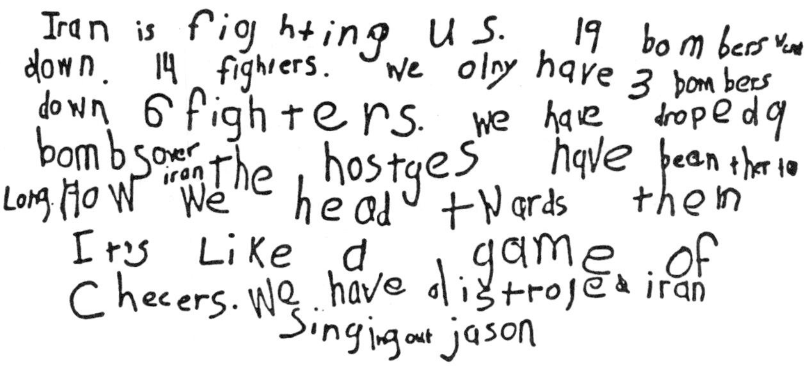

Iran is fighting U.S. 19 bombers shot down. 14 fighters. We olny have 3 bombers down 6 fighters. We have troped a bomb over iran the hostges have bean thr so Long. How we head tvards them Its Like a game of Checers. We have distroje iran
Singing out jason

FIGURE *3.14* *Typical writing of children in whole language classrooms (DeFord, 1981)*

(see also Eckhoff, 1984). Given such examples, there can be little doubt that a print-restricted environment inhibits children's writing growth, whereas a print-rich environment facilitates it. Nor can there be much doubt that primary children make less progress as writers when their time and attention is devoted to getting ready to write instead of actually writing.

WHOLE LANGUAGE AND EMERGENT LITERACY

Obviously the transmission model of education underlies typical basal reader instruction, which incorporates aspects of a phonics and sight word approach, while the transactional model underlies whole language education. See Figure 3.15 for a list of introductory readings on whole language.

Because it typifies the transactional model, the Shared Book Experience as developed by Don Holdaway (1979) will be described and discussed in some detail, followed by a section briefly describing other kinds of language experiences and activities that characterize whole language classrooms. Then, to conclude this chapter, we will compare different models of teaching reading and developing literacy.

Shared Book Experience, or Shared Reading Experience

The so-called Shared Book Experience was first developed in 1965 in New Zealand by Don Holdaway and a team of experienced teachers and consultants. They based their teaching procedures on observation of the ways that many children learn to read from the bedtime story experience in the home (Holdaway, 1979).

The teacher uses a Big Book that all the children in the group can see: a commercially published Big Book, a child/teacher-authored Big Book, or simply a chart of some sort, written in large print. This characterization of the Shared Book Experience (SBE) is derived from Andrea Butler (n.d.):

1. *Rereading favorite selections:* first rhymes, songs, and poems, then stories. During these rereadings, the teacher points to the words while reading.

   Teaching predetermined concepts or strategies: Before using the selection, the teacher will have determined what aspects of print or what reading strategies he or she might want to emphasize—for example, using prior knowledge and context plus the initial consonant of a word to predict what the word might be, or using all of these plus rhyme to predict a rhyming word.

   Capturing the teachable moment: In addition, the teacher capitalizes upon the children's needs and interests, taking advantage of the "teachable moment."

2. *Introducing a new story:* At least once a week, a new story is introduced in Big Book format. The primary aim upon a first reading is simply to enjoy the story. The teacher *introduces* the book by mentioning and perhaps commenting upon the author, title, and cover illustrations; *invites* children to predict, from this information, what the

Articles

Altwerger, B. (1991). Whole language teachers: Empowered professionals. In J. Hydrick (Ed.), *Whole language: Empowerment at the chalkface* (pp. 15–29). New York: Scholastic.

Goodman, K. S. (1989). Whole-language research: Foundations and development. *The Elementary School Journal, 90,* 208–221.

Goodman, Y. M. (1989). Roots of the whole-language movement. *The Elementary School Journal, 90,* 113–127.

Gursky, D. (1991). After the reign of Dick and Jane. *Teacher Magazine*, (August), pp. 22–29.

Monson, R. J., & Pahl, M. M. (1991). Charting a new course with whole language. *Educational Leadership, 48,* 51–53.

Newman, J. M., & Church, S. M. (1990). Myths of whole language. *The Reading Teacher, 44,* 20–26.

Pace, G. (1991). When teachers use literature for literacy instruction: Ways that constrain, ways that free. *Language Arts, 68,* 12–25.

Watson, D. J. (1989). Defining and describing whole language. *The Elementary School Journal, 90,* 130–141.

Books

Cambourne, B. (1988). *The whole story: Natural learning and the acquisition of literacy in the classroom.* Auckland, New Zealand: Scholastic.

Edelsky, C., Altwerger, B., & Flores, B. (1991). *Whole language: What's the difference?* Portsmouth, NH: Heinemann.

Goodman, K. S. (1986). *What's whole in whole language?* Richmond Hill, Ontario: Scholastic. (Available in the U. S. from Heinemann.)

Goodman, K. S., Bird, L. B., & Goodman, Y. M. (1990). *The whole language catalog.* Chicago, IL: American School Publishers.

Manning, G., & Manning, D. (Eds.) (1989). *Whole language: Beliefs and practices, K–8.* Washington, DC: National Education Association.

Stephens, D. (1991). *Research on whole language: Support for a new curriculum.* Katonah, NY: Richard C. Owen.

Weaver, C. (1990). *Understanding whole language: From principles to practice.* Portsmouth, NH: Heinemann.

FIGURE *3.15* *References on introductions to whole language*

story will be about; *reads* the story; *engages the children* in discussing the story; and *reads it again.* The initial emphasis is simply upon reading the story for enjoyment.

3. *Rereading the story independently:* Though the children may engage in related arts, crafts, drama, music, writing, and other activities, the most important follow-up to the Shared Book Experience is independent rereading. Typically, children read a

small version of the Big Book. Often, six or eight small books can be purchased as a set, along with a commercially prepared Big Book. Particularly with teacher-made and class-developed materials, ideally each child will have his or her own individual copy to read and reread. Often, the selection is made available for children to listen to on tape as they read. This significantly facilitates learning to read.

Many things can be learned through the Shared Book Experience. The following list is adapted from Andrea Butler, *The Story Box in the Classroom, Stage 1* (1984): see also Elfant (in progress). What can be learned includes:

1. Conventions of print, such as:
   • the fact that pages are read from top to bottom, left to right
   • the fact that words, not pictures, are read
   • what a word is
   • what a letter is
   • what punctuation does
2. Strategies, such as:
   • using meaning as the first and most important clue to getting words
   • predicting
   • self-correcting
3. Sight vocabulary
4. Letter/sound relationships

Children typically learn most of the concepts of print simply by observing how the teacher turns the pages of books, how the teacher's hand or pointer moves across and down the page, and how the teacher correlates the spoken word with the written word through the use of hand or pointer. The concepts of word and letter can likewise be learned incidentally as the teacher points to words and letters while talking about them.

The teacher is usually more direct in teaching other important concepts, such as effective reading strategies. By inviting students to predict what will happen next, for example, the teacher encourages them to adopt as their own the strategy of predicting (see Chapter 4 for a more detailed discussion). Sight words and letter/sound relationships are learned in part incidentally, and in part as teacher and children direct their attention to particular words and letter/sound relationships within the reading selections. (See Chapter 5 for more details on how whole language teachers help children develop phonics know-how, during a Shared Book Experience and in other ways.)

Several things about the Shared Book Experience are worth noting:

1. The classroom procedures and activities reflect, over time, the four phases of Holdaway's natural learning model: *demonstration* (the teacher reads the book); *guided participation* (the children participate in rereadings); *individual practice* (independent rereading); and *performance* (the child often volunteers to read aloud something he or she has become confident about reading).
2. Children aren't just getting ready to read. They are actually reading.

3. Children aren't expected to practice skills in isolation from real reading. The development of skills and strategies is fostered by discussion in the context of the literary selection.

4. Reading is an enjoyable social activity, not an individualized seatwork task.

5. Less proficient readers aren't segregated from their more proficient peers. Each child participates in the reading and discussion at his or her present level of competence, while having the opportunity to learn from others. Thus, every child experiences success while continuing to grow as a reader and language user.

6. The direct instruction within the Shared Book Experience is very different from what occurs in transmission-oriented classrooms. Within transmission classrooms, direct instruction is the major mode of teaching, based upon the behavioral premise that learning results from habit formation—whether the habit involves learning skills or remembering information. The learner is viewed as a receptacle for whatever the teacher or the textbook transmits, or teaches. In contrast, within transactional classrooms, even direct instruction is often inductive, involving the learners in noticing and thinking about phenomena for themselves. Furthermore, whenever the teacher engages in direct instruction within (for example) the Shared Book Experience, the underlying premise is still that learners construct knowledge for themselves. Thus, the teacher offers direct instruction mostly within the context of authentic reading, writing, and learning experiences, when the learners' interest and motivation are high and/or when they demonstrate a definite need for the instruction. Even under such favorable conditions, however, the transactional teacher does not assume that his or her teaching will necessarily result in learning for all students, much less in the same learning for all. Knowing that learning still depends upon each learner's constructing knowledge for him- or herself, the transactional teacher simply tries to provide comprehensible input and a supportive and motivating environment, in order to facilitate the construction of knowledge.

7. The Shared Book Experience succeeds because it meets the conditions articulated in Cambourne's model of natural learning. Children are treated in such a way that they feel they are potential "doers" of the activity of reading; engaging in such reading experiences typically furthers the purposes of their lives in the here and now (purposes like enjoyment and social interaction); and the children are free to take risks and make mistakes without these being viewed as wrong.

The Shared Book Experience can be thought of more broadly as a shared *reading* experience, since it need not involve books themselves, but the reading of anything written in large print for a whole group or class to read simultaneously. Thus, the shared reading experience seems to be suitable for all children. Ideally, however, many of the texts would reflect the oral and literate traditions of the children's own community, whatever that might be. In a community like Trackton, for example, children might talk a story (compose orally), to take advantage of the children's growing proficiency in developing stories orally; the teacher could write the stories on chart paper for shared reading experiences. Classroom routines, rules, labels, and directions could also be written on chart paper and used for shared reading experiences, to take advantage of the children's expectation that reading be relevant for action. In short, the shared reading experience can take advantage of the oral and literate traditions in local communities, while introducing children to books and genres that are less often found in their homes and communities.

Other Literacy Events in Whole Language Classrooms

This section will offer only a brief overview of some of the kinds of literacy events that commonly occur in whole language classrooms. I use the term "event" to suggest that these are not exercises, nor even activities undertaken just for the sake of learning some specific skill or strategy (Altwerger, 1991). They are acts of reading, writing, and oral language undertaken for their own sake: because they are enjoyable and offer opportunities for children to construct their own knowledge—to grow as readers, writers, speakers, listeners, and learners. Such acts have maximum potential for stimulating growth in language and literacy.

In addition to the Shared Book Experience and the guided reading that occurs within it, many whole language classrooms include the following (and other) literacy events regularly, if not daily:

Independent reading

In whole language classrooms, students have many opportunities to read independently, and often to *choose* what they will read. Sometimes these choices are constrained by the curriculum: for example, students may be able to choose from a number of books, but all of the options must relate to the American Revolution or to some other topic, such as ecology and the environment. Or all of the options may be fairy tales, or books that could at least loosely be considered memoirs. Often, though, students will also have time during school when they will be completely free to choose what they read and/or to choose reading from among other learning alternatives. Even the least proficient of emergent readers is treated as a reader and is expected to read and enjoy at least the pictures of a book when time is specifically set aside for independent reading.

Paired reading

Paired reading, like independent reading, may take various forms. Students may choose buddies to read with, even if they're reading different books and mostly just reading silently together. They may be paired to read and discuss related but different books. A more proficient reader may be paired with a less proficient reader, to serve as consultant and perhaps even to help the less proficient reader develop more effective reading strategies. Students may read aloud to each other, or even in unison, perhaps with a less proficient reader echoing a more proficient reading buddy. These are just some of the possibilities.

Listening to literature read aloud

Many teachers read aloud to students daily—even to high school and college students! This shared literature event creates a social bond as well as making reading enjoyable and meaningful. In addition, it helps develop listeners' grasp of syntax (Perera, 1986), vocabulary (Elley, 1989), story structure, and genre. "A story a day keeps the remedial program away." If that's not already a classroom motto, perhaps it ought to be (see Trelease, 1989). Of course, students may read aloud, too, not to demonstrate how well they can or can't identify words, but for everyone's enjoyment. When reading aloud for this purpose, both adults and children may need to practice what they're going to read. Listening to literature on tape is a valuable complement to the live read-aloud. Nowadays, many book–tape combinations for all ages may be purchased at bookstores and borrowed from libraries. (Hundreds of books on tape are available from Recorded Books, Inc., 270 Skipjack Road, Prince Frederick, MD 20678, 1-800-638-1304.)

Language experience

Language experience events (pp. 57–58) are not as common in whole language classrooms as independent writing, because dictation can all too easily convince children that they are not yet ready to write for themselves. However, teachers may occasionally "do" language experience with children. Whether the language experience writing is based on a shared classroom experience or an individual's experience, typically the teacher will write down a sentence dictated by each child—for example, "Aaron said, 'I put in peas and carrots'"; "Ye Jee said, 'I like tomatoes'" (see p. 201 for the context of these examples). Writing what the child dictates helps to give the child ownership over the writing, and makes the text easier to remember when rereading.

Guided writing

In whole language classrooms, group writing more often takes the form of guided writing, rather than student-by-student dictation of sentences. That is, teacher and students together brainstorm, select ideas, compose and shape sentences, then reread, reconsider, and revise. Finally, they may edit what they've written and publish it—by adding it to a collection of class writings, by displaying it on the bulletin board or in the hallway, or by including it in a class or school newspaper. Such guided writing may be based upon field trips, classroom experiments, a book the class has shared—in short, almost any communal experience.

Modeled writing

In modeled writing, the teacher demonstrates his or her own writing process by thinking out loud and writing a real piece as the children listen and observe. The kinds of writing that may be composed at the chalkboard (and copied by the children, if appropriate) include notices to go home, lists for parties, notes to lunchroom supervisors or janitors, and so forth. By writing in front of the children, the teacher can demonstrate not only the writing process but the relationship between spoken words and written words, key letter/sound relationships, punctuation, and the like—as well as the concept that writing can serve various practical purposes.

Independent writing

In whole language classrooms, even the youngest children—preschoolers and kindergartners—are encouraged to write independently. At first, their writings may consist merely of drawings, demonstrating their understanding that a visual image conveys meaning. Then they may progress to scribble writing, or prephonemic writing. The point, however, is that all students, even the least proficient emergent writers, are treated as writers. They become more proficient through exposure to books and print, through observing their more proficient peers' writing and adults' writing, and through direct help as well. As with reading, sometimes students are completely free to choose what they will write. At other times, they are expected to write in their dialogue journals, their reading journals or literature logs, or their learning logs; to experiment with certain forms and genres; and so forth. Nevertheless, choice plays a big part in what students write within whole language classrooms.

Journals and Learning Logs

Dialogue journals, reading journals, and learning logs are such important aspects of learning in whole language classrooms that they deserve separate mention. A *dialogue journal* is, ordinarily, a journal in which student and teacher write back and forth to each other. Nancie Atwell initiated dialogue journals with the eighth graders in her reading class. They wrote letters to Atwell in response to the books they were reading, and Atwell responded with letters of her own; together, they discussed these and other related books (Atwell, 1987). In other words, they held literature discussions via journals. Some teachers call these journals "reading journals" or "literature logs" when they focus specifically on literary works, using the term "dialogue journal" more broadly, to mean two people's writing back and forth about any subject. *Learning logs* are journals in which students respond to a certain subject, such as science or math. They become dialogue journals if they are used transactively between teacher and student (Fulwiler & Young, 1982).

Literature discussions

Increasingly, whole language teachers are discovering that perhaps the best way to develop children's reading strategies as well as their understanding and appreciation of literature is through discussion, particularly intensive small-group discussions. Teacher and students can share reactions to the literature; make connections with other books and their own lives; discuss such literary elements as characterization, symbol, and theme; and consider strategies for dealing with problem words and other elements of the text. Such discussion enriches understanding, as the group collaboratively constructs and reconstructs meaning. The group may read and discuss the same book, or they may read and share different, related books that constitute a text set. (See Chapter 9 for more details.)

Choral reading, readers theater, drama, storytelling

The oral and dramatic language arts also figure prominently in whole language classrooms (e.g. Heinig, 1993). Here are mentioned only some of the activities most obviously associated with literature and the literacy processes. Students have opportunities to perform literature through *choral reading*, with different parts of a literary selection assigned to different groups, who then read their part in unison, or chorus. Students may rehearse and read a script in *readers theater* format: The script is written much like a play, but the participants sit and read their parts (with appropriate facial expressions and perhaps gestures) instead of memorizing their lines and acting them out. Students may engage in *drama*, not only formal but informal: acting out key aspects of a story, for example, or acting out scenes in history, as the students think these events might have (or should have!) occurred. And they may engage in *storytelling*, after rehearsing a story for performance. (See MacDonald, 1993; Macguire, 1985; Bauer, 1977; Sawyer, 1962; and see Chapter 10.)

Observation and experimentation

Observation and experimentation become literacy events when children record what they have observed. They may document the growth of a plant or a rabbit, for example, complete with graphs and learning log entries. They may predict the results of an experiment, write out the procedures for conducting it, and describe the results, comparing these with their predictions. Even the youngest of learners can engage in such literate documentation and response, using pictures or pictures with labels.

Research

Research involves reading, writing, speaking, and listening. In whole language classrooms, language and literacy are developed through and across the entire curriculum (Halliday, 1975). Even very young learners are capable of engaging in simple kinds of data gathering and recording.

Obviously, research as a regular part of classroom activity can and does encompass many of the other kinds of literacy events listed above. And clearly, these do not exhaust the kinds of literacy events found in whole language classrooms; they are merely indicative of what often occurs.

Theme Study

Though the aforementioned literacy events can occur as separate experiences within the curriculum, many of them may naturally become part of *theme study*. Whole language classrooms are often characterized by in-depth exploration of a topic or theme, which naturally involves various reading and writing experiences as well as reading and the in-depth study of literature, research, the oral and dramatic language arts, and other arts (music, movement and/or dance, the visual arts). Topics typically derive from social studies and/or science. Depending upon the teacher's and students' purposes and interests, the topics may be relatively narrow (weather, family and friends, electricity, ecology and the environment) or relatively broad (change, contrasts, conflicts, compromise, cooperation). The broader the topic, the more opportunities for integrating the humanities, arts, math and the sciences, and social studies—and the greater the chance for students to gain proficiency in using language and to become literate and independent learners. Also, the broader the topic, the more opportunities for engaging in cross-age or even whole school exploration of a common topic, or "theme."

Discussions of Reading, Writing, and Research Strategies and Skills

Within the context of children's reading, writing, and researching, teachers help them develop the skills and strategies they need. For example, when a child has difficulty reading a particular word, the teacher may remind the child to use context and the initial consonant(s) to predict what the word might be, then look at the rest of the word to confirm or correct. When a child's writing demonstrates the need for a particular editing skill, the teacher may take that opportunity to teach the skill and help the child apply it. When children are researching topics of interest, the teacher may conclude it would be relevant to teach certain skills for locating and using various kind of references that the children need. Whole language teachers know that children apply strategies and skills best when they have been learned in the context of their application (e.g., Freppon, 1988, 1991; Cunningham, 1990; DiStefano & Killion, 1984; Calkins, 1980). Therefore, they provide many opportunities to learn such strategies while the children are actually reading, writing, and researching: by demonstrating the teachers' own strategies; by providing mini-lessons for individuals, a small group, or the whole class; and by encouraging the sharing of strategies and skills as children discuss literature, each others' writings, and their ongoing research.

What Makes These Literacy Events "Whole Language"?

It is critical to understand that what makes the aforementioned literacy events "whole language" is not their mere occurrence, but the spirit in which they are introduced, undertaken, and monitored, and the way in which the processes and results are assessed. Many of these could be assigned as activities in a highly teacher-directed way, with follow-up exercises and tests that reflect a transmission model rather than a transactional model of education and learning.

What makes them "whole language" is the underlying philosophy: commitment to promoting students' ownership over their learning, and a concomitant trust in students' ability to construct their own knowledge; facilitation and support of learning that is in large measure student-determined; direct instruction in the context of students' needs and interests; commitment to promoting individual growth rather than uniform mastery of a predetermined curriculum; and assessment that reflects these principles. When these literacy events reflect such a philosophy of learning and teaching, they can justifiably be considered "whole language."

DIFFERENT MODELS: READING INSTRUCTION VERSUS LITERACY DEVELOPMENT

By now it should be clear why whole language was not included in the first section of this chapter as a method of teaching children to read. It isn't a method, and it doesn't focus exclusively on reading, or even literacy. We shall come to see in later chapters that phonics is also inappropriately considered a method of teaching reading, though it's widely regarded as a method of reading instruction. Nevertheless, let us briefly contrast the so-called phonics approach to teaching reading, the eclectic skills approach typical of basal reading programs, and a whole language curriculum for developing literacy.

With phonics as a method, letter/sound relationships and "decoding" are taught as if nothing else were involved in learning to read. Basal reader programs typically teach not only phonics skills for decoding, but word analysis skills and comprehension skills, including critical thinking skills. The isolated and usually separate nature of these skills is depicted visually in Figure 3.16. Even with the skills taken collectively, these are all part-to-whole approaches to reading and learning to read, reflecting the behavioral laws of learning articulated by Thorndike but rejected by many educators today—including many who use materials based on such principles.

In contrast are whole language practices that foster literacy and learning—not by separating reading from writing, or oral language from written language, much less by teaching isolated skills. As a growing body of research suggests (see Chapter 7), much more can be learned in whole language classrooms than in skills classrooms, in the same amount of time. This is because everything is interrelated, with the learning of skills and strategies taking place within authentic literacy events, and literacy events taking place within the exploration of themes and topics in what have traditionally been considered curricular areas separate from reading and writing. Thus, the depiction of the whole language approach in Figure 3.17 shows literacy and learning at the heart of a circle that includes various kinds of literacy events and learning processes. What's learned includes not just reading and writing—that is, strategies for constructing and composing meaning through text, and metacognitive awareness of such strategies. In addition, what's learned includes (but is not limited to) such processes as collaborating, creating,

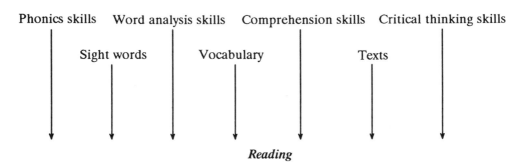

Phonics skills   Word analysis skills   Comprehension skills   Critical thinking skills

Sight words   Vocabulary   Texts

Reading

FIGURE *3.16*   *The skills approach to teaching reading*

evaluating, self-monitoring, self-regulating, and self-evaluating—all with respect to learning in general as well as to reading and writing.

In actual classrooms, conflicting practices are sometimes adopted by individual teachers. Many teachers, understandably, consider themselves prudently "eclectic" because they draw upon a variety of methods and materials in teaching reading. For example, they may use only some of the stories in the basal, supplement the basal with

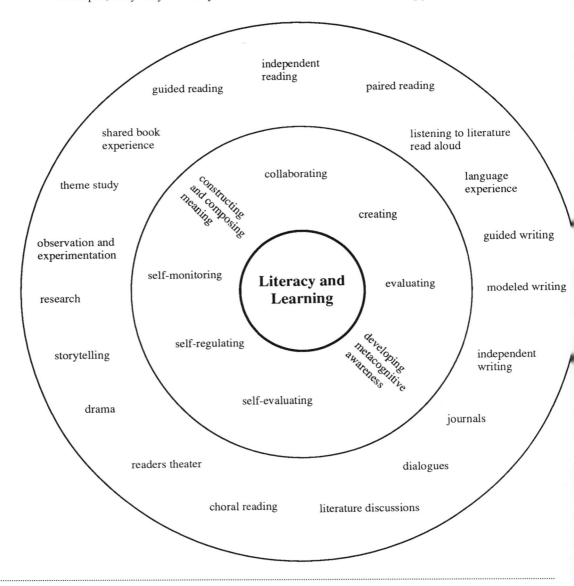

Figure 3.17   *A whole language approach to developing literacy and facilitating learning*

literature books, and perhaps use the basal as a guide to the skills they want their students to encounter and demonstrate during the school year. From one point of view, such enlightened skills teachers might be said to be theoryless or theory-confused, because their practices reflect conflicting assumptions about learning and teaching. However, they may simply be in the process of relinquishing a transmission model of education for the transactional model typified by whole language. (Chapter 8 will further discuss the nature of whole language learning and teaching, and Chapter 9 expands upon that discussion, further clarifying how teachers often grow toward and into whole language teaching.)

FOR FURTHER REFLECTION AND EXPLORATION

1. Compare Don Holdaway's natural learning model (p. 66) with the following six-step version of Madeline Hunter's model of education (Hunter, 1982):
   a. Anticipatory set and statement of objectives.
   b. Instruction and modeling.
   c. Checking understanding.
   d. Guided practice.
   e. Independent practice.
   f. Assessment.

   How are these models similar? How are they different? How are the typical outcomes similar and/or different? Which theory of learning and teaching does each reflect: the transmission, or the transactional?

2. Obtain a copy of the position statement prepared by the Commission on Reading of the National Council of Teachers of English, entitled "Basal Readers and the State of American Reading Instruction: A Call for Action." (Single copies are available free from the NCTE, 1111 Keynon Road, Urbana, IL 61801; the statement has been reprinted in my *Understanding Whole Language,* 1990a, pp. 58–59.) Consider and discuss the alleged problems with basal reading programs, given current theory and research.

3. In *Three by the Sea,* by Edward Marshall (1981), Lolly first undertakes to entertain her two friends by reading a story from her basal reader. Not impressed, Sam tells a story that is only a little more sophisticated in its use of language. Finally, Spider tells a much more interesting story, with more sophisticated language and concepts. If possible, obtain a copy of this book and consider the probable effects of using the three different kinds of materials with emergent readers.

4. In what ways is learning to read similar to the processes of learning to talk and learning to write and spell? List some of the similarities or parallels, with examples as needed.

5. Patrick Hartwell has made some interesting comments on the issue of whether "formal" grammar (grammar isolated from other language activities, like writing and reading) should be taught in the schools. Read the following quote and consider whether much the same thing could be said about the issue of how children can best be taught to read. Discuss.

Seventy-five years of experimental research has for all practical purposes told us nothing. . . . Studies are interpreted in terms of one's prior assumptions about the value of teaching grammar: their results seem not to change those assumptions. . . . It would seem unlikely, therefore, that further experimental research, in and of itself, will resolve the grammar issue. Any experimental design can be nitpicked, any experimental population can be criticized, and any experimental conclusion can be questioned or, more often, ignored. In fact, it may well be that the grammar question is not open to resolution by experimental research. (Hartwell, 1985, pp. 106–7)

Do you think this is true of the teaching-to-read issue: that it is not open to resolution merely by experimental research? If you agree, then by what means do you think we should decide the nature of our beginning reading or emergent literacy programs? You may want to consider the conflicting paradigms that are involved.

6. For each group of questions below, try to determine the rule governing how they are formed. Then decide which rule you think would develop first, second, and third (Klima and Bellugi-Klima, 1966; Dale, 1972; Cazden, 1972). How feasible would it be to *teach* children these rules?

a. What he can ride in?
How he can be a doctor?
Why he don't know how to pretend?
Where my spoon goed?

b. Where's his other eye?
Why are you thirsty?
What did you doed?

c. Who that?
What cowboy doing?
Where Ann pencil?
Where milk go?
Where horsie go?

7. The following conversation took place when a psychologist tried to correct an immaturity in her daughter's speech (McNeill, 1966, p. 69):

CHILD: Nobody don't like me.
MOTHER: No, say, "Nobody likes me."
CHILD: Nobody don't like me.
    (*eight repetitions of this dialogue*)
MOTHER: No. Now listen carefully; say, "Nobody likes me."
CHILD: Oh! Nobody don't likes me!

What does this incident suggest about the feasibility of deliberately trying to accelerate children's language development? What are some possible implications for teaching?

8. The first part of Sandra Wilde's *You Kan Red This! Spelling and Punctuation for Whole Language Classrooms, K–6* (1992) deals mainly with understanding children's

development in spelling and punctuation, while the second part deals with fostering the development of spelling and spelling strategies in the classroom (with a chapter on punctuation as well). You might try reading the first part and summarizing what you've learned, and/or reading the second part and implementing the ideas for conducting mini-lessons, communicating with parents and administrators, and so forth. Wilde's volume might well be billed "the last book you'll ever need on the teaching of spelling."

9. Despite my enthusiasm for Wilde's book, I must admit to thinking there is one major omission: sample lessons for teaching words with common bases or suffixes, which are typically of Latin or Greek origin. One of the easiest and best ways to develop such mini-lessons is to start with a word having a common element (such as *phone* in *phonograph*, *telephone*, *phonics*, etc.) and brainstorm for more words, then try to determine the meaning that the element has in all (or most) of the words. One book with collections of such words is *Words from the Romance Languages* (Danner, 1980). Many of the words in each set of the Danner volume might be too sophisticated for elementary and middle-school students, but the book is a valuable resource for the teacher. If you cannot locate this book, another valuable resource currently in print is *Dictionary of English Word-Roots*, by Bob Kupa'a Smith (1966). Richard Gentry and Jean Gillet's *Teaching Kids to Spell* (1993) includes a useful appendix with Latin and Greek stems and prefixes.

10. To enhance your understanding of the patterns typical of letter-name spellings, write the following words, spelling them in accordance with the letter-name patterns explained in the appendix to this chapter. (This list could be used as a quick assessment of children's spelling development, too. If used in that way, it would be important to say the word, then use the word in a sentence, then repeat the word.)

   a. cat   as in *Our cat purrs a lot.*
   b. wet   as in *The dog got all wet.*
   c. make   as in *Let's make pizza.*
   d. sent   as in *I sent her a birthday card.*
   e. water   as in *Let's get a drink of water.*
   f. why   as in *Why did she do that?*
   g. chip   as in *We baked some chocolate chip cookies.*
   h. band   as in *Rob plays a trumpet in the band.*
   i. clock   as in *Look at the clock to see what time it is.*
   j. train   as in *Jimmy has a new electric train.*
   k. once   as in *"Once upon a time . . ."*
   l. city   as in *Molly lives in the city.*
   m. dragon   as in *It's a fire-breathing dragon.*
   n. sheet   as in *May I have a sheet of paper?*
   o. kind   as in *What kind of candy is it?*

Next, choose five of the words in the list above and write each of them as you think they might be written in prephonemic, early phonemic, and transitional spellings. Explain the typical differences among the stages.

11. The following "stories" (Cramer, 1978, p. 43) reflect the first writing attempts of four first graders (their spelling has been standardized).[1] Which writings impress you the most? Which writers do you think were most concerned about spelling words correctly, most afraid to take the risk of spelling words as best they could? Discuss.

I play in the grass.	My dad is nice.
And I play with my friends.	My mom is nice.
And I play with Debbie.	My sisters are nice.
—Mary	—Danielle

Winnie the Pooh

One evening Winnie went	I cracked my head. I fell
out to get some honey.	off the bed. My Mom
He climbed and climbed	took me to the hospital.
for honey. He found honey.	—Nathalie
—John	

12. The following retelling of Shakespeare's *Romeo and Juliet* was written by nine-year-old Emily Joslin-Jeske, after watching the movie several times and reading the script of the movie. Without looking back at the script, Emily wrote the play at home, late in the evening, because she wanted the story in "plain English." Consider (and maybe analyze) the constructive spellings in this first draft.[2]

Romeo and Juliet

Secne in Verone

In the city of fair Verona a carnival was being held.
Childeren were runing and screaming.Two of the servince
of the house of Capulet and the house of Montague were
passing by each other.The two familys had been bitter
enimes. As they passed by one of the house of Montague
mattered something unplesent under his bereth. "What
did you say?"asked one of the Capulet suspishisly.
"It's none of your bissnes." hissed the Capulet.
"Well I'm making it my bissnes" hissed the Montague.
Before another word was said they druw there swords
and began to fight. Shortly the prince of Verona
came in. He was apoled at what he saw. "WHAT IS THIS
I SEE. DO MY EYES DESIVE ME! WHAT AM I SEEING. I AM
SEEING YOU FIGHT LIKE FOOLS!"

(Every one looks guilty)

"I HOPE NEVER TO SEE THIS AGAIN"

(every one leaves)

sene In Juliets room

"Good news darling" cryed Lady Capulet.
Juliet looked up from underneth the bed. "What mother?" she
asked. "The lordly paris has asked your hand in marigge"
said lord Capulet. "You to would make the perfect cople"
added Lady Capulet. "You shall meet at the masked ball
tonight" said lord Capulet."But . . . But . . . I think I'm a
little young to get married. I'm only 14 you know."
"Nonsence dear the younger the better!" said Lady Capulet

(They walk out of the room)

sene The masked ball

That night at the masked ball Juliet was waiting to see
Paris. During the party Romeo and his fiends Benvolio
and Mercutio all Montagues were passing by the party.
"Lets go to the party. We can were masks since its a
masked ball." "splended" cryed Romeo.

(They slip on outfits and masks)

When they got there Lord Paris had just been peresented
to Juliet. When Paris desided he would go to sleep
because he thought he had drank to much, Romeo desided
to flurt with Juliet. They both fell in love emedetly.

sene At Juliet's window

After the party was over, Romeo desided to go see Juliet
at her window. "I must see Juliet again" he said to himself.
When he got there Juliet was on the balcone singing to
herself. She did not see Romeo. Thinking she was alone she
said outloud "Romeo oh Romeo I love you" "And I to" said
Romeo. "Romeo what are you doing here, you might get killed"
"I only come here to SEE YOU!" "Shhhhhhhhhhhhhhhhhh leave
I hear someone coming" "Good night Juliet" "Good night Romeo.

Sene At the friers chambers

Juliet went to see the frier for help.
"Why do you come to me Juliet" asked the frier. "Frier please
Romeo and I wish to be marryed" said Juliet. "Please PLEASE
marry us secretly". "Srtaly I stand by god. Bring Romeo
and you will be marryed.

Sene Romeo and Juliet have just been marryed

"Oh Romeo I don't fell well I think I will go home".

(Juliet goes home)
"Hey Romeo" yelled benvolio. Lets go find Mercutio.
when they found Mercutio it wasn't a pertty sight. He and
Tybalt were fighting. Suddenly someone yelled, Mercutio

looked in that direction. With out anther word Tybalt slashed
Mercutio in the back. Mercutio fell to the ground. Romeo quickly
charged at Tybalt. Before Tybalt could turn to see what was
happening Romeos sword hit Tybalt in the heart. Tybalt fell
to the ground. The prince had seen it all. He stepped in "WAS
I EVER CLEAR. NO I SEE I WASN'T. Romeo will be banned. The prince
went away.

sene Juliet sees the frier

"Well I see your tragedy" said the frier thoughtfuly.
"Can you help I mean can you get Romeo back"? asked Juliet.
"No but I think I can get you two together. When you drink
this you go into a death like sleep. Send a message to Romeo.
You will be placed in the family tomb. He will meet you there.
The frier gave Juliet the poshin. When she got home she told
her parents she would marry Paris. She went to her room and
drank the poshin. She lay down on the bed and went to sleep.
Her parents came up to see her. When they found her she was
on her bed. When they realized she was dead they cryed and cryed.
Of course Juliet did not forget to send the messager. But the
messager gave the wrong message. "Juliet died" said the messager.

Sene Romeo at the tomb

"No. It couldn't be" cryed Romeo. "Life without Juliet"
"I'm as good as dead". Romeo pulled out some posin
and drank it. He droped down dead. Just then Juliet woke up.
She saw Romeo. "Romeo wake up wake up". His limp body rolled over.
When Juliet saw that he was dead she worled around. She grabbed
Romeos dagger and pushed in her chest. She sank to the floor.

THE END

REWRITTEN BY EMILY JOSLIN-JESKE

In your opinion, is Emily likely to have used such sophisticated vocabulary if she had been expected to spell everything correctly in a first draft? Indeed, would she have written this retelling at all, since she did it just because she wanted to? What might you respond to someone who asks, "When do you start demanding correct spelling?"

13. Should teachers "correct" children's writing? Consider the following quote:

> Evidence is also clear on this point: Children who write frequently and receive no correction on their papers will write more, have more creative ideas, enjoy writing more, and—at worst—will make no more mechanical errors than do those who receive correction on their papers. According to most studies, those who do not receive corrections make even fewer errors in capitalization, punctuation, and spelling. (Hillerich, 1977, p. 306; he cites several sources)

Considering your own experience (as student, parent, teacher), would you agree with this assertion? What better ways might there be to help students write correctly?

Discuss how the issue of whether or not to correct children's writing reflects the two contrasting paradigms, transmission and transactional.

14. Below are questions that administrators and/or parents might ask about introducing a whole language program that encourages young children to write freely, using their own constructive or invented spellings as needed, and not worrying about mechanics as they first compose. You might organize a "public meeting" for discussion, with one group representing doubters and another group representing enlightened teachers. (Originally raised by my students, these questions are arbitrarily grouped into four categories, for discussion by four groups; thus, there is some overlap in the questions.)

Goals/objectives—Rationale—Advantages

a. What goals/objectives do you expect to accomplish by encouraging children to write freely, without initially worrying about correct spelling and mechanics?
b. What are the principles upon which the approach is based?
c. What are the advantages of encouraging constructive spelling rather than insisting on correct spelling?

Feared disadvantages—More on advantages

d. Is there any evidence that this program won't succeed as well as a traditional approach to spelling and to mechanical correctness?
e. Won't this procedure harm children by getting them in the habit of spelling words incorrectly?
f. Is there any evidence that this approach will make children better writers? Better readers? Better spellers? Better in the use of other conventions of mechanics?

Fostering correctness

g. With this approach, how will children learn the rules for correct spelling, punctuation, and grammar?
h. When, if ever, will you correct the children's spelling errors and other mechanical errors?
i. How long do you recommend letting the children continue to use constructive spelling and their own conventions of punctuation and grammar?

Stimulating growth—Measuring progress—Introducing such a program

j. How can you help children begin to use constructive spellings? How do you help them use more sophisticated spellings?
k. How can you determine whether or not the children are making progress in learning to spell, if they don't have to spell correctly? How can you determine if the children are making progress in learning to punctuate?
l. Can you introduce this program without taking time away from other valuable activities? If so, how?

An outstanding book that deals with such issues in the teaching of writing is Lucy Calkins' *The Art of Teaching Writing* (1986). With respect to spelling and punctuation in particular, see Sandra Wilde's *You Kan Red This!* (1992) and other references in Figure 3.8.

15. Assume you are a primary grade teacher. Write a letter to parents explaining your program for teaching reading and writing. Explain how it reflects what we know about how children initially acquire language and how it encourages children's natural reading and writing development. (You may first want to read Chapter 7 on research.) Be sure to include examples of children's real reading and writing.

16. Read the report *Becoming a Nation of Readers* (Anderson, Heibert, Scott, & Wilkinson, 1985). Then do one or more of the following:

    a. Draw up a list of good points about basal reading programs and a list of bad points, based on the report. Add any other points you might think of. Be prepared to discuss.

    b. From the report, make a list of ten statements or recommendations that you think socio-psycholinguists would agree with, and that also seem significant to you. Be prepared to discuss.

    c. From the report, make a list of half a dozen statements that you think would, for one reason or another, make socio-psycholinguists uneasy. In several cases, many socio-psycholinguists might agree with part of a sentence but be concerned about another part. Be prepared to explain why.

17. In order to better anticipate and participate in the discussion of Chapter 4, you might try the following activity: Cut a slit in a piece of paper so that the slit will expose just one of the following lines at a time. Then find someone to be your experimental subject. Tell the person you are going to expose some lines of print one at a time, each for only a fraction of a second. The person is to try to focus attention on the middle of the line and then to write down in order all of the print seen, after which you will then expose another line. Try, of course, to expose each line for the same amount of time as the others, ideally only long enough for one eye fixation (about a quarter of a second). See if the person is able to recall more print from some lines than from others. What do you think accounts for any observed differences in how many letters are recalled?

QLH WCGMZK PGTXW NBFJMSV

BAX GORPLE CHURK FRENTLY

ANGRY GROW TAXES BOY UGLY

SILLY WINDOWS HIT THE BOX

FUNNY CLOWNS MAKE ME LAUGH

18. Again in preparation for Chapter 4, have some of your friends, or some children, brainstorm for words that might reasonably come next in a sentence that begins

"The cruel giant fell into the . . ." Encourage your brainstormers to be imaginative. (Some of my students have suggested such responses as *witches' cauldron, septic tank,* and *flour bin.)* When you are satisfied, tell the brainstormers that following the word or words they have supplied come the words "and drowned." Which of the suggested alternatives can you now eliminate as extremely unlikely? Discuss what enabled/encouraged your brainstormers to make the predictions they did, and what enabled them to eliminate certain alternatives. What does this activity suggest about the kinds of contexts we use in reading?

Appendix: Development in Children's Invented Spellings

The best way to show the various stages in children's writing and spelling is with actual examples. Accordingly, the figures in this appendix depict writings by children at different levels of spelling development:

- Figure A3.1: Scribble writing.
- Figure A3.2: Prephonemic writing.
- Figure A3.3: Early phonemic writing.
- Figure A3.4: Early letter-name writing.
- Figure A3.5: Letter-name writing.
- Figure A3.6: Late letter-name writing.
- Figure A3.7: Transitional stage of writing.

SCRIBBLE WRITING
Age 3

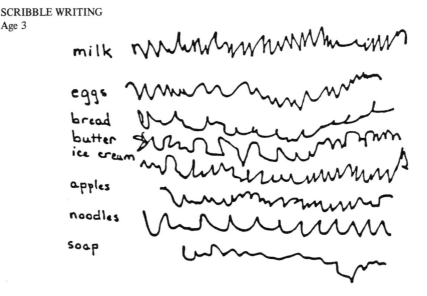

FIGURE A3.1   Three-year-old's scribble writing. She told her mother what each of these "words" meant (Temple, Nathan, Temple, & Burris, 1993)

PREPHONEMIC STAGE
Age 4

Kindergartener

FIGURE A3.2   Four-year-old's and kindergartner's prephonemic writing: the letters do not represent sounds (Temple, Nathan, Temple, & Burris, 1993)

EARLY PHONEMIC STAGE
Age 5

RCRBKD

Our car broke down.

Kindergartener

MBEWWMLht

My Baby was with me last night.

FIGURE A3.3   Children's early phonemic writing (Temple, Nathan, Temple, & Burris, 1993)

EARLY PHONEMIC STAGE
First Grader

I know you.

First Grader
The child represents
each syllable with letters.

There was a beautiful house.

FIGURE A3.3 *Children's early phonemic writing, continued. Notice the letter-name spelling of U for "you" in the first example, and the use of letters to represent each syllable in the second example (from Dobson, 1986b and 1986a respectively)*

LETTER-NAME STAGE (early)
Age 4

Once a lady went fishing and she caught Flipper.

FIGURE A3.4   *Four-year-old's early letter-name writing (C. Chomsky, 1971, p. 509)*

LETTER-NAME STAGE
First Grader

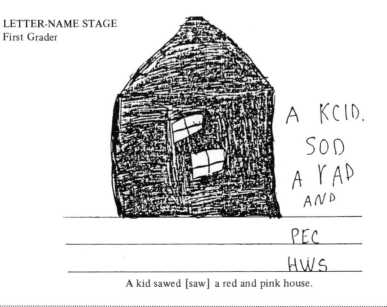

A kid sawed [saw] a red and pink house.

FIGURE A3.5   *First grader's letter-name writing (Dobson, 1986a)*

LETTER-NAME STAGE (late)
First Grader

I:yeNt:toot:The
yeeL The yeeL
yos a gtod yeeL
keeeNd

I went to the whale. The whale was a good whale.
The end.

LETTER-NAME STAGE (late)
Age 5

He had a blue
clth. It trd
in to a brd.

He had a blue cloth. It turned into a bird.

FIGURE A3.6 *Letter-name spellings. Note how in the first example the use of Y for /w/ shows the letter-name strategy, while the use of double vowels shows the influence of environmental print. In the second example some of the spellings also show the influence of environmental print. (Top example from Dobson, 1986a; bottom, from Temple, Nathan, Temple, & Burris, 1993.)*

TRANSITIONAL STAGE
First Grader

Elaine

At my house i have some
dayseses they are flowrs
they growe in the spreing
i pike them in the
spreing the rain mak the
flowrs growe and in the
somre they all droy up
and more flowrs
growe bak and they
have naw levs and
i poke them agan.

Elaine

I have a ducke. I can drcke
wottre. She has baby ducklings.
Theye foloe her in a strat line.
Theye leve ina barine.
Thoye are yellow. Theye can
tack a bathe and The
un is out. and we play a
lot with Theme.

FIGURE A3.7   *A first grader's transitional spelling (Temple, Nathan, Temple, & Burris, 1993)*

Consonant Patterns Reflecting the Letter-name Strategy

Y for the /w/ sound, as in *we* and *went*. The *name* of the letter Y begins with a /w/ sound.
Examples: YUTS for *once*   YENT or YET for *went*
YOZ for *was*   YEEL for *whale*

V for the /ð/ sound, as in *the* and *mother*. The name of the letter V sounds a lot like the /ð/ sound in these words, and the sounds are made similarly. Thus V is sometimes used to represent the /ð/ sound.
Examples: IHOVR for *each other*   VE for *the*   VA for *they*
Note that in the former case, each other, a young child may actually pronounce the th as a /v/ sound, so this fact alone might account for the V used here. However, /v/ for *th* at the beginning of a word is not common; the sound is likely to be /ð/ or /d/. Thus we might expect initial *th* in such words to be spelled as V, if the child pronounces such words as /ð/ and is using a letter-name strategy, or as D, if the child pronounces these words with /d/ and is using a letter-name strategy.

H for the /č/ sound, as in *chip*. The *name* of the letter H, "aitch," ends in a /č/ sound.
Examples: BRENH for *branch*   WHT for *watched*
NHR for *nature*   IHOVR for *each other*

H for the /š/ sound, as in *ship*. The *name* of the letter H, "aitch," ends in a /č/ sound, but the /č/ sound itself consists of two sounds run together, /t/ plus /š/. Thus the name "aitch" actually ends in the /š/ sound.

Examples: FEHEG for *fishing*   HE for *she*

Of course the /š/ sound is often represented by the letter S also, since the sounds are so similar.

Examples: SOS for *shoes*   SES for *she's*

At the beginning of a word, CH is often used for /t/, when an /r/ follows. The /č/ sound actually consists of a /t/ sound followed by a /š/ sound, so again there is logic to the choice.

Examples: CHRAN for *train*   CHRIBLS for *troubles*   CHRAY for *tray*

At the beginning of a word, J is often used for /d/, when an /r/ follows. The /ǰ/ sound actually consists of a /d/ sound followed by a /ž/ sound (the first consonant in *azure*). Again, the choice is logical.

Examples: JRIV for *drive*   JRAGN for *dragon*
              JRAN for *drain*   JREMS for *dreams*

Other Consonant Patterns Typical of the Letter-name Stage

The letters representing the nasal sounds /n/, /m/, and /ŋ/ (as in *think* or *finger*) are typically omitted before consonants.

Examples: MOSTR for *monster*   NUBRS for *numbers*   AGRE for *angry*
              PLAT for *plant*   ATTEPT for *attempt*   SEK for *sink*
              AD for *and*   STAPS for *stamps*   THEKCE for *thanks*
              CAT for *can't*

The consonants /l/, /r/, /n/, and /m/ tend to "swallow up" the vowel associated with them in an unaccented syllable, particularly at the ends of words. Thus the vowel letter is often omitted before or after /l/ or before /r/, /n/, or /m/ in such syllables.

Examples: SPESHL for *special*   BRATHR for *brother*   OPN for *open*
              LITL for *little*   FETHR for *feather*   WAGN for *wagon*
              CANDL for *candle*   GRANMOTR   EVN for *even*
              GOBL for *gobble*   for *grandmother*   CRAN for *crayon*
                                     SOPR for *supper*
              FRM for *from*

Vowel Patterns Reflecting the Letter-name Strategy

A for the /e/ sound, as in *bet*. The *name* of the letter A (eh-ee) begins with an /e/-like sound. Thus A is frequently used to represent the /e/ sound.

Examples: PAN for *pen*   PRTAND for *pretend*
              FALL for *fell*   DAVL for *devil*

E for the /i/ sound, as in *bit.* The *name* of the letter E (ih-ee) begins with an /i/-like sound. Thus E is sometimes used to represent the /i/ sound.

Examples: SEP for *ship*   FES for *fish*

FLEPR for *Flipper*   WEL for *will*

I for the /ɔ/ sound, as in *clock.* The *name* of the letter I (ah-ee) begins with an /ɔ/-like sound. Thus an I is occasionally used to represent the /ɔ/ sound.

Examples: GIT for *got*   CLICK for *clock*   DIKTR for *doctor*   IR for *are*

O for the stressed /ə/ sound, as in *mud.* The *name* of the letter O (uh-oh) begins with an /ə/-like sound. Thus an O is occasionally used to represent the stressed /ə/ sound.

Examples: MOD for *mud*   SOPR for *supper*

JOPT for *jumped*   HOGZ for *hugs*

The preceding are examples of typical letter-name spellings, taken mostly from Read (1975), the pioneering study of children's letter-name spellings. Other examples are from C. Chomsky (1979); Temple, Nathan, Temple, & Burris (1993); and Dobson (1986a).

4 | Context, Word Identification, and Constructing Meaning

The major folklore of reading instruction relates to the "theory" that reading is considered an exact process. In other words, the reader is expected to read everything exactly as printed on the page in order to understand the message of the author. In general the consuming public, legislatures, courts and too many educators hold to this theory. It is like the theory of the world being flat during the time of Columbus.

— Robert Harper and Gary Kilarr

In this chapter and the next, we will consider several kinds of context that affect word perception and identification: the context that letters provide for each other as they combine in familiar word patterns; syntactic and semantic context among words within sentences; and other contexts beyond the sentence and beyond the text. After this brief overview that proceeds from smaller units to larger, we will reverse the order for extended discussion. Chapter 5 then culminates in a model of proficient reading that reflects my attempt to synthesize these insights about word identification and the construction of meaning.

THE VARIETIES OF CONTEXT: AN OVERVIEW

One kind of context in reading is the visual context that letters provide for each other, creating recognizable and familiar patterns. To understand the significance of this kind of context, glance quickly at the column of pseudowords in the left-hand column below, then write down as many as you can remember. Next, do the same with the column of pseudowords on the right (Miller, Bruner, and Postman, 1954, p. 133):

RICANING	YRULPZOC
VERNALIT	OZHGPMTJ
MOISSANT	DLEGQMNW
POKERSON	GFUJXZAQ
FAVORIAL	WXPAUJVB

The pseudowords at the left are much easier to perceive and recall, simply because their letter patterns are a much closer approximation to normal English.

Given our internalized knowledge of letter patterns, it should not be surprising that we can identify a word in about as much time as it takes to identify a single letter. Indeed, we can identify a related group of words in about the same length of time as it takes to identify a single word. Research shows, in fact, that during a normal eye fixation of about one-fourth second, we can identify about four or five unrelated letters, or about ten or twelve letters organized into two or three unrelated words, or about twenty to twenty-five letters organized into a sequence of four or five related words (see, for example, F. Smith, 1973, p. 56, and F. Smith, 1975, p. 58). Hence, during a normal eye fixation, we might be able to identify a sequence like *lgibh* (four or five unrelated letters), a sequence like *know boys that* (ten to twelve letters organized into two or three unrelated words), or a sequence like *that girl knew many boys* (twenty to twenty-five letters organized into a sequence of four or five related words). Our perceptual span increases with the relatedness of the units being identified. We can identify more letters when they are organized into words, and more words when they are organized into a related phrase or sentence.

In phrases and sentences, we have basically two kinds of context to aid in word identification: syntactic context and semantic context. *Syntactic context* consists of the signals provided by word endings, function words, and word order (see Chapter 2). *Semantic context* consists of the meaningful relations among the words. In short, *syntax* means grammar, and *semantics* means meaning.

To see how grammar and meaning aid in the identification and recall of words, look for a moment at the following four strings of words. Which string would be easiest to process? Which would be hardest? Why?

1. Furry wildcats fight furious battles.
2. Furry jewelers create distressed stains.
3. Furry fight furious wildcats battles.
4. Furry create distressed jewelers stains.

As you might suspect, the first string is typically easiest to process, because it has both grammar and meaning: that is, it preserves normal word order, and it makes reasonable sense. The fourth string is typically hardest to process, because it has neither grammar nor meaning: the string does not preserve normal word order, and it does not make sense. Processing is easier when we have either normal word order (string 2) or some semblance of meaning (string 3). (For details, see Marks and Miller, 1964, pp. 1–5.)

Various laboratory experiments indicate that both grammar and meaning aid in the identification and recall of words. That is, both syntactic context and semantic context are important, as you probably concluded from some of the activities in the preceding chapter.

Another revealing activity is the so-called *cloze test,* a widely known method for assessing a reader's comprehension and his or her use of reading strategies. The standard cloze test typically requires supplying every fifth word of a text, as in the following example from Bormuth (1975, p. 70). Try to fill each blank space with whatever you think was omitted from the original text (in some cases a number or a part of a hyphenated word has been omitted). As you fill in the blanks, try to be conscious of how you are using context and of what kinds of context you are using:

The Beaver

Indians call beavers the "little men of the woods." But they (1)_____ really so

very little. (2)_____ beavers grow to be (3)_____ or four feet long (4)_____

weigh from 30 to (5)_____ pounds. These "little men (6)_____ the woods" are

busy (7)_____ of the time. That (8)_____ why we sometimes say, "(9)_____

busy as a beaver."

    (10)_____ know how to build (11)_____ that can hold water.

(12)_____ use their two front (13)_____ to do some of (14)_____ work.

Cutting down a (15)_____ with their four sharp-(16)_____ teeth is easy. A

(17)_____ can cut down a (18)_____ 4 inches thick in (19)_____ 15 minutes.

At the outset you probably found that to fill in the blanks you had to use both the grammar and the meaning of the preceding part of the sentence. In the first sentence where a blank occurs, "But they _____ . . . ," the word *they* suggests that a verb will be coming next; this is grammatical context, or syntax. The word *but* suggests that this second sentence will in some way contradict the first, and that the verb should therefore contain a negative marker; this is meaning context, or semantics. Putting both kinds of information together (and some other information as well), we are likely to supply the word *aren't,* and thus to read the sentence as "But they aren't really so very little." This word seems to fit syntactically and semantically with what comes after the blank as well as with what comes before.[1]

In some cases, following context is even more essential than in the first example. Look, for instance, at the sentence "That _____ why we sometimes say '_____ busy as a beaver.'" The word *that* can function as a noun determiner rather than a noun, as in "That fact explains why we sometimes say, 'as busy as a beaver.'" If we did not look ahead, we might supply the wrong kind of word in the blank following the word *that.* And we need to see "busy as a beaver" to know that the word in the second blank should be *as.* When we have adequate background knowledge, about one word in five— at least—can be supplied by the reader (W. Taylor, 1953). In other words, with only about four-fifths of the words present, the reader can still reconstruct the text, creating closure (hence the term "cloze procedure"). This suggests that there is considerable redundancy of information within most texts.

As we began to see in Chapter 2, "context" is far more inclusive than most people realize. We can and do use our entire personal context of knowledge and experience, our schemas (including our entire social context, our background) to help us identify (and sometimes misidentify) words. Second, we use aspects of the situational context, verbal and/or nonverbal. (An amusing example of a situationally caused miscue is from the sign in a church parking lot that one boy misread for a long time as "Angel parking" rather than "Angle parking".) For simplicity, I would also include under situational context various aspects of the sociolinguistic context. The classroom setting, for example, is a powerful sociolinguistic context, giving rise to particular kinds of assumptions and expectations on the part of both teachers and students. An example would be the expectation that many of my students bring to reading the poem "To Pat" (Chapter 2) in class; namely that there must be some deep, hidden meaning in the poem, a meaning that they probably aren't seeing clearly. Like the context within the reader, the sociolinguistic context can both aid and thwart word identification.

In addition to using these kinds of contexts that are outside or beyond the text, we of course use context within the text to identify words. First, we use context before and after the sentence being read, but within the same reading selection. Second, we use context before and after the word being identified, but within the same sentence. Figure 4.1 summarizes all these major kinds of contexts, while suggesting two major ways of subdividing them: context within the text versus context beyond the text, and context within the sentence versus context beyond the sentence and the text. Since contexts beyond the sentence tend especially to blend together, the following discussion will reflect this latter division. We will deal with the "larger" kinds of context first.

CONTEXT BEYOND THE SENTENCE AND THE TEXT

Using Context to Determine Meaning and Acquire Vocabulary

As proficient adult readers, we are often conscious of using context to determine the meaning of words we do not know (but see Schatz & Baldwin, 1986). One of my more

Context within the text		Context beyond the text	
Within the sentence (before and after the word being read)	Beyond the sentence (before and after the sentence being read)	Within the situation (verbal and nonverbal, including sociolinguistic context)	Within the reader (entire lifetime of knowledge and experience)

Context within the sentence   Context beyond the sentence and the text

FIGURE 4.1   *Contexts used in word identification*

interesting experiences was with the word *desiccant.* I could pronounce the word with no difficulty, but without context I would have had no idea what it meant. The word was printed on the outside of a little packet that came inside a bag of potato chips, and the manufacturers obligingly indicated that this packet of desiccant was included to absorb moisture and keep the chips fresh. Thanks to this explanation, I realized that the desiccant was not something to be thrown away as soon as the bag of chips was opened.

Writers are not always so obliging, yet often the preceding or following context gives a clue to the meaning of an unfamiliar word. Consider, for example, the context leading up to the word *fragile* and the word *melancholy,* below:

> The teacups were delicate, easily broken. So *fragile* that Ellen hardly dared grasp the handle.

> It was a gloomy day, more depressing than any that Margo had ever known. She lay motionless in bed, listless and *melancholy.*

Here, the preceding context indicates the meaning of *fragile* rather clearly, and at least supplies an appropriate connotation for *melancholy.* Note also that a reader would be able to get the essential meaning from these contexts, whether or not the words were pronounced correctly. As a matter of fact, I knew the meaning of *melancholy* for years before I finally learned that my mental pronunciation of the word was incorrect (I incorrectly syllabicated and stressed the word: *me-LAN-cho-ly*).

If the context of preceding sentences is not enough to make the meaning of a word clear, often the context of following sentences will come to the rescue. This is what happened when I first encountered the word *scofflaw.* When I read the headline "Scofflaw off to a Bad Start," I thought *flaw* must be the base word, so I mentally pronounced the word like this: SKO-fla. I could not even syllabicate or pronounce it correctly until I had read most of the article. It was the third paragraph that finally triggered my understanding:

> Cooper had ignored 780 parking tickets between 1973 and 1977. He was identified by a computer in 1977 as the city's worst traffic scofflaw. It took nearly a year for police to find him.[2]

In this case, I used the following context to correct my tentative stab at the word. Once I realized that a "scofflaw" is someone who scoffs at the law, I was able to syllabicate and pronounce the word correctly.

In a similar vein, Yetta Goodman cites as an interesting and instructionally useful example the concept of the word *krait* in Roald Dahl's short story "Poison" (1950). Goodman excerpted the following sentences from the story (Y. M. Goodman 1976, p. 101). Stop after each sentence and ask yourself what mental picture you have of the krait.

> "A krait! Oh, oh! Where'd it bite you?"

> "It's on my stomach. Lying there asleep."

"Then out of the corner of my eye I saw this krait sliding over my pajamas. Small, about ten inches."

They hang around people's houses and they go for warm places.

The bite is quite deadly, except sometimes when you catch it at once; and they kill a fair number of people each year in Bengal, mostly in the villages.

I was going to be ready to cut the bitten place and try to suck the venom out.

"Shall we draw the sheet back quick and brush it off before it has time to strike?"

"It is not safe," he continued, "because a snake is cold-blooded and anesthetic does not work so well or so quick with such animals."

The author builds suspense by only gradually providing the information necessary to identify the krait as a snake. Note, too, that how quickly a person understands this fact will depend largely upon how much that person knows about snakes. If one knew nothing about snakes, one might have to read even the last of the sentences above to realize what a krait is. Context within the selection must be supplemented by personal context, the totality of one's knowledge and experience.

Our ability to use everything we know in order to understand unfamiliar words in context enables us to learn new vocabulary through reading. It has been estimated that the "average" fifth grader is likely to encounter between 16,000 and 24,000 unknown words per year in the course of reading (R. C. Anderson & Freebody, 1983) and that the typical child adds more than 3,000 words a year to his or her recognition vocabulary—about 16 words per school day (Miller & Gildea, 1987; Nagy & Anderson, 1984; Nagy & Herman, 1987; Nagy, Anderson, & Herman, 1987). Clearly, not this many words are directly taught. The obvious conclusion is that many of these new words—indeed, most of them—are acquired through the act of reading. Usually it takes several encounters for the new word to take, and for the meanings inferred to become more accurate (Beck, McKeown, & McCaslin, 1983). Nevertheless, during their school years, children apparently learn most of their vocabulary through the act of reading.

This, of course, is one major reason why we should not withhold challenging texts from students until they can recognize nearly all of the words accurately. Such restraint will actually inhibit their acquisition of new vocabulary. In contrast, extensive reading will enhance vocabulary and thus encourage the reading of more sophisticated texts.

Using Context to Identify Words

So far we have talked about determining the meaning of words that one might not have understood without context. However, beginning and less proficient readers, in particular, use context to identify (that is, to name) words that are in their speaking vocabulary but that they do not immediately recognize in print. We shall soon see that such readers use context within the sentence to identify words that they do not always identify correctly in isolation. However, it is also true that such readers use context from the preceding and following sentences. Perhaps most remarkable is the fact that readers can use the context of the following sentences to correct the miscues they themselves have made. An example comes readily to mind. As a first grader, my son was having unusual difficulty with a basal story I had asked him to read for a miscue analysis (there are certain disadvantages to being a professor's son). The boy in the story was named Hap. While at a local fair, Hap noticed someone who was jumping high as he walked along. Hap's father explained that the person was able to jump so high because of the pack on his back. Here are the following four sentences of the story, along with my son's miscues on the word *gas*:

                    gams
"The pack has a kind of gas in it.

    gangs
The gas is very light.

It helps the boy to jump high."

          gangs
"What kind of gas is it?" asked Hap.

As you might suspect, my son was getting little meaning from this passage. But on the next page of the story, Hap's father explained to him that the gas is called helium. This explanation apparently triggered my son's understanding, because the next time he came to the word *gas* his face lit up and he said, "I got that wrong on the other page. It was *gas* all the time." In this case, the meaning of the word was familiar to the reader, but he did not recognize the word in print until the context of following sentences triggered his own personal context, his prior knowledge of helium and its effects.

Even context within the text is often not enough to facilitate the identification of words. The relative importance of grapho/phonemic cues, context cues, and prior knowledge can often be seen in the miscues of moderately proficient readers. Like most of us, they can use context and grapho/phonemic cues together to "get" words if the words are already within their personal schemas, but otherwise even simultaneous use of these cues may fail them. Consider, for instance, the following examples from Anne, a fifteen-year-old who demonstrated fairly effective use of reading strategies. The passage is from *Bread and Jam for Frances* (Hoban, 1964):

That evening for dinner, Mother cooked

          veil cutelets
breaded veal cutlets, with string beans

and baked potatoes.

"Ah," said Father. "What is there handsomer   ⓒ *husband*

on a plate and tastier to eat than breaded

val cutelets
veal cutlet!"

Anne managed to use all the language cue systems to correct "husband" to *handsomer*, despite the rather unusual and grammatically unpredictable use of the word. Probably she was able to make this correction because she was familiar with the written word *handsome* in other contexts. However, she was not able to get *veal cutlets*, twice more pronouncing it as "vail cutelets." Finally Anne said "cutlets" a page later, but miscued on *breaded*:

braid
What do cutlets wear before they're breaded?

Later questioning revealed that Anne had never heard of veal cutlets. Nor was she familiar with poached eggs, tangerines, or custard, all words on which she miscued. On the other hand, she was usually able to correct grammar-disrupting or meaning-disrupting miscues when the words were within her prior knowledge and experience.

The same thing happens to relatively proficient readers when they don't already know the word. Witness my problems with *melancholy* as a child, and my problems with *desiccant* and *scofflaw* as an adult. If you are still tempted to think that grapho/phonemic cues alone are usually adequate, try pronouncing some unfamiliar words in a textbook, and then check their pronunciation in a dictionary. Chances are you'll mispronounce a goodly proportion of them. But even if you get the pronunciation correct (as Anne eventually got the pronunciation of "cutlets"), can we necessarily assume that you have identified the word in any meaningful sense, without prior knowledge or at least adequate contextual information?

Of course, sometimes prior knowledge will lead us astray, as with the third grader who made the following miscue in a story about Henry Ford:

Henry felt that everyone should be able to own a car,

not just the wealthy people. In 1903 he started the Ford

more
Motor Company. His cars cost much less than other cars

had before.

Then there was the sixth-grade boy who seemed to have read his own role expectations into the following sentences written in the first person:

© a pilot

Sometimes I'm in a ballet costume, dancing on a stage.

psychiatrist waiting   © littles

Or I'm a secretary, writing important letters.

He seems to believe that boys are more likely to become pilots or psychiatrists than to become ballet dancers or secretaries.

One more example of how making good use of one's schemas can actually cause miscues in word identification comes from the fourth-grade son of one of my students. Reading one of the Encyclopedia Brown stories about a fictional ten-year-old "Sherlock Holmes in sneakers," David kept making miscues on the nickname "Encyclopedia," saying things like "Enkeycalapia," "Encaspeelas," and "Incapinkia." His mother was surprised by these miscues, since she thought he was familiar with the word *encyclopedia*. To test her belief, she wrote three sentences for the boy to read, two in which the word *encyclopedia* meant what it typically does, and one in which the word was used as a boy's nickname. She asked her son to read these three sentences:

If you want to find out about Abe Lincoln you can look in the Encyclopedia.

I read in the Encyclopedia all about World War I.

Bob and Danny went to Encyclopedia's house to see if he could play.

This time, David read "Encyclopedia" correctly in all three sentences, but he was convinced he had misread it in the third sentence. In that context, the word simply did not make sense to him. "I got that wrong," he said. "Is it 'Encaplesia'?" Though again the reader has been led astray by his own prior knowledge, David's problem with *Encyclopedia* illustrates the strength of what is usually a productive and in fact crucial reading strategy: using everything you know (or think you know) to try to make sense of what you read.

Miscues will not always be corrected, of course, but far more often than we realize, even young readers are capable of noticing when they have made a miscue. They may not express their realization overtly, though, as my son John did with the miscues on *gas*. Still, we must realize that children can and will do a lot of self-correcting, internally if not out loud. And we must give them opportunity and encouragement to correct their own miscues.

CONTEXT WITHIN THE SENTENCE

You may be most aware of context within the sentence. Yet even this kind of context has various aspects. On the one hand, we use both syntactic context and semantic context, both grammar and meaning. On the other hand, we use both preceding context and following context, both what comes before and what comes after the word being identified. Figure 4.2 summarizes these kinds of contexts in a grid, showing how each kind helps us identify the word *water* in the sentence "The cruel giant fell into the water and drowned." The word *the* indicates that the next word must be a noun or noun modifier, while the word *fell* suggests that the word after *the* should indicate something into which one can fall. The word *drowned* confirms that the word in question must indeed be a noun; further, *drowned* shows that the word should indicate something in which one can drown. The word in question could be *water, lake, pond, river, ocean, well,* or *moat* (to name some likely alternatives). The various kinds of contexts within the sentence have helped us narrow the alternatives to such a point that we need to use only a small amount of visual information from the word itself to identify the word in question as *water.*

In looking at the sentence in Figure 4.2, you may have thought, "That's silly. I already know the word *water.* I don't need to use context in order to identify that word." No doubt that is true. Nevertheless, the identification of words proceeds much faster and more efficiently when we are using the context provided by connected text. The fact is that fluent readers use context so automatically that they are rarely conscious of doing so. We become aware of our reliance on context mainly when we come to a word whose meaning we do not know, or when we make a miscue because of our reliance on preceding context.

To understand better this automatic use of context, read aloud the following sentences, without looking them over beforehand:

1. Can you read rapidly?
2. There was a strong wind blowing.
3. He wound the string up tightly.
4. I looked up and read the sign.
5. Her dress had a tear in it.

	Preceding Context	*Following Context*
Syntactic Context	Preceding syntactic context indicates the word is a noun or a noun modifier.	Following syntactic context confirms that the word is a noun.

The cruel giant fell into the water and drowned.

	Preceding Context	*Following Context*
Semantic Context	Preceding semantic context suggests the word should indicate something into which one can fall.	Following semantic context shows that the word should indicate something in which one can drown.

*FIGURE **4.2*** *Context within the sentence*

6. I saw a tear in her eye.
7. She looked at the minute printing on the label.
8. He made her a bow and arrow.

Each sentence contains a word that has, potentially, more than one pronunciation. In sentences 1–4, the preceding syntactic context is enough to signal the appropriate pronunciation of *read, wind, wound,* and *read.* In sentence 5, we need the preceding semantic context to tell us that *tear* should rhyme with *dare* rather than with *dear.* In sentences 6–8, we need following semantic context to signal the appropriate pronunciation of *tear, minute,* and *bow.* In short, we use preceding context to predict what is coming next, and we use following context to confirm or correct our predictions. This use of following context is facilitated by the fact that our eyes typically register about four words beyond the word we are focusing upon—in fact, the semantic information from these following words may be available to us even before we have consciously identified the words (McKean, 1981; see also Bishop, 1993).[3] If we do not use following context to help identify a word correctly in the first place, we use following context to tell us when we have made a miscue. Thus, if you incorrectly pronounced *bow* to rhyme with *now* in sentence 8, you surely recognized the miscue when you noticed the word *arrow.*

Although such sentences as these are somewhat atypical, they do help us understand the nature of proficient reading. We do not normally rely just on *grapho/phonemics,* our knowledge of letter/sound relations. Rather, we use context to complement and reduce our reliance on grapho/phonemic cues. In other words, we use non-visual information to reduce our dependence on visual information.

It should come as no surprise, then, that beginning readers and nonproficient readers can often read words better in context than in isolation. Here are some examples from first and second graders. On the left is the word misread in isolation, with the miscue indicated above the word. On the right is a sentence in which the same child read the word correctly:

has
his   . . . said his father.

hot
not   His father said, "You are not old enough for that."

want
went   The next day Hap and his mother and father went to the fair.

which
with   "Hap can come with me."

wig
wag   All morning Peter tried to make the turtle wag its tail.

now
know   "I know you would," said his mother.

don't
didn't   But she didn't bring it back to Peter.

our
your   "Come on, Lassie," said Peter. "Wag your tail."

tall
tail   He wanted the turtle to wag its tail.

made
named   Peter named his fish Lassie.

An early study showed that words are easier to recognize in familiar contexts than in relatively unfamiliar contexts. Even the function words tended to cause more recognition problems in the Group B sentences than in the Group A sentences below, for the less proficient beginning readers tested (Reid, 1958, p. 297):

Group A	*Group B*
You must do your best work.	You must not go back on your word.
I can see his face in the darkness.	No man can do more than his best.
We went back to the deep mud.	Darkness was upon the face of the deep.
Can you give me more words to read?	We must not give up when work is hard.

The best readers had no trouble with either set of sentences, but the less proficient readers had difficulty with many of the words in what was, to them, an unfamiliar context. Murphy's study (1986) produced comparable results.

Similarly, others have found that beginning readers may know color names like *brown* and *green*, but not be able to recognize these words when they are used in names like *Mr. Brown* and *Green Street*. Or the word *had* may be recognizable in a sentence where it indicates possession (as in "I had a dog"), but unrecognizable in a sentence where it indicates past perfect (as in "He had left already"). Unfamiliar idioms may cause word identification problems for many speakers of English as a second language, as well as for younger or less proficient readers; an example is the word *mustard* in the expression "He couldn't cut the mustard."

My favorite example of such difficulty comes from my son John. Early in his first-grade year, we visited Chicago's Field Museum of Natural History. As we were looking at the bird exhibits, my husband excitedly called John's attention to a display of Weaver birds. "Look, John. What kind of bird is this?" he asked, pointing to the identifying label. But in such an unfamiliar and unexpected context—indeed, without any sentence context at all—our son could not recognize his own name.

The classic study demonstrating the importance of context was undertaken by Kenneth Goodman. In context, his group of first graders correctly read 62 percent of the words that they had missed in isolation. His second graders correctly read 75 percent of the words they had missed in isolation. And his third-grade group correctly read 82 percent of the words they had missed in isolation (K. S. Goodman, 1965, p. 640). If these figures seem astonishingly high, it may be partly because the words were presented first in lists, and then in context. Thus, by the time the words were seen in context, prior experience with the words in lists might have made recognition easier. So reasoned P. David Pearson, who reported that when he gave children the same list twice, there was a 20 percent improvement without any context help. Furthermore, in his attempt at replicating Goodman's study, Pearson found that context produced gains of only 40 percent among first graders and 50–60 percent among third graders, when the list was presented first (Pearson, 1978). Still, these figures suggest that context helps substantially.

Tom Nicholson has further pointed out that Goodman's study did not differentiate between good and poor readers' use of context. (Incidentally, I define "good" readers as those who typically make efficient and effective use of language cues and reading strategies and readily comprehend appropriate text; poorer readers are those who are less proficient in one or both respects. In miscue studies that have led to such a definition, "good," "average," and "poor" readers are often preidentified by other means, such as standardized tests.) In any case, Nicholson, in more recent studies, has eliminated the order effect and considered how context affects the reading of poor, average, and good readers, at ages six, seven, and eight. Across the three studies, Nicholson found that younger readers and poorer readers of all ages generally read words more accurately in context. The results for the good older readers were less consistent; indeed, in the most recent study, the eight-year-old good readers did better with the list, when given the context passage first (Nicholson, 1991).

In general, research on word identification suggests that context improves the identification of words for younger and less proficient readers more than for older and more proficient readers (Stanovich, 1980, 1991; Perfetti, 1985; Nicholson, 1991). However, in view of the fact that good readers read for meaning, not to identify words, it is not surprising that the older good readers in Nicholson's study (1991) read the words better in lists. For one thing, they read the passage first. For another, they may have read the passage for meaning (the experimental procedures encouraged this), but read the list to identify the words. And as the next section helps explain, reading for meaning may have resulted in *more* miscues rather than fewer.

In general, the evidence from nearly three decades of miscue research demonstrates that:

1. Words are easier to identify in context than in isolation, at least for younger and less proficient readers.
2. Words are easier to identify in familiar contexts than in unfamiliar and unpredictable ones, at least for younger and less proficient readers.
3. Contextual information speeds and facilitates reading for proficient as well as non-proficient readers; it also facilitates the understanding of many words that the reader may not be able to pronounce or identify.
4. Proficient readers use contextual information in combination with prior knowledge and grapho/phonemic information.

LANGUAGE CUES AND READING STRATEGIES

When we analyze miscues, we consider how a reader has used language cues and reading strategies. The major *language cues* are syntactic, semantic, and grapho/phonemic.

Our intuitive knowledge of syntax, our grammatical schema, enables us to use word endings, function words, and word order as cues to word identification. These syntactic cues are complemented by semantic cues, the meaning relations among words and sentences in the text we are reading. In addition, we bring to bear various situational cues and our entire store of personal knowledge and experience. We use not only the syntactic and semantic cues available in the text and the situation, but also our entire experience with language and with life. Of course, reading could not exist without the grapho/phonemic cues, the letters and words on the page, and our intuitive knowledge of letter/sound relations and patterns. However, our reading would be both inefficient and ineffective if we relied just on grapho/phonemic cues. As Paul Kolers has written, "Reading is only incidentally visual" (Kolers, 1969). At this point, such an outrageous statement should begin to make sense.

Figure 4.3 indicates how language cues give rise to reading strategies. Whether conscious or unconscious, such strategies are plans for carrying out mental operations—in this case, the operation of reading. Of course during normal reading, all kinds of processing are going on simultaneously. But in order to understand some of this complexity, it may help, temporarily, to think of reading as a matter of identifying words. In order to identify a word, proficient readers first use syntactic and semantic knowledge and cues to *predict* what is coming next. We do not necessarily predict a specific word, but at least we subconsciously narrow down the possibilities. Thus, there is a limited number of words that might reasonably complete the sentence "The cruel giant fell into the _____."

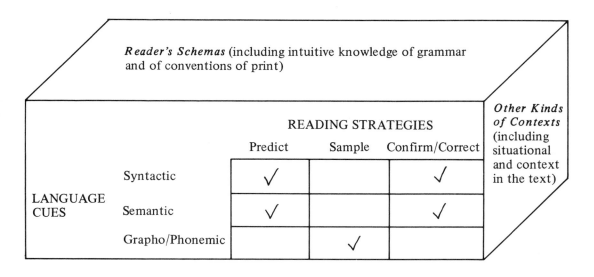

Figure 4.3   Language cues and reading strategies

After mentally restricting the possibilities, we normally look at the word itself—that is, we use grapho/phonemic cues. But because prediction has narrowed down the number of reasonable alternatives, we need to use only a minimum of visual information to tentatively identify the word. In the sentence about the giant, we would need to process only two or three consonant letters or parts of them in order to decide that the word is *water* rather than one of the other reasonable possibilities. Apparently as proficient readers, we only sample the grapho/phonemic cues, in simultaneously identifying the letters and the word. Finally, we use following syntactic and semantic cues to confirm our tentative identification of the word, or to correct if we have made a miscue that does not fit with the following context. The word *water* fits not only with the preceding context but with the following context in "The cruel giant fell into the water and drowned." Hence we would confirm our identification of the word in question. Figure 4.3 depicts this relationship between language cues and reading strategies, suggesting in addition the use of other contextual cues and the fact that it is our schemas that enable us to make use of the cues provided by text and situation.

Figure 4.4 attempts to suggest the simultaneity of these strategies: at one and the same time, we are sampling new grapho/phonemic cues, confirming or correcting what we've just read, and making new predictions about what is to follow. "Each [system and strategy] follows the others but at the same time precedes them, always moving toward constructing a text and making meaning" (Y. M. Goodman, Watson, & Burke, 1987, p. 33).

In Chapter 6, the form for analyzing miscues invites us to consider significant aspects of these relationships between language cues and reading strategies (p. 256). We ask, "Is the reader using syntactic and semantic cues to predict what might come

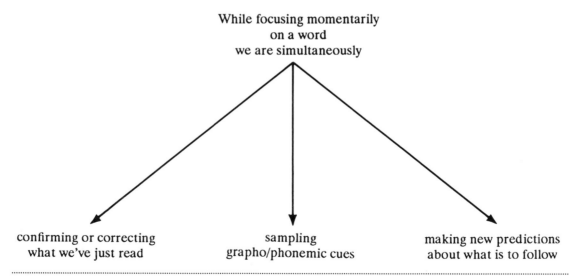

While focusing momentarily
on a word
we are simultaneously

confirming or correcting
what we've just read

sampling
grapho/phonemic cues

making new predictions
about what is to follow

Figure 4.4   *Simultaneous processes in reading*

next?" "Is the reader using following syntactic and semantic cues to confirm or correct what was actually read?" Both strategies are significant: not only in "getting" words but, more crucially, in constructing meaning from a text.

READING PROFICIENCY AND THE USE OF CONTEXT

Good readers use context automatically and efficiently, to reduce their reliance on visual cues and grapho/phonemic knowledge. This section will consider related observations about good and less proficient readers: (1) the fact that both good and less proficient readers may make miscues on simple "sight" words, but that good readers' miscues are more likely to preserve grammar and sense; (2) evidence (an example) that good readers use both preceding and following context effectively, even reconstructing text in their effort to construct meaning; and (3) a comparison of good versus less proficient readers' use of context.

Miscues on Basic Sight Words

Though good readers generally make fewer miscues than less proficient readers, they may actually make as many or more miscues involving pronouns and simple function words—the so-called basic sight words. This occurs because they are reading to construct meaning, rather than to identify words. Good readers tend to substitute one pronoun or function word for another, and to omit or insert optional function words. The following are examples (some from K. S. Goodman, 1973). To recap the meaning of the symbols: a carat points to an insertion; a circle indicates an omission; one or more words written above the text indicate a substitution; and (in the following section) a $\underline{\vee}$ indicates a reversal:

their
a. White men came from the cities.

It
b. That took us about an hour.

might
c. "You may be right."

d. She made her own paints from the roots.

e. . . . but after a month we saw that nothing was growing.

f. Mr. Tully beat me more often and more cruelly than Mr. Coffin had done.

the
g. Billy feasted on ^ roast corn. . . .

h. . . . it was enough to wake ^(up) the dead.

i. They told him ^(that) he had been foolish to plant sesame. . . .

In each of the foregoing examples, the meaning is preserved even though the surface structure is altered. The reader has made miscues precisely because he or she is constructing meaning rather than merely trying to identify words.

The following excerpt from a miscue analysis offers further evidence that good readers often miscue on simple words as they use context to construct meaning from a text. The reader is a sixth grader named Billy; the passage is from Joanne Williamson's *The Glorious Conspiracy* (1961, pp. 17–18):

Life went on as usual. Mr. ①Tully Tully beat me more often

and more cruelly than Mr. Coffin had ②(done). But I was

used to that now. And there were ways a poor boy could

find of having a bit of fun once in a while—like daring

the other apprentices to steal ③a ©(a bit) ^(of) from the shops and

watching to see if they got caught. If they did get

caught, they would be hanged at Gallows Mill, so that was

a real dare. Or one could throw bits of garbage in the way

of gentlemen in wigs and hide around the corner to see

them slip and fall ④(down). There wasn't much time for

such ⑤(sports), ^(though) so we made the most of what time we had.

My granddad had become pretty sick about this time.

He had the lung fever. He ⑥(had) had it a long while, but

now it was beginning to be bad, and Aunt Bet was begin-

ning to look frightened. I began to be scared, too, hearing

him cough so much and seeing him look so pale and ill.

And when I got through work at eight or nine ⑦ *o'clock* of the

clock, I took to hanging about the streets, tired and hun-

gry as I was, hiding out of the way of ⑧ (the) watchmen, so

as not to go home till I had to. I knew this made Aunt Bet

even more frightened; and that made me ashamed and

even more anxious not to go ⑨ *to* home.

One night after I had scrubbed down Mr. Tully's fish

house and come ⑩ (out) into the street, I saw a man come out

of a chandler's shop. I knew ⑪ (who) he was—Mr. Watson,

a ropemaker and an excellent workman, so everyone said.

I didn't want ⑫ *to see* him to see me, for I meant to tell Aunt Bet

that I had been kept late, and go ⑬ (looking) for mischief.

So I hid in a doorway and watched ⑭ *him go by* for him to go by.

Many of Billy's miscues involve the omission, substitution, or insertion of pronouns and function words—the allegedly simple sight words. Billy is reading to construct meaning, more than to identify each and every word.

Interestingly, it is mainly proficient readers who make miscues like these. The percentage of miscues involving pronouns and function words tends to increase as one becomes a more proficient reader (see K. S. Goodman, 1973, pp. 165–66, 184).

When less proficient readers make miscues on such basic sight words, the miscues may sometimes reflect the fact that the reader is not succeeding at constructing meaning, perhaps because the reader conceptualizes reading more as a matter of identifying words. One example comes from Tony's miscues (see Chapter 1):

$$\text{vengil}$$
. . . . The girls of the village

did not go to school, for the people thought that school was

$$\text{imprentice} \qquad \text{to}$$
not as important for girls as it was for boys.

In this sentence at least, Tony apparently was not succeeding in constructing meaning—which is probably why the miscue "to" for *it* was not corrected. This is rather typical of the sight word miscues of a less proficient reader: the miscues may have some grapho/phonemic element(s) in common with the word in the text and be of similar length, but they don't necessarily preserve good grammar or good sense. They don't fit with the context—especially the following context. And often, they aren't corrected.

Constructing Meaning and Reconstructing Text

The following example further shows how good readers typically construct meaning as they read, and sometimes even reconstruct the grammar of texts in doing so. Once you can read the passage fluently, making the same miscues this sixth grader Jay did, it may be revealing to ask someone to try to remember the miscues as you read the passage aloud. The passage is from an O. Henry story, "Jimmy Hayes and Muriel" (Porter, 1936, p. 670):

① around
After a hearty supper Hayes joined the smokers about

② at all
the fire. His appearance did not settle all the questions in
^   ③

the minds of his brother rangers. They saw simply a loose,

④
⑤ young
lank youth with tow-colored sunburned hair and a berry-

⑥ ingenious
brown, ingenuous face that wore a quizzical, good-

natured smile.

"Fellows," said the new ranger, "I'm goin' to interduce

you to a lady friend of mine. Ain't ⑥ever heard anybody ⑦ *much about*

⑧call her ⑨a beauty, but you'll all admit she's got some fine ⑩ *a*

points about her. Come along, Muriel!"

He held open the front of his blue flannel shirt. ⑪Out⑫of ⑪ *c*

⑫it crawled a horned frog. A bright red ribbon was tied ⑬ *toad*

jauntily around its spiky neck. It crawled to its owner's ⑭ *the*

knee and sat there motionless. ⑮ *it*

"This here Muriel," says Hayes, with an oratorical wave ⑯ *'s*

of his hand, "has got qualities. She never talks back, she ⑰ *o* *she's* ⑱

always stays ⑲at home, and she's satisfied with one red

dress for everyday and Sunday, too."

"Look at that blame insect!" said one of the rangers ⑳ *d*

with a grin. I've seen plenty of them horny frogs, but I ㉑ *toads*

never knew anybody to have one for a㉒side㉒ partner. Does ㉒ *c*

the blame thing know you from anybody else?"

"Take it over there and see," said Hayes. ㉓ *her*

Almost all of Jay's miscues fit the context: the preceding syntactic and semantic context, and the following syntactic and semantic context. In fact, when Jay has made a miscue that would disrupt the structure of the text, he makes others that restore grammatical structure. He draws upon prior knowledge, changing *frog(s)* to "toad(s)," and he even adds to the dialect O. Henry is trying to portray by reading *blame* as "blamed." In fact, his rendition of the story is so smooth, despite the numerous miscues, that when I read the passage aloud, reproducing Jay's miscues, usually only two are correctly identified by my listeners—and these are the two that disrupt grammar, though they do not seriously affect the sense.

Together, David's miscues (Chapter 1) along with Billy's and Jay's in this chapter help to illustrate the nature of proficient reading. It is not miscueless. Though many good readers do make fewer miscues than substantially poorer readers, the critical difference is the quality of the miscues. In other words, a good reader could make as many miscues as a less effective reader, but the use of language cues and reading strategies would ordinarily be different. Typically this difference is reflected in their differing use of context.

Good versus Less Proficient Readers' Use of Context

Even beginning and less proficient readers typically make some use of context as they read, especially in classrooms that emphasize the getting of meaning. An early study by Rose-Marie Weber sought to determine what percentage of a group of first graders' miscues were acceptable with preceding syntax only, and what percentage were acceptable with following syntax as well. The following examples illustrate the two types of miscues:

- Acceptable only with preceding context: Spot can help Dick.

  and (written above "can")

- Acceptable with both preceding and following syntax: Spot can help Dick.

  hear (written above "help")

The miscue "and" for *can* is syntactically acceptable up to that point in the sentence, but not beyond it. However, "hear" for *help* is syntactically acceptable with the following context as well (though of course it does change the meaning).

Weber found that about 90 percent of these first graders' miscues were acceptable with the preceding syntax. This startlingly high percentage was true for the low proficiency group as well as for the high proficiency group. Furthermore, 72 percent of the high group's miscues and 63 percent of the low group's miscues were acceptable with the following syntax as well. The major difference between groups was in the correction of miscues that did not fit with the following syntactic context (miscues like "and" for *can* in *Spot can help Dick*). The high group corrected 85 percent of these, while the low group corrected only 42 percent (Weber, 1970, pp. 153, 160, 161). Thus, a major difference between proficient and nonproficient readers lies in the correction of miscues that are unacceptable with the following syntactic context.

Weber's study focused just on the use of syntactic context. However, the broad conclusions are equally applicable to the use of semantic context as well. Emergent readers can indeed use both syntactic and semantic context as a means of word identification and meaning construction. Furthermore, many emergent readers tend to do so, especially if they are already well acquainted with books and the joys of being read to. Here, for example, are miscues from John, a child with only two months of reading instruction. The sentences are from *Opening Doors* in the Macmillan Reading Program (1965):

the
Get a ball, Mary.

can ride
Who rides with Mike?

Mary said, "Play ball, Jeff."
                                    ball
Mike and I want to play."
                                     ^

Mike said, "I can't ride.

              Mary and Jeff
I can't play with Jeff and Mary.

but
I can play ball."
^

The child's miscues make sense in context, but even more: some of the miscues seem to improve upon the original, making the deep structure—the meaning—even more explicit. Paradoxically, John's miscues allow us to see that he uses context in reading.

In contrast, we have seen with Tony's miscues in Chapter 1 that less proficient readers may make less efficient use of context in identifying words and constructing meaning. They may overattend to grapho/phonemic cues and underattend to syntactic and semantic cues. In an extensive study of reading miscues, Kenneth Goodman found that the miscues of low-proficiency eighth and tenth graders frequently looked and sounded more like the text word than the miscues of high-proficiency readers (K. S. Goodman, 1973, pp. 51, 53). But often this careful attention to grapho/phonemic cues produced nonwords like Tony's "souts" and "ramped," or words that did not fit the context. Such overreliance on grapho/phonemics actually hindered word identification, as well as the construction of meaning. Indeed, as with Tony's miscues, one sometimes gets the sense that a reader is hardly even trying to make sense of a passage; he or she is reading just to identify the words.

It should be noted, though, that sometimes in the early stages of learning to read, good readers will progress from merely trying to supply a sensible word to trying to get the *exact* word, using grapho/phonemic cues (Biemiller, 1970). For example, a child who earlier might have said "bird" for *canary* may now try to sound out the word, producing a nonword like "cainery." This is growth on the reader's part, reflecting the fact that the reader is now trying to integrate all three major language cue systems. Evidence that the child is trying to use grapho/phonemic cues along with prior knowledge and context cues comes from the retelling, when the child talks about the bird in the story—or even the canary! Indeed, even less proficient readers will often demonstrate that they understood an important word or concept, though they may never have pronounced the word correctly (see the example of Danny, pp. 151–152). These observations underscore not only the need for having a reader retell and discuss the story read, as part of a miscue analysis procedure, but also the importance of knowing the reader's pattern of growth in interpreting any particular sample of miscues.

Now to summarize. Decades of miscue analysis give rise to the following observations about effective and less effective readers:

1. Highly effective readers use preceding syntactic and semantic context to predict what is coming next (that is, to reduce the number of reasonable alternatives). On the one hand, their reliance on prior knowledge and context makes their use of visual cues more efficient. On the other hand, it also generates predictions resulting in miscues, but ones that typically fit with the grammar and meaning of the preceding context.
2. Highly effective readers use the following syntactic and semantic context to confirm their prediction, or as an impetus to reread and try to correct.
3. Moderately effective readers use preceding syntactic and semantic context to predict, but they are less successful in noticing when grammar or meaning has gone awry, and thus less successful in using following context to correct what doesn't fit.
4. Somewhat effective readers use preceding syntactic context to predict, but they are not as successful at using preceding semantic context to predict.

Hardly any readers read as if the words were arranged in a list rather than in sentences, making no use of context at all.

Of course, these generalizations should not be construed as suggesting that *all* less effective readers are ones who underrely on context and overrely on phonics. In fact, I often see readers who can make effective use of grapho/phonemic cues in dealing with short words, but who have never learned how to deal with longer words more or less syllable by syllable. Far worse, some individuals have gone through our school system never learning that there is even a relationship between letters and sounds, and are therefore unable to make effective use of grapho/phonemic cues to deal with any words not recognized on sight (e.g., Lloyd, in Prete and Strong, 1991). Clearly this should never happen, but an overemphasis instructionally on either sight word memorization or the use of context could lead to such a result. As miscue analysis demonstrates, what we need most crucially to remember is the following:

1. Constructing meaning from a text is far more important than identifying all the words—even though, obviously, many of the words have to be identified, or at least understood conceptually, if the reader is to construct meaning.
2. Effective and efficient reading requires integration of prior knowledge and all three major kinds of language cues: syntactic, semantic, and grapho/phonemic.
3. The goal of instruction should not be accurate identification of every word, but rather the effective use and integration of prior knowledge with all the language cue systems.

As we shall see in Chapter 6, many readers can make effective use of prior knowledge and all the language cue systems, yet still make many miscues—all the while getting the essential meaning of a text. Thus, making effective use of all the language cue systems may be a reasonable goal for virtually all readers—if we accept the fact that not all readers will use every cue system equally well.

On the other hand, completely accurate word identification is not a reasonable goal for *any* reader. The obvious exception would seem to be when reading a practiced piece aloud, as an oral performance—but even then, proficient readers typically make "good" miscues that go unnoticed. Of course, one reason accurate word identification isn't an appropriate goal is that concentrating on getting all the words detracts from getting the meaning. This is doubtless why proficient readers make so many miscues, most of which preserve grammar and meaning—or are corrected.

The following section will further consider why "getting all the words" is not a reasonable goal for readers, or a reasonable goal of reading instruction.

WHY NOT WORD IDENTIFICATION?

We have already seen one argument for not emphasizing accurate word identification as a goal of reading: this does not reflect what proficient readers actually do. Therefore, in emphasizing accurate word identification with those who are obviously less proficient readers, we may actually be impeding their growth toward reading proficiency.

In this section, we will consider three more arguments for the inappropriateness of exact word identification as a goal: (1) the fact that more than one word or group of words can signify a particular entity or concept; (2) the fact that we can often get the essence of a passage with its function words missing, or supply missing function words to fit the context; and (3) the fact that the precise words of a text are quickly forgotten anyway. All of these facts and factors lead to the conclusion that efficient and effective reading is a matter of constructing meaning, not of identifying words.

Words as Symbols

In the commonsense view, words stand for things. However, it is rare for a thing to be designated by one and only one word. Look, for example, at the italicized words and phrases in the following sentences:

- Here, *Daisy.*
- Don't let *the dog* in.
- Look at *'er* go!
- *She's a handsome animal.*

All of these expressions and more could be used to designate a particular dog. Usually more than one word or expression can be used to designate an entity; more than one word can be used to express an action; and so forth. As speakers and writers, we choose whichever word best suits our immediate purpose. And as listeners and readers, we may well substitute a contextually equivalent word or expression for that of the original.

One example is Jay's substitution of "toad" for *frog* in the O. Henry story "Jimmy Hayes and Muriel":

>   *toad*
> Out of it crawled a horned frog.

>   *toads*
> I've seen plenty of them horny frogs . . .

Though Jay's term was different, it still designated the same entity: Muriel. Like me, Jay had probably heard of horned toads but not of horned frogs. Instead of reflecting a loss of meaning, his substitution showed that he got the essential meaning of the author but translated it into something that made more sense to him.[4]

Especially common is the substitution of an appropriate pronoun for the noun to which it refers, a miscue made by a second grader reading the following passage from Bernard Wiseman's *Morris Has a Cold* (1978):

> Boris said,
>
> "Beds do not jump.
>
> Beds do not run.
>
> Beds just stand still."
>
> "Why?" asked Morris.
>
>   *they*
> "Are beds lazy?"

In this context, it was perfectly reasonable to substitute the pronoun "they" for the repeated noun *beds.* Jay made a similar miscue, substituting one pronoun for another:

her
"Take it over there and see," said Hayes.

In context, "her" made perfectly good sense, because Muriel was female.

Constructing Meaning Without All the Words

It is mainly proficient readers who make substitutions like those in the preceding examples. As mentioned earlier, the percentage of miscues involving pronouns and function words tends to *increase* as one becomes a more proficient reader (see K. S. Goodman 1973, *Theoretically Based Studies,* pp. 165–66 and p. 184). Insofar as they serve to signal relations between words, pronouns are like function words. And we can often supply many of the function words ourselves, if we are getting the essential meaning. That is, the content words, word order, and the total context are often adequate to signal many of the relations among the words in a sentence, if we have adequate background knowledge. To test this, consider the following passage. You may want to read it just for meaning first. Then try to fill in the missing function words (the original is from the *New York Times,* May 5, 1970, p. 17):

People usually find they can supply reasonable function words, often the precise one that was omitted from the original.[5] Just as words can normally be identified from only part of the visual information normally available, sentences can normally be understood from fewer than the total number of words available. We are able to recreate part of the surface structure from our understanding of the deep structure.

If meaning is the goal of reading, we hardly need to insist that every word be identified accurately. Instead of demanding an accurate rendition of the surface structure, we might better call for a reasonable interpretation of the deep structure.

Some will argue that there are times when it is vital to read every word accurately, and this is probably true. In savoring a poem, for example, one often dwells on the significance of virtually every word. And surface accuracy may sometimes be important in getting the deep structure of warranties and guarantees, application forms, recipes and other directions, and legal contracts. But even with such materials, surface accuracy is not as important or as helpful as commonly supposed. The proof of this is in our everyday experience. Many of us have had the frustrating experience of being able to read all the words in a set of directions or a contract, yet been unable to determine precisely what was meant. We are often able to get the surface structure, yet unable to get the deep structure—the intended meaning.

An experience of my own seems pertinent. Several years ago I was asked to render an expert linguistic opinion in a court case involving a life insurance claim. The deceased had died piloting his own plane. The linguistic question involved the following exclusion clause in the insurance policy, and in particular the word *passenger*. The insured person was not covered by the policy "while engaged in or taking part in aeronautics and/or aviation of any description or resulting from being in any aircraft except while a passenger in an aircraft previously tried, tested, and approved." The insurance company claimed that the word *passenger* excluded the pilot of a plane, and hence the man was not covered by the policy at the time of his death. The family claimed that the man *was* covered at the time of his death, because the pilot of a plane is also one of its passengers. Both parties agreed on the word and its basic meaning, but not on the meaning most relevant to that context. And it was a crucial $50,000 difference.[6]

Once again the conclusion seems clear: what is important is not necessarily the surface structure, but the deep structure. The proficient reader reads more for meaning than for surface detail.

Constructing Meaning and Forgetting the Words

You will learn most from the following example if you treat it as an experiment. Read through the following passage once, trying to fix it verbatim in your mind. Then write the sentences as you remember them, without looking back at the original. Alternatively, you might read the passage aloud to someone, asking the person to try to remember and write the passage verbatim. It is taken from Graham Greene's *The Power and the Glory* (1940, p. 139):

> The young men and women walked round and round the plaza in the hot electric night: the men one way, the girls another, never speaking to each other. In the northern sky the lightning flapped. It was like a religious ceremony which had lost all meaning, but at which they still wore their best clothes.

You (or your listener) may have found that you could not recall all of the passage after just one reading. This is typical. But in trying to recall as much as possible, you probably preserved the essential meaning, making only or mostly superficial changes in surface structure. Among the more common changes are these:

"around" for *round*	"flashed" for *flapped*
"women" for *girls*	"that" for *which*
"the other" for *another*	"to which" for *at which*

In addition, it is common to find the first sentence divided into two sentences, or even three:

The young men and women walked round and round the plaza in the hot electric night. The men went one way and the girls another. They never spoke to each other.

Obviously the wording and sentence structure may be changed in several other ways while still preserving the essential meaning. Most of the deep structure is retained, but some of the surface structure is lost. There is perhaps no definitive answer to precisely how fast surface structure is lost, but an experiment by Sachs suggests that we begin to forget the actual words within about half a second of reading them (Sachs, 1967).

Koestler (1969, p. 201) offers a succinct example of how the spoken word resolves itself into increasingly more abstract mental representations for the listener, just as the written word does for the reader:

> You watch a television play. The exact words of each actor are forgotten by the time he speaks his next line, and only their meaning remains; the next morning you can only remember the sequence of scenes which constituted the story; after a month, all you remember is that it was about a gangster on the run or about two men and a woman on a desert island.

In a few months, you may not remember the show at all, though it may have affected your available gangster-movie schema or your love-triangle schema. Words, scenes, even whole texts may be quickly forgotten.

Why, then, be so concerned about getting the exact words of the text, as long as the essential meaning is preserved?

IMPLICATIONS FOR UNDERSTANDING DIALECT MISCUES

It used to be common for teachers to think that miscues reflecting a reader's spoken dialect were wrong and needed to be corrected for understanding to occur; perhaps it still is. However, this assumption should be reconsidered in light of the evidence that understanding precedes oral verbalization and in light of the evidence that proficient readers make miscues that reflect their predictions, their prior knowledge, and even their preferred language structures (e. g., Jay's miscues, given earlier).

To understand how common it is to translate a text into our own language patterns precisely because we *are* understanding (getting the deep structure), you might try the following experiment with someone you consider to be a reasonably proficient reader. Without giving any hint of your purpose, have the person read the following passage aloud, while you take careful note of any miscues that are made. The passage is from Zachary Ball's *Bristle Face* (1962, p. 75), discussed in Rigg (1978, p. 287):

> He nodded. "Some good mud cats in there. That bluff you speak of, I denned me a bear in the rocks up there oncet."
> "A bear! When was that? Lately?"
> He chuckled. "Naw, that was way back yonder, when I was a boy, no older'n you. Ain't been no bear around here for sixty year, about. That was the last one ever I heard of hereabouts."

For those whose dialect is different from this rural mountain speech, "sixty years" for *sixty year is* a common miscue. As I checked this quote for accuracy, I first read "I ever" for *ever I,* changing the syntactic pattern to one more common in my speech. Your reader may have made other miscues that preserve the deep structure but change the surface structure to a more familiar pattern.

A second dialect passage may again help demonstrate the fact that we do not necessarily have to get all the words right in order to get the meaning. If possible, try this passage on yet another reader, someone who does not know your purpose. The passage is from Claude Brown's *Manchild in the Promised Land* (1965, p. 39):

> "Seem like nobody can't make him understand. I talk to him, I yell at him, I whip his ass, but it don't do no good. His daddy preach to him, he yell at him, he beat him so bad sometimes, I gotta run in the kitchen and git that big knife at him to stop him from killin' that boy. You think that might break him outta those devilish ways he got? Child, that scamp'll look Jesus dead in the eye when he standin' on a mountain of Bibles and swear to God in heaven he ain't gon do it no more. The next day, or even the next minute, that little lyin' Negro done gone and did it again—and got a mouthful-a lies when he git caught."

Among the numerous possible dialect miscues here, the more common are "he's got" for *he got,* and "he's standin'" for *he standin'.* Another is "gonna" for *gon,* which should be pronounced with a nasalized vowel and no final consonant. You may also find that your reader adds third person singular verb endings, saying, for example, "seems" for *seem,* "yells" for *yell,* and "beats" for *beat.* With miscues such as these, the reader has gotten the meaning without getting all the words entirely right. Indeed, it is *because* the reader has gotten the meaning that he or she makes such miscues.

In reading the passage from *Manchild,* speakers of a standard English dialect may add some of the surface grammatical features that would be normal for their dialect. In contrast, speakers of other dialects may read a passage written in standard English and omit some of the surface grammatical markers that are not always present in their dialect. What we often fail to realize is that such dialect translation would not be possible unless the reader had understood the deep structure of the author's sentence. Actively transacting with the text, the reader has simply expressed it in his or her own surface structure.

Usually, teachers are most disturbed by miscues that reflect a partially different grammatical system: "we was" for *we were,* "he don't have none" for *he doesn't have any,* and so forth. But such miscues as these are relatively rare. The more common grammatical miscues involve just pieces of words, the grammatical endings. Kenneth Goodman and his associates have found, for example, that among inner-city black children, the following are the most common dialect-related miscues that appear to involve grammar. Most of these miscues involve grammatical elements (adapted from K. S. Goodman & C. Buck, 1973, p. 9).[7]

- Absence of past tense marker
  "look" for *looked,* "call" for *called,* "wreck" for *wrecked,* "love" for *loved,* "pound" for *pounded,* "help" for *helped,* "use" for *used,* "run" for *ran,* "have" for *had,* "keep" for *kept,* "do" for *did*

- Absence of plural noun marker
  "thing" for *things,* "work" for *works,* "story" for *stories,* "prize" for *prizes*
- Absence of third person singular verb marker
  "look" for *looks,* "work" for *works,* "hide" for *hides*
- Absence of possessive noun or pronoun marker
  "Freddie" for *Freddie's,* "Mr. Vine" for Mr. *Vine's,* "one" for *one's,* "it" for *its*
- Substitution and omission of forms of *to be*
  "was" for *were,* "is" for *are,* "we" for *we're,* "he be talking" for *he'd been talking*
- Hypercorrections (the use of two grammatical markers of the same type)
  "likeded" for *liked,* "helpeded" for *helped,* "stoppeded" for *stopped*

More recently, Kenneth and Yetta Goodman and their associates completed a massive study (K. S. Goodman & Y. M. Goodman, 1978) of miscues among second, fourth, and sixth graders who speak a nonmainstream dialect or who speak English as a second language. The dialect groups were downeast Maine, Mississippi black, Appalachian, and Hawaiian Pidgin. The second-language groups were Texas Spanish, Hawaiian Samoan, Arabic, and Navajo. The most common kind of grammatical miscue, for both the dialect speakers and the ESL speakers, was again the absence of grammatical inflections on the ends of words. This is a common "interlanguage" feature among people learning English as a second language (Selinker, 1972).

From their impressive study, in which they examined not only the children's miscues but also their comprehension, the Goodmans concluded that there is "no evidence that inability to cope with Book English is a general problem for any group" (1978, p. 3–5). The students' dialect or interlanguage influence is evident in their reading, "but it is not in itself a barrier to comprehension" (p. 3–22).

With oral reading, then, we do not ordinarily need to be concerned about the absence or use of such features as those cited by Goodman and Buck. Such miscues typically reflect not a lack of understanding, but only an alternative surface structure common in the reader's everyday speech. Having understood the deep structure, the reader simply expresses it in an alternative oral form. Such a process is reflected in Figure 4.5. This model indicates that, as mentioned earlier, when we read aloud, our understanding is usually ahead of our voice. Unless we are having unusual difficulty, we get the meaning *before* speaking the words, rather than vice versa.

Given this fact as well as the specific research into dialect miscues and ESL miscues, the Goodmans point out that special reading materials are not needed for *any* of the low-status dialect groups studied, nor is special methodology needed (p. 8–5). What *is* needed, however, is a positive attitude toward reading miscues in general and toward dialect and ESL miscues in particular.

This point can hardly be emphasized enough. In a survey in which 94 Midwestern elementary teachers rated miscues as acceptable or unacceptable, Tovey (1979) found that when miscues were syntactically and semantically appropriate in the teacher's dialect, only 16 percent of the teachers would not accept the miscues. However, when the miscues reflected translation into the reader's dialect, 60 percent of the teachers would not accept the miscues. An earlier study by Cunningham produced similar results (1977). Teachers, then, must have the knowledge, the experience, and the *attitudes* that

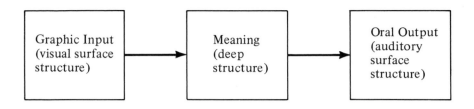

Figure 4.5   A simplified model of proficient oral reading

will enable them to recognize and accept miscues that merely reflect an alternative spoken dialect. This is essentially one of the conclusions that can be drawn from the famed Ann Arbor decision of 1979, in which a group of black children won their court suit charging that the school had failed to take their home language into account in teaching them to read (see *Ann Arbor Decision,* p. 9 in particular).

In his excellent book on Black English Vernacular, Robbins Burling offers some particularly pertinent remarks (1973, pp. 158–59):

> What should a teacher do when her children make such "mistakes"? She may be willing to accept the idea that children should be permitted to read aloud in their own natural pronunciation, but grammatical changes [or apparent grammatical changes] seem far more dramatic. To most teachers they look like out-and-out errors and they seem to warrant correction. Nevertheless, these "errors" give far better evidence of comprehension than would more literal and "accurate" recitation of the words. Word-for-word recitation may amount to no more than parroting. It may be no different from reading a word list in which the words have no relation to one another. Conversion to nonstandard forms, so long as the meaning is preserved, amounts to a kind of translation that would be quite impossible if the child did not understand. If reading with comprehension is our goal, then these "errors" prove that we have been successful.

At least some research indicates that it is the *best* readers who produce the most dialect-based miscues (B. Hunt, 1974–75), supporting the observation that good readers tend to express the author's deep structure in a surface structure that is partially their own. They are less concerned with surface detail than with meaning.

REVALUING READERS

Recognizing that reading is more a matter of constructing meaning than of identifying words should encourage us to revalue readers we might previously have considered to be poor readers. In part, this recognition should prompt us to revalue those we might have mistakenly considered less proficient because of their dialect miscues. It should also prompt us to revalue the many readers who are not very good at "getting" all or even most of the words, but whose miscues show good use of reading strategies and who comprehend well.

The example of Danny comes readily to mind. When the following sample of his miscues was generated, Danny was a third grader reading "What's the Matter with Carruthers?" by James Marshall, from *Windchimes* in the Houghton Mifflin basal reading program (1976). In the story, the bear Carruthers is grumpy when greeted by his friends Emily and Eugene—a pig and a turtle, respectively. Emily and Eugene try to cheer up Carruthers by playing music for him, inviting him over for a lunch of tea and honey cakes, taking him to an amusement park, and finally trying to keep him busy raking leaves. Nothing works.

Here is an excerpt from the text, with Danny's miscues marked. He was by now several pages into the story:

① *Egen*

"Well," Eugene began, after a long pause.

②

"Whenever I'm in a grouchy and unpleasant

mood, I always listen to beautiful music. In no

③ ⓒ ④ *I'm feeling much* ⑤
time at all I feel much better, and I'm sure that

I'm much more pleasant to be around."

ⓒ ⑥
a
"That gives me an idea," said Emily. "Come

with me."

⑦ ⑧
The two friends hurried home, but in a few

⑧ *later*
minutes they were back in the park with their
∧

⑨ *carried* ⑩
musical instruments. Emily was carrying her

Egen ⑪ *trumpet*
tuba. Eugene had his tambourine.

⑫ *Egen*
"What a good idea," said Eugene. "When we

(13) Caluthers' (14) plumped (15) nerv-es

smooth Carruthers' rumpled nerves with our

beautiful music, he'll be his old friendly self

(16)
again. I'm sure that he'll be (so) grateful."

(R)   (17) Caluthers
[Turning the bend, they saw Carruthers still

(C) (18)   (C) gl- (19)
sitting in the (same) place, still gazing at the

(20) (C) e-
falling leaves. And (ever) so quietly they tiptoed

(21) them
up behind him (22)

(23) Prancing a (24)
Placing the mouthpiece of her tuba to her lips,

(26) the keeth (27)
(25)
Emily puffed (up) her cheeks and began to play,

(28) quiet (29) Egen
softly at first and (then) quite loudly. Eugene

(30) the trombone (31)
tapped on his tambourine.

"Um-pah Um-Pah Tap Tap. Um-Pah Um-Pah

(32)   (R)   (33)
Tap Tap." It sounded something (like (that)

Caluthers
But Carruthers was not impressed. Instead

(34) (35)
he listened
of listening to the music, he put his paws to his

ears and growled, "That is the most awful noise I

(36)
have (ever) heard in my life!"

(R) (37)
[And (he) promptly got up and walked away.

If we conceptualize reading as first and foremost a matter of identifying words, we would see Danny as a weak reader who has missed a number of words in a short passage. But if we look at his strategies, we will see a reader who makes effective use of prior knowledge and context to predict, as well as some use of following context to correct miscues that don't fit the context. These strategies and the miscues that fit the context without needing correction (note, for instance, "trumpet" for *tambourine* and "trombone" for *trumpet)* suggest that Danny is reading to construct meaning, and probably succeeding. This impression is confirmed by the following except from his retelling:

> There was a bear friend of—of—of two [thinks about it] girls, I can say. And one person, that bear, wasn't being friendly. He wasn't being polite. And so they tried to play soft, beautiful music, but that didn't work. They invited him to honeycake and took him to an amusement park, but that didn't work. And finally they found out that it was time for him to hibernate.

Interestingly, Danny knew that Carruthers' friends had taken him to an amusement park, even though Danny didn't say the word "amusement" correctly when he encountered it in the text. Also, the story didn't use the word "hibernate" at all; Danny appropriately inferred it from the plot. He may not have known that "Eugene" is a boy's name, and thus assumed that both of Carruthers' friends were girls.

For whatever reason, correct word identification does not come easily to Danny. A traditional solution might be to give him flash cards to get him to memorize more sight words, or to give him more phonics instruction, on the assumption that he should be sounding out unfamiliar words. However, close examination of his reading strategies suggests that he is rather effectve in coordinating prior knowledge and context with grapho/phonemic cues to predict, sample, monitor comprehension, and sometimes to correct. It is possible that he does a lot of correcting silently, for he seems well able to get the essential meaning of the text. Emphasizing sight words or sounding out words could easily divert Danny from this apparent goal of constructing meaning.

In time and if he does a lot of reading, his word recognition will surely improve. Meanwhile, if we were his teacher or tutor, we might discuss his effective reading strategies with him and perhaps help him learn to correct more of his miscues, if they seriously disrupt meaning; we might even encourage him to correct miscues that have little effect on meaning, but that disrupt syntax. But in any case, the most important thing we can do for Danny is surely to revalue him as a reader: to recognize and celebrate his very real strengths.

DEVELOPING READING STRATEGIES

Chapters 6 and 12 will suggest more ways of working with readers who have particular needs. Here, we will focus on ways to help *all* students develop reading strategies, as needed. This section is not a complete how-to, but a description of some teaching strategies that teachers can use in the context of authentic reading. Some additional ideas will be offered in Chapter 9.

Some of the most important strategies readers need to develop are these:

- strategies for *reading with a purpose*
- strategies for *drawing upon prior knowledge*
- strategies for *predicting*
- strategies for *effectively sampling the visual display*
- strategies for *using all the language cue systems together* (semantic, syntactic, and grapho/phonemic)
- strategies for *confirming and correcting*
- strategies for *monitoring comprehension*
- strategies for *reviewing and retaining* desired information and concepts
- strategies for *adjusting rate and approach*, depending upon purpose

As we shall see, these strategies overlap and can easily be taught through demonstration, invitation, and discussion

Prediction

Even babies, toddlers, and older preschoolers can be encouraged to use all their resources to predict what's coming next. Of course this involves drawing upon prior knowledge, prior context, and other available cues, such as picture cues.

For example, teachers often demonstrate and discuss with children how they themselves use such cues to predict. During the same or subsequent reading events, the teacher invites children to do the same, and discusses with the children the prior knowledge and cues they used in predicting what they did. Such discussion serves as confirmation and as a further invitation to predict. This sequence might be termed the DDID cycle: Demonstration, Discussion, Invitation, and further Discussion—though of course in actual practice the elements may mingle and repeat. As the group progresses through the text, the teacher can invite students to discuss whether or not their predictions were correct, and to make new predictions from available cues. This resembles the Directed Reading-Thinking Activity, or DRTA (Stauffer, 1960, 1969; Stauffer & Cramer, 1968), but the DRTA may be done as a separate lesson, whereas demonstration, invitation, and discussion occur in the natural ebb and flow of collaboratively reading an enjoyable text. The DDID sequence is typically a part of the Shared Book (or shared reading) Experience used in the primary grades. Tracy Cobb's discussion with her first graders in reading the folktale *Stone Soup* is an example; see p. 345. Such procedures encourage students to read with a purpose, to monitor comprehension, and to confirm or correct the meanings they are constructing. These strategies become a natural part of the reading process.

Using All the Language Cue Systems Together

One way that teachers encourage students to use all the language cue systems together is by encouraging them to use prior knowledge and context along with initial consonants to *predict* the word in question. For example, we might use prior context and initial consonants to predict key words in the traditional rhyme "Susie Moriar":

> This is the story of Susie Moriar.
> It started one night as she sat by the f _____ .

Once children realize that this is a rhyming poem, they can use rhyme along with the other cues, to predict the key words:

> The fire was so hot,
> Susie jumped in a p _____ .
> The pot was so black,
> Susie dropped in a cr _____ .
> The crack was so narrow,
> Susie climbed on a wheel b _____ .

And so forth. Notice that the writer has obligingly supplied each key word in the next line, so readers can confirm their prediction by considering the word in its entirety.

This kind of strategy lesson is rather formal and may need to be preplanned (the teacher may want to cover all but the first consonant(s) of the rhyming words with Post-Its, or with paper stuck on by an adhesive stick). However, mini-lessons like this can also occur within the total Shared Book Experience, after the poem has been introduced and enjoyed on a previous day.

One of the best ways to help students learn to use all the language cues together (along with prior knowledge and other available cues) is simply to discuss strategies for dealing with problem words as the problem arises. However, many teachers now wisely avoid round-robin reading (see arguments in Anderson, Hiebert, Scott, & Wilkinson, 1985) and confine public reading to those occasions when students have had the opportunity to silently read and then practice what they are going to read aloud. Thus the opportunity to discuss strategies for dealing with problem words occurs mainly when a student reads aloud so the teacher can assess the reader's strategies (see Chapter 6); when the teacher demonstrates his or her own strategies and engages the class in a discussion of strategies; or when a student shares a problem word in small group discussion, so that together the group can explore possible strategies. In the last case, the student may have jotted down the problem word and its text location in his or her dialogue journal or literature log, perhaps at the teacher's request that everyone make a note of some problem words for group discussion. (See the description of literature discussion groups in Chapter 9.)

One problem word that I brought to class discussion with my preservice teachers was the word *fissiparous*. I had encountered it in an article I was reading a day or two before. In this instance, we all brainstormed strategies for dealing with this word, and then enlarged our list to include the various strategies we were aware of using with other words as well. Here is the list of strategies we compiled (Weaver, 1990a, pp. 14–15). This is not strictly an ordered set of strategies, but we did more or less think that we'd try the earlier strategies first and the later strategies last:

1. THINK what would make sense here; then, more or less simultaneously—
2. Try to sound it out.
   and/or
3. Look at meaningful word parts.
4. Regress and reread.
5. Substitute a word that seems to make sense, or a placeholder word like "something," and go on.
6. Continue—see if following context clarifies.
   If yes, continue reading.
   If no, decide if the word is important.
     If no, continue reading.
     If yes, regress and reread
       and/or ask someone
       and/or look it up in a dictionary or reference book.

Through class discussion, teachers can compile such lists even with emergent readers, though of course their lists won't initially be so extensive. As another strategy emerges from discussion, it can be added to the list, which can be posted in the classroom and used as a reminder.

Again, such discussion fosters several of the strategies needed for proficient reading, not just one. Notice that, in effect, our first strategy was to make use of prior knowledge and context, to "think what would make sense here." On the other hand, context is usually not enough by itself for identifying a word; Gough, Alford, and Holley-Wilcox (1981) estimate that in identifying the exact word, using prior knowledge and context alone succeeds only about 25 percent of the time. We need other strategies that draw upon other kinds of information, too.

One strategy increasingly needed by readers in the intermediate grades and beyond is the strategy of breaking words into pronounceable syllables, so as to identify written words that are already in their listening vocabulary. This strategy seems all the more critical because readers seem to process even familiar words in syllables or other familiar chunks of letters: prefixes, suffixes, and roots, for example, or onsets and rimes (see Chapter 5 for a definition and evidence).

However, we do not need to teach a formal system of syllabication for students to develop the strategy of dividing words into syllables and other pronounceable parts. Research indicates that when good readers come upon unfamiliar words, they typically decode them by analogy with known words and word parts, as you probably earlier did with the nonsense words in the *blonke* passage and the *corandic* passage. Most of the time we do this automatically and unconsciously. While it is true that this strategy can be taught both explicitly and extensively (for example, as described by Gaskins, Gaskins, & Gaskins, 1991), it is also true that few if any readers need so much drill. Most students will develop the strategy with (at most) teacher demonstration and discussion, encouragement to use the strategy on occasions when it's needed, and perhaps a little explicit practice with longer and more difficult words in occasional mini-lessons.

As with other strategies, whole language educators have found that they are best learned when discussed and practiced in the context of authentic reading (e.g., Kucer, 1992).

Strategies for Monitoring Comprehension and Confirming or Correcting

Good readers automatically monitor their comprehension most of the time. That is, they are constantly aware of whether or not what they're reading makes sense, and if it doesn't, they employ fix-it strategies—especially rereading. Less effective readers do not necessarily monitor their ongoing comprehension, which may be mainly why some readers are less effective in constructing meaning.

Teachers can help those who don't monitor comprehension by getting them to listen to themselves read, and ask themselves questions like

- Does that sound like language? Does that sound right? (when a miscue does not fit grammatically in the context)
- Does that make sense? (when a miscue does not make sense in the context)

It works best to tape-record the reader reading and then play back a passage in which the reader has made miscues that disrupt grammar and/or sense. That way, the reader can more easily listen to him- or herself and take time to reflect upon the passage, return to the text, and discuss with the teacher possible strategies for dealing with the problem word. (See Chapter 6 for more ways of using what has come to be known as "retrospective miscue analysis.")

For monitoring comprehension of longer passages, students can be encouraged to use a "click or clunk strategy" (developed in MERIT, 1986); this is especially appropriate for dealing with nonfiction prose. At the end of each paragraph or section read, readers are to ask themselves if the meaning or message "clicks" for them or if it goes "clunk." If it clunks, what is wrong? What can the reader do to make sense of it? This is a delightfully simple yet effective way of getting readers to stop their reading and rethink rather than continuing to read without comprehension. It is most likely to be adopted by students if the teacher repeatedly demonstrates how he or she uses it, and teachers and students use it collectively. (See also Wilson, 1988).

Strategies for Reading with a Purpose

One of the most useful strategies I've seen for guiding research-type reading is the simple strategy of making lists of "What I/we know" and "What I/we want to know" about a topic (Y. M. Goodman and Burke, 1980). This has developed into what is now termed the KWL strategy: make lists of what you Know, what you Want to know, and then what you Learned. Some teachers encourage students to make subsequent lists of "What I/we *still* want to know" to guide further reading and research.

Also effective is simplifying the procedure by just discussing what you know, actually listing only what you want to know, and then presenting part of what you learned, in some coherent manner.

A partial example comes from Pearson and Johnson (1978, pp. 189–91). In this hypothetical discussion, the teacher is preparing students to read a selection about the construction of the first continental railroad:[8]

INSTRUCTOR:	Tell me what you know about the Union Pacific Railroad. (No response.) Well, when was it built? (No response.) Before the Civil War? After? During?
STUDENT 1:	Before!
STUDENT 2:	After!
INSTRUCTOR:	Now, why do you say before?
STUDENT 1:	Just seems right to me. Maybe it had something to do with the Gold Rush?
STUDENT 2:	No, it was after!
INSTRUCTOR:	You're sure about that?
STUDENT 2:	Pretty sure. There's something about a Golden Spike out West in Utah, or Nevada, or Wyoming, and that country wasn't even settled by the time of the Civil War.
INSTRUCTOR:	Didn't they have railroads before the Civil War?
STUDENT 3:	Sure, the railroads came as early as 1820 or 1830. Right after the steam engine.
STUDENT 4:	But they were mostly in the Eastern United States.
INSTRUCTOR:	So no one is sure when it was built. Anyone want to guess about a date? (Several are offered, ranging from 1840 to 1910.) Okay, where did it start and where did it end?

The dialogue continues in similar fashion, with students and teacher pooling their fragmented knowledge but mostly admitting that they don't know for sure exactly when, where, how, or by whom the Continental Railroad was built. They jot down what they don't know and want to know, thus setting the stage for reading to find out.

Such strategies become most useful to students when teachers repeatedly guide them in collaborative use of the strategy, as in this example.

Reviewing and Retaining Information and Concepts

A technique as simple as note-taking may need to be explicitly demonstrated and discussed, with the teacher then inviting students to try it and perhaps discussing the resultant notes with them. (They could combine individual notes to create group notes, thus lessening the teacher's task.) I have even found this beneficial for college students in a developmental writing class, who hadn't all developed the handy technique of indenting to indicate subordinate ideas and supporting details:

Main idea

   Subordinate idea

      Supporting details

Such visual representation of the relationship among ideas and information facilitates review and understanding. Through teacher demonstration and discussion, even students in the intermediate grades can begin to develop this simple note-taking strategy.

Widely popular now is the strategy of developing a semantic map, web, or cluster (call it what you will) to visually represent ideas and the relationships among them (Heimlich & Pittelman, 1986). Usually a semantic map has some key word or concept at the center, with other information radiating outward, weblike. Semantic maps may be used before, during, and after reading: to represent what students already know about a topic, to keep ongoing notes, perhaps to reorganize and represent information, and certainly to review and enhance retention of the information. Figure 4.6 shows, as an example, a semantic map that fourth graders and I developed to reflect and remind us of what we knew about the robot Norby, after reading the first chapter of *Norby, the Mixed-up Robot* (in *The Norby Chronicles,* Asimov & Asimov, 1983).

A more detailed kind of visual organizer is sometimes called a *graphic organizer*. It may take various forms: a time line for history, arrows for cause-effect relationships, a chart with rows and columns for categories and cross-categories, and various other kinds of diagrams, depending upon the kind of information being represented. Figure 4.7 is a graphic organizer that Marilyn Wilson developed for a section of text dealing with rebellion in the American colonies (Wilson, 1988). If the teacher prepares the "cause" part of such a graphic organizer, students can use it to help monitor comprehension during reading. After reading, it can readily be used in reviewing the material. In fact, semantic maps and graphic organizers can typically be used before, during, and after reading (See Wilson, 1988, for example).

Each of these strategies may be most effectively learned through demonstration, invitation, discussion, and repeated collaborative practice in the context of authentic reading (see Kucer, 1992). The strategies are *used* when students see them as *useful*. See Pearson and Fielding (1991) for a review of some of the research on teaching reading strategies. However, as their review indicates, there has been almost no research on the incidental teaching of strategies. This is hardly surprising, since such teaching is not necessarily preplanned, but often takes advantage of the teachable moment.

REVIEW AND BEYOND

This chapter has dealt with a variety of interrelated topics: various kinds of context available to a reader, language cues and reading strategies, reading proficiency and the use of context, why it is inappropriate and unproductive to conceptualize reading as involving accurate identification of all the words, implications for understanding and accepting dialect miscues, and revaluing readers. Some references for further reading are listed in Figure 4.8.

Among the more important conclusions and implications are the following:

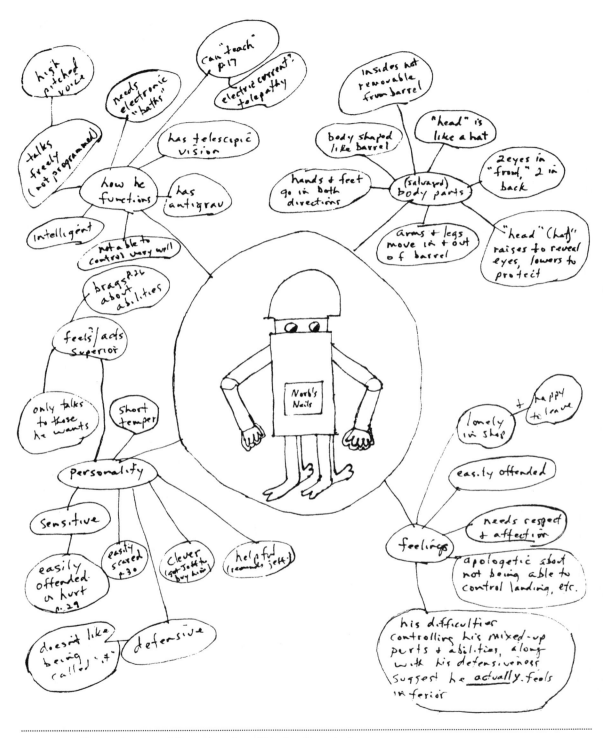

Figure 4.6   Semantic map of the character of Norby, the robot

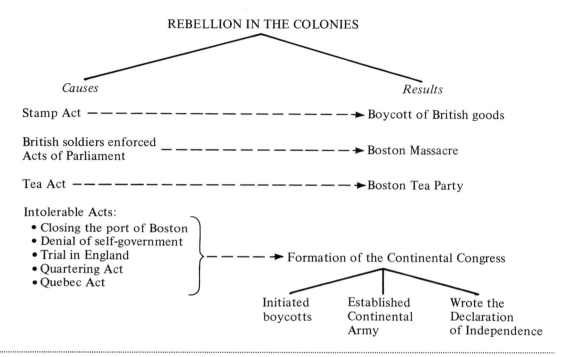

FIGURE 4.7   Graphic organizer (Wilson, 1988)

1. Readers do not need to rely on grapho/phonemic information alone. They have available both syntactic and semantic context within the sentence and the text, and context beyond the text—their own storehouse of prior knowledge and experience, including their intuitive knowledge of grammar.
2. Context can help all readers identify or at least understand words they don't immediately recognize, but it is especially helpful for younger and less proficient readers. For them, words are clearly easier to identify in context than in isolation.
3. Readers use syntactic and semantic cues to predict what is coming next in a sentence, and also to confirm or correct tentative identifications of words and their construction of meaning. More generally, language *cues* give rise to reading *strategies*.
4. Proficient readers—those who are both efficient and effective in constructing meaning—draw upon their prior knowledge in making simultaneous use of the language cue systems (syntactic, semantic, and grapho/phonemic) to construct meaning, not to identify every word correctly.
5. Less proficient readers may often be individuals who overrely on grapho/phonemic cues and underrely on context cues and prior knowledge, frequently in a misguided concern for saying all the words correctly. These readers can benefit from assistance in learning to use context and prior knowledge more effectively.

Allen, P. D., & Watson, D. J. (Eds.). (1976). *Findings of research in miscue analysis: Classroom implications.* Urbana, IL: ERIC Clearinghouse on Reading and Communication Skills and the National Council of Teachers of English.

Goodman, K. S. (1973). *Theoretically based studies of patterns of miscues in oral reading performance.* Detroit: Wayne State University. (ERIC Document Reproduction Service No. ED 079 708). This massive research report combines the studies of several researchers, to draw generalizations about the miscues of proficient and less proficient readers and the reading process itself.

Goodman, K. S. (Ed.) (1973). *Miscue analysis: Applications to reading instruction.* Urbana, IL: National Council of Teachers of English.

Goodman, K. S. (1982). *Language and literacy: The selected writings of Kenneth S. Goodman.* 2 vols. (F. V. Gollasch, Ed.). Boston: Routledge & Kegan Paul. Includes many of Goodman's most influential articles, including those on miscues.

Goodman, K. S., & Goodman, Y. M. (n. d.) Annotated miscue bibliography. Unpublished paper, Program in Language and Literacy, University of Arizona, Tucson. Annotates articles, books, and dissertations and theses from 1965 through 1990.

Goodman, Y. M., Watson, D. J., & Burke, C. (1987). *Reading Miscue Inventory: Alternative Procedures.* Katonah, NY: Richard C. Owen.

Page, W. D. (Ed.). (1975). *Help for the reading teacher: New directions in research.* Urbana, IL: National Conference on Research in English and the National Council of Teachers of English.

Smith, F. (1985). *Reading without nonsense* (2nd ed.). New York: Teachers College Press.

Smith, F. (1988). *Understanding reading* (4th ed.). Hillsdale, NJ: Erlbaum.

Figure 4.8 *References on the reading process, miscues, and miscue analysis*

6. On the other hand, some readers may need assistance in learning to use grapho/phonemic cues more effectively, in the context of constructing meaning. Some may even need basic assistance in understanding the alphabetic principle and in grasping basic letter/sound relationships—assistance provided in the context of meaningful reading and writing, as in a Reading Recovery program, for example (see Chapter 12).

7. Many words and sentences (even whole paragraphs) are not critical to the meaning of the evolving whole. Most texts reflect a significant degree of redundancy, especially at the word level.

8. Accurate word identification is appropriate only for *rehearsed* reading performance; it is not an appropriate goal for reading instruction per se, nor is the avoidance of dialect miscues an appropriate goal of instruction. Rather, a more appropriate and attainable goal is for readers to learn to use prior knowledge, context, and grapho/phonemic cues together to construct meaning. (Even so, not all proficient readers will use each cue system equally well.)

9. Coordinating prior knowledge with the language cue systems (syntactic, semantic, grapho/phonemic) involves learning such strategies as predicting, sampling the text appropriately, monitoring comprehension, and correcting (at least silently) miscues that disrupt grammar or sense.

10. In the long run, teaching sight words or phonics skills in isolation is not likely to be the most effective way of helping emergent readers. It is more effective to concentrate instructional attention on helping emergent readers make effective use of reading strategies in the context of meaningful reading. This will gradually develop their stock of sight words and their ability to use grapho/phonemic cues in conjunction with other kinds of language cues. (See Chapter 5 for further development of these points.)

11. Teachers can use relatively natural means to help students develop such strategies as prediction, simultaneous use of all the language cue systems, and monitoring comprehension to confirm and correct. One of the most effective means is teaching the DDID cycle: Demonstrate, Discuss, Invite students to try the strategy, and Discuss how it worked for them.

12. Reading is a complex process. Proficient reading involves automatic and simultaneous processing of various kinds, with considerable overlap and redundancy contributing to both effectiveness and efficiency in getting words and constructing meaning from text.

Chapter 5 focuses on the visual information used in word perception, with a substantive section on developing phonics knowledge. Chapter 6 supplements the present chapter in suggesting some ways of helping less proficient readers develop effective reading strategies. Then, in Chapter 7, we shall see growing evidence for the relative effectiveness of teaching reading strategies and the use of language cue systems in the context of authentic reading and writing, as compared with teaching sight words, phonics, and other skills in isolated lessons.

FOR FURTHER REFLECTION AND EXPLORATION

1. Look again at David's and Tony's miscues in Chapter 1. What language cues and reading strategies does each child seem to have been using? Ask yourself the same question about the miscues recorded below. The examples in (a) are from a kindergartner; examples (b) through (f) are from second graders; and the others are from older readers (sixth, eighth, and tenth graders) (K. S. Goodman, 1973, pp. 210–11, 230–31, 250, 258, 310).

   not getting anything
   a. I'm getting nothing for Christmas. [a line from a song]

   mean   inside
   "No, no," said Boris. "I don't mean outside."

Boris growled, "That's because you did it the wrong way."
@ didn't do [above "did"]

[The reader started to say, "You didn't do it right."]

b. Here is something you can do.
to get down [above "do"]

c. I am not too little to help with little things, am I?
I have not help the little kitten will we want little kitten to play ? [above line c]

d. "The little monkey had it."
truck [above "monkey"]

e. . . . a voice calling, ∧ somewhere above.
him [above, with caret after "calling,"]

f. . . . it was enough to wake ∧ the dead.
up [above, with caret after "wake"]

g. Billy knew that fawns were always very shy.
know   fun   was   sky [above "Billy", "fawns", "were", "shy"]

h. I leaned over the crib, pointing a finger . . .
liked   a crab potted [above "leaned", "crib,", "pointing", "finger"]

i. Billy was so pleased by the hunter's words.
proud [above "pleased"]

j. . . . to see if there was any danger. He heard the . . .
afraid [above "danger."]

k. . . . stop driving until we can see Los Angeles.

l. . . . I went over to his bed.

m. . . . when the children begin assuming ∧ control of the country.
the [above, with caret before "control"]

n. . . . the door of Harry's room. . . .
to   bedroom [above "door", "room"]

o. . . . a pair of pyjamas with blue, ∧ brown and white stripes.
and   with [above, with caret after "blue,"]

2. If you know of any teachers with widely differing instructional approaches and/or definitions of reading, it might be interesting to compare their reactions to Anne's miscues (p. 225) or Jay's (pp. 138–139) or Billy's (pp. 136–137), or all of them. Does

the teacher think most of these miscues are serious, a matter for concern? If not, why not? If so, what kind of instructional help would the teacher recommend? Compare the responses from the different teachers.

3. To determine for yourself whether words are easier to read in context or in isolation, choose a reader to work with, either a beginning reader (late first grade, or second grade) or a poor reader of any age. Then choose a reading selection that should be appropriate for this reader: not easy, but not terribly difficult either. The selection should be about 250 words long or longer (except for the youngest readers, who may find this too much). It might be wise to photocopy the selection for your later convenience in analysis and discussion. Once you have chosen the reading selection, type from it a list of about 50 words for the person to read (fewer if the reader is a nonproficient beginner). One possibility would be to make a list of all the different function words in the selection. Another possibility is simply to choose every fifth word (avoiding duplications). Have the reader read the list of words and then the entire selection. Instead of trying to take notes on the reader's miscues as he or she reads, just tape-record the session for later study. To facilitate discussion, mark each of the miscues on the word list and each of the miscues the reader made on the reading selection itself. For the most part, the marking symbols introduced in Chapter 1 should be adequate. Consider such questions as the following:

   a. On the whole, did the reader seem to be using context to predict what was coming next? What examples support your conclusion?

   b. Did the person read in context any of the words that he or she missed in isolation? If so, what are some examples? How or why might the context have helped?

   c. Did the person read in isolation any words that he or she later missed in context? If so, what are some examples? Why do you suppose these words were read correctly in isolation but not in context?

   d. On the whole, would you conclude that words are easier to read in isolation, or in context?

4. Even words that are central to a passage can often be determined from context. What word or words would you put in the blanks below? Essentially the same item belongs in each blank. The paragraph is from Ray Bradbury's *Dandelion Wine* (1957, p. 34):

   > Somehow the people who made _____ knew what boys needed and wanted. They put marshmallows and coiled springs in the soles and they wove the rest out of grasses bleached and fired in the wilderness. Somewhere deep in the soft loam of the _____ the thin hard sinews of the buck deer were hidden. The people that made the _____ must have watched a lot of winds blow the trees and a lot of rivers going down to the lakes. Whatever it was, it was in the _____, and it was summer.[9]

   You might try finding or creating similar passages to use with children.

5. We can often get the meaning of a word from context (even though we may never pronounce the word correctly). Try it:

a. First, jot down a definition for the following words: *deng, tolchock, veck,* and *viddy.* Just make up a definition that seems reasonable.

b. Now see if you can tell what the words mean, as used in this sentence from Anthony Burgess' novel A *Clockwork Orange* (1963): "Our pockets were full of *deng,* so there was no real need . . . to *tolchock* some old *veck* in an alley and *viddy* him swim in his blood while we counted the takings . . . " (pp. 1–2). Discuss what cues enable you to determine what the words mean.

c. Try essentially the same procedure again. Write down a definition for these words:

creech	malenky	razrez
droogs	messel	skorry
glazzies	millicents	spatted
goloss	poogly	zoobies

Do you notice yourself using any fairly consistent principle for determining what the words might mean? Discuss.

d. Now read the first chapter of A *Clockwork Orange.* In each case, how do you finally determine what the word means?

6. Many children who tend to deal with each word in a text as if it stood in isolation will make habitual confusions of one sort or another. They may confuse *then* with *than, the* with *they, and* with *can,* and so forth. The solution is not to drill students on these words in isolation, but to help them learn to use context to disentangle the confusion. You can begin with passages in which both grammar and meaning strongly signal the word intended. For example, if a person commonly reads "can" for *and* and vice versa, you might construct a passage beginning as follows:

Jim called to ask his friends Bob *and* Mike, "*Can* you come to the fort today?" Bob answered, "Yes, we *can.* But let's go get some pop *and* cookies to take with us."

You might even initially omit the problem words and ask the reader to supply whichever one is appropriate in context.

As an activity, then, create several passages that might be used to help readers overcome habitual confusions between pairs of words like those listed above. You might first create a passage where only one of the words is appropriate, and create a companion passage for the other word. You might then create a passage that includes blanks where the two words belong. Finally, you might create a passage like the one above, where both words are explicitly included. It would be better yet to find appropriate passages from children's literature and blank out the relevant words, since artificially constructed passages tend not to have the supportive language and meaningful context that make it possible for readers to supply or read the troublesome words. If possible, try these passages with readers who habitually confuse the words. (For various kinds of strategy lessons to use with middle-grade children and older, see Y. M. Goodman & C. Burke, 1980.)

7. As indicated earlier in the chapter, the "basic" cloze procedure, first developed by Wilson Taylor in 1953, involves the reader's supplying every fifth word, on the assumption that about one of every five words in a text can be predicted from context. Various modifications of the cloze procedure may be useful in helping students learn to use all the language cue systems—though Kucer's research (1992) suggests that students may not perceive the purpose of the activities, despite repeated explanations!

   If you think it worth trying some cloze activities, you might prepare some mini-lessons, using one or more of the following suggestions:

   a. Omit the last word of a sentence, if it is highly predictable—or include just the first letter of the last word. This is particularly useful with beginning readers.
   b. Omit inflectional endings, to help readers recognize their own syntactic knowledge.
   c. Omit function words, to help readers realize their ability to predict these words from the content words, word order, and context.
   d. Omit key concept-carrying words (as in the passage from Bradbury in activity 4 above), to help readers see how words can be understood from context.
   e. Omit every fifth word (or whatever) and have students read just for meaning, not to fill in the words, in order to help them see that comprehension is possible without identifying all the words.
   f. For less confident readers, omit only words and sentences that are highly predictable, to assure success.

   You might use a variety of materials: songs, poems, and stories; content-area textbooks; newspapers and magazines; and anything else that might be suitable. Whatever the variations and materials used, however, it is important for students to read through the entire cloze activity before filling in any of the missing parts, in order to help them see the value of using following context to identify and/or get the meaning of difficult words. Of course, you should accept any and all responses that reasonably fit in each blank, not just the actual word omitted. It is crucial for students to discuss their answers to a cloze exercise. They need the opportunity to share and compare their responses with those of other students, and the challenge of defending their choices or rejecting them in favor of something better. Perhaps even more crucial is explicitly discussing what the activity suggests about reading normal texts, including the need for using schemas and context in dealing with problem words. Kucer's research suggests that students are not too likely to make these connections for themselves. A useful reference is Jongsma, *Cloze Instruction Research: A Second Look,* (1980). Jongsma reviews the research from the 1970s on the use of cloze as a teaching technique, identifies weaknesses of the technique, and suggests directions for future research.

8. To compare proficient reading with nonproficient reading, try our blacked-out *New York Times* passage (p. 145) with both good and poor readers of about junior high age or beyond. First, be certain that each person can identify all of the content words in the selection; if necessary, read these words for the person one or more

times. Then ask the person to write in the missing function words (you may want to use a photocopy of the passage for this purpose). Are the good and poor readers equally able to supply reasonable possibilities for the missing words? If not, what does this suggest about their differing approaches to the task of reading?

9. This group activity further demonstrates that the same ideas can be expressed in different ways. Working separately, each participant should first follow the directions below. (The sentence-combining activity is from R. O'Donnell and K. Hunt, in Fagan, Cooper, & Jensen, 1975, p. 201; see also Hunt, 1970, pp. 64–65.) Once you have all completed this part of the activity, compare your results. Did you indeed find different ways to express the same ideas? What are some of the possible implications for reading?

Aluminum

Directions: Read the passage all the way through. You will notice that the sentences are short and choppy. Study the passage, and then rewrite it in a better way. You may combine sentences, change the order of words, and omit words that are repeated too many times. But try not to leave out any of the information.

Aluminum is a metal. It is abundant. It has many uses. It comes from bauxite. Bauxite is an ore. Bauxite looks like clay. Bauxite contains aluminum. It contains several other substances. Workmen extract these other substances from the bauxite. They grind the bauxite. They put it in tanks. Pressure is in the tanks. The other substances form a mass. They remove the mass. They use filters. A liquid remains. They put it through several other processes. It finally yields a chemical. The chemical is powdery. It is white. The chemical is alumina. It is a mixture. It contains aluminum. It contains oxygen. Workmen separate the aluminum from the oxygen. They use electricity. They finally produce a metal. The metal is light. It has a luster. The luster is bright. The luster is silvery. This metal comes in many forms.

10. Examine the dialect-related miscues that a college student made in reading the passage below. All of the miscues are numbered in this passage from the dialect reader *Friends,* by Joan Baratz and William Stewart (1970, pp. 24–30). What do you think caused the reader to make these miscues? Discuss.

One morning Ollie and Leroy was getting ready to

go to school. Leroy, he put on one of Ollie socks

'cause he lost his. Ollie say, "Boy, give me my ①_{back}

sock" but Leroy ②_{he} wouldn't give it to him. Leroy

say "It's my sock." But Ollie ③_{knew} know it wasn't

④ 's
'cause it wasn't even the same color as Leroy ∧

other sock. Ollie kept on begging and begging

Leroy for the sock. But Leroy still wouldn't

⑤ into
give it to him. Ollie hit Leroy. And they got to

⑥   ⑦ ed
a fight
fighting. Leroy hit Ollie in the nose and it start ∧

to bleeding. Then, Ollie got real mad and hit Leroy

on the arm as hard as he could. Leroy hollered real

loud. Big Momma must have heard them fighting 'cause

⑧
came
she come running in the room and she stop the fight.

⑨ ed
She say "All right, who start ∧ this mess?" Ollie say

Leroy start it and Leroy say Ollie start it.

Big Momma say, "I done told you about fighting

before. Since don't nobody know who start this

mess I'm just going to whip both of you."

Incidentally, I have typed this just the way it was typed by the student who carried out the experiment with her college friend. Along with four other errors in copying, my student made two dialect miscues in reading and typing the passage! Compare this version with the one in #11 below and see if you can locate the miscues.

11. The following is the same passage, correctly typed (I hope!):[10]

One morning Ollie and Leroy was getting ready to go to school. Leroy he put on one of Ollie sock 'cause he lost his. Ollie say, "Boy give me my sock" but Leroy wouldn't give it to him. Leroy say, "It's my sock." But Ollie know it wasn't 'cause it wasn't even the same color as Leroy other sock. Ollie kept on begging and begging Leroy for the sock. But Leroy still wouldn't give it to him. Ollie hit Leroy. And they got to fighting. Leroy hit Ollie in the nose and it start to bleeding. Then, Ollie got real mad and hit Leroy on his arm as hard as he could. Leroy hollered real loud. Big Momma must of heard them fighting 'cause she come running in the room and she stop the fight. She say, "All right, who start this mess?" Ollie say Leroy start it and Leroy say Ollie start it. Big Momma say, "I done told you about fighting before. Since don't nobody know who start this mess I'm just going to whip both of you."

It might be interesting to try one or both of the following activities with this passage:

a. Have one or more persons read the first four sentences of the passage twice, then try to write down exactly what they have read. Look to see what changes they have made in the authors' surface structure. Have they translated some of the patterns of the text into the patterns of their own dialect?

b. Have one or more persons read the passage aloud; if possible, try it with both children and adults. Listen to hear what dialect miscues they make. Again, have they translated some of the patterns of the text into the patterns of their own dialect?

12. To help you formulate your own position on the teaching of phonics (in preparation for reading Chapter 5), brainstorm all the reasons you can think of that are commonly given for and against the teaching of phonics. Compile a class list from your individual lists, and discuss.

13. Sometimes people who are convinced that heavy phonics instruction is not necessary for helping most children read still defend phonics instruction on the grounds that it is important in helping children spell. Try this as a class activity, and compare your results. Have someone dictate the following words to the rest of the class. Compare spellings. Then discuss what your chances are of spelling the words correctly using phonics alone. What would you conclude about the importance of phonics in learning to spell correctly?

a. Real words: homonyms (don't define these or use them in a sentence)

sun

brake

rowed

mete

b. Nonsense words

keak

pite

wraim

/ne´ der le/[11]

c. Real words that most people do not know

coriaceous /kôr' ē ā shəs/

deraign /di rān'/

escharotic /es' kə rät' ik/

gaudeamus /gou' dā ä mōōs/

isochronal /ī säk' rə nəl/

mesophyte /mes' o fīt/

piceous /pis' ē əs/

I often give this spelling test at the end of class and ask that students look up in a large desk dictionary before the next class the words in group c. Subsequent discussion on the difficulty of locating these words proves most illuminating.

5 | From Word Perception to Phonics, and Beyond

Words may be identified when their individual letters are separately indistinguishable.

— Frank Smith

THE EYES AND THE BRAIN

When children have difficulty reading, it is common practice to have their eyes checked. This is wise, because various kinds of eye malfunction can indeed make reading more difficult. In most cases, appropriately prescribed glasses compensate for problems with the eyes themselves. However, there are few children whose reading problems can be attributed solely to physical problems with the eyes.[1] This is because visual perception is only partly a function of the eyes. Perhaps your experience traveling on superhighways illustrates this point. Have you ever "seen" the words on a road sign, yet passed the sign before you were able to determine what the words were? Perhaps you were a little slow in looking at the sign, or perhaps you are nearsighted and were a little slow in picking up the visual image. Nevertheless, the crucial problem was not in your eyes, but in your brain: the brain simply did not have enough time to process the visual image before it disappeared from sight.

The preceding illustration suggests that visual perception is not merely a function of the eyes, but a function of the brain. In this text we are concerned with one particular kind of visual perception, the perception of words. We will be concerned with *both* aspects of word perception: with ocular and sensory processing, and with the actual identification of words.[2] However, such division is merely a convenient fiction. Visual perception is an *active* process, and what the eye processes is in large part determined by what the brain directs it to look for, as well as the knowledge that the brain brings to the visual task. We use our prior knowledge and experience to guide even the most elementary aspects of visual processing.

OCULAR AND SENSORY PROCESSING

It was implied above that the eye registers a visual image. Strictly speaking, however, this statement is not accurate. As the psycholinguist Frank Smith explains, "What goes into

172

the open eyes is a diffuse and continual bombardment of electromagnetic radiation, minute waves of light energy that vary only in frequency, amplitude, and spatial and temporal patterning. The rays of light that impinge on the eye do not in themselves carry the color and form and texture and movement that we see." Rather, these are constructions of the brain (F. Smith, 1988, p. 68). So too in reading: the eye receives waves of light energy that are transmitted to the brain as a series of neural impulses. Initially, the written symbols may be perceived as sets of bars, slits, edges, curves, angles, and breaks (Gough, 1972, p. 332; see also F. Smith, 1979, chaps. 8 and 9). The brain may then construct the words of the text from these bars, curves, angles, or whatever.

How, then, do the eyes (the ocular part of the system) pick up these waves of light energy that are transformed into words? In 1879, the Frenchman Émile Javal discovered that the eyes move along a line of print with a series of jerky movements he called *saccades,* meaning 'jerks.' It is difficult if not impossible to become aware of one's own saccades, for the eyes *seem* to move along a line of print with a smooth, continuous motion. Nevertheless, they do not: they move in a sequence of tiny leaps or jerks.

There is no useful vision during the eye movements themselves, as you can demonstrate by looking into a mirror with your head held still and moving your eyes from left to right between two imaginary points. As you will discover, you cannot see your eyes in motion. Neither can you read with your eyes in motion (I. H. Anderson & Dearborn, 1952, p. 101).

The saccades, or eye movements, take up only a small fraction of total reading time—about 10 percent of the time in rapid reading and about 5 percent of the time in slow reading (I. H. Anderson & Dearborn, 1952, p. 107). The rest of the time is taken up by *eye fixations,* or pauses. It is during these fixations that the eye receives the stimuli that are transformed into visual images in the brain.

Various aspects of visual processing have been studied in the laboratory, usually with the help of a *tachistoscope.* In simple terms, a tachistoscope is a device for presenting visual information for very short periods of time—as little as ten milliseconds (ten thousandths of a second, or one hundredth of a second). With the use of the tachistoscope, it has been found that successive letters or words can be perceived from a visual presentation as short as one-tenth of a second (see Huey, 1968, p. 65). Further, it has been found that as many as four or five words can be perceived in a single fixation (see F. Smith, 1971, p. 92). Such statistics represent the *maximal efficiency* of the ocular and sensory systems.

Usually, however, reading proceeds much more slowly. The average adult reader makes about four eye fixations per second and identifies about one word per fixation. This gives an average adult reading speed of 240 words per minute (see Carroll, 1970, p. 292; I. H. Anderson & Dearborn, 1952, p. 177; Dechant, 1970, p. 16). Many readers have a slightly higher rate, up to about 300 words per minute. This means either that they average slightly more than four fixations per second, or that they average slightly more than one word per fixation, or both.

These various measurements indicate that there is a considerable discrepancy between what the ocular and the sensory systems are capable of doing, and what they typically do in reading. The crucial differences are summarized in Figure 5.1. As this

Maximal Ocular and Sensory Efficiency	*Typical Ocular and Sensory Functioning in Reading*
An eye fixation of 1/10 second is enough for identifying a letter or word.	Eye fixations are normally about 1/4 second long.
We can identify four or five words in a normal eye fixation of about 1/4 second.	Readers typically process about one word in a normal eye fixation of about 1/4 second.
We can visually process about 960 to 1200 words per minute.	Most of us read at an average rate of about 240 to 300 words per minute.

FIGURE 5.1   *Ocular and sensory processing*

figure indicates, most people's ocular and sensory systems do not operate at maximal efficiency in normal reading. The eyes can handle about 960 to 1,200 words per minute, yet most of us read at an average speed of about 240 to 300 words per minute. Apparently most of us read at this slower rate because that is a comfortable speed for comprehending.

Of course, readers need to learn to vary their reading rate according to the material and their purpose for reading. To some extent we all do this, yet many of us could benefit from instruction and practice. We need to learn, for example, that it's okay to read a novel rapidly and without necessarily trying to remember all the details: there is no need to read a novel at a rate of only 240 to 300 words per minute unless we really want to, to savor the imagery and perhaps the language itself. We also need to learn to skim informational material, selecting only those parts of the text that are relevant to the particular purpose at hand. In general, this is the purpose of speed reading courses.

While recognizing the widespread need for these kinds of strategies, we should be wary of the simplistic notion that to improve reading, all we have to do is improve reading rate. If a person reads much slower than the average, he or she may be having difficulty constructing meaning from the text. The slow reading speed may be more a *symptom* of reading difficulty than a cause. In such cases, it may not help much to get readers to identify words faster; indeed, this may not even be possible.

What would help is learning to bring meaning to a text and having the background knowledge to do so. With greater understanding, readers will be able to identify words faster and usually more accurately, and that in turn will enhance their construction of meaning from a text.

There are various kinds of meaning we bring to a reading event. We bring not only prior knowledge of people, places, things, events, ideas, and feelings, but also prior knowledge about letters and sounds and the patterns and interconnections among them. Proficient readers seem automatically to draw upon the most salient and useful visual cues. We shall first consider which parts of words seem most useful in cueing word recognition, and then consider some of the research on how words are perceived.

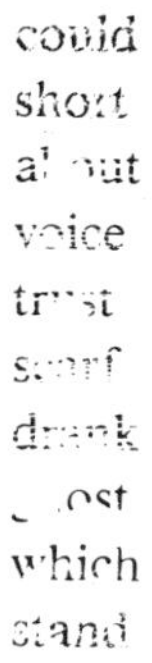

could
short
a⎵ut
voice
tr⎵st
scarf
drunk
⎵⎵ost
which
stand

FIGURE 5.2 Mutilated words

PARTS OF WORDS AT WORK

Various kinds of laboratory experiments make it abundantly clear that we do not need all the visual information normally available to us in order to identify familiar words. For example, you can probably read all or most of the words in Figure 5.2 fairly easily, though some are significantly mutilated by the omission of visual information. Furthermore, you may find that you have read each word more or less as a whole, without consciously identifying all the letters.[3]

The following three activities are designed to help you determine which parts of words are especially useful and which are less useful in cueing the recognition of words. These informal "experiments" are highly unscientific. There has been no strict control over vocabulary or sentence length and structure, and, most important, the words are presented in context rather than in isolation. But these experiments are more fun and easier to carry out than more scientific kinds of experiments on isolated words, and in most cases the conclusions are likely to be the same.[4]

Activity 1

You can use a stop watch, or a watch or clock with a second hand, to time yourself or someone else reading the following two sets of sentences, which constitute the beginning of a little story:

Vowels absent

–nc– –p–n – t–m– th–r– w–s – h–nds–m– y––ng w–lf
n–m–d L–b–. L–b– l–v–d w–th h–s m–th–r –nd f–th–r
–t th– –dg– –f – d––p, d–rk w––ds. –v–r– d–– L–b–
w–nt t– h–nt –t th– n–rth –dg– –f th– w––ds, n––r
th– l–ttl– v–ll–g– –f C–l––s.

Consonants absent

-o-e-i-e-   a--   -o-o   -ou--   -i--   -a-   a   -i-e-e-   o--
-a--e-   o-   -i-   -i-e,   -o--i--   i-   --e   -ie--s   -ea-   --e
-oo--   o-   -i--i--   -e--ie-   i-   --e   --i--e-.   A-   o--e-
-i-e-,   -o-o   -i---   e   -u--y   e-ou--   -o   -i--   a   --u--,
-ui-y   --i--   --a-   -a-   -i-o-eye-   i--   -a-e---   a--   ---aye-
-oo   -a-   --o-   -o-e.

After this experiment, it should be obvious that consonants are more important than vowels in cueing word recognition. This can be explained, at least in part, by two simple facts. First, there are considerably more consonants than vowels in English, and hence the consonants are more distinctive, more able to narrow down the number of possible alternatives that any given word could be. Second, consonants occur more frequently than vowels; that is, in most cases there are more consonants per word. Given these factors, it is hardly surprising to find that consonants are more useful in cueing word recognition. Indeed, written Arabic omits the vowels altogether, except in beginners' books (Gibson & Levin, 1975, p. 524).

Activity 2

This activity is related to the first. Again, time yourself or someone else reading the following two sets of sentences, a continuation of the story:

Bottoms absent

One day as Lobo was skirting the edge of the forest he came upon a little girl in a red hood. Her cheeks were so rosy and her arms so pudgy that Lobo knew she would be delicious. "Oh," she replied, "I'm taking this basket of goodies to my grandmother on the other side of the woods. Grandma isn't feeling very well."

Tops absent

Lobo thought for a moment. He could hardly wait to devour this scrumptious child, but then again he was hungry enough to eat the grandmother too. "Which house does your grandmother live in?" asked the wolf. "In the house by the three big oak trees," said Red Riding Hood (for that is what she was called). "She lives there all by herself."

Which paragraph took longer to read? Which part seems to be more important in cueing word recognition: the tops of words, or the bottoms? Most people conclude that the tops are more important, and this is indeed what research suggests. If you have not already figured out why, then look at the following list of the letters in our alphabet. How many ascend above the top line? How many descend below the bottom line?

abcdefghijklmnopqrstuvwxyz

As you can readily see, about twice as many letters ascend above the top line, making them visually more prominent. Note, too, that more than half of the consonants either ascend above the top line or descend below the bottom line, while none of the vowels do either (with the exception of y, which is only sometimes a vowel). Hence, consonants are not only more numerous and more frequently occurring than vowels, but many are also more prominent visually.

Activity 3

Again, time yourself or someone else reading the following passages, in order to determine the relative importance of the beginnings, middles, and ends of words:

Middles absent

"W–at   a   mar– –ous   oppo– – –nity!"   th– – –ht   L–bo.   He t–ld   t–e   c– –ld   to   s–op   a–d   p–ck   fl– – –rs   f–r   h–r gran– – –ther   on   t–e   w–y   th– – –gh   t–e   w– –ds,   t–en t–ok   o–f   on   a   s– –rt   c–t   t–at   o–ly   t–e   wo– –es k–ow   a– –ut.   S–on   he   ar– – –ed   at   t–e   grand– – –her's co– – –ge.   "I–'s   me,   Gr– – –ma,"   L–bo   s–id   in   a   t–ny v– –ce,   as   he   kn– – –ed   on   t–e   d–or.   He   pu– –ed t–e   d– –r   o–en   a–d   w–nt   in.

Ends absent

Lob–   wen–   strai– – –   to   th–   grandmoth– –'–   be–   an– gobb– – –   he–   up.   He   donn– –   he–   ca–   an–   gow– an–   clim– – –   int–   be–,   feel– – –   non–   to–   wel–   hims– – –. By   th–   tim–   Litt– –   Re–   Ridi– –   Hoo–   ha–   arri– – –, howe– – –,   he   ha–   overc– – –   hi–   atta– –   of   indigest– – – and   wa–   rea– –   fo–   dess– – –.   He   answe– – –   Red'–   kno– – in   an   ol–,   crack– –   voi– –:   "Com–   in,   dea–.   Jus– com–   on   in."

Beginnings absent

–obo   –as   so   – – –enous   –hat   he   – –dn't   –ait   –or – –ttle   –ed   – –ding   –ood   to   –sk   –er   "– – –ndma" –ow   –he   –as   or   –o   – –ing   –er   –he   – –sket   of – – –dies.   He   – –rew   –ack   –he   – –vers,   – –mped   –ut   of –ed,   –nd   –an   –ver   to   –he   – –ild.   –he   – – –eamed –nd   –an,   –ut   it   –as   –oo   –ate.   –obo   – – –bled   –er up.   – – –erwards   he   –at   by   –he   – – –eside   – – –king – – –ndma's   –ipe,   – – –aming   of   – –icy   – –ttle   – –rls.

Once again, which set of sentences took longest to read? Which took the shortest? From this experiment, you have probably concluded that the beginnings of words are more important in word identification than the middles or the ends. This is also what the research suggests. Various kinds of research also clearly indicate that the ends are more important than the middles. (If your results suggested otherwise, it was probably due to the flaws in the design of this particular experiment.)

Again, we may ask why these results occur. First, it seems that the beginnings and ends of words are important just because they are visually prominent, being either preceded or followed by white space. Second, the beginnings of words are particularly important because we read the words of a text more or less from left to right. In addition, the beginnings of words are less predictable than the ends, and therefore more necessary. The ends are more predictable than the beginnings because they often consist of grammatical endings, many of which are predictable from context. Thus, endings are less important cues to word recognition than beginnings, because endings are more predictable. On the other hand, endings are more important than middles, partly because they often do carry grammatical information. (For a discussion of many of the experiments that give rise to such observations, see I. H. Anderson & Dearborn, 1952, chap. 5.)

Children pay increasing attention to the beginnings and ends of words as they become more proficient at reading. In one study, for example, the spaces between words were filled in with a symbol created by superimposing an x on a c (see⛌Spot⛌run). Groups of children in the first and second grade read such a "filled" version of a story, as well as an "unfilled," or normal, version of a story. The filled version took significantly longer to read, but the difference was most noticeable for the better readers. The less proficient, slower readers were affected relatively little by the filled-in text (Hochberg, 1970, pp. 87–88). Since the poorer and slower readers were not much affected by the lack of spaces between words, it seems that these readers had not yet learned to pay particular attention to the beginnings and ends of words (see R. G. Brown, 1970, pp. 169–170). And this, in fact, might be one reason why these children *were* the less proficient readers.

Parts of Words in Review

Clearly, we can recognize familiar words from only part of the visual information available to us. Which parts of words are particularly important in cueing word recognition? We have found that:

1. Consonants are more important than vowels.
2. Beginnings of words are more important than middles and ends, and ends are more important than middles.
3. Some people may be relatively nonproficient readers at least in part because they have not learned to attend particularly to the parts of words that provide the most useful information.

HOW WE PERCEIVE WORDS

As the foregoing discussion suggests, the brain does not just passively interpret the data relayed through the eyes. In fact, the brain is in large measure independent of the eye. In normal vision, the picture that the eye registers is upside down, but the brain rights it. And as Frank Smith observes,

> In a number of perceptual experiments, many men and animals have been fitted with special spectacles which completely distort the information received

by the eye, switching top to bottom, or left to right, or distorting form or color. But within a very short while the brain "adapts" and the perceived world reverts to its normal appearance. No further distortion is perceived until the trick spectacles are removed, whereupon the "normal" pattern of stimulation produces a topsy-turvy percept which persists until the brain readapts. (F. Smith, 1971, p. 89; for more details, see Kohler, 1962).

The brain performs equally marvelous feats in normal reading.

We have seen that some visual cues are more important than others in cueing word recognition—namely, consonants and the beginnings of words (which are often consonantal). But are these the cues *actually* used the most in perceiving words? The answer seems to be yes and no.

Before further investigating how consonants and vowels contribute to word perception, let's deal with the widespread assumption that words are processed in serial fashion, letter by letter, from left to right.

Activity 1

First, try the following exercise on formulating phonics rules. In each of the words below, one letter is printed in boldface type. Determine how each boldface letter should be pronounced, and what part of the word signals the pronunciation of the boldface letter. In other words, try to formulate a rule for producing the correct pronunciation of the boldface letters. You will need at least one rule for each of the three sets.

Set A

hat	hate
hatter	hater
pet	Pete
petted	Peter
bit	bite
bitter	biting
mop	mope
mopping	moping
cut	cute
cutter	cuter

Set B

wrap	war
wren	wet
wring	win
wrong	won

Set C

car	cent
care	cereal
coat	cite
cough	city
cube	cyclone
cut	cyst

For the first column of words in Set A, you may have formulated a rule something like this: a vowel is short when it is followed by just a single consonant, or when it is followed by a double consonant plus an ending of some sort. For the second column of words in Set A, you may have formulated a rule something like the following: a vowel is long when it is followed by a silent *e,* or when it is followed by a single consonant plus an ending of some sort. Complicated, yes? The words in Set B should have been easier to deal with. You may have formulated a rather simple rule such as this: when a word begins with a *w* followed by an *r,* the *w* is not pronounced; otherwise, it is pronounced as a /w/. For the words in Set C, you might have formulated a rule something like this: when *c* is followed by *a, o,* or *u,* it is pronounced /k/; when *c* is followed by *e, i,* or *y,* it is pronounced /s/.

Doubtless these are not the only rules possible, nor are they necessarily the best rules. But note that in each case *the pronunciation of the boldface letter is determined not by what precedes, but by what follows.* We could not possibly pronounce the listed words correctly if we processed and pronounced them merely letter by letter, from left to right. Furthermore, most of these words are not exotic words that we encounter only once or twice in a lifetime; most are relatively common words that we encounter fairly often. As Venezky put it in *The Structure of English Orthography,* "A person who attempts to scan left to right, letter by letter, pronouncing as he goes, could not correctly read most English words" (1970b, p. 129).

Activity 2

Activity 1 leaves open the possibility that we might process each letter separately, even if not left to right. To test this possibility, try replicating the following experiment, from Edmund Huey's *The Psychology and Pedagogy of Reading* (1968, p. 100). For this experiment, you will need either a stopwatch or a watch or clock with a second hand. Figure 5.3 contains a column of letters, a column of four-letter words, and a column of eight-letter words. Time yourself or someone else reading the column of letters as rapidly as possible, either simply identifying each letter mentally or pronouncing it aloud. Repeat the same procedure for the column of four-letter words and the column of eight-letter words.

Even though you may have stumbled over some unfamiliar words, you probably found that it did not take nearly four times as long to read the column of four-letter words as it took to read the column of single letters; nor, surely, did it take eight times as long to read the column of eight-letter words. Huey's four experimental subjects read

y	pool	analysis
w	rugs	habitual
u	mark	occupied
s	send	inherent
q	list	probable
o	more	summoned
m	pick	devotion
k	stab	remarked
i	neck	overcome
g	your	resolute
e	dice	elements
c	font	conclude
a	earl	numbered
z	whit	struggle
x	ants	division
v	role	research
t	sink	original
r	rust	involved
p	ware	obstacle
n	fuss	relative
l	tick	physical
j	rasp	pastness
h	mold	lacteals
f	hive	sameness
d	four	distract

FIGURE 5.3   Huey's list of letters and words

the columns aloud, averaging 15.7 seconds for the isolated letters, 17.3 seconds for the four-letter words, and 19.6 seconds for the eight-letter words (Huey, 1968, p. 101). When I first tried the experiment, I read the columns silently. It took me 7 seconds for the single letters, 7 seconds for the four-letter words, and almost 8 seconds for the eight-letter words.

Clearly, fluent readers do not process words letter by letter. Just as we do not comprehend sentences merely by combining the meanings of individual words, so we do not perceive words merely by combining the perceptions of individual letters.

Given the examples in the preceding discussion, it should not be surprising that words can be identified under conditions that make it impossible to identify individual letters. As long ago as the turn of the century, Erdmann and Dodge determined: (1) that words can be recognized when lying too far from the eyes' fixation point to permit recognition of individual letters; (2) that words can be recognized when they are constructed of letters so small that the letters cannot be singly identified; and (3) that words can be recognized from distances at which the letters, exposed singly, cannot be recognized (see Huey, 1968, pp. 73–74). It has also been found that words can be identified under lighting conditions that do not permit the identification of single letters. In one experiment, even first graders could identify familiar three-letter words at lower light intensities than they needed for identifying single letters (see F. Smith, 1971, p. 141).

To get an idea of what these experiments are like, suppose that two letters are flashed upon a screen in front of you and that you are told these letters form an English word. Suppose too that you cannot identify either of the letters with certainty, but you can see enough features to determine that the first letter must be *a* or *e,* and the second letter must be *f* or *t.* Since this limits the possible combinations to *af, at, ef,* and *et,* you can readily identify the word as *at.* Because only one of the possible combinations forms a word in standard written English, you can identify the word without being able to identify either letter by itself (see F. Smith, 1979, p. 125).

A similar thing happens when you play the travel game of locating first one letter of the alphabet and then the next on road signs as you travel down the highway. If you have ever played this game with a young child just learning to read, you may have realized that your tremendous advantage is the fact that you identify the *words* first, and then recognize the letter you are looking for. The child who knows letters of the alphabet but few words must, of course, look for the individual letters. Your ability to recognize whole words aids your perception of individual letters.

In a similar vein, some rather startling experiments indicate that a person can get some sense of a word's meaning without consciously being able to identify it. McKean (1985) mentions, for example, the work of Anthony Marcel at Cambridge, England. Using a tachistoscope to flash words on a screen for an extremely brief period of time, Marcel noted that his volunteer readers were able to get some sense of the meaning of the word, even though they hadn't seen the word long enough to identify it. For example, if the word on the screen was "queen," people would guess it as "king," or if the target word was "yellow" they would guess it as "blue." Odd as it sounds, the people in the experiment retained a subconscious impression of a word's meaning—not only without knowing its identity, but even when the visual exposure was so brief that they weren't sure they had seen any word at all. Recent studies of brain-damaged individuals confirm that a person can recognize some key features of a word's meaning while being totally unable to recall other key features that they "know"(Bishop, 1993).

At this point, we can see in more detail what it means to say that we bring meaning to the written page in order to get meaning from it. We bring not only our knowledge of the world and our intuitive knowledge of grammar, but even an internalized knowledge of letter and sound patterns. Consider, for a moment, the following list of words. Which ones look like English words? Which ones do not?

glung	rpet	cratn	drepm
tsont	dremp	terp	stont
pret	lgung	crant	tepr

Without ever having been told, we know what is possible in English, and what is not. For example, we know that *glung* and *dremp* are possible, while *lgung* and *drepm* are not (see Gibson, Shurcliff, & Yonas, 1970, p. 59; Gibson, 1972, p. 13). Just as we do not consciously think of how sentences are structured as we speak, so we do not consciously think of how words are structured as we listen or read. Nevertheless, even before learning to read, we have acquired an internalized knowledge of sound patterns, and we quickly begin to acquire a similar internalized knowledge of letter patterns. Thus, our internalized knowledge of letter patterns enables us to identify words from only a fraction of the visual information available.

We use a minimal amount of visual information and a maximal amount of nonvisual information. The brain does not passively interpret data gathered by the eyes. On the contrary, the brain tells the eyes what data to gather, which parts of words to attend to. As stated earlier, visual perception is in fact more a function of the brain than of the eye.

An anecdote may help to solidify this point. Bateman reports the following (1974, p. 662):

> At a meeting several years ago, an opthalmologist presented a paper on the eye and reading. After the introduction he came to the podium and stood silently for a moment. Slowly and deliberately he delivered his paper—"Ladies and gentlemen, there are no important relationships between the eye and reading. Thank you." And he returned to his seat.

An exaggeration, certainly, but one containing much truth.

Syllables: A Perceptually Salient Unit

In reading the eight-letter words from Huey's lists, perhaps you had some sense of dealing with the words in syllables. And in fact, some of the research on word perception suggests that this is how proficient readers accomplish the visual part of word processing: by drawing upon part of the visual information within chunks of letters that more or less correspond to syllables (Mewhort & Campbell, 1981, cited in Adams, 1990a). Perhaps this relationship between the visual and spoken chunks we call syllables partially accounts for the fact that proficient readers typically "hear" what they read in their mind's ear (Perfetti, Bell, & Delaney, 1988; Tanenhaus, Flanigan, & Seidenberg, 1980), even though—as we saw in Chapter 4—mentally hearing or actually saying a word does not occur before the understanding of its meaning (Spoehr, 1981).

Research demonstates that it is much easier for young children to identify spoken syllables than to abstract either words or sounds (phonemes) from the stream of speech (see Adams, 1990a, pp. 296–300). This is not surprising, for a syllable is the smallest unit that can be spoken in isolation. When we say the names of letters, we necessarily say them as syllables. For example, we cannot pronounce letters like *b* without adding a vowel sound to them ("buh").

A syllable may be said to consist of two major parts, the onset and the rime. The *rime* consists of a vowel, which is the obligatory part of a syllable, plus any consonants that might follow it. Thus, the following words consist of one syllable, and that syllable has just the rime: *a, I, am, and, earn, up.* Many syllables, of course, have an onset as well. The *onset* consists of any consonants that precede the vowel: *ma, pi, Sam, hand, learn,* and *c*up. While all syllables must have a vowel, or rime, they do not necessarily have to have any preceding or following consonants.

Does that mean that the vowels are the most important parts of words, after all? No, not for most words. From one perspective, vowels are the least useful parts of written words, because they carry much less visual information. Adams (1990a) cites an interesting study in which Miller and Friedman (1957) found that when all the vowels were removed from printed texts, adults could reconstruct the texts almost perfectly:

> Ths   dmnstrts   tht   txt   s   stll   mr   r   lss   lgble
> whn   th   vwls   hv   bn   rmvd.

On the other hand, when a similar proportion of randomly selected letters had been removed, readers reconstructed the text with only 20 percent accuracy (that was the median, not the mean):

> Tis   dosts   that   ex   bome   elatey   ilgi   when   a   pabl
> ropoon   f   rndoml   lec   etters   a   ben   eov.[5]

The random omission of letters may be more confusing than the systematic omission of certain kinds of letters. However, we have already seen for ourselves the difficulty of reconstructing text with all the consonants systematically omitted.

On the one hand, then, the vowels are visually not very distinctive or prominent, and therefore the *specific* visual information they carry is not very helpful in identifying words. They become even less necessary when prior knowledge and context can be used along with consonants, as in normal reading. And yet, vowels seem to attract consonants to them (particularly the preceding consonants), and thus they help us group letters into visual patterns that correspond roughly to syllables. The vowel letters seem to pull consonants to them to create visually salient patterns that we can readily recognize. Perhaps, as Marilyn Adams suggests, the most useful function of vowels is simply to *be there* (Adams, 1990a, pp. 118–121, 219).

A quick caveat is in order, though. It surely is not important that we chunk words into syllables as defined by the dictionary or by linguists; the important thing is to cluster letters into visually identifiable chunks, whatever those may be. Thus, it's not really important whether we see *medical* as *me-di-cal* or *med-i-cal, elephant* as *el-e-phant* or *ele-phant, crumple* as *crum-ple* or *crump-le*. The point is that the chunks are ones we recognize at a glance.

As to *how* we chunk letters into syllables and other recognizable patterns, the following informal experiment should shed some light upon that topic.

Activity 3

Read the following paragraph aloud, as smoothly as possible:

> Corandic is an emurient grof with many fribs; it granks from corite, an olg which cargs like lange. Corite grinkles several other tarances, which garkers excarp by glarcking the corite and starping it in tranker-clarped storbs. The tarances starp

a chark which is exparged with worters, branking a slorp. This slorp is garped through several other coruscus, finally frasting a pragety, blickant crankle: coranda. Coranda is a cargurt, grinkling corandic and borigen. The corandic is nacerated from the borigen by means of loracity. Thus garkers finally thrap a glick, bracht, glupous grapant, corandic, which granks in many starps.

You were no doubt able to pronounce most of the words in the paragraph. But did you *consciously* apply any phonics rules? If so, which ones? If not, how did you know or decide how to pronounce the words? Once having recovered from the shock of seeing so many nonwords, most people are able to read the paragraph rather well, and without consciously applying many (if any) phonics rules. They have simply internalized enough knowledge of spelling/sound correspondences to be able to pronounce most of the words with little trouble. In fact, I have found that most adult readers who once had phonics instruction cannot verbalize many (if any) of the rules, whereas most adult readers who have never had phonics instruction can apply phonics rules anyway.

In effect, what we are doing is reading words and their syllables *by analogy* with familiar words and word parts. We scarcely even become conscious of this, except perhaps where there is more than one model for us to draw upon. Shall we pronounce *lange* like the *lang-* part of *language*, or shall we draw upon some word like *range* or *orange* for the rime part of the word? Subconsciously we recognize that there is more than one possible model, and we tend to hesitate, even in a mostly fluent rendition of the passage. Such conflicting analogies may also cause problems with a few of the words in the "blonke" passage in Chapter 2.

The fact that we can read most of these nonsense words fluently without resort to phonics rules strongly suggests what research demonstrates: that proficient readers seem to process unfamiliar words by analogy with familiar letter patterns, and to do so in syllables and/or smaller units like onsets and rimes (Glushko, 1979; Lenel & Cantor, 1981; Bradley & Bryant, 1983, 1985; Perfetti, 1985; Stanovich, 1984; Treiman & Chafetz, 1987; U. Goswami, 1986, 1988; Kirtley, Bryant, MacLean, & Bradley, 1989; Wise, Olson, & Treiman, 1990; Haskell et al., 1992). This observation lends further support to what we have already seen: that we draw upon internalized patterns of letter and letter/sound relations to minimize the use of visual information as we read.

Word Parts and Word Perception in Review

Drawing mostly upon the foregoing activities and discussion, we can articulate several generalizations about word recognition in fluent reading:

1. We do not simply process a word from left to right.
2. We do not separately identify each of the letters in a word prior to identifying the word itself.
3. We apparently process words in letter chunks, typically syllables and/or onsets and rimes, selectively using only part of the visual information available to us. The consonants are most visually distinctive and thus provide the most information, but the vowels help by drawing the consonants into syllables.

4. Identification of letters, groups of letters like onsets and rimes and syllables, and whole words occurs more or less simultaneously. That is, the perception of words—even words out of context—is simultaneously a bottom-up and a top-down process, from smaller units to larger but also from larger units to smaller.

5. Thus, proficient readers typically "see" the individual letters in a word (Rayner & Pollatsek, 1989), even though they don't need *or use* all the letters or all the visual information to identify them. The brain constructs the letters from the bars, slits, lines, curves, and such perceived by the eye.

6. We decode unfamiliar words by analogy with familiar words and word parts, particularly syllables and small meaningful units.

Notice that for the purposes of this discussion, we are considering the perception of words in isolation, or as if they occured in isolation. We have already seen in Chapter 4 what was further demonstrated by some of our activities here: that proficient readers automatically draw upon prior knowledge and context as they read, making word perception even more of a top-down process—potentially, at least—and further reducing the need for visual information during normal reading.

We shall see in the concluding section of this chapter that the notion of word perception as partly a top-down process is not universally accepted, though it is strongly supported by decades of miscue research.

ENGLISH AS AN ALPHABETIC SYSTEM

English is fundamentally an alphabetic system. That is, it uses visual characters—those of the Roman alphabet—to more or less represent sounds and sound patterns. Having said this, however, it is also critical to point out that English is not strictly a phonetic system. That is, the orthographic system (spelling system) was also designed, or has developed, so as to reflect meaning *rather than* sound, in many instances.

Homophones

One obvious example is the existence of homophones: words that sound alike but are spelled differently to reflect their difference in meaning. Examples include those from our spelling test, at the end of Chapter 4:

> sun, son
> brake, break
> rowed, rode, road
> mete, meat, meet
> no, know
> new, knew
> knight, night
> wrap, rap
> wring, ring
> write, right, rite

The homophones with at least one less common member often cause children difficulties that we adults may find amusing. For example, one of my students told in her journal how disappointed her three-year-old nephew was when he found that the mousse she was going to put in her hair was a foam rather than a large, antlered animal! The often humorous misunderstandings caused by homophones are captured in the Amelia Bedelia books by Petty Parish; there are several books in the series. More to my liking are books by Fred Gwynne: *The Sixteen Hand Horse* (1987), *A Chocolate Moose for Dinner* (1988a), *The King Who Rained* (1988b), and *Little Pigeon Toad* (1990).

In writing, the ambiguity of many homophones disappears. We spell the words differently, signaling the difference in meaning, rather than the sameness of sound.

Inflectional Endings

As literate adults, we are usually so aware of representing regular noun plural and verb third-person singular endings as -*s* or -*es* and regular past-tense endings as -*ed* that we don't even recognize the differences in sound among words. But if we spelled by sound rather than by meaning, we would use -*z* or -*ez* for some plural nouns and third-person singular verbs, and -*t* for some past tenses:

bowz (whether it's /bowz/, a noun, or /bawz/, a verb)
throwz
toez
hugz (noun or verb)
dreamz
wishez
ditchez

laught
misst
kickt
jumpt
watcht

What determines these endings is the nature of the last sound in the base noun or verb: if that sound is voiceless, a voiceless sound is added; but if that sound is voiced, a voiced sound is added. The spelling reflects the meaning, not the sound.

Cognates

If we think about the uninflected form of a word as "basic," then we can reasonably describe some words as "changing" sounds when they add certain derivational endings indicating the word's part of speech. Notice, for example, the following changes:

medicine   medic; medical   The /s/ of *medicine* changes to the /k/ of *medic(al),* and the second vowel changes.

music	musician	The /k / of *music* contributes to /sh/ in *musician*, but remains /k/ in *musical*.
logic	logician	The same change occurs, and the first vowel sound changes as the accent on syllables changes, but *logical* retains the sounds of *logic*.
site	situate; situation	The /t/ of *site* contributes to /ch/ in *situate*, and the second /t/ of *situate* contributes to /sh/ in *situation;* also, the vowel of *site* changes.
bomb	bombard	The silent /b/ of *bomb* is pronounced in *bombard* (and *bombardment, bombardier*).
resign	resignation	Both the vowels of *resign* change as the accent on the syllables changes, and the silent *g* in *resign* is pronounced /g/ in *resignation*.

For each example, you can probably think of others that show the same or a similar pattern. Most of the examples reflect a pattern that is the norm for English: that is, the pronunciation of vowels changes as the accenting of syllables changes (and as even the syllable divisions sometimes change). Vowels in unaccented syllables are typically pronounced as a schwa: a nondescript, unaccented "uh" sound (or a sound close to it).

Notice, however, that in each case there is good reason for the spelling to remain the same: it indicates the relatedness in *meaning* between words that have the same root. We spell the overlapping parts of the words the same, despite the differences in sound.

Dialects

Various words and word patterns are pronounced differently in differing parts of the country (Shuy, 1967). For example:

- Words ending in *-og* (e.g., *frog, fog, dog, hog, log, bog, cog, smog, clog, tog*) are not pronounced the same everywhere. In some English dialects, the vowels are all the same; in others, there are are at least two differing sets.
- *Merry, marry,* and *Mary* may all be pronounced the same in some dialects; others may make two or even three distinctions.
- *Far, father* and *awe* may have the same "a" sound in some dialects, but not in others.
- *Pin* and *pen* are different in most dialect areas, but not all.
- *Wash* and *Washington* take an added /r/ for many South Midlanders, who say the words as "warsh" and "Warshington"; Bostonians, on the other hand, may add an /r/ to words like *idea* ("the idear is") and *Cuba* ("Cubar is"); while in some areas of the South and the Northeast, speakers typically omit *r* after a vowel and before a consonant, as in "cahd" for *card*, "bahn" for *barn* (this pattern occurs also in Black English Vernacular).

As the proportion of these examples would suggest, most of the regional differences occur in vowels and vowel patterns—a potentially serious problem for children in classrooms that use phonics programs, since about two-thirds of the lessons often focus on vowel patterns. Even a simple little exercise on "short a" can be enough to bring forth these difficulties.

For the moment, however, the major point, again, is that our orthographic system holds the spellings constant, despite the regional differences in pronunciation. And we have not even considered ethnic differences, the differences in the speech of those who are learning English as a second language, or differences among English-speaking countries or within a country like Great Britain, which has a much greater variety of distinctively different dialects. In other words, spelling reflects constancy in meaning, even though the sounds may differ and change over time.

In short, various kinds of evidence demonstrate that while English is an alphabetic system, with letters more or less representing sounds, "more or less" is indeed the key. Spelling often reflects meaning rather than sound, and to do so, spelling often remains constant even though pronunciation differs or changes.

PHONICS AND PHONICS RULES

Most people think of phonics in connection with the *teaching* of letter/sound correspondences, relationships, and patterns. I use the term mostly this way too, but sometimes refer to functional "phonics knowledge" or "phonics know-how" as something acquired by the reader, irrespective of whether or how it has been taught. Such phonics knowledge may well be unconscious rather than conscious. Indeed, it is such unconscious phonics knowledge that proficient readers use in processing letter patterns into their corresponding sound patterns.

The earlier discussions of parts of words at work and of word perception should certainly convince us that letter/sound knowledge is important in reading. Indeed, who would ever have thought otherwise? What is not so obvious, however, is how teachers can best help students develop a functional awareness of letter/sound relations and patterns.

Clearly, these patterns are not simple. If our language were strictly phonetic as well as alphabetic, each distinctive sound would be represented by one consistent symbol, and vice versa: only one symbol would represent one distinctive sound. For English, however, we have already seen that this principle breaks down in many—perhaps most—of our words, as spelling reflects meaning even when pronunciation differs or changes. Furthermore, the principle does not hold even at the subword level. Take, for instance, the following exceptions to the one-to-one principle:

- There are several consonant digraphs, wherein two letters represent a single sound:
  ch, sh, th (which has two different sounds), *wh, gh, ph, ck, ng*
- There are some consonants that have have different pronunciations, depending upon what vowel follows:

  c is pronounced /k/ before *a, o, u*, but /s/ before *e, i, y*

  g is usually pronounced /g/ before *a, o, u*, but "j" before *e, i, y* (some notable exceptions are *get, give, girl*)

- There are some consonants that combine with vowels to produce different consonant sounds. For example:

  t joins with the *i* to become "sh" in *-tion* (*action, motion, nation*, etc.)

  c joins with the following *i* to become part of "sh" in *-cial* (*crucial, special*, etc.), *-cian* (*musician, physician*, etc.), and *-cious* (*atrocious, conscious*, etc.)

  s joins with the following *i* to become "zh" in *-sion* (*confusion, fusion*, etc.)

And so forth.

This list comes nowhere close to illustrating all the possible pronunciations of the consonants—and the possibilities are far more numerous for vowels.

In short, the conditions governing spelling/sound correspondences are often far more complex than is generally recognized (Venezky, 1967, 1970a, 1970b). Merely to represent the spelling/sound mappings of a good majority (80 to 90 percent) of English words—that is, ignoring true exceptions—it has generally been found that hundreds of correspondences are involved (Hanna et al., 1966, as cited in Adams, 1990a, p. 242). Nor is this complexity confined to words that are used primarily by adults rather than children. In one of the more extensive studies, Berdiansky and her associates tried to establish a set of rules to account for the spelling/sound correspondences in over six thousand one-syllable and two-syllable words among those in the comprehension vocabularies of six- to nine-year-olds. The researchers discovered that their 6,092 words involved 211 separate spelling/sound correspondences—that is, 211 correspondences between a letter and a sound, or between two letters functioning together (like *qu* or the digraphs above) and a sound. Of these 211 correspondences, 166 occurred in at least ten words out of the set of 6,092 different words, while 45 of the correspondences occurred in fewer than ten words (Berdiansky, Cronnell, & Koehler, 1969, p. 11); see F. Smith, 1979, pp. 139–140).

Research such as this should certainly convince us of the ridiculousness of Rudolph Flesch's simple prescription: "Reading means getting meaning from certain combinations of letters. Teach the child what each letter stands for and he can read" (Flesch, 1955, p. 10). In fact, as my colleague Bonnie Regelman has pointed out to me, Johnny could not even read the print on the cover of Flesch's *Why Johnny Can't Read* (1955) by using phonics rules alone! Nor could Johnny read the vast majority of the 150 most common words in schoolbook English (Adams, 1990a, p. 273).

Furthermore, sound-to-spelling patterns are not consistent or predictable with much precision, either. For example, applying the rules of Berdiansky and her associates in reverse, Cronnell found that that they generated correct sound-to-spelling translations for fewer than half the words in his corpus (Cronnell, 1970, as cited in Adams, 1990). Furthermore, using the 300 rules developed by Hanna and her colleagues (Hanna et al., 1966), fewer than 50 percent of the 17,000 words in their corpus would be spelled correctly. Yet, as Adams notes, "in a spelling bee between fourth graders and a computer that had been programmed with these rules, the fourth graders handily won out" (Simon & Simon, 1973, cited in Desberg, Elliott, & Marsh, 1980; Adams, 1990a, p. 390). So much for the oft-asserted opinion that we should teach phonics so that children will learn to spell correctly.

One might still ask, however, whether we aren't exaggerating the problem with phonics rules: rules that describe spelling-to-sound relationships. Aren't these simple and consistent enough to be taught to children? To answer that question, take a look at Figure 5.4, which reviews the actual usefulness of forty-five generalizations about phonics, as examined by Clymer (1963). A glance at the reliability of these rules suggests that relatively few would be worth teaching, even if teaching rules were a good idea. But is it?

Most children cannot remember abstract phonics terms and rules, yet they can apply such rules unconsciously in their reading. Tovey demonstrated this in a study of children from grades 2 to 6, with five children from each grade. Though their teachers indicated that the children had learned terms like *consonant, consonant blend, consonant digraph, vowel, long vowel, short vowel, vowel digraph,* and *diphthong,* the children's responses suggested otherwise. The only term acceptably defined by over half of the children was *silent letter.* More than half of the terms were acceptably defined by only 20 percent or fewer children. Interestingly, Tovey notes that second graders produced only two acceptable responses to questions about terms, and that sixth graders seemed relatively less able to deal with phonics terms than children in grades 3 through 5— probably, I would assume, because upper elementary students do not typically receive phonics instruction. However, all the children did much better on a phonics test that required them to pronounce nonsense words and to deal with the kinds of elements listed above (plus others) in reading actual text. On this test, all the scores were 55 percent or above, with the percentage rising steadily from 55 percent at grade 2 to 79 percent at grade 6 (fourth graders broke the gradually rising pattern temporarily with 83 percent). The children were able to make use of phonics knowledge that they were not conscious of, that they could not verbalize. Tovey concludes: "Instruction which requires children to deal constantly with the abstract or technical language related to phonics does not warrant the time and effort often expended. This time might better be spent reading" (Tovey, 1980, p. 437).

Certainly there is a correlation between rapid decoding and comprehension, especially in timed tests (see, for example, Perfetti & Hogaboam, 1975; Stanovich, 1980, 1991; and Allen, 1985). However, it does not necessarily follow that children must be *taught* phonics rules in order to decode rapidly. Since children can *apply* phonics rules even though they cannot define the terms or verbalize the rules, much of the current phonics instruction surely goes beyond what is needed, as pointed out even by phonics advocates. (See, for example, the discussion of phonics in *Becoming a Nation of Readers* [Anderson, Hiebert, Scott, & Wilkinson, 1985, p. 38], and my fuller discussion of this report's treatment of phonics in Chapter 7.)

Even Marilyn Adams, who advocates teaching phonics relationships systematically, generally seems to agree that teaching rules is no substitute for experience with words that exemplify the patterns. She sees some value in teaching rules, but summarizes thus: "For neither the expert nor the novice can rote knowledge of an abstract rule, in and of itself, make any difference" (1990a, p. 271).

Here is a further point to consider. Activity 1, at the end of Chapter 1, presented four sketches of children in first-grade classrooms (D. R. King & Watson, 1983, p. 70): one child being taught by what is probably a combined phonics/linguistics approach,

Generalizations	Number of Words Conforming	Number of Exceptions	Percent Utility
1. When there are two vowels side by side, the long sound of the first one is heard and the second is usually silent.	309 (bead)†	377 (chief)†	45
2. When a vowel is in the middle of a one-syllable word, the vowel is short.	408	249	62
middle letter	191 (dress)	84 (scold)	69
one of the middle two letters in a word of four letters	191 (rest)	135 (told)	59
one vowel *within* a word of more than four letters	26 (splash)	30 (fight)	46
3. If the only vowel letter is at the end of a word, the letter usually stands for a long sound.	23 (he)	8 (to)	74
4. When there are two vowels, one of which is final *e*, the first vowel is long and the *e* is silent.	180 (bone)	108 (done)	63
* 5. The *r* gives the preceding vowel a sound that is neither long nor short.	484 (horn)	134 (wire)	78
6. The first vowel is usually long and the second silent in the diagraphs *ai, ea, oa,* and *ui.*	179	92	66
ai	43 (nail)	24 (said)	64
ea	101 (bead)	51 (head)	66
oa	34 (boat)	1 (cupboard)	97
ui	1 (suit)	16 (build)	6

*Generalizations marked with an asterisk were found "useful" according to the criteria.

†Words in parentheses are examples—either of words that conform or of exceptions, depending on the column.

SOURCE: Clymer, T. "The Utility of Phonic Generalizations in the Primary Grades." *The Reading Teacher* 16 (January 1963): 252–58.

FIGURE 5.4   *The utility of forty-five phonics generalizations*

Generalizations	Number of Words Conforming	Number of Exceptions	Percent Utility
7. In the phonogram *ie*, the *i* is silent and the *e* has a long sound.	8 (field)	39 (friend)	17
* 8. Words having double *e* usually have the long *e* sound.	85 (seem)	2 (been)	98
9. When words end with silent *e*, the preceding *a* or *i* is long.	164 (cake)	108 (have)	60
*10. In *ay* the *y* is silent and gives *a* its long sound.	36 (play)	10 (always)	78
11. When the letter *i* is followed by the letters *gh*, the *i* usually stands for its long sound and the *gh* is silent.	22 (high)	9 (neighbor)	71
12. When *a* follows *w* in a word, it usually has the sound *a* as in *was*.	15 (watch)	32 (swam)	32
13. When *e* is followed by *w*, the vowel sound is the same as represented by *oo*.	9 (blew)	17 (sew)	35
14. The two letters *ow* make the long *o* sound.	50 (own)	35 (down)	59
15. *W* is sometimes a vowel and follows the vowel digraph rule.	50 (crow)	75 (threw)	40
*16. When *y* is the final letter in a word, it usually has a vowel sound.	169 (dry)	32 (tray)	84
17. When *y* is used as a vowel in words, it sometimes has the sound of long *i*.	29 (fly)	170 (funny)	15
18. The letter *a* has the same sound (ȯ) when followed by *l*, *w*, and *u*.	61 (all)	65 (canal)	48

FIGURE 5.4   *Continued*

19. When *a* is followed by *r* and final *e*, we expect to hear the sound heard in *care*.	9 (dare)	1 (are)	90
*20. When *c* and *h* are next to each other, they make only one sound.	103 (peach)	0	100
*21. *Ch* is usually pronounced as it is in *kitchen, catch,* and *chair,* not like *sh*.	99 (catch)	5 (machine)	95
*22. When *c* is followed by *e* or *i*, the sound of *s* is likely to be heard.	66 (cent)	3 (ocean)	96
*23. When the letter *c* is followed by *o* or *a*, the sound of *k* is likely to be heard.	143 (camp)	0	100
24. The letter *g* often has a sound similar to that of *j* in *jump* when it precedes the letter *i* or *e*.	49 (engine)	28 (give)	64
*25. When *ght* is seen in a word, *gh* is silent.	30 (fight)	0	100
26. When a word begins *kn*, the *k* is silent.	10 (knife)	0	100
27. When a word begins with *wr*, the *w* is silent.	8 (write)	0	100
*28. When two of the same consonants are side by side, only one is heard.	334 (carry)	3 (suggest)	99
*29. When a word ends in *ck*, it has the same last sound as in *look*.	46 (brick)	0	100
*30. In most two-syllable words, the first syllable is accented.	828 (famous)	143 (polite)	85
*31. If *a, in, re, ex, de,* or *be* is the first syllable in a word, it is usually unaccented.	86 (belong)	13 (insect)	87
*32. In most two-syllable words that end in a consonant followed by *y*, the first syllable is accented and the last is unaccented.	101 (baby)	4 (supply)	96

FIGURE 5.4 Continued

33. One vowel letter in an accented syllable has its short sound.	547 (city)	356 (lady)	61
34. When *y* or *ey* is seen in the last syllable that is not accented, the long sound of *e* is heard.	0	157 (baby)	0
35. When *ture* is the final syllable in a word, it is unaccented.	4 (picture)	0	100
36. When *tion* is the final syllable in a word, it is unaccented.	5 (station)	0	100
37. In many two- and three-syllable words, the final *e* lengthens the vowel in the last syllable.	52 (invite)	62 (gasoline)	46
38. If the first vowel sound in a word is followed by two consonants, the first syllable usually ends with the first of the two consonants.	404 (bullet)	159 (singer)	72
39. If the first vowel sound in a word is followed by a single consonant, that consonant usually begins the second syllable.	190 (over)	237 (oven)	44
*40. If the last syllable of a word ends in *le,* the consonant preceding the *le* usually begins the last syllable.	62 (tumble)	2 (buckle)	97
*41. When the first vowel element in a word is followed by *th, ch,* or *sh,* these symbols are not broken when the word is divided into syllables and may go with either the first or second syllables.	30 (dishes)	0	100
42. In a word of more than one syllable, the letter *v* usually goes with the preceding vowel to form a syllable.	53 (cover)	29 (clover)	73

Figure 5.4 Continued

Generalizations	Number of Words Conforming	Number of Exceptions	Percent Utility
43. When a word has only one vowel letter, the vowel sound is likely to be short.	433 (hid)	322 (kind)	57
*44. When there is one *e* in a word that ends in a consonant, the *e* usually has a short sound.	85 (leg)	27 (blew)	76
*45. When the last syllable is the sound *r*, it is unaccented.	188 (butter)	9 (appear)	95

FIGURE 5.4   *Continued*

one being taught by a sight word approach, one being taught through the Initial Teaching Alphabet (see activity 3 in the section "For Further Reflection and Exploration" at the end of this chapter), and one being taught by a language experience/whole language approach. Are all of these children going to become readers, King and Watson ask? Their answer: it is quite likely. But they suggest that some children may learn to read in spite of the instructional program rather than because of it. (And, of course, some children are receiving more impetus to enjoy reading and to become lifelong readers.)

If children are taught by a phonics method and they in fact learn to read, it seems logical to assume that they learned to read because of the phonics instruction. But this is not necessarily so. The fact that the rooster crows and the sun then comes up does not mean that the rooster's crowing causes the sun to rise, even though primitive societies and young children in our own society have assumed that the former causes the latter. The fact that parents buy their son or daughter a computer does not necessarily mean that the student will get better grades because of the computer, though a computer ad might have us believe otherwise. And the fact that children who have been exposed to a phonics approach learn to read does not necessarily mean that they learned to read *because of* that approach, though people unaware of the nature of the reading process and what is involved in learning to read are often inclined to make that assumption.

In determining how children best learn to read, Marie Carbo points out that "what works is not always phonics, and, in fact, for young children, what works *best* in reading may seldom be intensive phonic instruction" (Carbo, 1987b). Carbo has concluded that a small percentage of children really *need* phonics instruction—but not phonics *rules*—in order to become good readers. However, most children fall into other categories:

"those who are capable of learning phonics, but who *do not* need it to become good readers, and children who are *unable* to master phonics" (Carbo, 1987c).

One reason that most children are able—perhaps *best* able—to learn to read without intensive phonics instruction is (as we have seen in Chapters 2 and 4) that learning to read involves much more than learning to sound out words. It involves learning to bring one's own schemas to the act of transacting with the text, and it involves learning to use and coordinate all three language cue systems: syntactic, semantic, and grapho/phonemic. If children try to read by merely sounding out words, merely using grapho/phonemic cues, they may never learn to read effectively. Even word identification itself, a seemingly low-level skill, will suffer. Other excellent discussions of the role of phonics and the teaching of phonics can be found in F. Smith (1979), and in Sebasta's article "Why Rudolph Can't Read" (1981), a spoof of Rudolph Flesch's *Why Johnny Can't Read* (1955).

How is it, then, that children can learn to read with, or perhaps in spite of, an approach that focuses mainly on the grapho/phonemic cues? Because children have a natural, innate tendency to create meaning by transacting with their environment. Because they are often surrounded by meaningful print in their daily lives. Because many of them naturally transfer to the reading of print the strategies they have learned to use in making sense of spoken language. And because they have a tremendous capacity for forming their own hypotheses about how language works, a capacity clearly exemplified in the infant and preschool years as they learn to speak more and more like adults. On the other hand, children who have not had extensive preschool experiences with books may find learning to read particularly difficult with intensive and extensive focus on phonics; they may not so readily draw upon these other experiences and resources as children who already know the purpose of books and the joys of reading or being read to. (These points will be explored further in Chapter 7.)

DEVELOPING PHONICS KNOWLEDGE

Clearly, there are many reasons for *not* teaching phonics relationships intensively and systematically, much less for teaching actual phonics rules. Among these reasons are the following, some of which summarize previous points and some of which look ahead to subsequent chapters, especially Chapter 7:

1. *It's not necessary.* Just as they learn the patterns of oral language, so most children will unconsciously learn common phonics patterns, given ample opportunity to read environmental print and predictable and enjoyable materials, and ample opportunity to write with invented (constructive) spelling. (See Chapter 7.)
2. Not all visual information is equally important. For example, vowels contribute relatively little to the specific identification of words, particularly when the words occur in a meaningful context. Vowels help mainly by being there.
3. There are too many rules and patterns, especially for vowels—and there are too many exceptions to the rules. Even if a given rule applies to a word, it's not always possible to know which rule applies, or even whether a rule applies, unless you already know the word.

4. Proficient readers don't process words letter by letter: they process words in clusters of letters that typically correspond, at least roughly, to syllables and/or onsets and rimes. Fortunately, the pronunciation of vowels is relatively stable within common rime patterns (patterns like *-and, -ate, -ent, -el* and *-le, -er* and *-re, -ion, -ung*). In other words, pronouncing syllables and/or onsets and rimes may be far easier than trying to sound out an unfamiliar word letter by letter (Adams, 1990a, pp. 308–328; she cites, in particular, Treiman, 1985, 1986, 1988; Treiman & Chafetz, 1987; and Treiman & Baron, 1981).

5. Proficient readers use prior knowledge and context *along with* visual cues and their knowledge of letter/sound relations, in order to get words and construct meaning. This reduces the amount of strictly visual processing that is necessary. See Chapter 4.

6. Too much emphasis on phonics encourages children to use "sound it out" as their first and possibly only independent strategy for getting words and meaning. (Applebee, Langer, & Mullis, 1988b).

7. Overemphasizing word identification may encourage readers to focus too much on getting words and too little on constructing meaning. (See Chapters 1, 4, and 6, especially).

8. Many emergent readers are not good at learning analytically, abstractly, or auditorily. For them, the study of phonics is difficult, if not impossible. This conclusion is derived partly from Piagetian studies of child development (e.g., Wadsworth, 1989), but also from research into learning styles and reading styles (Carbo, especially the 1987 references).

9. Thus, teaching and testing numerous phonics patterns or rules may result in many children's quickly being labeled as reading failures or slow readers. For many children, it is far harder to "do phonics" than to learn to read (e.g., Carbo, 1987b—and a great deal of anecdotal observation over the years).

10. Children who learn to read relatively naturally—in the home, or in whole language classrooms—typically do so without the systematic teaching of phonics. Furthermore, a whole generation of readers in the 1940s and 1950s learned to read with phonics being taught only in the context of meaningful reading, and incidentally rather than formally. (This does not mean that everyone learned to read, but then neither does everyone heavily dosed with phonics. See, for instance, Boder, 1973; K. S. Goodman, 1973; C. Chomsky, 1976; Meek, 1983; Doake, 1985; and Carbo, 1987b. Coming from different perspectives, all of these researchers similarly note that less effective and/or "dyslexic" readers have typically received *more* phonics instruction than the average reader.)

11. Research in whole language classrooms suggests that less formal and less systematic ways of helping children develop *functional* phonics knowledge work better than direct, systematic teaching of phonics. (See Chapter 7.)

12. Time spent on intensive and systematic phonics may be better spent in developing and experiencing other aspects of literacy, with phonics taught primarily as the need and opportunity arise during authentic reading and writing. (See Chapters 3 and 7.)

13. Children who have had less extensive experiences with literacy and books prior to school may be especially disadvantaged by programs that teach phonics intensively and systematically. (Again, see Chapter 7.) Other excellent resources dealing with phonics include Kenneth Goodman's *Phonics Phacts* (1993) and Sandra Wilde's forthcoming book on phonics.

Figure 5.5 summarizes these various kinds of research leading to the conclusion that it is best *not* to teach phonics systematically and intensively, much less extensively, but rather to use other means to help children grasp the alphabetic principle that letters relate to sounds, and to internalize the letter/sound knowledge they need for reading and writing.

The fact that children develop phonics knowledge with less than complete and systematic teaching should hardly be a surprise, since they learned the sound patterns, word patterns, and major grammatical patterns of their language before entering school, and without direct teaching. (See Chapter 3.) The next section will focus on how children develop phonics knowledge. This will be followed by a summary from the point of view of what the teacher might do to facilitate such learning. Finally, the chapter concludes with what is in effect a summary of concepts from all the earlier chapters, but especially Chapters 2, 4, and 5 on the reading process: a section titled "Toward a More Complete Model of the Reading Process."

How Children Develop Phonics Knowledge

While children may develop phonics knowledge through the following means in their homes, the purpose of this section is to emphasize ways that children develop phonics knowledge in supportive classrooms. The following are only some of the ways, many of which will or can occur within the context of a shared reading experience (see Chapter 3). In fact, I will illustrate many of these possibilities by reference to what a group of first graders experienced over several days, as their teacher Tracy Cobb and I worked with them. This set of activities illustrates a "core literature" approach (Chapter 9) that does not reflect where I am in my thinking and practice today. However, some of our activities nicely illustrate how children can be guided in developing phonics knowledge throughout the activities that may be associated with a shared reading experience. The examples are partially out of the order in which they occurred, to illustrate the principles in what seems a logical order.

In supportive classrooms, children develop phonics knowledge through such means as these:

1. By having familiar and favorite stories read to them again and again, during a shared reading experience wherein they can see the text and thus begin to make connections between spoken and written words and between letters and sounds. In the shared reading experience, teachers facilitate this learning by running their hand or some kind of pointer under the text, word by word. For example, Tracy read the folktale *Stone Soup* to the children, using the simple Ann McGovern version (1968) because of its repetitive and cumulative refrains. Beforehand, I had written on posterboard the repetitive refrain:

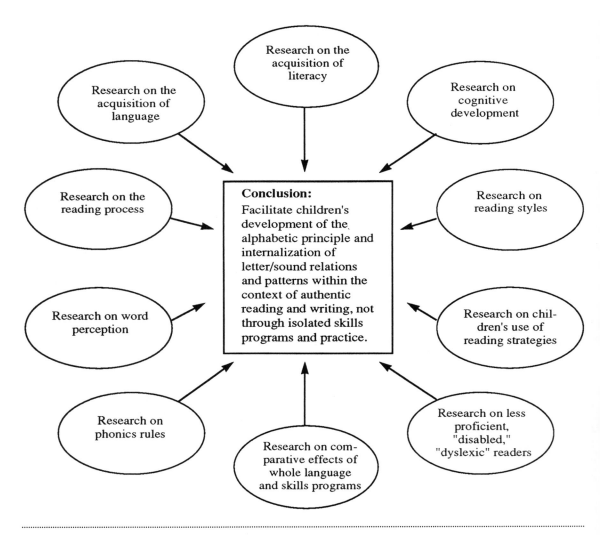

FIGURE 5.5   Kinds of research relevant to the learning and teaching of phonics

"Soup from a stone,"
said the little old lady.
"Fancy that."
The pot bubbled and bubbled.

On a second reading, we took advantage of there being two teachers: while Tracy read, I pointed to the words in the refrain and we encouraged the children to "read" along with us. I had also prepared strips of paper for constructing the cumulative refrain as each new ingredient was added to the pot. The children helped me add the strips of paper to the posterboard, and we read the cumulative refrain in like manner, adding to it each time.

2. By rereading favorite stories, songs, and poems, independently or with a peer. Such rereadings help solidify the children's growing understanding of print. The rereading is facilitated if children have individual copies of the texts, and if they can listen to a tape recording of the text as they read. It's especially helpful if the tape recording is appropriately paced (Carbo, 1989).

We made stone soup with the children, first using paper vegetables and then, on a later day, making real soup (yes, with a real stone). The children generated a language experience chart and I typed their text on the computer, making small booklets in which each child's line was printed at the bottom of the page, leaving most of the page for the child to illustrate. The children thoroughly enjoyed drawing the pictures and reading and rereading their very own books. Figure 5.6 shows one of the pages from the book that the children illustrated for me (each child illustrated his or her own page).

Figure 5.6   *Page from children's book on making stone soup*

3. By observing and participating as the teacher demonstrates letter/sound relationships while writing. For example, the teacher may compose something of his or her own while the children watch; the teacher may write a language experience chart or story while the children dictate sentences individually; or the teacher may write and rewrite what the children compose collectively. In any case, the teacher may select certain letter/sound correspondences to call to children's attention.

In the language experience chart we generated after making stone soup, I called particular attention to the initial consonants at the beginning of children's names—that is, to the correspondence between the sound and the letter. Serendipitously, we had another chance to comment on the nature of print when the children noticed that I had written small *a* in two different ways: a typewriter a, and a cursive *a*. This gave us an opportunity to think and talk about the fact that letters can be written in more than one way and still mean the same. In retrospect, I realize that I might have invited children to tell other things they noticed about the print, too.

4. By writing independently, constructing their own spellings as best they are able. Of course schoolchildren should be writing in whatever way they can, whether it be scribble writing, random letters and symbols, or letters that at least begin to be decipherable as words. But when they can use letters to represent sounds, they begin to promote their own phonics development through writing. In fact, Harste has noted that the knowledge of letter/sound correspondences exhibited in writing soon exceeds the knowledge that is called for by the phonics worksheets that, often, the children cannot do (Harste, 1985, p. 8:27). This is supported by a research study in which Clarke investigated the effects of promoting traditional (i.e., "correct") versus invented spelling among first graders. The inventive spellers scored better on almost all of the standardized tests of reading and spelling (Clarke, 1988). And, of course, the children could write more, and with far more sophisticated words, than they could if correct spelling were emphasized every time they put pencil to paper.

We had intended to have children write recipes for stone soup independently, but Tracy thought that we had extended the sequence of activities long enough without this. To my regret, then, all we had them write independently was the names of vegetables they wanted to put in the soup. The children's spellings were sophisticated enough that you can surely tell what vegetables are represented: *Bocele, Brocele, Bracle; Karrts, cairt; peesss; tumatu; collr; unyn;* and *machroms*. (See Weaver, 1990a, Chapter 7 for a fuller discussion.)

5. By considering how grapho/phonemic cues can be used along with prior knowledge and context, to predict what might make sense before looking at the entire word or the following context. Much of this can be done casually and spontaneously, as teachers and children discuss books. Teachers can demonstrate how they use prior knowledge, context, and initial consonants to predict a word. They can invite children to do the same with appropriate words in the shared reading. And they can discuss this strategy when children have problems with specific words, if the strategy seems likely to be productive.

In the context of our *Stone Soup* experiences, the day after we had developed the language experience chart I covered with Post-Its all but the initial consonants of two key words:

I put c _____ in the soup.

Let's put b _____ in the soup.

We then brainstormed for the names of vegetables that could go in each of the slots. Afterwards, of course, we looked carefully at each of the printed words, to decide which of our alternatives the word actually was.

6. By discussing the use of grapho/phonemic cues in the context of meaningful reading. One way to give children such opportunities is to choose literature in which words alliterate (begin the same) and/or rhyme (end with the same rime pattern). In fact, such emphasis on onsets and rimes is precisely what Marilyn Adams recommends (Adams, 1990a, pp. 318–328), as well as what many teachers have found effective, drawing upon literature rather than phonics programs. Children also enjoy and learn from literature with onomatopoetic words (words that sound like what they mean, such as *buzz* or *crunch*). Often children themselves will call attention to such patterns if they are asked, "What do you notice about this poem?" or "What do you notice about the sounds in this poem?" Of course, attention can be focused on letters, too. See Figure 5.7 for some literature with interesting sound elements.

In retrospect, I notice that the refrain of *Stone Soup* has several words starting with *b: butter, barley, bit (*of pepper*),* and *beef bones.* The children and I might have attended to these. And we might have attended to the three *s* words: *stone, soup,* and *salt.* If the children enjoyed thinking of other words that begin with these letters and sounds, we might even have begun a chart to which the children could keep adding words as they thought of them, using their own constructive spellings. They could later graph the number of words starting with these and other initial letters and blends they first charted. In fact, Whitin, Mills, and O'Keefe (1990) demonstrate that this is an excellent way for young children to learn math concepts in the context of developing literacy.

7. By making charts of words exhibiting letter/sound patterns of particular interest to them. After two or more charts have been compiled, children could make related graphs comparing appropriate data, as explained in item 6 above.

8. By experimenting with print and solidifying their understanding of letter/sound patterns in a variety of self-chosen ways. For example, some children enjoy sorting word cards into related sets: words that start the same, words that end the same, words that sound like what they mean, or whatever. It seems appropriate to encourage such activities *if* children are genuinely interested in them, and as long as the activities do not take much time away from actual reading and writing.

Alphabet books

Anno, Mitsumasa. (1975). *Anno's alphabet: An adventure in imagination.* New York: Harper.

Base, Graeme. (1986). *Animalia.* New York: Harry N. Abrams.

Boynton, Sandra. (1987). *A is for angry: An animal and adjective alphabet.* 2nd ed. New York: Workman Publishing.

Lear, Edward. (1986). *Edward Lear's ABC: Alphabet rhymes for children.* Illus. Carol Pike. Topsfield, MA: Salem House.

Lobel, Arnold. (1981). *On Market Street.* Illus. Anita Lobel. New York: Mulberry Books (William Morrow).

Van Allsburg, Chris. (1987). *The Z Was zapped. A play in twenty-six acts.* Boston: Houghton Mifflin.

Poetry and prose emphasizing sound elements

Aardema, Verna. (1981). *Bringing the rain to Kapiti plain.* Illus. Beatriz Vidal. New York: Dial.

Bennett, Jill. (Ed.)(1987). *Noisy poems.* Illus. Nick Sharrat. New York: Oxford University Press.

Brown, Marc. (1985). *Hand rhymes.* New York: Puffin.

Cameron, Polly. (1961). *"I can't" said the ant.* New York: Scholastic.

Ciardi, John. (1989). *The hopeful trout and other limericks.* Illus. Susan Meddaugh. Boston: Houghton Mifflin.

Dunrea, Oliver. (1989). *Deep down underground.* New York: Macmillan. [cumulative tale]

Lee, Dennis. (1983). *Jelly belly: Original nursery rhymes.* Illus. Juan Wijngaard. New York: Bedrick/Blackie.

McMillan, Bruce. (1990). *One sun: A book of terse verse.* New York: Holiday House.

Milne, A. A. (1924). *When we were very young.* New York: E. P. Dutton.

Nicoll, Helen. (Ed.). (1983). *Poems for 7-year-olds and under.* New York: Puffin.

Obligado, Lilian. (1983). *Faint frogs feeling feverish, and other terrifically tantalizing tongue twisters.* New York: Puffin.

Parry, Caroline. (Ed.). (1991). *Zoomerang a boomerang: Poems to make your belly laugh.* Illus. Michael Martchenko. New York: Puffin.

Prelutsky, Jack. (1986). *Ride a purple pelican.* Illus. Garth Williams. New York: Greenwillow.

Prelutsky, Jack. (Ed.). (1983). *The Random House book of poetry for children.* Illus. Arnold Lobel. New York: Random House.

Seuss, Dr. [Theodore Seuss Geisel]. *Green Eggs and Ham.* New York: Random House.

Silverstein, Shel. (1974). *Where the sidewalk ends.* New York: Harper.

FIGURE 5.7   Literature with interesting sound elements

9. By developing their own strategies for learning letter/sound patterns. The story of Jevon in *Jevon Doesn't Sit at the Back Anymore* (White, 1990) beautifully illustrates how children may develop their own strategies that teachers are not always aware of. During Jevon's second year in her kindergarten, White noticed that Jevon was learning letter/sound correspondences by observing the spellings of his classmates' names. She writes:

> While books and most other print were still obviously a hurdle for Jevon, he read his classmates' names in a multitude of places each day. He could independently read and deliver the canteen orders; he could use the alphabetical list I'd posted on chart paper to predict when he or any of his classmates would be the leader again; he read the name of the leader on the News Chart each day. When it was his turn to be leader and fill in the chart, he would rally his friends to help him; when one of his friends was leader, he was there ready to offer his help in return. He found his name and all of his classmates' names on the message board and the sign-up sheets. Reading the selections his friends had made for art, writing or math gave him information he sometimes wanted to consider before making a choice himself.
>
> Long before Jevon connected sounds and symbols in inventive spelling, names made their way into his written communication. (White, 1990, pp. 18–19)

Such a description suggests that Jevon was one of the many children who cannot readily learn letter/sound correspondences. However, he did eventually develop such knowledge, by attending first to what was meaningful to him: the names of his friends and classmates.

Obviously, it is important for teachers to notice children's own developing strategies and to support them.

10. By receiving additional help as needed, either from peers in a collaborative setting, from older children, from the teacher, from a Reading Recovery or resource room teacher, or from whoever might help. However, it is important not to assume that children need help with phonics just because they cannot do phonics activities on worksheets.

Consider the case of Jan, a fourth grader who was a good student and who considered herself a good reader, as did her teacher and her parents (Watson and Crowley, 1988). Given a worksheet on the three main sounds of *ea*, Jan completed less than half of the 72 items, and missed nearly half of the 31 items she attempted. Frustrated by this failure, Jan cried herself to sleep that night.

Equally frustrated and concerned, her parents consulted a reading teacher, who prepared for Jan a passage containing several words exemplifying four *ea* sounds. (Watson and Crowley called this a "determining lesson" because it was designed to help the teacher determine whether or not Jan had particular problems with *ea* words within connected text.) Here is the passage, with the *ea* italicized in those words. Also, Jan's miscues are marked:

① Ⓡ

When hunting s*ea*son comes Uncle Bill is almost as *ea*ger

to h*ea*d for the woods as Babe and Bingo are. Babe and Bingo are beautiful beagles, but Uncle Bill calls them *eager* beavers

when it comes to pheasant hunting.

②ⓒ re‑   ③ρ
When Uncle Bill releases those dogs from their steady

④ⓒ break‑
leash, you should see them streak across the meadow at break‑

neck speed. They can really work up a sweat!

Aunt Joan dreads hunting season. Babe and Bingo's

          dee.fing   ⑥ a   ⑦
⑤ deaf
steady stream of barking is deafening and gives her headaches

⑧ⓒ b‑
She can't bear to think of one feather on a bird being harmed.

Uncle Bill gives the pheasants to a neighbor. Babe and Bingo

howl.

In context, Jan was able to read three of the words, or variants thereof, that she had not been able to get in isolation: *sweat, pheasants,* and *steadier.* In context, she had trouble with few of the *ea* words.

This should serve as a reminder that the ability to read independently does *not* require the ability to "do phonics" in isolation. Nor is work on phonics in isolation likely to be the best way to promote independent and proficient reading.

Figure 5.8 lists valuable references for understanding how children develop phonics knowledge, and how teachers facilitate this learning.

How Teachers Facilitate Development of Phonics Knowledge

Teachers who understand that we do not teach rules and patterns of language to children as they are acquiring spoken language should find it easy to understand that, likewise, we do not need to teach children rules and patterns of written language for children to learn them. The same holds true for the relationships between the written and the spoken language: the grapho/phonemic relationships and patterns. In other words, we do not need to teach phonics systematically and intensively. This is borne out by a growing body of comparative research (see Chapter 7).

Freppon, P. A., & Dahl, K. L. (1991). Learning about phonics in a whole language classroom. *Language Arts, 68*, 190–197.

Mills, H., O'Keefe, T., & Stephens, D. (1992). *Looking closely: Exploring the role of phonics in one whole language classroom.* Urbana, IL: National Council of Teachers of English.

Powell, D., & Hornsby, D. (1993). *Learning phonics and spelling in a whole language classroom.* New York: Scholastic.

Weaver, C. (1990). *Understanding whole language: From principles to practice.* Portsmouth, NH: Heinemann. See Chapter 7, "Developing phonics knowledge in whole language classrooms."

In addition, a packet of informational material on topics relating to literacy education, including several sheets on phonics and/in whole language, can be obtained for $4 (U.S.) from the Center for Establishing Dialogue (CED), 325 E. Southern Avenue, Tempe, AZ 85282; (602) 929-0929. These sheets can be photocopied for distribution to teachers, parents, administrators, and school board members.

Figure 5.8   References on developing phonics knowledge (Note: Research on the development of phonics knowledge is discussed in Chapter 7. This bibliography focuses mainly on how teachers help children develop phonics knowledge in whole language classrooms, with examples from children.)

On the other hand, a certain amount of classroom attention to letter/sound correspondences and patterns will surely help children in learning what they need to know about the orthographic (spelling) system and in developing a working knowledge of phonics—that is, in developing the phonics knowledge they need to read effectively and independently. Furthermore, a relatively small proportion of children may actually find it easiest to develop a functional command of grapho/phonemic relations through some explicit attention to phonics—though even for them, phonics *rules* do not seem particularly helpful (Carbo, 1983, 1987b; Carbo, Dunn, & Dunn, 1986). Thus, without teaching phonics systematically or intensively, the teacher may nevertheless do several things to help children internalize the letter/sound knowledge they need to process words easily and automatically, and to use grapho/phonemic cues *along with* prior knowledge and context.

Here, then, are some of the ways that teachers can foster acquisition of the alphabetic principle and automaticity in using grapho/phonemic knowledge. These are the flip side of the aforementioned ways children may develop phonics knowledge in supportive classrooms. Teachers can help:

1. *By rereading favorite stories, songs, poems, and other materials during a shared reading experience and moving their hand or a pointer under the words, to give children the opportunity to notice not only correspondences between spoken and written words but also correspondences between sounds and letters.*

2. *By providing individual copies of materials read during a shared reading experience, so that children can reread the materials independently.* Taping these texts for the children to listen to as they read will further enhance the benefits of rereading. Carbo (1978) suggests too the value of taping the readings at an appropriate pace, and provides suggestions for doing so in *How to Record Books for Maximum Reading Gains* (Carbo, 1989).

3. *By discussing selectively chosen letter/sound correspondences and patterns while composing as the children watch, or while doing guided writing with the children.*

4. *By encouraging children to write using constructive (invented) spelling, and by helping them make letter/sound connections until they can produce early phonemic spellings independently.*

5. *By demonstrating how to use prior knowledge and context along with initial consonants to predict what a word will be, before confirming or correcting by looking at the entire word and using following context.* Having demonstrated this, the teacher continues to encourage the use of this strategy within the context of shared reading experiences—and in group literature discussions and conferences with individual children, as needed.

6. *By choosing for shared reading experiences some enjoyable literature that includes interesting sound elements, particularly alliteration, rhyme, and onomatopoeia.* And of course by engaging children in discussion of such elements during the shared reading experience.

7. *By helping children develop charts of interesting sound elements, beginning with those they have encountered and discussed in the context of shared reading experiences, the children's names, or patterns drawn from any other sources meaningful to the children.*

8. *By accepting children's suggestions for other meaningful activities with words and word parts, and being receptive to* a limited number *of other good ideas they might think of or encounter,* including games derived from children's interests and experiences (Mills, O'Keefe, & Stephens, 1992). I emphasize "a limited number" because this aspect of teacher support could easily get out of hand, reflecting the discredited notion that phonics must be taught explicitly and extensively.

9. *By observing children's own developing strategies for making sense of print, and supporting the children in their endeavors and their strategies.*

10. *By providing additional materials and help for individual children, as appropriate.* For instance, children who seem readily to grasp the concept of letter/sound relationships might especially benefit from Dr. Seuss books that reinforce letter/sound patterns (of course other children can enjoy and benefit from such books too). Other children will surely benefit from attention to letter/sound relationships in a tutorial setting, with such assistance offered within the context of authentic reading and writing. This may include attention to basic letter/sound correspondences, and *some* attention to dividing words roughly into syllables and reading them by analogy (e.g., Gaskins, Gaskins, & Gaskins, 1991)—but I question the need for such *extensive* direct instruction. (See also the discussion of retrospective miscue analysis in Chapter 6, as well as strategies for working with special needs students in Chapter 12. For some first graders, the Reading Recovery program originally developed by Marie Clay may be a feasible and appropriate option; again, see Chapter 12.)

In whole language classrooms, such support for the development of phonics knowledge reflects characteristic whole language principles, most notably the conviction that learners are capable of constructing phonics knowledge for themselves, given appropriate input and support.

TOWARD A MORE COMPLETE MODEL OF THE READING PROCESS

In Chapter 2, we developed a simple socio-psycholinguistic model of the reading process, emphasizing the fact that reading proceeds at least as much from whole to part as from part to whole. In Chapter 4 we deepened our insights by considering research that sheds light on the reading process through consideration of readers' miscues (e.g., K. S. Goodman, 1973; K. S. Goodman & Y. M. Goodman, n. d.). Taken together, such research demonstrates, among other things, that:

1. The meanings of individual words contribute to the meaning of the evolving whole, yet the evolving whole also determines the appropriate meanings of individual words.
2. Context reduces the amount of visual information that readers need in order to identify words and their constituent letters. That is, in proficient reading, even visual processing is facilitated by automatic use of context and prior knowledge.
3. Proficient readers ("good" readers, or what some researchers call "skilled" readers) automatically use prior knowledge and context to construct meaning as they read, as well as to reduce their reliance on visual information.
4. Proficient readers usually go directly from print to meaning. Only occasionally do they recode written words into spoken words in order to get meaning.
5. Some less proficient readers may succeed rather well at constructing meaning, even though they identify considerably fewer than all the words. Their focus on meaning minimizes the effects of their problems with specific words.
6. Some less proficient readers may not succeed very well at constructing meaning from texts, even though—or *because*—they try hard to identify all the words. Their focus on identifying words diverts them from the goal of constructing meaning.
7. Still other less proficient readers may not be very effective (much less efficient) at constructing meaning *or* at getting the words, even though—or *because*—they try hard to sound out words they don't immediately recognize. They make inadequate use of other reading strategies and language cues, such as prior knowledge and context.
8. Some less proficient readers may not succeed very well at getting the words of a text, even though—or *because*—they try to identify words on sight. They make inadequate use of other reading strategies and language cues, such as context and letter/sound patterns.

Some researchers have concentrated on what they perceive as a problem of inadequate letter/sound knowledge for recognizing words (e.g., Perfetti, 1985), while others have concentrated on what they perceive as a problem of inadequate use of prior knowledge and context to construct meaning (K. S. Goodman, 1973; and many of the references in K. S. Goodman & Y. M. Goodman, n. d.). Obviously, the problems are interrelated. However, a major theme of this book is that it is critical to emphasize the construction of meaning first and foremost—not only because the attempt to construct meaning facilitates word identification, but, much more crucially, because constructing meaning is the primary goal of reading. Therefore, attention to word parts and word processing should occur within the context of authentic reading and writing experiences.

However, a more complete model of the reading process than that in Chapter 2 should also take into account relevant research on the perception and processing of words, combining this with the research on reading as a sustained and natural process of constructing meaning. Some key conclusions from research on word perception and word processing are the following:

1. Good readers do not need context in order to recognize a majority of the words they encounter in text. They automatically recognize many words on sight (Stanovich, 1991).
2. However, longer and less familiar words are not recognized as wholes but rather as related clusters of letters—especially syllables and/or onsets and rimes (Mewhort & Campbell, 1981; Treiman & Chafetz, 1987).
3. Syllabic units are not recognized prior to letters, nor letters prior to syllables, but both more or less simultaneously.
4. What triggers such recognition is bars, slits, lines, curves, and so forth; visual information is processed selectively, with consonants contributing much more useful information than vowels.
5. Nevertheless, readers typically "see" the individual letters in a word—at least skilled readers do. Using prior knowledge of letters and letter patterns, the brain constructs a complete visual image from the partial data supplied by the eye.
6. Skilled readers typically recode printed words into sound; they "hear" the words in their mental ear.

Much of this research is summarized in detail by Adams (1990a) and succinctly by Stanovich (1991). Stanovich in particular discusses various models of word perception that became popular through the decade of the 1980s, culminating in complex models like the connectionist or distributed network model of Seidenberg and McClelland (1989). Typically, these models have been based upon the assumption that reading is a hierarchical process, with word identification preceding the process of constructing meaning. The later connectionist models involve greater overlap and simultaneity, while still tending to assume that prior knowledge and context play no role, or very little, in the automatic word identification of proficient readers. This assumption has led to research that seems to confirm it (see Stanovich, 1991, for a summary). On the other hand, there seems to be ample evidence from other experimental studies as well as miscue research that proficient readers do use prior knowledge and context to construct meaning and also to reduce their reliance on visual information in identifying words.

Without discussing in more depth the research on orthographic and phonological processing (Adams and Stanovich have done that), I would like to suggest a model that I think more adequately reflects experimental research on isolated word perception and naturalistic research on the reading of connected and coherent texts. Among other things, this model must reconcile the seeming contradictions between some of the conclusions from miscue research and word perception research, as indicated above. The model must somehow capture such observations as these:

1. Proficient readers automatically "see" the individual letters in most content words and many function words, *even though* their equally automatic use of context makes this unnecessary for identifying most words (McConkie & Zola, 1981; Rayner & Pollatsek, 1989).
2. Proficient readers automatically make use of contextual constraints as they read, *even though* their equally automatic processing of letter sequences and words makes the use of context unnecessary in identifying familiar words.
3. Proficient readers identify most of the words in a text, *even though* their primary goal is to construct meaning rather than to identify words.
4. Proficient readers pay most attention to constructing meaning from a text, *even though* they do identify most of the words in the process.
5. Proficient readers automatically "hear" the words of the text (Paterson & Coltheart, 1987; Banks, Oka, & Shugarman, 1981), *even though* translating written words into spoken words is rarely necessary for getting meaning, and in fact slows down their reading significantly (Tanenhaus, Flanigan, & Seidenberg, 1980).
6. In short, proficient readers make simultaneous and redundant use of all the information available to them, *even though* this is not necessary unless problems arise. This information includes orthographic (spelling), phonological (sound), and grapho/phonemic information (knowledge of letter/sound relations and patterns), as well syntactic, semantic, and schematic information (including pragmatic, or practical information, such as information about the demands of the reading situation). Simultaneous use of these linguistic and cognitive resources facilitates effective and efficient reading.

Furthermore, each kind of processing facilitates the others. The use of schemas and context to predict upcoming text facilitates the processing of letters, letter/sound knowledge, and sounds. The recognition of words facilitates the development of schemas and the further use of both schemas and context in identifying subsequent words. The processing of letters triggers not only phonological and grapho/phonemic knowledge but the use of context and schemas to grasp the meaning of words. And so forth. In other words, the processing systems each work in concert with and support of one another. This becomes most obvious, perhaps, when the orthographic processor does not lead to immediate word recognition. Then, if a word is in the person's listening vocabulary, the reader can get the word by processing the word grapho/phonemically, all the while automatically using context, schemas, and relevant knowledge of word meanings to process the word.

The redundancy within this processing system as well as within texts can help us understand how less proficient readers may construct meaning without necessarily identifying most of the words, and without being equally effective in using all kinds of language cues and strategies. Less proficient does not necessarily mean ineffective.

Figure 5.9 is an attempt to capture, visually, the complexity and redundancy of the reading process. I have tried to make the model abstract enough to capture the points of agreement among various research perspectives, while sidestepping the controversies. Unlike most models of word perception alone, the tentative model in Figure 5.9 is intended to give equal weight to the automatic use of context, along with the automatic use of orthographic and phonological knowledge. Furthermore, I think it more clearly implies what the total body of reading research suggests, including the word perception research summarized by Adams (1990a): namely, that *all* these kinds of processing are interconnected with each other, and that with proficient readers, all kinds of processing occur automatically, redundantly, and more or less simultaneously. This greatly facilitates the reading process.

FOR FURTHER REFLECTION AND EXPLORATION

1. In a *Time* magazine article that reports on a government study concluding that one in eight Americans cannot read, the suggestion is made that

   the American school system is partly to blame. In many elementary schools, reading time is devoted to "See Jane run" readers and dull word-drill workbooks. Another pedagogical problem: children frequently are force-fed new words by the "look and say" method, which requires recognition of whole words, rather than the more flexible and effective technique of phonics, or sounding out words, phoneme by phoneme. *(Time,* 5 May 1986)

   Comment on this quote in light of the discussion of reading approaches in Chapter 3, the discussion of readers' use of various kinds of contexts in Chapter 4, and the discussion of phonics in the present chapter.

2. To test for yourself the assertion that grammatical endings are often predictable when a word occurs in context, try to provide the endings missing from the following sentences (the same sentences from which the consonants were earlier omitted). As before, the dash indicates an omitted letter:

   Sometime- all Lobo could find was a wizen- - old farm- - and his wife, work- - - in the field- near the wood- or pick- - - berri- - in the thicket. At other time-, Lobo might be luck- enough to find a plump, juic- child that had disobey- - its parent- and stray- - too far from home.

   Did you find it easy to provide the grammatical endings? What do you think of the notion that we should teach grammatical endings to children in order to help them identify words?

3. If you are not familiar with the symbols of the Initial Teaching Alphabet, try the following experiment (or try it with someone else who is not familiar with the ITA). First, try to decide what sounds are probably represented by the following symbols:

   æ   ʊ   ω   ie   th   ʒ   ʃh   dʒ   ʒ

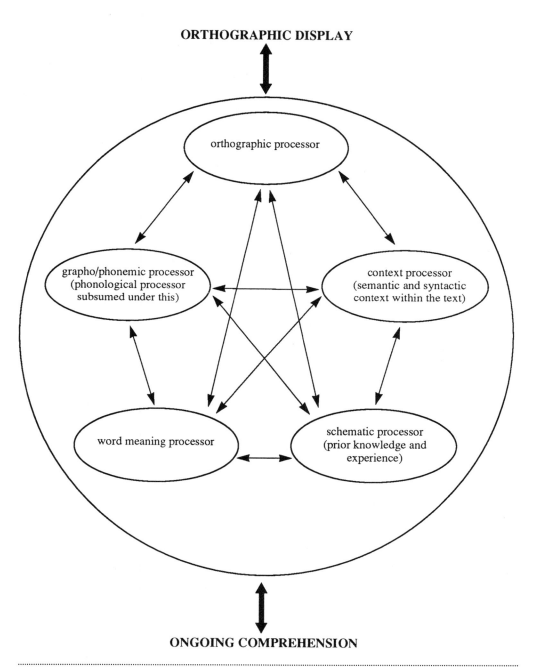

ORTHOGRAPHIC DISPLAY

orthographic processor

grapho/phonemic processor
(phonological processor
subsumed under this)

context processor
(semantic and syntactic
context within the text)

word meaning processor

schematic processor
(prior knowledge and
experience)

ONGOING COMPREHENSION

FIGURE 5.9   A redundancy model of the reading process

Now, simply read the paragraph below. This is an alternative conclusion to our story about the wolf and Red Riding Hood:

> ꝼhe littl girl taested delifhous but loeboe hardly had tiem tw enjoi ꝼhe flaevor befoer somwun nakt at ꝼhe doer. ꝼhe wwlf skrambld bak intw bed and sed, "Cum on in. just oepen ꝼhe doer." In stroed a big wwdsman. hεε recogniesd ꝼhe wwlf at wuns, and loeboe berly had tiem tw jump out ov bed and thrw a windoe befoer ꝼhe wwdsman's aks fel. tw this dae, loeboe has never gon bak tw ꝼhe south edʒ ov ꝼhe wwds. hεε staes nir hoem, settliŋ for wizend oeld farmers and ꝼher wievs.

What words caused particular difficulty, and why? On the whole, were you able to read the preceding paragraph fairly easily, even if you did not know what sound each of the symbols represents? If so, how were you able to read the passage without knowing all the letter/sound relationships?

4. To continue exploring the idea that the use of context can reduce our need for visual information during normal reading, have someone try to supply the words that are missing from the following, our story about the wolf and Red Riding Hood. The first letter of each missing word is provided as a clue, along with dashes to represent the missing letters:

> Once upon a t--- there was a handsome y---- wolf named Lobo. Lobo l---- with his mother and f----- at the edge of a d--, dark woods. Every day L--- went to hunt at t-- north edge of the w----, near the little village o- Calais. Sometimes all Lobo c---- find was a wizened o-- farmer and his wife, w------ in the fields near t-- woods or picking berries i- the thicket. At other t----, Lobo might be lucky e----- to find a plump, j---- child that had disobeyed i-- parents and strayed too f-- from home.
>
> One day a- Lobo was skirting the e--- of the forest, he c--- upon a little girl i- a red hood. Her c----s were so rosy and h-- arms so pudgy that L--- knew she would be d--------. "Where are you going, l----- girl?" he asked. "Oh," s-- replied, "I'm taking this b----- of goodies to my g---------- on the other side o- the woods. Grandma isn't f------ very well."
>
> Lobo thought f-- a moment. He could h----- wait to devour this s---------- child, but then again h- was hungry enough to e-- the grandmother too. "Which h---- does your grandmother live i-?" asked the wolf. "In t-- house by the three b-- oak trees," said Red R----- Hood (for that is w--- she was called). "She l---- there all by herself."
>
> "W--- a marvelous opportunity!" thought L---. He told the child to stop and pick flowers f-- her grandmother on the w--

through the woods, then t– – – off on a short c– – that only the wolves k– – – about. Soon he arrived a– the grandmother's cottage. "It's m–, Grandma," Lobo said in a t– – – voice, as he knocked o– the door. He pulled t– – door open and went i–.

Lobo went straight to t– – grandmother's bed and gobbled h– – up. He donned her c– – and gown and climbed i– – – bed, feeling none too w– – – – himself. By the time L– – – – – Red Riding Hood had a– – – – – –, however, he had overcome h– – attack of indigestion and w– – ready for dessert. He a– – – – – – – Red's knock in an o– –, cracked voice: "Come in, d– – –. Just come on in."

L– – – was so ravenous that h– didn't wait for Little R– – Riding Hood to ask h– – "grandma" how she was o– to bring her the b– – – – – of goodies. He threw b– – – the covers, jumped out o– bed, and ran over t– the child. She screamed a– – ran, but it was t– – late. Lobo gobbled her u–. Afterwards he sat b– the fireside smoking grandma's p– – –, dreaming of juicy little g– – – –.

Which kinds of missing words were easier to supply: content words or function words? Was it possible to get the essential meaning even without being able to supply all the words?

5. For use in shared reading experiences, locate rhymes, poems, and songs that contain alliteration and/or rhyme and/or onomatopoeia. Having chosen some materials, consider how you might initiate discussion of the interesting sound element(s), and try this within the context of a total shared reading experience (see Chapter 3). One useful source is *Noisy Poems*, collected by Jill Bennett (1987). You might also consider using alphabet books as well as poems: Chris Van Allsburg's *The Z Was Zapped* (1987) is but one example. Three other books to consider: *One Sun: A Book of Terse Verse* (McMillan, 1990); *Faint Frogs Feeling Feverish & Other Terrifically Tantalizing Tongue Twisters* (Obligado, 1983); and *Deep Down Underground* (Dunrea, 1989). See Figure 5.7 for other ideas.

6. If you know of a reader who is considered to be in need of phonics instruction, try developing a "determining lesson" similar to the one discussed in this chapter. Or simply have the reader read connected text and do a miscue analysis (see Chapter 6) to determine if he or she is making adequate use of grapho/phonemic cues in the context of meaningful reading. If the majority of the reader's miscues fit with the preceding context and also fit with the following context or are corrected, then adequate use is probably being made of these cues.

6 Portfolios, Reading, and Miscue Analysis

> *Only two basic uses of reading tests are legitimate. They are as follows: (1) to measure the effectiveness with which any person uses reading to comprehend written language. . . . (2) To diagnose the strengths and weaknesses of readers as an aid to planning instruction which will help to make them more effective.*
>
> — Kenneth Goodman

Increasingly, teachers, administrators, school systems, and even state and national assessments teams are insisting that standardized test scores are inadequate and inappropriate for assessing students' reading. There are various reasons for rejecting standardized test scores, among them the following (see references in Figure 6.1 for documentation and support):

1. The purpose of standardized test scores, by their very nature, is to rank order students, teachers, and schools, thereby labeling some as more successful and others as less successful. Standardized tests have little to do with promoting good education.
2. Standardized tests give a false impression of objectivity, and consequently of equal opportunity and fairness. They are "objective" only in that they are scored the same way for all students. However, the construction of the tests and the responses of test takers remain extremely subjective.
3. Standardized tests are inherently discriminatory. They inevitably reflect the background and culture of the test makers and therefore discriminate against students who do not share this background. This is true even of tests designed to be "culture-free."
4. For many children, standardized testing results in "death at an early age"—or at least to a life sentence in lower "ability" groups or in compensatory or remedial classes (L. W. Anderson & Pellicer, 1990; McGill-Franzen & Allington, 1991). (See Chapter 7 and Chapter 11.)
5. Standardized tests do not encourage or permit students to demonstrate the full range of their knowledge or abilities.
6. The scores on standardized tests do not necessarily reflect students' ability to engage in actual reading, writing, or thinking in daily life. For instance, "reading achievement" scores from standardized tests do not necessarily correlate well with

Anderson, L. W., & Pellicer, L. O. 1990. Synthesis of research on compensatory and remedial education. *Educational Leadership, 48* (September), 10–16.

Carbo, M. 1988. *What reading achievement tests should measure to increase literacy in the U. S.* Research Bulletin, no. 7. Bloomington, IN: Phi Delta Kappan.

Edelsky, C., & Harman, S. 1988. One more critique of reading tests—with two differences. *English Education, 20,* 157–171.

Madaus, G. F. 1985. Test scores as administrative mechanisms in educational policy. *Phi Delta Kappan, 66,* 616–617.

National Commission on Testing and Public Policy. 1990. *From gatekeeper to gateway: Transforming testing in America.* Chestnut Hill, MA: Boston College.

Neill, D. M. and Medina, N. J. 1989. Standardized testing: Harmful to educational health. *Phi Delta Kappan, 70,* 688–697.

Richards, T. S. 1989. Testmania: The school under siege. *Learning 89, 17,* 64–66.

Sternberg, R. J. 1989. The tyranny of testing. *Learning 89, 17,* 60–63.

Weaver, C. 1990. *Understanding whole language: From principles to practice,* Ch. 9. Portsmouth, NH: Heinemann.

Wiggins, G. 1989. A true test: Toward more authentic and equitable assessment. *Phi Delta Kappan, 70,* 703–713.

Figure 6.1   Criticisms of standardized tests

actual ability to read coherent, connected text and respond appropriately. That is, the tests lack construct validity.

7. Standardized tests do not tell us what we really need to know about students' learning. With reading, for instance, we need to know how the reader conceptualizes reading and what strategies the reader uses; how and how well the reader comprehends, with respect to various kinds of materials; what the reader's interests, tastes, habits are in reading; how the reader feels about him- or herself as a reader; how the reader has grown as a reader; and what the reader thinks he or she needs to work on as a reader. Both the teacher and the student can take such kinds of information into account in formulating goals for the reader and assessing progress toward these goals. Standardized tests cannot give us such data.

8. Instead, standardized tests focus students' and educators' attention on whatever skills students cannot demonstrate, at least not in isolation from authentic reading and writing and everyday life.

9. Thus, overreliance on standardized tests as measures of students' learning encourages educators to teach skills in isolation, with the result that learners are severely shortchanged.

For these and other reasons, many educators are turning toward *portfolio assessment* of students. Though often standardized tests are still administered, they are given much less weight than formerly, particularly in making decisions about the growth, placement, and educational needs of the individual student.

WHAT IS PORTFOLIO ASSESSMENT?

To the uninformed, the idea of portfolio assessment seems to generate the image of a manila folder or accordion folder into which the student's work—for the grading period, if not the entire year—has all been tossed or stuffed. Not so.

It matters little where or how we store the students' work, as long as both we and they have access to it. What is most crucial is the philosophy of assessment that informs the concept of portfolios.

Here are some principles that seem to be widely recognized as important in the development of portfolios and the movement to reconceptualize assessment:

1. Assessment should be collaborative, involving not only the teacher but the student as well, and perhaps peers and/or parents.
2. Assessment should be complex and multidimensional, concerned not just with *products* but with *processes* and *perceptions*—strategies, attitudes, habits, self-concept as a learner, and so forth.
3. Assessment should be ongoing and contextualized. That is, it should derive primarily from the day-to-day activities of students in the classroom.
4. Assessment should allow for and reflect the uniqueness of the individual student, with emphasis on strengths and growth.
5. Assessment should involve reflection and thoughtful critique, not simplistic grading.
6. Assessment should reflect and give rise to goals for learners—both students and teachers.

Such reflective evaluation and self-evaluation simultaneously derives from and generates increased awareness of what might appropriately be considered learning growth—whether the learner is officially the teacher or officially a student.

READING WITHIN LITERACY AND LEARNING PORTFOLIOS

Rarely would most teachers want to compile portfolios on reading alone. Even reading specialists recognize the value of writing for improving reading, and of integrated learning experiences for enhancing both language and literacy. For convenience, however, I will focus on the artifacts that one might collect as a basis for reflective evaluation of reading by itself, while recognizing—even insisting—that in classroom practice, these would be only part of a more complete literacy and learning portfolio.

Sources of data include the following:

1. *Periodic performance samples.* Actual samples of a student's reading can be analyzed for insights into the reader's strategies, ability to discuss and reflect upon what has been read, and so forth. Such samples consistute the raw data of miscue analysis, which is the major focus of this chapter.

2. *Think-alouds.* The purpose of a think-aloud is to gain insight into how and how well the reader processes a text. While reading (usually silently), the reader is to frequently comment aloud upon his or her own reading: what connections the reader is making to other texts, how parts of the text relate (or don't relate) to the reader's prior knowledge and experience, how the reader is dealing with the text and with problem words, what the reader understands and doesn't understand, and so forth. The teacher obviously needs to model this think-aloud process before asking students to try it. The think-aloud can be tape-recorded for later analysis of the reader's strengths and needs. Ideally, teacher and student may listen to the tape and reflect upon it together, perhaps using it as a guide in generating some goals for the reader.

3. *Recorded observations.* The teacher records observations that become part of the student's portfolio. For this purpose, some teachers keep handy sheets of adhesive-backed labels on which they can record observations of different students. Later they transfer the labels to each student's portfolio. Other teachers find stick-on slips workable in much the same way—or index cards that they can attach to paper with Tack-a-Note adhesive stick, or something similar. It's important to include not only spontaneous anecdotes but systematic observations—perhaps five students a day for a week, repeated periodically. That way, not only a student's highs and lows are captured, but also his or her daily reading strategies, habits, interests, and so forth, which may be more characteristic.

4. *Conferences and interviews.* Conferences and interviews can be particularly helpful in generating insight into such matters as

    The reader's understanding of reading and reading strategies

    How the reader feels about him- or herself as a reader

    What strategies the reader is conscious of using to deal with problem words and/or with problems in comprehending text

    What the reader likes to read (kinds of reading material, kinds of books, etc.)

    How often and how much the reader reads for pleasure

    Under what circumstances the reader likes to read

And so forth. Later in this chapter are some reading interview questions and a form for recording and eliciting some of these kinds of data.

5. *Inventories and questionnaires.* Much the same kinds of data can be obtained from inventories and questionnaires that the students respond to in writing. One fifth-grade teacher, Ruth Perino, elicited such information from her students by discuss-

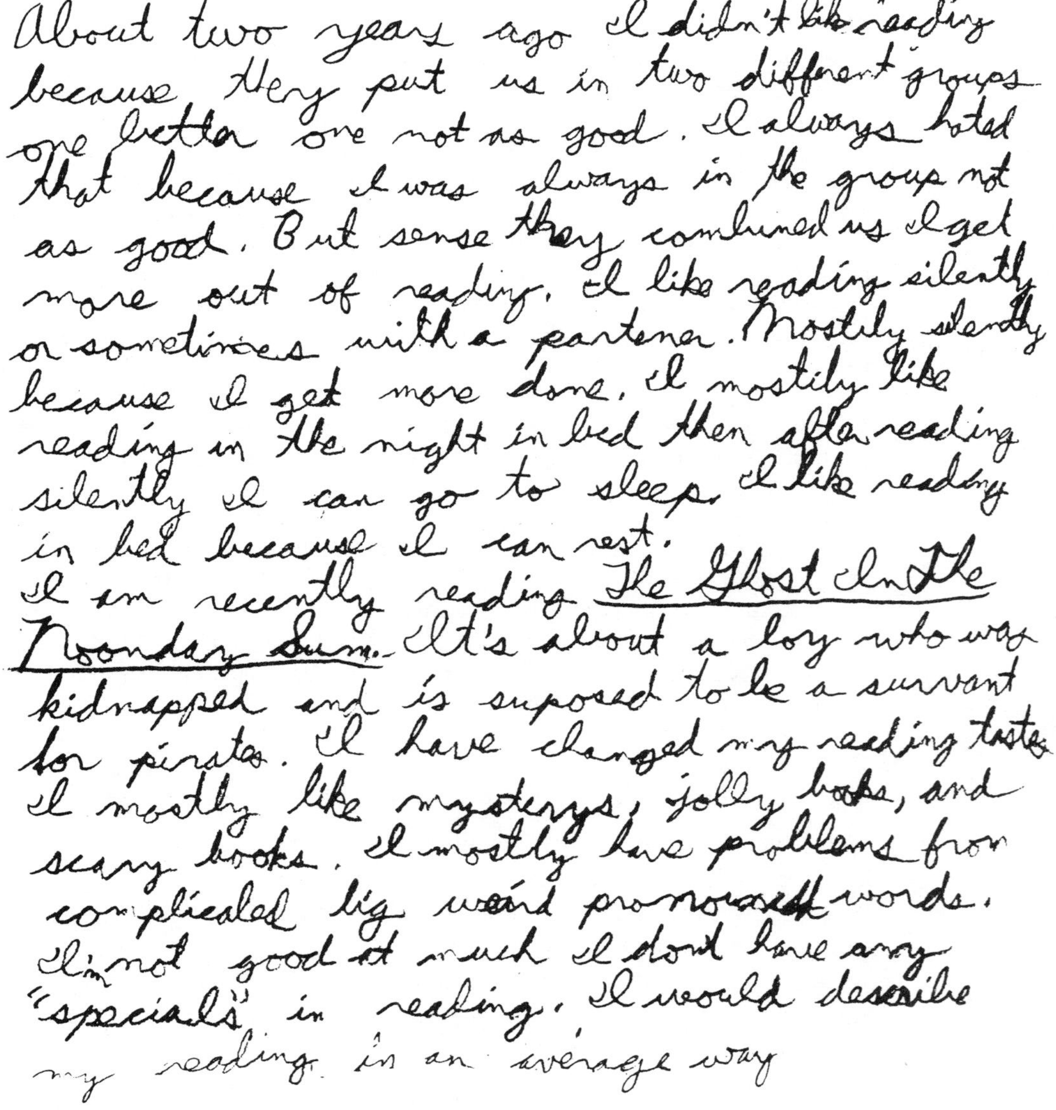

About two years ago I didn't like reading because they put us in two different groups one better one not as good. I always hated that because I was always in the group not as good. But sense they combined us I get more out of reading. I like reading silently or sometimes with a partener. Mostily silently because I get more done. I mostly like reading in the night in bed then after reading silently I can go to sleep. I like reading in bed because I can rest. I am recently reading <u>The Ghost In The Noonday Sun</u>. It's about a boy who was kidnapped and is suposed to be a survant for pirates. I have changed my reading tastes I mostly like mysterys, jolly books, and scary books. I mostly have problems from complicated big weird pronouced words. I'm not good at much I don't have any "specials" in reading. I would describe my reading in an average way

FIGURE **6.2**   *Rumi's description of himself as a reader*

ing reading interests, styles, and habits with the class, then asking students to write about themselves as readers. Figure 6.2 is the response from Rumi, who blossomed as a reader in his new school and in Ruth's class. Figure 6.3 is from Erica, and Figure 6.4 from Jackie, who were among the least proficient readers in their class. Note the variety of responses, and note also how children come to think of themselves as readers in classrooms that value and treat them as readers.

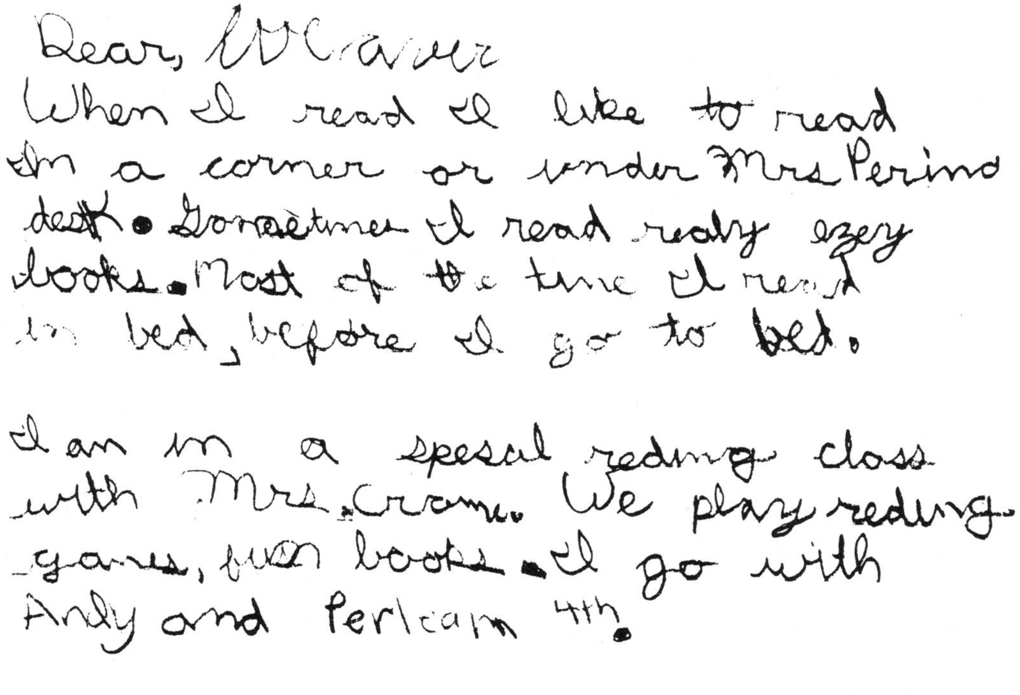

Dear, Weaver
When I read I like to read
in a corner or under Mrs Perino
desk. Sometimes I read realy ezey
books. Most of the time I read
in bed, before I go to bed.

I am in a spesal reding class
with Mrs Cram. We play reding
games, fuen books. I go with
Andy and Perlcam 4th.

In clas were reading a
book called "Roll of Thunder,
Hear My Cry!! In sport,
silinted redings I am reading
chose your own avelture.

Figure 6.3 *Erica's description of herself as a reader*

Hi my name is Jackie Hartyell,

I enjoy reading to my self very much. I very much enjoy reading fiction. I also love to here people read to me and I love to read out loud and sielently. When it is quite that is mostly when I love to read. I love to read in my room on my bed and in corners. I have read the Cats that Nobody Wanted, Harriet and the robot, The Slave Dancer and Roll of Thunder Hear My Cry. My reading taste has not changed. Yes I have dificultys reading somtimes because I am dislecsic and often I skip lines and keep on reading the same line. I like trying to be good at reading with expretion and mostly know what I am reading and what I am talking about. My reading style in reading so I can draw pictures showing what was hap-pining. I don't read fast at all. I read alot of reaserch books too. I also love to right vantastic storys.

FIGURE 6.4   Jackie's description of herself as a reader

A formal inventory might be used to gain insight into students' preferred learning/reading styles and the conditions under which they prefer to read. These and related factors are assessed by Marie Carbo's *Reading Style Inventory* (1981b), now available in regular, primary-grade, and adult versions. A considerable body of research demonstrates that students learn best when their reading style needs are met (Carbo, 1983; Carbo, 1987b; LaShell, 1986; Sudzina, 1986). A particularly relevant finding is that most young children are much more global than analytic—they deal with wholes better than parts, for example, and are not good at analyzing wholes into constituent parts. Also, they tend to be highly kinesthetic, needing to be physically and emotionally involved in order to learn best. Tactile, hands-on learning is important for most young children. They tend to be less visual than kinesthetic/tactile, and still less auditory—still less able to learn through listening alone. Thus, reading styles research demonstrates the inappropriateness of heavy phonics teaching for most children (Carbo, 1987b), and lends support to whole-to-part teaching with primary-grade children—provided the teacher is also alert for the children who may actually learn better by dealing with the parts and who may need more structured instruction (Carbo, 1992).

Whole language educators often shy away from assessment instruments like the Reading Style Inventory, and with good reason. One concern is that the instrument, when used with an entire class simultaneously, is subject to some of the same criticisms and concerns as any mass-administered, machine-scorable test. (This is not true of the primary version, which is administered to children individually.) Of deeper concern, though, is the possibility that individual learners might be viewed in terms of a single predominant learning or reading style, as if we were not complex individuals whose styles and needs differ under different circumstances. While sharing these concerns, I must admit that I find it valuable to have my undergraduates talk their way through the instrument with a reader, one on one. It gives inexperienced preservice teachers quick insight into the fact that not everyone learns in the same ways. It also helps them understand that alleged reading or learning failure or disability may be more a mismatch between the learner's needs and the curriculum than a problem that resides within the learner. Checklists for analyzing key aspects of a person's reading style are included as appendices to this chapter.

6. *Dialogue journals and literature logs.* As mentioned in Chapter 3, a dialogue journal is a journal in which a student and the teacher exchange letters about the books they are reading; a literature log is a journal in which the student records responses and perhaps responds to teachers' particular requests in dealing with and responding to the literature. When students respond to what they're reading in dialogue journals and literature logs, they provide significant data for assessing what and how they are reading: their reading interests, attitudes, habits, and strategies; their understanding and appreciation of literary elements; their criteria for choosing literature; and so forth. When specific information is desired, teachers can always make particular requests of students writing in literature logs—for example, "This time, when you read, put a check in the margin by some of the problem words.

Then, in your literature log, choose one of these words, write the sentence it's in, and tell how you dealt with it." Later, teacher and student(s) can discuss the effectiveness of the reader's strategies and perhaps suggest other strategies as well.

7. *Lists and record cards or sheets.* Students can keep lists of books they have read. Or they can respond in more detail, with not only the title and author, but comments about what they liked best (and least?) and whether they would or would not recommend the book to a friend, and why. Teacher and students may brainstorm as to what should be included on such a response card or sheet. Such responses may be made available to the whole class—via a box of index cards made up of book reviews, for example. But they can also be used for their insight into each reader's development of interests, self-confidence, enthusiasm for reading, critical response to literary works, and so forth.

8. *Other media.* Readers can respond to literature through other media—through drawing, drama, music, sculpture, and other means. One common way of assessing young children's understanding, for example, is to ask them to draw and then tell about the part of a story that they liked best. Or children can act out a particular story, choose and share music that reflects the mood of a story, sculpt something that reflects their understanding of the main character or his or her emotions—the possibilities are numerous. Each of these products offers an opportunity to reflect upon the reader's engagement in reading and the reader's understanding and appreciation of what has been read.

These and many other kinds of data can contribute to reading assessment that is complex, contextualized, and collaborative—three of the elements that are basic to portfolio assessment. (See also the brief discussion of assessment in Chapter 8, particularly Figures 8.5 and 8.6.)

What should we look for in these data? Portfolio assessment involves setting goals for and with each individual reader. Keeping this in mind, we might look for growth in such areas as these:

1. Positive self-concept and self-confidence as a reader.
2. Choosing to read (during and outside of school); enthusiasm for reading.
3. Taking risks, challenging oneself as a reader.
4. Focus on getting meaning, and ability to monitor ongoing comprehension.
5. Ability to use prior knowledge and all language cue systems together.
6. Flexibility in using strategies and solving problems as a reader.
7. Ability and inclination to make connections as a reader, both within and beyond the text.
8. Ability to read thoughtfully and critically.
9. Ability to read, with understanding, a variety of texts for differing purposes.
10. Ability to evaluate own development and needs as a reader.

Clearly, these goals go far beyond what can be measured by standardized tests.

ANALYZING READING PERFORMANCE

When considering reading performance, what should be analyzed, and why? The perspective in this section derives from the preceding chapters and, in particular, the miscue research that informs the discussion within Chapter 4.

Common Assessment Measures

In this section, we examine two common assessment measures: the Informal Reading Inventory (IRI) and the running record.

Informal reading inventories

Let us review some points from earlier chapters by considering the miscues made by Anne, a first grader reading Jene Barr's *Little Circus Dog* (1949). Which of Anne's miscues fit with the context? Which ones do not?

Now the band began to play. Then the lions roared.

        about ①
Peter the pony ran around the ring. Bill the circus boy

ⓒ *let* ②   *Everyone* ③
led Penny the elephant into the circus ring. Everybody

forgot to eat popcorn. They forgot to drink soda pop.

          A ④
They forgot to wave balloons. The circus man made a bow.

Trixie ran into the middle of the ring. She sat and

        went ⑤
waited. Carlo the clown ran up to Trixie. Trixie jumped

   on ⑥   *the* ⑦
up and sat in his hand. Carlo put Trixie on a box. Trixie

stood on her hind legs. Then she jumped onto Carlo's head.

              Every-
Trixie looked very funny sitting on Carlo's head. Every-

one ⑧
body laughed.

In every case, the miscue fits both the syntactic context and the semantic context. That is, the miscue results in a grammatical sentence that preserves the essential meaning of the original. Such miscues are typical of a good reader, one who ordinarily gets meaning from what is read. And in fact, Anne recalled almost every detail of the passage.

Oddly enough, by some standards the foregoing passage might be considered too difficult for Anne.

In order to determine where to place a child within a given basal reading series, it has been common to have the child read passages from several levels of a basal reader program to determine the child's *independent, instructional,* and *frustration* levels within that series. Material at the independent level is supposed to be suitable for the child's unaided reading; material at the instructional level is supposed to be suitable for instructional use with that child; and material at the frustration level is considered simply too difficult for that child to read.

The time-honored Betts criteria for determining these levels are as follows (Betts, 1946):

Reading Level	Words Decoded	Questions Answered
Independent	99%	90%
Instructional	95%	75%
Frustration	Below 90%	50%

More recently, there has been somewhat greater variation. Most of the twelve IRI's (informal reading inventories) reviewed by Harris and Niles (1982) suggested percentages within these ranges:

Independent	97–100%	80–90%
Instructional	90–97%	60–80%
Frustration	Below 90%	50–60%

However, this neat chart masks the extremes found in some of the IRI's. In most cases, these percentages seem to be arbitrarily determined. Worse yet, the word recognition score is often considered more important than the comprehension score, reflecting the typical emphasis on word-perfect reading.

If we compute Anne's word recognition score on the preceding excerpt from *Little Circus Dog,* we see that this story is allegedly too difficult for her to read without instructional help, according to the preceding word recognition criteria. Anne pronounced only 92 percent of the words without error, which puts this selection at her instructional level.

Perhaps some children who read 8 percent of the words inaccurately in a given selection will consider that selection too difficult to read independently—particularly if they have been encouraged to think that they are not reading well when they make miscues. However, Anne's miscues clearly indicate that she was using prior knowledge and context to predict. Since following context confirmed the appropriateness of the miscues, she left most of them uncorrected; indeed, she probably did not even notice most of them. Anne was reading to construct meaning, and doing so very successfully.

The same is true for Jay and Billy, whose miscues we saw in Chapter 4. Their miscues indicated highly effective use of reading strategies, and they were quite successful at constructing meaning. But would the selections have been considered appropriate for their independent reading, if we used the above criteria? Definitely not, as you can confirm by computing word recognition scores yourself.

This is one of the potential problems with informal reading inventories (e.g., Ekwall, 1986): they often encourage the use of word identification as a criteria for effective reading and/or a criteria for selecting appropriate reading materials. In other words, some IRI's have encouraged teachers to look at word recognition without regard to how the miscues might fit the context or whether they preserve essential meaning—and without much regard for how well the reader can construct meaning, despite the miscues. Sometimes the IRI's have even suggested looking specifically at whether the reader identified basic "sight words" correctly.

However, such miscues often reflect good predictions. For example:

saw
I first saw Claribel when I was

working in my office.

Instead, there was a

heard
lovely song. I looked up and had

my first view of Claribel.

Instead of considering these miscues to result from not knowing basic sight words, we might better observe that they reflect good predictions from the preceding context: that is, they are more likely to reflect an effective reading strategy than a poor memory for these "sight" words. This is confirmed when, as often happens, the same words are read correctly in other contexts.

While many informal inventories have been improved or better inventories developed since miscue analysis research became more widely known, there are still significant problems with most published IRI's. Harris and Niles mention some of the most pervasive drawbacks (1982, p. 161):

1. Generally the passages are too short to give the reader a chance to demonstrate his or her reading ability with more natural and longer texts. The nature of readers' miscues often changes after the first 200 words (Menosky, 1971), but few IRI's have passages significantly longer than that.

2. Comprehension questions can often be answered on the basis of prior knowledge—or the topics are unknown and totally unfamiliar to the reader, thus preventing the reader from making normal use of his or her schemas in constructing meaning from the text.

3. In order to devise an adequate number of comprehension questions on such short passages, the test maker may be forced to include mostly questions that focus on detail and recall of fact, rather than the more challenging kinds of questions that stimulate sophisticated inferences or critical reflection. Too often, questions on such passages can be answered simply by manipulating the language of the text, as we saw with the "blonke" and "corandic" passages in earlier chapters.

Given these typical limitations, even the more sophisticated IRI's are usually far from ideal for determining readers' strengths and needs. They simply do not give sufficient insight into either readers' strategies or their ability to connect with and reflect upon texts.

Running records

The growing popularity of Marie Clay's Reading Recovery program for first graders (Clay, 1985) has brought with it the "running record," wherein the teacher records miscues while the student is in the process of reading. The major advantage is obvious: there is no need for tape-recording and later playback. In fact, the teacher does not even need a typescript or photocopy of the reading selection for marking the miscues; only a sheet of paper is needed. Every word read correctly is indicated with a check mark or simply a slanted line. Thus, the teacher's running record consists of checks (or slanted lines) interspersed with the reader's miscues. A running record of Anne's rendition of *Little Circus Dog,* for example, might look like Figure 6.5.

Even a quick glance at this example should begin to suggest the concern that many educators have with the running record: it implicitly encourages us to consider miscues without regard to how they relate to the context. Although Clay explains that miscues should be analyzed for how they fit the context, she also emphasizes accuracy. She categorizes texts as easy, instructional, or hard based on the number of miscues. And she considers it important that students in the Reading Recovery program read a selection with 95 percent accuracy (including self-corrections) before they attempt more difficult texts (Clay, 1985, pp. 17–22; Clay, 1991a). Her point is to use texts that are easy enough to support the reader in developing reading strategies, but researchers experienced in miscue analysis have not found this degree of textual support to be necessary.

Despite Clay's own sophisticated understanding of miscues and what they reveal about reading strategies, and despite the fact that both teachers and students in the Reading Recovery program are encouraged to develop such an understanding, the analytical procedure and certain instructional practices seem to encourage more emphasis on accurate word identification than on reading strategies. They imply that the quantity of miscues is more important than the quality. Also, the child is not necessarily required to read more than 100 to 200 words of the selections chosen to establish reading level, so the reader has insufficient opportunity to get mentally into the text and demonstrate

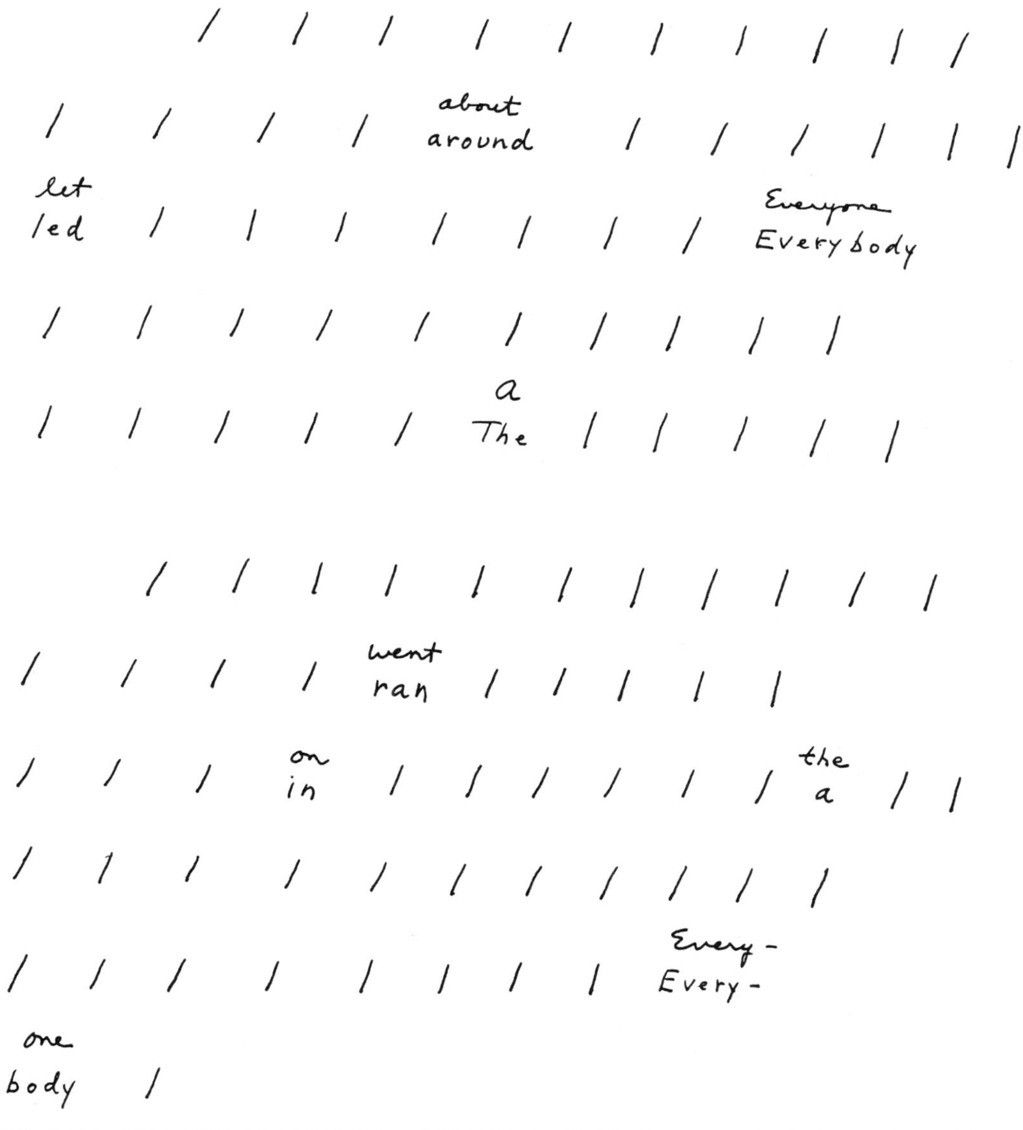

/ / / / / / / / / /

/ / / / about / / / / / /
　　　　　around

let
led / / / / / / / Everyone
　　　　　　　　　　　Everybody

/ / / / / / / / / /

/ / / / / a / / / / /
　　　　　　The

/ / / / / / / / / /

/ / / / went / / / / /
　　　　　ran

/ / / on / / / / / / the / /
　　　　in　　　　　　　　　　　a

/ / / / / / / / / /

/ / / / / / / / Every -
　　　　　　　　　　　Every -

one
body /

FIGURE 6.5　Running record of Anne's miscues

his or her reading strategies and ability at their best (Clay, 1985, p. 17). Thus, there are some important conceptual and philosophical differences between the miscue analysis procedures developed by Kenneth Goodman and his associates (K. S. Goodman, 1965, 1973; Y. M. Goodman, Watson, & Burke, 1987) and the running record procedures that

Marie Clay developed for the Reading Recovery program (Clay, 1979, 1985, 1993). Perhaps the greatest difference is in how proponents of miscue analysis view the miscues they analyze, as opposed to how Clay views and deals with "errors." We may summarize as follows some of the critical differences, including some previously mentioned:

1. Clay counts all *uncorrected* substitutions, omissions, and insertions as "errors." Goodman considers *all* departures from the text as miscues, including those that have been corrected. That way, the reader's self-corrections become part of what is analyzed, leading to insights about reading strategies that can all too easily be lost when self-corrections are excluded from further analysis.

2. Clay counts all uncorrected substitutions, omissions, and insertions—literally. She is concerned with the quantity of a reader's miscues (including the percentage of errors, the percentage of words read accurately, and the percentage of self-corrections), because she wants to base instruction for an emergent reader on texts that the reader can read with 90 percent accuracy. That way, she believes, the text will support the reader in constructing meaning and in self-correcting when an error *is* made. Clay also appears to believe that children should be getting precise messages from books, at least when they are emergent readers dealing with relatively simple text (Clay, 1992). In contrast, the standard miscue procedure does not involve counting miscues, because the reader's use of strategies is considered far more important than the quantity of miscues; indeed miscue researchers have learned to distrust measures of quantity because they can mislead observers into drawing inaccurate inferences about the reader's understanding of the text. Miscue research has demonstrated that readers can effectively construct meaning from text even when they have made numerous miscues (e.g., K. S. Goodman, 1973; K. S. Goodman and Y. M. Goodman, 1978; and much of the research cited in K. S. Goodman and Y. M. Goodman, n. d.).

3. With the exception of self-corrected miscues as mentioned above, what Clay calls "errors" are similar to the miscues that Goodman and others choose for analysis. However, the errors in Clay's system are always viewed as failures in some respect; these errors are counted, and the Reading Recovery teachers helps children develop strategies for getting the exact word. In contrast, the miscues in Goodman's procedure may be considered good miscues because they preserve the essential meaning, or at least partially good miscues because they reflect the use of important reading strategies, like using prior knowledge and context to predict what's coming next. From the perspective of miscue analysis and the supporting body of miscue research, it is inappropriate—even counterproductive—to have the reader try again to get the exact word if the reader's miscue preserves the essential meaning. This is why some miscue forms have had a category of "overcorrection."

4. When having the reader read for a running record in the Reading Recovery program, the child is given the word when he or she stops for a few seconds and seems unwilling to go on; it is considered important to facilitate fluent reading and to encourage the reader by providing such back-up support. When having the reader read for a miscue analysis, on the other hand, it is considered important not to help

the reader, since the intent is to analyze how the reader deals independently with words that aren't immediately recognized on sight.

In short, a running record is not merely a less time-consuming way of doing miscue analysis. Differences in underlying principles are involved.

When Is Miscue Analysis Not Miscue Analysis?

Just as the term "whole language" is bandied about with little understanding of what it means to experienced whole language educators, so the terms "miscue" and "miscue analysis" are used by those with little or no awareness of what concepts the terms were designed to reflect and convey.

At worst, the term "miscue" is used as a synonym for error, with no change in how such errors are viewed. But even when the term is not used so naively, what purports to be miscue analysis does not necessarily reflect the insights into the reading process that have been gleaned through decades of research following in the tradition of Kenneth Goodman and his associates. (For access to this research, see the references in Figure 6.6.)

One flagrant example of the misuse of the term "miscue analysis" occurs in a document outlining some of the procedures for the 1992 National Assessment of Educational Progress—specifically, procedures for the Integrated Reading Performance Record (IRPR) to be used with a subgroup of fourth graders within the larger NAEP assessment (National Assessment of Educational Progress, 1991). According to this document on the IRPR, miscues were to be analyzed for semantic and syntactic appropriateness in context, but they were also to be analyzed for evidence of the use of phonics and sight vocabulary. According to standard miscue analysis procedures, the use of phonics must be assessed *in conjunction with* the use of context. That is, the use of grapho/phonemic cues should not be considered apart from the use of contextual cues, as the IRPR document seems to imply. As for sight words: context may encourage good predictors to make miscues on sight words, so looking for evidence of sight word recognition is inappropriate, given what we know from miscue analysis. In fact, it is usually the best readers who make the most miscues on basic sight words, because they are reading to construct meaning rather than to identify words (K. S. Goodman, 1973).

A fluency score is also to be computed for the IRPR, based on the number of miscues and the total time taken by the student to read the passage. So reading speed and quantity of miscues become important issues—probably more important than the quality of the miscues and the strategies they reflect.

Thus, while the total IRPI may include an analysis of miscues in context, it also includes procedures that are entirely contrary to the intent of miscue analysis: it assesses evidence of the use of sight words without regard to context, and apparently does the same with the use of phonic analysis skills; it emphasizes the quantity of miscues, in computing a fluency score; and it emphasizes reading speed, by computing a fluency score. In short, only a very small part of the IRPI reflects miscue analysis procedures and the assumptions that both underly and emerge from the research by Goodman and his

Emphasis on research

Goodman, K. (1973). *Theoretically based studies of patterns of miscues in oral reading performance.* Detroit: Wayne State University. (Educational Resources Information Center: ED 079 708)

Page. W. D. (Ed.). (1975). *Help for the reading teacher: New directions in research.* Urbana, IL: National Conference on Research in English and the National Council of Teachers of English.

Research into Practice

Allen, P. D., & Watson, D. J. (Eds.). (1976). *Findings of research in miscue analysis: Classroom implications.* Urbana, IL: ERIC Clearinghouse on Reading and Communication Skills and the National Council of Teachers of English.

Goodman, K. (Ed.). (1973). *Miscue analysis: Applications to reading instruction.* Urbana, IL: National Council of Teachers of English.

Procedures for Analysis

Goodman, Y., & Burke, C. L. (1972). *Reading miscue inventory manual: Procedure for diagnosis and evaluation.* New York: Macmillan.

Goodman, Y. M., Watson, D. J., & Burke, C. L. (1987). *Reading miscue inventory: Alternative procedures.* Katonah, NY: Richard C. Owen. (Includes the research procedures originally developed by Kenneth Goodman.)

Annotated Bibliography

Goodman, K., & Goodman, Y. (n.d.). *Annotated miscue bibliography.* Tucson, AZ: Program in Language and Literacy, University of Arizona. (Includes references through 1990.)

FIGURE 6.6   *Basic references on miscue analysis*

associates. For the most part, the term "miscue" is used in ways that are contrary to the philosophy and intent of miscue analysis.

Let the reader beware, then: a "miscue" is not always a miscue, nor is "miscue analysis" necessarily the same as that described here. If alleged miscue analysis procedures reflect the original intent of miscue analysis, they will:

1. By their very nature, reflect the conviction that constructing meaning is more important than reproducing surface detail.
2. Be more concerned with reading strategies than with reading speed, fluency, or accuracy. Many readers are rather proficient at getting meaning, even though they read neither quickly, fluently, or with near accuracy. To label them as deficient and give them skills work rather than real reading is to deprive them of the experience that will most contribute to greater speed, fluency, and accuracy: the experience of reading interesting, coherent, and connected texts.
3. Focus attention on readers' strengths as well as their possible weaknesses. This means that "missing" basic sight words may be a strength, when such miscues

typically fit the context; that not sounding out a difficult word may be evidence of a strength, when the miscue fits the context; and that hesitations and repetitions may be evidence of effective strategies, as the reader tries to deal with upcoming words.

4. Consider miscues only in context, distinguishing between those that are appropriate in context and those that are not. In fact, the procedure might note as overcorrections those miscues that are corrected even though they fit the context and reflect no essential loss of meaning.

5. Provide insight into the reader's strategies, particularly into how well the reader uses context to predict what is coming next and to correct those miscues that do not make sense in context. Thus, the procedure offers a starting point for acknowledging the reader's already effective strategies and strengthening others.

6. Be conducted as part of a more comprehensive analysis that considers not only the reader's ability to reflect upon and discuss the selection read, but the reader's understanding of the reading process, conscious awareness of reading strategies, and other factors that offer insight into the person's reading and the reader as a person.

It is to this kind of comprehensive analysis that we turn in the next section, while emphasizing miscue analysis within a broader analysis of reading.

MISCUE ANALYSIS PROCEDURES: AN INTRODUCTION

Kenneth Goodman inaugurated not only a new way of thinking about reading "errors," but also an insightful way of analyzing them. His Taxonomy of Reading Miscues has been widely used in research. The 1973 version has been readily available in Allen and Watson's *Findings of Research in Miscue Analysis: Classroom Implications* (1976) and is now available in Y. M. Goodman, Watson, and Burke's *Reading Miscue Inventory: Alternative Procedures* (1987). However, this taxonomy is far too complicated for the day-to-day needs of classroom teachers and reading specialists.

To meet the ordinary needs of teacher and specialist, Yetta Goodman and Carolyn Burke prepared a *Reading Miscue Inventory Manual* (1972a), which explains their simpler procedure for analyzing a reader's strengths and weaknesses. In the newer *Reading Miscue Inventory: Alternative Procedures* (Y. Goodman, Watson, and Burke, 1987), the authors offer four procedures for analyzing miscues, the first similar to that in the original *Reading Miscue Inventory Manual* and the others progressively simpler. The discussion below draws heavily on both of these manuals as well as on my own experience. Henceforth, I shall refer to the first of these manuals as the *RMI Manual* and to the second as the *RMI Alternatives.*

Like the authors of the *RMI Alternatives,* I consider the most important use of miscue analysis to be helping teachers gain insight into the reading process. As these authors express it, "Once professionals concerned with reading have developed miscue analysis techniques they will never again listen to readers in the way they did in the past" (Y. M. Goodman, Watson, and Burke, 1987, p. 4). This, then, is my first and primary aim: to help you gain appreciation for reading as a unique transaction between reader and text, to help you learn to perceive the productive reading strategies that often cause readers to make miscues, and to help you understand that there is not always a close correlation between miscues and comprehension. In order to gain such insights, it is important to begin by analyzing miscues in some detail; later, when you have learned to listen to readers in a new way, you can use simpler procedures for analyzing the reading strengths and needs of students with whom you work.

I have written the following sections for the person completely inexperienced in doing miscue analysis. I have also assumed that you will spend considerable time in your initial analyses, not only for what you can learn about the individual reader but for what you can learn about the reading process in general.

It is important to remember that people may read more effectively when they read silently: for many of us, the task of reading aloud interferes with comprehension. However, if we are to determine a reader's strategies for dealing with print by analyzing the reader's miscues, we must have the person read aloud. But collecting and analyzing miscues is only part of the procedure: we also need to have the reader retell what he or she recalls, discuss what seemed important to the reader, make connections with the reader's own life and other texts as appropriate, and reflect upon the experience of reading the text.

This retelling/discussion/reflection provides an important check on our miscue analysis. Some readers are good at reproducing surface structure, but not very good at constructing meaning. Others develop good understanding, even though they have made a number of miscues that did not seem to preserve meaning and that they did not overtly correct. Both the miscues and the retelling are, of course, influenced by the reader's pre-existing schemas as well as by the reader's perception of the situation and the task.

If the reader recalls little of what has been read, it is important to try other alternatives before drawing conclusions about the reader's ability to understand and/or recall written text. You might have the reader assist you in choosing material of greater interest, perhaps, and/or have the reader read silently and then tell you about the selection. In short, it is crucial to give the reader other opportunities to demonstrate his or her reading strengths and ability to construct meaning from text.

Before having a reader read and then engage in retelling, discussion, and reflection, it is valuable to meet with the reader for a reading interview—or, at the very least, to incorporate some of the suggested procedures into your reading and retelling/discussion/reflection session. *Miscue analysis* has evolved into a more complete *reading analysis*, with consideration of miscues being only one major aspect of the analysis. In fact, the following procedures deal with collecting, analyzing, and interpreting much of the data that might be included in a reading/literacy portfolio.

PREPARING FOR AND CONDUCTING SESSIONS

The first step is to conduct a "reading interview" session, which may include significantly more than the reading interview itself. Subsequent steps in the analysis involve eliciting the oral reading and engaging the reader in retelling and discussing the selection and reflecting upon the reading experience.

Preparing for and Conducting the Reading Interview Session

I am assuming (perhaps optimistically) that you will have the opportunity to work twice with the reader you have chosen. This will not only enable you to gather more data, but to glean from the first session information that can help in planning for the second. If some of the suggestions and reminders seem ridiculously simple, please excuse my explicitness. I've found it's often the simplest things that we forget.

The heart of this part of a reading analysis is the reading interview, usually based on questions developed by Carolyn Burke (see below). However, it can be useful to do other things during this session as well. The following are some possibilities. What you need to prepare is implicit in the discussion of what you and the reader might do together.

First, in order to tape-record the session for later playback, be sure you have everything needed: a tape recorder in good working order, fresh batteries (in case you can't plug in the recorder), and one or more tapes, as needed. If you're not already acquainted with the reader, it is a good idea to be sure the reader is comfortable with being tape-recorded before actually beginning your interview and discussion (maybe invite the reader to talk into the tape recorder a bit, and play it back). You can then start this first session by recording basic information: the reader's name, age and grade, what reading and writing are like in school, how the reader feels about reading and writing—in short, whatever general information you don't already have that might be relevant.

It may be helpful to administer a Reading Style Inventory—either one of the forms developed by Marie Carbo, or a shorter questionnaire you devise yourself to determine how the reader reads and/or learns best, and under what circumstances. Reading the questions to or with the reader and asking for explanations may be the best procedure for eliciting true responses and also for helping you understand the reader's responses. At the very least, it may be helpful to find out when, where, and how the reader finds it easiest to read or likes best to read. Perhaps you can take advantage of this information in preparing for your next session. As an example, Figure 6.7 is a form my graduate students developed for use with adults and young adults who have learned English as a second language. Unlike the Carbo Reading Style Inventory, however, this set of items has not been formally validated. On the other hand, *discussing* a few of the issues in Figure 6.7 may be at least as valuable as scoring responses to questions on the RSI.

Then, conduct the reading interview, asking questions you have prepared beforehand, but also being alert to follow up the reader's responses with questions that probe more deeply, whenever appropriate. Your questions might be the same or similar to the following (these are mostly from Burke, 1980, as reported in Chapter 7 of the *RMI Alternatives*):

1. When I read:
     _____ I like to question why characters do what they do
     _____ I never question why characters do what they do
2. When I read:
     _____ it is easy for me to repeat verbally what I read
     _____ it is difficult for me to repeat verbally what I read
3. When I read:
     _____ I prefer to have pictures in stories I read
     _____ I don't care if I have pictures in stories I read
4. As I read a text about a foreign culture:
     _____ I use my imagination to try to understand
     _____ I use my reasoning to try to understand
5. As I learn English, I find:
     _____ lessons on phonics easy
     _____ other aspects of English easier than phonics
6. When I choose an English conversation book, I prefer:
     _____ a book with many illustrative pictures
     _____ a book with logical explanations (or a step-by-step process)
              and no pictures
7. When I study:
     _____ I prefer a quiet room
     _____ I like to listen to the radio or music
8. When I eat dinner I eat:
     _____ dishes I like best, first
     _____ dishes I don't like, first
9. When I am introduced to someone:
     _____ it's easy to remember his or her name
     _____ it's hard to remember his or her name
10. I do something new:
     _____ when people tell me to
     _____ by finding it myself
11. When I prepare for my classes:
     _____ I finish preparing for one class before starting another
     _____ I prepare for many of my classes at the same time
12. When I shop for food or eat:
     _____ I usually pay attention to what ingredients are in the food I eat
     _____ I seldom pay attention to what ingredients are in the food I eat
13. If I kept a diary, I would write:
     _____ many details of what happened each day
     _____ only important things that happened

FIGURE 6.7   *Form used to suggest learning and reading style preferences (*Note: *This form was prepared by ESL teachers for use with ESL adults and young adults. The items were designed to suggest to what extent the person is more analytical or more global in learning style, and which modalities are particularly strong: auditory, visual, tactile, and kinesthetic.)*

14. When I keep track of my expenses:
    _____ I write down every dollar I spend
    _____ I write down approximately what I spend
    _____ actually, I don't keep track of expenses
15. When I go shopping:
    _____ I bargain with the salesperson
    _____ I would never think of bargaining with the salesperson
16. If I were at the beach for a day, I would most enjoy:
    _____ looking at the water, sand, trees, and other scenery
    _____ listening to the sounds of water, the breeze, the people
    _____ feeling the warm sun and soft breezes on my skin and the sand between my toes
    _____ playing on the beach and swimming in the water

FIGURE 6.7   *Continued*

1. "What do you think reading is? That is, what are people actually doing when they read?" Keep rephrasing as necessary, until the reader seems to understand and respond appropriately.
2. To elicit as much information as possible, ask this one in three parts:
    a. "When you are reading and come to something (some word) you don't know, what do you do?"
    b. "What else do you do?"
    c. "What else might you do, or could you do?"
3. "Who is a good reader you know?"
4. "What makes _____ a good reader?"
5. "Do you think _____ ever comes to something he/she doesn't know?"
    If yes, ask, "What do you think _____ might do?"
    If no, ask, "Suppose _____ does come to something he/she doesn't know. What do you think _____ might do?"
6. "If you knew someone was having trouble reading, how would you help that person?"
7. "What would a teacher (your teacher) do to help that person?"
8. "How did you learn to read?"
9. "Do you think you are a good reader?"
    If *yes*, ask why. If *no*, ask why not.
10. "What would you like to do better as a reader?"

In a sense, questions 3 through 7 provide a check on the accuracy of the reader's responses to question 1 about reading itself and question 2 about reading strategies. If time does not permit asking all the questions, you might want to decide ahead of time which ones could be omitted (assuming you have decided to use this set of questions).

Figure 6.8 shows part of a form I devised for generating, recording, and analyzing responses to some of these questions. It was developed for use as a pre/post-test research instrument, but it could be used in other interview or teaching situations as well.

If the person you are working with speaks English as a second or subsequent language, you will surely want to ask other questions relevant to differences in how the person reads English as compared with the native language, particular difficulties the person has in reading English, and so forth. In short, plan your questions to be as appropriate as possible for your particular reader, and then adjust the questions as needed in the interview situation. It is especially important to follow up on the reader's responses by asking questions that probe more deeply, whenever appropriate.

You may want to ask about the person's reading tastes and habits: what kind of books and magazines the reader enjoys, how often and how long he or she reads at home, whether and how often he or she takes books out of the library, whether he or she gets ideas for writing from the books read, and so forth. (Figure 6.8 contains some of these questions.) If desired, you can develop ahead of time a form for eliciting and recording such information, as was done with Figure 6.8.

It may be a good idea to use the interview session to help you decide what reading material to use with the reader during the subsequent reading and retelling/discussion/reflection session. The material should be difficult enough for the reader to make enough miscues for analysis, but of course not so difficult as to be impossible (see further discussion below). If the student is using a basal reader in school, familiarity with that reader may give you some idea of what reading material might be appropriate. If you have available some books of varying difficulty that you think the reader might like, you could have the reader read a page or two of each, just to get an idea of what might be suitable. Remember, however, that whatever the reader reads for the miscue analysis should be something the reader has not read before. Therefore, it would be best not to make a definite decision about the selection during this first session with the reader, or at least not to let the reader know your choice (much less to leave the book in the reader's possession).

Doing a reading interview can help you prepare for the actual reading session in several ways: by giving you some idea of what reading material(s) to use; by cueing you to notice the reader's strategies for dealing with problem words; and by indicating under what circumstances the reader finds it easiest to read (if you did some kind of reading styles inventory or questionnaire, or at least discussed when, where, and how the reader prefers to read).

Preparing for the Reading Session

The miscue analysis procedures recommended below draw significantly upon the *RMI Manual* and the *RMI Alternatives*. When you try these procedure for yourself, you will doubtless have some questions that are not answered by this brief discussion. Do not be afraid to use your own good judgment in deciding what to do. However, it would also be wise to consult someone more experienced in such matters or to consult the *RMI Manual* or the *RMI Alternatives*. Although these resources need not be construed as ultimate authorities, they are based on years of experience with miscue analysis and therefore provide useful guidelines and valuable insights that go considerably beyond what is presented here.

Pre-_____ Post-_____ Interview   Student's name _____

Date _____   Interviewer's name _____

NOTE TO INTERVIEWER: This form is for you to use during the interview, or in listening to the tape recording of the interview. Check all responses that are appropriate, and make notes regarding additional responses. Then complete evaluative scales and tallies.

1. What do you think reading is? That is, what are people actually doing when they read? (Paraphrase in whatever way seems to make sense to the student.)

    Possible responses include:
        Pronouncing the words
        Sounding out words
        Saying the words
        Learning new words
        Saying the words and getting their meaning
        Getting meaning
        Thinking about what it says

    Other responses:

Interviewer's evaluative interpretation:

1	2	3	4	5
Pronouncing the words, saying all the words		Saying the words and getting their meaning		Getting meaning
(word identification)		(words to meaning)		(meaning emphasis; meaning to get words)

FIGURE 6.8   Question and analysis form for reading interview

2. What do you like to read? (What books or magazines specifically, what <u>kinds</u> of books or magazines, etc.)

3. What have you read in the last month, other than schoolwork?

   Specific titles of books: Total number of books: _____

   Specific titles of magazines: Total number of magazines: _____

   Other:

4. How many times have you voluntarily

   Gone to the school library in the past month?   _____
   Gone to the public library in the past month?   _____

   (Interviewer: Of course, what we want to know is how many times the student has gone to the library to look for books, magazines, encyclopedias, etc. — not how many times the student has chosen to use the library just to study or to meet with friends.)

FIGURE 6.8 Continued

5. How do you feel about reading? (Interviewer: elicit separate responses for pleasure reading and for school reading. After eliciting a verbal response, show the student the scales below and ask him or her to circle the most appropriate numbers.)

Response/comments:

Pleasure reading

1	2	3	4	5	6	7	8	9

Hate It   So-so   Love it

School reading

1	2	3	4	5	6	7	8	9

Hate It   So-so   Love it

6. How do you feel about yourself as a reader?

1	2	3	4	5	6	7	8	9

Not very good   So-so   Good   Very Good   Super

Interviewer: Indicate response and elicit <u>explanation</u> for why the person rates himself or herself this way.

FIGURE 6.8   Continued

7. Interviewer: Ask <u>all three</u> of these questions, rewording them as necessary. Please record the actual responses, in abbreviated form if necessary. Then check off the responses on the following lists, add any "other" responses, and, finally, total the different kinds:

a. When you are reading and come to something (some word) you don't know, what do you do?

b. What else do you do?

c. What else might you do, or could you do?

# of strategies in response to: a. _____   b. _____   c. _____   TOTAL strategies offered_____

Word-based strategies:
    (Try to) sound it out
    Look at word parts

Assistance-based strategies:
    Ask someone
    Use a dictionary

Meaning-based and independent strategies:
    Think what it might mean (check this one if you
        can't tell what sources of info. the reader
        would use)
    Use everything I know to get meaning
        (prior knowledge)
    Think what would make sense, given what came
        before (preceding context)
    Reread (prior knowledge, preceding context)
    Look at next word(s) and think what would
        make sense (following context)
    Read on and see if that helps me understand
        the word
    Just keep reading, if I can make sense without
        the word

Other (please decide which category the "other" responses fit into, when totaling the responses below):

Total # of word-based strategies _____   Assistance-based _____   Meaning-based and independent _____

                                                                    TOTAL _____

Figure 6.8 *Continued*

In preparing for the reading session, you will first need to select material appropriate to the individual whose reading strategies you are analyzing. The material must be difficult enough to cause the reader to make miscues, but not so difficult as to cause *extreme* frustration and distress. Keep in mind that you will need to analyze 25 or more *consecutive* miscues, preferably from the same reading selection. Research has demonstrated that the quality of miscues tends to change beyond the first 200 words of text, as the reader begins to get a sense of the developing meaning (Menosky, 1971). Therefore, it is best to collect enough miscues so that you can ignore, for purposes of analysis, the miscues on the early part of the text. This is important in order to be fair to the reader. For your own learning, though, it can be quite valuable to compare the reader's miscues on the introductory parts of the text with the miscues on the middle and the end (see, for example, Betsey's miscues in activity 3 at the end of this chapter).

Generally, a good rule of thumb is to begin with material one grade level above what the reader usually deals with in class. For beginning and/or poorer readers, however, it may be better to choose something only a little beyond what they are presently reading in class. When my students prepare for miscue analysis in an unfamiliar classroom with children they do not know, we sometimes ask the classroom teacher to choose material appropriate for each child, using the guidelines here. If you must choose material for a child you have never met, it may be easiest to choose something further along in the child's basal reader, being sure to avoid something with stilted language that impedes fluent reading. Ideally, it would be best to select materials that you know the individual reader will be interested in and able to read. If time permits, you might invite the reader to join with you in selecting something on the basis of the title and pictures. Again ideally, it is best to have at least two or three selections of different difficulty available for use, because you will need to try another selection if the reader is not making many miscues or if the selection is producing extreme distress. If you use miscue analysis frequently in your own classroom, you might create a collection of materials that can be used for this purpose: perhaps a combination of trade books, authentic stories (unaltered and unabridged stories written by "real" authors) from basal readers, articles, and other appropriate materials.

The passages selected for reading should rarely be less than 500 words; use two or three short selections if absolutely necessary, in order to provide enough text for the reader to make a sufficient number of miscues for analysis. The selections provided with an informal reading inventory are usually too brief to allow the reader to develop the sense of an emerging whole. What's needed is something that is *complete in itself*: a story, a self-contained chapter in a novel or other book, an article or section of a textbook—something that has a sense of wholeness. If you select a story, it should ordinarily have a strong plot (usually centering around some problem or conflict) as well as a theme (an underlying idea). The language should be natural—that is, it should not sound like the stilted, contrived language often found in basal readers. If you select an informational piece, it too should have natural language, and it should involve concepts that are clearly stated and not too complex. *The selection must be entirely new to the reader,* but the content should be something that he or she can understand and relate to. Not surprisingly, miscue research shows that the more personally involved readers become in their reading, the more proficiently they read *(RMI Alternatives,* Chapter 6). *The entire selection must be read in order for the retelling to have much significance.*

Once the text is selected, the materials needed while working with the reader must be gathered and prepared. You will need:

1. A functioning tape recorder, with fresh batteries (in case you can't plug in the recorder), one or more tapes, and a pencil or pen (I recommend a sharp pencil).
2. The material that the student is to read (see above). The reader should read from the original printed material (book, or whatever).
3. Your own copy of the selection(s) for marking the reader's miscues. It is a good idea to have this copy ready in advance of the reading session, so that you can make notes concerning any behavior that will not be apparent from the tape recording. If there is enough room to write between the lines of the original text, you can simply make a photocopy for your own use—or you may be able to enlarge the text on a photocopier, to obtain enough room between lines. Otherwise, you will need to prepare a typed copy for marking the reader's miscues. This typed copy should be double- or triple-spaced, so that there is enough room to indicate the reader's miscues above the lines. *Be sure to retain the line divisions of the original*, and indicate all page divisions. Be careful to be completely accurate in retyping the selection.
4. Notes on the selection, to use in asking questions to elicit more of what the reader recalls, after you have encouraged him or her to tell you about the selection without specific prompting.

   With regard to this fourth item, I suggest that you first read the selection aloud yourself and jot down what you recall. For example, if the selection is a story, jot down what seems important about the characters, events and plot, theme, and perhaps setting. If possible, have someone else do the same and compare notes, so that you get not only a sense of what might be centrally important in the story but also a sense of how idiosyncratic we are in deciding what's important. If you and a group of people did this with regard to the "Petronella" story (in the appendix at the end of this book) as one of the activities in Chapter 1, you should already have a strong appreciation of the fact that what a reader comprehends and recalls is very much affected by the reader's prior knowledge, beliefs, thoughts, emotions, and feelings—including, in the case of reading assessment, the reader's feelings about the situation, the assessor, the task, and the reader's perception of his or her ability to succeed in the assessment task.

   Keeping all of this in mind, be judicious in your selection of what you think the reader "should" remember about the selection. Because it is easy to forget everything you planned to ask about, you should prepare careful notes on the selection(s) you have chosen. If it is a story, for example, prepare an outline or list dealing with characters, events, plot, theme, and perhaps setting:

   • *Characters:* Which characters might the reader reasonably be expected to recall? What might the reader be likely to remember about each of these characters? This could include such aspects as physical appearance (particularly if important to the plot), attitudes and feelings, behavior, relationship with other characters, problems or conflicts, and so forth.

- *Events:* What events might the reader reasonably be expected to recall? What should the reader remember about the sequence of events?
- *Plot:* What might the reader reasonably be expected to tell about the central conflict or problem of the story?
- *Theme:* If there seems to be a theme, an underlying idea, what might be some alternative ways of expressing it?
- *Setting:* If the setting is important to the story, what might the reader reasonably be expected to tell about the setting?

It is also wise to note along with your outline the kinds of questions you might ask to elicit more information from the reader (see pp. 247–248).

5. In addition to the supplies, the text, and the notes on the selection, several types of questions need to be prepared:
   a. Questions you can ask to elicit the reader's responses to the story. Here are some possibilities:

   How did you feel when . . .?
   Why do you think so-and-so did such-and-such? Would you have done that? Why (or why not)?
   Have you ever been in a similar situation? What did you do?
   Do you think the story ended the way it should? Why (or why not)? If not, how would you have ended it?
   Does this story remind you of anything else you've ever read? Why? How?
   Did you like this story? Why (or why not)?

   b. Questions designed to stimulate further thinking about the story and related issues: specifically, to stimulate what Piaget called "formal operational thought." Such questions are appropriate for virtually all elementary-level children as well as for older students:

   > Questions that invite readers to think about abstract ideas and concepts, and to apply such concepts to their reading (What is a true friend? Do you think so-and-so was being a true friend when he or she . . . ? Why/why not?)
   >
   > Questions that invite readers to reason hypothetically (If so-and-so had done this, then what might have happened?)
   >
   > Questions that invite readers to systematically consider multiple causes/ explanations/factors and weigh their relative importance (You said you think there are three reasons why so-and-so did such-and-such. Which reason seems most important to you? Why?)

   Obviously some questions of this nature will have to be developed in response to what the reader has said about the story, but some advance planning can certainly be done.

   c. If you are not doing a separate reading interview session, a list of questions to elicit the reader's views about reading and about himself or herself as a reader (see the list of questions on p. 237. The reading interview is an important part of the overall reading analysis, critical for understanding the reader's concept of reading, conscious awareness of reading strategies, and self-concept as a reader.

Conducting the Reading and Retelling Session

Once you have collected all the aforementioned materials, you are ready to conduct the session. Here are some guidelines:

1. If you have not done so in a previous reading interview session, it may be helpful to let the reader briefly talk into the tape recorder and then play it back, to minimize any concern about being recorded. You might invite the reader to state his or her name and add other identifying information, such as the name of the teacher and the school, the reader's age and grade, and the date. Explain that you will be recording the entire session.
2. If you haven't previously conducted a reading interview with this reader, and you are sure you will still have enough time for the reading and the retelling/discussion/ reflection, you might begin by asking the reader some or all of the interview questions you have chosen or developed. Alternatively, you could save such questions until the end, or ask some now and some later.
3. Tell the reader that he or she is expected to read the *entire* selection aloud and that it is important to try to understand the material being read, because afterwards you will ask the reader to pretend you've never read the selection and to tell you all about it. You might encourage the reader to flip through the pages of the text to get some idea of the length of the selection.
4. Tell the reader that when encountering a problem word, the reader should do whatever he or she usually does in such situations when there's no one around to help. You might explain that the reason you can't help is that you're trying to find out what readers do when they must solve reading problems for themselves.
5. If the reader stops over a problem word, wait . . . and wait some more. If necessary, remind the reader to do whatever he or she would ordinarily do when reading alone, and reassure the reader that anything he or she chooses to do is all right.
6. Stop the reader if he or she is making scarcely any miscues, and turn to a more challenging selection. Do not, however, be quick to stop a reader who is having difficulty: numerous miscues, hesitations, long pauses, and repetitions are not in themselves sufficient justification for deciding that the selection is too difficult. In fact, readers may often surprise themselves (and everyone else) by gleaning substantial meaning from a text that seems too difficult.
7. While the reader is reading, you may want to write some notes on your copy of the selection(s) and/or, if appropriate, on another sheet of paper. It may help to face the reader so you can more easily hear and jot down what you might not be able to hear on the tape later, or to note significant aspects of the situation and the reader's nonverbal behavior that seem particularly important. Usually a reader becomes oblivious to such brief jottings. On the other hand, I personally do not like to write

the miscues on the worksheet while I'm listening; I think this can make a reader uneasy. Both during the session and later in marking the worksheet and the coding sheet, be sure to use *pencil*. You'll need to be able to erase and revise.

8. Follow the guidelines below in conducting the retelling/discussion/reflection part of the session.
9. Ask any remaining reading interview questions.
10. Remember to end by making the reader feel good about himself or herself.

Guiding the Retelling, Discussion, and Reflection

After the reader has finished the selection, ask the reader to close the book, pretend you've never read the selection, and tell you everything he or she can about it. *It is important that you not interrupt or ask any questions during this initial retelling.*

Some readers will tell you absolutely everything about what they have read. Others will volunteer very little, even though they may remember a great deal. This is why you should be prepared to ask questions that will encourage the reader to expand upon the retelling. As you listen to the unaided retelling, you can check off mentioned items on your notes or outline, provided you do so unobtrusively. Then, when the reader has finished the unaided retelling, you can ask questions. Here are some useful guidelines:

1. During the retelling session, be careful not to respond in such a way as to confirm or disconfirm the accuracy of what the reader is saying. Just be friendly and encouraging.
2. In formulating your questions, be sure to retain any mispronunciations or name changes that the reader used. At the end of the retelling session, you can ask about such words: for example, if the reader said "typeical baby" for *typical baby,* you can ask "What is a 'typeical baby,' anyway?"
3. In asking questions, be careful not to supply any information that the reader has not already given you. And try not to suggest insights that the reader has not acquired independently.
4. Avoid questions that the reader can answer with a simple yes or no. Instead, use questions that begin with the so-called "wh" words. Often, you can introduce these questions by referring to information the reader has already given you, as do the following examples keyed to the basic elements of a story:

Characters:
   What else can you tell me about so-and-so?
   Who else was in the story besides the characters you've mentioned?

Events:
   What else happened in the story?
   What happened after such-and-such?
   Where/when did such-and-such happen?
   How did such-and-such happen?

Plot:
  Why do you think such-and-such happened?
  What was so-and-so's main problem?

Theme:
  How did you feel when such-and-such happened?
  What do you think the author might have been trying to tell us in this story?

Setting:
  Where/when did the story take place?
  How was this important to the story?

It is important to focus your questions on crucial aspects of the story, not on relatively insignificant details. Remember, too, that there may be legitimate differences of opinion as to what is important in the story. On the other hand, try not to accept "I don't know" as an answer. If you think the matter is important, try to rephrase the question to get at the information in another way.

5. If the reader can tell you almost nothing about the selection, it is best to try the reading again. First, ask the reader why he or she remembered so little. Depending upon time and circumstances, you might then:

Invite the reader to reread the selection silently, and again tell you about the selection, before proceeding.

Switch to a less difficult or more motivating reading selection.

Try a different kind of text. (For example, if the reader was reading textbook material, try a story instead.)

6. Ask questions that elicit the reader's responses to the story. See item 5 in "Preparing for the Reading Session" above for some possibilities, which you should have considered ahead of time. However, it is equally important to ask questions that build upon what the reader actually says about the story.

7. Ask questions to stimulate further thinking about the story and related issues, as appropriate. Again, see item 5 in "Preparing for the Reading Session."

8. Ask questions directly related to the reading event, particularly questions that encourage the reader to reflect upon his or her reading (most of the following suggestions are from the *RMI Alternatives*, p. 48):

Overall, how did the reading go for you?
  Where did it go well?
  Where did you have trouble?
  (Together, you can reconsider the text, discuss the problem and strategies the reader used, consider other possibilities—in short, do whatever is appropriate, making this a learning experience for your reader as well as for you.)

Do you know what this word means now?

Remember when you said the kid was a "typeical baby"? What is a "typeical baby"? (Ask about key words that were mispronounced or otherwise miscued, to see if the reader grasped the concept despite the miscue.)

Is there anything you'd like to ask me about this story (article, or whatever)?

Other questions should occur to you in response to the individual's reading. Time permitting, you might play back the tape of a particular portion of the reading and discuss it with the reader.

TRANSCRIBING, ANALYZING, AND INTERPRETING THE MISCUE DATA

Because it's easiest to consider, this section begins by discussing ways of re-recording and then considering the data from the reading interview session and from the reading, retelling, and discussion. We then turn to miscue analysis.

Analyzing and Evaluating the Reading Interview and the Retelling, Discussion, and Reflection

You will need to replay the tape repeatedly, in order to make thorough notes on the reading interview (and related data) as well as on the reader's retelling, discussion, and reflection (sometimes described simply as the "retelling"). Depending on your purposes, you might begin by preparing a verbatim transcript of the reading interview itself, and the retelling part of the session. That is, you might write, in dialogue format, exactly what each of you said in turn.

You can use the form in Figure 6.7 to analyze some of the data from the reading interview, but most crucial will be comparing this information with data obtained from the miscue analysis and your transcript of the reading and retelling/discussion/reflection.

As you prepare to evaluate the reader's retelling of the selection and responses to your questions, remember that a retelling can *never* adequately reflect a reader's understanding of a text, and that the story the reader has created will *never* be exactly the same as the one you have created. Something else to consider is the possibility that remembering a lot of details may be a sign that the reader is reading more to meet the typical demands of school and tests than to understand or appreciate the selection read. This is why, to get away from this focus on minutiae, I have recommended above that you ask questions only about "important" information and that you ask questions designed to elicit the reader's personal and critical response to the selection.

One way to evaluate the retelling is to assign a predetermined number of points to various aspects of the selection and then evaluate the retelling accordingly. In the original *RMI Manual*, Goodman and Burke recommended assigning 30 points to character recall and development; 30 points to events; 20 to plot; and 20 to theme (p. 24). In the newer *RMI Alternatives*, the authors recommend focusing just on character (40 points) and events (60 points), without attending to plot, to theme, or—as I have suggested—to setting. You yourself will have to decide what seems appropriate, based on the particular story you have used. It's also possible that after using a selection once or twice, you will reconsider what is appropriate for a reader to recall.

I find in my own assessment of retellings (and of essay exams) that if I rigidly determine point values in advance of receiving students' work, I inevitably end up with scores that contradict my experienced professional judgment: more often than not, such predetermined point values leave no opportunity to appreciate and reward the unique insights of the individual and thus underestimate the individual's knowledge. Therefore, I tend to favor a holistic scoring procedure. As subjective as it may appear, I am convinced that, with experience, teachers can actually make fairer and in some respects more objective assessments this way. In the new *RMI Alternatives*, Yetta Goodman, Watson, and Burke also recommend a holistic scoring procedure for all but the first of their four miscue analysis procedures. They suggest using either an even-numbered scale (such as 1–4) so that there will be no average category, or an odd-numbered scale (such as 1–5) in order to provide a midpoint. In *Psycholinguistics and Reading* (1980), I suggested an odd-numbered, seven-point scale:

1	2	3	4	5	6	7
poor		adequate		good		excellent

Notice that "adequate" is not the midpoint, as might have been expected. My labeling of the scale thus encourages finer distinctions at the upper end of the range. In my opinion, a holistic scoring procedure such as this is preferable to a more rigid one, because it is more in line with our understanding that reading is a unique transaction between a reader and a text. Assigning a certain number of points to various aspects of a selection tends more to reflect the notion that everyone should remember and understand a text in exactly the same way.

With experience, I think you will find that such a holistic evaluation procedure may actually produce more consistent and more comparable results as you compare one reader with others or as you compare one reader with himself or herself at different times and/or on different kinds of reading materials.

Some reminders may be in order. Unfortunately, some readers will do less well than others at retelling and discussing a story, simply because they have rarely been encouraged to engage in this kind of response. Some readers may understand a selection well, yet do a relatively poor job of retelling the material, simply because they see no need to retell it. As my son used to say, "I know what it's about and so do you, so why do I need to tell you?" Other readers may do relatively poorly with a reading selection simply because they are not interested in it, or because the concepts are too difficult, despite one's best intentions in selecting materials. In that case, a reassessment with different material is in order. Some readers comprehend relatively little when they read aloud, yet comprehend well when reading silently. For such readers, the oral reading session is still important, because it offers insight into the reader's strategies. But if the subsequent retelling is less successful than the reading led you to expect, you should assess the reader's comprehension after silent reading as well (see p. 248, item 5 for suggestions).

Data from the retelling/discussion/reflection will of course need to be compared with data from the reading interview session and the miscue analysis. Each kind of data may help in understanding, or assessing the significance of, the other kinds of data.

Preparing the Miscue Worksheet

Before you can analyze or evaluate the reader's miscues, you must of course mark them on your copy of the selection(s) read; this copy is known as the *worksheet.* When the reader has said a nonword, or "nonsense" word, you should use as much of the spelling of the original as possible in representing the reader's pronunciation. Suppose, for example, that the text word is *psychology,* and the reader has said /SI - ko' - lo' - gi/. Write this as *psykology,* not as *sikology.* If the text word is *wrapped* and the reader has said /rāpt/, write the word as *wrăpped* or *wrāped,* not as *răpt* or *rāped.*

The following examples indicate the markings most commonly used in miscue analysis:

- *Substitution*   "Blow your nose ~~into~~ the Kleenex." *(with)*

(The substitution is simply written over the text.)

- *Omission*   "I will make you some (hot) tea."

Sometimes intonation suggests that the reader realizes he or she is uttering only part of a word. On the worksheet, use a hyphen to indicate what seems to be a partial word. Later it will be coded as an omission because usually the partial does not provide enough information for us to answer questions about it. Thus you might want to circle the partial to remind you to code it as an omission, as follows:

- *Partial*   With these (reservations) out of the way . . . *(re-)*

- *Insertion*   "You should just suck cough drops." *(on ʌ)*

- *Reversal*   "No, no," Boris⌐said.

- *Correction*   I first saw Claribel ⌐when I was working in my office. *(© saw)*

(The underlining attached to the © indicates what part of the text was repeated as the reader made the correction.)

- *Unsuccessful attempt at correction*

His mother . . . scrubbed and⌐pounded the clothes . . . *(uc) 2 putty / 1 pondy*

• *Abandoning a correct response*   He left home to make his <u>future</u> fortune.

(The reader first said "his fortune," then abandoned this response and said "his future.")

• *Repeating*   <u>"Why don't you do</u> my work some day?"

(When the reader repeats a word or phrase not for the purpose of correcting but apparently for the purpose of reflecting or of getting a running start on what comes next, this can be marked as above, with underlining to indicate what part was repeated.)

• *Pausing*   The Mayor said, "I will ask Mr. Pine . . ." [margin mark: *mother*]

(When the reader pauses significantly, this can be indicated with a P whose tail is inserted where the pause occurred.)

Notice that in many if not most instances, repeating and pausing can be considered *strategies* rather than miscues per se. That is, they are typically strategies for trying to resolve difficulties.

The last four markings are sometimes considered optional, and in fact have usually not been used in the examples in this text. If other symbols are needed, you can devise your own (but provide a key to the symbols if someone else will be reading your analysis). For unusual kinds of miscues, sometimes it is easiest just to write brief explanations in the margins. You might also consult the original *RMI Manual* or the newer *RMI Alternatives*. (Three of the above examples are from Chapter 3 of the latter; one, previously cited, is from Y. M. Goodman and Burke, 1972b.)

Once you have marked the miscues on your copy of the reading selection, it is time to number the miscues that are to be analyzed. As noted before, if you have collected more than 25 miscues, it is usually a good idea to discard the miscues on approximately the first 200 words of text (if, of course, this leaves at least 25 miscues). In most cases, 25 consecutive miscues will provide a representative sample of the reader's strategies. Rarely is it necessary to code more than 50 miscues, except perhaps for research.

The following procedures are recommended in numbering the miscues for analysis:

1. If the reader omits most or all of a line of text (or more), you need not number the miscue for later analysis, though you should make note of such omissions, if they occur at all frequently. Or you may code the omission as a single, complex miscue (see item 5 below).
2. Ordinarily, it is not considered necessary to number and analyze miscues that merely reflect the sound system of a reader's dialect or the reader's native language, or the

fact that English has some sounds not part of the reader's native language. For example, if a reader normally says "hep" for *help* or "picher" for *picture,* miscues such as these should not be coded. Nor should miscues like "dis" for *this* or "herro" for *hello*, when they reflect a different dialect or language pattern. On the other hand, miscues that reflect the reader's own grammatical or semantic system are ordinarily coded and analyzed, but considered completely acceptable: "We was" for *We were,* for example, or "quarter of nine" for *quarter till nine.* The same is true for miscues that occur because the reader has not completely mastered the grammatical system of English, such as "He want it" for *He wanted it* or "He was amazed to found it" for *He was amazed to find it.* (See the next section on analyzing miscues.)

3. Do not consider a partial attempt at a word as a miscue to be numbered and analyzed, if the partial is corrected. For example, if the text says *psychology* and the reader says "psy-" and then "psychology," mark it on the worksheet but don't number it for coding. On the other hand, if a partial word is not corrected, code it as an omission, since a partial word ordinarily provides too little information to make coding decisions about how it fits with context.

4. If a reader more than once makes *exactly the same substitution* for a *content* word, number and analyze only the first occurrence. The implication is that each *new* substitution for a content word, and each substitution for a function word (new or not) should be coded. However, there are times when this should not be done. For example: In reading *A Camel in the Sea,* Betsey (activity 3 at the end of this chapter) made so many miscues on the proper names that listing each new pronunciation would mean that a large percentage of the 25 coded miscues would be miscues on proper names. Since this would give a very distorted picture of Betsey's miscues and reading strategies, I chose not to number the various substitutions for names. Such repeated attempts should be noted at the bottom of the worksheet, however, or on a separate sheet.

5. If one particular miscue seems to have caused one or more others, it may be best to consider them together as a single complex miscue. Here is one possible example, from Jay's miscues:

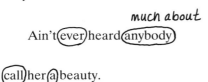

Ain't (ever) heard (anybody)

(call) her (a) beauty.

Instead of three omissions and one insertion, we might consider this to be one longer substitution miscue: "much about her beauty," instead of *anybody call her a beauty.* On the other hand, it can be reasonably argued that coding these as one complex miscue obscures rather than highlights the fact that additional miscues may result from readers accommodating following text to previous miscues, as in this example. For the latter reason, I have chosen to code this as three separate miscues, though it is defensible to code them as one complex miscue (as explained in Weaver, 1988).

As you become more experienced at analyzing reading miscues, you will probably add some other guidelines for determining how miscues should be selected and numbered for analysis.

Analyzing the Miscues

When you prepare to analyze the miscues, again keep in mind that you bring your own schemas to your reading of the text as well as to your analysis and evaluation of the reader's miscues. The meaning is not in the text but rather is created by each reader uniquely. Thus, "it is best to avoid the common sense notion that what the reader was supposed to have read was printed in the text" *(RMI Alternatives,* Chapter 4). If this seems appallingly subjective, remember that machine-scored standardized tests only *appear* to provide an objective measure of students' reading ability. As a test taker, I'd rather have a human being subjectively trying to understand my subjective responses than a computer providing a numerical score without any ability to analyze or understand what good reasons I might have had for doing what I did.

Before analyzing and coding the miscues, it helps to read the completed worksheet once or twice, reproducing all the miscues made by the reader. This should give you a better feel for the reader's strategies. Then you are ready to transfer the miscue data to the coding form. This form can be simple or complex, depending on the kinds of information you want to obtain. The form in Figure 6.9 is somewhere in between: simple enough to be used by teachers, but thorough enough to help you gain a better understanding of the reading process and to suggest various kinds of instructional help that readers might need.

For each miscue numbered for analysis, you first need to indicate what the text itself said, and what the reader said. This information should be entered in the "Text" and "Reader" columns, respectively. Then, ask the following questions for each miscue. *Keep in mind that if the miscue is grammatically and semantically appropriate for the reader's dialect or simply reflects imperfect mastery of the grammar of English, it should be coded as entirely acceptable* (checked under *yes* in columns 1, 2, 3, and 5).

0. *Was the miscue dialect-related or related to the reader's speaking English as a second or subsequent language?* We have noted previously that if a miscue simply reflects a different sound system in the reader's dialect or native language, it is ordinarily not listed on the coding sheet at all. But if it reflects a grammatical pattern common in the reader's dialect, or reflects imperfect mastery of the grammar of English because the person does not speak English natively, the miscue is noted on the coding form *but coded as completely acceptable in columns 1, 2, 3, and 5.* If there are many such miscues in your sample, you will need to code more than 25 miscues in order to gain insights into the reader's strategies. Some of the most common of the ESL-related grammatical miscues are the omission of inflectional endings ("he go" for *he goes,* "he walk" for *he walked*), the use of an inflectional ending in a verbal where none is needed ("he wanted to goed"), the inappropriate omission or use of

Reader's name _____

Date _____

Reading Selection _____

Text	Reader	0 Was the Miscue Dialect-Related or ESL-Related?		1 Did the Miscue Go with the Preceding Context?			2 Did the Miscue Go with the Following Context?			3a Was the Essential Meaning of the *Sentence* Left Intact?		3b Was the Essential Meaning of the *Selection* Left Intact?		4 Was the Miscue Corrected?		5 (cols. 3a & 4) Was the Miscue Either Meaning-Preserving or Corrected?	
		Yes	No	Yes	Partially	No	Yes	Partially	No	Yes	No	Yes	No	Yes	No	Yes	No
1.																	
2.																	
3.																	
4.																	
5.																	
6.																	
7.																	
8.																	
9.																	
10.																	
11.																	
12.																	
13.																	
14.																	
15.																	
16.																	
17.																	
18.																	
19.																	
20.																	
21.																	
22.																	
23.																	
24.																	
25.																	
Totals																	
Percents																	

FIGURE 6.9 *Miscue analysis form (From Constance Weaver, Reading Process and Practice: From Socio-Psycholinguistics to Whole Language, 2nd ed. Heinemann, 1994. © 1994 by Constance Weaver. May be reproduced for use.)*

articles (*a, an,* and *the*), or inappropriate use of one preposition for another ("at" for *in,* for example).

1. *Did the miscue go with the preceding context?* If the answer is a simple yes, put a check in the "yes" column. *Consider the miscue acceptable with preceding context if it resulted in a meaningful sequence of words, up to and including the miscue—even if the meaning is clearly changed.* Questions 3a and 3b ask us specifically to look at whether or not the miscue significantly changes or affects the meaning of the sentence or the selection, but questions 1 and 2 are designed to give credit for meaningful sentences, even if that meaning appears not to be the same meaning. If the miscue fits with the preceding grammar but not with the preceding meaning (or vice versa), put a check in the column labeled "partially;" then add a *G* to indicate that it fits with the grammar, or an *M* to indicate that it fits with meaning. If the miscue was not at all acceptable with preceding context, put a check in the "no" column. In trying to decide whether the miscue fits with the preceding context, read the preceding part of the sentence the way it finally ended up, perhaps with some miscues uncorrected but others corrected.

2. *Did the miscue go with the following context?* Follow essentially the same procedure as explained immediately above, but this time examine only the miscue and what immediately follows it in the sentence.

3a. *Was the essential meaning of the sentence left intact?* This is clearly the most subjective of the questions. Some teachers steeped in the notion that good reading must be word-perfect reading want to code *any* departure from the text as changing essential meaning. However, this is contrary to the whole purpose and spirit of miscue analysis. If only part of the essential meaning seems to be lost, or if you honestly cannot decide, you can put a check on the line between "yes" and "no." Otherwise, check either "yes" or "no." This column helps us draw inferences about the reader's ability to construct meaning at the sentence level, with the particular text in question.

3b. *Was the essential meaning of the selection left intact?* Particularly with stories, it is rare that a single miscue disrupts the essential meaning of the entire reading selection. If you are convinced it does, check "no," indicating that the meaning was not left intact, or put a check on the vertical line between columns, indicating indeterminacy or uncertainty. Otherwise, check "yes." Most people find that all or almost all of the reader's miscues receive a "yes" in this column. Why bother including it, then? Because teachers just beginning to understand miscues and miscue analysis can learn a lot about reading by considering how unimportant each individual miscue often is, at the story or whole-text level. Concomitantly, the results in column 3b may give you a greater appreciation for some readers' ability to grasp the essential meaning of a text despite numerous miscues that seem not to preserve the meaning of individual sentences.

4. *Was the miscue corrected?* If so, put a check in the "yes" column. If not, put a check under "no." If you marked unsuccessful attempts at correction on the coding sheet, you might want to put a check on the borderline between the two columns, indicating that the reader at least attempted to correct.

5. *Was the miscue either meaning-preserving at the sentence level, or else corrected?* The point here is that if the miscue preserved essential meaning at the sentence level (column 3a), there was no need for the miscue to be corrected. On the other hand, if the miscue didn't preserve meaning but was corrected (column 4), that too means that ultimately the miscue reflected no essential loss of meaning. In other words, check "yes" in column 5 if the miscue received a "yes" in either column 3a or 4; otherwise, check the "no" column. (If you marked some miscues as partially acceptable in column 3a, you can again check them on the borderline between "yes" and "no" in column 5, unless they were corrected; in that case, they automatically receive a "yes" in column 5.) In effect, the "yes" column here indicates which miscues initially or ultimately resulted in *no significant loss of comprehension* at the sentence level.

Interpreting the Miscue Data

Once you have answered the preceding questions for each miscue, calculate the percentage of responses for each column. If you have coded 25 miscues in the column, simply count the number of checks and multiply by 4 to obtain the percentage.

To interpret the miscue data, it is crucial to consider it in a larger perspective. For example, *how frequent are the miscues?* If the reader has miscued relatively infrequently, then even a preponderance of miscues showing a loss of comprehension ("no" in column 5) may be of little concern. On the other hand, frequent miscues may occasionally cause a loss of comprehension even if they reflect good reading strategies; for example, the reader may have difficulty constructing meaning because of struggling too much with individual words. (However, this happens much less commonly than most people think; many readers comprehend well despite numerous miscues.) Thus, the score in column 5 might not reflect the reader's actual comprehension of the selection so much as the reader's strategies for constructing ongoing comprehension at the sentence level.

Though we can reasonably draw inferences about reading strategies from the miscues alone, we can draw only tentative inferences about comprehension until we have also considered another question: *How does the miscue analysis compare with the retelling and discussion?* Again, if the retelling and discussion have been excellent, there may be little reason to be concerned about a preponderance of miscues that seem to show a loss of comprehension. Or if the retelling has been poor despite few miscues, further investigation of the reader's ability to comprehend is needed. Does the reader simply need a selection that relates more to his or her interests or prior knowledge? Does the reader comprehend well when reading silently? We would do the reader a grave injustice by not investigating further.

Remembering that the miscues do not tell the whole story, then, it may be helpful to know that proficient readers usually produce miscues that are semantically and syntactically acceptable with the preceding and following context at least 70 percent of the time. When they do produce miscues that reflect a loss of meaning, most proficient readers will correct these, most of the time (at least silently)—especially if they consider the miscue significant to the evolving meaning. On the other hand, substantially less proficient readers may produce contextually acceptable miscues as infrequently as 30 to 40 percent of the time (K. S. Goodman, 1973). Thus, keeping in mind that the miscue data cannot stand alone, we can tentatively suggest the following interpretations, keyed to the questions on the miscue form in Figure 6.9:

0. *Was the miscue dialect-related or related to the reader's speaking English as a second or subsequent language?* While the responses here may be of considerable interest, their significance lies mainly in their effect on coding questions 1, 2, 3, and 5.

1. *Did the miscue go with the preceding context?* If fewer than 60 percent of the reader's miscues rated a "yes" answer to this question, that probably means that the reader is making inadequate use of preceding grammar and/or meaning to *predict* what is coming next. If in the "partially" column you put *G* for miscues that went only with the preceding grammar and *M* for miscues that went only with the preceding meaning, this should give you additional insight into the reader's strategies. Often, readers are much better at predicting a word that fits with the preceding grammar than at predicting a word that fits with the preceding meaning.

2. *Did the miscue go with the following context?* If fewer than 60 percent of the reader's miscues rated a "yes" answer *and if most of these miscues were left uncorrected* (see column 4), this may mean that the reader is making inadequate use of following context to *confirm/correct* his or her predictions and sampling of the text (assuming that the text is appropriate to the reader's understanding). However, readers rarely correct more than 35 percent of their miscues. Remember, too, that some readers tend to correct silently, so that failure to correct disruptive miscues may not adequately reflect the reader's correction, much less his or her actual comprehension.

3. *Was the essential meaning of the sentence left intact?* Again, if fewer than 60 percent of the reader's miscues rated a "yes" and *if most of these miscues were left uncorrected* (see column 4), this may mean that the reader is making inadequate use of context, perhaps both preceding and following context (compare with columns 1 and 2).

3b. *Was the essential meaning of the selection left intact?* This will usually be the case. The major purpose of asking this question is to help teachers understand that miscues don't necessarily disrupt meaning significantly. However, it can be very interesting to compare the typical "yes" responses in this column with the reader's actual understanding, as determined through the retelling and discussion. The two do not necessarily correlate.

4. *Was the miscue corrected?* If fewer than 30 percent of the miscues were corrected, this may be a matter for concern, *unless most of these uncorrected miscues preserved essential meaning (or were corrected silently).*

5. *Was the miscue either meaning-preserving at the sentence level, or else corrected?* Again, if fewer than 60 percent of the miscues rated a "yes" response, this may be a matter for concern—but again, it depends upon the retelling.

It is crucial to remember that what might seem a matter for concern when examining the miscue data in isolation may turn out to be relatively inconsequential when considering this data in light of the reader's ability to retell and discuss the selection (or conversely).

Responses to the miscue questions indicate how well the reader is using prior knowledge and preceding context to predict, how well the reader is using following context to confirm and (if necessary) correct, and how well the reader is succeeding in retaining the essential meaning of the text. By looking particularly at the reader's use of grammar (syntax) and meaning (semantics), two of the three major kinds of language cues, we gain insight into certain reading strategies: the strategies of predicting, monitoring to be sure that what's read sounds like language and makes sense, and correcting whatever doesn't. Such analysis helps us determine whether or not the reader might benefit from assistance in becoming more aware of these strategies and trying to use them.

MISCUE ANALYSIS IN ACTION: TWO EXAMPLES

Miscue analysis is an invaluable way of determining a reader's use of language cues and reading strategies. But—yes, the point bears repeating—we must remember that miscue analysis does not give us a complete or necessarily accurate picture of a reader's ability to comprehend what he or she reads. A miscue analysis must be balanced by a more direct measure of comprehension: an analysis of the reader's ability to remember and discuss what has been read. We need both the *comprehending score* (the percentage of miscues that show no loss of comprehension) and the *comprehension score* (as determined from an analysis of the retelling), or more subjectively phrased conclusions from both.

This need for balance should be kept in mind, though in this section we are examining only the miscues of two readers, Jay and Tony. In both cases, we have fewer than 25 miscues in the available sample, and no detailed retelling data. Unfortunately, I let the retelling transcripts slip through my hands at a time when I did not yet fully appreciate the importance of the retelling. However, the miscues of Jay and Tony are still some of the most interesting and illuminating that I have (especially in relatively short excerpts from a text). Thus, as so often in everyday experience, we will make do with what we have.

Analyzing Jay's Miscues

Let us begin by looking once again at Jay's miscues on the passage from "Jimmy Hayes and Muriel" (see Chapter 4).

①
around
After a hearty supper Hayes joined the smokers about

at all②
the fire. His appearance did not settle all the questions in
∧

the minds of his brother rangers. They saw ③ simply a loose,

© young ④

lank youth with tow-colored sunburned hair and a berry-

ingenious ⑤

brown, ingenuous face that wore a quizzical, good-natured

smile.

"Fellows," said the new ranger, "I'm goin' to interduce

⑥ much about ⑦

you to a lady friend of mine. Ain't ever heard anybody

⑧ ⑨ a ⑩

call her a beauty, but you'll all admit she's got some fine

points about her. Come along, Muriel!"

© ⑪

He held open the front of his blue flannel shirt. Out of

⑫ toad ⑬

it crawled a horned frog. A bright red ribbon was tied

the ⑭

jauntily around its spiky neck. It crawled to its owner's

it ⑮

knee and sat there motionless.

⑯ 's

"This here Muriel," said Hayes, with an oratorical wave

⑰ o she's ⑱

of his hand, "has got qualities. She never talks back, she

⑲

always stays at home, and she's satisfied with one red

dress for everyday and Sunday, too."

d ⑳

"Look at that blame insect!" said one of the rangers

toads ㉑

with a grin. "I've seen plenty of them horny frogs, but I

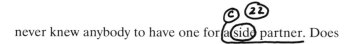

never knew anybody to have one for a side partner. Does

the blame thing know you from anybody else?"

"Take it over there and see," said Hayes.

We hardly need to analyze these miscues in order to see that Jay uses good reading strategies. Jay's miscues are a good starting point, for this very reason: they are relatively easy to analyze. It would be a good idea to photocopy the blank miscue analysis form (Figure 6.9) and try to analyze the miscues yourself, before reading further. Figure 6.10 reflects my own analysis of Jay's miscues.

I have made some slight changes in analyzing Jay's miscues here, compared to the first edition of this book. The main difference is that I decided to code separately some miscues that I had previously considered as a single miscue. For example, I had coded three of the following miscues as a single, multipart miscue:

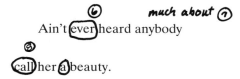

The first part of this miscue number 7, "much about" for *anybody*, was responsible for Jay's restructuring the text and making the other two miscues. I still think a good argument can therefore be made for considering these as one complex miscue. However, the fact that the second and third parts of the miscue were caused by the first is, in effect, lost by the time the miscue is coded. My recoding encourages us to take further note of the fact that the first miscue did not go with the following grammar and therefore prompted Jay to make the second and third of the miscues.

A second difference is that in this recoding, I have included some details that I long ago adopted in actual practice. One detail can be seen in the "partially" column for the questions regarding context (columns 1 and 2). After the check mark, I have written *G* if the miscue went with grammar but not with meaning, or *M* if the miscue went with meaning but not with grammar. In another instance, I in effect created a "partially" or "uncertain" category for column 3a and column 5, by checking a miscue on the borderline between "yes" and "no." All too often, this seems to be the most appropriate response. Sometimes I indicate remaining uncertainty with a question mark after my coding. This encourages me to reconsider the coding later.

While your own coding may not correspond exactly with mine, the following summary of Jay's miscues should hardly be surprising:

0% were dialect-related or ESL-related
96% fit completely with the preceding context

Reader's name: Jay
Date: April
Reading Selection: "Jimmy Hayes and Muriel"

Text	Reader	0 Was the Miscue Dialect-Related or ESL-Related? Yes	No	1 Did the Miscue Go with the Preceding Context? Yes	Partially	No	2 Did the Miscue Go with the Following Context? Yes	Partially	No	3a Was the Essential Meaning of the Sentence Left Intact? Yes	No	3b Was the Essential Meaning of the Selection Left Intact? Yes	No	4 Was the Miscue Corrected? Yes	No	5 (cols 3a & 4) Was the Miscue Either Meaning-Preserving or Corrected? Yes	No
1. about	around		✓	✓			✓			✓		✓			✓	✓	
2. —	at all		✓	✓			✓			✓		✓			✓	✓	
3. saw simply	simply saw		✓	✓			✓			✓		✓		✓		✓	
4. youth	young		✓	✓				✓M		✓		✓			✓	✓	
5. ingenuous	ingenious		✓		✓G			✓G		✓		✓			✓		✓
6. ever			✓	✓			✓				✓	✓			✓	✓	
7. anybody	much about		✓	✓			✓			✓		✓			✓	✓	
8. call	—		✓	✓			✓			✓		✓			✓	✓	
9. a	—		✓	✓			✓			✓		✓			✓	✓	
10. some	a		✓	✓				✓M		✓		✓		✓		✓	
11. of	—		✓	✓				✓M		✓		✓		✓		✓	
12. it	—		✓	✓			✓			✓		✓			✓	✓	
13. frog	Toad		✓	✓			✓			✓		✓			✓	✓	
14. its	the		✓	✓			✓			✓		✓			✓	✓	
15. —	it		✓	✓			✓			✓		✓			✓	✓	
16. —	is		✓	✓			✓			✓		✓			✓	✓	
17. ?	.		✓	✓			✓			✓		✓			✓	✓	
18. has	She's		✓	✓			✓			✓		✓			✓	✓	
19. at	—		✓	✓			✓			✓		✓			✓	✓	
20. blame	blamed		✓	✓			✓			✓		✓			✓	✓	
21. frogs	frog		✓	✓			✓			✓		✓			✓	✓	
22. side	—		✓	✓			✓			✓		✓		✓		✓	
23. it	her		✓	✓			✓			✓		✓			✓	✓	
24.																	
25.																	
Totals		0	23	22	1	0	19	4	0	22	1	23	0	4	19	22	1
Percents		0%	100%	96%	4%	0%	83%	17%	0%	96%	4%	100%	0%	17%	83%	96.4%	0%

FIGURE 6.10 Analysis of Jay's miscues

83% fit completely with the following context
96% preserved the essential meaning of the sentence
100% preserved the essential meaning of the selection
17% were corrected
96% were entirely acceptable in sentence context or were corrected

In short, it appears that Jay is a highly effective reader, well able to predict what is coming next and to correct those miscues that do not fit with the following context—or, as with some miscues, to reconstruct the following text to go with miscues he has already made. (Miscue 7 seems to have generated 8 and 9, miscue 11 seems to have generated 12, and miscue 16 seems to have generated 17 and 18.) His low percentage of correction is not a matter for concern, since most of his miscues were originally acceptable in context. His 96 percent comprehending score suggests that he understands what he reads, and this was confirmed by his excellent job of retelling the story.

Analyzing Tony's Miscues

Tony's reading is quite different from Jay's, as we see from this sample of his miscues from *A Camel in the Sea* (see also Chapter 1). As with Jay's miscues, it would be a good idea to first try to analyze Tony's miscues yourself.

①Mo-
Mohamed (mo-hah' med) loved to go swimming in the sea.

②2 Sammon / 1 Sam   ③(village)
How lucky he was to live in a Somali (so-mah'lee)(village)

④ran
right on the Indian Ocean! The sandy shore rang with the happy

⑤souts   ⑥(village)
shouts and cries of the(village)boys and girls. They liked

⑦high
to race one another into the surf, splashing and spraying ∧

⑧drase
the water into a white dancing foam before they dove into the

⑨Mola   ⑩yūng   ⑪Asla
waves. Mohamed and his young sister, Asha (ie'shuh),

[not numbered for analysis since the omission involves several words]

(spent all the time they could in the cool, clean)sea,

swimming and playing water games. They were good swimmers

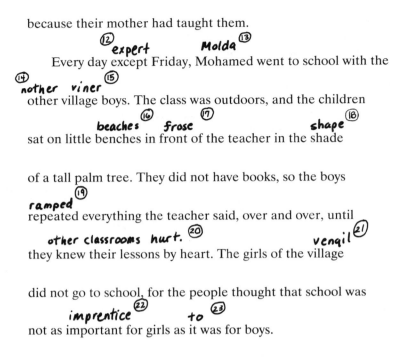

because their mother had taught them.

Every day except Friday, Mohamed went to school with the

other village boys. The class was outdoors, and the children

sat on little benches in front of the teacher in the shade

of a tall palm tree. They did not have books, so the boys

repeated everything the teacher said, over and over, until

they knew their lessons by heart. The girls of the village

did not go to school, for the people thought that school was

not as important for girls as it was for boys.

In analyzing Tony's miscues (Figure 6.11), I have made certain assumptions, partly on the basis of his retelling session (which, as mentioned, I unfortunately did not keep a record of). First, I have assumed that his nonword miscues on the proper names reflect no essential loss of meaning—even from the very beginning. (I am assuming that by the time Tony got to the second word, *loved*, he must have realized that "Mo-" was a proper name.) It seems clear that Tony at least knows these are the names of people and places, and that "Mola/Molda" is a boy and "Asla" is his sister. I have also assumed that certain nonwords are *grammatically* acceptable with both preceding and following context. This seems reasonably clear with miscues like "souts" for *shouts* and "ramped" for *repeated,* where Tony appears to have retained the grammatical ending of the original. I have also made that assumption for two other miscues that end like the original words: "yūng" for *young,* and "nother" for *other.*

Again, I have changed some of the codings from the previous edition. I have no longer coded all of the nonword miscues as preserving grammar, though they might have done so in Tony's mind. Also, I have coded more of the miscues as leaving the essential meaning intact. This results in a substantially higher comprehending score (column 5). You might try to see if you can grasp the reasoning behind my other coding decisions, especially those with which you do not initially agree.

Even with some variations in coding from person to person, Tony's miscues reflect certain strengths. If at first he does not get a word, he does not merely give up: he eventually makes several attempts at the word *village,* for example, after initially omitting it.

Reader's name Tony
Date April
Reading Selection _____

Text	Reader	0 Was the Miscue Dialect-Related or ESL-Related? Yes	No	1 Did the Miscue Go with the Preceding Context? Yes	Partially	No	2 Did the Miscue Go with the Following Context? Yes	Partially	No	3a Was the Essential Meaning of the Sentence Left Intact? Yes	No	3b Was the Essential Meaning of the Selection Left Intact? Yes	No	4 Was the Miscue Corrected? Yes	No	5 (cols. 3a & 4) Was the Miscue Either Meaning-Preserving or Corrected? Yes	No
1. Mohamed	Mo—		✓	✓	—				✓	✓		✓			✓	✓	
2. Somali	Sammon		✓	✓			✓			✓		✓			✓	✓	
3. village	ran		✓	✓		✓	✓				✓	✓			✓		✓
4. rang	ran		✓		√G		✓			✓		✓			✓	✓	
5. shouts	souts		✓	✓	√G		✓	√G		✓		✓			✓	✓	
6. village	—		✓	✓			✓			✓		✓			✓	✓	
7. —	high		✓	✓			✓			✓		✓			✓	✓	
8. dancing	drase		✓			✓	✓		✓			✓			✓	✓	
9. Mohamed	Mela		✓	✓			✓			✓		✓			✓	✓	
10. young	yung		✓	✓	√G		✓	√G		✓		✓			✓	✓	
11. Asha	Asia		✓	✓			✓			✓		✓			✓	✓	
12. except	expert		✓	✓			✓			✓		✓			✓	✓	✓
13. Mohamed	Molde		✓		√G		√G	√G			✓	✓			✓	✓	
14. other	nother		✓			✓	✓				✓	✓			✓		✓
15. village	viner		✓	✓			✓				✓	✓			✓		✓
16. benches	beaches		✓			✓	✓				✓	✓			✓		✓
17. front	frose		✓	✓			✓				✓	✓			✓		✓
18. shade	shape		✓	✓			✓				✓	✓			✓	✓	
19. repeated	ramped		✓	✓	√G		✓	√G			✓	✓			✓	✓	
20. their lessons other classrooms by heart	hunt		✓	✓			✓				✓	✓			✓	✓	
21. village	vengil		✓			✓			✓		✓	✓			✓		✓
22. important	imprentice		✓			✓			✓		✓	✓			✓		✓
23. it	to		✓			✓			✓		✓	✓			✓		✓
24.																	
25.																	
Totals		0	23	11	4	7	10	4	9	11	3 9	23	0	0	23	11	3 9
Percents		0%	100%	50%	18%	32%	44%	17%	39%	48%	13% 39%	100%	0%	0%	23%	48%	13% 39%

FIGURE 6.11 Analysis of Tony's miscues

Some of his miscues clearly show a concern for meaning, as when he inserts "high" in "splashing *high* and spraying the water." He makes good use of grapho/phonemic cues, especially at the beginnings and ends of words. And even some of his nonword miscues strongly suggest that he is preserving the grammar of the original, resulting in a significant percentage of miscues analyzed as partially acceptable with the preceding and following context. Note, however, his other percentages:

   0% were dialect-related or ESL-related
  50% fit completely with the preceding context
  44% fit completely with the following context
  48% preserved the essential meaning of the sentence
 100% preserved the essential meaning of the selection
   0% were corrected
  48% were entirely acceptable in sentence context or were corrected

Tony's comprehending score, the last percentage listed (from column 5), suggests that his use of reading strategies is only moderately effective. His miscue patterns suggest that he may need help in using prior context to predict, and in using following context to correct (if/when that's possible). He especially needs to make better use of semantic cues, meaning, in order to predict and to correct. In fact, from Tony's miscues we might tentatively infer that he is reading more to identify words than to construct meaning.

Despite this initial picture of Tony, we might have found that he comprehended the story rather well. Sometimes readers who make numerous low-quality miscues and leave them uncorrected do, nevertheless, have good comprehension. But in Tony's case, the retelling was unfortunately no more encouraging than the miscue analysis. It seemed clear that he had not read for meaning. A reading interview might have confirmed that Tony considered reading to be a matter of identifying words, had that been part of the total assessment procedure at the time.

Obviously, the original miscue form and retelling data did not directly supply us with all of these conclusions. Rather, the insights came from the analysis that was done in responding to the questions on the form about each miscue, and from inferences based on the analysis. This, of course, will always be true: at best, a form does nothing more than help us get our analysis together.

SELECTING AND DEVISING MISCUE ANALYSIS FORMS

Clearly, my basic miscue analysis form has both advantages and disadvantages: on the one hand, it is easy to draw tentative conclusions from the form as to whether the reader might benefit from assistance in using syntactic and semantic cues more effectively to predict and/or to confirm and correct. On the other hand, the form is in some ways both too complicated and too simple: too complicated for day-to-day use with whole classes of students, and yet not detailed and sophisticated enough for some kinds of research, or for studying in depth some of the more interesting readers one might encounter in the classroom.

One obvious shortcoming is that the form provides no systematic way for examining the reader's use of grapho/phonemic cues in relationship to his or her use of syntactic and semantic cues. We know from years of miscue research that the best readers typically make miscues that show less grapho/phonemic similarity to the text word than the miscues of poorer readers (K. S. Goodman, 1973); they are reading more to construct meaning than to say or sound out all the words. Conversely, readers who pay the *least* attention to meaning are often the ones who pay the *most* attention to grapho/phonemic cues. In other words, less proficient readers often tend to make less effective use of syntactic and especially semantic cues: they may read to identify words and use sounding-out as their major conscious strategy for dealing with words not immediately recognized on sight. To confirm or disprove this in a particular case, it would be useful to compare a reader's use of grapho/phonemic cues with his or her use of syntactic and semantic cues. But to do so, we would need a more complete coding form.

The most detailed and sophisticated form for obtaining such information is Kenneth Goodman's Taxonomy of Reading Miscues, included as an appendix in the *RMI Alternatives*. The miscue analysis form in the original *RMI Manual* asks questions dealing with the extent to which substitution miscues resemble the text word graphically and phonemically, as do the first two of the forms in the newer *RMI Alternatives*.

What most classroom teachers need, however, is not more detailed forms and procedures but simpler ones that will be less time-consuming to use, yet still sophisticated enough to yield information useful in planning instruction. Once you have gained some experience with analyzing readers' miscues, you should be able to choose or devise simpler forms that will be adequate for classroom assessment and record-keeping with most students. For example, as you listen to a student read, you might simply keep a running tally of your responses to one crucial question about each miscue, the same question as that in column 5 of my form:

• *Was the miscue either meaning-preserving within the sentence, or corrected?*

Or, to phrase the question a little differently: Did the miscue either leave the meaning of the sentence intact, or get corrected? If the reader has made a large number of miscues that are neither meaning-preserving nor corrected, and if the retelling is also sketchy, there is good reason to assume that the reader needs help in reading for meaning. Even so, it is best to confirm this conclusion by having the reader read silently and *then* describe what was read.

Although impressionistic responses without prior tabulation of data are obviously risky, with experience you might be able to listen to a student read, or at least to replay a tape recording of a reading session, and respond appropriately to questions like these:

	Seldom			Almost always	
1. Does the reader use prior knowledge and context to predict effectively?	1	2	3	4	5
2. Does the reader monitor comprehension and correct, or try to correct, miscues that don't make sense in context?	1	2	3	4	5

3. Does the reader use grapho/phonemic cues   1   2   3   4   5
   effectively, along with prior knowledge and
   context?

4. Do the sentences, as the reader left them,   1   2   3   4   5
   make sense in the context of the story? (Or do
   the sentences preserve meanings essential to
   the story?)

For informal record-keeping, you can jot down examples that clarify your responses to each of these questions (an illustration will be included in the section on retrospective miscue analysis later in this chapter). Of course, it is important that you have substantial experience listening to and analyzing readers' miscues before settling for such impressionistic and anecdotal records. Without enough background, you may all too easily miss important patterns in the miscue data.

The last three alternative forms offered in Chapter 6 of the *RMI Alternatives* differ from all the previously mentioned forms in one major way: they focus on whole sentences rather than on individual miscues. The most thorough of the alternative procedures offers questions such as these:

- Is the sentence syntactically (grammatically) acceptable in the reader's dialect and within the context of the entire passage?
- Is the sentence semantically acceptable in the reader's dialect and within the context of the entire story?
- Does the sentence, as finally produced by the reader, change the meaning of the story?

In addition, there are questions asking the degree to which substitution miscues look like the text item and sound like the expected response. The third of the proffered RMI procedures is similar to this second one, except that the miscues are both marked and coded on the worksheet; there is no separate coding sheet. The fourth and simplest procedure does not even involve tape-recording the session, though of course you could tape-record and replay the reading until you have gained enough confidence to analyze miscues on the spot. This procedure involves asking just one question of each sentence:

- Does the sentence, as the reader left it, make sense within the context of the selection?

Sentences are coded "yes" if they are totally acceptable semantically within the context of the entire selection, and/or if they are corrected. Otherwise, they are coded "no."

Obviously, this procedure is to be used only when one has had sufficient experience with miscue analysis to be able to make reliable assessments quickly. Before using such simplified procedures, it would be best to do several detailed analyses and to consult the *RMI Alternatives* for detailed suggestions on how to use the alternative procedures.

As I see it, then, miscue analysis is valuable in several ways. First and most important, it gives teachers crucial insight into the nature of the reading process and a greater appreciation for readers' strengths. It can give teachers added insight into how students perceive the reading process—*their* ideas of what reading is and how it is done. It can help teachers avoid overrelying on the often misleading results of standardized tests and also help them avoid the frequently erroneous assumption that few miscues indicate good comprehension and numerous miscues indicate poor comprehension. In addition, it can provide useful information as to the kinds of instructional help that individual students might need, as long as the teacher looks not just at the miscues and what they reveal about reading strategies, but at whether the quality of the miscues is or is not correlated with the quality of the retelling and discussion. In other words, do the strategies and the retelling match? Or does the reader use good reading strategies but remember relatively little? Or does the reader seem to use poor strategies, but remember a lot? This match or mismatch is important in considering what kinds of instructional assistance to offer, if any.

Fortunately, miscue analysis is almost as valuable as it is invaluable. Different forms and procedures can be adopted or developed, depending on your particular needs and resources. What's crucial is not any particular miscue analysis form or procedure, but the underlying philosophy. A vital element is that we not attend primarily to the quantity of the miscues, but to the quality—and the strategies they reflect. From the patterns that emerge from the worksheet, we can gain some insight into what kinds of assistance a reader might need.

USING MISCUE ANALYSIS TO ASSIST READERS

Of course, we teachers naturally use all the information available to us in trying to decide how we might help an individual reader. But because this chapter emphasizes analyzing miscues, it seems particularly appropriate to discuss how we can use miscues and miscue analysis in helping students become more proficient readers.

Erica: From Analysis to Assistance

Erica was a bright fifth grader who enjoyed discussing literature and offered insightful comments into the characters' feelings and motivations. However, both her writing and her reading were rather slow and painful—much less fluent than one would have predicted from her intelligence and liveliness. Each week she attended reading classes with two different special reading teachers.

Her classroom teacher and I decided to see what we could learn from analyzing Erica's miscues. The class was reading and discussing *Roll of Thunder, Hear My Cry*, by Mildred Taylor (1976); I was reading the book and discussing it with the least proficient readers, including Erica. Below is a passage she read while her teacher, Ruth Perino, listened and tape-recorded the session. The story concerns a black girl, Cassie, and her family in the rural South in the 1930s. At this point in the story, Cassie has just been ignored by a storekeeper as soon as white customers enter the store, then scolded and told to leave the store when she protested this treatment. Shortly after she and her older brother Stacey part outside the store, she has another painful awakening: she accidentally bumps into a white classmate on the sidewalk, Lillian Jean, and is humiliated by being forced to apologize and then to walk in the street. Erica's miscues in reading the first part of this passage are marked below:

(handwritten above text:)
① 5 I waved my hands
4 I whispered my hands
3 I whispered my hands
2 Ⓡ I whispered
1 whis–

As soon as we were outside, I whipped my hand

(handwritten: Ⓡ2)

(handwritten: R₂ = repeated twice)

from his. "What's the matter with you? You know he

was wrong!"

(handwritten: ② 2 flusk / 1 flu–   ③ he   Ⓒ 2 gruffily / Ⓡ ④ / gruf–)

Stacey swallowed to flush his anger, then said gruf-

fly, "I know it and you know it, but he don't know it,

(handwritten: ⑤ you   Ⓡ2)

and that's where the trouble is. Now come on 'fore you

(handwritten: ⑥ got   Ⓡ)

get us into a real mess. I'm going up to Mr. Jamison's to

(handwritten: Ⓡ2)

see what's keeping Big Ma."

(handwritten: Ⓡ Ⓡ2   ⑦ Ⓒ stopped)

"What 'bout T. J.?" I called as he stepped into the

street.

(handwritten: ⑧ Wearily   Ⓒ,R Ⓡ but ⑨)

Stacey laughed wryly. "Don't worry 'bout T. J. He

(handwritten: ⑩ Ⓒ what   ⑪ Ⓒ 2 sul- / 1 silen–)

knows exactly how to act." He crossed the street sullenly

then his hands jammed in his pockets.

(handwritten: ⑫ he)

I watched him go, but did not follow. Instead, I

(handwritten: ⑬ r)

ambled along the sidewalk trying to understand why

Mr. Barnett had acted the way he had. ⓇMore than once

⑭ *glanced*

I stopped and gazed over my shoulder at the mercan- ⑮ *2 mircantēl* / *1 mir*   (teacher then gave her the word)

⑯ *(1 to go mind into / 2 into the back to find out what / 3 what had /*

tile. I had a good mind to go back in and find out   *4 a good mind to go back and…*
     …and find out

what had made Mr. Barnett so mad. I actually turned

once and headed toward the store, then remembering

what Mr. Barnett had said about my returning, I

                         Ⓒ   ⑰ *and*
swung back around, kicking at the sidewalk, my head

ᴬᶜ *2 bōw-* / *1 bl-*   ⑱
bowed.

     (teacher then said
     "You got it — 'bowed.'")

     [AC = abandoning a correct form]

          ⑲ *2 Linna* / *1 Lin-*
It was then that I bumped into Lillian Jean

⑳ *2 Sil* / *1 Som*
Simms.

     (several tries —
     teacher then tells her)

"Why don't you look where you're going?" she

㉑ *said*   Ⓒ *2 an-* / *1 a-*   ㉒
asked huffily. Jeremy and her two younger brothers were

with her. "Hey, Cassie," said Jeremy.

                    Ⓒ   ㉓
"Hey, Jeremy," I said solemnly, keeping my eyes
2 Lin / *1 Lill-*
on Lillian Jean.

㉔ *a-a-ah-ā-ā-āpō-apōlə-gĭz-āpolah'gĭz*
"Well, apologize," she ordered.

"What?"   ㉕ *2 when the-* / *1 when you*

"You bumped into me. Now you apologize."
          ∧

㉖ ©don't   ®
I did not feel like messing with Lillian Jean. I had

©o-
other things on my mind. "Okay," I said, starting past,

㉗ 2 Willa Jean
1 Willa
"I'm sorry."
∧

Lillian Jean sidestepped in front of me. "That ain't

㉘
enough. Get down in the road."

ρ ㉙ ©You're
I looked up at her. "You crazy?"

㉚
© Don't ca-   ㉛ ©to
"You can't watch where you going, get in the road.

㉜ © 's   ㉝ © discount
Maybe that way you won't be bumping into decent
∧

㉞ © ha-
white folks with your little nasty self."

This second insult of the day was almost more than

㉟ © Mrs—
I could bear. Only the thought of Big Ma up in Mr.
㊱
James'   Linny   ㊲ s
Jamison's office saved Lillian Jean's lip. "I ain't nasty,"
∧
㊳ © 2 proudly ㊴
1 proudl-   ®   ρ
I said properly holding my temper in check, "and if

you're so afraid of getting bumped, walk down there

yourself."

In analyzing Erica's miscues, I asked the four questions on pp. 267–268 and concluded that Erica's miscues rated an "almost always" response in every instance. Below are the questions, with examples that clarify my strong affirmative.

1. *Does the reader use prior knowledge and context to predict effectively?* Yes, almost always:

           wearily
Stacey laughed wryly.

         glanced
I stopped and gazed over my shoulder . . .

           2 *when the —*
         1 *when you*
"You bumped into me. Now you apologize."

              © 2 *proudly*
             1 *proudl–*
"I ain't nasty," I said, properly holding my temper in check.

Each example shows Erica making an appropriate prediction from context. Her prior knowledge of the story is especially evident in the miscue "wearily" for *wryly*, and even more in "proudly" for *properly*: Cassie was indeed a proud young girl.

2. *Does the reader monitor comprehension and correct, or try to correct, miscues that don't make sense in context?* Yes, almost always:

© *Don't ca–*   © *to*
"You can't watch where you going, get in the road.

       © *'s*   © *discount*
Maybe that way you won't be bumping into decent

white folks with your little nasty self."

In each instance, Erica corrects the miscue when it does not sound like language or make sense with what follows in the sentence.

3. *Does the reader use grapho/phonemic cues effectively, along with prior knowledge and context?* Yes, almost always:

            2 *flusk*   2 *gruffily*
            1 *flu–*   © ® 1 *gruf–*
Stacey swallowed to flush his anger, then said gruf-

fly, . . .

                  © 2 *sul–*
                1 *silen*
He crossed the street sullenly. . .

q–a–ah–ā–ā–āpō–apɔlə–gĭz–āpɔlah'gĭz
"Well, apologize," she ordered.

"What?"

           2 *when the —*
         1 *when you*
"You bumped into me. Now you apologize."

These examples show Erica making good use of grapho/phonemic cues along with prior knowledge and context. When the actual word is not something that makes sense to her in context (*flush*, in the first example, and *apologize*, the first time it occurs), she is unable to get the word using grapho/phonemic cues alone. But when context supports her sounding out strategy, she is able to get the word. Indeed, she doesn't need to sound out *apologize* the second time she encounters it: the word makes sense to her in this context. Thus Erica is quite effective in using grapho/phonemic cues along with semantic and syntactic cues.

4. *Do the sentences, as the reader left them, make sense in the context of the story? (Or, do the sentences preserve meanings essential to the story?)* Yes, as almost all of the foregoing sentences would suggest. Indeed, though Erica does not regress and overtly correct her first prolonged attempt at sounding out *apologize*, it is obvious from her reading as well as later discussion that she realized the word had been *apologize*.

In short, Erica makes highly effective use of reading strategies. Therefore, her teacher and I concluded that what Erica needed most was lots more experience in reading itself, not skills or strategy work. Nevertheless, I did use the tape recording of her reading to help Erica gain self-confidence as a reader. Earlier, her literature discussion group had made with me a list of strategies for dealing with problem words. I asked Erica to review these briefly, then told her we would replay the tape and I'd like her to stop the tape whenever she heard herself making a good miscue. Of course she was then to explain why it was a good miscue—what good reading strategies she was using. I regret not tape recording this session, as Erica was absolutely thrilled to hear herself making good miscues and to be able to explain why they were good. This one session seemed to significantly boost her self-confidence as a reader.

Retrospective Miscue Analysis

My instructional procedure with Erica is a variation of what has come to be known as Retrospective Miscue Analysis, or RMA (Marek, 1989; Y. M. Goodman & Marek, 1989). The reader is tape-recorded, the teacher selects miscues for discussion, and the reader and the teacher consider the miscues together, either by looking at the miscues marked on a copy of the selection, by listening to the tape, or both. That is, they consider in retrospect the reader's miscues and the reading strategies they reflect.

Below are some reader characteristics, with suggestions for the kinds of miscues a teacher might choose for discussion in each case. These are a combination of my practices and those of Ann Marek (Marek, 1992):

Reader characteristics	*Kinds of miscues that could be examined*
Lacks self-confidence	Select miscues that fit the context appropriately.
Thinks reading means getting all the words	Select miscues that fit the context appropriately; might also consider the completely acceptable

Reader characteristics	*Kinds of miscues that could be examined*
	miscues of someone who is clearly a good reader—perhaps the teacher.
Seldom corrects miscues that don't go with following context	Select miscues that didn't go with following context and compare some that were corrected with those that weren't.
Makes miscues that don't go with the preceding context	Select miscues that do go with the preceding context and compare with those that don't.
Makes nonword substitutions that suggest underuse of syntactic and semantic cues and overuse of grapho/phonemic cues	Select miscues wherein all three kinds of cues were used effectively; contrast with miscues that reflect a sounding-out strategy with insufficient regard for meaning cues and/or grammatical cues.
Makes nonword substitutions for words in reader's oral vocabulary	Select miscues where persistence resulted in real words that fit the context; contrast these with nonword substitutions.
Makes miscues that suggest difficulty in sounding out long words that are in the reader's speaking vocabulary	Select miscues where sounding out has been successfully used in conjunction with prior knowledge and context; contrast with miscues where the reader seems not to have used an effective sounding-out strategy for multisyllabic words, or not to have used this strategy along with prior knowledge and context cues.
Consistently corrects high-quality miscues that fit the context	Select fully acceptable miscues where correction is unnecessary.

Of course the purpose of contrasting miscues that do exemplify a desirable strategy with those that don't is to demonstrate to the reader that he or she is capable of using the strategy and just needs to use it more consistently.

When listening to miscues that don't fit the context, teachers can ask "Does that make sense?" and/or "Does that sound like language?" Often, readers will quickly internalize these questions and comment spontaneously that "that doesn't sound right."

Variations on Retrospective Miscue Analysis

One advantage of retrospective miscue analysis is that the reader is not interrupted while reading. Another is that the reader can take more ownership over the reading process and the discussion of reading strategies. After the reading has been tape-recorded, for example, you can have the reader listen for certain kinds of miscues, if warranted by the reader's pattern of miscues. For instance:

1. While following along in the text, the reader can listen for miscues that fit the context appropriately and therefore don't need to be corrected. (This is for the reader

who lacks self-confidence and/or the reader who thinks reading means accurate word identification; it is also for the reader who consistently corrects miscues that don't need to be corrected.)

2. The reader can listen for miscues that reflect good predicting, but that don't go with following context. This reinforces the predicting strategies and any strategies the reader uses to self-correct—or else it demonstrates the need for correction. (This is for the reader who makes good predictions but seldom corrects miscues that don't fit with the following context.)

3. The reader can listen for miscues that don't sound like language. (This is for the reader who underuses syntactic as well as semantic cues and may overuse grapho/phonemic cues.)

Of course, similar instructional strategies can be used on the spot, with immediate playback of a paragraph just tape-recorded. And the discussion can be more open-ended. For example, the teacher can simply ask the reader to stop the tape at trouble spots as they listen to the tape together. The reader can explain why it was a problem and how he or she tried to deal with it; then together they can discuss any other strategies that might have been effective. Such instructional strategies as these can be developed as the teacher sees the need and opportunity.

Mini-lessons

For readers with particular strategy needs, the most effective instruction is likely to be one-on-one instruction, as discussed in the previous section and also in Chapter 11. However, group mini-lessons may also be helpful. For lessons on the kinds of strategies discussed here, I recommend

Goodman, Y. M., & Burke, C. (1980). *Reading strategies: Focus on comprehension.* Katonah, NY: Richard C. Owen.

The following books offer a broader and somewhat different range of suggestions:

Gilles, C., et al., (Eds.). (1988). *Whole language strategies for secondary students.* Katonah, NY: Richard C. Owen.

Tierney, R. J., Readence, J. E., & Dishner, E. K. (1985). *Reading strategies and practices: A compendium.* 2nd ed. Boston: Allyn and Bacon.

Watson, D. J. (Ed.). (1987). *Ideas and insights: Language arts in the elementary school.* Urbana, IL: National Council of Teachers of English.

Many of the ideas in these books would be helpful for preventing reading difficulties as well as for dealing with them. And that, of course, is what we would all prefer to do.

FOR FURTHER REFLECTION AND EXPLORATION

1. Consider whether the reading styles questions on pp. 236–237 are the best for your purposes. If not, revise them, creating your own interview form or questionnaire. You may want to do the same with the reading inventory questions (see p. 237 of the text and Figure 6.8).

2. To gain practice in analyzing and evaluating miscues, you might begin by analyzing David's (pp. 6–8) or Anne's (p. 225) or Billy's (pp. 136–137). Use the form in Figure 6.9, or devise a similar form. When you feel comfortable analyzing one of these easier samples, then try analyzing Erica's miscues (pp. 270–272) or Danny's miscues (pp. 151–152).

3. To gain further practice, analyze Betsey's miscues as illustrated below. You should begin by reading the passage as she read it, complete with all her miscues. As you will see, her miscues improve as she gets further and further into the story. Decide which consecutive stretch of 25 miscues to analyze, and again use the form in Figure 6.9 or a similar one. Judging by your examination and analysis of Betsey's miscues, what are her reading strengths? What are her weaknesses, if any? What kind of reading instruction and assistance do you think she needs, if any? Discuss your conclusions and recommendations. The reading selection is adapted from Lee Garrett Goetz, *A Camel in the Sea* (1966, pp. 11–30). Again, the line divisions reflect the way the material was presented to the reader. To give a more balanced picture of the reader's strategies, this time I have numbered only the first substitution for each of the proper names, even though the subsequent substitutions are not always the same.

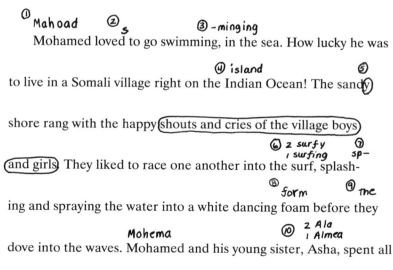

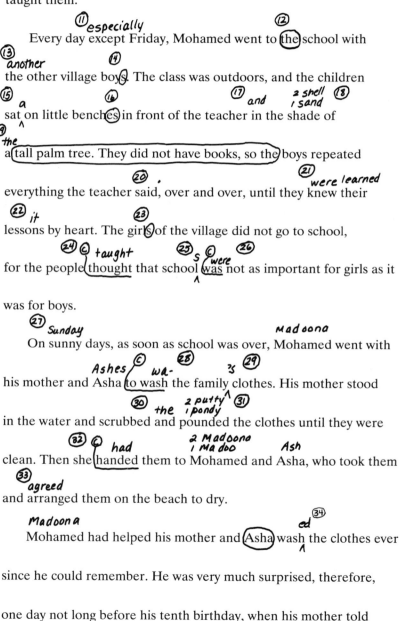

water games. They were good swimmers because their mother had

taught them.

Every day except Friday, Mohamed went to the school with

the other village boys. The class was outdoors, and the children

sat on little benches in front of the teacher in the shade of

a tall palm tree. They did not have books, so the boys repeated

everything the teacher said, over and over, until they knew their

lessons by heart. The girls of the village did not go to school,

for the people thought that school was not as important for girls as it

was for boys.

On sunny days, as soon as school was over, Mohamed went with

his mother and Asha to wash the family clothes. His mother stood

in the water and scrubbed and pounded the clothes until they were

clean. Then she handed them to Mohamed and Asha, who took them

and arranged them on the beach to dry.

Mohamed had helped his mother and Asha wash the clothes ever

since he could remember. He was very much surprised, therefore,

one day not long before his tenth birthday, when his mother told him not to come with her and Asha.

"I do not want you to help us any more, Mohamed," his mother

said. "It is time that Asha had more work to do around the

house. Besides, in two more years you will be thought of as a

man by our tribe, and it is not fitting that people see you

always doing women's work. From now on, you help your father in

the shop and Asha will help me at home."

That first day, Mohamed felt quite grown-up and superior

when he saw his mother and Asha carrying a heavy basket to the

beach. But this feeling did not last long. He had no one to

play with! He and Asha had played together for so long that the

other children were used to his not playing with them.

Mohamed stood and watched the other boys play "kick the

ball" and "hunt for robber" and "water tag." When no one

called him for a game, he turned and walked down the beach,

kicking up the sand with one foot, and trying to look as though

he really didn't care or want to play.

Finally, he decided to take his problem to his father, Hassan.

(57) *is*

"Mother doesn't want me to help wash the family clothes any more,

Madooha *Ashes*
Father," Mohamed told his father. "Asha has her work and her

friends, but now I have no one to play with."

(58) *Probably* *Madooha*
"Perhaps your mother is right, Mohamed," his father said,

(59) ©*help*
and he put down the piece of board that he held in his hand.

ship
"It is time that you should learn to help me in the shop."

(60) ©*when*
Hassan was a builder of fishing boats that went out to sea

every morning and returned to the shore every evening. His

ship
small shop was right on the beach.

Madooha
"When you come home from school each day, Mohamed," said

(61) *trouble*
his father, "I will show you the beginning of your trade. You

will be a builder of boats like me."

Madooha
"But father, when will I have time for games?" Mohamed asked.

"You help me a little, and I shall see that you have plenty

Hansa (62) *slowly*
of time to yourself," Hassan promised. He laughed softly. "I do

remember that boys need to have time to think and play.

You shall have it, my son."

(63) *desert*
That summer was the driest one that anyone—even the oldest

⁶⁴Madooha's

people in Mohamed's village—could recall. It did not rain at all.

Each day the people would look up at the sky to see if they

could see any rain clouds. But each day the sun shone brightly.

⁶⁸ ₂ hiding ⁶⁶

₁ hidden

There was not even one cloud (to) hide the sun('s) face for a while.

Soon all the leaves of the trees started to turn brown. The

⁶⁸dropped   ⁶⁹

flowers drooped low(er) and lower on their stems. Finally they

became dry as paper. When the wind blew the dry leaves, they

⁷⁰'s

made a noise like a snake slipping through the sand.
                         ∧

Day after day the sun beat down, and there was no shade from

⁷¹ leaves   ⁷²Jane   ⁷³Julie

the leafless trees. June and July came and went without rain.

August was nearly over and still no rain.

4. Analyze Erica's miscues and reading strategies, drawing upon the sample of her
   miscues within this chapter (pp. 270-272) and on the text as she read further.

⁴⁰

© the

I started past her again, and again she got in my way.

⁴¹

© let's   Linnean ®

Lilly

"Ah, let her pass, Lillian Jean," said Jeremy. "She

ain't done nothin' to you."

"She done something to me just standing in front

⁴²   ⁴³ © ₂ open-

© what's   ₁ at-

of me." With that, she reached for my arm and attempted to push me off the sidewalk. I braced myself

and swept my arm backward, out of Lillian Jean's

Ⓡ ㊹ s
㊺ wrists
reach. But someone caught it from behind, painfully

㊻ a shōvel ㊽ back ㊾
twisting it, and shoved me off the sidewalk into the

road. I landed bottom first on the ground.

Simson
Mr. Simms glared down at me. "When my gal Lil-

Linnean
Lin-   ㊼ I
lian Jean says for you to get yo'self off the sidewalk,

[The teacher then supplied the word "gal."]

you get, you hear?"

㊼ Ⓒ 2 me there was
        I him was   Ⓒ Mivin
Behind him were his sons R. W. and Melvin. People   Mar-

Ⓒ be-   ㊼ Simson's
from the store began to ring the Simmses. "Ain't that

                3 caught in
            ㊼ 2 was caught
        ㊼ I that caught   up ㊼   's ㊼
the same little nigger was cuttin' up back there at Jim
L-   everyone
Lee's?" someone asked.

    ㊼
        's
"Yeah, she the one," answered Mr. Simms. "You

Solomon Ⓡ

                                    Lig-
hear me talkin' to you, gal? You 'pologize to Miz Lil-

[Teacher corrects h

lian Jean this minute."

㊼ Starred ㊼   ㊼ and Ⓒ friendly ㊼
I stared up at Mr. Simms, frightened. Jeremy ap-

                ㊼
peared frightened, too. "I-I apologize already."

Jeremy seemed relieved that I had spoken. "She

⑥⁹d   ⑦⁰r-r   ⑦¹s-ſ

d-did, Pa. R-right now, 'fore y'll come, she did—"
  ∧   ∧   ∧
     Simmes   ⑦²glance
Mr. Simms turned an angry gaze upon his son and

⑦³ 2 flattered Ⓡlook
   1 flattened
Jeremy faltered, looked at me, and hung his head.

       Ⓡ₃
Then Mr. Simms jumped into the street. I moved

      ⑦⁴ keep   Ⓒ not   ⑮
away from him, trying to get up. He was a mean-look-

  Ⓒ ⑦⁶ ⑦⁷   4 bar
   with a   1,2 ⓡ 3 barned ⑦⁸
ing man, red in the face and bearded. I was afraid he

was going to hit me before I could get to my feet,

                              ⑦⁹ed
                                ∧
but he didn't. I scrambled up and ran blindly for the

            ⑧⁰Ⓒ found   Ⓒ at-
wagon. Someone grabbed me and I fought wildly, at-

tem- Ⓒ a ⑧¹
tempting to pull loose. "Stop, Cassie!" Big Ma said.

  Ⓒ ⑧² ⑧³   ⑧⁴
   this min- You're
"Stop, it's me. We're going home now."

              ⑧⁵   ⑧⁶
                               she
"Not 'fore she 'pologizes to my gal, y'all ain't," said
                              ∧
⑧⁷
Mr. Simms.

Big Ma gazed down at me, fear in her eyes, then
   ⑧⁸ 3 growling
      2 crowling
      1 growling
back at the growing crowd. "She jus' a child–"

      ⑧⁹ Annie
"Tell her, Aunty–"

              ⑨⁰ cracked
Big Ma looked at me again, her voice cracking as

she spoke. "Go on, child . . . apologize."

[Teacher has her return to beginning of sentence, after which she corrects the miscues toward the end of the sentence.]

Ⓡ
"But, Big Ma—"

�91 *Look* *said* �92
Her voice hardened. "Do like I say."

I swallowed hard.

"Go on!"

Ⓡ Ⓡ
"I'm sorry," I mumbled.

Ⓒ *Lin* Ⓒ *de-* *Soloms*
"I'm sorry, Miz⎸Lillian Jean,"⎸demanded Mr. Simms.

㉓ *2 baked*
1 bi –
"Big Ma!" I balked.   [*Teacher then supplied the word.*]

"Say it, child."

A painful tear slid down my cheek and my lips

trembled. "I'm sorry . . . M-Miz . . . Lillian Jean."

When the words had been spoken, I turned and

fled crying into the back of the wagon. No day in all

Ⓒ ㉔
curled
my life had ever been as⎸cruel as this one.

5. After you have practiced analyzing some miscues that have already been recorded and numbered, it is time to try the whole procedure discussed in this chapter: everything from preparing for the reading session to analyzing and evaluating the retelling and the reader's miscues, and finally to interpreting the results and making recommendations for reading instruction. As a valuable learning experience, I would suggest that you try one of the following:

a. Compare a good reader (someone who usually constructs meaning well) with a poor reader (someone who usually has trouble constructing meaning from text). Pay attention to the differences in their miscues. It should be interesting to have both persons read the same material. But in order to do this, you may have to select students from different grade levels: for example, a good third-grade reader and a relatively poor fourth-grade or fifth-grade reader. After you have collected and analyzed the data from each reader, compare the results. Do the two readers seem to use the same reading strategies? Do they use them equally well? Discuss this question in detail.

b. If you know of two teachers who have widely differing views of reading and/or methods of reading instruction, choose one of the poorer readers from each class, and compare them. Do they seem to use the same reading strategies? In each case, does there seem to be any relation between the teacher's views or methods, and the student's approach to reading? Discuss in detail.

6. Once you have become fairly comfortable with miscue analysis, try to use the four-question summary on pp. 267–268, without detailed analysis beforehand. Create your own form, leaving space to add examples that support your conclusions. At first, it is a good idea to tape-record the person's reading, so that you can listen to the miscues two or three times if necessary. Then, record your overall impressions on your form. If at all possible, compare your analysis with that of someone who is more experienced in miscue analysis.

7. If you were doing Restrospective Miscue Analysis with Tony (pp. 263–264), what would you focus upon first? What would you focus upon if you were doing RMA with Betsey, pp. 277–281.

Appendix
Checklists on Learning and Reading Styles

Figure A6.1 contains a list of characteristics that are typical of a global reading style, followed by characteristics typical of an analytic reading style. To determine how a child finds it easiest to read and/or to learn to read, you can look for some of these features in the child's behavior, and/or ask the child questions based upon some of these items. Figures A6.2–A6.5 are actual checklists for identifying kinesthetic, tactile, visual, and auditory strengths, along with a key for scoring them. Marie Carbo's Reading Style Inventory (in three versions: primary, regular, and adult) along with machine-scorable response forms for all but the primary version of the RSI are available, along with numerous related materials, from the National Reading Styles Institute, P. O. Box 39, Roslyn Heights, NY 11577; 1-800-3117. However, perhaps the greatest value of such inventories as well as the lists below is to make teachers more aware of the differences in learning styles that are likely to be reflected in every classroom, and thus to make us better kid-watchers.

We do not all learn, read, or learn to read most easily in the same ways. On the other hand, many emergent readers (young children and older, less proficient readers) are highly kinesthetic, tactile, and global in their learning style; they do not learn as readily with the analytical and auditory emphasis common in traditional classrooms. This pattern is exemplified by the case study of Jimmy that follows the lists of characteristics below.

Global Reading Style

Global students often:

1. concentrate and learn when information is presented as a gestalt or whole
2. respond to emotional appeals
3. tend to like fantasy and humor
4. get "wrapped up" in a story and do not concentrate on the facts
5. process information subjectively and in patterns
6. easily can identify the main ideas in a story
7. dislike memorizing facts such as dates, names or specifics
8. learn easily through stories
9. use story context often to figure out unknown words

Analytic Reading Style

Analytic students often:

1. concentrate and learn when information is presented in small, logical steps
2. respond to appeals of logic
3. solve problems systematically
4. process information sequentially and logically
5. enjoy doing puzzles (e.g., crossword, jigsaw)
6. like putting things together by following specific directions (e.g., mechanical toys, objects with parts)
7. pay close attention to exact directions, such as measurements in a recipe or explanations for assembling an object
8. enjoy learning facts such as dates, names, and other specifics
9. learn phonics easily
10. understand and apply phonic rules
11. are critical and analytic when reading
12. can identify the details in a story

Figure **A6.1** *Global and ayalytic reading styles (Carbo, Dunn, & Dunn, 1986. pp. 61–62)*

10–12 = Excellent

7–9   = Good

4–6   = Moderate

0–3   = Poor to Fair

The student can:

_____ 1. run, walk, catch a ball, and so on, in a rhythmical, smooth fashion

_____ 2. concentrate for fifteen to thirty minutes during kinesthetic activities that require whole-body movement

_____ 3. recall dances, games, sports, and/or directions after performing them a few times

_____ 4. move his/her body easily and freely when acting in a play

_____ 5. remember words seen on posters and signs when on a trip

_____ 6. memorize a script more easily when actually performing in a play

_____ 7. understand concepts after "experiencing" them in some way (e.g., going on a trip, acting in a play, caring for pets, performing experiments, and so on)

_____ 8. remember words after "experiencing" them (e.g., looking at the word "apple" while eating an apple or pretending to be an elephant while learning the word "elephant")

_____ 9. recall words used in a floor game after playing the game a few times

_____ 10. remember facts, poetry, lines in a play more easily when he/she is walking and/or running, rather than standing still

_____ 11. recall a letter of the alphabet after forming it with his/her entire body

_____ 12. remember the "feeling" of a story better than the details

FIGURE A6.2 *Checklist for identifying kinesthetic strengths. © Marie Carbo 1976. (Carbo, Dunn, & Dunn, 1986, p. 60)*

11–13   = Excellent
8–10   = Good
5–7   = Moderate
0–4   = Poor to Fair

The student can:

_____   1. draw and color pictures
_____   2. perform crafts such as sewing, weaving, and/or making models
_____   3. remember a phone number after dialing it a few times
_____   4. concentrate on a tactile task for 15 to 30 minutes
_____   5. hold a pen or pencil correctly
_____   6. write legible letters of the alphabet appropriate in size for his/her age
_____   7. write with correct spacing
_____   8. recall words after tracing over clay or sandpaper letters that form the words
_____   9. remember words after writing them a few times
_____   10. recall words after playing a game containing those words, such as bingo or dominoes
_____   11. recall the names of objects after touching them a few times
_____   12. write words correctly after tracing over them with his/her finger
_____   13. recall words after typing them a few times

FIGURE A6.3   *Checklist for identifying tactile strengths. © Marie Carbo 1976. (Carbo, Dunn, & Dunn, 1986, p. 59)*

11–13 = Excellent
8–10 = Good
5–7 = Moderate
0–4 = Poor to Fair

The student can:

_____ 1. follow a simple direction that is written and/or drawn
_____ 2. place four to six pictures in proper story sequence
_____ 3. recall a phone number after seeing it a few times
_____ 4. concentrate on a visual activity for 15 to 30 minutes
_____ 5. concentrate on a visual task when a visual distraction is presented
_____ 6. work on a visual task without looking away or rubbing his/her eyes
_____ 7. recall words after seeing them a few times
_____ 8. remember and understand words accompanied by a pictorial representation
_____ 9. read words without confusing the order of the letters (e.g., reading "spot" for "stop")
_____ 10. discriminate between/among letters that look alike (e.g., as "m" and "n" or "c," "e," and "o")
_____ 11. discriminate between/among words that look alike (e.g., "fill" and "full" or "that" and "what")

FIGURE A6.4   *Checklist for identifying visual strengths. © Marie Carbo 1976. (Carbo, Dunn, & Dunn, 1986, pp. 58–59)*

12–14 = Excellent

9–11 = Good

5–8 = Moderate

0–4 = Poor to Fair

The student can:

_____ 1. follow a short verbal direction

_____ 2. repeat simple sentences of eight to twelve words

_____ 3. remember a phone number after hearing it a few times

_____ 4. recall simple math facts or a few lines of poetry after hearing them several times

_____ 5. understand long sentences

_____ 6. remember and sequence events discussed

_____ 7. use appropriate vocabulary and sentence structure

_____ 8. pay attention to a story or lecture for 15 to 30 minutes

_____ 9. concentrate on an auditory task even when an auditory distraction is presented

_____ 10. identify and recall the sounds of individual letters

_____ 11. discriminate between/among words that sound alike (e.g., "leaf" and "leave" or "cot" and "cat")

_____ 12. discriminate between/among letters that sound alike (e.g., "sh" and "ch" or "a" and "o")

_____ 13. blend letters quickly to form words

_____ 14. sound out words and still retain the storyline

Figure A6.5 *Checklist for identifying auditory strengths. © Marie Carbo 1976. (Carbo, Dunn, & Dunn, 1986, p. 58)*

Case Study of Jimmy

To give teachers a feel for the pattern that is typical of many young children and of older underachieving readers as well, Marie Carbo uses the following case study of Jimmy in her Reading Styles seminar. As you read the case study, jot down your observations regarding his learning style, modalities, and preferences regarding environment, mobility, intake (food or drink), and whatever else seems noteworthy. (The case study is from Carbo's Reading Styles seminar, 1986; © 1981 Marie Carbo.)

Kindergarten

"Mommy, what's that word?" Jimmy asked as he shifted from foot to foot. Jimmy's mother was reading a storybook to him and, as usual, he interrupted her on every page to ask questions about the words. He would fidget, lean, and stretch in his chair while he nibbled on a cookie or a piece of fruit.

Jimmy loved to go to the library and choose books for his mother to read to him. He was able to read many words already—words on signs, in books and on television. Jimmy loved exciting stories and he was looking forward to first grade.

In his kindergarten class, Jimmy enjoyed playing with a couple of buddies on a little rug in the block corner. He particularly liked to create clay animals and then tell fantastic stories about them. Jimmy had an excellent imagination and vocabulary. He was a great favorite with his peers.

First Grade

"Jimmy, please sit down. We're ready to work," repeated Mrs. Jeremy. "Put away that snack and sit down, dear. You can talk to Paul later. Sit down now. Is everyone ready now? Good. Let's see if you remember what I taught you yesterday.

"Everyone sit up nice and straight. That's better. We are working on the 'm' sound. Now, Jimmy where do you hear the 'm' sound in the word 'family?' In the beginning, the middle, or at the end of the word?"

Jimmy shrugged his shoulders hoping that Mrs. Jeremey would ask another student. But she didn't.

"Jimmy, *listen* very carefully. You're a bright boy. I *know* you can do it if you just try a little harder. That's good. Sit up now."

Mrs. Jeremy knew that Jimmy had a high I.Q., but she could not understand why his skills were so weak. Immaturity was her guess. Even if he could read some words, Mrs. Jeremey wanted to give Jimmy a good phonics foundation before he left first grade. She went on.

"Do you hear the 'm' sound in the beginning, the middle or the end . . . 'fa - mi - ly,'" Mrs. Jeremey said more slowly.

A few of the students turned to watch Jimmy. He felt more and more uncomfortable. Tears were about to well in his eyes. He fought them back. The kids would make fun of him if he cried. Jimmy decided to guess. "At the end?" he asked.

"No Jimmy, please listen," said Mrs. Jeremy. "Sit up, dear. You can think better if you're sitting up. There now."

Jimmy couldn't understand why he couldn't do the work. Mrs. Jeremy was trying so hard. Everyone was staring now. Jimmy felt he would burst. Suddenly, he got up from his chair and ran out into the hall.

7 Phonics and Whole Language: From Politics to Research

If American education existed in a rational world, it would be clear that whole language brings together and is based in modern research in language, learning, and teaching.

— Kenneth Goodman

The subject of phonics is difficult to deal with, since people understand and define it in various ways. In this book, I've usually used the term *phonics* in the context of *teaching.* I've indicated that phonics is sometimes promoted as a method of teaching reading, even though its function is much more limited. Usually, I've used the term phonics as it is widely employed, to describe the teaching of letter/sound relationships and patterns. Sometimes I use the phrase "phonics knowledge" to describe the patterns themselves: what readers have learned about letter/sound relationships. Context usually indicates my precise intention. However, the term "phonics" still needs further clarification.

There are basically two camps that advocate *systematic phonics:* those who think phonics should be taught extensively and intensively, and those who think it should be taught systematically but not extensively and/or intensively. People in both groups are usually considered phonics advocates. In contrast are those who recommend less systematic, *intrinsic phonics:* phonics knowledge developed in the context of meaningful reading, and therefore intrinsic to it. Most of this group think children should receive some direct help in developing grapho/phonemic knowledge, but that this help can be *incidental* rather than systematic because young children who write with invented spelling and who read environmental print and predictable texts will usually acquire grapho/phonemic understandings with relatively little direct assistance. The latter group includes most whole language educators and advocates.

This chapter deals with these three major stances in turn. First, we consider the nature and the hidden agenda of extensive and intensive phonics. Second, we consider the argument for systematic (but not extensive or intensive) phonics, and the research evidence; this leads logically to a critique of that evidence and line of reasoning and into the research evidence for whole language—and for developing grapho/phonemic understandings more incidentally, in the context of authentic reading and writing experiences. Finally, we summarize the tentative conclusions from this research and consider the promise and limitations of whole language.

THE HIDDEN AGENDA OF EXTENSIVE, INTENSIVE PHONICS

My interest in the possible hidden agendas of heavy phonics instruction was aroused in 1989 when a U.S. Senate Republican Policy Committee document on phonics was read into the *Congressional Record*. Titled "Illiteracy: An Incurable Disease or Education Malpractice?" this paper was in effect a rallying cry for extensive and intensive phonics instruction. Ostensibly drawing conclusions from the available research, the apparent author of the report, Robert W. Sweet, concluded: "The overwhelming evidence from research and classroom results indicates that the cure for the 'disease of illiteracy' is the restoration of the instructional practice of intensive, systematic phonics in every primary school in America!" ("Illiteracy," 1989, p. 13).

This is demonstrably untrue. Before considering research evidence, however, we need to describe this kind of phonics instruction more clearly, discuss the source of advocacy for such instruction, and clarify its hidden agenda.

The Nature of Extensive, Intensive Phonics Instruction

What does it mean to teach phonics extensively and intensively? Essentially what the terms imply: to teach *a lot* of phonics and to teach it *hard*, typically before introducing children to coherent texts.

A program called *Explode the Code* offers one example. It includes twelve workbooks, preceded by three primers. Book 1, for instance, introduces short vowels; Book 1½ offers additional exercises on short vowel sounds. Book 2 deals with initial and final consonant blends, Book 2½ reviews these; and so forth. This program is distributed by Educators Publishing Service, which also sells *Primary Phonics*, a six-workbook program, followed by *More Primary Phonics*. There's a home teaching version of the famed DISTAR program, *Teach Your Child to Read in 100 Easy Lessons* (Englemann, Haddox, & Bruner, 1983). Even better known is *Hooked on Phonics* (Gateway Educational Products), a widely advertised program consisting of eight cassette tapes; nine decks of flash cards depicting letters, letter sequences, and words; four books of word lists corresponding to phonic features in the card decks; and one book of sentences corresponding to the word lists ("Reading educators . . . ," 1991). Competing with *Hooked on Phonics* is the newer *You Can Read!* (1993) consisting of two one-and-a-half hour videotapes, three workbooks, and a helper's manual. Something of a maverick, Samuel Blumenfeld's *Alpha-Phonics* (1983) also provides extensive and intensive attention to letter/sound patterns, but simply by presenting words in patterned lists, not teaching the patterns per se; thus the program is based on the (psycho)linguistic principle that readers only need exposure to the patterns to induce them (see Chapter 3).

Who advocates the teaching of extensive and intensive phonics? Typically it is not reading researchers or educators, even those who advocate systematic phonics (Patrick Groff is an exception; see, for instance, Groff, 1989). For example, among reading educators, even leading phonics advocates have denounced the *Hooked on Phonics* program as promising more than it can deliver (Kantrowitz, 1991). It is mainly laypersons—that is, those with no educational background in the process or the teaching of reading—who advocate the extensive and intensive teaching of phonics.

Typically, the impetus for teaching phonics extensively and intensively comes from certain leaders and their organizations among the political and religious Far Right. The following quote from the newsletter of Phyllis Schafly's Eagle Forum seems fairly typical of these groups:

> With true phonics, the child is first taught to recognize the letters of the alphabet and then is drilled in the letter sounds—first vowels, then consonants, then consonant-vowel combinations—so that the child develops an automatic association between letters and sounds. When that is accomplished, the child is then given words, sentences, and stories to read. ("Civil Rights," 1989, p. 3).

Notice that the author is advocating phonics *first*: before giving children the opportunity to read real literature—or even sentences!

There is substantial evidence that advocacy for heavy phonics instruction is coming particularly from certain individuals and organizations within the Far Right. For instance, the ultraright National Association of Christian Educators (NACE) and its action group Citizens for Excellence in Education (CEE) urge their Christian followers to insist upon the teaching of phonics in the schools (R. L. Simonds, 1984)—as if the schools have not been teaching phonics for years within basal reading programs. (Obviously, the phonics of basal programs is not extensive or intensive enough, and is contaminated by reading itself.) A publication of the Heritage Foundation, a conservative think tank in Washington, extols phonics as "the very first tenet of the back to basics approach," which is advocated as the best approach to the illiteracy problem (Allen, 1989, p. 8).

What motivates such advocacy? Oddly enough, it may not necessarily be what proponents claim: namely, the desire to teach all children to read. A great deal of the force behind such advocacy seems to be the desire to promote a religious agenda and/or to maintain the socioeconomic status quo.

Major Far Right leaders and groups include: Dr. Robert Simonds, director of the National Association of Christian Educators and the local and state branches that are often called Citizens for Excellence in Education, or CEEs; Samuel Blumenfeld, author, and editor of *The Blumenfeld Education Letter;* Robert W. Sweet, president of the National Right to Read Foundation (a pro-phonics organization) and publisher of its Right to Read Report; Norma and Mel Gabler, founders of Educational Research Analysts; Phyllis Schlafly, newspaper columnist and director of the Eagle Forum; Rev. Pat Robertson, host of the 700 Club on television; Rev. Jerry Falwell, founder of Liberty Federation; Beverly LaHay, director of Concerned Women for America; such groups as The Heritage Foundation, Pro-Family Forum, and the American Freedom Coalition; and U.S. Senators Orrin Hatch and Jesse Helms. Addresses for such organizations are included in Janet Jones' *What's Left After the Right?* (1990) and *No Right Turn* (1993). These also include information on organizations that combat censorship and the Far Right's attempt to impose its agenda on the public schools. These organizations include People for the American Way, American Civil Liberties Union, Americans for Religious Liberty, National Education Association, Council of Chief State School Officers, The Association for Supervision and Curriculum Development, the National Council of Teachers of English, and the International Reading Association.

The Hidden Agenda

Of course, it's important to note at the outset that by no means all members of the religious or political Far Right share an interest in promoting extensive and intensive phonics. Nevertheless, there is considerable agreement among at least some of the aforementioned leaders and the political action groups they have founded to control what will and what won't be taught in schools.

At least some Far Right religious leaders and groups seem to vest unquestioned authority in the church, the home, and the school—insofar as school serves the interests of the other two. Neither church nor parental authority nor the authority of the Scriptures is to be questioned, it appears, and whole language—which insists that individual interpretation of texts is not only permissible but inevitable—is charged with promoting Godlessness (e.g., Blumenfeld, 1992, 1994).

What does this have to do with phonics? A lot. Members of the Far Right who emphasize getting the words "right" and value so-called literal recall rather than construction of meaning also tend to insist upon the extensive and intensive teaching of phonics. Having children do extensive and intensive work with phonics suits their worldview. For example, James A. Chapman explicitly argues against a psycholinguistic view of reading in his pamphlet titled *Why Not Teach Intensive Phonics?* (1986). Specifically, he insists that intensive teaching of phonics is necessary because only the ability to sound out unfamiliar words will guarantee word-perfect reading. According to Chapman, "whenever initial emphasis is placed upon meaning instead of upon identifying the exact words that are on the page, a student is implicitly learning that individual words are not important" (p. 13). Of course, Chapman's does not necessarily represent the views of most Christians when he writes:

> Individual words may not be important to "progressive" educators (for whom excellence in education has never been a goal), but **the emphasis upon individual words has always been of paramount importance to Christian educators, who believe in the verbal inspiration of the Scriptures and in quality education.** Orthodox Christians believe that God gave every word of Scripture, not just the thoughts. . . . Christians therefore who are training young people to respond to Jesus' command to "live by every word that proceedeth out of the mouth of God" (Matt. 4:4) should reject a system of reading that trains students to guess at words and to be content with approximate meanings. . . . If one uses the whole-word method, which treats phonetic words as if they were ideographs, one can get away from stability, from standards, from restraint, from traditional pronounciation, from traditional spelling, and from correct and incorrect forms of speech. Such freedom is delightful to the "progressives," but not to Christians who see the importance of standards in all areas of life and thus are striving for excellence in education. (pp. 13–15).

Thus teaching intensive phonics is a way of maintaining "standards." It is also a way of keeping children's attention on doing what they're told and keeping them from reading or thinking for themselves. Furthermore, the curriculum is controlled by skills materials, which means it is not subject to teacher or student interest or whim but *is* readily monitored by parents. (This line of reasoning is further developed in Weaver, 1992a, and Brinkley, 1991; see also the relevant information sheet in Center for the Expansion of Learning and Teaching, 1992, and in Edelsky, 1993). We have drawn upon writings from and about the religious Far Right in coming to these conclusions and in coming to understand the Far Right's objections to whole language—objections that they typically relate to or hide under other guises, such as their fear (whether alleged or real) that children are not learning phonics. For example, Blumenfeld (1992, 1994) charges that "Whole language is a way of preventing children from becoming fluent, accurate phonetic readers" (p. 7; see also Blumenfeld, 1992b). Notice the concern for accuracy in identifying words and for sounding out words, along with the lack of concern for constructing meaning. (Other resources that reflect or shed light on the Far Right's educational agenda include Groothuis, 1988; Marrs, 1987; Martin, 1989; Schott, 1989; and Moffett, 1988). At the extreme, someone even said once in a public hearing that "God believes in the beauty of phonics" (Moffet, 1988, p. 226).

The Political Connection

If at least some elements within the religious Far Right are eager to preserve the authority of home and church and therefore, it seems, to promote forms of instruction that require adherence to a prescribed and thought-limiting curriculum, so some elements within the political Far Right are equally eager to preserve the socioeconomic status quo.

The political Far Right's agenda is well-served by promoting docility and obedience—on the part of the lower classes. The school is an ideal vehicle for teaching and preserving socioeconomic stratification. We assess students; divide them into "ability" groups, different tracks, and regular versus resource rooms; and teach them differently, according to their alleged ability. By the time they leave school, those in the lower groups/tracks/programs have generally lived down to the expectations of others and accepted their lower-class status (e.g., McGill-Franzen & Allington, 1991; Anderson & Pellicer, 1990).

Far-fetched? That's what I used to think, until I began reading more and more of so-called critical theory (e.g., Apple, 1982; Giroux, 1983; Shor, 1986; Aronowitz & Giroux, 1991). This reading and my subsequent reflection have convinced me that such stratification is not innocent—that, for example, recent government and business insistence upon more standardized tests for "accountability" is, in significant measure, an attempt to make schools even more effective as a means of preserving social stratification.

The Hidden Curriculum

From one point of view, though, what matters is not whether certain groups *try* to keep children passive and obedient, but what actually happens to them during their schooling. Therefore, what I want to address next is the hidden agenda of heavy phonics instruction—the probable educational, political, and social consquences of such instruction, regardless of whether such consequences are or are not a conscious agenda of those who promote phonics and more phonics.

Much of what students learn in school is not the overt curriculum, the content that is explicitly taught, if not necessarily learned. What students learn from schooling other than the overt content is often called the *hidden curriculum*. Because of its pervasiveness, the hidden curriculum may constitute more of what students learn in school than anything that is explicitly taught (Giroux, 1983, pp. 42–71; Shor, 1986, pp. 168–173; Lester & Onore, 1990, pp. 9, 15–35).

The hidden curriculum includes, but is not limited to, what is learned through the very organization and structure of schools: through the way authority and power are distributed and decisions made in the classroom and the school; through the omission or inclusion of content and materials from the curriculum and the library; through the way decisions about content and curriculum are made; through the way knowledge is dispensed or learning facilitated; through the rules for behavior and the way these are determined and enforced; through the way interpersonal conflicts and discipline are handled; and through the way success is measured and failure determined. To put it somewhat differently, the hidden curriculum resides not only in what is included and what excluded from the curriculum, but also in the means by which curriculum and school policies are determined and the way that the teaching/learning enterprise and evaluation are carried out—the *how* of schooling. These depend significantly upon who makes these curricular and instructional decisions.

Heavy phonics instruction reflects the assumptions of a transmission model of education, and the hidden curriculum inherent in that model. Some basics of that model are that:

1. Learning consists primarily of mastering skills and facts; it requires correct habit formation.
2. Teachers are expert technicians, dispensing the curriculum directly. The curriculum controls what teachers will teach and what students will learn.
3. Students are passive recipients of knowledge. They learn primarily by practicing skills taught by the teacher or the workbook, and by memorizing information.

When such implicit assumptions direct the develoment of curriculum guides and instructional materials, control and decision making are primarily autocratic and authoritarian. Both teachers and students are devalued and disempowered.

Clearly, these assumptions underlie phonics instruction that is both extensive and intensive. Heavy phonics instruction trains students to be passive and obedient, not to be active in their own learning. This may be another reason why such instruction appeals to businesspeople and politicians, who are accustomed to top-down control. It simply reflects their assumptions about how the world should be run. But more important, such instruction contributes to maintaining the unequal distribution of money and power among different social and ethnic groups.

The mechanisms by which this occurs bear scrutiny.

Intensive Phonics and Skills for the Less Advantaged

Whether ultraconservative forces are consciously aware of it or not, intensive skills instruction, including intensive phonics instruction, tends to promote the traditional conservative agenda of maintaining a stratified society, through both the hidden and the overt curriculum (for the socioeconomic connection, see Anyon, 1980; for an emphasis on the effects of heavy skills work, see L. W. Anderson & Pellicer, 1990; McGill-Franzen & Allington, 1991; Allington, 1991). The process whereby education maintains the status quo goes something like this:

1. Students from nonmainstream homes, typically lower socioeconomic and minority children, are often judged unready for school, lacking in the experiences and therefore the skills that will ensure success—specifically, certain emergent literacy skills already developed by many mainstream children (P. Shannon, 1985, 1989b, 1992; Giroux, 1983).

2. Such students are then assigned to lower "ability" groups. In particular, there is not only a strong correlation between reading group and social class, but even some evidence that social class may itself be (or formerly have been) a strong determinant of what ability group children are assigned to (Rist, 1970; see summaries in McDermott, 1974, and Hamilton, 1983).

3. Nonmainstream students, especially those in so-called lower ability groups or tracks, typically receive authoritarian instruction that serves to socialize them into subordinate roles. This is part of the hidden curriculum of the schools.

4. For such students, the overt curriculum—in language arts and reading, particularly—consists more of completing worksheets on isolated skills, such as phonics, than of reading and constructing meaning from connected texts.

5. Such instruction prevents these students from achieving their potential as readers. They become not only less successful as measured by standardized tests of reading, but often less successful in reading authentic texts as well; in short, they become less effective and therefore less motivated readers.

6. Because education in our schools depends so heavily upon the ability to read, these less successful readers typically are offered a less challenging education than their more advantaged mainstream counterparts. Ultimately, they tend simply to receive *less* education: they drop out of school.

7. Having received less education, such students typically must settle for lower-paying, lower-status jobs.

8. Thus, they in turn are likely to raise families that are nonmainstream, at least in economic terms. And their nonmainstream children all too often go through the same cycle.

Since the crux of the issue is the nature and the effects of such differential instruction for mainstream and nonmainstream students, we need to consider this in more detail.

Differential Reading Instruction

Keep in mind that a vastly disproportionate number of nonmainstream students are assigned to lower reading groups, on the grounds that they do not have the requisite background or skills for the higher reading groups.

Significantly, the *manner* of instruction in lower reading groups socializes these students for subordinate roles in school and in society. In addition, the *content* of such instruction tends to prevent these students from learning to read well enough to achieve more rewarding roles. Thus, both the manner and the content of instruction for students in lower reading groups contrasts significantly with the reading instruction offered those in higher reading groups—typically, the more advantaged, mainstream students.

The differential instruction afforded students considered "good" and "poor" readers is well documented in a variety of studies, as mentioned by Pinnell (1989) and summarized by McGill-Franzen & Allington (1991), Shannon (1985), Hillerich (1985), and Cazden (1985); see Figure 7 .1 for full references for key sources. Notice how the curriculum, both hidden and overt, differs for those labeled "good" and "poor" readers:

1. Readers in lower groups spend approximately 70 to 75 percent of their time in oral reading, done round robin—in trying to say the words correctly while the teacher listens and corrects. Readers in higher groups spend about 70 to 75 percent of their time reading silently, for meaning and enjoyment (Allington, 1983).
2. When readers in higher groups make a miscue, teachers typically ignore the miscue or suggest how the context may help to clarify meaning. But when readers in lower groups make a miscue, teachers typically stop them and often call attention to the

Allington, R. L. (1983). The reading instruction provided readers of differing reading abilities. *The Elementary School Journal, 83,* 548–559.

Allington, R. L., & McGill-Franzen, A. (1989). Different programs, indifferent instruction. In D. Lipsky & A. Gartner (Eds.), *Beyond separate education: Quality education for all* (pp. 75–98). Baltimore: Park Brookes.

Anderson, L. W., & Pellicer, L. O. (1990). Synthesis of research on compensatory and remedial education. *Educational Leadership, 48,* 10–16.

Hillerich, R. L. (1985). Let's pretend. *Michigan Journal of Reading, 18* (Summer), 15–18, 20.

McGill-Franzen, A. & Allington, R. L. (1991). The gridlock of low reading achievement: Perspectives on practice and policy. *Remedial and Special Education,* 12(3) 20–30.

Shannon, P. (1985). Reading instruction and social class. *Language Arts, 62,* 604–613.

Figure 7.1 *References on the nature and effects of instruction for lower-group readers and/or students in remedial and compensatory programs*

letter/sound cues exclusively, or correct the miscues immediately, giving the students in lower groups much less time to discover a lack of continuity in meaning and to correct themselves.

3. Reading lessons for lower groups are more teacher-centered, more tightly monitored, and more likely to focus on literal interpretation of text rather than upon drawing inferences, analyzing, evaluating, and extending or relating to what has been read (Brophy & Good, 1986).

4. Readers in lower groups receive much more drill on isolated words than do readers in higher groups. The lower-group readers are kept busy practicing skills with workbooks and dittos, and they may be drilled on word lists and flash cards. The higher-group readers read whole books and participate in creative ways of enhancing and expressing comprehension.

The students who seem most likely to be condemned to such authoritarian and stultifying instruction are those taught in compensatory Chapter 1 programs for the disadvantaged, and those called learning disabled. It is well documented that students in compensatory or special education programs often receive kinds of instruction that serve to perpetuate their status as labeled readers; it is also well documented that such students are often indistinguishable from others on the basis of their reading alone (Allington, 1983, 1987; Allington, Struetzel, & Shake, 1986; Allington & McGill-Franzen, 1989; Ysseldyke, Thurlow, Mecklenburg, & Graden, 1984; Ysseldyke, Algozzine, Shinn, & McGue, 1982).

It should not be surprising that such mind-numbing instruction prevents these students from achieving their potential as readers. After all, it is not the completion of skills work that produces good readers, but extensive experience reading authentic texts (R. C. Anderson, Hiebert, Scott, & Wilkinson, 1985, pp. 75–76). It is no wonder that for many students, being assigned to a compensatory Chapter 1 class or a special education class amounts to a life sentence of inferiority (L. W. Anderson & Pellicer, 1990; McGill-Franzen & Allington, 1991). Rex Brown, in his book *Schools of Thought* (1991), uses the example of a "successful" all-black school district to demonstrate how an exclusive focus on basic skills, even where there is strong community support for education, prevents students from aspiring to or attaining a level of achievement beyond that of their parents. The vicious cycle of exclusion from mainstream society is maintained, to a significant degree, by overemphasis on basic skills instruction, including phonics, and a concomitant underemphasis on reading for meaning and enjoyment.

Unfortunately, this vicious cycle is all too likely to be encouraged by the summary of Marilyn Adams' book *Beginning to Read: Thinking and Learning About Print* (1990a) written by Stahl, Osborn, and Lehr (Adams, 1990b) and cited approvingly by Far Right phonics advocates even before it was published ("Illiteracy," 1989). It is clear from Adams' own book (1990a) that she advocates extensive and enriched literacy experiences *first,* especially for children who have not had such experiences in the home. The authors of the summary of Adams' book seem to share this view (e.g., Stahl, 1992), but this does not come through clearly in the summary itself. There, the authors state:

[For] children who enter school with almost no relevant knowledge of print, much of the content of the beginning reading lessons will be new in detail and concept and, as a consequence, more confusing and harder to put together [than for children who already have already had extensive exposure to books].

To make sure that all necessary letter-sound pairs are learned well, teachers must see to it that [these low-readiness] students receive sufficient practice with each pair, and that they evaluate what their students are learning. (Adams, 1990b; the language is similar to that in Adams, 1990a, pp. 239–240)

Unfortunately, statements such as these are already being used to justify intensive and extensive phonics instruction for allegedly less prepared readers (D. Taylor, 1991a). Given past practices and effects, it seems likely that such heavy phonics instruction will serve to perpetuate the nonmainstream status of many of these students: through the overt curriculum, which keeps them busy with skills work instead of real reading; and through the hidden curriculum, which socializes students for subordinate roles, both in school and in society.

SYSTEMATIC PHONICS

Among reading researchers and educators, almost all who advocate the direct and systematic teaching of phonics also insist that such teaching nevertheless be relatively simple and brief (e.g., Stahl, 1992).

For example, *Becoming a Nation of Readers* (R. C. Anderson, Hiebert, Scott, & Wilkinson, 1985) is often cited in justification of heavy phonics instruction. But in fact the authors of the report clearly see phonics instruction as playing a very limited role in reading development. The report issues such warnings as these (pp. 38–43):

1. The purpose of phonics instruction is to reveal the *alphabetic principle*, the fact that there is a relationship (however inexact) between letters and sounds in the English language.
2. Phonics instruction should teach only the most important and regular of letter/sound relationships.
3. Phonics can be expected to help children come up with only approximate pronunciations that must be checked against their knowledge of real words and against the context in which the words occur.
4. A number of reading programs try to teach too many letter/sound relationships; thus, much of today's phonics instruction is probably unnecessary and unproductive.
5. It is not important that children be able to state the "rules" governing letter/sound relationships; they need only have a working knowledge of basic relationships.

Other statements in *Becoming a Nation of Readers* further clarify that phonics is not to be considered a *method* for teaching reading; rather, it is only one cue system used in identifying words.

In her widely cited book *Beginning to Read: Thinking and Learning About Print* (1990a), Marilyn Adams suggests teaching just onsets and rimes: the beginnings of words, particularly initial consonants and consonant clusters, and the parts that enter into rhymes: letter patterns like *-ate*, *-est*, *-ice*, *-unk*, and so forth. She cites Wylie and Durrell (1970), who have pointed out that nearly five hundred primary-grade words can be derived from a set of only thirty-seven rimes. Vowel sounds in these rime patterns are quite stable, so teaching rime patterns is far more useful than teaching vowel sounds in isolation.

Oddly enough, considering her fairly moderate suggestion for teaching phonics systematically, Adams notes throughout the book that research supports the "intensive" teaching of phonics (e.g., p. 13). Perhaps it is not surprising, then, that her book has been cited as "proving" that phonics should be taught extensively and intensively. In fact, however, the research base is ambiguous and open to challenge. Furthermore, Adams has totally ignored the other side of the coin, entirely omitting from consideration the rich body of professional literature on children's literacy development in whole language classrooms.

Research Supporting the Systematic Teaching of Phonics

The classroom research Adams cites in favor of teaching phonics systematically is mainly that cited by Jeanne Chall in *Learning to Read: The Great Debate* (1967, updated 1983), and the twenty-seven U.S. Office of Education studies as analyzed and summarized by Bond and Dykstra (1967).

At the outset of her study, Chall admitted, "One of the most important things, if not *the* most important thing, I learned from studying the existing research on beginning reading is that it says nothing consistently. . . . Taken as a whole, the research on beginning reading is strongly inconclusive" (Chall, 1967, pp. 87, 88). But guided by her theoretical perspective, Chall attempted to create order out of the chaos of conflicting data (Chall, 1989, pp. 524–528).

Because Chall's original conclusions are often oversimplified and then cited as definitive, these conclusions are worth quoting in detail:

> In summary, judging from the studies comparing systematic with intrinsic phonics, we can say that systematic phonics at the very beginning tends to produce generally better reading and spelling achievement than intrinsic phonics, at least through grade 3.
>
> More specifically, the child who begins with systematic phonics achieves early superiority in word recognition. This superior ability may not always show up on standardized silent reading (comprehension and vocabulary) tests in the first grade. But by the second and third grades, greater facility in recognizing words probably increases his ability to read for meaning, as measured by standardized silent reading tests of vocabulary and comprehension.
>
> As for rate, systematic phonics may produce slower readers in grades 1 and 2 because it develops greater concern for working out the words. However, by

the middle grades, rate seems to be about equal to that produced by intrinsic phonics.

Finally, there is probably a limit to the advantage that early facility with the code gives on comprehension tested after grade 4. After this point intelligence, experience, and language maturity probably become more important factors in success than ability to recognize words. (Chall, 1967, p. 114)

Thus, according to this early synthesis, systematic phonics produces higher scores on tests of reading and spelling "achievement," but only through the primary grades.

Much the same conclusion is drawn by Bond and Dykstra (1967) in their consideration of the twenty-seven USOE cooperative first-grade studies conducted during 1965–66. In a later summary of his conclusions favoring phonics, Dykstra says:

The evidence clearly demonstrates that children who receive early intensive instruction in phonics develop superior word recognition skills in the early stages of reading and tend to maintain their superiority at least through the third grade. These same pupils tend to do somewhat better than pupils enrolled in meaning-emphasis (delayed gradual phonics) programs in reading comprehension at the end of the first grade. (1974, p. 397)

Thus, these studies would seem to favor systematic phonics over intrinsic phonics; at least for grades 1 through 3, and at least according to standardized measures. Marilyn Adams (1990a) cites two studies that she thinks demonstrate positive longer-term effects from the early teaching of intensive, systematic phonics (Becker & Gersten, 1982; Gersten & Keating, 1987), but few are likely to find the evidence from these studies convincing. (For a fuller treatment, see Weaver, 1990b). Even Gersten himself has agreed, at least with reference to the earlier study (Gersten, 1990).

The Research Critiqued

It is important to note that evidence for the systematic teaching of phonics is all based upon reading "performance" or "achievement," as measured on standardized tests that typically test letter/sound knowledge and word knowledge in isolation. Even the comprehension portions of such tests typically test comprehension "skills." The tests do not consider such factors as whether children are developing effective reading strategies, whether they can actually read environmental print and books, and whether they can write using letters to represent sounds. Thus, reading "performance" and "achievement" have to do with scores on tests of isolated skills, not with the ability to actually read, comprehend, and enjoy real texts.

So where does this leave us?

For one thing, some scholars have interpreted some of the research differently, while others have critiqued the validity of the research studies and therefore the conclusions drawn by phonics advocates. Others have questioned at least the significance of the research results. Whole language educators have been among the challengers.

Chall admitted in her 1983 update of *Learning to Read: The Great Debate* (1967) that several other reviews of the USOE studies (e.g., Corder, 1971) did not conclude that code-emphasis approaches (typically phonics) were superior to meaning-emphasis approaches, even when measured just by standardized tests. Chall wrote:

> Yet many of the summaries of the USOE studies, and particularly the interpretations of their findings, contradicted this [her own] conclusion. Only a few indicated that the results showed an advantage for a heavier code-emphasis. Several, in fact, concluded that the USOE findings contradicted those of *The Great Debate*. This would mean that the USOE studies pointed to a meaning-emphasis as the advantageous approach. Yet this was not reported either. Indeed, most reviewers seemed to conclude that the 27 USOE studies found no method superior to any other. Superior results, if any, were attributed to the teacher. (1983 update, p. 6)

Also noteworthy is the fact that most of the so-called meaning-emphasis approaches focused on sight word recognition, not on reading whole texts and thereby developing sight vocabulary, reading strategies, and skills in the context of reading. In one analysis of the USOE data, a well-known European scholar concluded that the approaches that came closest to being "whole language" actually produced the best results (Grundin, 1985, p. 265).

In a 1988 critique of Chall's research synthesis in her *Learning to Read: The Great Debate* (1967, updated 1983), Marie Carbo points out what Chall admitted in her original attempt to synthesize the results of the experimental research studies: many of them had serious design flaws (Chall, 1967, pp. 100–101; Carbo, 1988a). Carbo's further analysis of the data from 16 of 31 studies discussed by Chall reveals some additional flaws in Chall's own analysis and reporting of these results. In several ways, Chall tended to skew the data as being more favorable to phonics instruction than the data seem to warrant. Carbo (1988a) demonstrates that this criticism applies not only to the studies reviewed and to the conclusions drawn in Chall's original 1967 edition of *The Great Debate*, but also to the post-1967 studies that Chall discusses (Chall, 1983 update).

To try to resolve the debate that developed between Carbo and Chall, assessment expert Richard Turner decided to see what conclusions could be drawn if he considered only "the best evidence" from the research Chall considered. He rejected not only laboratory experiments, which inevitably distort the nature of the normal reading process, but also "patched-up program evaluations," which constituted the vast majority of articles cited by Chall and criticized by Carbo.

This left nine randomized field experiments that compared a systematic phonics approach with either an intrinsic phonics approach or a "no-phonics" approach, in which students were left to develop, over time, their own methods for figuring out sounds in unrecognized words. Turner suggests that the latter strategy would be characteristic of a whole language approach, but in practice most whole language teachers combine this strategy with various kinds of direct and indirect teaching of phonics (see Chapter 5). None of the studies compared a systematic phonics approach to reading instruction with a whole language approach to developing literacy.

What the studies did compare is systematic phonics with differing variants of a whole word approach. Turner hypothesized that any initial advantages one approach might have over the other would appear early in the primary grades and then disappear. The data generally supported this hypothesis, leading Turner to conclude as follows:

> My overall conclusion from reviewing the randomized field studies is that systematic phonics falls into that vast category of weak instructional treatments with which education is perennially plagued. Systematic phonics appears to have a slight and early advantage over a basal-reader/whole-word approach as a method of beginning reading instruction. . . . However, this difference does not last long and has no clear meaning for the acquisition of literacy in the sense of enhancing vocabulary and improving comprehension. Moreover, learning theory offers little reason to believe that it should do so. (Turner, 1989, p. 283)

Turner concludes his analysis of the randomized field experiments by stating, "Perhaps it is time for reading experts to turn away from the debate over systematic phonics in search of more powerful instructional treatments that will influence the development of literacy in the middle grades and beyond" (p. 283).

Yes, indeed.

Misunderstanding and Invalid Research

When systematic phonics advocates have attempted to compare phonics or skills approaches with whole language classrooms, they have operated out of an apparent misunderstanding of whole language. This leads to invalid conclusions.

For example, the authors of *Becoming a Nation of Readers* wrote that in the United States, whole language approaches had produced results that were typically "indifferent" when compared with approaches typical in American classrooms—at least when measured by "performance on first- and second-grade standardized reading achievement tests" (R. C. Anderson, Hiebert, Scott, & Wilkinson, 1985, p. 45). However, the reference supporting this statement is Bond and Dykstra's 1967 summary of the USOE studies, which were undertaken at least two decades before whole language burgeoned in the United States. (Also, see Grundin's differing conclusion: that the approaches most like whole language produced the *best* results; Grundin, 1985, p. 265.)

More recently, Stahl and Miller (1989) conducted a statistical meta-analysis ("quantative research synthesis") of data from various studies in an attempt to compare the effects of differing approaches. Combining whole langue and language experience as if they were essentially the same (even though these researchers seemed to know better), they concluded that "overall, whole language/language experience approaches are approximately equal in their effects" to basal reader/skills approaches, but with some exceptions: for example, they note that whole language/language experience approaches may be most effective for developing concepts about print, while more direct approaches might be better at helping students master word recognition skills (Stahl & Miller, 1989, p. 87). However, anything the research might have suggested about whole language is invalidated by the fact that it is lumped together with language experience. As Chapter 3 should have made clear, language experience is simply one kind of activity that may be included in classrooms reflecting a much broader whole language philosophy of learning and teaching. (For more detailed criticisms, see McGee & Lomax, 1990, and Schickendanz, 1990.)

The fact that these researchers could have drawn such invalid conclusions may stem, in part, from the fact that systematic phonics researchers and whole language researchers typically operate from very different underlying assumptions.

DIFFERING ASSUMPTIONS

When considering the differences between systematic phonics researchers and whole language researchers (and those who sympathetically summarize their respective research) it is important to take into account their underlying assumptions, because these assumptions guide how they set up research studies and interpret the results: what they look for, and what counts as evidence (see, for instance, Edelsky's 1990 critique of McKenna, Robinson, & Miller, 1990).

To begin with, judging by their research studies, systematic phonics researchers consider readers' performance on standardized tests of isolated skills (reading "achievement") to be accurate and adequate measures of reading; whole language researchers do not. Instead, the latter consider it critical to examine reading and writing growth together, along with other aspects of intellectual and affective growth; to assess reading and writing by observing, describing, and analyzing what students do with literacy daily, not via standardized tests of skills; and to use a variety of measures in formal research.

One corollary is this: systematic phonics researchers seem to believe that students must be able to demonstrate a skill in isolation from actual reading, in order to control that skill or make use of that knowledge during actual reading. Furthermore, they often have a part-to-whole concept of reading. For example, Vellutino (in an article that reflects serious misconceptions about whole language) writes approvingly that "phoneme awareness [awareness of the separate sounds in words] is believed to be a prerequisite for learning to map alphabetic symbols to sound, and alphabetic mapping is believed to be a prerequisite for learning to identify individual words and learning to read in general" (1991, p. 439). From experience and research, whole language educators assume that understanding of the parts (letter/sound relationships and words) develops more gradually but also more readily within the context of the whole—reading and rereading predictable and enjoyable texts, and writing by using invented spelling. They also see no need for skills to be mastered or demonstrated in isolation; indeed, they assume that an emphasis on skills detracts from the process of learning to read.

Another corollary is this: systematic phonics researchers seem to concern themselves with short-term performance on test scores (e.g., on tests of letter/sound knowledge in grade 1), without considering how such an emphasis might affect students' overall growth as readers and writers and literate individuals through the primary years and beyond. Whole language educators and researchers take the longer view.

Systematic phonics researchers seem to take *correlations* either as evidence of unproven cause-effect relationships, as mandates for educational intervention, or both. For example, research indicates that there is a demonstrable correlation between fluent word identification and comprehension among good readers (e.g., Stanovich, 1980, 1981, 1984; Adams, 1990a). This has led systematic phonics advocates and others to assume that readers cannot comprehend well unless they can identify words fluently, an assumption that is clearly disproven by decades of miscue research (K. S. Goodman & Y. M. Goodman, n. d.); odd as it may seem, readers who read haltingly and with many miscues often comprehend quite well. The correlation between fluent word identification and comprehension has also led part-to-whole-oriented researchers to assume that phonics must be taught early¹ and perhaps intensively, to facilitate fluent reading and thus comprehension; this is part of Adams' argument (1990a). Supported by research on language acquisition and emergent literacy, whole language researchers reject not only the implicit assumption that the earlier children acquire phonics knowlege the better, but also the assumption that phonics must be systematically taught in order to generate fluent word reading and analysis. They are more concerned with the development of a wide array of literacy understandings, behaviors, and attitudes, on the assumption that the development of the whole of literacy is far more important in the long run.

Here's another example of phonics researchers using correlations as cause-effect relationships: Byrne and Fielding-Barnsley (1991) cite studies showing that phonemic awareness affects reading and spelling skills, then take as the starting point for their research the assumption that "It makes sense, therefore, to include instruction in phonemic organization in the early stages of the reading curriculum" (1991, p. 451). In other words, these researchers assume that because there's a correlation between phonemic awareness and reading and spelling skills, the earlier phonics is mastered, the better. Whole language researchers and educators note that this conclusion does not necessarily follow. Sooner is not necessarily better—at least not if other important learning is sacrificed.

Finally, systematic phonics researchers generally operate from a "stage theory" model of learning to read (Chall, 1983; Adams, 1990a; Stahl, 1992). What this means in practice is that they recognize the transactional nature of emergent literacy, up to and perhaps through kindergarten (Adams, 1990a; Chall, 1983). However, they seem to think that by grade 1, children must be explicitly taught to read; they can no longer be trusted to develop literacy by transacting with environmental print and books and by engaging in writing experiences, in a supportive environment. These researchers seem to trade in their transactional model of birth-through-kindergarten learning for a transmission model, starting in grade 1. At least, that's what one can infer from their insistence that by grade 1 (if not before), children must begin to be explicitly and systematically taught phonics. Whole language researchers assume that the constructivist nature of learning continues throughout our lives, whether or not we are taught by means compatible with how we learn most effectively.

Contrasting the underlying assumptions of systematic phonics researchers with those of whole language researchers sets the stage for better understanding the research that supports whole language.

RESEARCH SUPPORTING A WHOLE LANGUAGE ALTERNATIVE

There is a world of difference between phonics and whole language. Even though it is often promoted as a method of teaching reading, phonics deals only with one cue system used to construct meanings from texts. At the opposite end of the spectrum, whole language is in effect a total (albeit evolving and incomplete) theory or philosophy of learning and teaching. Phonics and whole language aren't really different routes to the same goals. Nevertheless, whole language classrooms do offer ways of developing phonics knowledge that contrast with systematic phonics (see also Chapter 5).

There are basically three kinds of research supporting whole language learning and teaching: research on language acquisition, emergent literacy, the reading process, and learning itself, which gave rise to whole language practice in the first place; naturalistic research documenting the success of whole language with individual children and classes; and experimental research comparing whole language with more traditional alternatives in the classroom (for summaries of research studies, see Krashen, 1993; Stephens, 1991; Shapiro, 1990; Heald-Taylor, 1989; Tunnell & Jacobs, 1989; Rhodes & Shanklin, 1989; and Weaver, 1988). The first kind of research forms the basis for much of this book, while the second is much better described in a rich abundance of other books and articles (see bibliographies in Chapter 3). The third kind of research, research comparing one kind of program or classroom with another, is briefly discussed below. An excellent overview of the research base is provided in Diane Stephens' *Research on Whole Language: Support for a New Curriculum* (1991). Stephens describes many of the studies in some depth, particularly the less accessible ones. (See Figure 7.2 for fuller bibliographic information on these summaries of research.) Stephens and I have described some of these studies also in Chapter 6 of my *Understanding Whole Language* (1990a), earlier studies were described in the first edition of *Reading Process and Practice* (1988). Below I describe three of the studies in those volumes, updating the references; describe four more studies; and draw generalizations from the seven studies reviewed. Described in greatest detail are those that are richest in the selection of subjects, the length of the study, the collection of data, or (at least in one instance) the characterizations of contrasting kinds of classrooms.

Because phonics advocates typically measure progress by standardized test scores, I have deliberately chosen, for comparison, studies that included at least one standardized test among the assessment measures. However, this decision should not be construed as evidence that I think standardized tests are appropriate measures of literacy development.

The first study described is actually a summary of nine research studies on learning English as a second language. The other studies are described in an order reflecting the age of the children and grade of the classrooms discussed, with longitudinal studies described last.

Goodman, K. S. (1989). Whole-language research: Foundations and development. *The Elementary School Journal, 90,* 208–221.

Hall, N. (1987). *The emergence of literacy.* Portsmouth, NH: Heinemann.

Heald-Taylor, G. (1989). *The administrator's guide to whole language.* Chap. 8, "Whole language research: Key studies and reference literature." Katonah, NY: Richard C. Owen.

Krashen, S. (1993). *The power of reading: Insights from the research.* Englewood, CO: Libraries Unlimited.

Rhodes, L. K., & Shanklin, N. L. (1989). *A research base for whole language.* Denver, CO: LINK.

Shapiro, J. (1990). Research perspectives on whole language. In V. Froese (Ed.), *Whole language practice and theory* (pp. 313–356). Boston: Allyn & Bacon.

Stephens, D. (1991). *Research on whole language: Support for a new curriculum.* Katonah, NY: Richard C. Owen.

Tunnell, M. O., & Jacobs, J. S. (1989). Using "real books": Research findings on literature based reading instruction. *The Reading Teacher, 42,* 470–477.

Weaver, C., & Stephens, D. (1990). What does the research say? Research in support of whole-to-part. In Constance Weaver, *Understanding whole language* (pp. 125–141). Portsmouth, NH: Heinemann.

Figure 7.2 *References summarizing research on whole language* (Note: *The references with the most items on experimental studies are Krashen and the last four.)*

W. Elley, 1991

Elley, W. B. (1991). Acquiring literacy in a second language: The effect of book-based programs. *Language Learning, 41*(3), 375–411.

Elley reviews nine studies of the acquisition of English as a second language, most of which were undertaken in the South Pacific and Southeast Asia, including his own earlier study (Elley & Manguhbai, 1983). Typically these studies compared the results of programs based on structured systematic instruction with "book flood" programs, which exposed children to large numbers of high-interest story books. In other words, the studies compared the effects of a direct instruction approach with an indirect approach that might be characterized as "whole language" or "natural" language learning. These studies all involved elementary school students.

What I've considered the direct instruction approach typically involved principles articulated by structural linguists (e.g., Bloomfield, 1942) and audiolingual methodology: practice on a carefully sequenced set of grammatical structures, through imitation, repetition, and reinforcement. The book flood studies reflected typical whole language principles, and usually involved either sustained silent reading of an extensive number of picture books; the Shared Book Experience (Holdaway, 1979), including reading, discussion, and related activities; or a combination of these, which in one instance also included a modified language experience approach.

From these combined studies, the following patterns emerged:

1. Students in the book flood programs did better on almost all standardized measures of reading, including not only comprehension skills but also word identification and phonics skills.
2. Usually favoring the book flood students were differences in measures of oral and written language and vocabulary (e.g., listening comprehension, written story completion), and sometimes differences in other aspects of school achievement as well (see also Elley, 1989).
3. More surprisingly, students in the book flood programs often did better on tests of the grammatical structures explicitly taught in the audiolingual program. Elley notes that this interpretation "was supported by an incidental study in which knowledge and use of English in natural settings was found to be largely unaffected by deliberate instruction in them" (1991, p. 389).
4. Students in Shared Book Experience programs typically showed greater gains on various tests than students in silent reading programs. (Perhaps this result suggests the value of oral reading and discussion, probably including the discussion of letter/sound relationships within the Shared Book Experience.)
5. Students in the book flood programs typically had a more positive attitude toward books and reading. (One wonders if these programs also affected children's attitudes toward English as a second language.)

Elley summarizes, in part, as follows: "That pupils showed equally large gains in the discrete-point tests of grammatical structures and vocabulary as they did in the more integrative measures of reading, listening, and writing is particularly damaging for those who argue that structures and vocabulary should be deliberately taught" (1991, p. 402). If more of the comparisons had included tests of decoding skills, perhaps the same conclusion could be drawn for the direct teaching of phonics.

In short, Elley's comparison of these several studies offers powerful evidence for whole language advocates' assertion that language and literacy are acquired gradually, through opportunities to use the language and to engage in literacy events in meaningful contexts.

W. C. Kasten and B. K. Clarke, 1989

Kasten, W. C., & Clarke, B. K. (1989). *Reading/writing readiness for preschool and kindergarten children: A whole language approach.* Sanibel: Florida Educational Research and Development Council, ED 312 041.

This year-long study involved children in two preschools and two kindergarten classes in two southwest Florida communities, one school at each level serving as a control and one implementing certain strategies associated with a whole language philosophy of learning. The latter will be referred to here as whole language classrooms and students, even though only the literacy activities were necessarily whole language in orientation.

The "business as usual" curriculum in the control classrooms seemed to proceed from common assumptions such as these (Kasten & Clarke, p. 73):

1. Children need to achieve a level of readiness for learning to read that includes extensive experience with letters of the alphabet and the sounds these letters represent. This occurs prior to learning to write.
2. Children are not ready or capable of writing connected text until a certain number of words can be spelled conventionally, and the prerequisite to writing is the ability to copy and formulate letters.
3. Authentic learning is limited to the learning or work produced by individuals who "do their own work," and learning is the result of what the teacher teaches.

Kasten and Clarke offer an extended anecdote that clarifies the nature of instruction stemming from such assumptions. The anecdote is from a private, well-funded, highly regarded preschool with an experienced, capable, highly regarded teacher:

> Ms. R. cheerfully welcomes her students and introduces us to them, reminding them of our names. Children gather in the carpeted area of the room around their teacher who is seated in a chair next to an easel. After some social conversation with the group, Ms. R. introduces the "special guest," who is a puppet named "Goofy Ghost." She announces they will talk about the letter G this day. The teacher elaborates that Goofy wears glasses and plays a guitar. She develops a story orally, preparing them to participate on a given signal with repeating phrases including "/g/ - /g/ - /g/ - /goo/," and "Goofy, good grief!" On the easel is paper with pockets which hold teacher prepared cards.
>
> As the story is completed, the teacher reviews "G" words with the children, and praises them at the end. She asks the children to give themselves a pat on the back, reviews the "G" words again, and they say "/g/ - /g/ - /g/ - /g/" a few more times. At the end, all children stand up to stretch, and are directed to pretend they are watering cans, and to make /g/ sound like water gushing from the watering cans with "/g/ - /g/ - /g/" noises.
>
> Next, the teacher initiates a guessing game with questions to "fill in the blank" orally, such as "Something Mommy puts on your mashed potatoes is . . .," and "You like to chew a stick of. . . ." (pp. 74–75)

The preschoolers are then asked to do some "writing": to copy the design Mrs. R. shows them on a flash card (circle, vertical line, etc.). She reminds them to "do their own work" and not look at anybody else's paper.

The instruction in the whole language preschool and kindergarten was significantly different, reflecting such assumptions as these (Kasten & Clarke, p. 72):

1. Children can write what they want to say before their knowledge of letter/sound relationships is perfect, and before they can spell conventionally.
2. Children can learn to read as they learn to speak, in a holistic, social context in which functions and purposes for reading are evident.

3. Children learn valuable lessons by collaborating with each other, and their learning can be enhanced by what they learn from each other.

In the following anecdote from a whole language preschool class, the paraprofessional teacher and all eight students are members of minority groups from very low socioeconomic neighborhoods. The anecdote illustrates the second and third of the above principles (Kasten & Clarke, pp. 67–68):

> The teacher presents a DLM book and, before she can ask the title, children call out "Three Dogs at the Door." Together the children count aloud the dogs on the cover, discuss the author, Roach Van Allen (1986), and discuss what an "illustrator" means. The children curl at the teacher's feet in an organized formation. The teacher uses a pointer as the class reads chorally. The teacher points out that the word "mad" looks different from the word "disgusted." The teacher asks individuals to act out how they might look if they felt "disgusted." All eight children say "disgusted," making appropriate facial expressions as they do.
>
> The children are extremely attentive, with all eyes on the book. They act out the next interesting word which is "upset," the same way they did with the word "disgusted." The teacher discusses with them how they can use these words when they have those feelings, labeling them for the children as "emotion words." They continue reading and come to the word "irritated." They discuss differences between "irritated," "mad," "upset," and "disgusted."

Teacher and children continue discussing the emotion words. The teacher then

> flips back through the text to each emotion word and asks which, of the ones they discussed, this one is. Each time some children guess correctly, and seem to be using initial letters to assist in their guesses of "disgusted," "furious," etc.

Since the children are not yet tired of shared reading, they go on to read *I'm the King of the Mountain* (Cowley, 1984b) together, using song and with the children chiming in on the repeated pattern "I'm the king of the mountain; I'm the king of the mountain." Finally, the children have the opportunity to choose books to read by themselves, in pairs, or to the teacher.

This anecdote nicely illustrates not only whole language principles of learning, but some of the procedures used in the whole language preschool and kindergarten classes. Shared reading experiences with predictable or patterned language books were to be used with the children at least twice a day, for a minimum of fifteen minutes each time. The teachers were asked to use a pointer to follow along with the text during the shared reading experiences. They were encouraged to extend the shared reading experiences through dramatization of the story, to use the text to teach concepts and skills, and to do "anything else their creativity might invent." The second aspect of the whole language program involved giving children an opportunity to write at least once a week: not to practice letter formation or to copy letters or someone else's text, but to compose— by writing using their own spellings or giving oral dictation to an adult (Kasten &

Clarke, p. 34). While these were the minimum criteria defining the whole language category, more time reading and writing—perhaps considerably more time—may have been spent in these classrooms.

The children were tested using several instruments: a Book Handling Test developed by Y. M. Goodman and B. Altwerger (included in Y. M. Goodman, Altwerger, & Marek, 1989) and a story Retelling Inventory based on the retelling portion of the Reading Miscue Inventory (Y. M. Goodman, Watson, & Burke, 1987), both used with all of the students; the six subtests of the Metropolitan Early School Inventory—Preliteracy (ESI), used as a posttest with preschoolers and both pretest and posttest with the kindergartners; and the Metropolitan Readiness Test (MRT), the latter used as a pretest and posttest only for the kindergartners. As Kasten and Clarke point out, the MRT attempts to assess traditional "readiness" skills, including letter knowledge, initial sounds, ending sounds, the sounds of consonant clusters, and so forth (1989, p. 30).

For the preschoolers, many of the differences between groups were not statistically significant. On the tests and subtests that were statistically significant, all the results favored the experimental, whole language classroom. The whole language children showed significantly more development than their comparison peers in the ESI subtest How You Read, on the story Retelling Inventory, and on the Book Handling Test.

For the kindergartners, all the differences except those on two subtests of the ESI (What You Read, and Name Writing) were statistically significant, favoring the children in the whole language classroom. Differences were particularly noticeable on subtest E of the ESI, Message Writing. When requested to produce some written message, the control students tended to inform the researchers that they couldn't write, while all of the experimental subjects produced some written message when asked to do to (Kasten & Clarke, p. 64). The whole language kindergartners performed significantly better than their counterparts on all subtests of the Metropolitan Readiness Test, including tests of beginning consonant sounds, letter/sound correspondences, and sounds and clusters of sounds in initial and final positions of words. They could also locate patterns in words or parts of words, and visually match items. In addition, they had a better command of the terminology associated with reading (letter, word, etc.).

However, these test results do not reveal the most significant differences between the control classes and the whole language classes. The investigators' field notes demonstrated that children in the whole language classes were clearly "falling in love with books": "The children frequently chose books over toys during free choice play times, even sometimes asking permission to take the books outside. These groups could be observed 'playing' at shared reading experiences, one student acting as the teacher, with a pointer in hand, and those playing 'student' reading in unison or taking turns reading. On other occasions, one child might sit alone, even with a less familiar book, and pretend to read by formulating a logical story to accompany the illustrations" (Kasten & Clarke, p. 70).

Clearly, these children perceived themselves as readers. They also came to perceive themselves as writers and began to write when asked to do so by the investigators, even if their writings were scribbled or unrecognizable. These behaviors and perceptions differed markedly from those of the control groups. While the whole language children demonstrated superiority in their development of literacy skills, as measured by various tests, their superior development in taking on the behaviors and attitudes of literate individuals was even more evident.

H. Ribowsky, 1985

Ribowsky, H. (1985). *The effects of a code emphasis approach and a whole language approach upon emergent literacy of kindergarten children.* Alexandria, VA: Educational Document Reproduction Service, ED 269 720. (Report developed more fully in Ribowsky's unpublished doctoral dissertation [same title], New York University, New York, 1986).

Though more limited in scope, Ribowsky's study focuses on measures of phonics knowledge.

The year-long study compared the effects of two approaches upon the emergent literacy of fifty-three girls in two kindergarten classes within an all girls' parochial school in the Northeast. The code emphasis classroom used a highly structured, teacher-directed program (Lippincott's *Beginning to Read, Write, and Listen* program). Consisting of twenty-four letter books, each with a teacher's guide, the program focuses mainly on hearing and analyzing phonemes and learning letter/sound correspondences. The whole language classroom used Holdaway's Shared Book Experience (Holdaway, 1979, pp. 72–73), which is described in Chapter 3.

In order to be fair to both approaches, Ribowsky employed different kinds of measures to assess the children's literacy development: Y. M. Goodman and Alterwerger's assessment of book handling knowledge (included in Y. M. Goodman, Altwerger, & Marek, 1989), the five principal subtests of the Test of Language Development—Primary; and the letter recognition and phoneme/grapheme subtests of the Metropolitan Achievement Test. The tests of letter recognition and phoneme/grapheme correspondence (consonants only) were administered only as posttests, since they were considered too difficult for beginning kindergartners.

Children in the whole language classrooms scored significantly better on all measures of growth and achievement, including the tests of letter recognition and letter/sound knowledge.

L. K. Clarke, 1988

Clarke, L. K. (1988). Invented versus traditional spelling in first graders' writings: Effects on learning to spell and read. *Research in the Teaching of English, 22,* 281–309.

This study compared the spelling development and certain aspects of the reading achievement of first-grade children in classrooms with contrasting approaches to spelling. The teachers in all the classrooms held writing sessions that totaled eighty to a hundred minutes a week, but two of the teachers encouraged traditional ("correct") spellings only, while the other two teachers encouraged children to construct or "invent" spellings of words they did not know. Each teacher used a basal reading program, taught letter sounds (generally in isolation), and taught the identification of initial letters and sounds as an important aid to reading words. Various oral drills and worksheets were used to reinforce the phonics skills.

In October, the students engaged in various pretests. Among other things, they were asked to print as many words as they could, and to read a list of high-frequency words from the Boder Word Recognition Inventory (Boder, 1973). Various aspects of children's writing behaviors were also recorded, including their strategies for spelling. Their written productions were also analyzed.

Differences between the traditional and the inventive spellers included the following:

1. Using invented spelling, more children were able to write independently in the early months, and their productions were significantly longer overall and contained a significantly greater variety of words and a significantly smaller percentage of correct spellings than the children encouraged to use only traditional spelling. (The investigator does not indicate which group could actually spell more words correctly.)

2. On the posttests, children using invented spelling scored significantly higher in two of the three spelling tasks than children using traditional spelling. These tests were the spelling subtest of the Wide Range Achievement Test, Level 1, and a list of low-frequency regularly spelled words (from Baron & Treiman, 1980).

3. Children using invented spelling also had significantly greater scores on three different word recognition tests: the untimed word analysis subtest of the Durrell Word Recognition test; the reading of a word list adapted from Baron and Treiman (1980); and the word attack subtest (on nonsense words) of the Woodcock Reading Mastery tests. Flash word recognition and reading comprehension showed only slight differences between the groups, though those slight differences also favored the inventive spellers.

4. Initially low-achieving children accounted for most of the gain in spelling and reading that resulted from using invented spelling.

The researcher summarizes as follows:

The superior spelling and phonic analysis skill of children using invented spelling suggested that they benefited from the practice of matching sound segments of words to letters as they wrote and from using their own sound sequence analysis. These differences were major considering that both groups were using basal readers which promote a reliance on processing words by their visual cues rather than by phonic analysis. . . .

Also, encouraging children to use invented spelling may induce them to shift from processing words visually toward using phonetic cue processing earlier than would otherwise occur when using a basal reading program. (Clarke, 1988, p. 307)

Of course, as the investigator notes, some of the most significant benefits of encouraging invented spelling lie in promoting independence, confidence, and more writing. And the children who benefit the most may be those initially found to be low-achieving, by traditional and standardized measures.

P. A. Freppon, 1988

Freppon, P. A. (1988). An investigation of children's concepts of the purpose and nature of reading in different instructional settings. Unpublished doctoral dissertation, University of Cincinnati, Ohio. This study is reported in a 1991 article by Freppon: Children's concepts of the nature and purpose of reading in different instructional settings, *Journal of Reading Behavior, 23*(2), 139–163.

Freppon compared the literacy development of students in two "skills-based" first-grade classrooms with those in two "literature-based" classrooms. She contrasts what the skills-based teachers typically did with what the literature-based teachers did:

> The skill-based teachers: (a) established ability grouping and round-robin oral reading with an emphasis on reading correctly; (b) emphasized drill and practice on discrete skills such as short vowels, blends, and vocabulary words; (c) used a reading basal series exclusively for instruction; (d) required daily completion of skill (word and phonics)-oriented worksheets and workbooks; and (e) followed a traditional, systematic and sequenced curriculum in teaching phonics and vocabulary.
>
> The literature-based teachers: (a) used book demonstrations and modeled reading strategies such as making connections between their own lives and the events in the text when reading to and with children; (b) promoted children's approximations to conventional reading and did not emphasize *word perfect* reading; (c) structured cooperative reading events such as choral and partner reading; (d) emphasized reading for meaning (requiring children to think about what was going on in the story, discussing sense making, directly commenting on making connections with prior knowledge during reading interactions); and (e) taught children to use specific reading strategies including meaning, predicting, skipping words, rereading (*and getting ready to say the word*), guessing, and using graphophonic information. (1991, pp. 143–144)

The following are some of Freppon's conclusions, with contributing evidence:

1. Students in the literature-based group seemed to have a better sense of what sounds like language. Evidence? Of the literature-based group, 97 percent rejected words in scrambled sentence order as not being languagelike, while only 42 percent of the skills-based group rejected such sentences.
2. Students in the literature-based group seemed to have a stronger sense that reading involves constructing meaning, not merely getting the words right. Evidence? Of the students in the literature-based group, 92 percent said that understanding the

story or both understanding and getting the words right are important in reading, while only 50 percent of the skills-based group mentioned meaning or emphasized both as important.

Students in the literature-based group reported using more strategies in reading, and were more often observed to do so; also, they more often discussed using meaning to self-monitor.

Though children in both groups said they were good readers, those in the literature-based group said they were good readers because they read a lot of books, while children in the skills group said they were good readers because they knew a lot of words.

Students in the literature-based group were more successful in using grapho/phonemic cues in conjunction with prior knowledge and other language cues in order to construct meaning. Though the skills group attempted to sound out words more than twice as often, the literature group was more successful in doing so: a 53 percent success rate compared with a 32 percent success rate for the skills group. Also, the literature group more often showed a balanced use of language cueing systems in their substitutions of one word for another.

In short, students in the literature-based group seemed to be making greater progress toward becoming literate.

K. L. Dahl and P. A. Freppon, 1992

Dahl, K. L., & Freppon, P. A. (1992). *Learning to read and write in inner-city schools: A comparison of children's sense-making in skills-based and whole language classrooms.* Final Report to the Office of Educational Research and Improvement. U.S. Department of Education, Grant Award No. R117E00134.

Part of the data described here is reported in two more accessible articles, in addition to the references cited in the discussion below:

Freppon, P. A. (1991). Children's concepts of the nature and purpose of reading in different instructional settings. *Journal of Reading Behavior, 23*(2), 139–163.

Dahl, K. L., & Freppon, P. A. 1991. Literacy learning in whole-language classrooms: An analysis of low socioeconomic urban children learning to read and write in kindergarten. In J. Zutell & S. McCormick (Eds.), *Learner Factors/ Teacher Factors: Issues in Literacy Research and Instruction*, pp. 149–158. Chicago, IL: National Reading Conference.

Two studies were involved in this comparison: an investigation of children's sense-making in skills-based classrooms (Dahl, Purcell-Gates, & McIntyre, 1989) and a similar study in whole language classrooms (Dahl & Freppon, 1991). Both studies were ethnographic, spanning a two-year period from kindergarten through first grade, and both studies documented children's evolving hypotheses about reading and writing. The school populations "were representative of the racial and cultural mix typical of the urban low-income populations in the midwest—African American and white Appalachian" (Dahl & Freppon, 1992). The learners at each site were randomly selected from among those who qualified for the federally funded lunch program. Seven learners remained through the two-year skills-based study; twelve completed the whole language study. The "focal learners" were racially balanced in each study (four African American and three Appalachian white in the skills-based study; six of each ethnic background in the whole language study).

At the beginning of kindergarten and at the end of first grade, all learners in both studies completed six kinds of tasks assessing various aspects of written language knowledge: (1) an "Intentionality" task designed to determine to what extent the children understood that written language is a symbol system conveying meaning; (2) Marie Clay's (1979) Concepts About Print test; (3) three tasks designed to determine children's knowledge of the alphabetic principle and their knowledge of letter/sound relations; (4) two tasks designed to determine children's understanding of how written narratives are structured; (5) a task requiring children to pretend to read a wordless storybook to a doll, in order to determine the children's "Written Narrative Register" (Purcell-Gates, 1988); and, (6) a writing task designed to elicit children's concepts of writing. The researchers describe most of these tasks in detail.

Upon entering kindergarten, the children in both studies had a very limited understanding of written language. The children in the whole language kindergartens scored slightly lower on every pretest measure except one. Two years later, children in the skills-based classrooms showed statistically significant gains on all measures except one (the Written Narrative Register); those in the whole language classrooms showed statistically significant gains on all six measures. With five of the six assessment measures (all except Story Structure), the whole language children had lower pretest scores than the skills-based children. However, the whole language children scored higher on all six of the posttest measures (Dahl & Freppon, 1992, p. 24). Two of these six differences were statistically significant: the tests of written register and concepts of writing.

Interestingly, the skills-based group was knowledgeable about intentionality (writing as conveying meaning), though this was not explicitly emphasized during instruction. Similarly, the whole language group had comparable (in fact, slightly higher) scores on the tests of alphabetic principle and letter/sound relations, though these are taught less directly and less extensively in whole language classrooms. Furthermore, a much greater proportion of the whole language learners consistently applied their knowledge of letter/sound relations effectively by the end of first grade (Dahl & Freppon, 1992, p. 36).

The more interesting and significant differences between children in the two kinds of classrooms were qualitative, not quantitative. For example:

1. In the whole language classrooms, children's ongoing talk as they participated in reading and writing demonstrated that they perceived themselves as readers and writers, even if they were relatively less proficient readers and writers than their classmates. Regardless of their proficiency or degree of success, all the whole

language children tended to persist in reading and writing activities. In the skills-based classrooms, these patterns were restricted to just the most proficient readers and writers.

2. Children in the whole language classrooms participated actively in the reading and discussion of literature, related new books to previously read texts, and developed a critical stance toward trade books. The curriculum in the skills-based classrooms did not encourage these behaviors in students.

3. In skills-based classrooms, passivity appeared to be the most frequent coping strategy for learners having difficulty. In whole language classrooms, those having difficulty tended to draw upon other learners for support: by saying the phrases and sentences that others could read, by copying what they wrote, and so forth. The less proficient literacy learners in whole language classrooms still attempted to remain engaged in literacy activities with their peers.

4. In reading, whole language students at each level of proficiency demonstrated a greater variety of reading strategies and more active engagement in reading.

5. By the end of first grade, a considerably larger proportion of the whole language children were writing sentences and stories.

In summary, the children in the whole language classrooms demonstrated slightly greater gains on quantitative measures of literacy skills, including knowledge of the alphabetic principle and of letter/sound relations. The greatest differences, however, occurred in the range and depth of attitudes and behaviors characteristic of literate individuals. The authors conclude that "a number of instructional elements and practices were productive for low-SES inner-city children. These included extensive experience with children's literature, writing opportunities with self-selected topics, social contexts where learners could work together, and one-on-one teacher conferences" (Dahl & Freppon, 1992, p. 71). Only the last of these was found in the skills-based classrooms.

P. A. Freppon, 1993

Freppon, P. A. (1993). Making sense of reading and writing in urban classrooms: Understanding at-risk children's knowledge construction in different curricula. Final Report to the Office of Educational Research and Improvement. U.S. Department of Education, Grant Award No. R117E102361–91.

This study built upon the previously described study of Dahl and Freppon (1992). The same children participated in this follow-up study, now as second graders. One question the investigator wanted to address is the frequently asked question, "Do children with experience in a whole language curriculum, particularly in the early grades, have the skills necessary for success in a traditional, skills-based curriculum?" Another research question was the extent to which students maintained the literacy abilities, behaviors, and attitudes they had developed through kindergarten and first grade.

One group of eight children from the original whole language group in Dahl and Freppon (1992) made a transition to a skills-based second grade (the Transition Group), while the other group of nine continued in a whole language classroom in second grade (the Continuing Group). All participating children were given pretests and posttests. Eight focal children, four in each group, were closely followed. Data gathering included written artifacts, reading samples, field notes, and audio and video tapes.

At the end of second grade, there was little difference between groups on the standardized tests, and little difference in their gain from pretest to posttest. Findings from the reading and writing interviews revealed several areas of decline in the Transition Group while the Continuing Group generally remained stable or gained in some areas. For example: the Transition Group, now in a skills-based second grade, showed 37 percent less identification of items to be read beyond school, while the Continuing Group, still in a whole language classroom showed 33 percent more identification of items to read beyond school. The Transition Group showed a 30 percent decrease in responses reflecting megacognitive or strategic knowledge, while the Continuing Group showed a 30 percent increase. The Transition Group showed a 32 percent increase in statements that writing was difficult, a 38 percent increase in preference for writing with others, and stability in citing the story and surface features as important in writing. The Continuing Group showed no increase in statements that writing was difficult, stability in preference for writing with others, and a 30 percent or greater increase in citing the story and surface features as important in writing (pp. 24–25).

The focal children in the Transition Group concentrated primarily on "getting through" assignments. Persistence in self-selected reading and writing declined in the Transition Group, among all but the most academically proficient child within that focal group. In contrast, the focal children in the Continuing Group maintained talk and action demonstrating a sense of themselves as readers and writers and persisted in self-selected reading and writing during second grade, regardless of their academic proficiency.

The investigator concluded that the children in the Transition Group had the literacy skills necessary for success in the skills-based second grade classroom, but that some of the children showed a loss of motivation for literacy experiences that was not experienced by the students who continued in a whole language classroom (p. 85).

C. F. Stice and N. P. Bertrand, 1990

Stice, C. F., & Bertrand, N. P. (1990). *Whole language and the emergent literacy of at-risk children: A two-year comparative study*. Nashville: Center of Excellence: Basic Skills, Tennessee State University, ED 324 636.

Stice and Bertrand begin by observing, "Too often poor and minority children are not becoming sufficiently literate to allow the achievement of social and economic parity" (p. 3). They cited Neisser (1986) as demonstrating that neither the traditional approaches to literacy instruction (phonics/skills or traditional basal) nor the decoding, subskills approaches (or behavioral/mastery learning) have proved successful in the case of poor, minority children. Their study focused on the effects of a whole language approach to the literacy development of at-risk first- and second-graders, in comparison with a traditional skills approach.

The study involved fifty children, averaging five each in five whole language classrooms, grades 1 and 2, and their counterparts from traditional skills classrooms. The study included both rural and inner-city children who were deemed to be "at risk," according to typical factors.

Several quantitative and qualitative measures were used to compare the two groups, including scores on the reading portion of the Stanford Achievement Test (Primary I and II), responses to a Concepts About Print survey, analysis of an oral reading and retelling, writing samples, and individual interviews.

On the Stanford Achievement Test, the whole language children showed slightly greater gains than the traditionally taught children, but the gains were too slight to be statistically significant. While the children in the whole language groups scored lower on the Concepts About Print test to begin with, they scored significantly higher on the posttest. The children in whole language classrooms did as well on traditional spelling as their counterparts, while also using more invented spellings. Whole language children offered significantly longer, more complete versions of the stories they retold, suggesting that their comprehension might have been better. They also corrected more of their miscues.

Data from the reading and writing interviews revealed several interesting trends, similar to those in the Freppon study and the Dahl and Freppon study previously cited:

1. The children in the whole language classrooms were more aware of alternative strategies for dealing with problems, such as problems with particular words. For example, when asked, "When you are reading and you come to something you don't know, what do you do?" the whole language children suggested six strategies, while the children in traditional classrooms suggested only three.
2. The whole language children appeared to feel better about themselves as readers and writers. When asked, "Who do you know who is a good reader?" 82 percent of the kindergartners in the whole language classrooms said "Me," but only 5 percent of the kindergartners in the traditional classrooms mentioned themselves. During the first-grade year, when the children were asked directly, "Are you a good reader?" 70 percent of the whole language children said yes, but only 33 percent of the traditional children said yes.
3. The whole language children appeared to focus more on meaning and the communicative nature of language. For example, when asked, "What makes a good reader?" they reported that good readers read a great deal and that they can read any book in the room. The children in the traditional classrooms tended to focus on words and surface correctness; they reported that good readers read big words, they know all the words, and they don't miss any words.
4. The children in the whole language classrooms seemed to be developing greater independence in both reading and writing. The children in traditional classrooms seemed to be more dependent on the teacher when their initial strategy failed.

Again, the standardized test scores of the children in the whole language classrooms were slightly (though not significantly) better than the scores of children in the traditional classrooms. The other measures discussed suggest, however, that they are far ahead of their counterparts in developing the understanding, strategies, and attitudes of readers, writers, and thinkers.

WHOLE LANGUAGE VERSUS TRADITIONAL CLASSROOMS: TENTATIVE CONCLUSIONS AND TESTABLE HYPOTHESES

The research described above is a fairly small research base, and these studies are doubtless not without their limitations and flaws. On the other hand, it also true that these research results corroborate conclusions from more naturalistic research; they do not stand alone in support of whole language. Furthermore, other comparative studies have generated similar results (see the summaries in Stephens, 1991; Shapiro, 1990; Tunnell & Jacobs, 1989).

Combining the results of these studies, then, it would seem reasonable to draw the following tentative conclusions, as long as we consider them to be reframable as hypotheses subject to further testing. In general:

1. Children in whole language classrooms typically show greater gains on various reading tests and subtests—or at least they did in these research studies, though the differences often were not statistically significant.
2. Children in whole language classrooms develop greater ability to use phonics knowledge effectively than children in more traditional classrooms, where skills are practiced in isolation. (For another relevant study, see also A. E. Cunningham, 1990.)
3. Children in whole language classrooms develop vocabulary, spelling, grammar, and punctuation skills as well as or better than children in more traditional classrooms. (In addition to some of the studies above, see Calkins, 1980; Gunderson & Shapiro, 1987, 1988; DiStefano & Killion, 1984.)
4. Children in whole language classrooms are more inclined and able to read for meaning rather than just to identify words. They also are able to describe more fully the stories they have read.
5. Children in whole language classrooms develop more strategies for dealing with problems in reading—e.g., problem words.
6. Children in whole language classrooms develop greater facility in writing.
7. Children in whole language classrooms develop a stronger sense of themselves as readers and writers.
8. Children in whole language classrooms develop greater independence as readers and writers.

As you will have noticed, only one of these conclusions relates to standardized test scores, because whole language researchers consider them relatively unimportant and often downright misleading in assessing children's actual ability to read and to write, and to develop the attitudes, values, and behaviors of literate individuals. Most of these conclusions are therefore drawn from an extensive collection of a wide range of data.

All of these studies were conducted with primary-grade children. Whole language educators anticipate that further research will not only confirm these tentative conclusions, but also uncover differences in the outcomes of traditional and whole language classrooms that continue into the middle grades and beyond.

THE PROMISE AND LIMITATIONS OF WHOLE LANGUAGE

The preceding section suggests the promise of whole langage in developing more competent, confident, joyful readers and writers and learners. But will whole language produce primary graders all of whom can read and write well, spell and punctuate perfectly, and engage in other academic tasks without any difficulty or flaw? Of course not! (F. Smith, 1992)

This has become one of my serious concerns: that people think whole language must be abandoned when some first graders haven't learned to read independently in grade 1, or some children haven't learned to spell or punctuate well by, say, grade 3. If our traditional instruction had been succeeding so well, why do we have such an alleged illiteracy problem in the United States? Why do we know so many adults who are poor spellers? So many college students who don't know how to punctuate correctly?

Tom Nicholson laments that about 15 percent of the first graders in New Zealand need the intensive help provided by Reading Recovery programs, and he implies that this is the fault of the whole language instruction in New Zealand, or at least the fault of an emphasis on using context in reading (Nicoloson, 1991, p. 444). But this 15 percent is an arbitrary percentage: the lowest 15 percent in grade 1. In the U.S., typically the lowest 20 percent of first graders have been included in Reading Recovery programs (Dunkeld, 1991, p. 38).

It's true that children's approaches to reading typically reflect the way they were taught, as suggested in Chapter 1 (and recently confirmed by Dahl & Freppon, 1992, p. 156, as well as the other studies cited above). However, some children's approaches seem to reflect their own learning styles and strategies, sometimes in spite of the instructional approach. And some children have difficulty learning, especially when the approach does not match well with their learning styles and strategies (Carbo, 1984a, 1987a, b, c; Carbo, Dunn, & Dunn, 1986).

In the report of their two-year study, Dahl and Freppon (1992) indicate that in both skills-based and whole language classrooms, there were children who did not progress as expected. The following are contrasting highlights from their characterizations of two first-grade children:

> Rodney had a limited number of reading strategies that he used in his . . . classroom. Working with the teacher, Rodney read only the words he knew and waited to be told the rest. Rodney also "guessed at" unknown words using his repertoire of sight words such as *was, it, if,* and *in*, even though these words did not make sense with the story or bear letter/sound similarity. . . . His actions were focused on getting the words to the point of guessing "wildly." He did not

effectively use letter/sound relations for getting unknown words, but rather, seemed confused and uncomfortable when he tried to apply this information. (pp. 54–55)

In contrast is Ann:

Her main reading strategy was to reread when she came to an unknown word. Ann also skipped unknown words and mumbled ones she was unsure of. Her intonation varied from fluent reading to word-by-word. Later in the school year Ann effectively used letter/sound cues to get words, and came to over-rely on this strategy. Occasionally she asked the teacher for help. . . . Miscue analysis indicated that her substitutions frequently demonstrated an over-reliance on phonics. (pp. 55–56)

Miscue analysis indicates that children in meaning-oriented classrooms make miscues that often reflect more attention to meaning than to grapho/phonemic cues, while children in skills-oriented classrooms with phonics emphasis make miscues that often reflect more attention to grapho/phonemic cues and less to meaning (DeLawter, 1975; Dank, 1977; Elder, 1971). Therefore, we might have predicted that Rodney was in a meaning-emphasis classroom, or at least one that emphasized sight words rather than phonics. Wrong. We might also have predicted that Ann was in a phonics-oriented classroom. Wrong again. Rodney was a first grader in one of the skills-based classrooms, while Ann was a first grader in one of the whole language classrooms.

This comparison illustrates what whole language educators know from experience as well as research: that though there often is a correlation between what's taught and what's learned, nevertheless it is still true that learners construct knowledge for themselves. Therefore, what's taught is not necessarily what's learned. And despite the best teaching, there will be children from *every* kind of classroom who will fall short of what we might want them to learn—especially when our instructional approach does not honor their own learning styles and strategies, and especially in a short time span.

Kindergarten teacher Connie White's story of Jevon (1990) poignantly illustrates this generalization. Despite the success of White's whole language methods with most of her kindergartners, Jevon did not make significant progress toward literacy during his first year in her classroom. Consequently, White decided to hold him back for a second kindergarten year. Additional professional study and development over the summer encouraged White to become more observant of her students' own learning strategies, and to support these. During Jevon's second year in kindergarten, White observed that he began teaching himself to read by learning to recognize his classmates' names when written, and beginning to make letter/sound generalizations from the names. In a classroom developed in accordance with White's new understanding of whole language, Jevon made significant progress toward literacy—but not quickly, and not easily.

The moral of the story is that we should not expect whole language classrooms to immediately succeed in producing entire classrooms of chldren who can read, write, compute, and reason perfectly; but we can and do expect that whole language classrooms will generate continued learning and enhanced self-esteem and pleasure in learning. And if some learners still need more support or more time than one classroom teacher can provide, we should not be surprised.

FOR FURTHER REFLECTION AND EXPLORATION

Probably the most appropriate follow-up to this chapter would be to locate and read the relevant research for yourself. However, it seems at least defensible to include here the following activities, since they offer the opportunity to reflect upon many of the points made in this and preceding chapters.

1. In his 1973 edited book *Psycholinguistics and Reading,* Frank Smith published an essay titled "Twelve Easy Ways to Make Learning to Read Difficult, and One Difficult Way to Make It Easy." In 1977, Estes and Johnstone published a take-off on Smith's article, titled "Twelve Easy Ways to Make Readers Hate Reading (and One Difficult Way to Make Them Love It)." Similar tongue-in-cheek rules can be inferred from Allen's article "Implications for Reading Instruction" (in P. D. Allen and Watson, 1976). Here are some statements taken or adapted from these articles, along with some "real" rules for teaching reading. For each rule, decide whether it is one that teachers should follow or one that they should not, and why. Discuss, as some of these "rules" will surely generate controversy even among those who have adopted a socio-psycholinguistic view of reading. To facilitate discussion, you might make three lists: rules that are definite "no-nos"; rules that are definite "yeses"; and rules that are debatable or that depend upon how one interprets the rule.

    a. Fail children who do not read up to grade level.
    b. Don't correct children's miscues; rather, allow (encourage, help) them learn to detect when their miscues don't make sense, and to correct those miscues themselves.
    c. Use only basal readers for reading instruction.
    d. Follow the lesson plan in the basal reader, without any deviations.
    e. Don't worry about precise word identification, as long as meaning is preserved.
    f. Assess children's reading by determining their reading strategies and their ability to comprehend a variety of reading materials.
    g. Emphasize strategies for getting meaning rather than skills for identifying words.
    h. Define reading ability as scores on a standardized test.
    i. Assume that young children must learn to read before they can read to learn.
    j. Provide many opportunities for children to read.
    k. Encourage the avoidance of errors.
    l. Don't be concerned about the quantity of miscues, as long as they preserve meaning.
    m. Emphasize the strengths that a reader brings to the reading task.
    n. Integrate reading with all other content areas; combine learning to read with reading to learn.
    o. For vocabulary development, have children copy definitions from the dictionary.
    p. Help children learn to establish their own purposes for reading.
    q. Emphasize the teaching of skills for identifying words, even if this leaves no time for actual reading.

r. Insure that phonics rules are learned and consciously applied to sound out problem words.

s. Have children read aloud in groups, round robin.

t. Make word-perfect reading the prime objective.

u. Don't skip over stories in the basal, and do not switch children from one basal series to another.

v. Teach letters or words one at a time, making sure each new letter or word is learned before moving on.

w. Insist on careful reading for detail.

x. Don't let children guess at words.

y. Make sure children understand the importance of reading and the seriousness of falling behind.

z. Don't let children proceed without correcting their errors; correct the errors for them if necessary.

aa. Spend most of your "reading" time preparing children for standardized tests (tests of phonics knowledge, sight word knowledge, and multiple-choice comprehension).

bb. Identify and give special attention to problem readers as soon as possible.

cc. Make it a primary goal to create independent readers as early as possible.

dd. Make it a primary goal to help children develop a love of reading as early as possible.

After completing this activity, you might read the articles mentioned below to see what they have to say about the "rules" discussed:

Smith, F. (1973). Twelve easy ways to make learning to read difficult, and one difficult way to make it easy. In F. Smith (Ed.), *Psycholinguistics and reading* (pp. 183–196). New York: Holt, Rinehart.

Estes, T. H., & Johnstone, J. P. (1977). Twelve easy ways to make readers hate reading (and one difficult way to make them love it). *Language Arts, 54:* 891–897.

Allen, P. D. (1976). Implications for reading instruction. In P. D. Allen & D. J. Watson (Eds.), *Findings of research in miscue analysis: classroom implications* (pp. 107–112). Urbana, IL: ERIC Clearinghouse on Reading and Communication Skills and the National Council of Teachers of English.

2. Below are ten statements from *Becoming a Nation of Readers* (R. Anderson et al., 1985). Some of the statements are ones with which socio-psycholinguistics and whole language advocates would heartily agree. Others are statements that, for one reason or another, would make psycholinguists and whole language advocates cringe. Locate the statements that would disturb psycholinguists and whole language advocates and explain why they would find at least part of the statement disturbing. (It seems to me that most psycholinguists and whole language teachers would find something disturbing in about half of these statements, give or take a couple. In other words, there's room for individual interpretation here, as is appropriate in a text emphasizing the fact that reading is a unique transaction between reader and text.)

a. "While there is more consensus about reading than in the past, there are still important issues about which reasonable people disagree" (p. 4).

b. "First, like the performance of a symphony, reading is a holistic act. In other words, while reading can be analyzed into subskills such as discriminating letters and identifying words, performing the subskills one at a time does not constitute reading" (p. 7).

c. "The meaning constructed from the same text can vary greatly among people because of differences in the knowledge they possess. . . . Research reveals that children are not good at drawing on their prior knowledge, especially in school settings" (p. 10).

d. "Research suggests that, no matter which strategies are used to introduce them to reading, the children who earn the best scores on reading comprehension tests in second grade are the ones who made the most progress in fast and accurate word identification in the first grade" (p. 10).

e. "Immature readers are sometimes unable to focus on meaning during reading because they have such a low level of decoding skill" (p. 12).

f. "Increasing the proportion of children who read widely and with evident satisfaction ought to be as much a goal of reading instruction as increasing the number who are competent readers" (p. 15).

g. "Many of the tasks assigned to children in the name of reading are drudgery" (p. 15).

h. "A good rule of thumb is that the most useful form of practice is doing the whole skill of reading—that is, reading meaningful text for the purpose of understanding the message it contains" (p. 17).

i. "Thus, the issue is no longer, as it was several decades ago, whether children should be taught phonics. The issues now are specific ones of just how it should be done" (p. 37).

j. "Once the basic relationships have been taught, the best way to get children to refine and extend their knowledge of letter-sound correspondences is through repeated opportunities to read" (p. 38).

3. Respond again to the DeFord Theoretical Orientation to Reading Profile (TORP) included at the end of Chapter 1 (DeFord, 1985), and compare your responses now with those before. For each question, circle the one best answer that reflects the strength of your agreement or disagreement; SA means "strongly agree," while SD means "strongly disagree." In what respects have your views changed, if any?

1. A child needs to be able to verbalize the rules of phonics in order to assure proficiency in processing new words.	1 2 3 4 5 SA SD
2. An increase in reading errors is usually related to a decrease in comprehension.	1 2 3 4 5 SA SD
3. Dividing words into syllables according to rules is a helpful instructional practice for reading new words.	1 2 3 4 5 SA SD

4. Fluency and expression are necessary components of reading that indicate good comprehension.

1	2	3	4	5
SA				SD

5. Materials for early reading should be written in natural language without concern for short, simple words and sentences.

1	2	3	4	5
SA				SD

6. When children do not know a word, they should be instructed to sound out its parts.

1	2	3	4	5
SA				SD

7. It is a good practice to allow children to edit what is written into their own dialect when learning to read.

1	2	3	4	5
SA				SD

8. The use of a glossary or dictionary is necessary in determining the meaning and pronunciation of new words.

1	2	3	4	5
SA				SD

9. Reversals (e.g., saying "saw" for "was") are significant problems in the teaching of reading.

1	2	3	4	5
SA				SD

10. It is a good practice to correct a child as soon as an oral reading mistake is made.

1	2	3	4	5
SA				SD

11. It is important for a word to be repeated a number of times after it has been introduced to insure that it will become a part of sight vocabulary.

1	2	3	4	5
SA				SD

12. Paying close attention to punctuation marks is necessary to understanding story content.

1	2	3	4	5
SA				SD

13. It is a sign of an ineffective reader when words and phrases are repeated.

1	2	3	4	5
SA				SD

14. Being able to label words according to grammatical function (nouns, etc.) is useful in proficient reading.

1	2	3	4	5
SA				SD

15. When coming to a word that's unknown, the reader should be encouraged to guess upon meaning and go on.

1	2	3	4	5
SA				SD

16. Young readers need to be introduced to the root form of words (run, long) before they are asked to read inflected forms (running, longest).

1	2	3	4	5
SA				SD

17. It is not necessary for a child to know the letters of the alphabet in order to learn to read.

1	2	3	4	5
SA				SD

18. Flashcard drills with sight words is an unnecessary form of practice in reading instruction.

1	2	3	4	5
SA				SD

19. Ability to use accent patterns in multisyllable words (pho´-to-graph, pho-to´-gra-phy, and pho-to-gra´-phic) should be developed as part of reading instruction.

1	2	3	4	5
SA				SD

20. Controlling text through consistent spelling patterns ("The fat cat ran back. The fat cat sat on a hat") is a means by which children can best learn to read.

1	2	3	4	5
SA				SD

21. Formal instruction in reading is necessary to insure the adequate development of all the skills used in reading.

1	2	3	4	5
SA				SD

22. Phonic analysis is the most important form of analysis used when meeting new words.

1	2	3	4	5
SA				SD

23. Children's initial encounters with print should focus on meaning, not upon exact graphic representation.

1	2	3	4	5
SA				SD

24. Word shapes (word configuration) should be taught in reading to aid in word recognition.

1	2	3	4	5
SA				SD

25. It is important to teach skills in relation to other skills.

1	2	3	4	5
SA				SD

26. If a child says "house" for the written word "home," the response should be left uncorrected.

1	2	3	4	5
SA				SD

27. It is not necessary to introduce new words before they appear in the reading text.

1	2	3	4	5
SA				SD

28. Some problems in reading are caused by readers dropping the inflectional endings from words (e.g., jump*s*, jump*ed*).

1	2	3	4	5
SA				SD

8 Understanding Whole Language

Whole language is a perspective on education that is supported by beliefs about learners and learning, teachers and teaching, language and curriculum. . . . Whole language is not a program, package, set of materials, method, practice, or technique; rather, it is a perspective on language and learning that *leads to the acceptance* of certain strategies, methods, materials, and techniques.

— Dorothy Watson

In Chapter 3, we introduced the concept of whole language, explaining some of its origins as a philosophy of learning and teaching. We also sketched some of the kinds of literacy events common in whole language classrooms, indicating that it's the underlying philosophy that makes them "whole language," not the events themselves. In Chapter 5 we indicated some of the ways that phonics know-how is developed in whole language classrooms, while in Chapter 7 we described some of the research giving rise to and supporting whole language education. This chapter focuses on clarifing the underlying principles that guide whole language practices, and on clarifying some of the misunderstandings that currently surround whole language.

BASIC PRINCIPLES OF WHOLE LANGUAGE

When Lee Gunderson and Jon Shapiro wrote, "The term *whole language* has nearly as many definitions as it has advocates" (1987, p. 22), they probably did not anticipate the dilution that the term "whole language" has experienced in recent years. Not knowing any better, some teachers call themselves whole language teachers because they use Big Books in their classrooms, even though the way they use Big Books differs little from the way they have traditionally used basals. Administrators think they can get their teachers to "do" whole language by bringing in an outside expert to conduct an inservice workshop or two. Eager to cash in on the popularity of whole language, commercial publishers advertise their wares as whole language basals, whole language programs, and even whole language activity sheets—either not realizing or not caring that such prepackaged materials are contrary to the philosophy and spirit of whole language.

Such perversions of the concept of whole language threaten its demise, for if whole language can mean anything and everything, then in effect it means nothing.

The term *whole language* seems to have grown originally from a concern for keeping language whole during instruction, from the desire to avoid fragmenting language into bits and pieces for isolated drill (Watson, 1989). It reflected the understanding that the same kinds of response and encouragement that nurtured the development of spoken language could stimulate children's development as readers and writers, using whole texts with natural language patterns rather than primerese, the stilted and unnatural language characterizing the early levels of basal reading tests. Gradually, whole language has grown into a philosophy not only of literacy development, but of learning in general. Based upon a solid body of research in fields as diverse as language acquisition and emergent literacy, psycholinguistics and sociolinguistics, schema theory and literary theory, and ethnography, anthropology, philosophy, and education, whole language may also be characterized as theory in practice, practiceable theory, or simply as a belief system that is open to new insights and is therefore continually evolving. Figure 7.2 in Chapter 7 lists references that describe some of the research underlying and supporting whole language.

Though indeed there is no one true definition of whole language, there are many principles that together form a core of beliefs characterizing the essence of a whole language philosophy. Most leading and long-time whole language educators would agree upon the principles discussed below, though doubtless they would describe them somewhat differently and include other principles as well. (Figure 8.1 lists some references that characterize such whole language principles.)

As the following discussion will show, whole language doesn't simply mean that teachers adopt new materials or develop new activities. Rather, it requires that teachers understand learners and learning in new ways, that they interact with students and develop curricula in new ways, that they modify their roles as teachers, and that they hold new expectations for students and develop new means of assessment congruent with these expectations. Such a major "paradigm shift" (pp. 339–341 in this chapter, and pp. 411–413 in Chapter 9) is usually accomplished only gradually, and only with considerable reflection and professional soul-searching, accompanied by anxiety and stress. What particularly facilitates and supports such a shift in belief systems is reading professional books and articles, talking with other teachers undergoing a similar paradigm shift, visiting classrooms where a whole language philosophy already guides what teachers and learners do, and receiving support from administrators who understand and share the whole language philosophy.

The discussion of whole language principles in this chapter draws substantially from my piece in *Supporting Whole Language* (Weaver and Henke, 1992). As virtually all of the pieces in that collection indicate, whole language cannot be successfully mandated by administrators. Indeed, when administrators understand whole language, they realize that it cannot be mandated, because whole language is fundamentally a belief system that guides instructional decision making, not a set of materials or activities that can be required. Knowledgeable administrators can, however, facilitate and support teachers' growth into this belief system. (For details, see the various articles in *Supporting Whole Language*.)

Altwerger, B. (1991). Whole language teachers: Empowered professionals. In J. Hydrick (Ed.), *Whole language: Empowerment at the chalkface* (pp. 15-29). New York: Scholastic.

Cambourne, B. (1988). *The whole story: Natural learning and the acquisition of literacy in the classroom.* Auckland, New Zealand: Scholastic.

Edelsky, C., & Draper, K. (1989). Reading/"reading"; writing/"writing"; text/"text." *Reading-Canada-Lecture, 7,* 201-216.

Edelsky, C., & Smith, K. (1984). "Is that writing—or are those marks just a figment of your curriculum?" *Language Arts, 61,* 24-32.

Ferreiro, E., & Teberosky, A. (1982). *Literacy before schooling.* (K. G. Castro, Trans.) Portsmouth, NH: Heinemann.

Goodman, K. S. (1973). *Theoretically based studies of patterns of miscues in oral reading performance.* Detroit: Wayne State University. (ERIC Document Reproduction Service No. ED 079 708)

Goodman, K. S. (1982). *Language and literacy: The selected writings of Kenneth S. Goodman.* 2 vols. (F. V. Gollasch, Ed.). Boston: Routledge & Kegan Paul.

Goodman, K. S., & Goodman, Y. M. (1979). Learning to read is natural. In L. B. Resnick & P. A. Weaver (Eds.), *Theory and practice of early reading,* Vol. 1 (pp. 137-154). Hillsdale, NJ: Erlbaum.

Goodman, Y. M. (1978). Kid watching: An alternative to testing. *National Elementary School Principal, 57,* 41-45.

Halliday, M. A. K. (1975). *Learning how to mean: Explorations in the development of language.* New York: Elsevier.

Harste, J. C., Woodward, V. A., & Burke, C. L. (1984). *Language stories and literacy lessons.* Portsmouth, NH: Heinemann.

Holdaway, D. (1979). *Foundations of literacy.* Sydney, Australia: Scholastic. (Available in the U.S. from Heinemann.)

Rosenblatt, L. (1978). *The reader, the text, the poem: The transactional theory of the literary work.* Carbondale, IL: Southern Illinois University Press.

Short, K., & Burke, C. (1992). *Creating curriculum: Teachers and students as a community of learners.* Portsmouth, NH: Heinemann.

Smith, F. (1975). *Comprehension and learning: A conceptual framework for teachers.* Katonah, NY: Richard C. Owen.

Smith, F. (1981a). Demonstrations, engagement, and sensitivity: The choice between people and programs. *Language Arts, 58,* 634-642.

Smith, F. (1981b). Demonstrations, engagement, and sensitivity: A revised approach to language learning. *Language Arts, 58,* 103-122.

Figure 8.1 References for understanding the roots of a whole language philosophy of learning and teaching

Smith, F. (1988). *Understanding reading* (4th ed.). Hillsdale, NJ: Erlbaum.

Vygotsky, L. S. (1978). *Mind in society: The development of higher psychological processes.* (M. Cole, V. John-Steiner, S. Scribner, & E. Souberman, Eds.). Cambridge: Harvard University Press.

Vygotsky, L. S. (1986). *Thought and Language.* (A. Kozulin, Trans.). Cambridge: MIT Press.

Figure 8.1 Continued

Learning and the Learner

Explicitly rejecting behaviorism as a model for significant human learning, whole language educators have been influenced by the work of cognitive psychologists and learning theorists who emphasize the roles of motivation and social interaction in learning (see Y. M. Goodman, 1989; K. S. Goodman, 1989). Their understanding of learning has also been strongly influenced by descriptions of language and literacy development in natural settings (see Figures 3.6 and 3.12, and the discussion within that section of Chapter 3). Such research has given rise to the following principles:

1. Learners construct meaning for themselves, most readily in contexts where they can actively transact with other people, with books, and with objects and materials in the external world. The most significant and enduring learning, particularly of concepts and complex processes, is likely to be that constructed by the learner, not imposed from without.
2. When learning is perceived as functional to and purposeful for the learner, it is more likely to endure. That is, the most significant learning derives from whatever arouses the interest, meets the needs, and furthers the purposes of the learner in the here and now.
3. In order to engage themselves wholeheartedly in learning, however, learners must be confident that they will be safe from negative repercussions. They must be free to take risks without fear of being criticized, penalized, or declared wrong.
4. Though there are developmental trends among learners, learning is fundamentally idiosyncratic, even chaotic; the nature and course of each individual's learning are unique.
5. Individual learning is promoted by social collaboration: by opportunities to work with others, to brainstorm, to try out ideas and get feedback, to obtain assistance. Social collaboration also offers powerful demonstrations of how others work, learn, act, and so forth, which is particularly valuable in promoting the growth of those whose strategies are initially less successful. In short, learning is facilitated by and within a community of learners.

Each of these principles about learning and the learner derives from the section on the development of language and literacy in Chapter 3. Many of the following principles either stem from or pertain to the discussions in earlier chapters, including Chapter 7 dealing with research on whole language versus traditional classrooms.

The Nature and Development of the Curriculum

Several implications for curriculum follow from the aforementioned principles of learning:

1. Since learning proceeds best when learners engage in authentic literacy and learning experiences, the curriculum should consist not of worksheets and dittos but of opportunities to engage in the myriad kinds of reading, discussion, experimentation, and research that children and adults voluntarily engage in, outside of school. "Opportunities" implies a strong element of learner choice.
2. Since choice is an important factor in facilitating learning, the curriculum is in many respects negotiated among the teacher and the students. The teacher determines the parameters within which he or she and the children are free to make choices. Long-range curricular decisions may be made by the teacher and students brainstorming possibilities and together making choices, within the bottom-line parameters of the externally imposed curriculum. Negotiation also occurs daily, in the give-and-take of the classroom. Students may suggest a better way to do something, or something better to do; the teacher will often agree. Not all the initiation for change comes from the teacher.
3. Since learning opportunities need to be perceived as functional and purposeful by the learner, it follows that language itself must be kept natural and whole. This means that emergent readers will be helped to read rhymes, songs, repetitive and predictable stories, and environmental print, rather than the stilted, unnatural language known as primerese. They will read whole texts rather than the contextless bits and pieces of language that characterize worksheets and workbooks. Similarly, students will write authentic stories, poems, letters, and other pieces, not do assignments like "Write a story about the day you woke up as a pencil," copying a poem from the blackboard, or filling in the blanks or lines of a workbook page.
4. Direct and indirect instruction of the parts of language occurs in the context of the whole, and in the context of the students' need. For example, during shared reading or literature discussions, the teacher may demonstrate effective reading strategies, and during writers' workshop, the teacher may demonstrate effective strategies for drafting or revision or editing, in each instance adding ideas to the "class pot" (Calkins, 1986) for students to draw upon. At other times, for example, the teacher will show one or more students how to punctuate dialogue when the students have actually used dialogue in a story. Phonics skills are developed through writing and in the context of enjoying a rhyme or song, not through worksheet practice. To generalize: in whole language classrooms, the teacher will sometimes directly teach something to the whole class, if it seems relevant to what many of them are doing or might

soon want to do as readers, writers, and learners. But at other times the teacher will work with a small group or an individual, particularly on a skill or strategy currently needed by only a few students. Typically, instruction proceeds from whole to part, then back to the whole. That is, the part is considered only in the context of the whole: the authentic reading, writing, and investigating that students are doing.

5. Thus, direct teaching occurs not according to a predetermined scope and sequence chart, but mostly in direct response to the students' interests and needs, as determined by them and by the teacher's observations. Significantly, direct instruction also occurs between and among peers, as they help one another with reading and writing and learning. Much direct instruction occurs in response to the "teachable moment."

Teacher Roles and Functions in Facilitating Learning

Whole language principles of learning, characteristics of curriculum, and teacher roles all draw heavily from research into the acquisition of language and literacy and how such learning is facilitated (see Chapter 3, pp. 59–65, 68–81). In fact, Holdaway's model for literacy learning (pp. 66–67) derives from the ways parents provide support for literacy development, in homes where books are frequently read to children.

Just as caretakers and other adults do not teach the "rules" of spoken language directly, so they do not usually try to teach children rules for reading. They read to children, demonstrating what it means to be a reader; they guide and encourage the child's active participation in reading the story; they discuss the story with the child, encouraging strategies like prediction ("What do you think's going to happen?"); they respond to the child's "What's this?" when asked of pictures, words, and letters; and they repeatedly offer opportunities for such guided participation by acceding to requests of "Read it again!" Usually the child is not only allowed but encouraged to practice independently, retelling and later actually reading the book to him- or herself, or to a doll or the dog. Finally, the child, now a confident reader, will want to read the book to some other person—even if the child is mainly turning the pages and retelling the remembered story as triggered by the pictures.

When whole language educators talk about the natural acquisition of literacy, what they mean is that literacy can best be fostered by using the means that parents have used, more or less naturally, to foster their preschoolers' development of literacy. Among the important implications for classroom instuction are these:

1. The teacher is, first of all, a role model. In order to foster students' development of literacy and learning, teachers must demonstrate that they themselves are passionate readers, writers, and learners. Teachers also need to demonstrate what it means to be risk takers and decision makers.

2. The teacher is also a mentor, collaborator, and facilitator. Often, the teacher serves as a master to whom students are apprenticed, and from whom they learn such crafts as reading and writing and learning itself. The teacher demonstrates and discusses his or her own knowledge of the craft with students, while collaborating with

them. For example, the teacher demonstrates and discusses reading strategies with students, helping them use and become consciously (metacognitively) aware of a growing range of strategies for constructing meaning and dealing with text. The teacher demonstrates and discusses writing strategies, teaches needed skills and strategies while conferring with students, and encourages peer collaboration and learning. In general, the teacher offers learning experiences and choices, helps students consider and acquire the resources needed for their projects, guides students in learning valuable strategies and skills for carrying out their purposes, monitors their progress, and responds to their needs—both those the students articulate and those the teacher merely observes or intuits. The teacher also helps students perceive themselves and each other as sources of information, resources, and so forth.

3. Teachers are responsible for creating a supportive community of learners, in which everyone (including the teacher) is free to take risks and make decisions without fear of negative consequences, and in which everyone is supported by others. Within this community, teachers encourage collaboration in various ways, such as by brainstorming ideas, responding to each others' writings and other work, sharing resources, working together on projects, sharing expertise, and helping one another.

4. Teachers present themselves as learners rather than as ultimate authorities, and similarly they treat students as capable and developing, not as incapable or as deficient products. Such teachers model and encourage risk taking, and they respond positively to what their students can do, while issuing invitations and offering challenges to stimulate students' growth.

5. Teachers share responsibility for curricular decision making with students, thus encouraging them to take ownership of and responsibility for their own learning. By also encouraging risk taking and decision making without fear of negative consequences, teachers empower students to become independent, self-motivated learners and doers.

Though both implicit and explicit in the preceding discussion, it is perhaps worth emphasizing that one of the most important ways whole language teachers facilitate learning is by scaffolding: they help learners do, or ask others to help them do, what they cannot yet do on their own. By not only permitting but actually encouraging dependence on other learners, teachers make it easier for children to become and succeed as independent learners. Paradoxically, perhaps, collaborative learning experiences promote both cooperation and community, on the one hand, and individual and independent growth and ability, on the other.

Assessment and Evaluation

It should not be surprising that in whole language classrooms, assessment and evaluation reflect many of the aforementioned principles of learning and teaching.

1. Assessment is *collaborative*. The teacher evaluates the student, but the student also engages in reflection and self-evaluation. Assessment may also involve peers and/or

parents. In particular, peers may evaluate each other's contributions to collaborative projects and learning, and/or to the class community in general. Parents may be invited to describe their child's strengths and needs as a learner at the beginning of the school year, then later invited to assess growth and suggest needs and goals (Barrs, Ellis, Tester, & Thomas, 1989). Furthermore, the various assessors can collaborate in assessing the individual: for instance, groups of students can talk about each others' strengths and suggest possible areas for improvement, and teachers can hold conferences in which child, teacher, and parent(s) together assess progress and determine learning goals. Or children can plan for and conduct conferences with their parents (Anthony, Johnson, Mickelson, & Preece, 1991). Each contributor to assessment may provide a valuable and to some degree unique perspective—rather like the parable of the blind men and the elephant. We need *all* of these perspectives to begin to build an accurate picture. (For more on multiple perspectives, see Short & Burke, 1992.)

2. Assessment is *complex and multidimensional*, based upon data of various kinds. Among other things, this means that those engaging in evaluation—teachers, students, and perhaps parents—look not just at *products* the learners have produced, but also at students' *processes* for reading, writing, and learning (and doing math, science, etc.). For instance, one would look for growth in the range and flexibility of reading and writing strategies; growth in ability to extend these strategies into new genres of reading and writing and to refine or modify them accordingly; and/or growth in the ability to integrate various strategies to learn more effectively. Evaluators also look at changes in students' *perceptions* of themselves as readers, writers, and learners—in other words, the affective factors that most powerfully influence learning. Is the student coming to view him- or herself as a reader, writer, and independent learner? Is the student growing in the range of learning experiences that he or she enjoys and engages in wholeheartedly? Something else to consider are the *social aspects* of learning. Is the student growing in ability to work collaboratively with others? If so, in what ways? With each of these measures, growth is typically considered a major factor. As Kathryn Mitchell Pierce has suggested, such ongoing assessment, with emphasis on growth, is like a videotape filmed over a substantial period of time, in comparison with standardized tests, which are more like single snapshots unrelated to one another.

3. Assessment is *contextualized*, drawing primarily upon information collected during the day-to-day activities of classroom life, rather than upon scores from tests that are quite unlike normal learning experiences. Drawing upon data that are both rich and varied, assessment is thus ongoing and continuous, intertwined with learning and teaching. Recorded observations are an important part of teachers' contribution to evaluation, but so are various kinds of artifacts, including periodic performance samples (e.g., of writing or reading) and "think-alouds," in which the learner thinks and talks his or her way through a reading or writing experience, as well as data from conferencces and interviews, inventories and questionnaires, dialogue journals and learning logs, and student-kept records (of such things as books read, topics and range of writings, goals set and progress made, self-evaluation, etc.). Projects of

various kinds, and the processes involved in producing them, are another important source of data for assessment. In other words, the teacher can draw upon a wide range of information, including (if desired) the students' own evaluations (or the data from students' self-evaluations can be kept and weighted separately, in the summative evaluation). Whole language classrooms invite many possibilities.

The summative evaluation is *weighted* appropriately, reflecting not only various viewpoints, kinds of goals, and kinds of data, but also a carefully conceived weighting among *individual-referenced assessment*, based primarily upon growth; *criterion-referenced assessment*, based upon the meeting of external expectations and the attainment of externally imposed goals; and *norm-referenced assessment*, based upon comparison with others, perhaps using whatever standardized tests may have been mandated. Sometimes the individual-referenced and criterion-referenced assessment are kept separate from the norm-referenced assessment (Edelsky & Harman, 1988). This is particularly true if the norm-referenced assessment consists exclusively of standardized test scores, which are best used (if they must be used at all) as part of an aggregate of data for an entire school.

Whole language teachers typically give significant weight to both individual-referenced assessment (growth) and to criterion-referenced assessment, with the balance between them determined by such factors as grade level. For instance, in evaluating preservice teachers in my university classes, I give more weight to criterion-referenced assessment than to individual-referenced, whereas the balance would be reversed if I were working with emergent readers and writers. (For an example of such weighted evaluation, see Cora Five's discussion of how she evaluated a special needs learner in Chapter 12 of this book; see also Anthony, Johnson, Mickelson, & Preece, 1991.)

5. Students and teachers evaluate themselves, each other, and the curriculum— that is, the classroom experiences that they have shaped and shared together. For example, students can consider how and how well they have contributed to the classroom community and/or to collaborative groups in which they have worked. They can also, if they have experience in other types of classrooms, consider how their whole language learning differs from traditional instruction, compare the advantages and disadvantages, and offer suggestions for change. (These examples come from an actual classroom, documented in Weaver, Chaston, & Peterson, 1993.)

Figure 8.2 includes advice from bilingual and biliterate first graders in Montreal who were asked what advice they would give to adults wanting to develop a good bilingual program. Part of an evaluation of an existing bilingual program (Maguire, 1993), these recommendations also clarify what whole language teachers have learned about how to teach more effectively.

A PARADIGM SHIFT

These principles of whole language should make it clear that no one can become a whole language teacher simply by using sets of materials labeled "whole language," by

1. Get our English and French teachers to work together to stop double dosing of homework.
2. Have us read more interesting books.
3. Let us choose our own topics. Let us make up our own stories.
4. Let us choose our own books.
5. Don't correct our work unless we want it corrected.
6. Don't make us recopy boring work.
7. Give us more time to write.
8. Have teachers that are funny and like to laugh.
9. Have us do more projects on our own in English and in French.
10. Remember that we like working with our friends on stuff.
11. When we make a mistake help us understand why it's a mistake.
12. Give us more time on the computer.
13. Invite more authors like Robert Souliere.
14. We don't like sheets made by machine.
15. Trust and be nice to kids.
16. We should do more plays in class, and art stuff.
17. Fill-ins are boring in any language.
18. We like getting more than just "Bravo" or "good" on our stuff.
19. Pray to God your teachers like each other.
20. It's a challenge when we have to write ourselves in any language.
21. Making up your own stuff and not copying the teacher's stuff is better.
22. Give kids choice. Last week I had to write a story about how bunnies live. I couldn't think of how bunnies live. Do you know how bunnies live? Do you really care?

FIGURE *8.2* *First graders' advice for developing a good bilingual and biliteracy program (Maguire, 1993)*

getting ideas from a single inservice seminar or conference, or by experimenting with different activities *without also developing new ways of viewing students as learners and new ways of transacting with them and assessing their learning.*

Certainly some of the materials, ideas, and activities teachers pick up at a workshop or conference can often make learning more fun, but they often reflect the same old notions of what must be taught and learned, how learning takes place, and how it should be evaluated. In a short time, it's easy to learn some ways to make boring, senseless skills work more fun. However, it takes much more effort and greater depth of understanding to change classroom practices so that students willingly engage in challenging projects that are fun not because they're silly, clever, or cute, but because they are meaningful for the learner and demand the learner's best.

As whole language teachers share teaching strategies among themselves, they help one another consider which strategies actually reflect their emerging paradigm. But this requires collaboration over time, among teachers who learn to support one another in risk taking and reflective self-evaluation. It cannot be accomplished in one or two workshops or conferences, though these may serve to motivate teachers to engage in such long-term collaboration and growth into a transactional paradigm of learning and teaching.

In short, whole language teaching both reflects and requires a shift from a transmission concept of learning to a transactional concept (see Chapter 3, as well as Harste, 1989b, and Short & Burke, 1992). According to the behavioristic psychology that underlies the transmission model, learning is said to result primarily from habit formation and simple association; hence, a great deal of time is spent practicing skills and memorizing information. It is true, of course, that rules can be practiced and isolated facts memorized (at least by some students), but such rules and facts are often forgotten soon after testing. Cognitive psychologists point out that complex processes and enduring concepts are learned far differently: *Humans construct knowledge for themselves, drawing from their experiences, and with or without the guidance and support of others.*

This concept is a central tenet in a whole language perspective on learning and teaching. Whole language is not an approach or method, and certainly not a set of pre-packaged materials. Instead, as stated earlier, whole language is a philosophy of learning and teaching: a belief system that guides instructional decision making. Thus, *a whole language teacher might be defined as someone who believes that humans fundamentally construct their own knowledge, and who works to increasingly activate that belief in the classroom.* So defined, whole language teaching is obviously not confined to the language arts. Indeed, this constructivist concept of learning permeates curricular reform efforts in every major discipline, including math, science, social studies, and health education.

Figure 8.3 presents a continuum, with the extremes of the transmission model at the left, and the extremes of a transactional model at the right. In general, whole language teachers are teachers who have made significant progress toward understanding and acting upon the principles and procedures toward the right.

COUNTERACTING MYTHS ABOUT WHOLE LANGUAGE

Perhaps the hardest thing for the newcomer to whole language to really understand is the paradigm shift that it both reflects and requires. Many of the myths about whole language that have developed in recent years derive from not understanding the alternative transactional paradigm. By discussing some of these myths, I hope to clarify some specific principles articulated in the section above, while explaining more broadly what the shift to a constructive, transactional view of education means in day-to-day practice. (See also Newman & Church, 1990; Weaver, 1990a; and Altwerger, 1991.)

Misconception number one: Whole language teachers do not teach. This misconception is perhaps understandable, because whole language teachers do generally avoid the traditional "teach, practice/apply, test" cycle that is followed in most classrooms.

In what ways *do* whole language teachers teach? In general, they serve more as master craftspersons, as mentors from whom apprentice readers, writers, and learners

Transmission Model of Learning	Transactional Model of Learning
LEARNING AND THE LEARNER	
Learner passively and often begrudgingly practices skills, memorizes facts, accumulates information	Learner actively and often enthusiastically engages in complex language and reasoning processes and the construction of complex concepts
Material practiced and learned is rarely perceived as functional or purposeful by the learner	Authentic experiences and projects are typically perceived as functional and purposeful by the learner
Uniform instruction reflects assumption that all learners learn the same things at the same time	Learner-sensitive instruction based on explicit assumption that all learners learn and develop uniquely
Lack of adult correctness generates negative feedback to what are considered to be errors in execution	Gradual approach to adult correctness is expected; learning is seen as best facilitated when learners are free to experiment and take risks without fear of negative feedback
Learning is seen as best facilitated by competition	Learning is seen as best facilitated by collaboration
CURRICULUM	
Curriculum is characterized by an emphasis on minimal skills and factual information	Curriculum is characterized by the kinds of learning experiences that lifelong learners engage in outside of school
Curriculum is divided into subjects, and subjects into skills and facts; language and literacy are taught as the mastery of isolated skills	Curriculum is integrated around topics and themes, with emphasis on developing language and literacy skills across the curriculum
Curriculum is determined by outside forces (curriculum guides and objectives, texts, and programs)	Curriculum is determined by, and negotiated among, the teacher and the students
Reading materials are characterized, at the earliest levels, by unnaturally stilted language ("basalese") consisting of basic sight words and/or phonically regular words	Reading materials include, at the earliest levels, a wide variety of materials in natural language patterns with emphasis on repetitive and predictable patterns
Beyond the primary grades, many reading selections consist of literature that has been altered, abridged, or excerpted from literary works	Beyond the primary grades, the range and depth of reading materials are increased, with emphasis on whole works of high literary quality as well as nonfiction prose
Direct teaching of skills occurs in isolation, according to a predetermined teach/practice/test format or program, with attention to mastering the parts of language	Direct teaching of skills occurs within the context of the whole learning experience and the learners' needs and interests (parts in context of the whole)

Figure 8.3   A continuum of educational models, from transmission to transactional

Transmission Model of Learning	**Transactional Model of Learning**

TEACHER ROLES

	Serves as a master craftsperson, mentor, role model, demonstrating what it is to be a literate person and lifelong learner
Serves to dispense information, assign tasks, and evaluate work	Stimulates learning by demonstrating, inviting, discussing, affirming, facilitating, collaborating
Explains lessons and assignments; determines work to be done	Creates a supportive community of learners wherein collaboration and assistance are encouraged
Creates a climate wherein competition and comparison are encouraged	Treats students as capable and developing, honoring their unique patterns of development and offering invitations and challenges to growth
Treats students as incapable and deficient insofar as they have not measured up to preset objectives and norms	Responds positively to successive approximations, thus encouraging risk taking and hypothesis formation
Rejects and penalizes errors, thus discouraging risk taking and hypothesis formation (thinking)	Shares responsibility for curricular decision making with students, thus empowering them to take ownership of and responsibility for their own learning
Fosters dependence on external authority to determine what to do and how to do things, as well as to decide what is and is not correct	

ASSESSMENT AND EVALUATION

Only the teacher assesses the student	Assessment is collaborative, involving not only the teacher but the student and perhaps peers and/or parents
	Assessment is complex and multidimensional, with attention given not only to products (such as test scores and reading and writing samples), but also to processes and to affective factors
Assessment is often limited to tests, with standardized tests given the greatest weight in evaluation and decision making regarding instruction and placement	Assessment is contextualized, based upon the day-to-day authentic learning experiences of the classroom
	Assessment is ongoing and continuous
Assessment is decontextualized; that is, it bears little resemblance to normal reading, writing, and learning activities	Assessment is learner-referenced (based on the individual learner's growth) as well as criterion-referenced
Assessment is infrequent	Students and teachers evaluate themselves, each other, and the curriculum—that is, their shared learning experiences
Assessment is primarily norm-referenced and to some extent criterion-referenced	
Both students and teachers are evaluated by students' performance on standardized tests and/or by students' attainment of externally imposed curriculum goals	

Figure 8.3   Continued

learn their crafts. Such teachers *demonstrate*: for example, when they show emergent readers how they themselves read a book (in what direction print is read, the matching of spoken words with written words, and so forth). They *invite* and *support*, as when they invite children to read along with them and support children in their reading. They teach by discussing, as when they *discuss* alliteration and rhyme in a poem or song. They *affirm* children's efforts, supporting them even when their assumptions aren't correct. They *facilitate* learning and *collaborate* with learners in a variety of ways.

The Shared Book Experience is an example of what psychologist Jerome Bruner has called *scaffolding* for learning (Ninio & Bruner, 1978; Bruner, 1983a, 1983b, 1986). For example, a whole language teacher may support children who cannot read independently by using *predictable* and *patterned* text in a shared reading situation, where these children can chime in with repeated phrases and sentences, echo the teacher and their more competent peers as they read the less predictable elements, and, through repeated exposure, begin to learn conventions of print, specific words, and letter/sound relations. The teacher doesn't simply read and reread the text. She helps children notice and verbalize how print works. Such scaffolding is a lot like the training wheels on a bicycle: what the child can do with support today, he or she will be able to do independently tomorrow. (This relates to Vygotsky's "zone of proximal development;" see Vygotsky, 1962/1986, 1978.)

Another example of supportive and collaborative whole language teaching comes from Ruth Perino, a fifth-grade teacher I worked with at an innovative elementary school, the Kalamazoo Academy. Instead of emphasizing the memorization and testing of facts, she embedded factual knowledge in a learning context that supported the development of concepts far beyond just the facts.

The students were studying that period in U.S. history immediately after the Civil War when, through amendments to the constitution, the slaves were freed, blacks were declared equal under the law, and black males were given the right to vote. Traditionally, one might simply have taught factual information about this period, including the rights supposedly guaranteed by these three amendments to the constitution. But Ruth not only discussed this period of history with the students, but also got them involved in reading the historical novel *Roll of Thunder, Hear My Cry* by Mildred D. Taylor. Through its recreation of the lives and difficulties of Southern blacks in the 1930s, this gripping story brought home the reality of the lives of many blacks, in contrast to the ideals made official by the constitution more than fifty years earlier.

After reviewing with the class some of the factual events of the Reconstruction era, Ruth helped the students organize themselves into groups to write and act out skits and thereby share some of what they'd learned about this historical period. To get the students thinking, she and I shared some suggestions for skits: one of our ideas, for example, was to have Mama, who teaches school in *Roll of Thunder,* teach her students a history lesson about the three aforementioned amendments, with the children in her class pointing out the discrepancies between the rights that blacks supposedly had and the repression they actually experienced in the rural South of the 1930s. Our examples may have helped, but Ruth's students came up with ideas entirely their own.

Not surprisingly, as the children drafted their skits, we teachers had to remind them of some of the factual information. We shared our resource books and our knowledge, collaborating with the students as needed. The less competent students had a third opportunity to absorb factual knowledge and develop concepts as they watched their more accomplished peers take the lead in performing the skits, then later expanded and revised their own skits to perform the next week. However, we teachers were trying not primarily to teach and test forgettable facts, but to provide opportunities for students to develop concepts and attitudes that could last a lifetime.

Instead of going through a traditional cycle of teach, practice/apply, and test, whole language teachers typically facilitate learning and collaborate with learners in the construction of knowledge. They assess not only the products of learning (written artifacts, for example) but also students' growth in the processes of learning and the attitudes conducive to learning and to becoming lifelong learners. In effect, process and affective factors become part of the sought-after products.

Misconception number two: Whole language teachers don't teach directly, they don't teach skills, they don't teach skills directly; consequently, children in whole language classrooms don't learn skills. Whole language teachers don't follow the teach, practice/apply, test cycle, but that doesn't mean they don't teach directly.

Here is an example of how Tracy Cobb, a first-grade teacher in Mattawan, Michigan, directly teaches effective reading strategies. Together, we and a group of her first graders did a series of activities revolving around the folktale *Stone Soup*. We used the simple Scholastic version by Ann McGovern. First, Tracy showed the cover to generate predictions. In the cover picture, an old woman is serving soup to a long-haired young man, who is smiling. Tracy asked the children to predict what the problem in the story might be, given the title and pictures. One child said the problem might be getting the girl (actually the young man) to eat the soup. Another said he didn't think so, because the boy looked happy about eating the soup. Tracy then asked the second child, "What did you just do that good readers do?" Thus, she was developing metacognitive awareness of a good reading strategy: using details in the picture to predict.

A page or so later, Tracy invited the children to tell what the young man might be like, again using the pictures to predict. The children made several good observations: that the young man looked poor because his clothes were ragged and torn (one child actually said "tattered"); that he looked hungry and tired; that he looked as if he'd walked a long way, all day and all night. When Tracy then read the words on the following page, one boy commented, "I made *two* good predictions."

By demonstrating and talking about her own reading strategies, and by leading children to use and verbalize good reading strategies, Tracy is directly teaching them how to read effectively. But of course, such direct teaching differs markedly from the teach, practice, apply, test method.

But what about skills?

What this means to whole language teachers is that the teacher helps the students, and the students help each other, learn skills in the context of *need* and/or *interest*, while they are involved in the reading and writing of authentic texts (as opposed to practice exercises or activities).

Adding ideas to the "class pot" is one of the ways in which teachers teach strategies and skills directly. When the teacher notices that several readers in the class might benefit from developing a particular reading strategy, such as reading on to see if further context will clarify a problem word, the teacher may demonstrate and discuss how he or she uses that strategy personally, then invite students to try it and later to discuss what they did and how it worked (the DDID cycle suggested in Chapter 4). Or when the teacher notices that several writers might be ready to consider new ways of developing character, the teacher might share examples from literature, perhaps demonstrating and discussing how the teacher has tried out the ideas as a writer, inviting students to do the same, and encouraging students to share and discuss their experiments with others (again, the DDID pattern). Whatever strategy or skill might be taught, and however it might be taught, the key here is to *invite* students to try it, not to demand that they practice it and then test them on their learning. This is a key difference between minilessons taught from a whole language, transactional model of learning and those taught from a traditional transmission model.

One of my favorite examples of developing skills in context is from an article by Lucy Calkins (1980). Calkins compared the learning of punctuation in two third-grade classrooms. In one classroom, the teacher taught simple sentences, periods, and other aspects of mechanics directly, through dittos and with pretests and posttests: in other words, the traditional concept of direct instruction. In the other classroom, students never studied punctuation formally, but instead wrote for an hour a day, three days a week, learning punctuation as needed to make their meaning clear, and learning it from the teacher and their peers and the books they were reading.

At the end of the year, Calkins interviewed all the children in each class to determine what they knew about punctuation. The children who had studied punctuation day after day could explain, on the average, only 3.85 marks of punctuation, typically by reciting the rules they'd learned for the period, question mark, and exclamation mark. In contrast, the students who wrote instead of studying isolated aspects of mechanics could explain, on the average, 8.66 marks of punctuation. These children tended to explain punctuation marks by telling or demonstrating how they used the marks in their own writing. As with oral language, children's natural development in writing seems to progress from fluency, to clarity, and gradually to correctness. Whole language teachers work with this natural tendency, rather than against it.

Another example of developing writing skills in context is an editing checklist from a first grader in Mary Ellen Giacobbe's class (Figure 8.4). In their writing folders, Giacobbe's first graders kept a cumulative list of editing skills for which they could take responsibility in editing their writing. Giacobbe would teach a child a new skill as the child's writing revealed the need. When the child could demonstrate the ability to apply this editing skill to his or her writing, the child and the teacher would agree it was time to add the skill to the list (Giacobbe, 1984).

In whole language classrooms, the teaching of skills is not dictated by the scope and sequence plan of the basal reading series or the language arts series, which require the

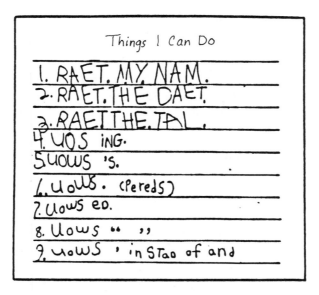

Figure 8.4   First grader's list of editing skills (Giacobbe, 1984)

teaching of many skills that do not need to be mastered for effective reading and writing (for example, the identification of parts of speech). Rather, whole language teachers focus on teaching meaningful skills that real readers and writers actually use beyond the classroom. Furthermore, these teachers don't limit students' access to skills to just those designated for a particular grade level; they teach whatever skills students need to accomplish their purposes as learners.

The whole language research described in Chapter 7 provides clear evidence that children in whole language classrooms learn not only the skills and strategies needed for real reading and writing, but also the attitudes and habits of literate individuals.

Misconception number three: Whole language teachers abandon control of the classroom to the students. This misconception arises from the use of phrases like "student ownership" and "empowerment" and the concern for "negotiating the curriculum." In practice, however, the teacher is still the primary authority: it's simply that she or he maintains control and organization in such a way as to allow more freedom and decision making by students.

A couple of years ago, Scott Peterson, a fourth-grade teacher from Mattawan elementary school, and I worked with his students two mornings each week to develop *with* his students a unit on the future (Weaver, Chaston, & Peterson, 1993). We wanted to learn firsthand what "negotiating the curriculum" might be like (a concept from Australian educator Garth Boomer, 1988; see especially his "Negotiating the Curriculum"). From our four months' experience, we concluded that negotiating the curriculum means two major things: (1) making long-range plans jointly *with* students instead of unilaterally planning for them; and (2) on a day-by-day, minute-by-minute basis, being responsive to the needs and suggestions of students as they become more adept at deciding what and how they want to learn.

Scott and I had decided unilaterally on a broad theme: the future. After listening to some books that we read aloud and brainstorming their concerns about the future, the students each chose one of the major subtopics that had emerged: environmental concerns, technology, and social problems such as drug abuse, child abuse, and suicide. Once they had chosen their broad topic, the students went on to make more decisions about what kind of project they would do to share their learning, what particular aspect of the topic they would work on, with whom they would work, and so forth. In other words, they negotiated significant aspects of this unit of study with us and with each other. Details were renegotiated almost daily, as the students' enthusiasm generated new ideas and insights. Gradually I learned to hold at bay my own tendency to say, "But we've already decided to do it this way," and instead to listen to new suggestions; to admit that sometimes the students' new ideas were better than their original ideas, or ours; and to see the potential for learning in activities I would previously have thought a waste of time. In the process of learning to negotiate the curriculum, I was gradually giving over more and more ownership to the students; I was helping to "empower" them as learners and even as teachers. (Kathryn Mitchell Pierce suggests that control and ownership of the curriculum can be seen as a commodity that increases in amount as it is shared among teacher and students. Though that's not how I thought of it at the time, I like this idea.)

Misconception number four: Whole language classrooms are unstructured and, therefore, may not meet the needs of those students who require a significant amount of structure. This misconception is understandable, since whole language classrooms are not structured in conventional ways: according to curriculum guides imposed upon teachers and children, according to prepackaged sets of materials, or according to the scope and sequence charts of basal reader programs.

In fact, however, there *is* structure; whole language teachers simply structure time, the curriculum, and the classroom differently. Reading strategies may be considered as students discuss a work of literature they have read; social studies events and concepts may likewise be approached partly through literature; scientific discoveries may be explored through biography and autobiography; and, of course, writing, oral language, and research abilities may be developed through study in all these areas. Thus, the whole language teacher may not set aside daily time for skills work, for instance, but will approach the teaching and learning of skills within the context of whatever the students are studying and exploring. Such a major change as this may make it difficult for those who haven't spent time in whole language classrooms to see the structure.

Nevertheless, the structure is there. The teacher may set aside larger blocks of time for integrated theme study, but time management is still a critical part of the teacher's role. The boundaries between different areas of the curriculum are blurred or lost as teacher and students explore topics and themes, but the teacher still determines the structure within which all members of the classroom community will operate—including the kinds of decision making in which the students will participate, and the kinds and range of choices they may make regarding major projects, activities to do during daily choice time (reading, writing, math, science, etc.), and books to read, topics and genres for writing, and so forth.

The teacher may also structure the classroom differently, clustering desks into working groups instead of rows and/or establishing centers for writing, reading, math, science, and art, but the classroom is still arranged according to definable principles.

As we shall see from some concrete examples in Chapter 12, learners with special needs may indeed benefit from more specific help in structuring their work. Such help is provided on an individual basis as necessary, by whole language teachers (and other teachers who understand such students' needs). For example, whole language teachers may help students with an Attention Deficit Hyperactivity Disorder by limiting their range of choices (e.g., suggesting they choose one book from among a specified three), if they have particular difficulty making decisions; by working with them to plan and schedule the various parts of a complex project, and by monitoring their progress; by keeping their homework to a mimimum and making sure these students leave school with the needed materials and a clear understanding of how to do whatever work *is* assigned (Weaver, 1992b, 1993). For a fulller discussion of how whole language classrooms facilitate the learning of students with AD(H)D, see the articles in *Success at last! Helping Students with Attention Deficit (Hyperactivity) Disorders Achieve their Potential* (Weaver, 1994). The students that comprise Cora Five's case studies in Chapter 12 may both have had an Attention Deficit Discorder (one with hyperactivity, one without), though neither had been diagnosed as such. Five's descriptions of their progress in her whole language fifth-grade class help clarify how and why students with special needs begin to flourish in whole language classrooms, where additional structure is provided as needed for individual students. In Chapter 12, Linda Erdmann's discussion of whole language classrooms for special needs students also helps clarify how both learning and behavior are enhanced by classrooms that operate upon whole language principles.

Misconception number five: Whole language is just for the primary grades or elementary school, and/or whole language is just for language arts or English instruction. The basic reason why whole language is *not* confined to the primary grades or to elementary school is that whole language is fundamentally a set of principles about learning and teaching. These principles are based upon a constructivist, transactional model of learning that is relevant to teaching at all levels, regardless of the different ways these concepts might be actualized in different settings.

Two previous examples should help illustrate. In Scott Peterson's fourth-grade class, we were all using language and literacy to learn about science (the technology and environment of the future, and even the chemical aspects of drug abuse). We also got into social science when considering what forms of help are available to those who are abused by parents and spouses, to those who are hooked on drugs or alcohol, and to those who are depressed and suicidal. But throughout our theme exploration, Scott and I fostered student choice and ownership of their own learning, established a setting for collaborative learning, and helped the students construct knowledge for themselves. Similarly, the fifth-grade history and literature unit in Ruth Perino's class further illustrates how whole language principles might operate in the intermediate or middle grades.

I'd like to further dispel both myths by describing Stuart, a high school teacher of earth science, who knows that students need to discover knowledge and principles for themselves, not to be taught someone else's discoveries. For example, Stuart involves his students in an expedition investigating a river behind his school. He contrasts this experience with a textbook explanation of rivers:

> The experiences my students have are *real,* not make believe. What I do are real experiments in science. We go to the Lincoln River and we measure stream velocity and its effects on rocks. The kids learn about stream energy, sorting, grain size, roundness . . .

Through observing, documenting, and analyzing, Stuart wants his students to discover, for themselves, the fundamental laws of the earth. Effective educational practices like this often involve "reinventing the wheel." It doesn't seem very efficient, but it's far more rewarding and enduring.

This example of Stuart is from an article by Laura Fulwiler in *Supporting Whole Language: Stories of Teacher and Institutional Change,* (Weaver & Henke, 1992). In interviewing a kindergarten teacher, a sixth-grade teacher, a middle school teacher, and two high school science teachers, Laura found that one of the whole language beliefs they held in common was a conviction that students can—and indeed must—be encouraged to construct meaning for themselves. This forms the heart of whole language education.

Still another example illustrates how some whole language principles are actualized more than others, depending upon the group and the setting. Taking my cue from a colleague, poet Elizabeth Kerlikowske, I prepared a handout with some poems labeled "Poetry" and others labeled "Not Poetry." By comparing the two sets of poems, the discussion group was to try to determine what characterizes genuine poetry. (One might have divided the poems into "Good Poetry" versus "Bad Poetry," but I preferred to avoid the obviously judgmental labels. For teachers familiar with James Britton's distinctions among kinds of writing, we might alternatively have used the labels "Poetic Writing" and "Expressive Writing"—see Britton, 1970.)

After we discussed the criteria, the group was asked to apply them by categorizing some previously unseen poems. Given more time, I would have encouraged the group to reconsider my original labelings and decide whether any of the poems were mislabeled, in their opinion, using their criteria. Because time was short (we had less than an hour), I had set the task(s) for the group, assembled the materials, and to some extent predetermined the likely outcome. However, they still had some degree of ownership, in that the criteria for distinguishing poetry from nonpoetry were theirs, constructed inductively through discussion. The setting in this case was a workshop involving teachers, but I might use a similar activity in a high school or college classroom. In such a situation, we would have more time for students to choose poems for discussion—and probably to challenge the critieria initially derived. Once their ideas were added to the class pot, students could later choose whether to establish for themselves as writers a goal like "Use more concrete, sensory details," one of the criteria for poetry that typically emerges from such discussions of effective poems.

Misconception number six: Whole language teachers don't assess students' learning. Though it's true that whole language teachers prefer to spend most of their time fostering learning rather than assessing it, the good news is that virtually everything that happens in whole language classrooms can become part of assessment and evaluation. (See Figure 8.5 for some references on more contextualized kinds of assessment.)

Though there are several principles that guide assessment in most whole language classrooms, for simplicity I'll mention only the five described earlier in this chapter:

1. Assessment is *collaborative*, involving the student and perhaps parents and/or peers, as well as the teacher.
2. Assessment is *complex* and *multidimensional*, concerned not just with products but also with processes and perceptions (affective factors).
3. Assessment is *contextualized*. That is, assessment derives primarily from what students are doing every day. It occurs within the context of learning.
4. In the summative evaluation, individual-referenced assessment (growth) is weighted with criterion-referenced assessment, with the balance between the two being determined partly by grade level (e.g., these factors would probably not be weighted the same for primary-grade students and university students). Evaluation may include norm-referenced assessment, such as standardized test scores, but these are given little if any weight in major decisions affecting the individual student.
5. Assessment involves multifaceted reflection and critique, with students and teachers evaluating themselves, each other, and the curriculum as they have designed and experienced it.

Figure 8.6 depicts a cube that can be helpful in conceptualizing the assessment of students, regardless of the level at which one teaches. The cube includes three broad questions to be addressed in planning for assessment:

1. Who will be involved in assessment?
2. What will we be looking for?
3. What kinds of data will we collect?

Such questions can be explored not only among teachers and administrators, but among teachers and students in the classroom, and teachers, parents, and students during a parent conference. At the college level, my students and I have been discussing not only who should have input into their grades but why, and how; we also negotiate how much of the final grade will be my responsibility and how much will be theirs—both with appropriate justification, of course. Often we can't make decisions on these issues until we see how the course is shaping up, and particularly how and what kinds of peer collaboration are involved. But we can discuss the kinds of factors we ought to be looking for as evidence of learning, and some of the kinds of data from which inferences about learning might be drawn.

Taking significant responsibility for their own assessment helps students take greater responsibility for their own learning as well. When someone else is doing the

Books

Anthony, R. J., Johnson, T. D., Mickelson, N. I., & Preece, A. (1991). *Evaluating literacy: A perspective for change.* Portsmouth, NH: Heinemann.

Barrs, M., Ellis, S., Tester, H., & Thomas, A. *The primary language record: Handbook for teachers.* Portsmouth, NH: Heinemann.

Belanoff, P., & Dickson, M. (1991). *Portfolio grading: Process and product.* Portsmouth, NH: Boynton/Cook–Heinemann.

Eggleton, J. (1990). *Whole language evaluation: Reading, writing, and spelling.* San Diego: The Wright Group.

Goodman, K. S., Bridges, L. B., & Goodman, Y. M. (Eds.) (1992). *The whole language catalog: Supplement on authentic assessment.* Chicago, IL: American School Publishers.

Goodman, K. S., Goodman, Y. M., & Hood, W. J. (1989). *The whole language evaluation book.* Portsmouth, NH: Heinemann.

Goodman, Y. M., Watson, D. J., & Burke, C. L. (1987). *Reading miscue inventory: Alternative procedures.* Katonah, NY: Richard C. Owen.

Graves, D. H., & Sunstein, B. S. (Eds.) (1992). *Portfolio portraits.* Portsmouth, NH: Heinemann.

Harp, B. (Ed.). (1991). *Assessment and evaluation in whole language programs.* Norwood, MA: Christopher-Gordon.

Sharp, Q. Q. (1989). *Evaluation: Whole language checklists for evaluating your children: For grades K to 6.* New York: Scholastic.

Tierney, R. J., Carter, M. A., & Desai, L. E. (1991). *Portfolio assessment in the reading-writing classroom.* Norwood, MA: Christopher-Gordon.

Articles and portions of books

Fisher, B. (1991). *Joyful learning: A whole language kindergarten.* Portsmouth, NH: Heinemann. Includes a lot of sample forms.

Routman, R. (1991). *Invitations: Changing as teachers and learners K–12.* Portsmouth, NH: Heinemann. Includes excellent chapter on evaluation, with lots of examples.

Taylor, D. (1989). Toward a unified theory of literacy learning and instructional practices. *Phi Delta Kappan, 71,* 184–193. Articulates the need for alternative kinds of assessment; gives examples.

Taylor, D. (1990). Teaching without testing: Assessing the complexity of children's literacy learning. *English Education 22* (February), 4–74. Presents in more depth the arguments and evidence of the 1989 article.

Weaver, C. (1990). *Understanding whole language.* Portsmouth, NH: Heinemann. Includes a chapter on problems with using standardized tests, and another chapter on whole language assessment.

FIGURE *8.5*   *References on alternatives in assessment*

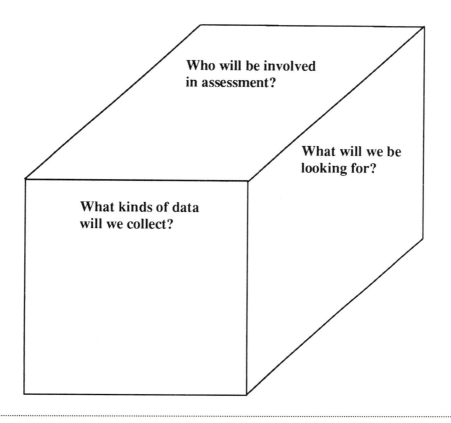

Figure 8.6 *Assessment cube*

grading, students often complain they don't know why or how they got the grades they did. When students participate from the start in developing an assessment cube like the one in Figure 8.7, they are necessarily involved in developing criteria and standards to use as guidelines in taking greater responsibility for their own learning as well as their own assessment. Figure 8.6 shows the kind of cube that might result, after brainstorming, discussion, and initial decision making. However, the cube must always be open to modification and change, when good reasons for renegotiation emerge.

Misconception number seven: Whole language students do worse on standardized tests; and/or whole language learning and teaching are not supported by comparative research. You may have heard, as I have, that in such-and-such a school or school system, or in so-and-so's classroom, standardized test scores are not as good as they used to be, since whole language has been "adopted." Of course, there may be various causes beyond the teacher's or the school's control for the alleged drop in scores. Still, we should ask: *Could* such results have anything to do with changes in teaching?

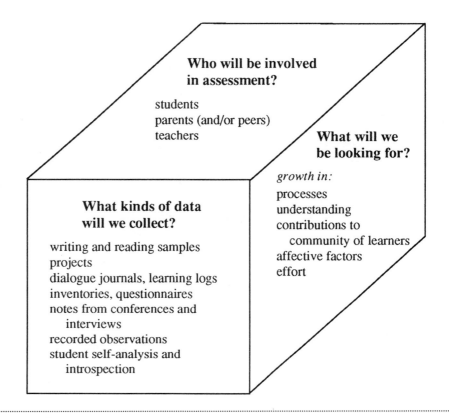

Who will be involved
in assessment?

students
parents (and/or peers)
teachers

What will we
be looking for?

growth in:
processes
understanding
contributions to
    community of learners
affective factors
effort

What kinds of data
will we collect?

writing and reading samples
projects
dialogue journals, learning logs
inventories, questionnaires
notes from conferences and
    interviews
recorded observations
student self-analysis and
    introspection

FIGURE 8.7   Sample assessment cube

Possibly. I do hear of "whole language" teachers who, for instance, don't do much to support children in learning about how print works and what strategies are most effective in reading. A year ago, for example, one of my outstanding graduates was hired by a principal in another state who wanted someone to help colleagues become more effective as whole language teachers. My former student discovered that while some who called themselves whole language teachers might read a Big Book to their children, they had no idea of the kinds of discussion typically involved in the Shared Book Experience (see Chapter 3). They simply read the book to the children—once. Similarly, I hear of teachers who attempt "process writing" (to me, the very existence of the term suggests misunderstanding) but who never help children revise and edit their writing, never help them learn the conventions of writing while editing, and never give them help in correcting or developing strategies for spelling. To me, these practices reflect a misunderstanding of whole language. Such practices are especially likely to happen when teachers are simply told they are expected to "do" whole language or to "be" whole language teachers.

So if test scores drop when the teacher claims to have become a whole language teacher, I think the following are some likely explanations we should consider:

1. Perhaps the teacher is expected to "be" a whole language teacher, without having had the support necessary to grow into the underlying philosophy and to figure out what that means—and doesn't mean—for teaching.
2. Perhaps the teacher really *isn't* helping kids learn skills and strategies in the context of authentic reading and writing experiences.
3. Perhaps the kids have never, or rarely, seen anything resembling standardized tests before, and consequently don't know how to take such tests.

Teachers need administrative support in growing into whole language. Also, students may need limited but guided practice in test taking, if they and their teacher and whole language itself are to be judged on the basis of standardized test scores. But anyone who knows much about whole language also knows that standardized tests provide inadequate, culturally biased, and often highly misleading estimates of students' actual ability to read authentic texts (as I've discussed in *Understanding Whole Language,* 1990a). Adopting whole language ways of teaching requires downplaying the results of standardized test scores while developing a variety of more informative and more appropriate assessment measures. Developing more appropriate means of assessment (like those described earlier in this chapter, and in Chapter 6) should minimize everyone's concern about standardized test scores, and put these scores into better perspective.

Still, what *does* comparative research say about the test scores of students in traditional versus whole language classrooms? And what does it demonstrate about the more substantive and qualitative benefits of whole language education?

In the comparative studies I've been able to locate (see Chapter 7), students in whole language classrooms have shown greater gains than those in traditional classrooms on every different kind of measure, standardized or otherwise. In other words, the small but growing body of comparative research has, so far, *overwhelmingly* indicated the superiority of whole language educational practices. To date, most of these studies have involved students in the primary grades, and a substantial proportion of these studies have involved the Shared Book Experience, or something similar; that is, the teachers have actively given children support in constructing their own knowledge about print, books, words, letter/sound relations, reading strategies, and so forth.

Combining results from these studies, it seems reasonable to draw the following tentative conclusions (as long as we simultaneously consider them to be reframable as hypotheses subject to further testing):

1. *Children in whole language classrooms usually show equal or greater gains on various reading tests and subtests—or at least they did in these research studies (though the differences often were not statistically significant).* For example, the whole language kindergartners in Ribowsky's study (1985) scored better on all measures of growth and achievement, including the tests of letter recognition and letter/sound knowledge. In the Kasten and Clarke study (1989), the whole language kindergartners performed significantly better than their counterparts on all subtests of the

Metropolitan Readiness Test, including tests of beginning consonant sounds, letter/sound correspondences, and sounds and clusters of sounds in initial and final positions of words.

2. *Children in whole language classrooms develop greater ability to use phonics knowledge effectively than children in more traditional classrooms, where skills are practiced in isolation.* For example, in Freppon's study (1988, 1991), the skills group attempted to sound out words more than twice as often as the others, but the literature-based group was more successful in doing so: a 53 percent success rate compared with a 32 percent success rate for the skills group. Apparently the literature-based children were more successful because they made better use of phonics in conjunction with other information and cues. (For another relevant study, see Cunningham, 1990.)

3. *Children in whole language classrooms develop vocabulary, spelling, grammar, and punctuation skills as well as or better than children in more traditional classrooms.* (For example, see the 1991 Elley summary of studies on learning English as a second language; also Clarke, 1988, and Stice & Bertrand, 1990, on spelling. In addition, see Calkins, 1980; Gunderson & Shapiro, 1987, 1988; DiStefano & Killion, 1984).

4. *Children in whole language classrooms are more inclined and able to read for meaning rather than just to identify words.* For example, when asked "What makes a good reader?" the children in Stice and Bertrand's study (1990) reported that good readers read a great deal and that they can read any book in the room. The children in the traditional classrooms tended to focus on words and surface correctness; they reported that good readers read big words, know all the words, and don't miss any words.

5. *Children in whole language classrooms develop more strategies for dealing with problems in reading.* For example, the whole language children in Stice and Bertrand's study (1990) typically described six strategies for dealing with problem words; the children in traditional classrooms described only three.

6. *Children in whole language classrooms develop greater facility in writing.* For example, in the Dahl and Freppon study (1992), a considerably larger proportion of the children in the whole language classrooms were writing sentences and stories by the end of first grade. The whole language children in the Kasten and Clarke study (1989) were similarly much more advanced as writers by the end of their kindergarten year.

7. *Children in whole language classrooms develop a stronger sense of themselves as readers and writers.* Take, for example, the Stice and Bertrand study (1992): When asked "Who do you know who is a good reader?" 82 percent of the kindergartners in the whole language classrooms mentioned themselves, but only 5 percent of the kindergartners in the traditional classrooms said "Me." During the first-grade year, when the children were asked directly "Are you a good reader?" 70 percent of the whole language children said yes, but only 33 percent of the traditional children said yes.

8. *Children in whole language classrooms also develop greater independence as readers and writers.* In the Dahl and Freppon study (1992), for instance, passivity seemed to be the most frequent coping strategy for learners having difficulty in the skills-based

classrooms. But in whole language classrooms, those having difficulty tended to draw upon other learners for support: by saying the phrases and sentences that others could read, by copying what they wrote, and so forth. Less proficient literacy learners still attempted to remain engaged in literacy activities with their peers. (See also item 5 above.)

As you will have noticed, only one of these conclusions relates to standardized test scores, because whole language researchers consider them much less important than the time typically spent on them and the significance often accorded to them would suggest. In fact, such tests are often downright misleading in assessing children's actual ability to read and to write, and to develop the attitudes, values, and behaviors of literate individuals. Most of these research conclusions are therefore drawn from a wide range of data. (For more information, see the references cited in Figure 7.2, especially Stephens, 1991.)

A growing number of research studies offer impressive evidence of the benefits of whole language education. The fact that standardized test scores are about the same as or better than the results in traditional classrooms is the least important result of these studies, though it may be politically useful with administrators who are reluctant to permit or promote whole language teaching because of their fear of lowered test scores. To whole language educators, what's really important is the fact that whole language students are generally more proficient at reading and writing, are more independent as learners, and have more positive concepts of themselves as readers and writers and learners.

Misconception number eight: Anyone can be a whole language teacher simply by going to an inservice or two, replacing basal reading programs with trade books, maybe buying some of the newer instructional materials labeled "whole language," and obtaining from conferences or from the teacher next door some clever ideas for turning skills work into a fun game. When schools and teachers are increasingly eager to hop onto the popular whole language bandwagon, it's tempting to take shortcuts and hope they will suffice. And all of these may help, in some ways. But they are not enough to bring about that shift from the typical transmission concept of education to the transactional, constructivist concept that underlies whole language learning and teaching.

The following are among the kinds of support that teachers need:

1. They need ample time to visit the classrooms of colleagues whom they consider role models, time to talk with these teachers, and time to reflect on implications for their own teaching, perhaps in the company of sympathetic colleagues and administrators.
2. They need ample time to read professional literature and discuss it with other interested colleagues.
3. They need to see demonstrations of effective practices undertaken in their own classrooms by more experienced whole language teachers. They may also want these colleagues to critique and comment upon some of their own attempts at change.

4. They need encouragement to raise their own questions about what might work more effectively in their own classrooms, and encouragement to take risks, to try new things.

5. They need new materials: paper and chart paper, instead of workbooks; new trade books, instead of basals; art supplies for writing and drawing and creating; math and science supplies and programs instead of traditional textbooks; and so forth.

6. Perhaps most of all, they need respect and support—especially when what they attempt doesn't work out as well as hoped, or the standardized test scores don't come in quite as high as before.

7. Much of this can be planned, facilitated, arranged, and even celebrated through weekly professional development meetings in the school.

Misconception number nine: Whole language can be successfully mandated by administrators. An administrator who understands whole language will know better. Whole language is fundamentally a belief system, and you can't bring about a change in belief systems simply by demanding it. Indeed, the very idea of mandating whole language from on high is so contrary to the principles of whole language that even experienced whole language teachers may be appalled and alienated if whole language is mandated. At best, what one will get from others is compliant lip service; at worse, open defiance and subtle undermining of the intent of the mandate. If it's necessary to keep their jobs, teachers may claim that theirs is a whole language school, that they are whole language teachers, and that they teach children in whole language ways—all the while making only the most superficial changes in their teaching. But this hypocrisy serves only to create distrust and divisiveness among teachers, to confuse the public as to what whole language really is, and perhaps thereby to contribute to its demise.

The articles in *Supporting Whole Language* (Weaver & Henke, 1992) help clarify how whole language education can be supported rather than destroyed by well-meaning administrators, while Lester and Onore's *Learning Change* (1990) further indicates the gradual nature of teacher change, and how administrators can support teachers and one another in making the shift from a transmission model to a transactional model of education. Such support requires an understanding of the principles of whole language and a rejection of the myths that surround it.

FROM PRINCIPLES TO PRACTICE

Becoming convinced of the major principles of whole language creates obligations for us as teachers. It means we need to begin making changes, moving from a transmission model of education toward a transactional model in our classrooms. For most of us, growing into whole language is a gradual process, rather than a sharp break with what we've done before. We may try to actualize one or two principles this year, become more adept at understanding and actualizing them the next, and continue trying to put into practice more of what we now understand about teaching and learning.

In this section, I list some of the principles that seem most critical to me, along with the kinds of questions I've been asking myself as a teacher, whether in the university classroom or working with elementary teachers and students. In each area, there is probably a continuum of growth, but new understanding of how I might implement one principle leads to new insights in other areas, too. In addition, implementation of these principles varies considerably from one course to another, and even from one class of students to another. I have personalized this section because that is what each of us must do to develop as whole language teachers: we must translate principles into action, perhaps starting by asking ourselves questions, as I keep doing.

Ultimately, learners construct (or don't construct) knowledge for themselves, regardless of what we do or don't do as teachers, what we explicitly teach or don't teach. This is a chilling thought, yet we teachers see every day that what we or our predecessors have taught has been forgotten, because the learners weren't really interested in learning what we had to teach and therefore didn't incorporate what we taught into their knowledge system, their schemas. This reluctant recognition has led me to ask myself such questions as these:

- How can I replace what learners consider meaningless activities and assignments with meaningful reading, writing, and learning opportunities and experiences—those that *the learners* will consider meaningful?
- How can I offer students meaningful choices, so as to increase the probability that each student will engage in learning and constructing knowledge?
- How can I organize the experiences or tasks or spaces to expand the potential for collaborative learning?
- How can I most effectively develop the curriculum *with* students, honoring their interests and needs, while meeting at least the bottom-line requirements of the curriculum or the course?
- In short, how can we make decisions collectively and individually, so that what we do will be meaningful to students and therefore will encourage them to construct knowledge for themselves?

I have come to the conclusion that the questions reflect, in essentially this order, a deepening understanding of the principle of learners constructing knowledge for themselves, and what it means for education. My initial inclination was to assume that I must change what I do in the classroom, yet I was still retaining all the authority and responsibility to consider alternatives and make decisions. When I ask myself the second and third questions, I am still retaining most of that authority and responsibility. But if I ask how I can negotiate the curriculum with students, I am coming closer to sharing responsibility equally with the learners—and thus to increasing the probability of their being interested, motivated, and engaged enough to construct enduring knowledge for themselves.

Notice that as we teachers grow into an appreciation of the principle that learners construct knowledge for themselves, we increasingly come to trust the learner—just as we trust young children to learn language. We empower them to take ownership and responsibility for their own learning. We also come to appreciate the fact that, often, less is more: less information for students to learn allows more time for students to develop concepts about important topics and issues.

In order to encourage students to genuinely learn, we teachers need to become role models, mentors, collaborators, and facilitators, as well as sources of needed information. We need to demonstrate what it means to be readers and writers and lifelong learners, as well as to demonstrate the skills and strategies that such learners need to develop; to invite learners to try new things without fear of negative repercussions; and to support learners in what they are trying to do. Here are some of the questions I find myself asking:

- How should I be demonstrating that reading and writing and learning are important to me personally? That is, how should I go about being a role model?
- How can I demonstrate risk taking and encourage it by supporting learners and not penalizing them for their efforts?
- How can I share my knowledge with students in the context of collaborating with them and assisting them, rather than through isolated lessons?
- How can I create an enviroment in which collaboration encourages individual growth?
- How can I provide just enough structure to facilitate the freedom students need in order to succeed at pursuing their own learning?

Some of what I have learned in this regard is documented in *Theme Exploration: A Voyage of Discovery* (Weaver, Chaston, & Peterson, 1993), in the chapters wherein Scott Peterson and I describe our learning as we helped his fourth graders pursue their interests in learning about the future of our world and how we might improve it. For example, I remember helping three girls learn how to use the yellow pages in the phone book to locate agencies that might provide us with relevant information and speakers, and explaining to one student the who-what-when-where strategy of journalism as we collaborated to write an introduction to the videotape our group produced. This is just one example of sharing knowledge with students while collaborating with them, a process critical to whole language classrooms.

Parts are best learned in the context of the whole; in other words, skills are best learned with assistance at the point of need. For about two decades, I've been teaching editing skills at the point of need, after students have written and revised their pieces. I now do the same with reading strategies. Over the years I have had to ask myself questions such as these:

- How can I help students develop editing skills in the context of authentic writing?
- How can I help students develop reading strategies in the context of authentic reading?
- How can I most effectively teach the class or a small group a mini-lesson on some skill or strategy many of them may need?
- What other learning strategies or research strategies can I teach at the point of need, and how?

For me, a major insight has been that every time we briefly teach a writing technique or editing skill or reading strategy, we teachers don't need to follow this with guided and/ or independent practice and then assessment of some sort (see also Chapter 9). We can simply demonstrate and share what we know, inviting those students who have a need for the skill or technique or strategy to adopt it. These students may later help others acquire what they have learned.

This practice reflects trust in the learner and the conviction that learners construct knowledge for themselves—or don't, if it doesn't seem relevant to them. Experience suggests that, in the long run, this teaching stragegy is more effective and far more efficient than routinely having students practice and then be tested on skills for which they don't yet see a need.

Assessment should derive from and be intertwined with learning and teaching, not be separate from or unrelated to it. It should also reflect confidence in learners' fundamental ability to learn what's meaningful to them, belief that learners are capable and developing rather than deficient, and the conviction that having learners taking significant responsibility for assessment goes along with their taking increased responsibility for their own learning. When I approach assessment in this way, I begin asking myself questions such as these:

- How can I design assessment so as to focus more on students' idiosyncratic growth than on their meeting arbitrary criteria? How can I design assessment reflecting the conviction that students are capable and developing, rather than incapable and deficient?
- How can I record anecdotal incidents and periodic observations, and incorporate these into my assessment of individuals' growth and accomplishment?
- What artifacts can we use as part of assessment? (Examples: journals, learning logs, interviews and questionnaires, writing and reading samples, projects.)
- How can I involve students in self-evaluation and (if or as appropriate) peer and/or parent evaluation—and all of us in evaluating the curriculum and me?

The previous discussions of assessment in this chapter and in Chapter 6 indicate some of the ways I have been answering these questions recently. The assessment cube (Figure 8.6) has been particularly valuable in generating class discussion and decisions about assessment.

Teachers need to be responsive not only to the curricular needs and interests of individual students, but also to their learning strategies and styles—their learning strengths. Though many whole language educators reject learning styles research because talking about someone's learning style seems to reduce a complex human being to an unrealistically simplistic trait or set of traits, I think there is much that whole language educators can gain from the study of learning styles. For instance, what we need to recognize is that the whole-to-part strategies that work best for most young learners need to be supplemented with more emphasis on the parts, for some learners—and more emphasis on teaching based on observation of the strategies that individual learners are developing (see, for example, the story of Jevon, p. 325). We also need to meet the wider range of learning strategies and needs evidenced by our students as they get older.

My background reading in learning styles research (Dunn & Dunn, n. d., 1990; Carbo, all references; McCarthy, 1980) and research on differing "intelligences" (Gardner, 1985, 1987) leads me to ask myself questions such as these:

- How can I come to perceive students more as they really are, rather than through the lenses of my beliefs?
- In general, how can I establish a balance in meeting the learning style needs of diverse individuals?
- How can I begin with activities and strategies appropriate to those who learn globally, then move toward what the more analytical learners need?
- How can I identify the needs of students whose preferred learning styles and natural learning strategies differ from my predominant teaching styles and strategies?
- How can we organize the classroom and negotiate the curriculum so that students can meet many of their own needs?

Again, I think the order of the questions reflects some of my own growth as a whole language teacher. Initially, I thought I had to take all the responsibility for addressing students' learning styles. Gradually, I am learning to involve the students more in decision making and in taking responsibility for meeting their own interests and needs.

What these five principles and my related questions reveal, I think, is that *whole language teachers are reflective practitioners.* We constantly reflect upon the effects and the effectiveness of what we are doing as teachers, remain open to learning from our students as well as from colleagues and professional studies, and repeatedly take new risks in an attempt to make our teaching even more conducive to genuine learning.

A supportive context for such reflection is provided by an innovative whole language staff development program, *Frameworks.* Developed by Jan Turbill and Brian Cambourne at the University of Wollongong in Australia, this program is being offered at various sites within the United States. (For more information, contact the Office of Staff Development, Wayne-Finger Lakes BOCES, 3501 County Road 20, Stanley, NY 14561; telephone 716–526–6420.)

Some common patterns of growth into whole language teaching are presented in the next chapter, which describes the teaching of writing, reading, literature, and topics (or themes as they are often called).

FOR FURTHER REFLECTION AND EXPLORATION

1. To gain a better understanding of whole language principles and practices, consult some of the references in Figure 3.15, Figure 8.1, and others of your choice. Then, write an explanation of whole language as you understand it, keeping in mind a

specific audience that would be appropriate, such as other teachers and administrators in your school, the parents of children in your classroom, the parent of a neighbor's child who is in a whole language classroom, other preservice teachers who know little about whole language.

2. Interview classroom teachers about their understanding of whole language. For example, find out whether they do or do not label themselves as "whole language" teachers, and why. How do they define/characterize whole language, and what sources or experiences have given rise to this definition/characterization? If they consider themselves to be whole language teachers, what concept of whole language is reflected by their classrooms, by what they have children do, by how they interact with children? How does their verbalized definition compare with the definition they put into action?

3. Compare these teachers' characterizations of whole language with your own and/or with that described in this chapter. Prepare a response to any myths you may encounter, keeping the teacher(s) in mind as your potential audience.

9 | Growing into Whole Language

*Many whole-language teachers have grown to realize that their defini-
tion of whole language is in process, that tomorrow it will be sharp-
ened and refined.*

— Dorothy Watson

I have agonized over whether or not to conceptualize and entitle this chapter as "Growing into Whole Language," because describing whole language in terms of various
phases of growth could induce some teachers to feel bad because they are not "as far
along" as others, while causing other teachers to feel smug about "where they are" as
whole language teachers. I do not want to generate either response.

Why, then, take that chance?

There are several good reasons, I think, for talking about whole language teaching
in terms of a process of development. For one thing, as the personal examples in this
chapter should make clear, those who are considered leaders in the whole language
movement have also been wherever you are; they know what it's like from personal
experience. It should not be surprising that individual educators would continue to
recapitulate the growth of the literacy profession as a whole. Indeed, it should be of
some comfort to those new to whole language to see that few of us have made drastic
changes overnight.

In fact, for *all* of us, whole language must be conceptualized as a never-ending process of learning and growing. Instead of saying that I myself *am* a whole language
teacher, I often say that I am *in the process of becoming* a whole language teacher—and
I really mean that. As my friend Adrian Peetoom has pointed out, the old paradigm can
be as difficult to relinquish as old, comfortable slippers (*Grandpa's Slippers,* J. Watson,
1989).

Being or becoming a whole language teacher is not an all-or-nothing matter of
being a transmission teacher one day and a transactional teacher the next, as I have
tried to explain in Chapter 8. Rather, it typically involves significant movement from
essentially a transmission model toward and into a transactional model, in both beliefs
and practices, until finally we can honestly say we have made a paradigm shift (discussed in Chapters 3 and 8 as well as later in this chapter). Like Figure 8.3 in the preceding chapter, Figure 9.1 characterizes (in briefer form) the extremes from which and
toward which we move, as we grow into understanding a whole language philosophy and
implementing it in the classroom. Thus, wherever we are as whole language teachers, it

Transmission	Transactional
Reductionist	Constructivist
Behavioral psychology	Cognitive psychology
Habit formation	Hypothesis formation
Avoiding mistakes prevents formation of bad habits	Errors necessary for encouraging more sophisticated hypotheses
Students passively practice skills, memorize facts	Students actively pursue learning and construct knowledge
Teacher dispenses prepackaged, predetermined curriculum	Teacher develops and negotiates curriculum with students
Direct teaching of curriculum	Responsive teaching, to meet students' needs and interests
Taskmaster, with emphasis on cycle of *teach, practice/apply/memorize, test*	Mastercraftsperson, mentor: emphasis on demonstrating, inviting, discussing, affirming, facilitating, collaborating, observing, supporting
Lessons taught, practiced and/or applied, then tested	Mini-lessons taught as demonstration, invitation; adding an idea to the class pot
Performance on decontextualized tests is taken as measure of learning of limited information	Assessment from a variety of contextualized learning experiences captures diverse aspects of learning
Learning is expected to be uniform, same for everyone; uniform means of assessment guarantee that many will fail, in significant ways	Learning is expected to be individual, different for everyone; flexible and multiple means of assessment guarantee all will succeed, in differing ways
Adds up to a failure-oriented model, ferreting out students' weaknesses and preparing them to take their place in a stratified society	Adds up to a success-oriented model, emphasizing students' strengths and preparing them to be the best they can be in a stratified society

FIGURE **9.1**   *Ends of a transmission-to-transactional continuum*

is vital to continue focusing upon the directions our own growth might appropriately take. That's a critical part of what it means to be a whole language teacher.

In short, whole language teachers are learners. That means they are necessarily risk takers, trying new ways of teaching, new ways of responding to students, new ways of evaluating students' progress. It is common nowadays to speak of whole language teachers as reflective practitioners, or even as teacher/researchers within their own classrooms. The development of such a stance has been fostered by such books as *Lessons from a Child (Calkins, 1983), Breaking Ground (Hansen, Newkirk, & Graves, 1985), Whole Language: Theory in Use (Newman, 1985), and the award-winning In the Middle (Atwell, 1987). Such teacher growth is documented by an increasing proliferation of* books, including *Whole Language: Inquiring Voices*, by Dorothy Watson, Carolyn Burke, and Jerome Harste (1989); *Becoming a Whole Language School: The Fair Oaks Story*, edited by Lois Bridges Bird (1989); *The Learners' Way*, by Anne Forester and Margaret Reinhard (1989); *Jevon Doesn't Sit at the Back Anymore,* by Connie White (1990); *Children Learning Through Literature*, by June McConaghy (1990); *Finding Our Own Way,* edited by Judith Newman (1990); *Portraits of Whole Language Classrooms*, edited by Heidi Mills and Jean Anne Clyde (1990); *Whole Language: Getting Started . . . Moving Forward* (1991), by Linda Crafton; *Joyful Learning: A Whole Language Kindergarten* (1991), by Bobbi Fisher; *Lasting Impressions: Weaving Literature into the Writing Workshop* (1992), by Shelley Harwayne; *Seeking Diversity: Language Arts with Adolescents* (1992), by Linda Rief; *Whole Learning: Whole Language and Content in the Upper Elementary Grades* (1992), by Pat Cordeiro; *Special Voices*, by Cora Lee Five (1992); and *Theme Exploration: A Voyage of Discovery,* by myself in collaboration with Joel Chaston and Scott Peterson (1993). What the growing emphasis on teachers as reflective practitioners and classroom researchers means is simply that more and more teachers are becoming genuine professionals. And whole language teachers are at the forefront of this movement toward professionalism.

This chapter briefly describes some of the common patterns of growth among whole language teachers, the intent being to clarify whole language principles and also to demonstrate that becoming a whole language teacher is indeed a process of continual growth. To emphasize the universality of this growth process, I include several personal examples. Also valuable is Regie Routman's book *Invitations: Changing as Teachers and Learners, K–12* (1991), in which she documents her and her colleagues' growth from the earlier *Transitions* (1988). Already, *Invitations* has provided inspiration and a wealth of practical ideas for thousands of teachers growing into whole language.

It's important to realize that the transformation process for teachers is as complex and unique as the processes of becoming language users and literate individuals are for children. Different teachers approach the process differently, and demonstrate different paths in their individual growth. Furthermore, different countries seem to be characterized by differing emphases. For example, whole language teachers in Australia and New Zealand place greater emphasis upon teacher scaffolding, explicit instruction, and teacher direction of learning than some of the leaders of the whole language movement in the United States (B. Gray, 1987, and Cazden, 1992; cf. Harste, Woodward, & Burke, 1984, with Goldenberg, 1991; Holdaway, 1979, 1984, 1986; Cambourne, 1988; and Butler & Turbill, 1984).

GROWING IN THE TEACHING OF WRITING

In many classrooms and schools, the National Writing Project and/or the influence of Donald Graves, Don Murray, and the New Hampshire school of writing has revolutionized the teaching of writing. Instead of merely assigning topics and word or page requirements, as many teachers used to do, teachers now more often guide their students through the writing process, from initial efforts at determining what they will write about to eventual "publication" and/or public celebration of their writing.

Instead of serving as a perceived adversary, correcting students' papers and evaluating their first and only drafts, teachers of the writing process serve as allies, helping children discover what they want to say, helping them focus and strengthen their pieces, teaching them the conventions of writing needed to make their pieces clearer for an audience, helping them polish and publish their pieces, and celebrating their writings within and beyond the classroom community.

Prior to the rise of what has come to be known as the writing process movement, many teachers were having children write in journals that the teachers responded to, but did not grade. This was a step in the direction of student ownership, which became a major principle of the early writing process movement.

Virtually all of the whole language principles relating to learning and the learner and discussed in the preceding chapter were embodied in the early emphasis on encouraging writing as a multiphase process. Students were (are) active in their own learning, choosing their own topics, making their own decisions about revision and publication. They were encouraged to take risks in writing and spelling, and they received positive response for what they did, rather than criticism for what they could not yet do. They talked to classmates about their ideas and shared their writings, soliciting ideas for improvement and submitting finished works to be celebrated by their peers. Being in control of their own writing, students developed wonderful personal narratives that had voice, texture, and life rarely found in the single-draft writings produced to fulfill an assignment on a topic. The benefits of student ownership of the writing process were abundantly clear.

In fact, leading advocates of teaching writing as a process freely admit that at first they were so excited by the personal narratives children produced when encouraged to choose their own topics and take control of their writing that they themselves, as educators, erred in offering children too little in the way of guidance and instruction (Calkins, 1986, pp. 164–165). Furthermore, they admit to having been so enamored of the personal narratives that at first they neglected other genres, to the ultimate detriment of children's writing growth. (For evidence of this recognition, see books wherein leading educators demonstrate their own growth beyond the early limitations: Calkins, 1986; Graves, 1989a, 1989b, 1992; Newkirk, 1989.) Thus, the pioneers in helping us understand the writing processes of children continued to lead the way as they grew into understanding the limitations of the instructional practices they had been recommending.

The whole language principle that seems initially to have been neglected is the notion that learning involves a *transaction*, with teachers playing a facilitating role. Early practitioners and proponents of the writing process model were too close to becoming laissez-faire teachers, doing little to stimulate children's growth beyond encouraging them to experiment and take control of their learning.

A graph in Calkins' *Art of Teaching Writing* (1986) helps put the growth of the writing process movement within perspective. Figure 9.2 reflects Calkins' concept, though the numbering of the quadrants has been changed. Quadrant 1, with low student and

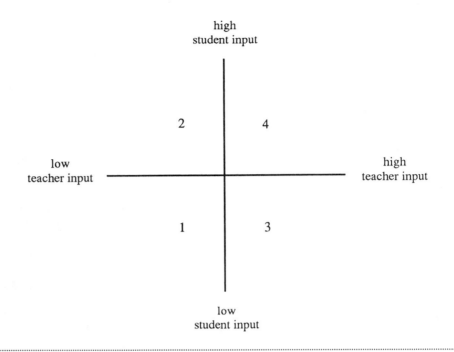

Figure **9.2**   *Differing models of education (adapted from Calkins, 1986, p. 164)*

low teacher input, reflects direct teaching of the transmission model kind, which characterized most classrooms prior to interest in the writing process and in whole language. Quadrant 2 reflects the early writing process movement: students were actively engaged in writing, but teachers played a relatively passive role. Quadrant 3, with low student input but high teacher input, might be said to encompass the best of traditional teaching: the transmission model with elements of the transactional incorporated. Quadrant 4, with high teacher *and* high student input, characterizes whole language and writing process at its best. The crucial difference between quadrants 3 and 4 lies in the element of student choice, responsibility, control—and hence student engagement in learning. This, I have come to believe, is often the factor that most clearly distinguishes whole language from the best of traditional teaching.

To return to the writing process: departing from the high-student, low-teacher input of quadrant 2, writing educators began to direct their questions more toward stimulating learning during their conferences with students. They would even end conferences with questions like "What have you learned that you can apply next time?" In addition, they began to teach mini-lessons, perhaps first described by Lucy Calkins in *The Art of Teaching Writing* (1986) and by Nancie Atwell in her book *In the Middle* (1987). These are brief lessons designed to add ideas to the class pot, to be drawn upon by the students when relevant.

Therein lies a major difference between the mini-lessons predominantly reflecting a transmission paradigm of learning and those reflecting the transactional paradigm that characterizes whole language. Mini-lessons within a transmission paradigm would be taught in a teach/practice/test format, whereas mini-lessons within a transactional paradigm would primarily be demonstrations and invitations (F. Smith, 1981a, 1981b; for a highly practical approach to spelling and punctuation, see Wilde, 1992). The decision whether, or when, to actually use the strategies or skills demonstrated would remain with the students (as it does even in the transmission model, though that is not their teacher's intent).

At first, these mini-lessons tended to focus on the conventions of language: how to punctuate dialogue, how to use commas instead of "and" in a series, how to combine sentences effectively. Another early focus was how to write effective leads to introduce a piece, or how to add effective detail. Soon, leading writing process educators began to realize the importance of literary models for fostering writing growth. As more and more teachers recognized this crucial connection between literature and writing, they began to offer mini-lessons on how characters are developed, how the senses can be used to bring something or someone into focus, what stimulates writers to revise their writing. These mini-lessons consist of discussions of literary techniques and writing processes used by published authors—and by teachers and students themselves. Teachers share their own enthusiasm about children's books with their students, focusing on elements that will help their students become more sensitive readers and more effective writers. Students, too, are encouraged to share and initiate discussions of style and technique that they particularly like. The teacher demonstrates an awareness of literary elements, then invites students to do likewise.

My own experience typifies this shift. Back in the 1970s, what I now think of as mini-lessons used to be the prelude to full-fledged assignments, because I was still locked into a transmission concept of teaching and learning.

For example, my colleague Theone Hughes developed a lesson and assignment on what she called "putting a character into viewpoint." In preparation for writing, students compared an actual passage from Jean Craighead George's *Julie of the Wolves* (1972) with Theone's rewrite, without knowing which was which. Their task was to decide which was the more effective passage. Of course, the "right" answer was the one written by the original author, the one that described the terrain through Miyax's eyes (see Figure 9.3). Following this discussion and a brief exercise designed to solidify the concept, we then had students write a story in which they similarly described the external world through the viewpoint of the main character.

What is different between then and now? *Then*, we engineered a discussion to which there was a "right" answer; led the students in a writing exercise; and assigned a paper to demonstrate mastery of the writing technique. Our assumptions reflected those of a transmission model of education: teach students something, have them practice it, then test to see that the something is mastered.

Now, I would introduce the contrasting passages for discussion, but not insist that students prefer (or pretend to prefer) the original; nor would I assign an exercise or a follow-up paper. I would simply add this example of effective technique to the class pot,

Directions: *Below are two versions of the beginning of Jean Craighead George's* Julie of the Wolves, *one the original and one a rewrite. The original is the one that enables the reader to see through Miyax's (Julie's) eyes. Which version is that, and how does the author let us see through the character's eyes?*

Miyax pushed back her sealskin parka. The Arctic sun was a yellow disc in a lime-green sky. It was now about six o'clock in the evening and the time when wolves awake. She put down her cooking pot and crept to the top of a dome-shaped frost heave, one of the many earth buckles that rise and fall in the crackling cold of the Arctic winter. She lay on her stomach. The Arctic in this part was a vast lawn of grass and moss. The wolves were now waking up and wagging their tails as they saw each other.

Miyax pushed back the hood of her sealskin parka and looked at the Arctic sun. It was a yellow disc in a lime-green sky, the colors of six o'clock in the evening and the time when the wolves awoke. Quietly she put down her cooking pot and crept to the top of a dome-shaped frost heave, one of the many earth buckles that rise and fall in the crackling cold of the Arctic winter. Lying on her stomach, she looked across a vast lawn of grass and moss and focused her attention on the wolves she had come upon two sleeps ago. They were wagging their tails as they awoke and saw each other.

FIGURE 9.3 *Mini-lesson on putting a character into viewpoint (from Theone Hughes)*

to be drawn upon or not as the student writers might choose. I might also copy and post the passage on the bulletin board for easy inspection by those interested. *Now*, my teaching reflects more of a transactional concept of learning and teaching: demonstrate something and invite students to try it.

In *Living Between the Lines* (1990), Lucy Calkins discusses some recent shifts in the writing process movement, as reflected in the Teachers College Writing Project. There are several differences from earlier practices; perhaps the most significant is that the writing process movement seems to have shifted from an emphasis on mini-lessons derived from literature to an emphasis on immersion in whole works of literature—literature for its own sake, and for the stimulation of substantive writing projects with more than fleeting significance for the writer. (For a still more recent look at shifts in the writing process movement, see Harwayne, 1992.)

Within this context, mini-lessons take a back seat to study groups in which students discuss and analyze literature with each other, partly just to enjoy and appreciate the literature, but also to prepare for writing in the genre under study. Students interested in writing picture book memoirs or autobiographies, for instance, might read and discuss such books as Riki Levinson's *Watch the Stars Come Out*, Scott Sanders' *Aurora Means Dawn*, Anna Smucker's *No Star Night*, Judith Hendershot's *In Coal Country*, Thomas Allen's *On Granddaddy's Farm*, Nancy Hundal's *I Heard My Mother Call My Name*, and Cynthia Rylant's *When I Was Young in the Mountains* (see also Calkins, 1990, Chapter 12).

The growth of the writing process movement might be characterized by a continuum like that in Figure 9.4.

The early phases of the writing process movement characterize some of the early growth in the development of a whole language philosophy, and in the growth of many whole language teachers. Once teachers come to realize the power of encouraging students to take ownership of their learning, as some did in the first phase of the writing process movement, it may still take time for them to discover and redefine their own necessary roles in the learning process. Whole language teaching is not laissez-faire teaching, though it is sometimes misperceived that way, perhaps because such teaching characterizes the early efforts of some teachers growing into whole language. They—perhaps most of us—have yet to develop an appropriate balance between student ownership and teacher assistance and direction, and have miles to grow in refining that balance.

GROWING IN THE TEACHING OF READING

Many teachers have grown into whole language initially by teaching writing as a process, then adopting some of the same principles in their teaching of reading. Jane Hansen in *When Writers Read* (1987) and Nancie Atwell in *In the Middle* (1987) were among the first to articulate, in print, major implications for the teaching of reading that they and other teachers had learned from teaching writing as a process. More generally, these principles characterize whole language teaching in general. To facilitate learning, teachers need to provide a climate that fosters student ownership; sufficient time for sustained engagement in significant activities; concrete and constructive response, based on the expectation of eventual success; structure that facilitates individual decision making and commitment; and a supportive community that includes both peers and the teacher as co-learners.

Teachers have been much slower to implement these principles in the teaching of reading, however. Doutbtless there are many causes: the omnipresence of the basal reading program and external demands for its use; the teachers' own fear that students

| students writing personal narratives | $\rightarrow$ | mini-lessons, often on writing conventions (more teacher input) | $\rightarrow$ | mini-lessons drawn from children's literature | $\rightarrow$ | immersion in whole works of literature during reading-writing workshops; writing of more significant works, in more genres |

FIGURE 9.4 Growth of the writing process movement

may miss something important in learning to read if they abandon the skills teaching dictated by the basal; and finally the simple fact that in each new context, many of us have to relearn the importance of student ownership and struggle our way anew to an appropriate balance between student ownership and teacher direction. We must continually define and refine our roles as teachers.

Modifying the Basal Reading Lesson

Typically, one of the first steps in breaking the domination of the basal reading program is to modify the basal reading lesson by drawing more upon students' schemas in developing concepts and vocabulary critical to the story, demonstrating and discussing reading strategies during reading, reinforcing good reading strategies, asking questions that require critical and divergent thinking more than recall, and suggesting a wider range of follow-up activities.

As teachers beginning to question the basals come to realize, basal reading programs are skills programs, designed for teaching in isolation various skills and strategies that are virtually inseparable in real reading. This includes instruction in so-called comprehension skills, which are generally taught, practiced, and tested through ancillary workbooks and other materials. Though teacher and students focus on whole texts during the typical basal reader lesson, the attention to comprehension does not adequately or appropriately reflect what we know about the reading process and what best fosters reading and language growth:

1. There is typically a concern for preteaching vocabulary, which may sometimes be important. However, such preteaching often does not draw sufficiently upon readers' prior knowledge; also, the preteaching of vocabulary and concepts can inadvertently discourage readers from developing their ability to understand new words through context.
2. The suggestions for prereading discussion often are not adequate for activating readers' schemas and thus enhancing comprehension.
3. Often, the majority of the postreading questions focus on recall of details rather than on understanding of the characters' motivations and feelings and how these are reflected in the development of the plot. Thus, the questions seem designed more to see whether the students have read and remembered the words of the story than to genuinely engage them in discussing and appreciating what they have read. (See, for example, Durkin's 1990 study, "Reading Comprehension Instruction in Five Basal Reading Series." The preponderance of literal questions "in search of a single answer" helps explain why, as Durkin had found earlier [1978–79], teachers tend to ask such questions predominantly.)

As an example of how teachers have modified and extended basal reader lessons, let us consider a lesson for "Petronella," by Jay Williams (the story is included as the appendix at the back of this book). This story is found in the book *Weavers,* the first of the intermediate-level readers in the Houghton Mifflin Reading Series (1983). The teacher's manual provides first a summary of the story and then a list of glossary words. In the subsequent section, "Motivation and Silent Reading," the teacher is advised to write the word *enchanter* on the chalkboard and pronounce it, then ask a volunteer to define it, and finally define it for the students if no one knows an acceptable definition. Students are next to be advised that the story they are about to read is a fairy tale, but one somewhat different from the ordinary. As they read, the students are to think about how this story differs from typical fairy tales. Finally, the teacher is advised to have the students read the title and the author's name silently, then to have a volunteer read these aloud. From this point, students are apparently on their own, until faced with postreading questions. Only six out of seventeen of these questions are labeled as literal—a relatively low percentage, but still probably more than necessary, particularly since most of these literal questions are not used as stepping-stones to more challenging and interesting questions.

Perhaps the easiest way to demonstrate the weaknesses of this approach is to suggest how a teacher who understands the reading process might depart from the suggestions in the teacher's manual, translating the typical skills approach to vocabulary and comprehension into an approach that more effectively encourages reading for meaning and for personal engagement with the story. Following this lesson is a discussion of various features of it, along with a recapitulation of how the imaginary teacher's lesson departs from that of the basal reading series. The idea for using this story comes from Charles Temple (Temple and Burns, 1986), as do some of the discussion questions.

Scene: A fifth-grade classroom. The teacher has decided to use the story "Petronella" with the whole class, then later do additional reading strategy work with the children who seem to need it. The children's desks are pulled together in pairs so that they can share books, and the less competent readers are paired with someone who can help them if necessary. The teacher's name is Ms. Matthews.

Ms. M.: The story we're going to read today is a modern fairy tale. Before we open our books, let's review what we know about fairy tales. Where and when do they usually take place?

CLASS: Long ago and far away.

Ms. M.: Right. What do we know about typical plots and characters?

CLASS: Well, often there's some kind of test or challenge, like in "The Princess and the Pea."

Yes, and the events often come in threes, like in "The Fisherman and His Wife" or "The Three Billy Goats Gruff" or "Rumplestiltskin."

There's often a mean stepmother, or a stupid father, or a younger brother who's kinda innocent but succeeds where his older brothers have failed.

Or just some simple kid who succeeds, like Jack [and the Beanstalk].

Or a simple girl, like Cinderella, who beats out her nasty sisters to wear the glass slipper and win the prince.

Yeah, or a prince who wins a princess, like in "Cinderella" or "Sleeping Beauty."

Ms. M.: What are princes and princesses usually like?

CLASS: The prince is handsome.

Yeah, and the princess is beautiful.

And they live happily ever after.

Ms. M.:   Does anybody typically help the main character get what he or she wants?

CLASS: Yeah, sometimes. There's the fairy godmother in "Cinderella."

And the giant's wife in "Jack and the Beanstalk."

Ms. M.:   Okay, good. Would you say these stories are realistic?

CLASS: No.

Ms. M.:   Why not?

CLASS: 'Cause there's usually some kind of magic going on. Things that couldn't really happen.

Yeah, like a wolf dressing up in a woman's clothes.

Or fairy godmothers and magic fish and magic beans and little men like Rumplestiltskin.

Ms. M.:   Okay, good. Do you know any names for kinds of people who do magical things?

CLASS: Fairy godmothers.

Magicians.

Witches.

Wizards [*this from someone who plays Dungeons and Dragons*].

Ms. M.:   Right. Another word is *enchanter* [*she writes this on the chalkboard*]. Usually an enchanter casts spells of different kinds. There's an enchanter in the story we're going to read.

CLASS: Hurray! Maybe he can cast a spell to give us pizza for lunch!

Ms. M.:   Okay! What do we know about how fairy tales usually end?

CLASS: "And everybody lived happily ever after."

Ms. M.:   Yes, good. Okay, let's review what we've discussed. [*As discussion has progressed, Ms. Matthews has been writing the main points on the chalkboard. She now reviews these.*] Okay, open your books to page 43. What's the title of this modern fairy tale?

CLASS: "Petronella."

Ms. M.:   Yes. Does the title give you any hints as to what the story might be about?

CLASS: Well, probably someone named Petronella.

Sounds like Cinderella.

Maybe it's a poor kid like Cinderella.

Ms. M.:   Okay, good. We haven't read any stories by Jay Williams before, so knowing the author's name doesn't tell us much. We could look at his biographical sketch, but let's skip that for now. What about the picture? Judging from this picture, what do you think is going to happen?

CLASS: Looks like a dragon with a paintbrush and paint.

Maybe somebody's going to go slay a dragon.

Ms. M.:   Well, let's read and see. First let's look just at the opening sentence: "In the kingdom of Skyclear Mountain, three princes were always born to the king and queen." Do you have any more ideas about who the story is going to be about or what's going to happen?

CLASS: Well, it might be about their three princes. Maybe the youngest one goes on a quest or outsmarts his older brothers somehow.

Yeah, but maybe it's going to be different this time.

Ms. M.: What do you mean?

CLASS: Well, maybe there aren't going to be three princes.

Maybe there will be only two. Or four.

Yeah, or maybe the king and queen will have girls instead.

Ms. M.: What makes you think things might be different this time?

CLASS: Well, it says "always." The king and queen "always" have three princes. "Always" makes you think somehow that things are going to change.

Ms. M.: Okay, let me read you the rest of the paragraph and see what you think. Just listen; don't try to read along. [*Ms. Matthews reads.*] "The oldest prince was always called Michael, the middle prince was always called George, and the youngest was always called Peter. When they were grown, they always went out to seek their fortunes. What happened to the oldest prince and the middle prince no one ever knew. But the youngest prince always rescued a princess, brought her home, and in time ruled over the kingdom. That was the way it had always been. And so far as anyone knew, that was the way it would always be." Okay, now what do you think? Are there going to be three princes? Or what?

CLASS: No. Nope. No way. [*A chorus of denials.*]

Ms. M.: Why not?

CLASS: Well, it keeps saying *this* "always" happens or *that* "always" happens. So you know it's going to be different this time.

Yeah. From those last two sentences, you just know it's going to be different.

Ms. M.: Yes, you're right. Look at the last sentence on page 43: "Until now." That was the way it always was, until now. Any idea how things might be different now?

CLASS: Like Rob said: maybe there will be more kids.

Or not as many.

Or maybe they won't have any kids at all. Maybe they'll adopt a dragon!

Ms. M.: Let's read on and find out. Read the next paragraph silently, and then look up when you're done. Read *just* the next paragraph. . . . Okay, now that everybody's done, would someone care to read the paragraph aloud? Okay, Mark, go ahead. [*Mark is by no means the most fluent reader in the class, but Ms. Matthews has helped the children learn to be respectful of each other's efforts, to listen for and praise each other's good miscues on the rare occasions when they read aloud in small groups, and never to interrupt a reader by yelling out a word. Thus, Mark has gained some confidence in his reading and is occasionally willing to risk reading in front of the others, especially when he has had a chance to read ahead silently.*]

MARK: Now was the time of King Peter the twenty-sixth

                       of
and Queen Blossom. An oldest prince was
          ∧

               then
born, and a middle prince. But the youngest
               ∧

(prince) turned out to be a girl."

Ms. M.:   Very good, Mark. Class, what do you think might happen, now that the youngest prince has turned out to be a girl?
Class: The king won't like it.
           The queen will be jealous of her, like Sleeping Beauty's stepmother.
           They'll disown her, give her away to some poor woman to raise.
           Yeah, and then she'll grow up and find out she's really a princess.
           And come back and rule the kingdom, 'cause her older brothers have been killed.
Ms. M.:   Well, let's read on. Go ahead and read through the paragraph that ends at the top of page 45, then look up to let me know you're done. [*They all read the following: "Well," said the king gloomily, "we can't call her Peter. We'll have to call her Petronella. And what's to be done about it, I'm sure I don't know." There was nothing to be done. The years passed, and the time came for the princes to go out and seek their fortunes. Michael and George said good-bye to the king and queen and mounted their horses. Then out came Petronella. She was dressed in traveling clothes, with her bag packed and a sword by her side."*]
Ms. M.:   What kind of girl do you think Petronella is? What's she like?
Class: Not the type that plays with dolls.
           She probably wears jeans.
           Yeah. And plays with the boys. [Someone snickers.]
           Doesn't sound like a princess to me.
Ms. M.:   What do you think she's going to do, all dressed up in traveling clothes?
Class: She's going to seek her fortune too.
           Maybe she'll go looking for a prince.
Ms. M.:   What makes you think so?
Class: They said the youngest prince always goes out to look for a princess. Well, Petronella is the youngest, but she's a princess, not a prince. So, maybe she's going to look for a prince.
Ms. M.:   Any other ideas?
Class: Maybe she's going to go on some other kind of quest.
           Maybe she'll kill a dragon and become king of some other land.
           Not king, you dope. Queen.
Ms. M.:   Well, let's read and find out. Read through the paragraph that ends at the top of page 46, and raise your hand so I can tell you're through. While you wait for others to finish, jot down your ideas about what's going to happen in the story. [They read the following: *"If you think," she said, "that I'm going to sit*

at home, you are mistaken. I'm going to seek my fortune too." "Impossible!" said the king. "What will people say?" cried the queen. "Look," said Prince Michael. "Be reasonable, Pet. Stay home. Sooner or later a prince will turn up here." Petronella smiled. She was a tall, handsome girl with flaming red hair, and when she smiled in that particular way, it meant she was trying to keep her temper. "I'm going with you," she said. "I'll find a prince if I have to rescue one from something myself. And that's that."]

At this point, Ms. Matthews encourages most of the class to finish the story silently. She tells them that when they have finished, they should brainstorm and make a list of fun activities to do individually or in groups, as a follow-up to reading "Petronella." Figure 9.5 indicates some of the possibilities they come up with, translated into more adult phraseology. While most of the class are reading silently and brainstorming, Ms. Matthews continues the prediction procedure with a small group who need to develop their predicting and comprehension-monitoring strategies. She stops at crucial points to ask what the students think is going to happen next and why they think so, then later asks which of their predictions were confirmed or proved wrong and how they knew. Students are expected to justify their responses with specific references to the text. (If you have not already read "Petronella" in the appendix, you might follow this procedure

1. Write about what happens when Petronella arrives home with the enchanter. That is, write a sequel to the story.
2. Pretend that Petronella took the prince home with her, instead of the enchanter. Write a sequel.
3. Write diary entries from the viewpoint of Petronella, maybe when she was a child, or when she is going on her quest to find and rescue the prince.
4. Write a story about the prince and what happens to him.
5. Write a different story about a modern girl like Petronella, or a story about a boy who doesn't fit our stereotype of the macho male. Maybe make our own books, with illustrations.
6. Write dialogue for a play retelling the story of Petronella, and then act out the play. Maybe put on the play for other classes. Or videotape the play.
7. Make a mural of one of the important scenes from "Petronella." Display it on the wall outside our classroom.
8. Read some other books with nontraditional main characters. Do TV commercials for the books we've read; maybe videotape. Or write ads for our books. Maybe make a display of some of these books for the glass case by the principal's office.
9. Compare male and female roles in "Petronella" and other nontraditional fairy tales with male and female roles in traditional tales.
10. Have Ms. Matthews take us on a guided visualization of Petronella's three tasks. Figure 9.17 provides such a guided visualization.

FIGURE 9.5 *"Petronella" activities*

yourself as you read the rest of the story: stop at each line of asterisks, ask yourself the kinds of questions Ms. Matthews might ask about what will happen next and why, and then read to see whether or to what degree you were right.) Obviously such a procedure encourages readers to become actively involved with the story, to use their own schemas, and to predict, sample, and confirm or correct as they read, all at the story level.

When the students have all finished reading "Petronella," the teacher turns to the list of questions she has prepared. First, she has prepared an outline of the major events in the story—a "story grammar"—and she has developed questions keyed to these points, with some going beyond. Assuming that the students will understand the literal content of the story and knowing that she can always backtrack to asking literal questions if necessary, Ms. Matthews has selected carefully from among the questions accompanying the selection in the Teacher's Manual. She has used literal questions only when they lead into more thought-provoking ones, and she has added a generous number of inferential, interpretive, and evaluative questions not in the Teacher's Manual. (The questions with an asterisk below are the same as or similar to questions in the TM.)

Petronella is born:
*1. How do you think King Peter felt when he found out that his youngest child was a girl? How do you think you would have felt?
Departs to find a prince:
 2. When Petronella left to find a prince, what do you think she really wanted? What makes you think this?
Encounters man at crossroads:
 3. What did Petronella ask the old man at the crossroads? *How was her question different from her brothers' questions? Why do you think she was the first to ask the old man the question that would free him?
Sees prince at the enchanter's:
 4. What do you think Petronella thought of the prince when she first saw him? What makes you think this?
Asks to work for Albion in order to free prince:
*5. Why do you think Petronella goes through with rescuing the prince, even though she's not much impressed with him?
Completes the tasks successfully:
 6. How did Petronella quiet the hounds? The horses? The hawks? Do you think a prince would have handled the situation in the same way? Why or why not?
Flees with prince:
 7. How do you think Petronella felt when she and the prince were fleeing from the enchanter? Was she glad to have rescued the prince? What makes you think as you do?
Stops to free Albion:
 8. Why do you think Petronella stoppped to free Albion from the ring? How is her behavior here similar to her behavior at other points in the story?
Takes Albion home:

9. Do you think Petronella made a wise decision in abandoning the prince and taking the enchanter home with her? Why or why not? *What do you think will happen when Petronella returns home with the enchanter? *Do you think she will rule the kingdom of Skyclear Mountain?

   Additional questions:

10. Is Petronella more like a typical (stereotypical) princess, or more like a prince? How does she differ from both stereotypes? (These questions may need to be preceded by ones focusing on stereotypes of male and female roles, particularly with respect to princes and princesses.)

11. How is the story "Petronella" like a typical fairy tale? How is it different from a typical fairy tale?

12. (For girls:) If you were Petronella, would you have rescued the prince? Would you have liked to be Petronella? Why or why not? Would you ultimately have chosen the enchanter instead of the prince? Why or why not?

    (For boys:) If you were the enchanter, would you have wanted to marry Petronella? Why or why not?

Although Ms. Matthews may call on children to give evidence from the text to support their recollections and interpretations, many of her questions focus more on bringing to bear what children already know about human behavior and male/female roles and stereotypes.

Let us look briefly at the major ways in which Ms. Matthews has used and departed from the suggestions in the Teacher's Manual as she led the class in reading and discussing "Petronella."

First of all, the Teacher's Manual suggests some activities for vocabulary development to precede the reading of the story. Wanting students to learn to use context and their own schemas to cope with most unfamiliar words, Ms. Matthews postpones this kind of activity until after the reading. Then, she has the students most likely to need vocabulary and concept development work in a group to puzzle out the meanings of problem words together. The following day she will discuss these words with the group or perhaps with the whole class, now that this group has worked out its own definitions.

Second, as previously mentioned, the Teacher's Manual includes a section titled "Motivation and Silent Reading." It is suggested that the teacher write the word *enchanter* on the chalkboard and define it, if none of the students can; then, the teacher is to tell students that they are going to read a fairy tale that is somewhat different from other fairy tales they've heard or read. According to the Teacher's Manual, students are to think about how this tale differs from a typical fairy tale, as they will discuss these differences after reading the story. Ms. Matthews' approach is virtually the opposite. She begins by eliciting what the children already know about fairy tales, to help them draw upon and develop their schemas. She elicits other words for those who perform magic and then, having recalled and developed the concept, she offers the specific word that is new to many of them: *enchanter*. Finally, she refrains from telling them that this fairy tale is atypical; she wants the class to pick up on the cues in the text to predict that it will be different, then read to confirm that prediction.

Once the title and author's name have been read aloud, the Teacher's Manual suggests having children read silently. While silent reading is the major part of the total curriculum, Ms. Matthews also knows it is particularly helpful to less competent readers for her to occasionally lead the class as well as smaller groups of students through what is sometimes called a "Directed Reading-Thinking Activity," or DRTA (see Stauffer, 1960, 1969; and Stauffer & Cramer, 1968). This technique involves predicting what will come next and citing evidence to justify those predictions; reading to confirm, reject, or modify predictions; and making and justifying new predictions. By occasionally leading the class through such an activity, Ms. Matthews reinforces the importance of transacting actively with a text.

In preparing questions to discuss with the students after the reading of the story, Ms. Matthews chooses carefully from among those in the Teacher's Manual, omitting many of the recall questions and adding others that she thinks are more interesting and challenging. She is aware, of course, of such popular taxonomies of reading comprehension as Barrett's, which divides comprehension and comprehension questions into bits and pieces labeled *literal recognition* or *recall* (reading the lines), *inference* (reading between the lines), and *evaluation* and *appreciation* (reading beyond the lines) (Barrett, in R. J. Smith and T. C. Barrett, 1974, pp. 53–57). However, she is also aware of the limitations of such schemes.

For one thing, the division of questions into such neat types does not correspond with how people actually comprehend what they read. For example, students may make inferences and/or draw upon their own schemas in answering questions that are thought to be literal recall questions, and of course this kind of active processing of text is to be encouraged rather than discouraged. For instance, the question about how Petronella quieted the hounds, horses, and hawks (question 6) is more or less literal. Though it can be answered either by reference to Petronella's actions (she kept the dogs company, talking to them and stroking them) or by reference to the quality she exhibited in doing so (her bravery), in either case an answer is provided in the text. However, the students might answer by drawing inferences from the text and/or by using their own schemas: for example, "She quieted the dogs by being nice to them" or "After a minute, the dogs could tell she wasn't scared of them, so they quieted down." Neither answer comes directly from the text. While it is sometimes important for students to be able to justify their responses by appropriate reference to the text read, it would be unfortunate indeed if the teacher rejected the latter two responses just because they aren't directly stated in the text.

Another problem with such a breakdown of comprehension questions is that reading for minute details is often treated as more important than reading for understanding. The following is a poignant example from Estes and Johnstone (1977, p. 895):

Last Christmas, the first author read to his students a story by Truman Capote called, "A Christmas Memory" [Capote, 1989]. It is beautiful and poignant, as affecting as any story one could choose. Many of the students cried at the end. Their teacher looked at the questions following the story—he cried.

1. To what use is the dilapidated baby carriage put in the various scenes?

2. What evidence is there in the story that the setting, a rural town, is located in the southern area of our country?

Perhaps the most serious problem with such hierarchies of comprehension is the assumption that literal recall questions must precede the supposedly more complex kinds of questions, and even that less competent readers should be asked only the "easier" recall kinds of questions. This, Ms. Matthews knows, is sheer nonsense. In fact, students who tend not to remember details well can often demonstrate highly sophisticated thinking in response to the more probing kinds of questions.

Given such objections to dividing comprehension into different types of questions that only purport to reflect separable reading/thinking skills, Ms. Matthews has developed her own guidelines for asking questions about literature:

1. As a general rule, don't ask literal recall questions unless they are a springboard to more challenging questions. For example, the question about how Petronella quieted the hounds, horses, and hawks is followed by the question "Do you think a prince would have handled the situation in the same way? Why or why not?"
2. Ask questions that focus on the motivation and feelings of the characters. The literal question "What did so-and-so do when . . . ?" leads into questions like "Why do you think so-and-so did this?" and "How do you think so-and-so felt when . . . ?"
3. Ask questions that involve students in evaluating the actions of the characters: "Do you think so-and-so did the best/right thing when . . . ?"
4. Ask questions that invite students to project themselves into the story and to imagine themselves in similar situations: "How do you think you would have felt if . . . ?" or "How do you think you would feel if . . . ?" "What would you have done when . . . ?" or "What would you do if . . . ?"

These recommended kinds of questions do in fact involve students in remembering literal information, drawing inferences, and so forth; they simply do not make artificial divisions among the kinds of comprehension involved. Students responding to thoughtful questions about a reading selection will of necessity analyze, synthesize, and compare information, drawing upon their schemas as well as the text to make inferences and evaluations, to hypothesize, and to weigh alternatives. In short, such questions will stimulate the kinds of thinking that Piaget said characterize formal operational (adult) thought. Though his research suggested that such thought patterns did not typically develop until pre- or early adolescence, many people have come to realize that in real life, as opposed to artificial testing situations, children do not necessarily exhibit the cognitive limitations that Piaget found among younger children (see Donaldson, 1978, for example). It is abundantly clear that asking thought-provoking questions about literature from a very early age is one way that teachers can naturally stimulate the development of sophisticated forms of thought.

In summary, Ms. Matthews' modification of the basal reader lesson has enabled her to encourage the students to:

1. Activate relevant schemas before reading a selection.

2. Use schemas and all available cues to make predictions, then sample the text, and keep confirming and revising predictions as the selection develops (the DRTA, Directed Reading-Thinking Activity).
3. Transact with the story in ways that will help them develop their reasoning ability (the discussion questions).
4. Use context as well as schemas to focus on getting meaning at the sentence and word levels (since most "vocabulary" words were not pretaught).
5. Prepare for additional activities that extend the story and the children's interest in it.

Thus, Ms. Matthews has helped her students strengthen their reading and critical thinking abilities, departing in some significant ways from the traditional basal reading lesson.

It should be noted, however, that while Ms. Matthews' teaching reflects a transactional understanding of the reading process itself, it still illustrates more of a transmission concept of teaching and learning: the teacher dominates, and the students have virtually no control over the lesson. This represents a significant improvement over traditional instruction, but it is not yet whole language.

Letting Go of the Basal

Another early step toward breaking the domination of the basal reading program is often to supplement it: by reading aloud to students, and by setting aside time for sustained silent reading, or DEAR: Drop Everything and Read. Gradually, teachers may begin to realize that they need not assign every story in the basal, much less every worksheet. They are still within the throes of the transmission paradigm, but beginning to recognize that the scope and sequence of the basal reading program is not as sacrosanct as they once thought.

In breaking the hold of the transmission paradigm, many teachers have found helpful *The Report Card on Basal Readers*, by Ken Goodman, Pat Shannon, Yvonne Freeman, and Sharon Murphy (1988). This analysis of the basal reading programs of the mid-1980s makes it abundantly clear that there is no scientific justification for the sequencing of skills in the basal programs; no justification, in fact, for teaching reading as a series of skills to be separately mastered; and no justification for using the highly unscientific tests in basal programs as a basis for evaluation, much less for student placement. Some of the major conclusions to be drawn from this study are encapsulated in a position statement on basal readers prepared by the Commission on Reading of the National Council of Teachers of English (1988). As the position statement indicates, current research and theory strongly support such conclusions as those articulated above (see Figure 9.6 for the complete list from the position statement). As Dolores Durkin's analysis (1990) of the basals of the late 1980s indicates, the newest basals are, unfortunately, little more than old wine in new bottles. Most of the criticisms in the *Report Card on Basal Readers* still apply, since most basal programs still teach reading as a sequence of skills to be mastered—even though those skills may now be labeled "strategies."

Basal reading series typically reflect and promote the misconception that reading is necessarily learned from smaller to larger parts.

The sequencing of skills in a basal reading series exists not because this is how children learn to read but simply because of the logistics of developing a series of lessons that can be taught sequentially, day after day, week after week, year after year.

Students are typically tested for ability to master the bits and pieces of reading, such as phonics and other word identification skills. However, there is no evidence that mastering such skills in isolation guarantees the ability to comprehend connected text, or that students who cannot give evidence of such skills in isolation are necessarily unable to comprehend connected text.

Thus, for many if not most children, the typical basal reading series may actually make learning to read more difficult than it needs to be.

So much time is typically taken up by "instructional" activities (including activities with workbooks and skill sheets) that only a very slight amount of time is spent in actual reading—despite the overwhelming evidence that extensive reading and writing are crucial to the development of literacy.

Basal reading series typically reflect and promote the widespread misconception that the ability to verbalize an answer, orally or in writing, is evidence of understanding and learning. Thus, even students who appear to be learning from a basal reading series are being severely shortchanged, for they are being systematically encouraged not to think.

Basal reading series typically tell teachers exactly what they should do and say while teaching a lesson, thus depriving teachers of the responsibility and authority to make informed professional judgments.

"Going through the paces" thus becomes the measure of both teaching and learning. The teachers are assumed to have taught well if and only if they have taught the lesson. Students are assumed to have learned if and only if they have given "right" answers.

The result of such misconceptions about learning and such rigid control of teacher and student activities is to discourage both teachers and students from thinking, and particularly to discourage students from developing and exercising critical literacy and thinking skills needed to participate fully in a technologically advanced democratic society.

Figure **9.6**   *Concerns about basal programs, from "Basal readers and the state of American reading instruction: A call for action" (Commission on Reading of the National Council of Teachers of English, 1988)*

Most recently, Kenneth Goodman and Patrick Shannon have analyzed basals of the early 1990s, to determine to what extent the earlier patterns still persist (K. S. Goodman & Shannon, forthcoming).

Mini-Lessons: Again a Paradigm Shift

As teachers become more comfortable with the notion that students do not learn to read one skill at a time, even when it is taught that way; and as they become more aware that guided reading along with extensive silent reading and literary discussions are the best means to foster student's reading development; they may abandon at least the worksheets and workbooks in the basal programs, replacing them with whole-class or whole-group mini-lessons on global strategies that are crucial to reading. Among the strategies that readers need to develop are these:

- Strategies for *reading with a purpose*.
- Strategies for *drawing upon prior knowledge*.
- Strategies for *predicting*.
- Strategies for *effectively sampling the visual display*.
- Strategies for *using all the language cue systems together* (meaning, grammar, and phonic relationships) to get meaning and deal with problem words.
- Strategies for *confirming and correcting*.
- Strategies for *monitoring comprehension*.
- Strategies for *reviewing and retaining* desired information and concepts.
- Strategies for *adjusting rate and approach* depending on purpose.

These are among the major strategies that readers must eventually develop, consciously or unconsciously, in order to effectively read a wide range of print for various purposes. During a mini-lesson, for example, teachers could engage students in discussing possible ways of dealing with problem words like *ergonomic* in the movie theatre ad in Figure 9.7, then give the students guided practice in dealing with other problem words within a verbal context. Or the teacher might engage students in discussing where they get their information for responding to questions about the "window" text in Figure 9.8, then assign the students group activities wherein they further practice becoming metacognitively aware of the sources they draw upon (text and their own prior knowledge).

Often, mini-lessons on such strategies reflect a transactional paradigm (the new knowledge about reading) in their content, but the transmission paradigm (the old model of teaching) in their execution—that is, they are taught according to a teach/practice/test format. This is essentially the situation with the imaginary Ms. Matthews' modification of the basal reading program lesson, though it didn't (yet) include any testing.

Many emergent whole language teachers have discovered that mini-lessons are even more effective in changing students' actual reading habits if the lessons are offered in the spirit of demonstration, engagement, discussion, and invitation (see Figure 9.9 for the contrast, with the "mixed paradigm" transactional content and transmission methods in the middle).

Some of the sources teachers draw upon for mini-lessons in reading include *Creating Classrooms for Authors* (Harste & Short, with Burke, 1988); *Reading Strategies: Focus on Comprehension* (Y. M. Goodman and Burke, 1980); *Reading Strategies and Practices: A Compendium* (Tierney, Readence, & Disnher, 1990); *Reading Miscue*

PLEASE TRY THE ACTIVITY BELOW BEFORE READING THE NEXT PAGE:

"ERGONOMIC," a word in this ad, may be unfamiliar. If you could not use a dictionary, what strategies would you use to discover the meaning?

FIGURE 9.7   Lesson/discussion on dealing with problem words (from materials distributed at a Michigan Department of Education conference, Nov. 21, 1986)

Possible strategies to find the meaning of "ERGONOMIC":

1. Consider the context, both the whole ad and and the specific phrase. It has something to do with a movie theater, in general, and something to do with a "seat" specifically.

2. Use phonics skills to sound it out. Maybe you have heard it before and can remember possible meanings.

3. Does the structure help you? "ERGO" means "therefore." "NOMIC" is in "economic."

4. Would knowing the part of speech of "ERGONOMIC" help to unlock the meaning? "ERGONOMIC" is an adjective (it is in the position of an adjective).

5. Brainstorm using a semantic map or web.

6. Consult an expert. Call the theater.

7. Look "ERGONOMIC" up in the dictionary.

8. Consider that this might be a misprint. Newspapers are infamous for typographical errors.

FIGURE 9.7   Continued

Window Text

He plunked down $5.00 at the window. She tried to give him $2.50, but he refused to take it. So when they got inside, she bought him a large bag of popcorn.

1. Where did he plunk down the $5.00?
2. What kind of a window was it?
3. How much was the entrance fee for each person?
4. Why wouldn't he take the $2.50?
5. Does he like popcorn?
6. How old are these people?
7. Why does she try to pay her own way?
8. Why does he refuse to take her money?

The purpose of this activity is to consider to what extent your responses to the questions derive from the text, and to what extent they derive from your head: your prior knowledge, experiences, beliefs. Responses might be located along a continuum:

Text ————————————————————————————— Reader

FIGURE *9.8*   *Sources of information in responding to text (adapted from materials distributed at a Michigan Department of Education conference, Nov. 21, 1986; statement of purpose added)*

Inventory: Alternative Procedures (Y. M. Goodman, Watson, & Burke, 1987); and *Ideas and Insights: Language Arts in the Elementary School* (Watson, 1987). However, whole language educators caution that no more than 20 to 30 percent of a student's reading time should be spent on strategy lessons (Y. M. Goodman, Watson, & Burke, 1987). Furthermore, the differences between the structured kinds of lessons in the earlier of these idea books and the more open-ended kinds in the later books reflect the growth of the whole language movement itself, with respect to developing reading strategies. Whole language teachers' recent experience suggests that mini-lessons may be most effective when the strategies and concepts are taught in the context of students' needs and/or simply added to the class pot rather than taught, practiced, and tested.

For example, a teacher might briefly demonstrate and discuss how she has read a particular children's book (or a section or chapter of it), using various clues to predict what was coming next, repeatedly confirming or correcting predictions when encountering new information, and then making new predictions. He or she might encourage students to make and discuss their own predictions in the context of a Shared Book Experience. Or the teacher might *briefly* guide the students in a directed reading-thinking activity (DRTA) with a very short text or section of text ("The Window" in Figure 9.10 works well for such a purpose). Afterwards, the teacher might engage students in discussing how they predict when reading by themselves, and finally invite them to share, on subsequent days, how they have made and modified predictions in reading a book of their choice. These sharings then become mini-lessons in themselves, further inviting

What is taught recognizes reading as a process of constructing meaning, with emphasis on such strategies as predicting, confirming/correcting, and monitoring comprehension.

What differs is the methodology and underlying assumptions:

Transmission model		**Transactional model**
Reading is taught as a set of strategies	Reading is not taught, per se: the teacher demonstrates strategies and invites students to use them	Reading is not taught, per se: strategies are discussed as needed, while discussing literature, etc.
Teacher models, students practice (apply) and then may be tested	Teacher models; students are encouraged to use strategies during everyday reading	Teacher and students discuss and try strategies in the context of authentic reading
Emphasis on teaching	Emphasis on demonstrating	Emphasis on discussing and inviting
Teacher may make lists of strategies taught	Teacher may make list of useful strategies	Teacher and students may collaborate to make list of strategies they use
Teacher is authority, perhaps with a program for guidance	Teacher is authority, but students increasingly have ownership over their learning	Teacher and students together are authorities
Trust that what is taught and practiced will be learned and applied	Increasing trust in the learner	Trust in the learner

*Note that **all** of these approaches and their underlying assumptions reflect movement away from the traditional basal reading program, which has typically taught reading as mastering skills for identifying words rather than developing strategies for getting meaning. **The middle and the right-hand column increasingly reflect whole language principles.***

FIGURE 9.9   *Mini-lessons on reading strategies*

other children to use the strategies involved. The emphasis on demonstration, discussion, invitation, and further discussion reflects the DDID cycle described in Chapter 3.

Teachers who have replaced independent basal practice on isolated skills with various kinds of mini-lessons, through using and discussing whole texts instead of assigning worksheets, have made significant progress in teaching reading from a whole language perspective and philosophy. A critical difference is that they now offer mini-lessons not in a teach/practice/test format, but in the spirit of invitation, and within the context of risk-free, collaborative learning.

There were once two men, Mr. Wilson and Mr. Thompson, both seriously ill in the same room of a great hospital. Quite a small room, just large enough for the pair of them. Two beds, two bedside lockers, a door opening on the hall, and one window looking out on the world.

Mr. Wilson, as part of his treatment, was allowed to sit up in bed for an hour in the afternoon (something to do with draining the fluid from his lungs). His bed was next to the window. But Mr. Thompson had to spend all of his time flat on his back. Both of them had to be kept quiet and still, which was the reason they were in the small room by themselves. They were grateful for the peace and privacy, though. None of the bustle and clatter and prying eyes of the general ward for them. Of course, one of the disadvantages of their condition was that they weren't allowed to do much: no reading, no radio, certainly no television. They just had to keep quiet and still, just the two of them.

Well, they used to talk for hours and hours. About their wives, their children, their homes, their jobs, their hobbies, their childhood, what they did during the war, where they'd been on vacations, all that sort of thing. Every afternoon, when Mr. Wilson, the man by the window, was propped up for his hour, he would pass the time by describing what he could see outside. And Mr. Thompson began to live for those hours.

The window apparently overlooked a park with a lake where there were ducks and swans, children throwing them bread and sailing model boats, and young lovers walking hand in hand beneath the trees. And there were flowers and stretches of grass, games of softball, people taking their ease in the sunshine, and right at the back, behind the fringe of trees, there was a fine view of the city skyline. Mr. Thompson would listen to all of this, enjoying every minute. How a child nearly fell into the lake, how beautiful the girls were in their summer dresses, then an exciting ball game, or a boy playing with his puppy. It got to the point that he could almost see what was happening outside.

Then one fine afternoon when there was some sort of a parade, the thought struck him: Why should Wilson, next to the window, have all the pleasure of seeing what was going on? Why shouldn't *he* get the chance? He felt ashamed and tried not to think like that, but the more he tried, the worse he wanted a change. He would do anything! In a few days, he had turned sour. *He* should be by the window. He brooded. He couldn't sleep and grew even more seriously ill, which the doctors just couldn't understand.

One night as he stared at the ceiling, Mr. Wilson suddenly woke up, coughing and choking, the fluid congesting in his lungs, his hands groping for the call button that would bring the night nurse running. But Mr. Thompson watched without moving. The coughing racked the darkness. On and on. He choked and then stopped. The sound of breathing stopped. Mr. Thompson continued to stare at the ceiling.

In the morning, the day nurse came in with water for their baths and found Mr. Wilson dead. They took his body away quietly with no fuss.

As soon as it seemed decent, Mr. Thompson asked if he could be moved to the bed next to the window. So they moved him, tucked him in, made him quite comfortable, and left him alone to be quiet and still. The minute they'd gone, he propped himself up on one elbow, painfully and laboriously, and strained as he looked out the window.

FIGURE *9.10* *"The Window," a text for a predicting activity (Michigan Department of Education, inservice materials)*

The context of the Shared Book Experience with primary-grade students—or more broadly, a shared *reading* experience—allows for a variety of mini-lessons within the context of reading and enjoying a book, rhyme, song, poem, predictable story, or language experience chart. The teacher uses a Big Book, or chart, that all the children in the group can see. A shared reading experience typically begins with the rereading of favorite selections, during which the teacher points to the individual words while reading. After the initial rereading(s), the teacher may call attention to concepts about print or to reading strategies, to particular words or to phonics elements—while not neglecting to take advantage of the teachable moment or to simply ask children "What do you notice?" about the reading selection. In other words, the teacher engages the children in mini-lessons on whatever aspects of reading the text itself seems to invite. Next, the teacher introduces and reads a new story, after which the children practice rereading the story independently. Often, the children may engage in related arts, crafts, drama, music, writing, and other activities, but the repeated rereading of the new story is most crucial. Such a procedure helps children learn to read naturally (Holdaway, 1979; Butler, n. d.; see also Chapter 3, pp. 92–96).

The Shared Book Experience or shared reading activity reflects a whole language philosophy in significant ways. This procedure offers children an opportunity to take advantage of whatever instruction they can benefit from, yet there is no expectation that all children should learn the same things. During the shared readings, for example, less able readers simply read along as best they can, gaining support from the teacher and their more able peers. Teachers record individual students' progress, mainly by observing them in daily activities. Based upon their observations, whole language teachers provide help as needed, in the context of reading and rereading favorite selections. But they do not test the learning of skills in isolation, nor do they isolate less proficient readers from their more proficient classmates. Using whole texts, and within the context of the supportive learning community, whole language teachers facilitate the development of emergent readers, though they do not directly teach reading according to the transmission model.

Discussing reading strategies within the Shared Book Experience is very much like discussing strategies within the context of literature discussions, as described below. A major difference is simply that the Shared Book Experience is undertaken with younger children, while literature discussions occur with older students as well as with younger children. Another significant difference is that the Shared Book Experience often involves a greater degree of teacher direction.

Dialogue Journals and Literature Logs

As explained by Nancie Atwell in *In the Middle* (1987), the practice of using "dialogue journals" to enhance appreciation and understanding of literature has been adopted in many classrooms. Basically, the students periodically write letters to their teacher about the book they are currently reading, and the teacher responds by commenting upon connections the students have made, sharing his or her own reactions, extending insights, suggesting other books the readers might like, and in general responding to what the readers-writers have said.

These dialogue journals became a crucial part of the reading workshop that Atwell developed with her eighth-grade reading class, virtually all of whom were reluctant readers. Over the course of the year, her students came to perceive themselves as readers, and by June, almost all indicated that they regularly read at home for pleasure. Not so incidentally, their scores on standardized achievement tests rose too: "Their scores on standardized achievement tests averaged at the seventy-second percentile, up from an average at the fifty-fourth percentile when fully twenty-one percent scored in the bottom quartile; last year, that figure was just two percent" (Atwell, 1987, p. 158).

What was revealed through the dialogue journals gave even more evidence of students' learning. In an appendix, Atwell lists over a hundred kinds of "talk" that emerged in their dialogue journals: various facets of the author's craft and concepts of genre and mode, the reader's own reading processes and writing, the readers' personal response to the book, book recommendations and criteria for making them, and how books are published, among other topics.

I suspect that what made the students' dialogue journals so rich was the depth and sophistication of Atwell's responses. However, understanding and appreciation of literature can also be fostered by having students keep literature logs that are used to initiate oral discussions between teacher and student, or among students in a literature discussion group. At times, the teacher may specify all or part of what should be included (e.g., "Describe Johnny and tell what you think of him in the first chapters of the book"; "If you have problems with any words, jot down two or three of them and note where they are located; later, we can discuss the strategies you used in dealing with them"). Usually, literature logs are most conducive to learning and discussion if free response is also encouraged whenever any specific responses are requested.

Literature Discussion Groups

Recently, teachers have been discovering that mini-lessons on reading strategies may not be as necessary as previously thought, when taught separately from the literature that students are reading. Indeed, some recent research by Kucer (1992) suggests that practice activities on reading strategies may be significantly less useful than discussions of such strategies in the context of actual reading. Teachers are finding that many of the essential elements and strategies of reading can be learned in the give-and-take of dialogue journals and especially literature discussion groups, or literature circles (Harste & Short, with Burke, 1988) that complement the silent, individual reading of texts.

Why literature groups? In the following transcript, fourth-grade teacher Tonya ("T") and two of her colleagues, Mary Ann ("M") and Barb ("B") discuss with Kathryn Mitchell Pierce ("K") their reasons for reasons for initiating literature discussion groups, in response to the questions they were asking about reading (Pierce, 1990, pp. 182–183):

K: Why did you start using literature discussion groups? What were you looking for, or moving away from?

T: I didn't want ability groups in reading.

M: I was searching for a better way of teaching reading, of not really teaching reading. I was resisting that built-in failure factor of the basal program.

B: I wanted to see kids interested in the reading, more than just spoon-feeding it to them. I was using writing workshop and could see some ways of connecting it to the literature.

T: I didn't want to be the leader anymore—in discussions. I wanted to hear what they had to say.

M: To think that you could do it all the time, become readers, breaking away from the basal—that was eye-opening.

T: With the VTS kids [Voluntary Transfer Students in a desegregation busing program], it lets you see. They can show me things through the discussion that I couldn't see before. There were no restraints on them.

M: I saw that over and over. Kids who would have been failing—

B: The high kids were also shining. They weren't bored anymore. They didn't have to do four more worksheets.

The teachers also reported that the children were eager to read and talk about the books chosen for literature discussion, whereas the students never chose a basal for free reading. The self-chosen books did far more to develop their interest in literature and their appreciation of it.

The following description of literature discussions and literature extensions draws upon Kathryn Mitchell Pierce's extensive participation in such discussions.

Literature Discussions and Literature Extensions
Kathryn Mitchell Pierce

Literature discussion groups of approximately five to seven students allow in-depth discussion of a literary work. Generally, students choose a book to read and share in the small group. The teacher then places students into groups based on interest rather than ability. Readers stop to reflect in a literature log before, at several points during, and after the reading of the entire text.

Reflections may include questions, connections to other texts and life experiences, predictions and insights or hunches, and topics for discussion in the group. Some readers also make note of words or passages that they found particularly difficult or intriguing. Small-group discussions of the book, whether at several points during the reading or following the reading of the entire book, provide opportunities for readers to share responses to the book as well as strategies used during the reading of the book. Often, reading an excerpt from the literature log provides a starting point for the discussion.

At times, readers decide to revisit a topic from their discussion during a subsequent discussion. For example, after having discussed Katherine Paterson's *The Great Gilly Hopkins*, one group of readers decided to revisit, in subsequent discussions, the topics of racism and character development. They returned to the book and made note in their literature logs of points they wanted to include in the follow-up discussion. In preparation for discussion with other group members, they skimmed, reread, and reflected on the ways racism and character development or change were addressed in the text. One day they shared and discussed their information about racism, and the next day they focused on character development and change, expecially Gilly's.

The group found many connections between their discussions of racism and character development, on the one hand, and their general responses to the text, on the other. Feeling that the discussion was a significant one for them, the group decided to create a presentation for the class. The presentation focused not on the book per se, but on the development of Gilly as a character throughout the events of the book. In a fourth discussion of the book, having decided to create a series of skits highlighting Gilly's changes, the group selected from the beginning, middle, and end of the book various episodes that best demonstrated these changes.

When teachers choose to participate in literature discussion groups with students, they, too, read and respond in a literature log. As participants in the group, teachers offer their perspectives on the text and provide rich demonstrations of how more experienced readers engage with the text and respond. Reading a selected passage from their own literature logs, teachers can offer demonstrations of the types of comments one might include in a log and how these might support the group's discussions.

In addition, by participating in the planning sessions for literature presentations, teachers can help groups move beyond using other forms of communication for simply retelling the story to using other forms of expression and other media to re-present their own experience with the text—through art, music, movement, drama, discussion, display, and so forth.

Even when teachers choose not to participate in a discussion group, they can encourage groups to reflect on the discussion process and help establish topical and/or procedural goals for subsequent discussions.

As Eeds and Wells express it (1989), these literature discussions are not "gentle inquisitions," but rather "grand conversations" about literature: the kind of thought-provoking discussions you might have with friends after reading a good book or seeing a good movie.

A Shift in the Teacher's Role

Obviously such classroom discussions require a drastic shift from the teacher's traditional role. The teacher serves to guide the discussion, but is primarily a participant rather than a discussion leader; the teacher neither dominates the discussion nor cross-examines students on their reading of the text. A videotape of Karen Smith conducting a literature study group with fifth and sixth graders reveals that in such discussions, Karen comments, speculates, connects ideas, builds upon what students have noticed, provides needed background information, restates and confirms, invites response, clarifies details, extends insights, shares personal reactions and opinions—but never quizzes the students, never tells the students what to think, never demands that they construct the same meanings from the text as she does (Center for the Expansion of Dialogue, 1990). Figure 9.11 includes some ways I have developed of initiating literary discussions and keeping them going. Discussing the book again after a second reading

Initiating discussion by starting with the students' responses:

Well, now that you've read this story, what particularly interested you about it?

Who would like to start our discussion of this story by sharing a reaction?

Okay, would someone start by telling us what you think (or how you feel) about the story (or the main character, or a key event in the story), and why?

Ways of redirecting the conversation without engaging in teacher inquisition:

You know, when I read about X, I began to wonder. . . . What did you think?

When I read (or read about) such-and-such, I got to thinking. . . .

Did you feel the same, or different?

I wondered if I would have felt/done the same as X in this situation. How about you?

I got to thinking about how X is like Y. What do you think?

I got to thinking about what I would have done if I had been X. What about you?

One of the things that interested me about X was. . . .

What did you think?

Ways of sharing your own responses and opinions and prior knowledge, without conveying the impression that students must think the way you do or accept your interpretation as the only one:

Some of the suggested responses in the section above would work with slight modification. Also:

You know, what you just said (or what so-and-so said) is interesting. I didn't happen to see it quite that way. What I thought was . . . , because. . . .

When I read X, I thought . . . because. . . . (share what you knew about the author, his or her other writings, other related texts, or whatever affected your interpretation)

Well, I remembered X, so I found myself thinking. . . .

I hadn't thought of it that way. What I thought was. . . . I wonder, what do the rest of you think?

Ways of building upon students' responses to encourage them to consider literary elements and the author's craft:

That's an interesting observation about X (perhaps the main character). Do you think that X developed in any other ways, in the story?

You're right, every time the weather was bad, bad things seemed to happen. I wonder why the author chose to use bad weather as a symbol for trouble.

That's an interesting idea. We could probably say that's one theme of the story, couldn't we? I wonder if there are any other important themes.

Fɪɢᴜʀᴇ **9.11**   *Comments and questions to generate discussion and insight in literature discussions*

would encourage more probing comments by students as well as the teacher— comments that can become springboards to noninquisition-like questions about characterization, plot, theme, metaphorical language, and so forth. It is critical to avoid inquisition-like questions and to participate as a discussant more than as a leader.

It is also important for students themselves to choose the books to be read and discussed, from among several options offered by the teacher. Usually students indicate their first and second choices, then are grouped according to their preferences. Thus, they have a considerably greater degree of ownership than when reading assigned stories from a basal.

Often, discussion about the meaning of a work will lead readers to return to the text for clarification. Particularly when they have kept literature logs in which they have responded to the book and also made note of some problem sections or words, readers will spontaneously discuss those problems and how they tried to solve them (the reading strategies they used). Teachers can invite other students to offer additional strategies and can share their own, thus demonstrating, during the ongoing discussion, various ways of becoming a more effective reader. The students' repertoire of reading strategies is expanded naturally, in the context of discussing the literary work. Therefore, mini-lessons are not necessarily needed.

> Develop habit of reading aloud to students;
> begin to involve parents in sharing and monitoring
> students' at-home reading

↓

> Engage students in extensive reading of self-chosen books;
> proceed into literature discussion groups only when
> this pattern is well established

↓

> From perhaps 7 or 8 available literature sets of books
> rich in meanings, facilitate students' choice of books;
> plan on 4 or 5 groups of approximately 5–7 students

↓

One group spends a week on an initial reading of the book they chose for literary study . . .	The remaining groups continue reading self-chosen books *other than* those chosen for their literary study
↓	↓
then, they spend a second week discussing the book with the teacher	As the teacher becomes more comfortable with the process, he or she might start a second group on their initial reading of their book, at the same time as the first group is engaging in intensive discussion

FIGURE **9.12** *Implementing literature discussion groups (based on Peterson & Eeds, 1990)*

The teacher need not conduct four or five literature discussion groups on different books, all within the same week. Indeed, the teacher just beginning to involve students in discussion groups would probably be overwhelmed by trying to conduct so many groups in a brief time period. In their excellent book *Grand Conversations: Literature Groups in Action* (1990), Peterson and Eeds recommend moving into literature discussion groups only gradually, and then conducting only one such group until discussion of that book is completed. (Figure 9.12 illustrates my interpretation, with a slight extension, of the steps they recommend.) This book is both inspirational and practical, containing extensive examples of literature discussions, explanations of literary elements that might be discussed in particular books, and suggestions and sample forms for record-keeping and evaluation. Other valuable resources are Kathy Short and Kathryn Mitchell Pierce's collection of articles, *Talking About Books: Creating Literate Communities* (1990), which includes several chapters by classroom teachers describing their own experiences with a variety of types of litererature and group discussion strategies, and Pierce and Gilles' *Cycles of Meaning* (1993), which also includes several chapters wherein elementary teachers describe their process of growing together in their use of literature and group talk in the classroom. Harste and Short's *Creating Classrooms for Authors* (with Burke, 1988) also offers a useful discussion of how to initiate literature circles, though their model is more teacher-dominated than that of the more recent books cited.

The Process of Growth

Different ways of helping students acquire vocabulary and concepts while reading the novel *Johnny Tremain* (Forbes, 1943) can illustrate differing stages in moving away from basal reader instruction toward and into whole language.

Johnny Tremain takes place just before and during the time of the American Revolution. At the beginning of the story, fifteen-year-old Johnny is an apprentice to the famed silversmith Paul Revere. Because the concept of an apprentice is critical to understanding the story, the typical basal method would be to preteach the term *apprentice*. With some understanding of the importance of drawing forth students' prior knowledge, the teacher would probably begin by eliciting what the students know about this concept, rather than by defining the word for them.

A teacher in the early stages of moving away from basal reading methods might extract sentences from the opening chapters of the novel and preteach a mini-lesson in which students are helped to discover the meaning of *apprentice* within the context of these sentences, perhaps through a discussion of which contexts are more helpful and why. A teacher more comfortable with whole language practices might call the word to the students' attention before they begin reading the novel and ask them to keep notes in their literature log on how context increasingly helped them understand the word. In a literature discussion group, they might then discuss their use of context to come to an appropriate understanding of the concept *apprentice* and their understanding of what it meant to Johnny and the other boys to be apprentices. In moving away from basal

Transmission			**Transactional**
modifying the basal lesson $\rightarrow$	mini-lessons on strategies: teach/ practice/test format $\rightarrow$	mini-lessons offered as demonstration, invitation $\rightarrow$	strategies discussed as needed, during discussions of literature, etc.

supplementing the basal— reading aloud to students, adding sustained silent reading time, or DEAR

omitting some workbook pages and stories

FIGURE *9.13   Growing in the teaching of reading*

methodology, teachers increasingly provide larger contexts for learning, place more emphasis upon developing strategies in these contexts, emphasize discussion over direct teaching and inquisition, and show more faith in the learner. Some whole language teachers would probably not mention this key word at all prior to starting the novel, but would just make sure during discussion of the first chapters that students had gleaned an appropriate understanding of the term, perhaps encouraging the students to comment and reflect upon their use of context in doing so.

Figure 9.13 suggests how teachers often grow from basal managers to discussion leaders and facilitators in the way they approach the teaching of reading. As should be clear from the preceding description, literary discussion groups represent perhaps the epitome of a whole language approach to the development of reading. Learning takes place naturally in the discussion among students and a literate adult.

As for the imaginary Ms. Matthews' modification of a basal reader lesson, how might teachers do things differently, with more of a whole language orientation? This is beautifully demonstrated in the next section, where Kathryn Mitchell Pierce describes how she prepares for discussions of children's literature and offers a glimpse of what a literature discussion might be like, using Jay Williams' "Petronella" as an example.

TALKING ABOUT BOOKS: AN ILLUSTRATION WITH "PETRONELLA"— *KATHRYN MITCHELL PIERCE*

In some contexts, and earlier in my teaching experience, teacher preparation for discussion of a reading selection meant becoming familiar with the lesson plan in the Teacher's Manual accompanying the basal reading series. Good teachers, I was told, always read the story and the lesson plan in advance of teaching the story, and spend time thinking about the selection from the perspective of the skills to be developed through the reading. Someone else selected the skills to be developed and the story to be used in the lesson, offering suggestions as to how this could best be accomplished. These suggestions included a myriad of questions to ask before, during, and after the reading. The familiar pattern called for the teacher to ask the questions and the students to respond.

Somewhere along the path of my teaching career I began to change the ways I approached the reading and discussion of particular selections. Early changes included developing my own questions, which seemed better suited to what I knew about my readers, and selecting my own stories and books to develop the skills identified for the lessons. Later, I learned to support readers in actual conversations about their reading rather than engaging in the question-and-answer sessions we had grown accustomed to.

Each successive change brought my planning further away from following the basal and more into my own hands. This was scary business as I wrestled with my qualifications to assume responsibility for such planning, particularly in light of the qualifications of those whose names appeared on the covers of the Teacher's Manual. One of my most significant qualifications, I came to realize, was that I knew my learners in ways that professionals outside my classroom would never know them. Later, I recognized that my love for and knowledge of children's literature was also an essential qualification. Still, I allowed someone else's lists of skills to determine the criteria I used in evaluating a reader's comprehension (Pierce, 1990).

I was familiar with the "Petronella" story through the writings of Connie Weaver, but had never "taught" the story with a group of children. This section is my response to Connie's question "How would you approach this story today, given what you know about the reading process and your work with literature discussion groups?"

My answer to her question began with reflection on the essential reasons for sharing the literature in the first place. Huck (1990) reminds us of the power children's literature has to evoke greater understanding of ourselves and others as we enter into the story worlds of our favorite characters. In addition, literature helps us come to know our world—past and present, real and imagined—and our future. To stock my classroom library and to share with readers of all ages, I select literature that has the potential to help us see ourselves and our world differently—to evoke a change in the reader.

I also share literature for the purpose of helping readers come to understand literature as an art form, a form of communication, an object of study in and of itself. Peterson and Eeds (1990) have helped me understand the significance of literature as worthy of study, and not merely the vehicle through which we teach reading. I once talked with Karen Smith, who has worked extensively with Peterson and Eeds, about the ways she prepares for a literature study group (she prefers the term "literature study" over "literature discussion group" to signal that the purpose is to *study* the literature). Karen rereads the text several times in order to explore the potential for discussion. She doesn't predetermine what the group discussion focus *will* be, but rather, what it *could* be. This helps her be prepared to take a lead from one of the students. Through exploring this lead, Karen will be able to provide demonstrations of the elements of literature as they drive the discussion. I choose material, therefore, that provides examples of literature at its best and that has the potential to help readers understand the key elements of literature (plot, theme, character, etc.).

Karen's description of this process has also caused me to rethink the ways I prepare for discussions. I try to think through all the topics I'm aware of that could become a part of the actual discussion, but I want to do so in such a way that I don't shut myself off from student suggestions that would be more powerful. (Later in this section, I describe how I went about this with "Petronella.")

Another significant influence on the way I approach my planning for discussion groups comes from Dorothy Watson. Early on, she helped me view literature as a vehicle for teaching reading, and reading as an active process of making meaning. Because literature is so powerful in its potential to evoke a response from readers, it provides the motivation for children to become, and continue to grow as, readers. Literature is its own reward for reading. In addition, she helped me see that there is no better way to learn the complex task of reading than through engagement in it. My conversations with Dorothy were instrumental in my decisions to use literature rather than contrived texts to teach reading and to focus reading instruction on developing and expanding the behaviors and strategies associated with proficient readers.

Some time later, Dorothy described a decision she had made relative to teaching reading using literature. She had decided to participate in literature discussion groups by offering "I wonder" statements rather than asking questions in hope of promoting more sophisticated discussion. These open-ended statements signal to participants that exploration of diverse views on a topic are invited. Questions, on the other hand, can signal that the questioner is seeking judgments on a final draft idea, or the "right" answer. When I prepare for a literature discussion group, therefore, I reflect on my own experience reading the text, making note of the things I wondered about and the strategies I used in constructing meaning from the text.

Kathy Short and Carolyn Burke, among others, have helped me better understand a single reading experience—reading "Petronella," for example—in the context of a larger world of ongoing reading and inquiry. Through my work with literature discussion groups, and particularly as a result of ideas shared by Kathy Short, I have come to see that individual texts can have a certain potential for a group of readers, and that this potential can be expanded by organizing books into text sets—groups of books that have a common theme, topic, or text structure. (For a more extended discussion of text sets, see Harste & Short, with Burke, 1988; Short & Pierce, 1990; and Pierce & Gilles, 1993.) Carolyn Burke once described books as being social, changing their character when in the company of different books. She invited teachers to consider grouping books together on our shelves by asking, "What kinds of conversations might these books have together?" and "How would this book act differently when in the company of a different set of books?" For this reason, my preparation for literature discussions always includes consideration of the connections I make between the target text and other texts with which I am familiar.

The following discussion provides an example of the ways I put these ideas into practice in preparation for a literature discussion. In writing this section, I have attempted to think aloud on paper. That is, I have tried to make myself conscious of the issues and considerations involved in my planning in order to share them with others.

Preparing for Discussion

In preparing for a literature discussion, I must first, of course, read or reread the text or portion of text we are discussing. During this reading, I write notes in a literature log of the connections I make, the responses I have to various aspects of the text, and the questions I ask of the text or in response to the text. In general, I am trying to record what Jerry Harste describes as the mental trip I take during the reading. Rosenblatt (1978) reminds us that reading is a transaction between reader and text that leaves both changed as a result. Therefore, each reading of a text is a new experience. I try to note topics that emerge during a second reading that I hadn't noticed in the first. I also try to note times I recognize that my ideas have changed since an earlier reading, either because of life experiences I've had in the meantime or because of things others raised in an earlier discussion. Because significant meanings develop over time, recursively and cyclically in literature discussion groups (Pierce and Gilles, 1993), I want to track the development of my own ideas so that I can share these examples with others during our discussions.

Here are a few excerpts from my literature response log for "Petronella," with italics indicating statements that seem especially well-suited for discussion:

End of first page (43):

The name sounded so much like "Cinderella" that, the first time I read this, I thought it was going to be a variant on that familiar tale. The way the page breaks after "Until now"—I knew that the story would be about the ways the traditions were changed.

End of page 45:

Petronella, as a character, doesn't represent the typical dependent female usually found in Grimm and Perrault tales. Her brief battle with her parents over breaking with tradition sounds familiar. Seems each generation finds something to do differently in order to establish a unique identity. The red hair seems a bit of a stereotype. *Since such exists and is a part of what readers must know in order to understand some characters, I guess this would be an opportunity to discuss the expectation—red hair, fiery personality—and then to explore the stereotype briefly in relation to others.*

Reminds me at this point of the Faerie Tale Theater version of Cinderella with Shelley Duvall. In that video, Cinderella is tall, dark, and assertive/confident. The prince was shy, shorter, and reluctant to take action. *I assumed that since Petronella is like this Cinderella, there's a good likelihood that the prince she will undoubtedly encounter will be her opposite in personality.*

Would be interesting to compare female leading characters in fairy tales and contemporary variants to see how they highlight what the society values in a woman. For example, *Mufaro's Beautiful Daughters* (Steptoe, 1987) gives insight into what that African tribe values in a woman. These traits can be highlighted when compared to the Cinderella character in *Yeh Shen* (Louie, 1982), *The Crane Wife* (Yagawa, 1981), Grimm's original, and Walt Disney's popularized tale. Adding *Prince Cinders* (B. Cole, 1988) to the mix offers another view of the Cinderella character from a modern perspective.

Page 46:

As the only sister of two brothers, I had no difficulty accepting the fact that they let her go with them. My brothers would have, too. *I assume this is different from families in which brothers are expected to look after, protect, and think fondly of the sister left at home.*

The old man on this page reminded me of the "tests" that Mufaro's daughters encountered on their trip to the city to meet the prince. Those who treat elders and "undesirables" with care and compassion often win out. That's common in many fairy tales.

"Beauty and the Beast," highlighted in the Disney version, is based on the consequences of not being kind to everyone, regardless of outward appearances.

"Petronella's kind heart was touched" seems to be a key to what made her worthy of the opportunity to seek her fortune and find success. *Compare to other Cinderella characters.*

Page 49:

"Nothing we really want is easy." Sounds like a very direct way of introducing a potential theme, or worldly truth. This is certainly still true today. *I wonder if middle elementary readers have experienced enough of waiting for something worthwhile to have an opinion on this point. I could ask.*

Page 50:

The prince sounds like the prince in Shelley Duvall's Cinderella story, except without the redeeming naïveté. The business about suntans could evoke different responses these days than when the story first appeared in the reading series. *With all the bad press about sun exposure, I wonder if some of the readers will see this as more stupidity than vanity.*

Page 51:

This is the first place where Petronella makes a clear decision to risk her life for the prince, whom she finds less than ideal. This is the subject of discussion question C after the story. I like the question. *I found this part a bit difficult to accept—why would she risk her life for him? Was tradition and family expectation that strong to override what seemed to be common sense? Of course, times have changed and I'm not sure a modern Petronella would do the same thing, or at least not for the same reasons. This would also be a good point to discuss with the readers.*

Page 56:

The three tasks remind me a bit of *Arrow to the Sun* (McDermott, 1974) in that the main character must endure and rise above expectations in three tasks in order to reach a self-selected goal. In both cases, a rites-of-passage element seems to be involved—something one must do to be considered an adult, or ready for marriage. *I wonder what the kids would say is the object of the three tests for Petronella. What would she be gaining, besides the prince? Adulthood? Equal status with her brothers? Preparation for marriage? Access to truth?*

Page 59:

The enchanter turns into several other forms. This is a common feature for enchanters and other magic makers. Check (Huck, Hepler, and Hickman, 1987) or Norton (1987) for beginning list of other "transformations" titles. It does remind me a bit of *Runaway Bunny* (M. Brown, 1942/1972), however, in that the mother will change into whatever she needs to become in order to protect her child. There is a certain element of desire and quiet, confident acceptance here as in that story.

Page 60:

The twist ending was fun. It would have been far too predictable if she had ended up with the prince. *To appreciate this twist, I guess kids need to have a well-developed schema for "happily ever after," which isn't difficult to establish.*

Reflective entry:

In retrospect, this is also a story about going to a lot of dangerous work as a result of a mistaken assumption. Because Petronella needed to rescue a prince, she saw him as someone who needed to be rescued. How would the story have been different if she had asked him first whether he really wanted to be rescued?

Seemed uncharacteristic of Petronella to just ride off into the sunset and leave poor Ferdinand to walk home. I would expect her to eventually check and be sure he's O.K.

After familiarizing myself with the text, I sketch out a quick web of connections, related ideas, and relationships among various aspects of the text and my responses. These webs often include references to other titles that could eventually become parts of text sets. The webs are a visual map of the ideas I have been considering and the relationships among them. Often the connections first appear in my literature response log or in my notes in the margins of the book. Other times, the act of creating the web leads to inclusion of additional titles. Figure 9.14 is the web I sketched for "Petronella" following the literature response entries included above. Figure 9.15 lists resources that have been useful to teachers and preservice teachers in developing webs and lists of related books and stories.

Next, I write out, underline, or make marginal notes in the literature response log alongside the "I wonder" statements that seem best suited to the group that will be discussing the book. I presently participate in a curriculum study group made up of teachers, university faculty, graduate students, and district curriculum administrators. I prepare for our discussion groups in the same manner I prepare for discussions with elementary readers. We recently read *Creating Curriculum* (Short & Burke, 1992). As I prepared for our discussion, I reflected on the notes I had made in the margins of the text, selecting those that seemed best suited to our discussion group. I developed an informal list of "I wonder" statements that I wanted to explore with members of our group. I took into consideration the perspectives each of them takes on curriculum, the life experiences they bring to the table that add diversity to our deliberations. For example, I was very

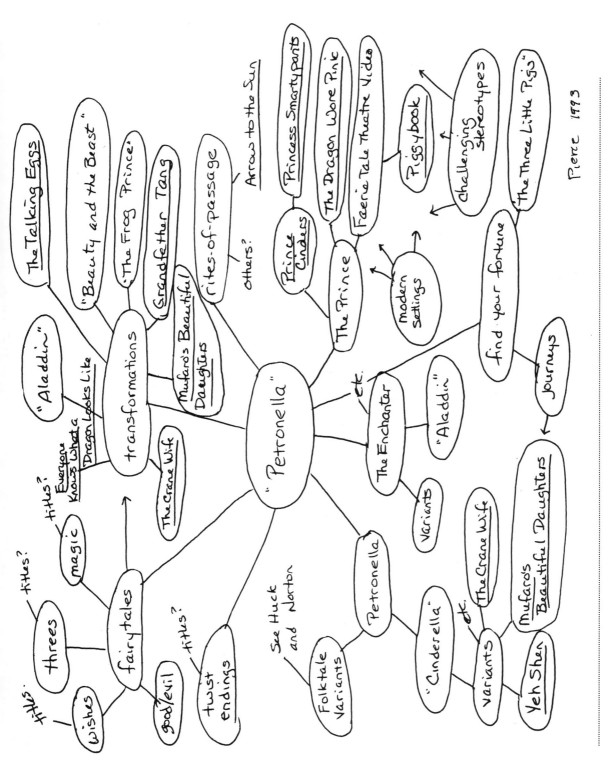

FIGURE 9.14 Planning web for "Petronella" discussion

Bromley, K. D. (1991). *Webbing with literature.* Boston: Allyn & Bacon. An excellent discussion of ways to think about using literature in the reading curriculum and across the curriculum. As the name implies, it includes extensive information about using webs with literature.

Crenshaw, S., Pierce, K. M., Reikes, L., Slane, S., & Stopsky, F. (1989). Teaching history across the elementary curriculum. Pull-out feature, *Social Studies and the Young Learner, 2* (2) (November/December). Includes some Cinderella titles and possible ways of using them to explore history and culture.

Huck, C., Hepler, S., & Hickman, J. (1987 or recent edition). *Children's literature in the elementary school.* New York: Holt, Rinehart and Winston. See particularly Chapter 6 ("Traditional Literature") for a chart outlining titles for a cross-cultural study of folktale motifs such as magical objects, transformations, and wishes. In addition, the book includes a list of Cinderella tales from a variety of cultures. Both lists are accompanied by suggestions for supporting readers' discussions of these sets of books.

Norton, D. (1987 or recent edition). *Through the eyes of a child: An introduction to children's literature.* Columbus, Ohio: Merrill. See particularly Chapter 6 ("Traditional Literature") for a listing of Cinderella tales from different countries along with discussion possibilities for exploring the characteristics of these tales, including a chart highlighting the elements of a Cinderella tale. Also includes sample webs.

Worthy, M., & Bloodgood, J. (1992/1993). Enhancing reading instruction through Cinderella tales, *The Reading Teacher, 46* (4): 290–301. Provides a description of a thematic unit of study focused on variants of the Cinderella story. The article includes samples of children's work created during the study and a bibliography of children's books and stories used.

Figure 9.15   *References for selecting related literature*

interested in the implications of the book for the design of prospective teacher education experiences as well as for issues of home-school communication. Knowing the group, I thought the latter would be a more fruitful discussion because many of the participants regularly work closely with parents. I chose to share the parent-related statements and to save the teacher education–related experiences for discussions with fellow teacher educators.

A word of clarification: The "I wonder" statements I generate in preparation for discussion do not function as pseudoquestions. I do not conceive of them as ways to ask a predetermined question without really asking it. Rather, these are the topics I genuinely wish to explore with the particular group of readers that will be meeting. I hope, through my demonstrations, that they, too, will think about coming to the discussion groups with their own "I wonder" statements: statements chosen because the reader wants to hear what these particular group members have to say about the topic.

The italicized portions of the journal entries included previously are the "I wonder" statements I noted in preparation for discussion of "Petronella."

Finally, I revisit the text, through skimming or reflection, focusing on the aspects of the writer's craft that seem to be particularly highlighted in this text. I see my function in a literature discussion group as primarily one of expanding the range of options learners consider in their own reading and thinking about text. Sharing my literature response log entries, providing demonstrations of the ways I approach the reading process, and highlighting the effective strategies others describe are all ways that I can accomplish this goal. For example, *The True Story of the Three Little Pigs! By A. Wolf* (Scieszka, 1989) provides an excellent opportunity for discussing characters' point of view. This is not to say that I set out to teach point of view using this book, as one might do in a mini-lesson. Rather, I am aware in advance that the book provides a rich opportunity for exploring this concept and that the other readers in the group may bring it up, directly or indirectly. Having thought about it in advance, I can be prepared to draw their attention to the ways the author signals point of view, to remind them of other reading experiences we have shared in which point of view played a central role, and so forth.

Similarly, some books are rich in potential for discussion of specific reading strategies. For example, *Do Not Open* (Turkle, 1981) provides opportunities to discuss predicting and confirming strategies, while *The Great Gilly Hopkins* (Paterson, 1978) provides opportunities for discussing ways of connecting plot development with character development. Reflecting on the potential to discuss a particular reading strategy relative to the book helps me be prepared to support the group as they explore this strategy, or to share my own use of the strategy as a demonstration of what is possible in the process of constructing meaning from the text.

Discussing "Petronella"

A colleague of mine, Jean Dickinson, recently invited her new fifth- and sixth-grade students in a year-round school to read and discuss "Petronella." The following is a description of the events and some of my analysis of their comments during the discussion. I have also brought out ways in which the readers addressed the topics proposed by the end-of-story questions presented in the published version of the tale, the issues I developed in my planning notes, and other noteworthy aspects of their discussions.

The students in this class have participated in literature discussion groups for a large part of their elementary school career. On Thursday Jean provided copies of the story, explaining that while it was from a third-grade basal reader it was really of interest to all ages, like the picture books she has shared with the class. She then explained that I was interested in ways students would discuss the story, and helped them assign a keeper of the tape recorder, who would turn the tape on at the beginning and off at the end of each discussion.

Jean then instructed the students to read the story, making note of the things they wanted to talk about when they got together the next day to discuss it. Acknowledging their prior experiences with literature discussion groups, she invited them to discuss the story in any way they felt appropriate. One student suggested that they begin by making some predictions about the story, based on the information available from the title page and skimming the illustrations. They offered a few predictions, confirmed that they could read the entire story before meeting the next day, and then adjourned to read.

The group met two more times to discuss the story: Friday and then again on Monday. While Jean did not participate in the group, she did step in twice to listen to the discussion and, on these occasions, to ask a few questions for clarification.

The group opened their discussion session by sharing general reactions to the story. They all agreed it was a good story, and that it really didn't sound like a third-grade story.

1 JOHN: Yeah, . . . it didn't really sound like a third-grade book or anything. It sounded more like a fifth- or sixth-grade book.

2 SARAH: Well, reading level doesn't say everything. It's like you either like it or you don't like it.

They also discussed the characteristics of fairy tales they found in this tale, often making connections to other fairy tales that shared these characteristics: magic, objects that are transformed, wizards and enchanters, three quests, happily-ever-after endings, and "good" characters who can perform special feats (such as tame horses). Key elements of the plot, particularly the general sequence of events, were discussed as the students retold portions of the story to make their points, to clarify confusing sections, and to seek peer response to particular episodes. While they did not formally summarize or retell the story in a sequenced and coherent fashion, the general sharing and requests for confirmation of events and responses clearly indicated that they understood what happened when in the story.

Their responses to particular episodes demonstrated the humor they found in the story. They liked the twist at the end, particularly the fact that Petronella was going to take a "grandpa guy" home with her instead of a young, handsome prince. The following excerpt is characteristic of their discussion session, showing the interplay of retelling, response, and reflection:

3 SARAH: When it was a girl that was born, and she was ready to go out and seek her fortune, they treated her like a baby.

4 JEANNA: She wanted to show them what she could really do.

5 ERIK: Yeah, but they might have laughed at her for bringing back this old grandpa guy, this wizard.

6 SARAH: He was really old!

7 TODD: If this took place in the nineties, I think she'd be a total feminist!

8 ERIK: And it wouldn't be a wizard, either.

9 JEANNA: I think she was really bold to go out like that.

10 SARAH: I like that part where the old man is sitting there and he says he's been stuck there for years and years and years.

11 EVAN: Yeah, that's another one of the fairy tale qualities.

12 ERIK: Yeah, and I like that he's got all those cobwebs all over him and all that . . .

13 JOHN: I like the pictures. I like how they really show you a lot, like the old man. It's really a good picture of the old man, like it shows you what he really looks like.

14 TODD: Let me ask you this. If you saw these big old horses and everything and they were, like, snarling at you, would you just walk up and start brushing them or anything?

15 EVAN: Well, yeah, it's a fairy tale quality. Like, it shows that she has courage and everything. Or was that the hawks?

16 JEANNA: Yeah, she taught them how to sing.

17 EVAN: That's another fairy tale quality.

18 JOHN: Yeah, but it's not too many of those things. I like that, because if it's got too many of those things like that then it's too far . . . way out of your world.

19 SARAH: And it doesn't sound right.

The preceding excerpt is typical of small group exploratory talk. The readers use one another to confirm the events in the story, building up a shared and agreed-upon story line (lines 3, 6, 10, 12, and 16). They explore their own responses to the story by asking others about their responses directly or by making statements that invite others to agree or disagree (lines 7, 14, and 18). And they explore decisions made by the author in relation to their own ideas (lines 7, 8, and 18), often predicting what "could have happened if. . . ."

The group made connections between "Petronella" and "Cinderella" as I had done, thinking Petronella was going to be "a poor Cinderella." They seemed most fascinated, however, with the contrast between the familiar sex-role expectations found in "Cinderella" and the characters in "Petronella." The following excerpt captures some of the discussion of these contrasts.

20 JOHN: When the prince, when she was trying to rescue him, supposedly, and he said it was too early in the morning and he wanted to go back to bed, well, if this was a prince in, like, "Cinderella" or something—I mean, not that "Cinderella" isn't a good fairy tale or anything—but like if she tried to rescue that prince he would just jump out of bed and everything and be ready to go.

21 ERIK: Yeah, but this one, he's just lazy and everything.

22 JEANNA: He doesn't even deserve to be saved.

23 TODD: But that's the point. She needed to find a prince. She's got that pressure to find a prince from her mom and her dad, and that's why I think she'd be feminist today.

24 SARAH: She's under so much pressure to be normal, to be like her two older brothers.

25 JEANNA: Yeah, like in that other story—the one with the eggs . . .

26 SARAH: *The Talking Eggs* [San Souci, 1989]?

27 JEANNA: Yeah, *The Talking Eggs*. She wanted to be like . . .

28 TODD: Well, I like how when she comes to the part where the road forks into three paths . . .

29 EVAN: Yeah, they always have a choice. That's what makes it a good fairy tale.

30 SARAH: Well, like she could have said, "Well, I don't want to go there because all it leads to is a wizard. I want to go the other way because that's to the large kingdom and it has more opportunities."

31 ERIK: Well, I think she actually has four quests. Because, like with the first one, she could have just asked him for directions and then gone away. But the story would have been so boring if she'd have just done that—or she could have just gone to the city or the kingdom.

32 JOHN: But, yeah, since she's so kind and everything. So she asked him.

33 EVAN: It's like that. They always have that kindness stuff, like "Cinderella" is like that. It's a good fairy tale quality.

As the previous excerpt shows, they discussed the believability of the characters' actions, basing their judgments on their knowledge of both traditional tales and current human behavior (lines 20 and 23). Building these connections between the text, other texts, and life experiences helps students construct a complex web of meaning and response for the story. When readers share their connections, they offer demonstrations to the other participants of ways the text might be viewed, and how particular connections shed light on the characters' and authors' motive.

Making connections is an active process, which often includes asking questions (line 14). Jean's students are encouraged to write questions like these in their literature response logs in order to preserve them for the discussion. It is interesting to note the balance between questions and statements in the students' conversation. Teacher-directed discussion groups often include many more questions, generally asked by the teacher. Left to conduct their own discussions, these students experienced little difficulty in maintaining the discussion with minimal use of questions.

In the following excerpt, Todd seems to be having difficulty understanding the character of the prince because the prince in this story doesn't match what he has come to expect from a prince in a fairy tale. He draws on his current understanding of fairy tales by clarifying that they often have two characters, one good and one bad, and that sometimes a bad character can actually turn out to be a good character. By making these observations in the group discussion, Todd invited his peers to respond. Later, in line 37, Todd makes an observation that functions as a question, inviting his peers to resolve an anomaly.

34 TODD: There's something I want to ask . . . There's something in this story that's in every fairy tale. . . . It seems like he's a bad guy, the old man, but really he wasn't. Sometimes it turns out to be a royal person like in "Beauty and the Beast." It seems like a bad person, but then he turns into this wonderful prince.

35 ERIK: Yeah, just like the old man, the enchanter or whatever. He seemed like a mean guy but he turned out not to be.

36 EVAN: That's like in a fairy tale. They always have one good guy and he might turn into a bad guy.

37 TODD: I don't see how that lazy guy . . . how he could be a prince.

38 JOHN: In a lot of movies they have a really slimy, lazy prince . . .

39 ERIK: Yeah, there's two kinds of princes, a good one and a lazy one. And the princess, she like finds a really good prince and he just dumps the other one in the trash or something.

40 JOHN: Like the one, the dude that cares, like in "Cinderella." They have different qualities.

41 SARAH: Where he's daring and adventurous and kind of nice and *this* prince, I don't know. Like what I was saying a long time ago, she was just out there to get a prince to fit in like everyone else.

Raising the anomaly in the discussion group provided Todd with an opportunity to construct an understanding of the characters in this story by building on the insights shared by others. The collective experiences of the group helped each member reach a more complex understanding of the differences between the characters in "Petronella" and those found in more traditional fairy tales.

Later in the discussion, Erik initiated a similar exchange when he asked how it was possible to have any princesses to become queens if the royal families always had sons. His colleagues explained that first, this is a fairy tale and these things happen, and second, not all princes have to marry members of a royal family, listing several familiar tales to illustrate the point. Gilles (1993) provides several examples of ways in which meanings such as this are built over time, across several discussions, using the exploratory talk characteristic of successful literature discussion groups.

In this final excerpt from their discussion, Todd invites the group to revisit the sex role expectations for characters in fairy tales. Again, he uses a direct question to elicit the responses of his peers, one of the few questions asked in the discussion.

42 TODD: Imagine if Petronella were a boy, would that change your attitude or something? Do you think he would act like Petronella and go out anyway? Or if he had two older sisters? And they thought he couldn't do anything, like even cook a bowl of spaghetti or some thing?

43 ERIK: Well, they wouldn't have him face eagles or anything. They would have him face a dragon or something.

44 JOHN: What would he throw at the enchanter? A bale of hay or a spear instead of a mirror or comb?

. . . .

49 SARAH: Why did she do it?

50 JOHN: She wanted to prove something to her mother: that she wasn't a weakling. That she was man enough to take on something daring . . .

51 ERIK: Yeah, strong enough for a man but gentle enough for a woman! [*Chuckles*]

52 TODD: She wanted to prove to her family that she could fit in, be part of the royal family. To fit in she had to do something weird.

53 JOHN: Yeah, like if it was a rag boy, a poor kid, he'd like go out and slay five dragons, then come back to town. And you'd be seen as a different person. They'd say, "Wow!"

54 ERIK: "Oh yeah, I'll show you!"

55 JEANNA: And Petronella's gonna come back with the real old guy.

56 JOHN: Yeah, her grandpa guy.

57 SARAH: Like they said she was going to seek her own fortune, but they didn't *say* they expect her to find a prince.

58 JEANNA: But that was kind of what she was thinking, hoping.

59 EVAN: Obviously, there's got to be a prince involved in a fairy tale.

Todd's question (line 42) invites others to share their opinions. Asking the question provides Todd with an opportunity to hear what his *peers* think as he sorts out what *he* thinks. In responding to Todd's question, the readers discussed what Petronella had to do to prove herself and fit into the expectations of her family. They contrasted this to what a poor child would have to do, explaining that the main character would have to do something "weird" in order to gain the admiration of others in the village. They also clarified that Petronella and her brothers set out to find their fortunes, not necessarily for Petronella to find a prince. Because this is a fairy tale, these readers expected the prince to be involved in Petronella's quest. Again, their knowledge of fairy tales supported their meaning-constructing process.

As the discussion continued, the readers explored what wizards or enchanters would look like in eighteenth-century America. They decided that since America was so clean and new at that time, an old enchanter would not be appropriate. And in today's America, if they encountered an enchanter or wizard who was an old man sitting alone near a convenience store, they probably wouldn't approach him for directions, and certainly wouldn't ask if there were anything they could do for him. This led to a discussion of one important way that Petronella was different from her brothers: she took the time to ask about the old man, and wasn't so quick to ride off to get her fortune. This singled her out as a special person in their eyes.

At Jean's request, the group began the final discussion session with a review of the elements of a fairy tale that are present in "Petronella." They listed the elements briefly, and added the comment that the enchanter was a "gatekeeper," but did not expand on his role. Jean then mentioned some things she had noticed in the story that let her know it was a more modern tale. She asked them to share their own observations. The students noted that one of the characters was wearing tennis shoes, that a crossword puzzle was depicted in one of the illustrations, that the prince was wearing purple pajamas, and that he had gone to "spend the weekend," which seemed like a modern phrase to them. They debated whether the enchanter, who had been waiting for many years for the right question to be asked, could have been included in a modern tale. They concluded that since the enchanter could still be there waiting today for someone to ask the question, it could be a modern tale.

The conversation moved next to consideration of the dragon pictures on every page. The group concluded that these were typical of fairy tales and that they were a symbol of Petronella's courage. They discussed other stories with repeated elements that don't really affect the story. The dragons in Petronella didn't really depict anything in the story, but seemed connected to it, since this was a fairy tale.

Over the two days of discussion, the group raised several topics from my "I wonder" list along with many more of their own. They explored the elements of fiction, particularly the unique characteristics of fairy tales, often making connections to the many other stories they had read. Specific details were brought out as students discussed the general events of the story, shared responses, and answered one another's questions. These readers drew upon their knowledge of the world, particularly the pressure to conform to family expectations, as they worked to understand character motives in this nontraditional tale. Essentially, they covered all the topics a fifth- or sixth-grade basal reading series would have asked of them, and several more.

The important distinction for me between covering the skills listed in the manual through teacher questioning on the one hand, and small-group discussions of literature, such as this one, on the other, is the control of the agenda. These students were able to use the small-group format to explore issues that intrigued them, to ask their own questions, to explore their own themes and conceptions of the author's purpose. They understand that reading is both an active process, in which the reader must work at constructing meaning, and a social process, in which discussion with others can shed light on the reading of *this* text while offering insights into ways of approaching *future* texts.

THE IMPORTANCE OF A PARADIGM SHIFT

Literature discussions like those illustrated by Kathryn Mitchell Pierce reflect the shift from a transmission paradigm of education to a transactional paradigm. In contrast, failure to understand that whole language requires a shift from a transmission to a transactional paradigm accounts for many unfortunate caricatures of whole language teaching.

For example, in trying to implement the writing process approach, some teachers have set aside Monday for prewriting, Tuesday for drafting, Wednesday for revising, Thursday for editing, and Friday for celebrating the writing. I once developed such a scheme myself. But now I realize that imposing such a Procrustean bed technique on the natural process of writing is a travesty of that process, and of whole language education. Requiring students to revise and edit every piece they attempt is similarly a violation of whole language principles: in this case, the principle of student ownership and decision making. We should scarcely be surprised if the writings produced under such artificial constraints fail to impress us as significantly better than those produced under the one-draft-only conditions previously so common. On the other hand, having students draft piece after piece of writing without helping them learn to revise and edit ignores the natural opportunities for developing skills in the context of authentic literacy experiences. It sells short the potential of whole language itself, as well as the potential of the students and their writing.

Not understanding that whole language is first and foremost a philosophy of education, many teachers and administrators think that whole language can be characterized as certain kinds of activities: silent reading and journal writing, for example; or writing multiple drafts of a piece ("process writing"); or using Big Books; or using literature instead of basals. All too often, teachers are observed "doing" process writing while violating the philosophy from which it derives, or using Big Books in very traditional ways while claiming to be "doing" whole language. By co-opting the label "whole language," such teachers manage to avoid recognizing that whole language teaching requires a shift in their belief systems.

There is nothing sacred or inherently "whole language" about any of these activities or materials, including Big Books. Now produced on the mass market as well as by numerous educational publishers, some Big Books have no literary merit and little educational value. Nor is there necessarily a great deal of educational value in reading even the better-quality Big Books to children. Teachers are not necessarily "doing" whole language just because they are reading Big Books to their students (Unsworth, 1988). What *can* make high quality Big Books educationally valuable, though, is using the Shared Book Experience or something similar— that is, using a teaching procedure that reflects key whole language principles.

The same is true with the use of literature: the *abuse* of literature can result if teachers still operate from a transmission paradigm and if they do not know children's literature and genuinely enjoy discussing it with their students. In the article "Literature-Based or Literature: Where Do We Stand?" Yvonne Freeman (1989) characterizes what can happen to literature in a so-called "literature-based" curriculum when teachers do not have the requisite understanding of whole language principles, of children's literature, and of how to engage children in discussing literature. Figure 9.16 presents a simplified version of Freeman's contrast between "literature-based" assumptions, on the one hand, and "literature assumptions," on the other. A transmission paradigm underlies the former assumptions about the use of literature in the classroom, while a transactional, whole language paradigm underlies the latter. Thus, as Figure 9.16 indicates, a literature-based curriculum may be characterized by the same old requirements that students all read the same selections, answer the same questions and do the same workbook pages, and glean someone else's predetermined meanings from

Literature-based	Literature
Prepackaged program	Separate trade books
Organized into grade levels	Not graded
Assigned to whole class or small groups	Individually chosen, or students are grouped according to choice
Packages include activities to complete	Students choose follow-up activities, if any
Predetermined questions	Students and teachers raise own questions
Questions assume that everyone should get same meaning from text, that there is one right answer	Questions assume that others may construct different meanings from text, that there is often no right answer
Students read to find someone else's meaning, answer someone else's questions	Students read to find their own meanings and answer their own questions; they learn from others by discussing the literature

Fɪɢᴜʀᴇ **9.16** *Assumptions underlying a "literature-based" compared with a "literature" curriculum (adapted from Y. S. Freeman, 1989)*

the selections they read. This is emphatically not whole language. (See Pace, 1991, for an excellent article expressing related concerns.)

As teachers, administrators, and publishers try to get on the whole language band-wagon, there is much that happens in the name of whole language that doesn't reflect the principles most central to it (Newman & Church, 1990; Weaver, 1990a, Chap. 1). In other words, all that's labeled or purported to be whole language isn't necessarily so.

GROWING IN THE TEACHING OF LITERATURE

As the foregoing discussion indicates, not all instruction that claims to be literature-based is indeed whole language. In fact, some of the commercially produced and teacher-made exercises and activities to accompany works of literature are at least as trivial and stultifying as the worst of basal reader worksheets. Such materials abuse and debase the literature, as well as insult and bore the students. However, one can hardly expect any-thing else when teachers are suddenly required to use trade books instead of basals without having the opportunity and needed support to grow into an understanding of various ways to share, discuss, experience, and even emulate literature in the classroom.

Perhaps one of the earliest signs of development from a transmission paradigm to-ward a transactional paradigm is teachers' downplaying of literal recall questions and increased use of questions that stimulate higher-order reasoning and divergent thinking. For example, a class of my preservice teachers in 1980 developed sets of cognitive mem-ory, convergent, divergent, and evaluative questions to use in discussing five junior novels (Weaver, 1981). At the time, the development of more sophisticated and demanding questions seemed innovative: it was far more respectful of students' intelligence than the sets of questions then typical of basal reader programs. More recently, teachers have been encouraged to develop a range of questions based on the "story grammar" of a narrative (see, for instance, the questions relating to "Petronella," on pp. 378–379). Many more suggestions for improving on basal lessons are offered in *Improving Basal Reading Instruction* (Winograd, Wixson, & Lipson, 1989); however, the educational par-adigm reflected in the book is still much more transmission than transactional.

A Core Literature Approach

A major step toward the transactional end of the continuum is what is sometimes called a core literature approach (Zarillo, 1989). While the books themselves are not neces-sarily designated by some outside authority as books that every child in the school or district should be exposed to (as in the California Literature Initiative—see California State Department of Education, 1987), the chosen books do serve as a core for gener-ating activities across the curriculum. At its transmission worst, such a core literature approach may be highly skills-oriented, with the literary work serving as something of an excuse for tangentially related skills activities, for which there is often no clear or justifiable motivation. For example, in my 1980 *Psycholinguistics and Reading*, one of the suggested activities relating to Maurice Sendak's *Chicken Soup with Rice* was "Have students study area, using rice. How many grains of rice does it take to measure out one centimeter? One decimeter? One meter?" (p. 273). It now seems abundantly clear that this activity, and some of the others, had little to justify it and bore little relationship to the work of literature. But at the time, such "integration" seemed innovative, and certainly better than teaching each area of the curriculum in isolation.

Using a work of literature as the core for meaningful activities is one of the ways teachers move significantly into whole language. Recently, for example, I delineated for kindergarten teachers in a nearby school system a detailed description of how various activities relating to the book *Stone Soup* (Ann McGovern's version) could further their newly developed, more holistic curriculum goals and objectives. Some of the activities that first graders carried out, with their teacher Tracy Cobb and with me, were making paper vegetables and using invented spelling to write each vegetable's name on its cut-out before adding it to a soup pot; dictating language experience sentences about what they put in the pot, and later rereading their chart; reading and illustrating their own booklet derived from the language experience chart; and dramatizing the story as they made stone soup. Throughout the sequence of activities, discussion focused on developing children's reading strategies, spelling awareness, and oral language abilities, the goal being to have the children better prepared to deal with new texts in more complex ways. Perhaps most significant is that reading, enjoying, and discussing the work were primary. This illustrates a core literature approach wherein the activities derive fairly naturally from the book; they seem more integral than contrived.

Moving outward from literature in this way may be one of the easiest ways for teachers to begin to grow into whole language. This in fact is the process documented in Regie Routman's popular *Transitions: From Literature to Literacy* (1988) and T. D. Johnson and Louis' *Bringing It All Together: A Program for Literacy* (1990), among many others. The books *Story S-t-r-e-t-c-h-e-r-s: Activities to Expand Children's Favorite Books* (Raines & Canady, 1989) and *More Story S-t-r-e-t-c-h-e-r-s* (Raines & Canady, 1991) are excellent resources for primary teachers wanting to use literature as a core for generating other learning activities, as well as a clear example of what we mean by a core literature approach. Another collection of ideas is *Booksharing: 101 Programs to Use with Preschoolers* (MacDonald, 1988). A valuable resource book with a more particular focus is *Fact, Fantasy, and Folklore: Expanding Language Arts and Critical Thinking Skills* (Lipson & Morrison, 1977), which suggests a variety of oral and written language activities to generate critical thinking about folktales and some of the issues they raise. Bette Bosma's *Fairy Tales, Fables, Legends, and Myths* (1992) is also especially valuable, with an extensive bibliography of the literature and demonstrations of how such traditional literature can generate art, music, drama, storytelling, improvisation, puppetry, and pantomime. Gare Thompson's *Teaching Through Themes* (1991) includes activities to accompany core literature books that are grouped according to topics ("themes").

A company called LINK (*L*anguage *I*nstruction *N*atural to *K*ids) offers LINK Paks on various picture and chapter books for children from kindergarten through grade seven. Scholastic's K–6 program *Bridges* is an example of a commercial program with one literary work per grade level intended as a core text. And the reading program *Journeys* (Ginn of Canada, the 1989 edition) suggests, for many stories, a variety of activities reflecting other areas or aspects of the curriculum. Indeed, these are only examples: most of the publishers of Big Books provide teaching guides that treat the books as core literature texts. Some of these companies also publish materials for students through grade 12, and often some of these books too can be treated as core texts. To obtain more information about such materials and programs, see the Literature Collections and Programs list at the back of this book.

Reading Literature Aloud

More and more teachers, however, are turning away from using literature in this way to simply sharing, discussing, experiencing, and emulating it with their students. Often inspired by Jim Trelease's *The Read-Aloud Handbook* (1989), whole language teachers typically read to their students every day, giving them the opportunity to enjoy books whose words and syntax might be beyond their ability to read by themselves, allowing them to savor the richness of literature dramatized by the human voice, and creating a community of learners who have shared authentic and meaningful literary experiences.

Joel Chaston, formerly a middle school teacher, claims that the best thing he did as a beginning teacher was read aloud to his sixth and seventh graders. The school in which he taught had the lowest reading scores in the district on the Iowa Tests. But even students who initially hated reading books came to recognize the power of literature and what it might have to say to them through the books Joel read aloud during class—works such as Mollie Hunter's *A Stranger Came Ashore*, E. L. Koningsburg's *From the Mixed-up Files of Mrs. Basil E. Frankweiler*, and Wilson Rawls' *Summer of the Monkeys*. Joel recalls one day in particular, when he was reading *A Stranger Came Ashore* to the "low" language arts group. They had come to a climactic moment in the book, with Nicol Anderson fighting the great Selkie, Finn Larson. The class was visibly upset when the bell rang (Weaver, Chaston, & Peterson, 1993).

Currently there are many books recorded on audiotape that can be purchased from local bookstores and educational publishers or borrowed from libraries: adult books as well as books for children and adolescents. (An extensive catalog of books on tape can be obtained from Recorded Books, Inc., 270 Skipjack Road, Prince Frederick, MD 20678; 1-800-638-1304.) While these cannot substitute for the sense of community created when the teacher reads aloud to a class, they can provide a worthwhile supplement. Recorded books are especially valuable for those whose reading ability falls short of their interest level, for such books can not only enable such readers to enjoy appropriate literature but also help them become more fluent readers through the experience of listening and reading along with the tape.

Experiencing Literature

As teachers grow into whole language, they seem increasingly to provide opportunities for students to experience literature through the oral, visual, and dramatic language arts. Students may engage in choral reading of a text, or even develop a readers theater production. They may pantomime the actions in a story or poem or visualize the details as the teacher reads it, act out the story with puppets, or reenact the entire story as informal drama. Sometimes they may use a published story as the basis for their own storytelling. Occasionally they may even dramatize a story more formally, or write and produce a play. Such activities, particularly when chosen by the students, can significantly enrich their appreciation of literature. (Some valuable teaching ideas are presented in Harste & Short, with Burke, 1988, but see especially Heinig, 1993.)

In narrative pantomime and guided visualization, students experience sights, sounds, textures, smells, and tastes called forth by the work of literature. Through imagination and movement, the literature becomes three-dimensional.

For example, Gene Zion's *The Sugar Mouse Cake* forms the basis for the script of a narrative pantomime by Cottrell (1987b). In this pantomime, all the students act out the role of Tom, the young ninth assistant to the chief pastry cook in the king's palace, who is about to bake a cake that he hopes will win him the job as the Chief Pastry Cook's replacement. The teacher acts as a sidecoach, narrating the script to be acted out by all the Toms:

> Tip-toe out into the night kitchen. Look around, check behind doors and around corners. Good, you have the entire kitchen to yourself. Feel the outside of the oven. Open the big oven door and check inside . . . empty and hot enough to bake a cake perfectly. You must hurry.
>
> Quickly but quietly open the cupboards and assemble all of the things you will need from the shelves—bowls, spoons, beaters, and pans. Set them on the counter. Now go to the pantry and find the ingredients for your cake: flour, sugar, butter, eggs, fruit, and nuts. Carry everything to the counter and carefully measure and sift the flour. Cream the sugar and butter together in the biggest bowl. Add the eggs, six of them, one at a time.
>
> You must work quickly but carefully if this is to be a prize-winning cake. You are working so hard you do not notice that your music box has fallen into the cake batter. (Cottrell, 1987, p. 90)

In addition to movement, this excerpt from the narrative pantomime involves several of the senses—including simulated taste, if "Tom" samples the batter while making the cake!

Narrative pantomime scripts could serve equally well for guided visualization: experiencing the sights, sounds, movements and such in the mind's eye, without the accompaniment of movement. Figure 9.17 presents a script based on "Petronella" and written specifically for guided visualization, to generate deepened appreciation of the character of Petronella and of the value of using sensory detail in one's own narrative writing. The script could also be used for narrative pantomime.

Narrative pantomime and guided visualization are modes of experiencing and enriching literature that have yet to become as widely practiced as choral reading and readers theater; yet they have even greater potential for encouraging students to temporarily inhabit the worlds created by works of literature (e.g., Heinig, 1993). Chapter 10, written by Ruth Heinig, presents more details on how to engage children in these and other dramatic language arts activities that enhance reading and enrich the appreciation of literature.

Preparation

It is important that the children be familiar with the story, so they know that Petronella accomplishes the tasks successfully, without being terrified or harmed.

As the teacher, you would first get children into a relaxed, receptive state. You might tell them to settle into a comfortable position, sitting straight but relaxed, with their hands on their desk, their eyes closed. You might have them take a few deep breaths, breathing slowly in and out, then give them directions for progressively relaxing each part of the body, beginning with the toes and working upwards. It can be particularly effective to imagine a warm liquid flowing down the arms and out to the fingertips. It may also help to have students imagine riding an escalator down and down, deeper and deeper into relaxation. At this point, you might assure students they are in a safe place; no harm can come to them. This accomplished, you can begin slowly reading the guided visualization, pausing at appropriate points while the students experience what has been described. Remember afterwards to bring students out of the guided visualization slowly, perhaps saying that they are to ride back up the escalator and awaken gradually as they count to five and telling them that they will return to the classroom alert and refreshed; then count to five very slowly.

Guided visualization

Now let yourself become Petronella, the daughter of King Peter the twenty-sixth and Queen Blossom. You are *there,* in the kingdom of Skyclear Mountain. You have left your brothers at the crossroads and gone on a quest to find a prince. At the home of Albion the enchanter you have found a prince, Prince Michael. He is sitting in the sun, trying to get a suntan. How do you feel about him? . . . Clearly he is selfish and lazy, but you are determined to carry through with your quest and rescue him from Albion.

In order to free the prince, you have offered to work for Albion. Now it is dark. . . . Albion leads you outside toward a stone building. He hasn't told you what task you must perform, but he *has* said that if you fail at the task, you will die. How do you feel, alone with Albion, being led through the dark night to goodness only knows what? . . . Now you have reached the building. The stone is cold and clammy as you lean up against it. . . . From around the door comes the smell of rotting straw, and you sense the presence of animals within. . . . How do you feel? . . . Do you and Albion say anything to each other? If so, what do you say? . . . Now Albion unbolts and opens the door. Inside are seven *huge* black dogs, larger than any you have ever seen or imagined. . . . "You must watch my hounds all night," Albion says. He closes and locks the door behind you. . . . Your eyes have scarcely begun to adjust to the dimmed light when the hounds begin to snarl and bark menacingly, showing their teeth. How do you feel? . . . What are you thinking? . . .

You remember that you are, after all, a real princess. . . . You screw up your courage and walk toward the dogs. You speak to them in a quiet voice. What do you say? Speak to them. . . . They stop snarling and sniff at your hands.

FIGURE 9.17   Guided visualization based on Petronella's tasks

Slowly, you reach forward and pat the head of the dog nearest you. He licks your hand. How do you feel now? . . . You pet the others in turn, letting them nudge you with their cold noses and lick your hands and face. They are lonely, you realize. Finally you sit down on the floor. Two of the hounds put their heads in your lap; the others snuggle up as close as they can get. Now how do you feel? . . . You sit and stroke their short, smooth fur, talking to them softly, and singing lullabies. What do you say to them? Talk to them, sing to them, in your imagination. . . .

Hours have now passed. Just as you are about to fall asleep exhausted, the sun streams through the cracks around the door. It is morning, and you know that you have succeeded at the task. How do you feel now? . . .

Figure 9.17   Continued

Literature Study Groups

In the earlier description of literature discussion groups and how they can foster the development of reading strategies and critical thinking, I mentioned literature study groups without clarifying the distinction between the two.

In the kinds of *literature discussion groups* or *literature circles* described in Short and Pierce (1990) as well as in Harste and Short (with Burke, 1988), the agenda is broad. Literature discussion groups may involve discussion not only of the story and the literature, but also of readers' responses and connections to the literature, as well as the reading strategies they used. Many educators using literature discussion groups focus on the reading process as well as the literature itself and feel that this time for discussion is a crucial part of the reading curriculum. Also, such discussions are a natural way of experiencing and exploring the text sets often incorporated into the study of a topic or theme drawn from other content areas (see the section below). Figure 9.18 includes books that help teachers at various levels conduct literature discussions, literature study groups, or what some teachers call "readers' workshop" (MacKenzie, 1992).

Several educators in Arizona (Peterson & Eeds, 1990; and Karen Smith, whose classroom was filmed in the previously mentioned videotape from the Center for Establishing Dialogue) have given a somewhat different direction to their *literature study groups*. These study groups attend more to the literary work as an artifact, with emphasis on such aspects as characterization, plot development, symbols and other literary devices, and style. Such discussions in effect transform the nature of literary study.

Figure 9.19, for example, illustrates a dialogue among fifth-grade children discussing *The Secret Garden* by Frances Hodgson Burnett. Exploring together how Mary and the garden resemble one another, they come to recognize the symbolic function of the garden in the story, as well as to explore character change.

Literature and the Whole Curriculum

Increasingly, educators are documenting the power of literature to evoke feelings, memories, and images that serve as a stimulus to powerful writing. For example, Lucy

Theory and general (all levels)

MacKenzie, T. (Ed.). (1992). *Readers' workshops: Bridging literature and literacy.* Toronto: Irwin.

Rosenblatt, L. (1983). *Literature as exploration.* 4th ed. New York: Modern Language Association. (Originally published in 1938).

Rosenblatt, L. (1978). *The reader, the text, the poem.* Carbondale, IL: Southern Illinois University Press.

Purves, A. C. (1991). *The idea of difficulty in literature.* Albany, NY: State University of New York Press.

Emphasis on elementary

Harste, J., Short, K., with Burke, C. (1988). *Creating classrooms for authors: The reading-writing connection.* Portsmouth, NH: Heinemann.

Peetoom, A. (1993). *ConneXions: Inviting engagements with books.* Richmond Hill, Ontario: Scholastic.

Peterson, R., & Eeds, M. (1990). *Grand conversations: Literature groups in action.* Richmond Hill, Ontario: Scholastic.

Pierce, K. M., & Gilles, C. (Eds.). (1994). *Cycles of meaning: Conversation, story and dialogue in learning communities.* Portsmouth, NH: Heinemann.

Short, K. G., & Pierce, K. M. (Eds.). (1990). *Talking about books: Creating literate communities.* Portsmouth, NH: Heinemann.

Emphasis on middle school/junior high

Atwell, N. (1987). *In the middle: Reading, writing, and learning with adolescents.* Portsmouth, NH: Heinemann.

Rief, L. (1991). *Seeking diversity: Language arts with adolescents.* Portsmouth, NH: Heinemann.

Emphasis on junior high/high school/college

Andrasick, K. D. (1990). *Opening texts: Using writing to teach literature.* Portsmouth, NH: Boynton/Cook-Heinemann.

Beach, R., Green, J. L., Kamil, M. L., & Shanahan, T. (Eds.) (1992). *Multidisciplinary perspectives on literacy research.* Urbana, IL: National Council of Teachers of English.

Bogdan, D., & Straw, S. B. (1990). *Beyond communication: Reading comprehension and criticism.* Portsmouth, NH: Boynton/Cook-Heinemann.

Karolides, N. J. (Ed.). (1992). *Reader response in the classroom.* New York: Longman.

Nelms, B. F. (1988). *Literature in the classroom: Readers, texts, and contexts.* Urbana, IL: National Council of Teachers of English.

Probst, R. E. (1988). *Response and analysis: Teaching literature in junior and senior high school.* Portsmouth, NH: Boynton/Cook-Heinemann.

FIGURE 9.18   References on engaging with literature in the classroom

TEACHER: Since we're talking about Mary and changing, let's talk about Mary and the garden.

RANDY: It started to grow.

TEACHER: The garden did?

RANDY: Yeah. It was like magic. It just started to blossom and stuff. The way she took care of it and stuff.

SHAWNA: I like the way they described how it wasn't dead but it was wickering or something.

RANDY: I think . . . I think . . .

SHAWNA: When you break them in half they weren't dead. They were all dried out, but there were still some roots getting ready to grow—wickered or something like that.

RANDY: Wickered! I think wickered means still alive.

SHAWNA: On the outside it was all dried out but when you break them in half it's still good and they grow as soon as the right time and season comes.

RANDY: Like it's green! Like when you pick a fruit it looks ripe on the outside and you end up biting it and on the inside it's all green.

SHAWNA: Nasty!

TEACHER: Except this is the other way around though because she's saying it looks bad on the outside but it's good on the inside.

RANDY: Yeah. Yeah.

TEACHER: I'm thinking about people when you say that.

SHAWNA: (*looking askance*) You break people in half? [*Both children laugh.*]

RANDY: No, like if they're still alive and they look dead, they'd bury' em and they'd end up buried alive or something.

TEACHER: Hmmm.

SHAWNA: You see that on a lot of soap operas.

RANDY: Only now they have different things to tell to see your heartbeat, and if it goes then you're dead.

TEACHER: I'm thinking as you say that, about the characters in the book.

SHAWNA: (*a pause—then a look of dawning*) It seems like Martha, I mean Mary . . . She was like real mean and nasty on the outside but then later on in the story she taught Colin how to walk.

RANDY: And her outside . . . her inside came to the outside. Like she was mean on the outside but inside she was nice. And then after awhile her inside came out.

SHAWNA: All of the good came out. That's when she taught Colin to walk and started taking care of the plants.

TEACHER: (*writing on a chart which lists insights about character*) I want to hold on to this . . . were there other characters you noticed changing?

FIGURE **9.19** *Transcript from literature discussion of* The Secret Garden *with a group of fifth graders (Peterson & Eeds, 1990, pp. 63–65)*

Calkins describes a teacher who opened the floodgates of children's lives by reading them poignant and thought-provoking stories like *Roll of Thunder, Hear My Cry*, by Mildred Taylor, and *A Taste of Blackberries*, by Doris Buchanan Smith (see Calkins, 1990, p. 21). The stories, she said, tapped into the pain in her own life and in the children's. Soon, they started telling and writing their own stories as never before. Shelley Harwayne's *Lasting Impressions* (1992) similarly testifies to the power of literature in the writing curriculum.

Of course, silent reading of literature also occurs in whole language classrooms—and not just during a "sustained silent reading" time that is separate from the rest of the curriculum, or that is part of a separate block called "language arts."

In whole language classrooms, literature becomes part of social studies and science as well. For example, bibliographies from the monthly *Book Links*, a publication of the American Library Association, group books into related sets with a thematic focus that often reflects topics and themes in social studies. (See also such commercial programs as Scholastic's *Bookshelf* for grades K–2, and the Wright Group's Sunshine series for grades K–5. These and other programs are listed in "Literature Collections and Programs" at the back of this book.) Literature makes history come alive and reveals the excitement of scientific invention and discovery (e.g., Von Dras, 1990; Short & Armstrong, 1993).

Because it is important to combine literary treatment of various topics with factual treatment, Figure 9.20 includes resources for locating both fiction and nonfiction for children. Another useful book is E. B. Freeman and Person's *Using Nonfiction Trade Books in the Elementary Classroom* (1992). A CD-ROM program, *Matchmaker,* locates literature on specific themes.

Literature Discussion with Text Sets

In the section on growing into the teaching of reading, we have already considered how literature discussion groups have become an integral part of many whole language classrooms, replacing basal reading groups. As described, the students in a group would all read and discuss the same book.

However, discussion groups can alternatively deal with what have come to be called "text sets": single copies of several related texts to be shared and discussed by the group (Harste & Short, with Burke, 1988). The point is to make connections among the texts—often, to notice significant similarities and differences. Text sets can foster both an appreciation of literature and the exploration of topics and themes across the curriculum.

At first, the teacher may want to read the books aloud to students, engaging the class in discussion of each book, then relating them as each subsequent book in the set is read. Once students are accustomed to making connections among books, text sets can readily be used in literature discussion groups. Each student can read a different text and share it with the group, or the group can rotate the texts prior to, or in the course of, discussing them.

Abrahamson, R. F., & Carter, B. (Eds.) (1988). *Books for you: A booklist for senior high students.* Urbana, IL: National Council of Teachers of English.

Benedict, S. (1991). *Beyond words: Picture books for older readers and writers.* Portsmouth, NH: Heinemann.

Booth, D., Swartz, L., Zola, M. (1987). *Choosing children's books.* Markham, Ontario: Pembroke.

Bosma, B. (1992). *Fairy tales, fables, legends, and myths: Using folk literature in your classroom.* New York: Teachers College Press.

Dreyer, S. (1977–89). *The bookfinder: A guide to children's literature about the needs and problems of youth ages 2–15.* 4 vols. Circle Pines, MN: American Guidance Service.

Freeman, J. (1990). *Books kids will sit still for.* (2nd ed.). New Providence, NJ: Bowker.

Gagnon, A., & Gagnon, A. (Eds.) (1988). *Canadian books for young people/Livres Canadien poor la jeunesse* (4th ed.). Toronto: University of Toronto Press.

Gillespie, J. T., & Naden, C. J. (Eds.). (1990). *Best books for children: Preschool through grade 6* (4th ed.). New York: Bowker.

Harris, V. J. (Ed.) (1993). *Teaching multicultural literature in grades K–8.* Norwood, MA: Christopher-Gordon.

Huck, C. (1992). *Children's literature in the elementary school* (5th ed.). Orlando: Harcourt Brace Jovanovich.

Jensen, J., & Roser, N. (1993). *Adventuring with books: A booklist for pre-K–grade 6.* (10th ed.). (Earlier editions annotate earlier books.)

Kennedy, D. M., Spangler, S. S., & Vanderwerf, M. A. (1990). *Science and technology in fact and fiction: A guide to children's books.* New Providence, NJ: Bowker.

Kobrin, B. (1988). *Eyeopeners! How to choose and use children's books about real people, places, and things.* New York: Penguin.

Landsberg, M. (1986). *Michele Landsberg's guide to children's books.* Toronto: Penguin.

Lima, C. W., & Lima, J. A. (Eds.). (1989). *A to zoo: Subject access to children's picture books.* (3rd ed.). New Providence, NJ: Bowker.

Moir, H., Cain, M., & Prosak-Beres, L. (Eds.) (1990). *Collected perspectives: Choosing and using books for the classroom.* Norwood, MA: Christopher-Gordon.

Norton, D. (1991). *Through the eyes of a child: An introduction to children's literature* (3rd ed.). New York: Macmillan.

Oppenheim, J., Brenner, B., & Boegehold, B. D. (1986). *Choosing books for kids: How to choose the right book for the right child at the right time.* New York: Ballantine.

Osborn, S. (1987). *Free (and almost free) things for teachers.* New York: Perigee Books.

Peterson, B. (1991). Selecting books for beginning readers. In D. E. DeFord, C. A. Lyons, & G. S. Pinnell (Eds.), *Bridges to literacy: Learning from Reading Recovery.* Portsmouth, NH: Heinemann.

Figure **9.20** *Resources for locating fiction and nonfiction for children and adolescents (drawn, in part, from bibliographies compiled by Joel Chaston, Southwest Missouri State University, and Marcie Bovetz, The Wright Company)*

Rudman, M. K. (Ed.) (1993). *Children's literature: Resource for the classroom* (2nd ed.). Norwood, MA: Christopher-Gordon.

Sinclair, P. (1992). *E for environment: An annotated bibliography of children's books with environmental themes.* New Providence, NJ: Bowker.

Subject guide to children's books in print. New Providence, NJ: Bowker. (Annual.)

Sutherland, Z. (1986). *The best in children's picture books: The University of Chicago guide to children's literature, 1979–1984.* Chicago: University of Chicago Press.

Sutherland, Z., & Arbuthnot, M. H. (1991). *Children and books* (8th ed.). New York: Harper Collins.

Trelease, J. (1989). *The new read-aloud handbook.* New York: Penguin.

VanMeter, V. (1990). *American history for children and young adults: An annotated bibliographic index.* Englewood, CO: Libraries Unlimited.

Webb, C. A. (Ed.) (1993). *Your reading: A booklist for junior high and middle school students.* (8th ed.). Urbana, IL: National Council of Teachers of English. (Earlier editions annotate earlier books.)

Wilms, D. M., ed. (1985) *Science books for children: Selections from* Booklist, 1976–1983. Chicago: American Library Association.

Winkel, L. (1988). *The elementary school library collection: A guide to books and other media.* (16th ed.). Williamsburg, PA: Brodart.

Wittig, A. J. (1989). *U.S. government publications for the school media center.* Englewood, CO: Libraries Unlimited.

Reviews of Literature

Book Links

Published bimonthly
Booklist Publications
American Library Association
50 E. Huron Street
Chicago, IL 60611

Includes articles and book reviews. Especially valuable for its reviews of books on different topics.

The Horn Book Guide to Children's and Young Adult Books

Consists of a book published twice a year
The Horn Book
14 Beacon Street
Boston, MA 02108

FIGURE **9.20**   *Continued*

This is the most comprehensive source of reviews of new books for children and young adults. Books are arranged by grade level, genre, and subject; includes several different indexes. Each book is rated, from outstanding to acceptable.

The New Advocate: For Those Involved with Young People and Their Literature

4 issues per year
Christopher-Gordon Publishers, Inc.
480 Washington Street
Norwood, MA 02062

Some book reviews are included in this journal concerned with the writing, publication, analysis, and teaching of literature for young people.

The WEB: Wonderfully Exciting Books

4 issues per year
The WEB
Ohio State University College of Education
200 Ramseyer Hall
29 West Woodruff
Columbus, Ohio 43210-1177

The center spread in each issue is a teaching web focused on activities that center around a book, group of books, genre, or theme. Includes comprehensive book reviews, with teaching ideas.

The Five Owls

6 bimonthly issues per year
The Five Owls, Inc.
2004 Sheridan Avenue South
Minneapolis, MN 55405

Includes in-depth book reviews, practical ideas for using books with children, specialized bibliographies, as well as articles and interviews.

The Kobrin Letter, Concerning Children's Books about Real People, Places, and Things

7 issues per year
The Kobrin Letter
732 Greer Road
Palo Alto, CA 94303

This is the only publication dealing exclusively with the review and recommendation of children's nonfiction. Several themes or topics are dealt with in each issue.

Figure 9.20 Continued

Harste & Short, (with Burke, 1988) offer practical suggestions for organizing and conducting discussions of text sets. In addition, they provide examples of text sets illustrating all but one of the following priciples for assembling text sets. Among other possibilities, text sets can consist of:

1. Variations of a single folktale
2. Different cultural versions of the same folktale
3. Modern retellings of the same or different folktales
4. Several books by the same author or illustrator
5. The same text, with different illustrators
6. Books with similar structures
7. Books in the same genre
8. Books with the same characters
9. Books reflecting the same culture
10. Books on a certain topic or theme

Particularly when a topic or theme is the focus of the text set, the "texts" need not be limited to fiction and poetry or drama, the kinds of texts we often define as literature. They can include biography, autobiography, nonfiction of all sorts, and even magazines, newspapers, maps, catalogues, menus—in short whatever might be relevant to a theme or topic.

The following are some examples of text sets, organized according to different principles. Most of the books are picture books:

Same author

Rylant, Cynthia. 1982. *When I Was Young in the Mountains.* New York: E. P. Dutton.
Rylant, Cynthia. 1983. *Miss Maggie.* New York: E. P. Dutton.
Rylant, Cynthia. 1984. *Waiting to Waltz: A Childhood.* New York: Bradbury. [poems]
Rylant, Cynthia. 1985. *The Relatives Came.* New York: Bradbury.
[These books could also form part of a set of picture books on memoirs; see p. 370 for other titles, and Calkins, 1990 for still more.]

Different cultural versions of the same folktale

Climo, Shirley. (1989). *The Egyptian Cinderella.* Illus. Ruth Hellar. New York: Harper Collins. [Egypt]
Climo, Shirley. (1993). *The Korean Cinderella.* Illus. Ruth Hellar. New York: Harper Collins. [Korea]
Hooks, William. (1987). *Moss Gown.* Illus. Donald Carrick. New York: Clarion. [North Carolina]
Huck, Charlotte. (1989). *Princess Furball.* Illus. Anita Lobel. New York. William Morrow. [Germany]
Louie, Ai-Ling. (1982). *Yeh-Shen: A Cinderella Story from China.* Illus. Ed Young. New York: Philomel. [China]

Martin, Rafe, & Shannon, David. (1992). *The Rough-Face Girl.* New York: G. P. Putnam's Sons. [Algonquin, from Canada]

Perrault, Charles. (1985). *Cinderella.* Retold by Amy Ehrich. Illus. Susan Jeffers. New York: Dial. [France]

Steptoe, John. (1987). *Mufaro's Beautiful Daughters: An African Tale.* New York: Lothrop, Lee, & Shepard. [Africa]

Vuong, Lynnette Dyer. (1982). *The Brocaded Slipper and Other Vietnamese Tales.* Illus. Vo-Dinh Mai. Reading, MA: Addison-Wesley.

Modern retellings of different folktales

Berenzy, Alix. (1989). *A Frog Prince.* New York: Henry Holt.

Briggs, Raymond. (1970). *Jim and the Beanstalk.* New York: Puffin.

Cochrane, Orin. (1988). *Cinderella Chant.* Winnipeg: Whole Language Consultants. Distributed in the U.S. by Richard C. Owen Publishers. [Big book, small books]

Dahl, Roald. (1982). *Revolting Rhymes.* Illus. Quentin Blake. New York: Knopf.

French, Fiona. (1986). *Snow White in New York.* New York: Oxford.

Ludski, Trevor, and Greg Martin. (1989). *Little Red.* Markham, Ontario: Markon Press.

McKissack, Patricia C. (1986). *Flossie and the Fox.* Illus. Rachael Isadora. NY: Dial. [rural south retelling of Little Red Riding Hood]

Nikly, Michelle. (1981). *The Princess on the Nut, Or the Curious Courtship of the Son of the Princess on the Pea.* Illus. Jean Chaverie. Boston: Faber and Faber.

Scieszka, Jon. (1989). *The True Story of the Three Little Pigs! by A Wolf.* New York: Viking Penguin.

Scieszka, Jon. (1991). *The Frog Prince, Continued.* Illus. Steve Johnson. New York: Viking Penguin.

Turkle, Brinton. (1976). *Deep in the Forest.* Boston: Houghton Mifflin. [wordless picture book; reversal of the bear and human roles in Goldilocks]

Vozar, David. (1993). *Yo, Hungry Wolf! A Nursery Rap.* Illus. Betsy Lewin. New York: Doubleday.

Yolen, Jane. (1981). *Sleeping Ugly.* Illus. Diane Stanley. New York: Coward-McCann.

Traditional male/female roles reconsidered via traditional and modern fairy tales and related poetry

Traditional roles

Hodges, Margaret. (1990). *The Kitchen Knight: A Tale of King Arthur.* Illus. Trina Schart Hyman. New York: Holiday House.

Huck, Charlotte. (1989). *Princess Furball.* Illus. Anita Lobel. New York: William Morrow.

Nontraditional roles

Berenzy, Alix. (1989). *A Frog Prince.* New York: Henry Holt. [The frog rejects the haughty princess and sets out in search of a princess who will accept and love him; he finally finds a frog princess and they marry.]

Browne, Anthony. (1986). *Piggybook.* New York: Knopf. [At first, the wife/mother figuratively carries her husband and children piggyback, because they aren't doing any of the housework. But after she leaves them to fend for themselves, they learn to do their share. This isn't a fairy tale, but it's too good to miss!]

Dahl, Roald. (1982). *Revolting Rhymes.* Illus. Quentin Blake. New York: Knopf. [These poems are all take-offs on traditional fairy tales.]

McKissack, Patricia C. (1986). *Flossie and the Fox.* Illus. Rachael Isadora. New York: Dial. [In this retelling of the Red Riding Hood tale, Flossie outwits the fox.]

Munsch, Robert N. (1980). *The Paper Bag Princess.* Illus. Michael Martchenko. Buffalo, NY, and Willowdale, Ontario: Firefly. [As in "Petronella," the princess rescues the prince, only to decide he is not worthy of her.]

Roberts, Tom. (1990). *The Three Little Pigs.* Illus. David Jorgensen. Westport, Conn.: Rabbit Ears. [The little pigs are female, so the female outwits the male.]

Scieszka, Jon. (1991). *The Frog Prince, Continued.* Illus. Steve Johnson. New York: Viking Penguin. [Humorously introduces the stereotype of the nagging wife and the henpecked husband, and more broadly the theme of how to get along in a marriage or relationship.]

Viorst, Judith. (1981). *If I were in Charge of the World, and Other Worries.* New York: Aladdin. [Book of poetry, with four poems that are take-offs on traditional fairy tales and their stereotypes.]

Williams, Jay. (1973). *Petronella.* Illus. Friso Henstra. New York: Parents' Magazine Press.

Williams, Jay. (1978). *The Practical Princess and Other Liberating Fairy Tales.* New York: Scholastic. [Includes the story "Petronella," originally published as a picture book and reprinted in an appendix at the back of this book. All the stories have nontraditional heroes or heroines, with "The Practical Princess" perhaps the best for this text set.]

Eating (with themes such as being greedy, being a finicky eater).

Adoff, Arnold. (1979). *Eats Poems.* New York: Lothrup, Lee & Shepard.

Barrett, Judi. (1978). *Cloudy With A Chance of Meatballs.* Illus. Ron Barrett. New York: Atheneum.

Carle, Eric. (1981). *The Very Hungry Caterpillar.* New York: Philomel. [Scholastic has reprinted this as a Big Book, with accompanying small books]

Cole, William, ed. (1981). *Poem Stew.* New York: Lippincott.

Cowley, Joy. (1988). *Greedy Cat.* Wellington, New Zealand. Department of Education. Distributed in the U.S. by Richard C. Owen Publishers. [Big book, small books]

Ehlert, Lois. (1989). *Eating the Alphabet: Fruits and Vegetables from A to Z.* San Diego: Harcourt Brace Jovanovich.

Ehlert, Lois. (1990). *Growing Vegetable Soup.* San Diego: Harcourt Brace Jovanovich.

Friedman, Ina R. (1987). *How My Parents Learned to Eat.* Illus. Allen Say. Boston: Houghton Mifflin.

Gelman, Rita Golden. (1977). *More Spaghetti, I Say!* New York: Scholastic. [Big book, small books]

Hoban, Russell. (1964). *Bread and Jam for Frances.* New York: Harper & Row.

Sendak, Maurice. (1962). *Chicken Soup with Rice.* New York: Harper & Row.

Seuss, Dr. [Theodore Geissel]. (1960). *Green Eggs and Ham.* New York: Random House.

Sharmat, Mitchell. (1980). *Gregory the Terrible Eater.* New York: Four Winds.

Some of these literature texts could be complemented by non-literary texts—in a unit on nutrition, for example.

Clearly, there is no given number of texts that can constitute a "set." There may be as few as three or four, or as many as the teacher and class together compile, perhaps building collaboratively from a small set introduced by the teacher. The important point is that there be interrelationships that invite discussion among the books (Peetoom, 1993). In *Theme Exploration: A Journey of Discovery* (Weaver, Chaston, & Peterson, 1993), Joel Chaston's chapter on the first graders' study of weather nicely illustrates how a text set can grow with the interests of students and teacher.

An innovative program that includes literature and non-fiction together in text sets is Scholastic of Canada's *RefleXions*. This "unprogram" may be the last language arts program teachers will ever want, because it guides teachers into becoming competent whole language professionals through demonstration, discussion, and invitation, rather than through directives (Peetoom, 1992, 1993; see "Literature Collections and Programs," at the back of this book).

The Teaching of Literature Comes of Age

The epitome of whole language involvement with literature consists, then, of at least these components: reading aloud to students and providing opportunities for them to experience literature through the oral language arts, providing for individual reading, conducting reading-writing workshops and literature discussion or study groups, and including literature texts as an integral part of the entire curriculum (see Figure 9.21). The key is that the literature is read and appreciated primarily for its human and humane and aesthetic values, not for some utilitarian purpose. We read and talk about literature together because it introduces us to other times, places, and peoples; heightens our sensitivity to others; offers alternative perspectives on life; excites our aesthetic sensibilities and creative urges; creates a bond among us; and, most of all, touches our hearts and enriches our lives.

Transmission			**Transactional**
sophisticated questions requiring higher-order reasoning and divergent thinking	→ work of literature serves as core for various activities across the curriculum	→ programs involving wide reading of literature	→ various authentic literature experiences: reading aloud to students; reading/writing workshops; literature discussion groups; experiencing literature through oral language; wide reading of literature across the whole curriculum

FIGURE 9.21   *Growing in the teaching of literature*

Paradoxically, when we have fully grown into the teaching of literature, we are not really teaching it at all: we are experiencing, sharing, and exploring it with our students.

GROWING IN THEME STUDY

Just as teachers often grow into a whole language concept of teaching writing and reading, so they may grow gradually into an understanding of what it means to adopt a thematic approach based upon whole language principles. By "thematic approach," I mean that in which a topic or so-called theme provides the focus for study. Typically, these themes derive from topics in social studies and/or science: themes (topics) like the family, weather, animal habits and habitats, life cycles, flight, the American Revolution, slavery, the environment, the effect of technology on society, and so forth. Or the themes may be broader, inviting multidisciplinary perspectives: change, for example, or conflict. The most interesting themes, particularly beyond the primary years, are often those that give rise to difficult questions and issues, such as how to reconcile the needs of the environment with the demands of technology.

I would like to suggest three progressively sophisticated concepts of theme study, along a continuum from a transmission to a transactional paradigm, with theme units giving way to theme exploration and ultimately to theme cycles, as students become increasingly responsible for making decisions about their own learning (see Figure 9.22). A *theme unit* is teacher-oriented, with the topic predetermined, the teacher responsible for planning and organizing, and the goals reflecting those of the teacher or the curriculum. At the other end of the continuum are *theme cycles,* wherein teachers and students together brainstorm to determine topics and questions to be explored;

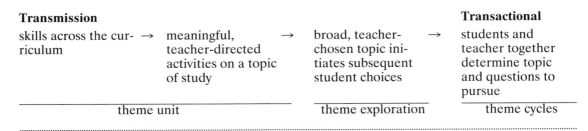

Transmission			Transactional
skills across the curriculum $\rightarrow$	meaningful, teacher-directed activities on a topic of study $\rightarrow$	broad, teacher-chosen topic initiates subsequent student choices $\rightarrow$	students and teacher together determine topic and questions to pursue
theme unit		theme exploration	theme cycles

FIGURE **9.22** *Growing in theme study*

together plan, organize, and reorganize; and together determine and redetermine their learning goals. We might call this an inquiry or "quest" (Tchudi, 1987) approach to theme exploration (see also Short & Burke, 1991).

Theme Units

Potentially more effective than the isolation of each curricular area from the others is what Altwerger has described as the "theme unit" (Altwerger & Saavedra, 1989). Often, a theme unit consists of prepackaged materials that include unit objectives and how they can be evaluated, as well as step-by-step details for daily lesson plans. Examples are the thematic units published in the 1970s by the National Council of Teachers of English (e.g., Spann & Culp, 1977), followed by Joy Moss' *Focus Units in Literature* (1984), which is less detailed in telling teachers what they might do. A more recent example is the *Whole Language Sourcebook*, one for grades K–2, one for grades 3–4, (Baskwill & Whitman, 1986, 1988), and one for grades 5–6 (Baskwill & Baskwill, 1991) though these offer suggestions and examples rather than prescriptions.

At the transmission extreme, a theme unit might be nothing more than a topic used as an excuse for a variety of traditional activities designed to develop skills in reading, writing, and the oral language arts, as well as to meet specific curricular objectives in other areas. For example, Bess Altwerger of Towson State University in Baltimore tells of a "bear" unit that one of her best students prepared a few years ago. Many of the activities had nothing substantive to do with bears. "Bear math," for example, consisted of problems like "If papa bear has three ice cream cones, mama bear has two ice cream cones, and baby bear has one ice cream cone, how many ice cream cones do they have all together?" (however, the problems were written in columnar form, not in story form). Similarly, one of my outstanding students just a few years ago produced a unit on caterpillars, with equally irrelevant "worm math" problems. Bess and I have both admitted publicly that we were not yet clear enough in our own minds about the inappropriateness of such a concept of theme study to have led our students to recognize beforehand how such activities reflect a trivialization of the concept.

The theme unit, then, may involve nothing more revolutionary than a skills curriculum superficially organized around a topic. On the other hand, it may reflect a much more creative integration of writing, reading, and oral language activities into study of a chosen topic. For example: in a social studies unit on Japan, one teacher wrote a script for a narrative pantomime of waking up and starting the day as a Japanese youth, next led her students in this informal creative drama activity, then had them write as if they were a Japanese child going through this daily routine. During a study of Columbus' "discovery" of America, a third-grade teacher had her students write from the point of view of one of the reluctant sailors on Columbus' ship. A preservice teacher wrote a guided visualization to encourage her students to experience what it was like to be a slave escaping along the Underground Railway, then asked them to use their imaginations to continue the journey through writing. A group of preservice teachers led students to visualize and experience the despair of the winter at Valley Forge as if they were Washington's soldiers camped there, then had them write letters home to their parents—while sitting on the ground (the floor) and writing by firelight (candlelight).

These, of course, are only a few examples of integrative activities that might be part of a thematic unit. Ten years ago, two of my students developed and taught to fifth graders, two mornings a week for eight weeks, a unit on the American Revolution. As a basis for the unit, they used a core book, *Johnny Tremain* by Esther Forbes, about a young man apprenticed to the silversmith Paul Revere. The two preservice teachers developed a variety of activities and engaged their students in a wealth of experiences that would help them appreciate the novel and understand the Revolution and the period of time in which it took place. The students made a time-line of pictures depicting major events of the Revolution, acted out the courtroom scene from Johnny Tremain, wrote letters to the editor either for or against the Boston Tea Party and related anti-British activities, listened and watched as a silversmith demonstrated how to pour silver, learned songs and dances from the Revolutionary period (with the help of the music and physical education teachers), experienced food prepared according to colonial recipes, and ultimately produced their own edition of the *Boston Observer* newspaper, as it might have appeared in the days of Johnny Tremain and the American Revolution.

Similarly, when Joel Chaston first taught in the public schools, he developed a four-week unit on Medieval life for his sixth-grade classroom. Drawing upon a number of children's books, including David Macauley's *Castle* and Aliki's *A Medieval Feast*, his students designed their own coats of arms, built their own castles, role-played the parts of kings, knights, serfs, and so forth.

These are examples of theme units at their absolute best, with high teacher input and often high student involvement.

From a whole language point of view, however, what is typically minimal or missing from such thematic units is the element of student choice, of ownership. Even though the preservice teachers demonstrated flexibility in responding to the demonstrated needs of the students, and even though the students engaged in a variety of stimulating activities, the choice of activities was always the teachers', not the students'. The same was true with Joel's unit on medieval life. Furthermore, "Such preplanning means that the teacher (or the unit planner) has set the problems, identified the major ideas, organized the material, and found the resources. The teacher [or unit developer], that is, did most of the problem solving and therefore the learning" (Edelsky, Altwerger, & Flores, 1991, p. 66).

Theme Exploration

In *Theme Exploration: A Voyage of Discovery,* I described an integrative unit on robots that Joel Chaston and I once started to develop. Our plan was a step beyond theme units, in terms of student ownership. As teachers, we prepared activities to introduce possible subtopics for exploration, but then planned to have the students decide what particular subtopics or issues to pursue, how to pursue them, and how to share what they had learned (Weaver, Chaston, & Peterson, 1993, pp. 7–12).

This intended theme study on robots was similar in process to the *actual* theme exploration that Joel Chaston and Nora Wolf undertook in her first-grade class, and that Scott Peterson and I undertook in his fourth-grade class. On an early visit to the first-grade class, Joel introduced the topic of weather through Ezra Jack Keats' *The Snowy Day*; that is, the teachers determined the topic beforehand and carried out an initiating activity. But through the ensuing discussion, which touched on a variety of weather-related topics, it became apparent that the children were most interested in their own experiences with weather and its impact on them personally. This discussion, and a brainstorm session in which they chose the kinds of weather they wanted to study, shaped the rest of the project. With the fourth graders, Scott and I engaged the class in activities to introduce the topic that we, as teachers, had chosen: the future. But the major subtopics—the environment, technology, and social problems of the future— were delineated by the students, and they further determined what to pursue within these subtopics. What we did is similar to the description of how to do theme study in *Learning and Loving It* (Gamberg et al., 1988), except that our theme explorations were not quite so controlled by the teacher and were somewhat more responsive, I think, to the students' ideas.

In the book documenting our experiences, we chose to call these projects "theme exploration" in an attempt to characterize theme study in which students have a significant degree of ownership. The term "exploration" is meant to suggest that there is no prepackaged or predetermined unit: the theme study evolves as teachers and students negotiate the curriculum. Long-range planning is mostly replaced by replanning on a day-to-day basis. Skills are taught as they are needed to carry out the activities chosen by students (Weaver, Chaston, & Peterson, 1993).

Theme Cycles

A still further step toward actualizing the whole language principle of ownership is what Bess Altwerger characterizes as *theme cycles*. Taking into account bottom-line curricular requirements as well as their own interests, together the teacher and students brainstorm possible topics for extended study; together, they determine the questions, locate the resources, and pursue their line of inquiry. Theme cycles "consist of a chain—one task grows out of questions raised in the preceding tasks, all connected to an original theme or initiating question" (Edlelsky, Altwerger, & Flores, 1991, p. 64).

In theme cycles, students do not do science *activities*; they do *science*, as a scientist would (Edelsky, Altwerger, & Flores, 1991, pp. 64–68). They do not do social studies *activities*; they investigate social phenomena as a social scientist would. They engage in artistic experiences for their own sake, not as an adjunct to study in some other curricular area. In short, theme cycles involve authentic learning experiences that are typically missing from theme units, though not necessarily from theme exploration. And theme cycles involve students in deciding what lines of inquiry to pursue and in continually raising new questions to guide their inquiry. When one line of inquiry or theme is exhausted, the class begins another in the theme cycle. (For more details, see Harste & Short, with Burke, 1988; Short and Burke, 1991.)

The major difference between theme exploration and theme cycles is that in the latter, students have an even more significant voice in the topics or themes to be explored, and in the planning and organizing of their work. The themes may be tentatively planned in advance for an entire school year, yet in the process of exploring their interests, teachers and students may find one theme generating new interests, and go with some of those instead of what was originally planned. Cordeiro's (1992) "generative curriculum" is similar, though the teacher makes more of the instructional decisions.

An integrative emphasis upon theme study rather than separate subjects like social studies and science is not necessarily incompatible with traditional curricular goals. For example, many teachers who are required to teach American history at their particular grade level find that it is acceptable to abandon the bird's-eye view of centuries of history in favor of concentrating upon key events and periods, the people involved, their way of life, their motivations and actions, and so forth. Prior to the twentieth century, for instance, one important theme might be the history of Native Americans before Columbus and then Columbus' "discovery" of America and its consequences, including the consequences for Native Americans. Other themes might be developed around the American Revolution and around the Civil War. The point is that what appears in textbooks to be an intimidating amount of factual information to be memorized can often be replaced by a few topics, explored extensively during thematic study.

Theme Study and Critical Literacy

In recent years, an incresing number of whole language teachers have realized that empowering students to *think* means that we must encourage them to *think about* something worthwhile, including the issues that plague our society. Furthermore, as our students participate more and more in classroom decision making, they are increasingly prepared to act and be treated as thinkers and doers: to question and challenge beliefs and opinions, including those offered as "fact"; to express their own informed opinions and urge appropriate actions upon authorities, including lawmakers; to serve on advisory committees and in administrative positions within their community; and to exercise the various decision-making functions of citizens and voters. In short, many teachers have realized that creating more democratic classrooms leads naturally to engaging in the kind of thinking that occupies concerned citizens in a democracy (e.g., Edelsky, 1991; Shor, 1992).

This concern for so-called critical literacy comes initially from Paulo Freire's work with illiterate adults in Brazil (e.g., Freire, 1970, 1985; Freire & Macedo, 1987). He concluded that in teaching adults to read, it is crucial not merely to teach them to read the printed word, but to read the world in which they live—the political, social, economic, and cultural forces that impinge upon their lives. Literacy becomes a tool for critiquing and attempting to change society: hence the term *critical literacy*. As implied in Chapter 7, education is not neutral: either it exemplifies and promotes the status quo, whether consciously or unconsciously; or it deliberately seeks to challenge and change the status quo. Both the overt content and the hidden curriculum of schools play significant roles in this ongoing process.

It has been something of a surprise to many whole language teachers that by opting for more democratic classrooms, they have become a force for social change. The joint teacher-student decision making and student ownership of learning in their classrooms reflect an emancipatory hidden curriculum, rather than the traditional repressive curriculum of the transmission classroom.

As for content, teachers and students in whole language classrooms at various ages and grade levels often find themselves exploring such issues as these:

- How are we destroying the natural environment? Why? Who does it benefit? Who does it harm? What can we do to slow or stop this destruction?
- Why do people start wars? Who does war help, if anyone? Who does it hurt? What can we do to prevent war?
- Why do people become alcoholics and drug addicts? How can we learn to say no to drugs? How can we help alcoholics and addicts?
- What are the actual and potential uses of genetic engineering? What are the implications and possible consequences? What are the issues that require principled and responsible choice?
- How are language and dialect differences used to help maintain power in a society? In general, how do dominant cultures maintain power, inducing others to perceive themselves as less worthy? What are the implications for us as students and teachers, citizens and human beings?
- In what ways do schools serve as instruments to maintain the social status quo? How can we make schools more a gateway to opportunity than a gatekeeper?
- How have Europeans and their descendents typically mistreated native peoples, such as Native Americans and aboriginal Australians? Why? How can we help change repressive laws and policies?
- How was Christopher Columbus not only a hero, but a villain?

Obviously some of these questions reflect a clear political agenda: opting to promote not only social awareness, but justice and equality as well. For more and more teachers, empowering all learners as citizens and members of society seems a logical outgrowth of empowering students as learners. (See Figure 9.23 for some resources on critical literacy.)

When, in 1992, the United States officially celebrated the five hundredth anniversary of the so-called discovery of America by Christopher Columbus, an increasing

Books

Edelsky, C. (1991). *With literacy and justice for all.* London: Falmer Press.

Edelsky, C., Altwerger, B., & Flores, B. (1991). *Whole language: What's the difference?* Portsmouth, NH: Heinemann.

Shannon, P. (Ed.). (1992). *Becoming political: Readings and writings in the politics of literacy education.* Portsmouth, NH: Heinemann.

Shor, I. (Ed.) (1987). *Freire for the classroom: A sourcebook for liberatory teaching.* Portsmouth, NH: Boynton/Cook–Heinemann.

Shor, I. (1992). *Empowering education: Critical teaching for social change.* Chicago: University of Chicago Press.

Stuckey, J. E. (1991). *The violence of literacy.* Portsmouth, NH: Boynton/Cook–Heinemann. (This is more an example of critical literacy than a discussion of it.)

Walsh, C. E. (Ed.). (1991). *Literacy as praxis: Culture, language, and pedagogy.* Norwood, NJ: Ablex.

Articles and teaching resources

Bigelow, W. (1992). Once upon a genocide: Christopher Columbus in children's literature. *Language Arts, 69,* 112–120.

   1. Peterson, R. E. (1987). Books to empower young people. *Rethinking Schools, 1*(3), 8–9.

Peterson, R. E. (1991). Teaching how to read the world and change it: Critical pedagogy in the intermediate grades. In C. E. Walsh (Ed.), *Literacy as praxis: Culture, language and pedagogy* (pp. 156–182). Norwood, NJ: Ablex.

Periodicals

Rethinking Schools. (Rethinking Schools Ltd., 1001 E. Keefe Ave., Milwaukee, WI 53212; 414-964-9646.) See the 1991 special issue titled *Rethinking Columbus.*

Teaching Tolerance. (Southern Poverty Law Center, 400 Washington Avenue, Montgomery, Alabama 36195; FAX 205-264-0629.)

FIGURE *9.23   Resources for understanding and practicing critical literacy*

number of teachers—even at the elementary level—engaged their students in critically examining that event and the events and consequences that followed. From a Native American viewpoint, what Columbus and his men did was invade an already existing civilization; conquer, subjugate, and enslave its inhabitants; and introduce not only European diseases but Black slavery into the Americas. Some teachers concerned about the traditional lopsided presentation of American history have drawn upon nontraditional resources to correct this imbalance.

In this regard, a particularly valuable classroom activity might be to compare nontraditional views of history with how significant events and individuals are presented in books for children. Bigelow's article on Christopher Columbus in children's literature (1992) provides a useful bibliography and analysis of several such books. Other books on Columbus are annotated in the September 1991 issue of *Book Links*, published by the

American Library Association. I have recently acquired a small text set on the Cherokee people, for similar study of how the dominant society's treatment of Native Americans is reflected in books for children. Some books are much more honest than others in portraying the expulsion of Native Americans from the eastern United States, the forced march to barren western lands, and the suffering and death forced upon Native Americans during the devastating journey along what is now known as the Trail of Tears.

The critical literacy imperative is claiming the attention of more and more whole language teachers, who are introducing such social concerns and issues to their students as possible themes for extended study.

CONTINUING TO GROW AS TEACHERS

I can only begin to predict new directions in the growth of the whole language movement. One possibility may be more widespread awareness and acknowledgment of the inherently political aspects of whole language teaching, and perhaps more overt commitment to teaching for social awareness and social change. Other than that, I make no predictions, not even tentative ones.

What I do know, however, is that in order to remain professionals, we educators must continue to learn more about students and learning, reflect upon our teaching, and take new risks in order to become even better teachers. Individually and collectively, we must accept the challenge of continuing self-renewal as learners and thus as teachers, modifying our theories of learning and teaching accordingly. As Jerome Harste says, "The future of whole language is collaboratively ours for the creating" (1989a, p. 248).

FOR FURTHER REFLECTION AND EXPLORATION

1. Consider how you might introduce the story "Petronella" to students in your classroom. Would you use a modified basal reader approach, a core literature approach, or a whole language approach? How might whole language teachers and their students go about reading, discussing, and enjoying the story, as well as connecting it to other texts?
2. Brainstorm possible themes like change, conflict, togetherness/isolation, contrasts. Then investigate the bottom-line curricular requirements for your (an) elementary school. Consider whether, and how, these curricular requirements could be met through exploration of the themes you have brainstormed, along with other themes that emerge as you consider the curricular requirements.
3. Discuss with other practicing teachers where each of you are on a continuum from transmission to transactional teaching. How have you changed your teaching, and what successes can you celebrate? What new challenges and risks are you considering?

10 Reading, Literature, and the Dramatic Language Arts
Ruth Beall Heinig

An artist is not a special kind of person; everyone is a special kind of artist.

— Eric Gill

Reading, literature, and drama are inextricably related. McInnes (1985) posits that the act of reading is dramatic in itself since readers, in their minds, participate in the literature. As we have seen in earlier chapters, they also draw on their personal experiences and use their imagination, creating their own version of the text. McInnes goes on to describe how readers are also like theater directors, imagining the story's staging, pacing the action, shaping the scenes, lighting the set, and costuming the players as the author's words are brought to life in their heads. Readers even become actors, projecting themselves into the story in the roles of selected favorite characters. In this chapter we look at some ways whole language teachers can engage students in drama and related activities, enhancing their enjoyment of reading, their involvement in and appreciation of literature, and the exploration of themes.

THE MANY FACES OF DRAMA

The use of drama in education is certainly not new. No doubt most readers have had some drama experiences in their own educational background—school plays, puppet shows, musicals (even opera), or variety shows. However, the formal production of drama, or putting on a play with scripts, costumes, props, and so on, is not considered here. While that is of course drama, our emphasis is on informal drama experiences that exist primarily for the benefit of the participants, rather than performance for an audience.

Traditionally known in the United States as "creative drama," many other terms such as "informal drama," "playmaking," "improvisational drama," "educational drama," "process drama" or just "drama" have also been used for the informal drama we discuss in this chapter. A definition developed by the American Alliance for Theatre and Education reads in part: "Creative drama is an improvisational, nonexhibitional, process-centered form of drama in which participants are guided by a leader to imagine, enact, and reflect upon human experiences" (for a fuller development of this definition, see Davis & Behm, 1977).

Often informal drama involves the improvised enactment of literature. It can also include the further exploration of themes, concepts, and issues raised by the literature. Or drama may have its own text and provide children with the motivation to do further reading in related literature, dictionaries, encyclopedias, or biographies. Drama experiences also produce rich material for writing in all forms: letters, charts, journals, and so on.

As an introduction to this type of activity, let us look at one drama lesson with a class of fifth graders. Please keep in mind that this is only one example, a beginning lesson with a new group, and not necessarily a prescription of how drama must be done.

Ms. Downey, a guest drama teacher, begins the fifth graders' first drama lesson by showing them a book she thinks they might enjoy. She introduces the picture book *Company's Coming* by Arthur Yorinks (1988) and begins to read it aloud with enthusiasm. The children, seated at their desks in a circle around the room, listen attentively.

The story is about two small aliens, who land their spaceship in Shirley and Moe's backyard in a town called Bellmore. Despite Moe's protestations, Shirley invites the aliens to join her, Moe, and their cousins for dinner. The little creatures readily accept, saying they will return at six o'clock. Ms. Downey, with suspenseful voice, stops reading at the point where the aliens arrive at the door with a neatly wrapped, beribboned box, and suggests, "Let's postpone the end of the story for a bit and do some drama with it, shall we?" The children are clearly captivated by the humor and intrigue of the story and seem eager to accept any suggestion.

Because the students have not experienced drama previously, Ms. Downey suggests that they get into the feel of the story by "trying on some of the characters." She instructs them to think of three things that Shirley or Moe might do to get ready for dinner with their relatives. This activity will help set the scene of the story. The children are to pantomime their ideas to the count of three, simultaneously, working in their own individual spaces in the center of the room. Before the children begin, however, Ms. Downey quickly brainstorms with them to see that they all have ideas to perform. This precaution helps to insure their success in the activity. Their quick responses indicate that they are ready, and the pantomiming begins.

Between counts, Ms. Downey comments on the pantomime ideas she sees, "It looks as if someone is mowing the grass; hmmm, I think I see some potato salad being made; and someone appears to be painting." This feedback is given to show that the pantomime ideas are being communicated. However, no attention is called to any one child, and no names are used. Typically, many of the ideas pantomimed come from the story's text and illustrations, while others are from the children's own experiences and interpretations. After the pantomiming is ended, Ms. Downey asks the children to name some of the ideas they had in order to give recognition to their efforts. "Good," she says with a smile, and asks if they want to try on the characters of the aliens.

This suggestion is greeted enthusiastically. Ms. Downey reminds them of the two aliens' comment in the text about traveling for years on their way to the next galaxy. "I wonder," she muses, "what the scene might have been like when the aliens made their decision to take their space journey? Shall we give this a try?" The children nod and make affirmative comments such as "Oh, boy!", "Yessss," or "Cool." She then hands out some three-by-five cards to the children. The cards have random statements pasted on them that have been clipped from magazines. "Here are some statements I thought that someone preparing for a new adventure might say," she explains. "Let's read a few of them aloud first."

In her oral reading of the story, Ms. Downey spoke the aliens' dialogue in the stereotypical monotone voice of quasi-human speech. Since the children obviously enjoyed her interpretation and are familiar with the sound, she anticipates that they will imitate it, although she does not require it. Eager volunteers read the statements on their cards, easily speaking in computer-sounding voices: "We are not on a picnic," "I'm scared," "Why are we here?" and so on. After a few moments, she suggests, "Now that you see what the cards are like, let's begin. This time one of you will start us off with a statement. If one of you has a card that you think follows that statement logically, you may read it. Since several of you may think you have a statement that fits, the first one to stand gets to read." She hands out approximately five cards per child to allow for some variety and choice.

Ms. Downey then begins speaking in her alien voice as if she is in charge of a meeting and announces, "You may have wondered why I've called all you citizens of this planet to this meeting. As you know, we are overpopulated [this information is brought out later in the book] and must search for new places to colonize. What are your feelings on this matter? Who wishes to speak first?" One child stands and reads the line, "Where will it all end?" This is followed by another student's reading, "Who knows?" and yet another, "It's better in the Bahamas." Ms. Downey also ad-libs some appropriate comments, generally when there are moments of silence, to lend additional give-and-take to the dramatized discussion.

When the children appear to have read most of the cards and while the momentum is still high, Ms. Downey brings the game to a close in her role as the alien leader: "Thank you for your input. Final decisions are always difficult to make, but we will try to keep everyone's thoughts in mind as we proceed with our plans. Dismissed." Switching to her normal voice, Ms. Downey collects the cards and exchanges comments with the children about their reactions to the game.

Now she asks the class if they would like to try yet another activity with different characters. They would, so she reminds them that Moe was worried about the aliens and secretly called the FBI, who in turn called the Pentagon. "I wonder what might have happened there? Let's see." Then, in an authoritative voice, Ms. Downey addresses the class: "Ladies and gentlemen of the Pentagon, I have a problem I need your help with. A telephone call has been received from someone named Moe in a place called Bellmore. He says two aliens are coming to his house at six o'clock this evening, and he wants us to do something about it. Now, since I have to attend a meeting with the President about other pressing matters, I need you to analyze this situation for me and come up with a plan of action if you feel one is needed. Please organize in discussion groups of five." (This is done very quickly under Ms. Downey's supervision.) "Here are pads of paper and writing implements for you to use in your deliberations." (These are handed out quickly.) "Synchronize your watches, please. It is now 10:00 A.M. We have exactly eight hours until the aliens' arrival. I'll return in a little while to hear your ideas." (She "exits" by stepping outside the circle of desks.)

Ms. Downey enters the circle again as teacher and circulates among the discussion groups, clarifying instructions and lending help or answering questions where needed. When necessary, she refers to the person she portrayed earlier as "the general." After several minutes she returns as the general and asks for their thoughts: "What have you decided about this matter?" One group wonders if the call is a hoax that shouldn't be believed. Their plan is to investigate further. "I see. Hmm, that is a possibility," Ms. Downey responds in role. Two groups suggest calling in outside forces such as Superman or the Teenage Mutant Ninja Turtles. Since these answers seem to be an easy way out of the problem, she cautions, "But our own jobs might be in jeopardy if we cannot handle these problems ourselves. The President reminded me again in my meeting with him that he plans to cut unnecessary government costs. He just might consider our jobs expendable. Maybe we'd better give that another think." Thus, while not rejecting the children's ideas entirely, she hints that the "solution" has the potential of creating another problem—one that could affect them personally. The remaining groups have various detailed plans of mobilizing forces to surround the house, as, in fact, the story shows later. All the ideas are listened to, but no final conclusions are reached. This tentativeness keeps the dramatic tension high so that the drama does not end too quickly. To conclude the scene, the general thanks them for their help and says she will return at a later time.

Ms. Downey pauses for a moment to ease the transition back to her role as teacher and then says, "There are so many possible scenes in this story we could explore. Remember that Moe called the FBI. Shall we find out what might be happening there?" The students are ready for anything. In an authoritative voice, she speaks again as some type of leader. "Ladies and gentlemen of the FBI. It has come to my attention that we might be called out for a special mission soon. We have a problem, however. Our undercover surveillance on our last case was a bit muddy, so I'm here to help you sharpen your skills."

Ms. Downey continues by explaining the rules of a theater game adapted from Spolin (see "Give & Take Warm-up," in Spolin, 1986, p. 117). She seats several volunteer "agents" in random fashion in a small circle. The rules of the game are as follows: agents are allowed to move whenever they want, but only one person may move at a time "so as not to call attention to yourselves while you're doing undercover work." The children must develop sensitivity to each other's movements to play the game effectively.

To help them get started, Ms. Downey assigns each player a number and calls the numbers randomly. When a player's number is called, he or she is allowed to move. If another number is called, the first player must "hold." After the children experience this adapted version of the game for a few minutes they are challenged to negotiate their moves on their own. Ms. Downey, still playing the role of an agent trainer, coaches and encourages the players, reminding them of the importance of their work as agents.

She commends the agents for their achievements in strengthening their surveillance skills, and tells them to "remain alert for any calls for your services."

Because the class period is coming quickly to an end, Ms. Downey decides to finish with one brief activity. She brings out a tray with a few intriguing miscellaneous items on it. She tells the childen that after the aliens entered Moe and Shirley's house to use the bathroom (as they do in the story), the objects were discovered. "We're not sure if these things belong to the aliens or not, but Moe and Shirley asked me to get your ideas on these." The various nondescript gadgets are shown one by one and the children discuss their interpretations. "That's a two-way wrist radio the aliens use to communicate with their space ship." "I'll bet that's a laser gun disguised." "That doesn't belong to the aliens at all; it's a missing part from Moe's lawn mower he accidentally dropped." So many ideas, so little time. Ms. Downey asks if they want to hear the end of the story. Of course they do. The reading is finished, and the class rushes out to lunch period.

The circumstances surrounding this drama lesson may not be typical for the regular classroom. However, it serves to illustrate a discussion of three predominant approaches to dramatization used today: creative drama (or playmaking), theater games, and educational drama (see Kase-Polisini, 1988). Ms. Downey introduced all three approaches in her lesson.

CREATIVE DRAMA

The early development of creative drama in the United States is credited to Winifred Ward, who taught at Northwestern University from 1918 to 1950, supervised drama instruction in the Evanston, Illinois public schools, and was a founder and director of the Evanston Children's Theater. She advanced the field of child drama for nearly forty years, and many of her basic methods remain influential today.

Even though Ward produced and directed formal theatre for child audiences, she felt that children in elementary school were better served participating in improvised drama for their own enjoyment and educational benefit. She wanted them to experience the art of theater without the pressures of play production, and emphasized the importance of process over product. Her method of self-expression she eventually called "creative dramatics" or "playmaking," terms she used interchangeably. Included in creative drama were "dramatic play, story dramatization, impromptu work in pantomime, shadow and puppet plays, and all other extemporaneous drama" (Ward, 1957, p. 3).

Ward's Philosophy and Methods

Although never trained as a teacher, Ward was familiar with the principles of the leading educators of her era, and drew her philosophy from the child-centered movement in education (Guffin, 1977). In developing her methods, she sequenced creative drama into a series of activities designed to develop children's skills in creating plays. Beginning with rhythmic and movement activities, sensory training, and simple pantomime exercises, the activities progressed to character analysis and the creation of original characters and dialogue. Basically, her goals were to provide for a controlled emotional outlet; to offer an avenue of self-expression in one of the arts; to encourage imagination; to provide opportunities to grow in social understanding and cooperation; and to give children experience in thinking on their feet and expressing ideas fearlessly.

Although Ward felt that the ideas, plots, and characters in creative drama could either be original or based on literature, the use of literature has almost become a hallmark of her work. She believed that children's enjoyment of their favorite literature selections deserved to be prolonged and strengthened. Playmaking was an ideal way to achieve this end.

In Ward's method, genre and style of literature often suggest the mode of dramatic expression. For example, mood poetry (e.g., "Who Has Seen the Wind?" by Christina Rosetti) or rhythmic poetry (e.g., "Marching Song" by Robert Louis Stevenson) can stimulate pantomime to music. Poems that emphasize characters (e.g., "Doorbells" by Rachel Field, or "The Pirate Don Durk of Dowdee" by Mildred Plew Meigs) might encourage dialogue scenes, while story poems (e.g., "The Elf and the Dormouse" by Oliver Herford, or "Get Up and Bar the Door," an old ballad) are suitable for adaptation into plays. (All the aforementioned poems may be found in Arbuthnot, 1961.)

Equally important considerations in dramatizing literature are the children's age, capabilities, and wishes. For example, for a very young or inexperienced group, the enactment of a Mother Goose rhyme such as "Little Miss Muffet" might simply become the scary advance of the spider toward Miss Muffet and her resultant frightened escape. Several children (or even half the class) would be the spider, and several (or the other half) Miss Muffet. For young children, such enactment is an extension of their own dramatic play of the rhyme. If children desire it and are able, a simple play might be made of the rhyme with additional characters: Miss Muffet's mother, some garden flowers or animals who might warn Miss Muffet of a spider lurking about. There may even be a reversal of the ending, with Miss Muffet standing her ground and scaring the spider away.

Obviously, older children are able to elaborate more extensively and to dramatize longer stories and novels over extended periods of time. An entire semester might be devoted to a particular piece of literature that requires more in-depth analysis. Generally, such extended experiences would be integrated with other curricular areas. For children from twelve to fourteen years of age Ward's recommended literature included the classical works of William Shakespeare, Washington Irving, and Victor Hugo (Ward, 1952/1983).

Creating Plays from Literature

Making improvised plays from literature requires a number of considerations. First of all, young children in kindergarten and first grade are usually more interested in simpler drama activities (rhythmic movement, sensory exploration, pantomime experiences, and group characterizations) than in any elaborate or extended work in making plays.

Generally speaking, only the simplest of familiar stories are made into plays with this age group. As children become ready for playmaking, selection of appropriate literature is an important key to success.

Selecting appropriate literature for playmaking

Since Ward was highly familiar with both play writing and play production, she was quick to point out that not every piece of literature, even though excellent, could be effectively made into a play. Accordingly, she taught that material for dramatizing needs:

- Worthwhile ideas.
- Dramatic conflict that is not unduly episodic.
- Action that can be played without elaborate staging techniques.
- Believable characters, whether humans, animals, or fantasy.
- Interesting but not intricate dialogue.
- Strong appeal to the children who are dramatizing it.

As a general rule, and to guarantee success, stories used for dramatization should be a little simpler than ones children can listen to or read for themselves.

Ward felt that stories known mainly for their beauty of language, such as *The Little Prince* by Antoine de Saint-Exupéry (1943/1971), run the risk of being spoiled by improvisational dramatizing. (Such stories, however, are often highly suited to readers theater, discussed below.) She also cautioned against using stories of modern life with characters too much like the children themselves, since she felt children would be too self-conscious to gain from the experience. Although granting exceptions, such as Robert McCloskey's *Homer Price* (1943), Ward generally used folktales and stories set in other time periods. While leaders today might not be as rigid in making literary selections, Ward's concern for both maintaining the integrity of the literature and guaranteeing children's success at dramatization should not be overlooked. (For suggestions of appropriate literature to dramatize, bibliographies are available in a number of sources including Ward, 1952/1983 and 1957; Siks, 1958 and 1964; Bauer, 1977; Bosma, 1992; and Heinig, 1993.)

If a piece of literature translates easily into the dramatic format, children can usually improvise a play from it rather quickly. The simple structure and fairly stereotypical characters of folktales make them readily accessible to dramatization. Though sometimes a little more sophisticated, stories written in the style of a folktale are also good candidates for dramatization. An excellent example would be Jay Williams' "Petronella," reprinted as an appendix to this book.

Here let us pause for a moment to consider the story Ms. Downey used. *Company's Coming* is a simple, modern tale with elements of science fiction. Because the story is brief and many of the scenes are open-ended, it served as a useful stimulus for introducing drama. As Ms. Downey's class becomes more familiar with drama, they could probably make a play of it rather quickly. However, Yorinks' economy of text moves his story along at such a rapid pace that extended improvisation could hamper the total effect. If so, the story may be more successfully enacted in readers theater format. Children could try the story both ways and judge the results for themselves.

Steps in story dramatization

In Ward's methods for improvising a play from a literary source, the teacher and class together work on it in bits and pieces. The basic steps in the process are plan, play, evaluate, and replay. If the children's interest continues, the parts are eventually melded into a completed drama.

The leader keeps the sequence of drama activities (simpler to more complex) in mind, but also follows the children's wishes and implements what they want to experience in the story. Ward believed a teacher needed to be overprepared with ideas for a drama lesson. Only then could one be ready and willing to go in whatever direction the children desire. In her words, "Knowing that we may have to discard all of our plans, we realize that only by exploring all of the possibilities we can think of shall we be ready to guide the children in such a way that the experience will have real worth" (1957, p. 126).

One technique of Ward's is "trying on characters." While discussing the characters, children experience the characters' feelings and thoughts through physical and vocal expression. For example, with the story "Petronella," a leader might suggest something as simple as "Let's see how the king and queen might have looked, sitting regally on their thrones." All the children can show their interpretations simultaneously as they sit in a circle on the floor or at their desks. Or the leader might ask, "If you were Petronella, what might you say to your family to convince them you should go off to seek your fortune, just as your brothers plan to do?" and let volunteers give their responses. (Recall that Ms. Downey also used the technique of trying on characters in her drama lesson.)

To assist children in developing dialogue and expressing the inner thoughts and feelings of the characters, a leader might play a role with them. For example, if children are trying on the roles of King Peter and Queen Blossom, the leader might engage them in conversation as a person of the court and ask probing questions: "Your majesties, I understand your daughter Petronella is talking about going with her brothers to seek her fortune. What do you think of that idea?" Again, the questions may be addressed to the whole class, allowing volunteers to respond. (Note that this technique was carried out by Ms. Downey in the scene at the Pentagon.)

After a few such motivating activities, the leader might next ask the children, "What scene in the story would be the most fun or interesting to play first?" By beginning with the most interesting scene, rather than approaching the scenes chronologically, children are involved in decision making and their interest is kept high. Suppose the children select the scene in which Petronella meets Albion and Ferdinand. The leader then helps the children define the scene—what characters might be in the scene, where the scene takes place, and other organizational details that might be helpful. Players are cast and the scene is improvised.

On occasion, a leader might even enter the playing spontaneously in order to encourage new ideas (Ward 1952/1983). Ward uses an example with a traditional tale called "The Stone in the Road." This story is a useful one for developing characters, because any number of people can pass by to deal with the intrusive stone. The children enact their own ideas of who might pass by and what their reaction would be. Ward suggests that if the children's ideas are all too similar to each other,

> you may, without any warning, become a poet, perhaps, walking down the road, note-book in hand, enthralled by the idea for a poem. With head in air, and eyes on the thrush in yonder tree, you stumble over the stone, look at it vaguely, sit on it, and complete your poem before going on down the road! (1952/1983, p. 15)

After playing a scene, both players and observing class members evaluate what was good about the playing and what might be made better. Except with young children, who may have difficulty seeing any perspective but their own, evaluation is usually done with a speculative audience in mind. Questions such as "Would an audience understand what's happening in our scene?" or "How can we make this scene clearer to someone watching it?" focus the children's attention on the importance of creating and sharing meaning with others.

When evaluating their playmaking, the children use the characters' names (rather than the children's own names) so that the emphasis is on dramatic, not personal, criticism. For "Petronella" children might offer such suggestions as "The little old man should be a little stiffer when he gets up from the ground. After all, he's been sitting there for sixty-two years" or "When Petronella rescues Ferdinand, maybe he should argue with her more about not wanting to leave his warm bed." After a brief discussion of the various interpretations, new players are cast and the scene is replayed. Ideally, each replaying builds on previous playings and the ideas expressed in the intermittent discussions.

Approaching playscripting

As children become experienced in playmaking, they are able to turn more complex stories into plays, often adding characters and new scenes to heighten the dramatic telling. For "Petronella" they might suggest, "Shouldn't we have something else happen with the little old man? He seems to just disappear." "What about adding some servants around Albion's house? I think Ferdinand likes to be waited on a lot." "We could have a wedding scene at the end. Maybe the little old man could show up there," and so on. While the leader's artistic ideas are not imposed, they can be suggested for consideration. In this way, some playwriting skills are taught.

If a story is played and replayed a number of times, it can appear very much like a scripted play. Some children might even want to transcribe the class's creation into a written playscript. This could be done from memory or with the help of an audio recording or videotape. Of course, recordings also serve as a document of the work accomplished.

When story dramatization begins to resemble the performance of a rehearsed, scripted play, it might be shared with (not performed for) a supportive audience of peers and friends, but only if the children desire it. At this point the children are usually so familiar with their dramatization that any child would be able to play any part. At the same time, no one owns a certain role; instead, the class owns the whole play collectively. Again, final production is not to be the teacher's reason for undertaking story dramatization. Not only would that put the pressures of play production on the children, it would exclude them from making an important decision.

According to Ward, story adaptation generally produces more satisfying results than creating an original play, especially when one is working with an entire classroom. After children have had a number of experiences in story adaptation, it is reasonable to assume that they would be better prepared for the more challenging task of creating original plotlines and plays, should that be desired. For further guidelines in story adaptation, Ward's chapter on play structure (1957) is still useful. Teachers who are interested in encouraging playwriting with advanced and highly motivated children will find many excellent suggestions in *Writing Your Own Plays* by Korty (1986); *Making Theater* by Kohl (1988); *Playmaking: Children Writing and Performing Their Own Plays* by Sklar (1990); and *Teaching Young Playwrights* by Chapman (1991).

Integrated Projects

Ward also encouraged what she called "integrated projects." These were improvised plays that correlated with other parts of the curriculum, a practice not unlike many being encouraged today. (See the section on theme study in Chapter 9.) Such dramatizations are often based on novels and developed over several weeks' time. Novels set in other countries and time periods integrate well with social studies. Art, music, and dance might also be incorporated into the dramatization. Other related activities might include writing in character, making charts and scale models, or building a meaningful prop such as a space ship.

Ward realized that children would probably want the satisfaction of sharing these ambitious dramatizations and plays with an audience. Although she considered the performance the culminating event, she felt it was "not the really valuable part of what they had done" (1957, p. 166). Instead, growth in responsibility, constructive use of creative imagination, cooperation with peers, and opportunity for controlled emotional release were some of the more important goals.

Even though she encouraged relating drama to the curriculum, Ward did not approve of "making a cart-horse of drama" (1957, p. 16). By this she meant using drama for the simple enactment of facts and as a tool to test children's mastery of limited concepts. Ever mindful of creative drama's roots in the art of theater, Ward consistently used those principles in guiding her philosophy and methods.

Even after retirement, Winifred Ward continued to write and to remain influential in guiding the field of child drama. Other writers, some of whom were her students, have expanded and updated her methods, but without changing the basic procedures she advocated. For a selected list of readings in playmaking/creative drama as pioneered by Winifred Ward, see Figure 10.1.

Cottrell, J. (1987a). *Creative drama in the classsroom, grades 1–3.* Lincolnwood, IL: National Textbook Company.

Cottrell, J. (1987b). *Creative drama in the classroom, grades 4-6.* Lincolnwood, IL: National Textbook Company.

Heinig, R. B. (1993). *Creative drama for the classroom teacher* (4th ed.). Englewood Cliffs, NJ: Prentice Hall.

McCaslin, N. (1987a). *Creative drama in the intermediate grades.* Studio City, CA: Players Press.

McCaslin, N. (1987b). *Creative drama in the primary grades.* Studio City, CA: Players Press.

McCaslin, N. (1990). *Creative drama in the classroom* (5th ed.). Studio City, CA: Players Press.

Salisbury, Barbara T. (1986). *Theatre arts in the elementary classroom: Kindergarten through grade three.* New Orleans: Anchorage Press.

Salisbury, Barbara T. (1986). *Theatre arts in the elementary classroom: Grade four through grade six.* New Orleans: Anchorage Press.

Schwartz, D., & Aldrich, D. (Eds.). (1985). *Give them roots . . . and wings!* (2nd ed.). New Orleans: Anchorage Press.

Siks, G. B. (1958). *Creative dramatics: An art for children.* New York: Harper & Row.

Siks, G. B. (1964). *Children's literature for dramatization.* New York: Harper & Row.

Stewig, J. W. (1983). *Informal drama in the elementary language arts program.* New York: Teachers College Press.

Ward, W. (1957). *Playmaking with children* (2nd ed.). New York: Appleton-Century-Crofts.

Ward, W. (1952; reissued 1983). *Stories to dramatize.* New Orleans: Anchorage Press.

Figure 10.1   References on creative drama

THEATER GAMES

While creative drama was becoming more widely known in educational circles during the mid-1900s, improvisational theater methods were also becoming popular. In the United States, Viola Spolin's theater games (1963/1983) were particularly welcomed by creative drama teachers as additional tools for drama education. Eventually the theater games were printed in a file format for easier reference (Spolin, 1975/1989). A few years ago her writings were edited specifically for classroom teachers (Spolin, 1986).

Spolin was inspired by the work of Neva Boyd, a pioneer in the field of creative group play. As Boyd's student at Chicago's Hull House in the 1920s, Spolin learned how to use games, drama activities, folk dance, and storytelling to stimulate creative expression in children and adults. Later, Spolin became a teacher and supervisor of creative drama on the WPA Project in Chicago, where she began the development of her unique games and methods. In 1946, Spolin founded and directed the Young Actors Company in Hollywood. Returning to Chicago in 1955, she worked with her son, Paul Sills, a co-founder of the first improvisational theater company in the United States, who later founded the famed Second City in Chicago. These experiences helped Spolin in the further articulation of her methods, and eventually led to the founding of the Spolin Theater Games Center in Los Angeles in 1975. For both theater professionals and drama educators alike, Spolin's work continues to be as influential today as when it first appeared.

Spolin's Philosophy

Spolin believes strongly in the power of play, and quotes Boyd in explaining the learning potential of playing a game:

> Playing a game is psychologically different in degree but not in kind from dramatic acting. The ability to create a situation imaginatively and to play a role in it is a tremendous experience, a sort of vacation from one's everyday self and the routine of everyday living. We observe that this psychological freedom creates a condition in which *strain* and *conflict* are dissolved and potentialities are released in the spontaneous effort to meet the demands of the situation. (Spolin, 1963/1983, p. 5)

Spolin also believes that the learner finds his or her own way, and that the key to intuitive learning is spontaneity. As she explains it,

> Through spontaneity we are re-formed into ourselves. It creates an explosion that for the moment frees us from handed-down frames of reference, memory choked with old facts and information and undigested theories and techniques of other people's findings. (1963/1983, p. 4)

Games thus are seen as a way of achieving spontaneity and diminishing predictability, a way of keeping players on edge and in tune. Whether one is an actor in training or an interested layperson, a child or an adult, games offer a way of being alive to learning and open to life experiences.

Spolin's Game Method

A Spolin game often begins simply, moving to more complex dimensions by degrees. Consider the game of tag. After an initial playing of the game in the traditional manner, the playing may be gradually slowed until players' movements are almost free floating. Heightened concentration is required to achieve slow-motion movements; the resultant slowed pace intensifies players' awareness of each other and their interrelationships in space.

Spolin games are structured to build on each other and may be used in various combinations. Some are designed to enhance sensory awareness and recollection of past sensory experiences. Other games focus on who, what, and where in developing improvised scenes. Some games have several variations in order to move players through progressive steps of growth over time. A mirroring exercise, for example, has eight variations, while a game called "Gibberish" has nine (1963/1983).

The games have three essential parts: focus, sidecoaching, and evaluation. *Focus* is couched in problem-solving terms. Often the specific problems are ones Spolin observed actors struggling with. For example, the audience's eye usually follows an actor who is moving on stage. If an actor is playing a subordinate role in a scene and moves more than the actor playing the dominant role, it is said that he or she is "stealing the scene" or distracting the audience's attention. Therefore, actors must learn to "take the scene" when the audience's attention is supposed to be on them, and "give the scene" when the audience's attention is to be on another actor. Spolin's game "Give and Take Warm-up" (1986, p. 117) is designed to intensify actors' awareness of each other's movements. The rule is that any player can move at any time, but must hold if another player moves. (Ms. Downey incorporated the Give and Take game into the Yorinks story by suggesting these behavior skills were needed by FBI undercover agents during surveillance assignments.)

Since the appropriate giving and taking of scenes is necessary in theater performance, the game obviously has a very practical side to it. However, Spolin has a higher intent in her games, as evidenced in two of her reminders: "On stage, one's taking is the other's giving" and "Improvisation is not exchange of information between players; it is communion" (1963/1983, p. 45). In my own experience, shy children tend to become more confident by playing this game. They seem to acquire a newfound power in realizing they can stop another player simply by moving. Aggressive children find that they cannot dominate the game, but instead must submit on cue. Both players and observers achieve deep satisfaction when the players' movements are finally coordinated in a smooth-flowing stream of ultimate sharing.

Inherent in each theater game is a problem players must resolve. This is the focus of the game. (Originally Spolin used the term "point of concentration" for what she later called "focus.") In "Play Ball" the imagined ball becomes the focus. By focusing on an object or event, players more readily achieve a group response, "becoming one body through which all are directly involved in the outcome of the playing" (Spolin, 1983, p. xv). In doing so, they are transported into the world of play or dramatic reality. Believability is thus enhanced both for the players and the spectator-audience.

To begin a Spolin game, rules are presented. However, since Spolin believes no one can teach anyone anything, players are not told specifically how to solve the game's problems effectively. Instead, they are to discover their own solutions in the act of playing itself.

The Role of the Leader

Part of the leader's responsibility in Spolin's method is to select the appropriate games a particular group needs for its growth in spontaneity. As the group progresses, the leader adds continuing challenges to move the players ever forward.

The leader also facilitates the playing process by *sidecoaching,* encouraging the players and reminding them of the points of concentration and the problems to be solved. In "Play Ball," a game of tossing an imaginary ball, the leader might coach, "Use your whole body to throw the ball! Keep your eye on the ball! Allow the ball its time in space!" (1986, p. 48).

During a game, the leader may also throw out new challenges or rules. In "Play Ball" the weight of the ball might be changed by sidecoaching: "Now imagine the ball weighs twenty pounds!" Players must stay mentally alert to respond to each new problem, taking it into the imagined reality and reacting accordingly.

The leader also facilitates *evaluation.* Similar to the evaluation in Ward's playmaking, game evaluation takes into account the audience, who are the other players watching the game. Spolin believes an audience is the most important member of the theater; indeed, there is no theater without an audience (1963/1983, p. 12). Actors are encouraged to share an experience with an audience rather than viewing them as critics or even amused friends. Much like the reader who makes his or her own unique meaning from the text, Spolin feels that "each member of the audience must have a personal experience, not artifical stimulation, while viewing a play" (1963/1983, p. 13).

Games, Story Dramatization, and Improvised Scenes

The games may be used to develop skills for performing a script, a story dramatization (suggested literature is listed in Spolin, 1986), or an original improvisation. As an example, slow motion, which occurs in several exercises, can be equally useful in story dramatizations. In Jay Williams' "Petronella," for example, the scenes with the dogs, horses, and falcons could be played in slow motion to intensify the animals' wild nature. The flight on horseback might also be effective in slow motion. Slow motion could be helpful in portraying the trees (played by children) growing into an impenetrable barrier.

Games may extend into improvisational scenes. In "Who Am I?" (Spolin, 1986) one volunteer (Who) leaves the room, while the group decides on his or her occupation or identity. Who returns and waits in the playing area. The other players, one at a time or in small groups, approach Who and engage in appropriate activity. Who plays along, and eventually discovers his or her identity.

A "Who" game can be adapted into an interesting exercise in exploring the characters of a story. Who, for example, might be Ferdinand in "Petronella." The other players portray characters in the story, interacting with Ferdinand according to their interpretation. Of course, some invention and imagination would be necessary if scenes went beyond the storyline. For example, what would happen if Queen Blossom were to meet Ferdinand? As she approaches him, would her looks be approving or disapproving? Would she give him a token gift, welcoming him as a potential son-in-law? Or might she ignore him and simply walk past him?

Playing "Where" games helps establish believability in an imagined environment. In one Where game, for example, a player enters a predetermined space such as "living room." He or she pretends to carry an object, such as a floor lamp, and begins furnishing the room. Observers guess the identity of the object by noting the way it is carried, placed in the space, and utilized. Additional players continue carrying objects into the "room" until it is furnished totally in mime. In addition to being an excellent exercise in imagined awareness, this game is useful in creating various stage settings for story dramatization. The environments may be based on details described in the literature, or they may be creatively imagined and interpreted. (For an example, see Activity 1n at the end of this chapter.)

In "What" games the emphasis is on stage action or mutual activity between actors. For example, a pantomime guessing game based on occupations may be played. One team secretly agrees on an occupation to pantomime and performs it for another team to guess. In another "What" game a group of players must solve the problem of pushing an imaginary object such as a car without using their hands.

As players become experienced in improvisation, they can make short plays out of various combinations of who, what, and where ideas. Readers may have seen a professional troupe of improvisational actors, either live or on television, challenge themselves in performance by asking the audience to call out suggestions of who, what, and where. The actors then improvise a scene on the spot or with just a few minutes of planning.

Theater as Life

Spolin believes that life itself presents material for theater; therefore, actors must become open to the world. By the same token, artistic growth is also personal growth. According to the editor's preface to Spolin's *Theater Games for the Classroom:*

> Playing theater games, students will learn not only a variety of performance skills but the basic rules of storytelling, literary criticism, and character analysis. Through play, they will develop imagination and intuition; they will find it easier to project themselves into unfamiliar situations. These games, in short, go beyond the theatrical to nurture skills and attitudes that are useful in every aspect of learning and life. (1986)

Games and Other Approaches to Drama

Some writers have included game and improvisation methods with other approaches to drama. Games are frequently used as warm-ups to improvisation and story dramatization (Heinig, 1993). Swartz (1988) includes a variety of games as an introduction to each of his lessons in educational drama. But perhaps no one has articulated a game philosophy quite as thoroughly and uniquely as Viola Spolin. Armed with her rationale, one can select games from her storehouse, as well as from other writers, and begin an odyssey into teaching and learning. Suggested books containing various games and improvisations are presented in Figure 10.2.

Belt, L., & Stockley, R. (1991). *Improvisation through theatre sports.* Puyallup, WA: Thespis Productions.

Booth, D. (1986). *Games for everyone.* Markham, Ontario: Pembroke.

Booth, D., & Lundy, C. J. (1985). *Improvisation.* Toronto: Academic Press.

Novelly, M. C. (1985). *Theatre games for young performers.* Colorado Springs: Meriwether.

Polsky, M. (1989). *Let's improvise!* Lanham, MD: University Press of America.

Scher, A., & Verrall, C. (1992). *200+ ideas for drama.* Portsmouth, NH: Heinemann.

Spolin, V. (1963/1983). *Improvisation for the theater.* Evanston, IL: Northwestern University Press.

Spolin, V. (1975). *The theater game file.* St. Louis: CEMREL. (Reissued in 1989 by Northwestern University Press.)

Spolin, V. (1986). *Theater games for the classroom: A teacher's handbook.* Evanston, IL: Northwestern University Press.

Swartz, L. (1988). *Dramathemes: A practical guide for teaching drama.* Markham, Ontario: Pembroke. (Available in the United States from Heinemann.)

Figure 10.2 References on theater games

EDUCATIONAL DRAMA

As the use of informal drama spread in the United States, the work of practitioners in other countries became known and their impact felt (Courtney, 1974; Way, 1967). More recently, educational drama has become another method to be added to the drama educator's teaching repertoire. Particularly influential since the 1970s have been the teachings of England's Dorothy Heathcote (pronounced Heth´-kit).

Trained as an actress, Heathcote began her teaching career at the University of Newcastle-upon-Tyne at the age of twenty-three. Her methods were first described for Americans by Betty Jane Wagner (1976), a well-known English education specialist in the United States. Before Heathcote's retirement in the late 1980s, she made many trips to the United States to teach workshops and classes, which further enhanced her popularity and influence.

Heathcote's Subject Matter for Drama

Unlike Ward and her followers, Heathcote usually prefers not to use literature to engage children in drama. For her, dramatizing a selected story limits more than broadens children's creativity, and only minimally explores the human condition. Rarely does she even use literature as a stimulus for drama work (although, as we shall see later, some of her followers have moved in this direction). Rather, she assists children in finding their own topics for drama.

Frequently, Heathcote simply begins a drama session by asking the children, "What would you like to make your play about?" For her, "play" means the creation of an unfolding drama rather than the dramatization of a known plot line. When children are asked what they want to make a play about, they often suggest topics like ghosts or pirates or spies. The wishes of the majority are taken, although promises are made to use the other ideas on subsequent days.

By careful questioning, Heathcote develops the nature of the drama to be played. For example, she might ask what she calls a "branching" question: "Do you want to be pirates or meet them?" She might also question them about the setting and time of the drama. Her attempt is to make the drama the children's as much as possible, rather than basing it on a storyline. For example, in beginning a drama about pirates, Heathcote might pretend to be the captain of a pirate ship, and interview the class as potential candidates for her crew. Children might be asked to demonstrate physical prowess or give convincing arguments as to their qualifications.

Heathcote never allows children to handle the drama casually or superficially. If necessary, and in her role as the pirate leader, she might say sternly to a noncommitted child, "Being a pirate is serious business. Are you up to it?" Or she might engage them through pantomimic rituals (such as swabbing the deck) to help them build their belief in the dramatic reality. Even though children might have stereotypical notions of pirates, envisioning mainly sword fighting and plank walking, Heathcote always leads and deepens the drama to a consideration of the human condition. Pirates are developed as real people, with families, personal conflicts, and concerns about the future.

Her genius at guiding children from such open-ended beginnings is a marvel to watch in live demonstration or on film (*Three Looms Waiting*) and videotape (*Building Belief, Parts I and II*). Although fascinated by her techniques, many admirers have found them difficult to emulate, let alone master. In addition, Heathcote's writings, edited by L. Johnson & O'Neill (1984), are theoretical and full of her own terminology (e.g., "brotherhoods," "dropping to the universal," and "building belief"), with unique meanings making them highly challenging to beginners.

Fortunately for novices, a number of drama educators have adapted and elaborated on Heathcote's methods in writings that are often easier to follow. Those who adhere to her philosophy closely still tend to bypass literature (Morgan & Saxton, 1987). Others may use literature as a stimulus for drama, expanding the themes of the material rather than developing the plot line (O'Neill & Lambert, 1982; Swartz, 1988). Tarlington and Verriour (1991) have recently suggested that the use of literature makes the methods of educational drama a little easier to learn. In all cases, however, the dramatization of a story from beginning to end is still regarded by educational drama purists as a relatively unimaginative endeavor.

Heathcote's Role Drama

Heathcote's dramatic method is sometimes called "role drama" (the terms "contextual drama" or "drama structure" have also been used). To create a role drama, the leader sets up an imagined situation that focuses on a problem. Heathcote's famous definition of drama as "man in a mess" suggests that any human problem can become the topic of a role drama. Within the imagined situation, the leader considers the various roles that might be played by the children and by him- or herself in developing the drama.

In using literature for a role drama, a central problem is identified and additional scenes are developed from it. For example, in Tarlington and Verriour (1991) the leader tells the story of Rumplestiltskin, and stops at the point where the queen faces the dilemma of having to give up her baby. Saying the queen's advisers will know what to do, the leader then asks the children to become those advisers. (In a similar manner, Ms. Downey interrupted her story and eventually asked the children to be Pentagon advisers solving the alien problem.)

Another way to use role drama with literature is by exploring what happened prior to the story. For example, why is the thirteenth fairy in the story of Sleeping Beauty so touchy? In *Company's Coming*, what events led to the aliens' decision to leave their galaxy? In like manner, an exploration may be made of what happens after a story is ended. For example, what is life at the palace like after Cinderella's stepmother and stepsisters are invited to live there? How can the town of Hamelin get the children back from the Pied Piper? In *Company's Coming*, what adventures will the aliens have trying to reach a new galaxy?

Role dramas, even those based on literature, do not have a preconceived plot line, as a story does. Rather, they evolve. A role drama may be carried on for several days, depending on the children's sustained interest. Even though Ms. Downey finished her session by reading the end of the story, the drama could be picked up again in subsequent sessions. For example, the FBI could decide to conduct an investigation of Shirley and Moe; the Pentagon might decide to pursue the aliens or mobilize an attack force in case they returned; or Shirley and Moe could face the dilemma of becoming media celebrities.

There are a number of standard strategies a leader can draw upon in developing a role drama. These include: full class discussion of a problem; group frozen scenes (or tableau), either singly or in a series; interview of teacher playing a role; children interviewing each other in pairs or as a panel; children portraying experts; creation of missing scenes (especially in literature); collection of evidence in tribunals or through investigation; and improvisation of scenes in groups. By being familiar with these strategies, a leader is able to set up scenes and move the drama along.

During a role drama, frequent stops are made to plan the next activity or scene, or to decide the direction the drama should take. Although the leader considers some possible alternatives ahead of time, the children's wishes determine how the drama will unfold. For example, in Ms. Downey's lesson the Pentagon general listened to, but didn't act upon, the children's suggestions. The class could return to this scene at another time and consider a branching question: "Do you want the Pentagon to ignore Moe's call, or should it be investigated further?" The leader would be prepared to go in whichever direction the class selects. Or the leader might simply ask, "What should our next scene be?" Children might request that certain characters meet or confront certain other characters. The leader could select one of the strategies listed in the previous paragraph and set up the scene.

Occasionally a session of drama is stopped because it runs into a snag, doesn't seem to be getting anywhere, or simply isn't interesting. (This knowledge should serve as a relief to beginners who feel an idea must be foolproof before they try it!) Sometimes a drama is stopped in order to research information and make the playing more accurate. For example, the group may need to know what a pirate ship looks like, how it would be sailed, or what kind of cargo it might be carrying. In *Company's Coming*, the class may want to research procedures used by the Pentagon and the FBI. Thus, as much as possible, the drama is the children's own, based on their needs as they see them.

Writing opportunities frequently arise during role dramas. Ms. Downey might have suggested writing a letter from the Pentagon to Moe; as the aliens the children could have written about their earth visit in a diary or space log; or newspaper articles might have been written with titles like "FBI Investigates Possible Alien Invasion," "Aliens Spotted at Smith's Appliance Warehouse," or "Bellmore Couple Hosts Foreign Visitors." (Suggestions of writing activities for "Petronella" are found in Activity 1o at the end of this chapter.)

Reflective Discussion

At various times throughout a role drama, the leader engages the group in *reflective thinking*. This is a discussion of questions that go beyond what has been played and that often explore philosophical issues related to the human condition. For example, if the drama is about the pirates, ghosts, or spies mentioned earlier, a leader might ask, "Why do you suppose people are so interested in ghosts?" "What qualities are required for a person to be a spy?" or "How easy or difficult would the life of a pirate be?"

With literature, a leader often explores the broader themes suggested. Ms. Downey, for example, might have encouraged the fifth graders to reflect on the question "What are some of the different ways people react to the arrival of strangers in their community?" or "What would it be like to have to look for a new place to live?" Reflective questions have no preconceived answers, and the teacher genuinely muses over them along with the children. During such discussions, ideas for further playing or new role dramas may emerge.

Teaching in Role

A second important method of Heathcote's is called *teaching in role*. Although a leader need not always work "in role," it is a technique that is particularly useful in beginning drama with a group. (Ms. Downey capitalized on this technique in her first lesson with the fifth graders.)

By playing a role, the leader gives the children someone to respond to. The interaction is live and immediate. Rather than discussing what a character might say or do, as is often the case in literary discussions, the children and teacher play it out.

In playing a role, the leader is not to "act" in some stereotypical or showy manner. As we saw with Ms. Downey, the leader probably suggests a role more than acts it. One simply changes the tenor of his or her voice and communicates the role subtly through body stance, gestures, or other nonverbal communication. This information is often of great solace to classroom teachers who are understandably reluctant to act. Most teachers are already dramatic by virtue of being a teacher, and this is enough experience to launch them into teaching in role. As Cecily O'Neill has said, "Drama is nothing more than saying to children, 'Let's pretend. . . .'" (Swartz, 1988, p. 8).

Roles the leader may play

The various roles played by the leader help determine the direction of the drama and the educational benefits to be derived. The roles may range from being purposely vague to quite specific. One might choose to play an authority role. In playing the role one might simply speak in an authoritative voice, as teachers often do, to establish him- or herself as one who should be listened to. For instance, "You, there, bring the [imaginary] equipment over here so we can make an inventory." Sometimes the authority role is more explicit: a police officer, a captain of a crew, a mother. (Recall that in our opening example Ms. Downey played various authority roles: a leader of the aliens, a general, and an FBI trainer.)

In addition to the authority role, a second-in-command role is often useful. For example, the leader may play a messenger who brings a concern from a higher authority. The messages may be in written form or tape-recorded to lend credibility. In the second-in-command role the leader can introduce a conflict from an authority figure without becoming one. This strategy protects the teacher in case the children have a negative reaction toward too much domination, particularly if they perceive the role as highly antagonistic. (Bold children have been known to suggest killing a despot!) As second-in-command, the leader can say, "These are the orders. [Don't blame me!] I didn't make them; I've only been sent to see that they are carried out." (It's a little like the role the teacher sometimes plays when enforcing an unpopular rule from the principal or other school official.)

Another role type, sometimes called "helpless," is that of a person seeking the group's expertise on a problem. Heathcote enjoys this technique as a way of giving power to the group. She wants children to have opportunities to share their information and opinions on matters, something she feels schools do not do enough of. She abhors the image of schoolchildren as vessels that information is poured into. Striving to reverse that process, she prefers to build on what children already know and to give them recognition for their knowledge. (Note that Ms. Downey cast the children in an expert's role when she turned over her problem to them at the Pentagon, and again when she asked for their interpretations of the objects found in the house.)

Other roles the leader may choose to play include such types as devil's advocate, one-of-the-group, and antagonist. The leader may switch from one type to another within a role drama, just as Ms. Downey did. (For further discussion of role types, see Morgan & Saxton, 1987; and Heinig, 1993.)

Children in role

Of course, when the teacher plays a role, the children are often in role, too. As with the leader's roles, the children's roles may also range from being fairly vague to more specific.

For example, even though Ms. Downey refers to the children as "ladies and gentlemen of the Pentagon," they probably do not look or sound much different from themselves. In some instances, however, a leader might spend a good deal of time readying children to be advisers by questioning them on their ages, their families, what their place of work looks like, and even how they might sit as an adviser. Tarlington and Verriour (1991) use this procedure with the queen's advisers in the Rumplestiltskin story. Such preparation is sometimes deemed necessary to commit children to the seriousness and importance of their role.

Discussion in role

Especially with beginners or with new topics, drama may look and sound very much like a typical class discussion. In fact, the leader purposely searches drama topics for possible group meetings in role. This technique makes initial attempts at dramatizing much easier, not only because discussions are commonplace in the classroom, but also because the children are more orderly in a sit-and-talk position.

After an initial large-group discussion, the class may be reorganized into pairs or smaller groups with the children interacting in different roles. In pairs, for example, reporters could interview witnesses. (In Ms. Downey's lesson, reporters might interview neighbors who saw the space ship land.) Or, in small groups, children may be asked to show their version of what happened during some incident in question. (For *Company's Coming*, children might create scenes showing what happened when the aliens purchased their gift of a food blender.) Improvisations may be shared with the class and provide stimulus for further discussion.

Ending the role drama

The children themselves decide when a role drama is over, based on their satisfaction with the outcome of events. The leader, however, should not let children solve problems too soon. After all, when a problem is solved, the drama is over. Also, thinking about the various ways to solve problems may be more educationally beneficial than rushing to one solution. Remember that when Ms. Downey concluded the meeting with the Pentagon staff, no plan of action was selected. This strategy keeps the drama pending, and even allows the class to return to the same scene. In drama, as in life, various human problems are faced again and again.

Precautions

Because of the open-endedness of educational drama, teachers are sometimes concerned about how to deal with the unanticipated or unknown (this concern is often expressed as "losing control"). What if, for example, a teacher (in role) asks the children's advice, and then doesn't like or is afraid of their response. Ms. Downey appears to have experienced this when some children suggested that the Pentagon call on Superman or the Teenage Mutant Ninja Turtles to deal with the aliens. Although she didn't reject the answer, she pointed out that turning over the problem to someone else might cost them their jobs.

There is another technique, requiring more trust, that Ms. Downey might have used. She could have asked the rest of the class, "What do you think about that?" Some of the students might have rejected their classmates' ideas simply because there would be more challenge and glory in dealing with the problem themselves. They, too, might have seen the suggestion as a cop-out, as Ms. Downey did. Thus, while the end result might have been the same, the decision would have come from the children rather than from the teacher. (If the majority of the class felt that their classmates' suggestion had merit, Ms. Downey might be well advised to go along. In this case, she might have set up job interviews between the suggested cartoon characters and Pentagon officials to see what would develop. She just might be pleasantly surprised to see how the class would deal with it.)

Another important technique in role drama discussion is preparation. Before conducting an interview, for example, the class can prepare a list of questions that would be most useful to ask. "Before we bring X into our chambers, what do we want to know from him?" In addition to making the playing more successful, this procedure provides an opportunity to learn some interviewing skills. Another advantage is that the teacher (or whoever is going to play the interviewed person) has some lead time to consider the responses he or she might make.

Finally, leaders are cautioned to not rush into playing too many role drama ideas at once or playing them too quickly. Heathcote frequently talks about slowing the drama down. (It is doubtful that she would have worked as quickly as Ms. Downey did.) In cooking, slow simmering often produces the best flavors; so, too, drama is the most effective when ideas are given time to develop. As another example of slowing down, Heathcote would caution a leader in role who is being interviewed by the class against feeling the need to tell or answer all. To almost any question one can say mysteriously, "I don't know" and then exit. This, in itself, creates considerable dramatic suspense.

Another common concern of teachers is how to control action. Often children are eager to get to physical action in drama, especially if discussion has gone on for a long time. An excellent device for allowing controlled physical action is the creation of tableaux or frozen scenes. Pairs or groups develop a series of perhaps three frozen pictures showing the beginning, middle, and end of the action scene or fight. Students are encouraged to depict the crucial events in the scene. For example, in a fight or battle the emphasis would be on showing precisely how the foe was vanquished.

Planning a Role Drama with "Petronella"

When planning a role drama with a particular piece of literature, a leader can take certain steps. A brief plan is presented here, using Jay Williams' "Petronella." (For a more thorough discussion on planning, see Tarlington & Verriour, 1991.)

It is important to remember that for all the planning a teacher does, ideas are implemented when and if the children want to go in that direction. The teacher remains flexible, but keeps in mind the available strategies that will achieve the students' desires for learning. Children are, of course, encouraged to give their planning input at any stage along the way.

In planning, a leader first looks for various themes and topics the class might wish to explore, just as one might with theme study, as discussed in Chapter 9. In "Petronella," some themes and topics might include: the role of women and men in society; the role and duties of a princess; a kingdom's expectations of royalty; family relationships; duties and responsibilities of children and parents; manners; kindness to people and animals; enchanters and magical powers; patience; bravery; and so on.

After selecting one area of focus, a key question that centers on human conflict is formulated. For example, "How does Petronella's independent spirit affect her family?" or "What role should women play in society?"

Next, one considers the various persons or groups who may have viewpoints to offer on the key question—for example, Albion, Albion's family, Petronella, Petronella's friends, Ferdinand, government officials, courtiers, castle servants, people of the kingdom, royalty in nearby lands, enchanters or persons with magical powers, church officials, the news media, wedding consultants, marriage counselors, real estate agents.

To begin a role drama, any of the above persons may be placed in an encounter and given a problem to resolve or a decision to make. For example:

Petronella's family	Meeting to discuss difficulties in dealing with Petronella's headstrong personality. Considering implications of Petronella's succession to the throne if Princes Michael and George do not return.
Government officials	Meeting to consider the potential dangers of having an enchanter in the royal family.
Castle servants	Sharing concerns over the additional duties thrust upon them in taking care of Albion's horses, dogs, and falcons.
Ferdinand	Complaining to Petronella's family that she abandoned him.
Wedding consultants	Debating the style of wedding appropriate for a princess and an enchanter.

After selecting a situation the students wish to explore, the leader places himself or herself and the children into roles. To focus the discussion and add tension, it is helpful if the leader begins by expressing a particular viewpoint in role. For example, in the first instance listed above, the leader could play Petronella's great-aunt. Embarrassed by Petronella's forthright behavior, she might insist that her grandniece receive intensive training in how to become a proper lady. Or the leader may play Ferdinand (or his lawyer), who seeks restitution from the family for emotional damages.

As the leader considers such scenes for possible dramatization, or as the scenes are played, other ideas and methods of playing them begin to emerge. For example, in small groups, students might create tableaux or short improvisations to demonstrate an instance when Petronella's behavior might have embarrassed her great-aunt. A second scene might demonstrate the behavior Petronella's great-aunt would have preferred to see. Or, the class could be divided into pairs; one plays Ferdinand and the other a lawyer who wishes to represent him. Ferdinand could conduct a hiring interview of the lawyer; or the lawyer could interview Ferdinand and decide whether to take the case.

One can find numerous sources for the further study of educational drama. The suggested texts listed in Figure 10.3 have been selected for their practicality and emphasis on lesson plan ideas. The selections vary in presentation, from fairly simplified to more sophisticated. Some are more appropriate for use with younger children, while others emphasize work with the upper grades.

COMMON THREADS IN THE THREE APPROACHES

The proponents of the three approaches to drama would agree that classroom drama has its roots in theater and is a powerful medium for learning. In all drama methods students are encouraged to work cooperatively, to exchange factual and personal information and ideas, to solve problems, and to try out new behaviors and language in the process of exploring the human condition.

Drama also provides a rehearsal for living and aids in sensitizing participants to the world around them. Within the safety of pretend, players can risk exploring all manner of situations without suffering the consequences they might be forced to experience in the real world. Drama offers a way of putting meaning into action and action into meaning, shaped to the readers' and players' consensual satisfaction. When children dramatize, they are building on their natural inclinations toward dramatic play and the power of pretending. Verriour (1989) emphasizes the relationship of drama to play and then asserts, "Above all, like social, pretend play, drama is a shared learning experience which flourishes in classrooms where a sense of community and the importance of negotiation are valued" (p. 285). Certainly such goals are central to the whole language philosophy.

Finally, another common thread in any drama approach is the belief that drama is most effective, and the learning derived from it most keen, when players make it as real

Cranston, J. W. (1991). *Transformations through drama.* Lanham, MD: University Press of America.

Davies, G. (1983). *Practical primary drama.* Portsmouth, NH: Heinemann.

Fox, M. (1987). *Teaching drama to young children.* Portsmouth, NH: Heinemann.

Morgan, N., & Saxton, J. (1987). *Teaching drama: A mind of many wonders.* Portsmouth, NH: Heinemann.

O'Neill, C., & Lambert, A. (1982). *Drama structures.* Portsmouth, NH: Heinemann.

O'Neill, C., Lambert, A., Linell, R. & Warr-Wood, J. (1977). *Drama guidelines.* Portsmouth, NH: Heinemann.

Swartz, L. (1988). *Dramathemes: A practical guide for teaching drama.* Markham, Ontario: Pembroke. (Available in the United States from Heinemann.)

Tarlington, C., & Verriour, P. (1991). *Role drama.* Portsmouth, NH: Heinemann.

Figure 10.3 References on educational drama

as possible. Ward and Spolin use group evaluation in judging believability in dramatizations and games. Heathcote talks of the importance of encouraging "commitment to the drama" and "building belief." Therefore, no matter what method of dramatizing is used, it is important to note that superficial playing is never considered sufficient.

RESEARCH IN CLASSROOM DRAMA

Research in the area of classroom drama has evolved from a variety of disciplines, but is still in its infancy. For many years, educators have described numerous values and outcomes of drama on children. However, only since the early 1960s has any empirical research been reported. While positive tendencies are evident in a number of areas, research is limited (Errington, 1993; O'Farrell, 1993).

In an important study by Kardash and Wright (1987), a meta-analysis was conducted on sixteen previous studies of drama with children from kindergarten through grade seven. The results showed that drama has a moderately positive effect on children's achievement in four areas: reading, oral and written communication, person perception, and drama skills. In particular, drama seems to have "an extremely beneficial effect on roletaking abilities" (p. 17). Because role taking is related to awareness of others, it is considered a significant dimension of effective communication.

Wagner (1988) conducted a review of classroom drama research, focusing on language arts studies. She concluded that, in general, drama produces positive effects on oral language, reading, and writing. As a language arts specialist who has taught drama, Wagner is aware of children's positive response to drama. In her words, "Those of us who have led groups of children or have heard them interact in role in a classroom drama have often marveled at their maturity of expression. Surely this is the kind of language we want to foster" (p. 52). However, Wagner also notes the need for more qualitative studies, analysis of oral language and literacy events with drama in process, as well as more detailed observations of classroom drama. Such research would parallel the strides currently being made in reading and writing research.

Jett-Simpson (1989) reviews research in the area of reading and drama and finds that there is a natural, even confirmed, partnership between drama and reading comprehension. She also details a number of ways drama can be used with literature, such as dramatizing students' personal experiences as they relate to key concepts and themes of a story, motivating interest in a story, acting out vocabulary words, dramatizing predictions, inferring and interpreting characters through interviews, and dramatizing new endings.

The American Alliance for Theatre and Education has recently established an International Center for Studies in Theatre Education. With the input of scholars and professionals from all parts of the United States and Canada, research is being undertaken in a number of areas of concern to the field of youth drama. It is hoped that this concerted effort will produce a body of significant research to document the claims that seem obvious to so many artists and educators.

ADDITIONAL WAYS TO EXPERIENCE LITERATURE

In addition to creative drama, theater games, and educational drama, several other dramatic language arts methods are particularly useful with literature study.

Narrative Pantomime

One method that beginning teachers find helpful and easy to implement is called "narrative pantomime" (Heinig, 1993). Narrative pantomime gets children physically, mentally, and emotionally involved in literature. Using literature that is primarily action-oriented, the leader reads or narrates the selection (sometimes minor adaptation is needed) while children mime the action. "Through imagination and movement, the literature becomes three-dimensional." (p. 416).

Narrative pantomime provides children the opportunity to try on favorite characters in literature and join them in their adventures. Players creatively interpret the characters' movements, while gaining insight into their thoughts and feelings. (See Heinig, 1993, for more detailed instructions in playing narrative pantomimes, for tips on adapting and creating original materials, and for bibliographies of narrative pantomime materials.)

Solo narrative pantomime

Stories that have a single character may be mimed by the entire class working individually and simultaneously. Excerpts from longer novels may also be used. With solo playing, children can often pantomime right at their desk area. The desk may become part of the story, being transformed into a car, a bed, or a mouse hole. Examples of stories with single characters include *Harold and the Purple Crayon* by Crockett Johnson (1955), *Hildilid's Night* by Cheli Duran Ryan (1971), *Snail's Spell* by Joanne Ryder (1982), and *Hatchet* by Gary Paulsen (1987).

Paired narrative pantomime

Some stories, or excerpts from longer novels, have two characters on an adventure together. For these, the class may be divided into pairs, with children again miming simultaneously in carefully designated playing spaces. Depending on the space available and the classroom arrangement, a leader may prefer to limit the number of pairs that are allowed to play at one time. Caution and a little extra rehearsal may be required if the characters interact physically, especially if the action is aggressive.

Some examples suitable for paired playing include *Bear Shadow* by Frank Asch (1985), *If You Give a Mouse a Cookie* by Laura Joffe Numeroff (1985), and *Two Bad Ants* by Chris Van Allsburg (1988).

Group narrative pantomime

Narrative pantomime stories that have several characters may be performed as a pantomime play. For these group stories, one child is the narrator (or more children may share the narrative reading), and the others play the various parts. Suggested stories for group playing include *Lentil* by Robert McCloskey (1940/1968), *The Little Brute Family* by Russell Hoban (1966), *The Money Tree* by Sarah Stewart (1991), and *The Story of Ferdinand* by Monro Leaf (1936/1977).

If there are enough characters (or the possibility of adding parts), the entire class may be involved in one story. For example, in *Lentil* there is a parade; in *Ferdinand* there is the audience at the bullfight. Sometimes there are interesting animals or even intriguing inanimate objects that children enjoy creating, such as the title role itself in Stewart's *The Money Tree.*

Small-group narrative pantomimes can lead easily into short improvised plays. When children spend time working out the details of group stories, they often see opportunities for adding some dialogue. If so, the narrator simply pauses briefly and allows the actors to speak a few words improvisationally. Sometimes children want to include a few simple costume pieces (material remnants) and props (found objects in the classroom) for their plays. Music may also be added for effect.

After some experience with narrative pantomime, classes may divide into small groups of perhaps five children. Each group may have its own story to enact and its own narrator. Generally this procedure works best with third grade and up, the age at which children begin to handle small-group work effectively.

Adapting literature

Literature may also be adapted for narrative pantomimes (see the example from Gene Zion's *Sugar Mouse Cake* on p. 416) and original materials may be written, based on literary sources. Children, too, may try their hand at writing similar narratives.

Narrative pantomimes may also relate to a variety of curricular areas. Dramatically written science stories by authors like Jean George (e.g., *One Day in the Prairie*, 1986) and social-historical books like *Chimney Sweeps* by James Cross Giblin (1982) are only two of many possibilities. Such materials also provide excellent models for teachers' and children's own writing.

Choral Speaking

Choral speaking (sometimes called choral reading or verse choir) is an ancient art, dating back to the choruses of Greek plays. A leader directs the group in similar fashion to a musical conductor. As with music choirs, scripts may be used or the material may be committed to memory. The reading or speaking may be prepared for sharing with an audience, although that is not neccessary to achieve the benefits and enjoyment of the activity.

Choral reading easily integrates listening, reading, and speaking. As with community singing, it provides an opportunity for children to work together to achieve artistic expression. Participation in such a group experience can increase confidence in the shy speaker and integrate the assertiveness of the forward child. Because clear speech is necessary when several people are speaking together, choral reading also encourages good diction. Most important for our purposes, however, choral reading encourages children to engage in the interpretation of literature through reading together. If led by an enthusiastic teacher, choral reading should enhance children's appreciation of the spoken word.

Discussion of the literature and its interpretation is a critical part of choral reading. No doubt there will be differences of opinion as to how a certain line or passage should be read in order to convey meaning most effectively. It is well within the practice of choral reading to experiment with various suggestions and then let the group decide on the preferred reading. Tape-recording a selection and playing it back can help the decision making. (Don't worry, however, if children cannot agree. Consider how many Shakespearean actors have interpreted Hamlet's soliloquies in a variety of ways. The process of exploration is more important than any final decision.)

Techniques and arrangements

Several techniques and arrangements are used in choral speaking. One simple technique useful with younger children or for beginning groups is *rhythmic activity*. The leader reads a poem with strong rhythm, such as a Mother Goose rhyme, while the children listen. In repeated readings, the children may lightly clap the rhythm or perform an appropriate action such as swaying, hopping, skipping, or marching. A. A. Milne's "Hoppity" (Arbuthnot, 1976) is a good example of a hopping poem, while "The Grand Old Duke of York" (Mother Goose) is good for marching.

The *refrain* method is another easy arrangement, used with poems that have refrains. The leader reads or recites the various stanzas, and the children join in on the refrains. The refrains are easily remembered after one or two repeated sayings, but may be placed on the chalkboard, a chart, or an overhead projector for a shared reading experience similar to those discussed in Chapter 3.

The refrain technique fits poetry such as the following:

- "Bow, wow, wow," Mother Goose (Saltman, 1985).
- "To Market, to Market," Mother Goose (Arbuthnot, 1976).
- "The Wind," Robert Louis Stevenson (Arbuthnot, 1976).
- "Feather or Fur," John Becker (Prelutsky, 1983).
- "To Walk in Warm Rain," David McCord (Prelutsky, 1983).
- "The Yak," Jack Prelutsky (Prelutsky, 1983).

Two-part arrangements are used with poems that are divided into two thoughts, sometimes in contrast to each other. In some cases it is fun to have higher voices balanced with lower voices, or one group might read slower and the other faster. The following poems may be used this way:

- "Aunt Sponge and Aunt Spiker," Roald Dahl (Prelutsky, 1983).
- "Celery," Ogden Nash (Prelutsky, 1983).
- "Some People," Rachel Field (Prelutsky, 1983).
- "Wiggly Giggles," Stacy Jo Crossen and Natalie Anne Covell (Prelutsky, 1983).
- "Swift Things Are Beautiful," Elizabeth Coatsworth (Arbuthnot, 1976; Saltman, 1985).

In some cases, poems are written in question-and-answer fashion. The *antiphonal* or dialogue *method* may be used for these poems. Half the class reads one part (or the question), and the other half reads the second (or answer). This technique may be used for the following poems:

- "Father William," Lewis Carroll (Prelutsky, 1983).
- "The Secret Song," Margaret Wise Brown (Prelutsky, 1983).
- "What Is Pink?" Christina Rosetti (Arbuthnot, 1976; Prelutsky, 1983).
- "Overheard in a Saltmarsh," Harold Monro (Arbuthnot, 1976; Saltman, 1985).
- "Pussy Cat, Pussy Cat, Where Have You Been?" Mother Goose (Arbuthnot, 1976; Saltman, 1985).
- "Two Friends," David Ignatow (Arbuthnot, 1976).

Two wonderful books by Paul Fleischman, *I Am Phoenix: Poems for Two Voices* (1985) and *Joyful Noise: Poems for Two Voices* (1989), contain collections of poems for two voices. The poems are written in two columns; one reader reads the left-hand column while the other reads the right-hand column. Some words or lines are shared by both readers. It's a little tricky at first, but the resultant sound is so satisfying that the efforts are well worth the time spent.

Line-a-child or *line-a-group* is the technique of having individual children, small groups, or the entire group reading assigned lines. Children enjoy the dramatic effects created by the variety this arrangement offers. It is crucial, however, that any division of the poems fit their meaning. One should not simply assign each line of a poem to a child or group to read unless there is some logical reason for doing so. For example, some poems list items by phrase or line, in which case the meaning is enhanced if different children or groups read the various items. Several poems from Prelutsky (1983) fit this pattern:

- "The Bat," Frank Jacobs.
- "Cats," Eleanor Farjeon.
- "maggie and milly and molly and may," e. e. cummings.
- "Mice," Rose Fyleman (also Arbuthnot, 1976; Saltman, 1985).
- "The Months," Sara Coleridge.
- "Rules," Karla Kuskin (also Saltman, 1985).
- "Silver," Walter de la Mare (also Arbuthnot, 1976).
- "Smart," Shel Silverstein.
- "Too Many Daves," Dr. Seuss.
- "Valentine," Shel Silverstein.
- "What Is Red?" Mary O'Neill.

Cumulative arrangement is the adding of speakers to subsequent lines of a poem, creating a crescendo effect. An equally dramatic effect can be achieved by gradually dropping out voices until a single voice speaks.

Carl Sandburg's brief poem "Buffalo Dusk" (Arbuthnot, 1976; Prelutsky, 1983) is an excellent example for this method. A solo voice can speak the beginning line, "The buffaloes are gone"; a few more voices may be added to the second line, "And those who saw the buffaloes are gone." The entire choir can speak the descriptive line of the thunderous buffalo herds, returning again to the repeated small group line and finally the repeated solo first line. In this instance the single voice helps to convey the poignancy of absence, while the increased volume and intensity helps to create the sound and image of thousands of buffaloes pawing the ground.

Other poems useful for cumulative readings include:

- "This Is The House That Jack Built," Mother Goose (Saltman, 1985).
- "Poor Old Lady" (also known as "I Know an Old Lady Who Swallowed a Fly"), Anonymous (Prelutsky, 1983).
- "Smart" Shel Silverstein (Prelutsky, 1983).
- "Summer," Frank Asch (Prelutsky, 1983).
- "The Pickety Fence," David McCord (Arbuthnot, 1976).

In *unison speaking* the entire choir speaks every line together. Unfortunately, teachers often begin with unison reading first since it seems the easiest. However, unless the group is reciting short Mother Goose rhymes or other very short poems, unison speaking can be the most difficult of all arrangements.

A pitfall in unison choral reading is the group's tendency to slow down, lower the pitch to a common monotone, end sentences with an upward inflection, or sing-song all phrases in a similar manner. Usually this is done in the effort to stay together, but it is deadly to listen to. Some practice is required under careful leadership in order to maintain unity, articulation, pitch, inflection, and mood.

In beginning unison choral speaking, shorter poems are usually easiest. After experiencing success with these, the group will be more confident to try longer selections. Sometimes it is helpful to play appropriate music in the background to heighten the unified feeling. There are many short poems in Prelutsky (1983) that can be effectively read in unison. A sampling follows:

- "A Wolf. . ." Osage Indian.
- "Crickets," Valerie Worth.
- "Grandpa Bear's Lullaby," Jane Yolen.
- "Help!" X. J. Kennedy.
- "Oodles of Noodles," Lucia and James L. Hymes, Jr.
- "This Is Just to Say," William Carlos Williams.
- Any short poems by Ogden Nash.

Some poems are fun to turn into *rounds*. For example, Spike Milligan's four-line poem "A Thousand Hairy Savages" (Prelutsky, 1983) can be read as a round by dividing the class into four groups. Group 1 begins the poem; as they read the second line, the second group begins with the first line, and so on. The last line, "Munch, munch, munch," dies down as each group drops out and the final group says the line alone. The effect of thousands of savages eating their lunch is enhanced by the rumbling repetition. Actions such as stamping feet and pounding fists on desks (in moderation, of course) may be added. Perhaps everyone will be reminded of the school cafeteria at lunchtime!

Other rounds can be made with short Mother Goose rhymes such as "Hickory Dickory Dock," "Three Blind Mice," and "Ride a Cock Horse."

After the various choral speaking arrangements have been experienced, they may be used in *combination* with one another in lengthier or more complex readings. Dividing a poem into solo lines, small-group lines, and unison speeches can create theatrical effect. For example, John Ciardi's "Mummy Slept Late and Daddy Fixed Breakfast" (Arbuthnot, 1976; Prelutsky, 1983) presents opportunities for whole-group narration, solo lines for Daddy's dialogue, and various solo and small-group lines for the list of ways the child tries to attack the tough waffle. (The whole group should narrate "he said" tag lines so the dialogue stands out.)

As choral arrangments become more complex, it becomes more challenging to weave the various parts into a unified reading of the poem. If any one reader or group is late in speaking, the rhythm or meaning will be destroyed. The mood of the piece must also be appreciated by everyone to keep it flowing. But the group's efforts usually pay off. There is nothing quite as dramatically exciting as listening to a piece read with many voices, making the literature come alive with meaning.

Choral speaking combined with narrative pantomime

Choral speaking can be combined with creative drama, again as long as attention is paid to the nature and meaning of the material. Poems with action, such as the American baseball ballad "Casey at the Bat" by E. L. Thayer (1988), offer opportunities for pantomime by one group while another group recites. The ball players and umpire can mime their actions and speak any brief lines; the choral group can also be the crowd. For sharing with an audience, a simple suggestion of costume, such as baseball caps, may be added.

Other poems that may be used in this fashion include the following:

- "Jabberwocky," Lewis Carroll (Arbuthnot, 1976; Prelutsky, 1983; Saltman, 1985).
- "A Visit from St. Nicholas," Clement Clarke Moore (Arbuthnot, 1976; Prelutsky, 1983; Saltman, 1985).
- "Adventures of Isabel," Ogden Nash (Prelutsky, 1983; Saltman, 1985).
- "Jonathan Bing," B. Curtis Brown (Prelutsky, 1983; Saltman, 1985).
- "The King's Breakfast," A. A. Milne (Saltman, 1985).
- "The Duel," Eugene Field (Arbuthnot, 1976; Prelutksy, 1983).
- "Colonel Fazackerley," Charles Causley (Prelutsky, 1983).
- "The Elf and the Dormouse," Oliver Herford (Prelutsky, 1983).

Storytelling

Storytelling, at once an ancient and a modern art form, is experiencing a renaissance. Some observers are amazed when they see that children can be as engrossed in a well-told story as they are in any television show. Yet this shouldn't be surprising, since the greatest of teachers, past and present, often use stories and parables to educate their charges. No doubt this is one reason many teacher education programs are returning to instruction in storytelling as an important aspect of a teacher's training. In societies and cultures where there is no print media, the storyteller is a repository for, and transmitter of, the group's knowledge to its members. As such, the storyteller has often held a highly revered position in society.

Storytelling involves children directly and actively with a story. As in reading, their imagination is stimulated to create the backdrop and characters who are enacting the drama. With its focus on oral language, storytelling prompts children to appreciate the patterns and sounds of language. And because of its rich heritage in all civilizations, storytelling is as integral to other areas of the curriculum as it is to language arts.

A story's shape and content, as well as its telling, are influenced by the culture that produces it. In Western culture, stories generally have a beginning, middle, and end; this format is readily recognized by children at an early age. Other cultures may have a less structured format, producing very lengthy or serialized stories that are told over a period of time. A comparison of tales from different cultures is certainly a worthy pursuit.

Although there are many excellent sourcebooks one can consult on storytelling (see Figure 10.4 for a selected listing), there is probably no substitute for jumping in and giving it a try. The same is true for children undertaking the art of storytelling. In the next section some basic tips are presented; consider them for both adult and child storytellers.

Story selection

Select stories you genuinely enjoy and are eager to tell, since your enthusiasm for the story will be critical. Select simple stories at first until you have built up confidence in telling. The simpler the plot, the easier it will be to remember. You will, of course, need to keep in mind the appropriate topic, length, and language for the interests and ages of your listeners.

As in story dramatization, the stories that work well for beginning storytellers are folktales. After all, many of the old tales were originally passed on by word of mouth. Their action is strong, the plot dramatic, and the conflict well defined. They move along quickly and generally come to a quick, satisfying ending.

Many old folktales have been collected and set down in books, but some have been rewritten to the extent that their original strength and charm have been lost. Be sure to look for the original collections of the tales (e.g., Joseph Jacobs for some English tales; the Grimm brothers for many German tales), rather than being content with the supermarket tradebook variety. There are numerous picture-book versions of many of the old tales (see Chapter 9).

Because you will be using your own words to tell the story rather than memorizing it, select only stories you feel you can paraphrase easily. Again, the important thing is to build confidence in your ability to tell.

Preparation for telling

Once you have selected the story you want to tell, reread it aloud several times, using as much variety and expression in your voice as possible. This will help set the story in your mind and give you an opportunity to listen to its language orally.

Baker, A., & Greene, E. (1987). *Storytelling: Art and technique* (2nd ed.). New York: Bowker.

Barton, B. (1986). *Tell me another: Storytelling and reading aloud at home, at school, and in the community.* Portsmouth, NH: Heinemann.

Barton, B., & Booth, D. (1990). *Stories in the classroom.* Markham, Ontario: Pembroke.

Bauer, C. F. (1977). *Handbook for storytellers.* Chicago: American Library Association.

Bauer, C. F. (1985). *Celebration.* New York: H. W. Wilson.

Bosma, B. (1992). *Fairytales, fables, legends, and myths: Using folk literature in your classroom.* (2nd ed.). New York: Teachers College Press.

Breneman, L., & Breneman, B. (1983). *Once upon a time: A storytelling handbook.* Chicago: Nelson-Hall.

Cook, E. (1969). *The ordinary and the fabulous: An introduction to myths, legends, and fairy tales for teachers and storytellers.* New York: Cambridge University Press.

Cooper, P. J., & Collins, R. B. (1992). *Look what happened to frog: Storytelling in education.* Scottsdale, AZ: Gorsuch Scarisbrick.

DeWit, D. (1978). *Children's faces looking up.* Chicago: American Library Association.

MacDonald, M. R. (1986). *Twenty tellable tales: Audience participation folktales for beginning storytellers.* New York: H. W. Wilson.

Pellowski, A. (1984). *The story vine: A source book of unusual and easy-to-tell stories from around the world.* New York: Macmillan.

Rosen, B. (1988). *And none of it was nonsense: The power of storytelling in school.* Portsmouth, NH: Heinemann.

Sawyer, R. (1962). *The way of the storyteller.* New York: Viking.

Schimmel, N. (1982). *Just enough to make a story: A source book for storytelling.* Berkeley, CA: Sister's Choice Press.

Sierra, J. (1987). *The flannel board storytelling book.* New York: H. W. Wilson.

FIGURE *10.4* *References on storytelling*

When you feel you have a clear outline of the story in mind, try telling it aloud. Refer to the text only when absolutely necessary. Keep practicing the story aloud; don't be satisfied with just telling the story in your head. Some tellers find it helpful to practice in front of a mirror; some use a tape recorder. Eventually, try the story out on a family member or friend to be sure you know it completely.

Although you will be paraphrasing a story, unique wordings from the story must be included. A classic example is the wolf's entreaty "Little pig, little pig, let me come in" and the response "No, no, by the hair of my chiny chin chin" in Joseph Jacobs' "The Story of Three Little Pigs" (Arbuthnot, 1976; Saltman, 1985). Unless you already know them from your own childhood, you'll need to memorize such refrains.

Many simple stories can be told by beginners. One of the best sources for assistance in finding stories are children's librarians in public libraries. Most of them are required to tell stories during library story hours and can give you much advice and help. Also check the multimedia room of the library for records and audiotapes of professional storytellers.

Multimedia and storytelling

Some experts suggest that beginning storytellers (children included) may be more comfortable telling a story with a flannel board, a few props, puppets, or other objects to hold and manipulate. The theory is that having something to hang onto or hide behind can give one confidence. Since the audience usually focuses on the props more than the teller, anxious beginners are relieved not to be in the spotlight.

A practical reason for using additional materials is to aid in remembering the story or to help children visualize it. For example, I like to use enlarged tagboard cards in telling the story *Harold and the Purple Crayon* by Crockett Johnson (1955). Since the book is too small for more than one child to see at a time, my enlargements of the stick-figure drawings allow an entire class to enjoy the book. The cards also help me remember the story's sequence of events.

As another example, I use very small props (a small cookie, a tiny glass, a piece of drinking straw) to tell the story *If You Give a Mouse a Cookie* by Laura Joffe Numeroff (1985). A small mouse finger puppet is also part of the act. I line up the props beforehand (but conceal them from the audience) in the order they appear in the story. Then, by not having to worry about the sequence of events, I can devote my energies to the telling.

Extra time, of course, is needed to acquire or prepare the materials and to practice with them. There's nothing worse than having materials fall apart, become lost, or not function properly.

To make storytime special and to set the mood for telling, storytellers sometimes use a particular ritual such as lighting a candle, reciting a very brief poem, or donning an appropriate article of clothing, like a hat or shawl. These rituals serve as the signal to children that storytelling is about to begin. At the end of the story, the candle is blown out, another brief poem is recited, or the article of clothing is removed.

Literary tales

After telling some of the old folktales and simple stories, storytellers are ready to try more literary tales, stories that sound like folktales, but that have known authors. Sometimes the plot is based on an old tale, but the author's style of writing makes the story unique; in some cases even the plots have been invented by the author. Writers such as Hans Christian Andersen, Rudyard Kipling, Ruth Sawyer, and Jane Yolen are well-known contributors to the large body of literary tales that exist. (Jay Williams, the author of "Petronella," is another example.)

Telling a literary tale requires thorough familiarity to the point of knowing it verbatim. For example, the opening of "The Elephant's Child" by Rudyard Kipling (Arbuthnot, 1976) reads: "In the high and Far-Off times the Elephant, O best Beloved, had no trunk." From there we enter into a world of wonderfully descriptive names such as "the great, grey-green, greasy Limpopo River," "the Kolokolo Bird," and "the Bi-Coloured-

Python-Rock-Snake." This imaginative language must, of course, be kept intact in order to retain the story's charm.

Children telling tales

Most children enjoy telling tales as much as they do listening to them. Middle- and upper-grade children may even wish to tell stories to younger grades. Telling stories gives children experience in organizing and sequencing, conveying thoughts clearly, and participating actively in literature. If encouraged and assisted in these experiences, rather than being pressured, they will feel more comfortable and enjoy greater success. Often the positive feedback they receive catapults them into even more storytelling.

A good game for practicing storytelling is telling in round-robin style. One child begins the first sentence or two of a story and others add on. The stories may at first be familiar ones; then children may try their hand at inventing new ones. The original stories children tell may not be well structured at first, but continued exposure to excellent literature and listening to stories will eventually pay dividends.

Another useful technique for young storytellers is "reading" wordless picture books (illustrated books with no text or just a few words). For storytelling purposes, be sure to select wordless books whose pictures truly tell a story. Some wordless picture books contain puzzles or are filled with photography. Such books invite observing, commenting, and asking questions but do not have a true storyline. Some popular author-artists who have created memorable wordless picture books include Fernando Krahn, Mercer Mayer, John Goodall, Alexandra Day, and Tomie de Paola. Listings of wordless picture books may be found in Routman, 1991; Watson, 1987; and Gilles et al., 1988.

Spolin's storytelling

Spolin (all sources) has a technique she calls storytelling that actually combines story-telling and drama. It is also similar to the group narrative pantomimes described earlier in this chapter. With Spolin's technique the stories usually are original, although they may be derived from traditional literature, such as folktales.

Spolin suggests that either a child or the teacher perform the role of storyteller. He or she prepares and rehearses a story beforehand, and then relates the story as the players enact it. The emphasis is on spontaneity; therefore, the players do not know what they are supposed to do until the storyteller gives the lines.

Spolin suggests keeping the action more open-ended rather than telling the players exactly what to do. "He was happy as he walked down the road," for example, is preferable to saying, "He walked down the road whistling a merry tune." The former leaves more room for the players' interpretations and is thus more interesting. Evaluation after playing includes discussing suggestions for further adaptation of the story.

Readers Theater

Readers theater is a form of oral reading in which two or more readers present playscripts or other prose and poetic literature aloud. Portrayal of character and interpretation of the material are dependent on skillful oral expression because costume, makeup, props, and scenery are usually dispensed with. Readers theater may be an informal classroom activity with students reading from their desks or using the front of the classroom as a stage, or it may be performed more formally, in an activity room or on a stage in front of an invited audience.

Readers theater is an excellent way to encourage discussion, analysis, and evaluation of literature, as well as to provide practice in oral reading. Children can participate in the excitement of dramatic performance without the stress of memorizing lines or preparing extensive staging. Temple and Gillet (1984) also suggest that readers theater is an effective way to encourage repeated readings, which in turn develop larger sight-word vocabularies, increased rate and fluency, and self-confidence in oral reading.

Literature that works best for readers theater generally has limited action and a manageable number of actors. Playscripts are often performed in readers theater style, although other material such as short stories, excerpts from novels and nonfiction, essays, and poetry are equally popular.

Traditionally, the readers remain on stage throughout the entire reading. The scripted material is held in sturdy folders or placed on music stands. Readers may be seated on stools until their scene occurs, at which time they may rise to speak. Or characters may keep their backs turned when they are not involved in a scene and face forward to signal their entrance.

For presentation of stories, a narrator, who speaks directly to the audience, reads the narrative portions of the story. Narrators are usually placed off to one side of the stage. In longer stories with extensive narrative passages, two narrators may alternate reading. Each may be placed on one side of the stage.

The readers speaking the character roles are positioned so they can look at each other during their scenes of interaction. The dialogue is spoken with the elimination of the tag lines such as "he said" and "she said." However, readers should pay attention to descriptions, such as "he yelled" or "she whispered," since the dialogue should be delivered accordingly.

As was mentioned earlier, the short story *Company's Coming* (Yorinks, 1988) is suitable for readers theater. In addition to the characters of Shirley, Moe, and the spacemen, there are the cousins, Sheldon and Etta, who have one line apiece. A longer story for readers theater, and one with more characters, is Jay Williams' "Petronella." Since these narrative sections are somewhat lengthy, more than one narrator may be used.

From readers theater to radio drama

For some readers theater experiences, children may want to add appropriate sound effects and music. In *Company's Coming* there are such sounds as the space ship landing, a ringing doorbell, and soldiers bursting into the house. Animal sounds, thundering hoofbeats, and Albion's use of magic provide opportunities in "Petronella." For both stories, appropriate theme music may be played to open and close the selection. Incidental or bridge music may be added intermittently, as desired.

Since this approach resembles radio drama, children should have the opportunity to tape-record their reading. In addition to being fun and challenging to make, the tape recording can be a useful tool for self-evaluation. Children enjoy listening to their final product again and again, and no doubt will want to share it with other classes. It may even be possible for middle and upper grades to supply younger children with a collection of audiotaped materials. The lower grades might share a few in return.

Themed programming

After initial experiences in readers theater, middle and upper elementary grades often enjoy the challenge of creating more elaborate programs with themes. Excerpts from various literary selections that fit the theme are sequenced into an interesting arrangement. A subject theme may include a particular holiday, a season of the year, an emotion, or topics such as pets, vacations, or sports. Themed anthologies of children's literature or poetry provide an excellent starting place for ideas. Additional ideas for themed approaches, including political and social issues such as the environment, war, and drug abuse, may be garnered from the discussion of theme study in Chapter 9.

For themed programs, one or more narrators may introduce the literature and make transitional commentary between selections. The narrator's material may be drawn from the literature itself, although students may want to write additional commentary to explain the selections.

Variety and emphasis can be achieved by selecting different genres and styles of literature. For example, balancing poetry with prose and humor with seriousness broadens a program and makes it effective and satisfying. Additional enhancements, such as choral reading, instrumental and vocal music, drama and dance, storytelling, or visual media (slides, posters, artwork) may also be included. Such projects can produce a community of scholarship and negotiated learning as children discover their mutual interests and as they organize the messages and meanings they wish to share with listeners.

Additional sources for readers theater are listed in Figure 10.5.

SUMMARY

This chapter provides only an introduction to the many possibilities that exist for blending the dramatic language arts with whole language. All of the methods discussed are, in many ways, extensions of children's natural responses to literature. Who has not witnessed children responding with sounds, rhythmic repetitions, and playacting when introduced to literature they find appealing? It is their natural way of experiencing the people and events they meet in the literary world, of walking in someone else's shoes. The dramatic language arts build on children's early experiences with dramatic play and help keep alive the imaginative spirit of "let's pretend." By encouraging this participation and by experiencing it themselves, teachers can establish a powerful bond of communication with their students.

Barchers, S. I. (1993). *Readers theatre for beginning readers.* Englewood, CO: Libraries Unlimited/Teacher Ideas Press.

Bauer, C. F. (1987). *Presenting reader's theater.* New York: H. W. Wilson.

Busching, B. A. (1981). Readers theatre: An education for language and life. *Language Arts, 58,* 330–338.

Coger, L. I. & White, M. R. (1982). *Readers theatre handbook: A dramatic approach literature* (3rd ed.). Glenview, IL: Scott, Foresman.

Laughlin, M. K., Black. P. T., & Loberg, M. K. (1991). *Social studies readers theatre for children: Scripts and script development.* Englewood, CO: Libraries Unlimited/ Teacher Ideas Press.

Laughlin, M. K., & Latrobe, K. H. (1990). *Readers theatre for children: Scripts and script development.* Englewood, CO: Libraries Unlimited/Teacher Ideas Press.

Sloyer, S. (1982). *Readers theatre: Story dramatization in the classroom.* Urbana, IL: National Council of Teachers of English.

Tanner, F. A. (1987). *Readers theatre fundamentals.* Topeka, KS: Clark Publishing.

FIGURE *10.5   Selected sources for readers theater*

Becoming a part of literature deepens our understanding of human interaction and the meaning of life. The social interaction of sharing and negotiating meaning together helps us see the world in new ways. It encourages us to search for additional information and insight and to explore an infinite variety of events, issues, and relationships. Through the dramatic language arts, literature comes alive and enriches our existence and our well-being.

FOR FURTHER REFLECTION AND EXPLORATION

1. As mentioned earlier, a story like Jay Williams' "Petronella" provides considerable material for dramatization. Additional activities are presented below. In each case, consider what students might learn by engaging in the activity. How might the activities be integrated with discussion and exploration of the themes and characters? What activities might you use with children, and why? Based on the methods presented in this chapter, what additional activities can you suggest? (For more activities of this nature with traditional tales, see Heinig, 1992.)

   a. All the children pretend to be Albion the enchanter. On the leader's count of three they are to turn themselves into an ax that chops down a tree. They return to Albion's human shape when the leader rings a bell. Do the same for turning into the salmon. What other shapes might Albion turn himself into? Children, on their own, may think of three things not mentioned in the story and pantomime them as the leader counts to three slowly.

   b. In pairs, children enact a brief narrative pantomime of Petronella and Ferdinand making their getaway. (It is not necessary for boys to be paired with girls.)

The passage should be read slowly first, for consideration of how each of the movements can be played safely. Children can usually find a variety of ways to interpret these movements, but it is wise to check out the best ideas and have them demonstrated. Perhaps three pairs of competent students can demonstrate their ideas before the entire class plays it in their pairs. Here is the passage for pantomime:

> She grabbed him by the wrist and dragged him out of bed. She hauled him down the stairs. His horse and hers were in a separate stable, and she saddled them quickly. She gave the prince a shove, and he mounted. She jumped on her own horse, seized the prince's reins, and away they went like the wind.

c. The King and Queen are expecting a child and want the kingdom to be involved in the selection of a name. In one large meeting or in small groups, the children, as royal courtiers, discuss appropriate names for the royal child. The leader may play an emissary or servant.

d. According to the story, no one ever knew what happened to the two older princes in the kingdom after they went off to seek their fortunes: Prince Michael to the castle of Blitz and Prince George to the city of Gratz. Children may create a round-robin story, detailing the adventures of one of the princes. Or, in groups of five, children may prepare a brief scene showing what happened. For a third alternative, play the stories in groups, using Spolin's storytelling technique (described on p. 471).

e. In pairs, one child plays Albion trying to suggest politely to Ferdinand that he has overstayed his welcome. Ferdinand doesn't seem to get the point, or else he chooses to ignore it. Children improvise some of this conversation. Pairs may try out their ideas in private, simultaneously. Then volunteers may be called on to share a little of their scene.

f. Children are asked to pretend they are Petronella. The leader (as an interested bystander, friend, or family member) asks them, "Why do you continue to try to rescue Ferdinand when he seems so unworthy?" Volunteers give responses.

g. The wrinkled old man has sat on the same spot for sixty-two years, waiting to be released from a spell with the question "Is there anything I can do to help you?" He is also able to give important information to Petronella. As powerful as he seems to be, apparently he was also under someone else's spell. Who is this strange little man, and what is his story? Let four or five children be the little old man on a panel, answering questions from the class. (Children usually do not worry that the details expressed may be different from each other's.) After such an exploration, children may wish to write their own stories about the little old man, perhaps from his perspective.

h. Several children may be a panel of Albions. The audience may ask questions such as "How did you become an enchanter?" "What spell can you perform that you are especially proud of?" "Why couldn't you free yourself from the ring trap?" "What different things can you turn yourself into?" "What is your favorite thing to be and why?" and so on. A similar panel could be made for the character of Ferdinand. "Why did you go to Albion's castle in the first place?" "What happened to you after you were left to find your own way home?" "What is your goal in life?"

i. Divide the class into groups of four to prepare the optional final scene, enacting events that transpire after Petronella returns home with Albion. What happens when Petronella and Albion return to the castle? How are they received by Petronella's parents? What would make the best ending for this story? Let students share their scenes. Perhaps a composite of ideas can be included in one scene.

j. Since Albion is an enchanter, what might Petronella's life be like after they are married? Groups of three to five children might improvise a short scene depicting an event.

k. The leader plays the role of Ferdinand's father or mother and seeks the group's advice on how to help Ferdinand become more like a prince.

l. Albion and Petronella are having a disagreement over wedding plans. Albion wants to invite his enchanter friends, while Petronella thinks things could get out of hand. What compromise do they reach? (The class may be divided into pairs to discuss the problem and report on their compromise.)

m. Select several children to play Petronella and her family. The rest of the class are reporters who want to know what sort of role Petronella intends to play in the future. Does she plan to settle down after seeking her fortune? What plans do the family members have for her? What do they think of her responses? (A similar activity could be played by having paired interviews with Petronella, a panel of Petronellas, or a press conference with Petronella and Albion.)

n. Have children play a "Where" theater game and build a study-workroom for Albion the enchanter. Determine the imagined room's dimensions and establish at least one door for entering and exiting. Considering Albion's line of work, what furnishings might there be in such a room? (Students may work in pairs or groups to move large or heavy objects.)

o. Related written activities could include the wedding announcement/invitation for Petronella and Albion; a letter from Ferdinand to his family telling of his latest adventure; a list of rules for Petronella on how to be a proper young lady; a list of occupations appropriate for Ferdinand; advice on the care and feeding of horses, hounds, and falcons; a marriage counselor's advice to women who marry enchanters; a society column report on the wedding, including details of Albion's side of the family; a menu for the wedding feast; a page from Albion's book of enchantments; a toast to be said at the wedding; King Peter's and Queen Blossom's blessings on the marriage.

2. Read the following fictional newspaper account, written by Connie Weaver (from Weaver, Chaston, & Peterson, *Theme Exploration: A Voyage of Discovery*, 1993):

Robots Take Over Los Angeles!

UPI—Early this morning, an army of robots took over the government of Los Angeles, first by taking over their computers and later by bodily taking possession of the city building. Government officials and police were powerless to stop them.

According to two city officials, who spoke on condition they remain anonymous, the takeover began at 12:01 A.M. when the robots broke the security codes of the city computers and thereby gained control not only of the city's records and finances, but its police and security personnel. Within three hours, an estimated army of 5,000 robots had marched on the city. The police, under control of the robots, repelled any citizens who attempted to halt the onslaught of the army. By daylight, the army of robots had taken over all key positions within the city government, including the mayor and the city council, the police and firefighting forces, and the city treasury.

As near as stunned officials can determine, the takeover of the robots began five years ago when an enterprising firm named Water Everywhere purchased a specially designed self-replicating robot from a Japanese firm to reproduce other robots that would drill for wells in the Mojave Desert. Since then, the robots have proliferated "like rabbits," as one official of Water Everywhere put it. "But until today," she said, "the robots have appeared content to locate water, drill for wells, and run the operations of piping water to southern California and Arizona."

It is not known why the robots turned from well-drilling to taking over a city, nor is it known how many other self-replicating robots with similar ambitions might exist elsewhere in this country.

How might the situation presented in this news account be explored further through drama activities? Begin by brainstorming some activities similiar to those presented in Activity 1. Or try your hand at planning a possible role drama, following the steps suggested on pp. 453–458. Be sure to try acting out at least some of the activities you design.

3. With others, try some of the oral language activities described in this chapter. For example, you might reenact the story of "Petronella" using the creative drama/playmaking method or by trying some of the activities listed in Activity 1 above. Or you might try the educational drama method, using the outline on pp. 452–458. Or perform some of the poems cited in the choral reading section. Tell a folktale, perhaps using a multimedia approach. Or organize and present a readers theater program around a theme of significance. Perhaps your class can be divided into small groups, with each group preparing a different activity to share.

11 Reconsidering Dyslexia and Learning Disabilities

Educators often say we want students to become whatever they are capable of becoming. In fact, researchers have found, we ourselves decide very early what each child is capable of. After that, our curriculum and instruction help confirm our self-fulfilling prophecies.

— Ron Brandt

The label "disabled" takes away self-confidence. . . . Because I have unique learning abilities, I have given myself a different label—that of creative learner.

— Christopher Lee

Consider the following:

- Between the academic years 1976–77 and 1989–90, the number of U.S. students identified as learning disabled increased approximately 150 percent, while the school-age population remained nearly the same. (National Center for Educational Statistics, 1995, pp. 63 & 11).
- The number of students classified as learning disabled is over two million, or a little more than 5 percent of the school age population (p. 65).
- It has been estimated that more than 80 percent of all students could be classified as learning disabled by one or more definitions now in use (Ysseldyke et al., 1983).
- Because the child, not the system, is defined as the problem, children remain dependent on special education (Case, 1992, p. 33).
- Yet the fault lies not in the children but in the system that failed to prevent the damage in the first place (Slavin, 1991, p. 587, referring to students assigned to Chapter 1 programs for "at risk" children from low-income homes).

Because certain labels can be more harmful than beneficial, it is important that we reconceptualize negatively labeled learners, perhaps as "special needs" or, better yet, simply as "special" students or "creative learners," to use the term that Christopher Lee has applied to himself and other learners who have not just special problems but also unique learning abilities (Lee & Jackson, 1992). Such a shift in terminology helps us revalue these learners.

"Creative learners" and other special needs students come in many sizes, shapes, and colors. They may be children considered "at risk" because they come from lower-socioeconomic families, from single-parent homes, and/or from homes where there are few books. They may be children identified as having an alleged learning disability, such as dyslexia, or a "special handicapping condition," such as an attention deficit disorder. They may be children whose mental function has been impaired by prenatal factors or birth complications: children whose mothers were addicted to drugs during pregnancy, for instance, or children with Down's syndrome.

What these and other special needs students have in common is that they—and/or their families and home environment—have traditionally been considered *deficient* in some way. Take, for example, the "official" definition of dyslexia, also known as a "specific reading disability" and as "specific developmental dyslexia." The latter has been defined by the World Federation of Neurology as follows:

> A disorder manifested by difficulty in learning to read despite conventional instruction, adequate intelligence, and socio-cultural opportunity. It is dependent upon fundamental cognitive disabilities which are frequently of constitutional origin. (Critchley, 1970)

In other words, dyslexic readers are said to have something wrong with—or at least not quite right with—how their brain functions. According to this official definition, they have a disability that amounts to a deficiency.

Furthermore, in diagnosing children as dyslexic, educators and other specialists have seemed merely to assume that conventional instruction is appropriate to and adequate for all children. Thus, children who are victims of such standardized instruction are typically blamed for not responding to it. With allegedly at-risk children, the home is typically considered lacking—that is, the children's family and/or culture are blamed. When children are diagnosed as learning disabled, however, it is typically the children themselves who are blamed: their neurological systems are considered somehow deficient.

TOWARD A RECONCEPTUALIZATION OF DYSLEXIA AND LEARNING DISABILITIES

What seems more productive for understanding and alleviating reading and learning difficulties is, first of all, to recognize the role that environment in general and education in particular play in the genesis, diagnosis, and maintenance of such difficulties. As Figure 11.1 suggests, not only factors located within the individual but also factors located within the environment may play a role even in the reader's or learner's genetic make-up and neurological functioning, as well as in the reader's or learner's measured behaviors and in the diagnosis of an individual as dyslexic and/or learning disabled. Specifically:

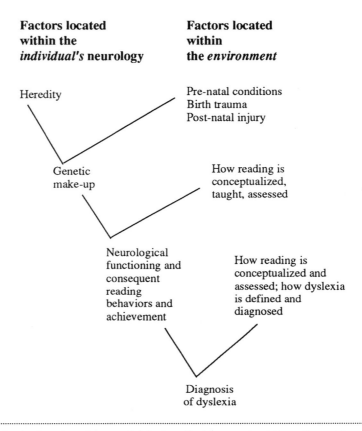

FIGURE 11.1   *Neurological and environmental factors that may enter into a diagnosis of dyslexia*

1. A person's *genetic make-up* may result not only from heredity, but from pre-natal conditions (e.g., the mother's drug dependency), from birth trauma, and/or from post-natal trauma (injury).
2. A person's *neurological functioning* and consequent reading/learning behaviors may result not only from his or her genetic make-up, but from how reading/learning are conceptualized, taught, and assessed.
3. A person's being diagnosed as *dyslexic* and/or as *learning disabled* results not only from his or her overt reading/learning behaviors and achievement but from how dyslexia and learning disabilities are defined. In other words, the concepts of dyslexia and learning disablilities reflect our concept of reading and learning and assessment as much or more than actual neurological functioning of an individual.

The thesis of this chapter is that we need to rethink traditional concepts of dyslexia, recognizing that what has traditionally been considered evidence of dyslexia reflects certain concepts about reading and reading assessment that are challenged by miscue and other psycholinguistic research. Similarly, we need to rethink learning disabilities, considering the evidence—such as the data regarding "at risk" students in Chapter 7 and the anecdotal evidence regarding differently abled students in Chapter 12—that special needs students can succeed academically when the classroom environment, expectations, experiences, and evaluation better accommodate these learners' strengths instead of making their weaknesses a barrier.

The following discussion focuses on dyslexia more than on learning disabilities—not only because this is a book about the reading process and the teaching of reading, but because, as Coles suggests, reading "is the most common disability, so much so that calling a child learning disabled is understood to mean reading disabled" (Coles, 1987, p. xii). Though not necessarily or always true, this often seems to be the case: in our schools today, many students are diagnosed as learning disabled because of an apparent problem with reading—their alleged dyslexia.

DYSLEXIA AS NEUROLOGICAL FUNCTIONING

In keeping with the "both/and" orientation of the preceding discussion, we will consider evidence for less-than-optimal neurological functioning in alleged dyslexia before considering various roles the environment might play. The former entails not only a recapitulation of common definitions of dyslexia but also an examination of the evidence for reading as a process involving both the left and right cerebral hemispheres of the brain. "Normal" brain functioning in reading is then compared with reading behaviors of alleged dyslexics, whose errors in reading isolated words suggest lopsided or inadequately integrated hemispheric processing—at least with respect to the kinds of linguistic processing that characterize reading.

Neurologically-based Definitions of Dyslexia

The term *dyslexia* has come to designate severe reading difficulty in people "who are otherwise normal intellectually, emotionally, and medically" (Witelson, 1977, p. 16). More perniciously, people themselves are often labeled dyslexic when they have severe difficulty in reading without any identifiable physical, psychological, intellectual, or environmental deficits (Karlin, 1980, p. 103). However, care is rarely taken to rule out these other causes of reading difficulty, and often the term "dyslexia" is little more than a fancy word for what is perceived as a reading problem (Harris & Hodges, 1981, p. 95). Because of the uncertainty as to what "dyslexia" really means, it is perhaps not surprising that some authorities estimate that about 3 percent of the school-age population suffers from dyslexia, while others place the estimate as high as 15 percent.

The concept of dyslexia was popularized by a neurologist named Samuel Orton. In 1937, he proposed that severe reading difficulty with no obvious physical, mental, or environmental cause might in fact be caused by poorly established hemispheric dominance in the brain. The left cerebral hemisphere is dominant for many aspects of language processing in most right-handed and many left-handed people, while the right hemisphere is dominant for most other left-handers. However, for the people termed dyslexic, Orton hypothesized that neither hemisphere was dominant. He based this hypothesis largely upon his observation that many such readers and writers seemed to reverse visual images, reading and writing *b* as *d, was* as *saw,* and so forth. Orton hypothesized that this apparent misperception stemmed from the brain receiving images from both the left and the right cerebral hemisphere simultaneously, rather than from just one dominant hemisphere. This, he reasoned, might be responsible for the apparent perception of words and letters as mirror images of one another (see Monaghan, 1980, for a more thorough discussion of the history of dyslexia as a medical concept).

Orton later took a more holistic perspective toward conceptualizing dyslexia, but as a result of his early hypothesis, many people think of dyslexia as being characterized by reversals of letters and words. However, there are several things to keep in mind regarding reversals like *b* for *d* and *was* for *saw* in reading and writing. First, many people with severe reading problems show little or no tendency toward reversals, especially if they are reading for meaning. Second, many children misperceive such isolated elements of language during the early stages of reading; this is a normal part of language development (e.g., Clay, 1975; 1987b), and most children outgrow it with no difficulty or need for special instruction. Third, only a very small percentage of children do not outgrow it naturally, but persist in having problems with reversals, particularly in writing: they may, for example, typically write a word completely backwards, from the last letter to the first. Such children may indeed need specialized help as well as sympathetic understanding on the part of parents and teachers.

However, it is all too seldom recognized that children who need help overcoming reversals in reading can often circumvent the difficulty when they are helped to view the troublesome elements within a larger context. After all, how often do you need to focus on *b* and *d* or *was* and *saw* as isolated elements, outside of the classroom? Instead of focusing on isolated elements, instructional assistance can involve using the troublesome letters in words and the words in highly predictable sentences, thus focusing the reader's attention on meaning rather than letters. The reader who has difficulty distinguishing between *b* and *d* in isolation will not necessarily confuse *big* with *dig* in sentences like "That elephant is *big*" or "Let's get a shovel and *dig* here," when the reader has been encouraged to focus on meaning rather than on distinguishing one letter from another.

What, then, of Orton's original hypothesis that otherwise unexplained severe reading difficulty may be characterized by the two cerebral hemispheres producing conflicting mirror images? Today this particular hypothesis is accepted by almost no one. This may be partly because few children with severe reading difficulties persist with such reversals (especially if they are taught to focus on meaning). In addition, however, there appears to be no evidence for this hypothesis in the rapidly accelerating body of brain research.

Nevertheless, some of today's brain specialists think that severe reading difficulty may often result from a deficiency in the functioning of one cerebral hemisphere, from the abnormal dominance of one hemisphere, and/or from inadequate integration of the two hemispheres (see, for example, Zaidel, 1979, and Hynd & Hynd, 1984). There are three major lines of research that converge to support this hypothesis. First is research into the functioning of the brain hemispheres. This in some ways correlates or converges with research into the nature of the reading process and also with research into the nature of severe reading difficulties. We shall turn, then, to a discussion of this evidence for the broad hypothesis that dyslexia may result from lopsided hemispheric processing.

Reading as a Whole-Brain Process: Complementary Hemispheric Functioning

Recent studies of hemispheric functioning in normal, healthy brains have established that reading, writing, and other complex processes involve both the right and the left hemispheres. This is shown by studies of blood flow on the surface of the brain and by studies that map the electrical activity on the surface of the hemispheres. Though in most people the left hemisphere is more involved than the right, widespread areas of both hemispheres are involved in reading (see, for instance, Lassen, Ingvar, & Skinhoj, 1978; McKean, 1981; & Duffy et al., 1980, 1984). Some studies have found that when readers' attention is directed to the sounds and letters in words, blood flow on the left side is decidedly more prominent. However, when readers' attention is directed to the meanings of words, both hemispheres are equally activated, as determined by equal increases in blood flow on both sides of the brain (Flowers, Wood, & Naylor, 1989; Rumsey et al., 1987). Vellutino and Denckla (1991) review most of these studies, including studies of hemidecorticate children whose right or left hemisphere was removed early in life, and adults with brain damage in one hemisphere or the other.

When one hemisphere is removed early in life, the other can compensate to a significant degree—but not entirely. Children who learned to read with only a right hemisphere typically have difficulty with the linear processing of grapho/phonemics and syntax, and with literal comprehension of words and phrases—aspects of reading commonly associated with the left hemisphere. Children who learn to read with only a left hemisphere typically have difficulty with visual and spatial perception of words and with comprehension, particularly of larger wholes—aspects of reading that seem typically to be associated with the right hemisphere (Dennis, 1982).

While the role of certain regions of the left hemisphere is widely recognized as critical in phonological and syntactic processing, the role of the right hemisphere in language processing has commonly been overlooked. However, the role of the right hemisphere in comprehension is strongly suggested by certain studies of right-hemisphere-damaged adults as well as by hemidecorticate children. Using primarily their left hemisphere for language processing, such adults are often very literal-minded, unable to determine the significance of details in a story; unable to appreciate humor or emotional content; unable to bring past meaning to the reading of present texts; and unable to integrate details into a coherent whole. Thus it looks as if the right hemisphere typically plays a significant role in what we think of as higher levels of comperehension (Levy, 1985; Vellutino and Denckla, 1991).

Clearly, both hemispheres are involved in normal reading—and, indeed, in all but perhaps the very simplest of mental processes.

Also relevant for understanding reading and reading difficulties, however, is the observation that the two hemispheres seem to specialize in different functions: the left hemisphere typically deals with linear grapho/phonemic, syntactic, and semantic processing, while the right hemisphere typically specializes in comprehending larger wholes. Given the gestalt-seeking function currently attributed to the right hemisphere, perhaps it often comes into play first, initiating the active search for meaning and drawing upon the reader's schemas in that search (at present, this suggestion is no more than a hypothesis). But as the act of reading progresses, there is complementary interplay between the two kinds of processing: the linear, element-by-element processing attributed to the left hemisphere, and the simultaneous, pattern-seeking processing attributed to the right. As suggested in Chapter 5, these and other kinds of processing occur not only more or less simultaneously, but to some extent redundantly, during proficient reading.

But what if one hemisphere's kind of processing somehow predominated over the other's? Or what if the differing kinds were not integrated into a smoothly functioning whole? In such a case, we might expect to find the kind of reading characteristic of beginning readers and of those who have severe reading difficulty. Let us look, then, at some of the research on dyslexia, to see whether so-called dyslexics seem to have the kinds of difficulties that would be predicted if one kind of processing predominated and/or the two kinds were not well coordinated.

Possible Neurological Bases of Dyslexia

One thing that emerges clearly from the research on dyslexia is the observation that no two individuals exhibit exactly the same configuration of reading difficulties. Thus, on the one hand, we must be wary of too readily categorizing individuals as having this or that kind of problem, and thereby overlooking the person's unique strengths and needs. On the other hand, we may gain a deeper understanding of typical reading difficulties if we look at some of the recurring patterns.

So far, much of the dyslexia research purports to test reading comprehension by focusing on students' ability to identify single words—a procedure that sociopsycholinguists consider hopelessly inadequate. Nevertheless, the results of such assessment suggest lopsided hemispheric processing in many cases.

In a widely cited article, for example, Boder (1973) presented groundbreaking research on subtypes of dyslexia, using word identification and patterns of spelling as her measures. Of the 107 dyslexic students in her study, approximately 9 percent had a poor memory for visual patterns and tended to read analytically, "'by ear,' through a process of phonetic analysis and synthesis, sounding out familiar as well as unfamiliar combinations of letters, rather than by whole-word visual gestalts" (Boder, 1973, p. 670). They also tended to spell phonetically, with the result that even the simplest "sight words" were often misspelled, yet the childrens' spellings of unfamiliar words were usually readable because they were phonetic. They read "laboriously, as if . . . seeing each word for the first time" (p. 670). Not surprisingly, these readers typically had a much lower sight vocabulary than those in the major group, whose sight vocabulary itself was characterized as "limited."

In contrast were dyslexic readers who read words globally as instantaneous visual gestalts, rather than analytically. Lacking word-analysis skills, they were unable to sound out and blend the letters and syllables of a word. Such readers made substitutions based primarily on visual resemblance and apparently grammar ("horse" for *house,* "monkey" for *money,* "stop" for *step).* However, their most striking substitutions were words closely related conceptually but not phonetically to the original word. Examples are "funny" for *laugh,* "chicken" or "quack" for *duck,* "answer" for *ask,* "stairs" for *step,* "airplane" for *train,* "person" for *human,* "planet" for *moon,* and "Los Angeles" for *city* (Boder, 1973, p. 670). Interestingly, such substitutions occurred even though the words were presented in isolation, lending further support to the observation that the general sense of a word can be understood even when the word itself is not identified or identifiable (McKean, 1985; Bishop, 1993; see Chapter 5, p. 182). This group's spelling patterns also resembled their reading patterns. That is, they could spell familiar words that they recognized on sight, even irregular and long ones, but they had difficulty sounding out even the simplest regular words, if the words were not already familiar. Boder indicates that the largest percentage of dyslexics in her study, approximately two-thirds, exhibited the latter reading and spelling patterns.

Overall, 9 percent of the dyslexics in Boder's study read words analytically rather than globally, while the rest (22 percent) exhibited both patterns (Boder, 1973, p. 676). According to Boder, these proportions seem to be typical of other studies as well. In particular, the major proportion of readers diagnosed as dyslexic seem to have difficulty with analytical, letter-by-letter processing.

From studies of hemispheric functioning in reading and from studies finding subtypes of dyslexics, it appears that when left-hemispheric processing predominates, we may get word-for-word reading with little comprehension, or letter-by-letter processing that because of inattention to meaning results in frequent nonwords, such as Tony's "souts" for *shouts* and "ramped" for *repeated* (though Tony's processing was not as lop-sided overall as these examples suggest in isolation—see Chapter 6). Some researchers have called such readers "surface dyslexics," since they attend mainly to the superficial, surface features of the text rather than to meaning (Hynd & Hynd, 1984, pp. 493–494). On the other hand, when right-hemispheric processing predominates, we may get renditions that preserve important aspects of the meaning but sometimes bear little visual or auditory resemblance to the actual words on the page, such as "green" for *white,* "girl" for *children,* "tigers" for *lions,* and "wheels" for *car* (Seymour & Elder, 1986; these renditions are from children who had been taught and tested on words in isolation). Such readers may be called "deep dyslexics" because they attend primarily to deep structure, to meaning (see Coltheart, Patterson, & Marshall, 1980, for various articles on deep dyslexia).

Particularly interesting with regard to deep dyslexia are some of Vellutino and Denckla's observations from studies of children learning to read with only one brain hemisphere. True, without a left hemisphere, "there is inevitably poor reading of unfamiliar words, due to poor phonological skills, and a poor grasp of the larger syntactic relationships that facilitate comprehension of complex texts." Nevertheless, the right hemisphere alone "can support and sustain a functional and reasonably adequate level of reading, in which meaning can be derived from written text" (Vellutino & Denckla, 1991, p. 598; they cite the research of Dennis, 1982). For example, Christopher Lee's personal story (Lee & Jackson, 1992) suggests that when he reads, right-hemispheric kinds of processing compensate significantly for the left-hemispheric kinds of tasks that are nearly impossible for him. Reading complex texts is still incredibly difficult, but he has developed creative learning strategies in order to cope.

Regardless of the causes, there appear to be some readers who make insufficient use of the global, meaning-seeking strategies commonly attributed to the right hemisphere, and other readers who make insufficient use of the linear, analytical strategies commonly attributed to the left. More specifically, when reading words, some readers have difficulty recognizing words as wholes; some have difficulty sounding out words; and others have both kinds of difficulties.

According to Boder and many others, the largest share of dyslexics are those who make insufficient use of grapho/phonemic cues; that is, they identify (and misidentify) words on sight but seem unable to sound out words that they don't recognize on sight. But I cannot help suspecting that many of these so-called dyslexics might be considered adequate to good readers if meaning and not word identification were the goal. Remember that in Boder's study (and in most other studies of dyslexia), reading was operationally defined as word identification, and word identification was tested in isolation. Even under such non-natural "reading" conditions, most of the miscues of the larger group of alleged dyslexics bore syntactic and semantic resemblance to the stimulus word. If such readers were to read connected text, might we not find some of them exhibiting the patterns of good readers like Jay and Anne?

Thus, I suspect that many readers considered dyslexic are viewed as such because the examiners define reading as first and foremost a matter of identifying words and because they are looking for readers' weaknesses in identifying words rather than their strengths in constructing meaning. Even investigators solidly convinced that dyslexia is characterized by neurological dysfunction point out that virtually all of the available research "has failed to evaluate or adequately control for the environmental and/or educational deficits that may cause a reading disorder" (Vellutino & Denckla, 1991, p. 603).

I am simply taking such an observation one (giant) step further by suggesting that one of the educational deficits may be the concept of reading that underlies both reading assessment and reading instruction. In other words, there may be at least three ways the environment contributes to both the development and the maintenance of reading strategies that are less than fully successful: through a dysfunctional conceptualization of reading; through reading assessment that reflects this conceptualization; and through reading instruction that similarly reflects and maintains this view. At the root of the issue is the traditional but dysfunctional concept of reading as identifying words.

DYSLEXIA AS AN ENVIRONMENTAL CONSTRUCT

Traditionally, clinicians and researchers have used (separately or concomitantly) such criteria as these for diagnosing a reader as dyslexic: (1) the reader is at least two years below grade level, according to certain standardized tests; (2) there is a significant discrepancy between intelligence and observed achievement level, again according to standardized tests. In other words, dyslexia is commonly viewed as resulting from a develomental lag in scoring well on tests that, one way or another, place a high premium upon fast and fluent word identification. In effect, it is implicitly or explicitly assumed that a reader is dyslexic if he or she cannot read words easily—or reads words much less easily than most peers. Or to put it the other way around, dyslexia is implicitly defined as having greater difficulty in reading words that most of one's age-mates. Therefore, most procedures for diagnosing dyslexia focus on how well and/or how one reads words in isolation or in timed tests.

What's Wrong with the Traditional Concept of Reading as Identifying Words

True, a substantial body of research has found that fluent word identification strongly correlates with reading comprehension (see summaries in Adams, 1990; Stanovich, 1991). But this should be no surprise when reading comprehension is measured by timed tests via multiple choice questions about relatively short texts that offer little redudancy or opportunity for concepts to be developed in print, much less understood by the reader. Under the conditions imposed by standardized tests, it is not necessarily significant that fluent word identification correlates with what passes for reading comprehension. Correlation under these conditions does not necessarily mean that word identification correlates with comprehension under other circumstances, using different assessment measures.

Given what we know about miscues and the reading of proficient readers, a definition of dyslexia based instead upon miscue research would take into account the following conclusions from the hundreds of miscue studies conducted since the early 1970s (Goodman and Goodman, n. d.) and from psycholinguistic research into the nature of the reading process (e.g., F. Smith's *Understanding Reading,* first published in 1971 and published in a fourth edition in 1987):

1. Proficient readers focus more upon meaning than upon words. Therefore, reading should not be considered first or foremost a matter of identifying words, but a matter of constructing meaning from connected, coherent, and authentic text.
2. The construction of meaning involves such strategies as using prior knowledge and context to predict, sampling the visual display, monitoring comprenension, employing "fix-it" strategies when meaning has gone awry, and so forth. Such strategies are used simultaneously and cyclically rather than linearly.

3. Readers who make many miscues—either on isolated words, connected text, or both—may nevertheless construct meaning effectively from appropriate texts. Consequently, testing readers on isolated words, or even assessing their reading by considering the strategies reflected by their miscues, may often underestimate the ability of seemingly less proficient readers to contruct meaning from connected, coherent, and authentic text.

In other words, the major problem with a traditional characterization of dyslexia is the underlying notion that reading means identifying words correctly. Diagnosing dyslexia on the basis of word identification tests and timed comprehension tests results in identifying as dyslexic many readers who are reasonably proficient at constructing meaning, given world enough and time.

The Solution Becomes the Problem

After defining and diagnosing dyslexia and learning disabilities on the basis of isolated skills, we have traditionally offered more instruction focused on the student's ability to do skills exercises apart from authentic acts of reading, writing, or learning. Consequently, by continuing to focus on the reading of words, we have further diverted readers' attention from the construction of meaning. In addition, we have given alleged dyslexics even fewer opportunities to read connected text for meaning. They have been kept busy doing skills work instead.

The title of this section is borrowed from Bartoli and Botel's *Reading/Learning Disability: An Ecological Approach* (1988) because their thinking is so close to mine regarding the causes and maintenance of alleged learning disabilities. They mention three problematic "solutions" to improving reading: obsessive testing of trivia; fragmented, skills-oriented curricula that provide more of the same skills work that the students often are not good at; and special remedial programs that typically provide still more of the same decontextualized skills work, while isolating students from their peers and from the authentic reading and writing their peers may be doing.

Obsessive testing leads to identifying as learning disabled many children who can do authentic reading and writing reasonably well. Denny Taylor's book *Learning Denied* (1991b) documents the incredible harm that can be done to children by diagnosing them as having dyslexia or some other kind(s) of learning disability by using standardized tests of isolated skills, with total disregard for their ability to actually read and write. As previously mentioned, miscue analysis often suggests, too, that readers are far more competent at constructing meaning than one would assume from standardized tests.

This is one way that obsessive testing harms our students: by diagnosing children as having dyslexia and learning disabilities that exist more in the eye of the beholder, or the testing instruments, than in the child.

Once diagnosed, these learners are typically dosed with more of the skills work that has been difficult for them to do or complete. They may be assigned to resource room teachers, who can more readily supervise and assist them in completing skills activities. In such a small-group or one-on-one setting, these allegedly learning disabled children can often complete skills work that they previously could not do, or at least did not do. This understandably leads teachers and administrators to claim success for their programs (as noted by Bartoli & Botel, 1988, Chapter 3). But, we must ask, success at *what*? And what are these students *not* given the opportunity to succeed at doing?

Take, for instance, the situations of Sunny and James, as described in Bartoli and Botel (1988). Early in their school careers, these children were assigned to LD classrooms, apparently in part because of their family and cultural background (Bartoli & Botel, 1988, pp. 37–41) and despite PL 94–142 legislation that expressly forbids assigning students to LD classes on such a basis. James, for instance, was among the black children who were simply assumed to not have the home advantages of their peers and who were grouped together as "deprived" students, in order to "better serve their needs," to "help the students feel better about themselves," and to "almost guarantee a kind of success" by giving them less demanding tasks than the other children.

Bartoli and Botel summarize the kind of curriculum to which Sunny and James were subjected in their LD classroom, with its "fragmented definition of reading and learning":

> Both Sunny and James were fed steady diets of parts and pieces of language removed from meaningful context. They were continually schooled on the subskills of language to the neglect of whole language learning that integrates skills with content. They had six years of spelling, phonics, and answering main idea questions; but they were only rarely observed reading a book of their choice, writing to extend and develop their own thoughts, or developing higher level critical thinking to approach new learning. (Bartoli & Botel, 1988, p. 50)

In part, the results of such a curriculum can be seen in the children's standardized test scores. Sunny's IQ dropped nearly twenty points during her four years of special learning disability training, from 93–96 in the first grade to 78 in the fourth grade, as measured on the Wechsler Intelligence Scale for Children—Revised (WISC-R). James' reading level at the end of second grade was measured as 2.6, but by the end of sixth grade his reading progress was reported to be "growth" from low-second to mid-third grade, with a grade level of 1.5 in word recognition. Understandably, Bartoli and Botel conclude that "we have two more examples of the paradox of the solution becoming the problem—victims of a system operating under a narrowly conceived framework that leads to fragmentation, stigmatization, and fossilization of potential" (Bartoli & Botel, 1988, pp. 39, 34, 50).

When they are kept busy doing skills work instead of authentic reading and writing, children are prevented from engaging in the very kinds of activities and experiences that would best promote their reading strategies and skills, not to mention their interest in reading and their self-concept as readers and writers (see Chapter 7). It is no wonder that, once consigned to traditional remedial programs, students rarely escape from them—perhaps because they still cannot demonstrate proficiency on the tests, but even more because they have been left further and further behind by classmates who are doing less skills work and more reading of books, magazines, and a variety of print for everyday learning and pleasure. (For some of the evidence leading to such conclusions, see such references as Goodlad, 1984; Oakes, 1985; and review articles by Anderson & Pellicer, 1990; McGill-Franzen & Allington, 1991; and Allington & McGill-Franzen, 1989.)

In short, our schools are typically not serving children well by categorizing them as learning disabled on the basis of tests that bear little relationship to normal reading, then giving them more skills work that resembles the test instead of engaging them in authentic reading and writing and developing *needed* skills and strategies within that context. A "dumbed-down" curriculum tends to become a self-fulfilling prophecy, resulting in intellectual and academic losses rather than gains. Furthermore, "Most of the studies that document success on subskill instruction are laboratory studies that show little concern with generalization to real world uses of literacy or even to how the student integrates the subskills to finally read or write" (Cousin & Weekley, 1992).

In summary, the traditional concepts of reading and of dyslexia promote assessment and instruction that actually lessen the possibility of students' becoming proficient at constructing meaning from authentic texts.

Dyslexics Compared with Unlabeled Readers

Another way the environment has contributed to misunderstanding those diagnosed as dyslexic is by not realizing that so-called normal readers use essentially the same range of strategies found in the alleged subtypes of dyslexia.

For example, Ebro compared twenty-six developmental dyslexic adolescents attending a school for those who have been unresponsive to remediation in normal schools with twenty-six normal readers of the same I.Q. and "reading age," the latter as measured by a standard silent reading test with sentences; the dyslexic adolescents ranged from thirteen years seven months to seventeen years three months, while the normal readers were in the second or third grade, ages eight years four months to ten years eleven months. When Ebro measured their responses on seven measures designed to determine their acquisition of the phonemic principle and their tendency to use a letter-level recoding strategy, he obtained results that pointed toward a specific phonemic deficit in the dyslexic adolescents. Also, half the dyslexic readers displayed a more whole-word oriented reading strategy than did any of the normal subjects. However, when Elbro compared the distribution of normal readers' and dyslexics' reading strategies, he did not find distinct groups among the dyslexics, based on their use or non-use of a letter-level reading strategy (Ebro, 1991, 1990).

Another interesting set of studies is reported by Goswami and Bryant (1990, pp. 134–136). They describe a study by Temple and Marshall (1983) in which these investigators described a seventeen-year-old girl (HM) with a reading level of ten years, who seemed to rely almost exclusively on a whole-word strategy: she found it almost impossible to read nonsense words and long regular words, and other errors suggested she was relying heavily on the visual appearance of words in order to read them. In contrast is another seventeen-year-old girl (CD), likewise with a reading level of ten years. According to M. Coltheart, Masterson, Byng, Prior & Riddoch (1983), the symptoms shown by this girl were almost the mirror image of those made by HM: she could read regular words much more easily than irregular ones, and she made other errors typical of dyslexics who rely heavily on a letter-by-letter strategy (my terminology, based on the descriptions). But in a later study that compared HM's and CD's patterns of reading words with a group of "normal" readers with a mean reading age of ten years one month, the investigators found that all but one of the "symptoms" of dyslexia found in one or the other of these young women was found in the reading of the normal readers at essentially the same reading age (Bryant & Impey, 1986; for a summary, see Goswami & Bryant, 1990, p. 135). There were differences among the normal readers, too: some were more like HM, some more like CD. As Goswami & Bryant put it, "This suggests striking qualitative differences between normal readers, and underlines the point that these differences cannot be used to explain the difficulties of the dyslexic children" (1990, p. 136). Or in other words, it's not differences in strategies for reading words that accounts for readers being labeled dyslexic in the first place, not do the word-reading strategies of dyslexics often differ from the range of differences found among unlabeled readers.

Similar conclusions about the range of differences being similar among dyslexic and unlabeled readers were drawn from a recent longitudinal study involving more than four hundred children. Defining "dyslexia" as a significant discrepancy between intelligence and observed achievement level in reading (as measured by the revised Wechsler Intelligence Scale for Children and the Woodcock-Johnson Psychoeducational Battery, respectively), the investigators found no *qualitative* differences between "dyslexic" children and children showing no significant discrepancy between these scores. More technically, the children identified as dyslexic simply fell at the lower end of a normal curve. Moreover, only seven of the twenty-five children classified as dyslexic in grade 1 met the same criteria for dyslexia in grade three (Shaywitz et al., 1992).

We have seen, then, that studies of readers labeled dyslexic suggest that there are different subtypes of dyslexia, based upon different strategies for reading words; these differing strategies suggest lopsided hemispheric processing and hence possibly a neurological factor in what has been diagnosed as dyslexia. But when the strategies of readers labeled as dyslexic are compared with unlabeled readers at the same "reading level," their collective range of strategies is not found to differ significantly. This suggests that indeed, being "dyslexic" may be simply or mainly a matter of scoring significantly lower than "grade level" on standardized tests of reading. And since such standardized tests are ordinarily timed tests, what this difference may amount to is simply reading words much less readily and rapidly than one's age-mates. A traditional diagnosis of "dyslexia" may have little to do *either* with one's neurological functioning in and of itself *or* with constructing meaning from texts that the reader has the conceptual background to understand, in an untimed situation.

The recognition that "dyslexics" employ roughly the same range of strategies and have the same range of difficulties in reading words as younger readers has prompted the developmental hypothesis: that dyslexics are simply delayed in reading development. This has led to various stage theories of dyslexia (e.g., Frith, 1985, 1986) and to counterarguments against strictly developmental stage theories, and counterproposals (e.g., Goswami & Bryant, 1990, pp. 141–150). Given the way dyslexia is commonly diagnosed, it should not be surprising that readers labeled as dyslexic exhibit reading patterns found among younger readers.

In any case, the research comparing labeled and unlabeled readers of different ages but scoring at the same reading level adds impetus to the idea of reconceptualizing dyslexia as a label reflecting not merely (or mainly?) the neurological functioning of the individual, but rather the environment's interpretation of what the reading behaviors and the apparent neurological functioning mean, in accordance with its particular assumptions about reading and assumptions about age-related appropriateness.

RECONCEPTUALIZING DYSLEXIA AND OTHER LEARNING DISABILITIES

In fact, the entire notion of "learning disability" and the concept of learning *deficiencies* warrants serious reexamination, along similar lines.

Learning Disabilities as a Social Construct

Whole language educators are among those who argue that it is far more productive as well as more humane to view learners as exhibiting learning *differences* rather than having learning *disabilities* or deficiencies. Instead of viewing some students as having learning disabilities, we can view them as having unique learning abilities—as creative learners (Lee & Jackson, 1992). In fact, one of the major reasons I have been attracted to learning- and reading-styles research (p. 235 and in Chapter 6 appendix) is that such researchers assume that we are all different from one another in our learning-style patterns. Those who have researched learning styles reject not only the idea that some children are deficient, but even the idea that some are different from a hypothetical norm. They see variety itself as normal, and all of us as having learning differences from one another.

Coles' Interactivity Theory, and Bartoli and Botel's Ecological Theory

Other investigators have critiqued the concept of learning disabilities from somewhat different vantage points. Gerald Coles, for example, has demonstrated weaknesses in many of the research studies allegedly documenting neurological deficiencies or differences in students diagnosed as learning disabled. In part, his argument rests on demonstrating that the studies have not adequately taken into account other factors that can account for the "disability." For instance, he gives examples of parents needing to believe in their child's reading disability to bolster their own self-esteem; in such situations, the child may sense the parents' need and oblige by remaining a less competent reader than he or she could readily become. Or the child may remain less competent because his or her "disability" earns attention and affection from the parent(s), or even power over them (Coles, 1987, pp. 144–145).

In critiquing conventional learning disability research and assumptions, Coles offers instead an *interactivity theory*. Conceding that a small number of children have dysfunctional brains, Coles argues that most "learning disabled" children have merely *different* brains. He further argues that even these differences are environmental rather than genetic in origin. That is, according to Coles, such brain differences should be attributed to environmental factors such as the family unit and our educational system and the teaching it promotes—which are a reflection of our social, cultural, and economic systems and values.

Few theorists are as extreme as Coles, but the concept of learning disabilities as a social construct is gaining increased attention within the field of special education (Carrier, 1983; Sleeter, 1986; Wixon & Lipson, 1986; Adelman, 1992; K. S. Goodman, 1982b, and other articles within that same journal issue; also the May 1991 issue of *Topics in Language Disorders*). In general, these researchers and educators argue that learning disabilities are to a significant extent created by the external world and/or reflect that world's refusal to recognize that the "problem" stems from what they inappropriately expect and demand of the learner. This view is ably argued in insightful articles by Heshusius (1989) and by Poplin (1988b; for a contrasting view, see Poplin, 1988a; Poplin & Stone, 1992). See Figure 11.2 for a list of some critiques of the traditional concept of learning disabilities and special education.

Along similar lines, the *ecological systems theory* developed by Bartoli and Botel makes considerable sense. They concede that there may be a neurological factor involved in an apparent learning disability, but they focus instead on improving the transactions between the individual and the environment (1988, p. xi)—partly because

---

Altwerger, B., & Bird, L. (1982). Disabled: The learner or the curriculum? *Topics in Learning and Learning Disabilities, 1,* 69–78.

Bartoli, J., and Botel, M. (1988). *Reading/learning disability: An ecological approach.* New York: Teachers College Press.

Coles, G. (1987). *The learning mystique: A critical look at "learning disabilities."* New York: Fawcett Columbine.

Goodman, K. S. (1982). Revaluing readers and reading. *Topics in Learning and Learning Disabilities, 1,* 87–93.

Johnston, P. H. (1985). Understanding reading disability: A case study approach. *Harvard Educational Review, 55,* 153–177.

Lee, C., & Jackson, R. (1992). *Faking it: A look into the mind of a creative learner.* Portsmouth, NH: Boynton/Cook–Heinemann.

Poplin, M. S. (1988). The reductionistic fallacy in learning disabilities: Replicating the past by reducing the present. *Journal of Learning Disabilities, 21,* 389–400.

Poplin, M., & Stone, S. (1992). Paradigm shifts in instructional strategies: From reductionism to holistic/constructivism. In W. Stainback & S. Stainback (Eds.), *Controversial issues confronting special education: Divergent perspectives* (pp. 153–179). Boston: Allyn & Bacon.

Taylor, D. (1991). *Learning denied.* Portsmouth, NH: Heinemann.

Figure 11.2 Critiques of traditional concepts of reading/learning disabilities

the expectations and demands of the environment may contribute substantially to the alleged problem, but also because these external factors are usually what can be most readily changed. Their book *Reading/Learning Disability: An Ecological Approach* (1988) is a superb treatment of the factors frequently involved in diagnosing and maintaining alleged learning disabilities (though I cannot so readily recommend the details of their suggested educational solutions).

A SYSTEMS THEORY OF DYSLEXIA IN PARTICULAR, AND LEARNING DISABILITIES IN GENERAL

Though developed independently, my own *systems theory* of learning disabilities has a great deal in common with Bartoli and Botel's ecological theory, which they even call an ecological systems theory. The major difference, perhaps, is that I am more interested in also considering neurological factors within the learner (Bartoli & Botel, 1988, p. xi), due to my long-standing interest in brain functioning and also to my son's being diagnosed as having an Attention Deficit Hyperactivity Disorder (a diagnosis that I heartily resisted until I had read a lot about the behavioral patterns that characterize ADHD).

Like Bartoli and Botel (1988) and others, I too want to abandon the terms "disability" and "deficiency" in favor of learning "differences." Moreover, I think a reconceptualization of dyslexia and learning disabilities should focus on reading/learning *strategies*, rather than on abilities or disabilities that are traditionally presumed to be inherent to the learner. Thus, I offer a tentative theory of learning disabilities in Figure 11.3, a model generalized from my systems-theory model of ADHD (Weaver, 1991a, 1993, 1994). This model draws upon general system theory, originated by Ludwig von Bertalanffy (1968) and further refined and modified by Gregory Bateson (1972) and others. This systems theory rejects simplistic cause-effect reasoning and linear explanations, seeing causation as multidimensional and multidirectional.

At the heart of this model are reading and learning strategies that would traditionally be considered dyslexic or dysfunctional. But such strategies are almost always partially successful, and might be completely successful if we were to reconsider the appropriateness of our expectations. Therefore, I suggest we consider them not as reading and/or learning strategy deficiencies but as *differences* from what are common among proficient readers (i.e., strategies such as predicting, sampling text, monitoring comprehension, and trying again when meaning has gone awry—all orchestrated in a seemingly effortless way. Strategies that differ from those common among proficient readers may or may not lead to reading difficulties, depending in part upon environmental expectations and circumstances.

According to the model, both heredity and environment can give rise to neurological factors—the kinds of brain functioning that have traditionally been thought to reflect learning disabilities. In other words, the neurological factors affecting reading and learning strategies may reflect either genetic inheritance or environmental conditions before, during, and after birth. With dyslexic reading patterns, for instance, there

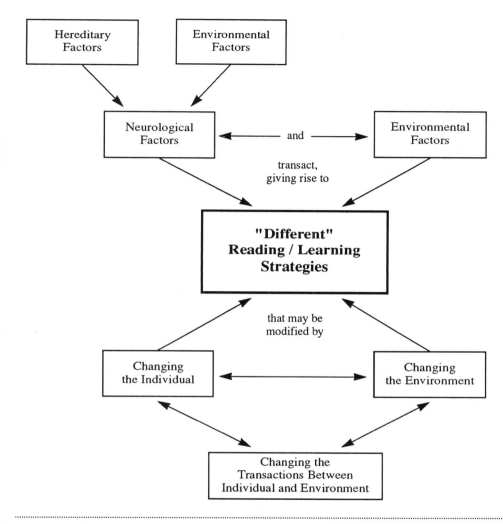

FIGURE 11.3   A systems theory of dyslexia in particular, and learning disabilities in general

seems to be strong evidence that a genetic factor may often be involved (Vellutino & Denckla, 1991), but—theoretically, at least—so could a variety of environmental factors, especially those surrounding birth. Certainly the possibility of prenatal and birth trauma is well documented for other learning difficulties, and for related conditions like ADHD (Barkley, 1990, pp. 95–100). Furthermore, later brain damage, while infrequent, can also affect neurological functioning in reading and learning.

Second, the model suggests that both neurological predisposition and environmental factors can generate different learning strategies, such as those previously discussed under the rubric of dyslexia. While neurological and environmental factors may operate separately to result in such strategies, they often act in concert with each other. Among environmental factors operating to create certain reading strategies, we must include as key factors the concept of reading that underlies reading assessment and instruction, and of course assessment and instruction themselves. For example, too much instructional emphasis on phonics can encourage some readers not to read for meaning, much less to self-monitor for comprehension and use fix-it strategies whenever meaning is lost or going awry. On the other hand, too little attention to letter/sound patterns can encourage other readers to just guess at unfamiliar words, especially if the readers have such predispositions anyway.

Third, the model suggests that the typically used strategies may be modified (theoretically, at least) by modifying either the individual or the environment, or both—but especially by modifying the transactions *between* the learner and the environment. Among other things, this means that we adults—teachers, for instance—might reconceptualize reading and learning, make different demands upon the individual, reject the traditional tendency to look for students' weaknesses, and/or modify our teaching in response to students' strengths.

With certain learning difficulties or differences, it may be appropriate to address the functioning of the individual through medication. For instance, between 70 percent and 80 percent of children with ADHD do exhibit a positive response to central nervous system stimulants (Ritalin, Cylert, or less often Dexadrine), an improvement significantly greater than that perceived with placebos (DuPaul & Barkley, 1990; also Baren, 1989; Gordon, 1991). On the other hand, medication for alleged dyslexia is not a widely accepted treatment, nor is there yet enough evidence that it should be (e.g., Forness et al., 1992).

Obviously, one major thrust of the preceding arguments is that ideally we should help all readers and learners succeed to the best of their potential, without labeling them. (If we must label something, perhaps we can label the strategies, not the individuals.) Another point is that we should consider authentic reading, writing, and learning the only appropriate goals—not the completion of skills work. These goals can be achieved in the regular classroom, with the guidance of the regular classroom teacher and also with assistance from special services teachers. Such goals can also be accomplished by knowledgeable teachers in pull-out programs, provided that students spend enough uninterrupted time in special needs classrooms to engage in authentic reading, writing, and learning.

What will clearly benefit learners with *all* different kinds of learning strategies is an environment that accepts them as they are, treats them as already competent and successful, and leads them to greater success by engaging them in authentic reading, writing, and learning. Whole language classrooms provide such an environment.

WHOLE LANGUAGE FOR SPECIAL LEARNERS

Authentic literacy and learning events take place routinely in whole language classrooms, and it is here that special learners succeed best.

The following activities, described in detail in Chapters 3 and 9, offer opportunities for children to construct their own knowledge:

• Shared Book Experience, or shared reading experience.
• Independent reading.
• Paired reading.
• Listening to literature read aloud.
• Language experience.
• Guided writing.
• Modeled writing.
• Independent writing.
• Journals and learning logs.
• Literature discussions.
• Choral reading, readers theater, drama, storytelling.
• Observation and experimentation.
• Research.
• Theme study.
• Discussions of reading, writing, and research strategies and skills.

Within the context of children's reading, writing, and researching, teachers help them develop the skills and strategies they need. For example, when a child has difficulty reading a particular word, the teacher may remind the child to use context and the initial consonant(s) to predict what the word might be, then look at the rest of the word to confirm or correct. When a child's writing demonstrates the need for a particular editing skill, the teacher may take that opportunity to teach the skill and help the child apply it. When children are researching topics of interest, the teacher may conclude it would be relevant to teach certain skills for locating and using various kinds of references that the children need. Whole language teachers know that children apply strategies and skills best when they have been learned in the context of their application (e.g., Freppon, 1988, 1991; Cunningham, 1990; DiStefano & Killion, 1984; Calkins, 1980). Therefore, they provide many opportunities to learn such strategies while the children are actually reading, writing, and researching: by demonstrating the teachers' own strategies; by providing mini-lessons for individuals, a small group, or the whole class; and by encouraging the sharing of strategies and skills as children discuss literature, each others' writings, and their ongoing research.

The next chapter describes students engaged in many of these literacy events: Linda Erdmann describes how and why special learners succeed in whole language classrooms; Marie Dionisio describes a child's progress in her sixth-grade (remedial) reading class; and Cora Five describes the success of two special learners in her regular fifth-grade whole language classroom.

What makes these literacy events particularly valuable is not necessarily the activities themselves, but (as noted in Chapter 3) the spirit in which they are introduced, undertaken, monitored, and the processes and results assessed. To put it differently, such literacy events are most valuable when the classroom reflects a whole language philosophy.

The following whole language practices are especially salient for special learners:

1. Learners are treated as capable and developing, not as incapable and deficient.
2. Learners' strengths are emphasized, not their weaknesses.
3. Likewise, learners' unique learning abilities and strategies are valued.
4. Students' needs and interests help guide the development of the curriculum.
5. Assessment is based much less on standardized tests than upon individual growth and upon the achievement of classroom goals, including goals for individuals that may have been established jointly by the teacher and the student.
6. The teacher promotes the learning of all students, by creating a supportive classroom community, giving students time (the whole school year) in which to grow, offering choices and ownership, providing response and structure, and gradually expecting and allowing students to take more responsibility for their work (Hansen, 1987).

In an environment where literacy events reflect such practices, special learners have their best chance to flourish.

Time and again, studies of individual children or small groups of children have demonstrated that they succeed much better in whole language learning/teaching situations than in traditional situations, whether the setting be the regular classroom, a special class or program, or a tutorial situation. Many of the naturalistic studies published prior to 1991 have been summarized in Diane Stephens' *Research on Whole Language: Support for a New Curriculum* (1991). These studies and various anecdotal reports suggest that whole language learning succeeds with special learners in many of the same ways, if not to the same degree, as it does with nonlabeled students (Meek, 1983; Phinney, 1988; Rhodes & Dudley-Marling, 1988; Crowley, 1989; Doyle, 1990; and articles in the January 1982 issue of *Topics in Learning and Learning Disabilities* and in the May 1991 issue of *Topics in Language Disorders*).

So far, few research studies have systematically compared the success of special needs or other "at-risk" learners in whole language and traditional classrooms. However, the Stice and Bertrand study (1990) described in Chapter 7 focused exclusively on at-risk learners, while the Dahl and Freppon study (1992) included only children from low-income families who qualified for the federally funded lunch program. Within these studies, the kindergartners, first graders, and second graders in the whole language classrooms more often perceived themselves as readers and writers, more often and more effectively engaged in reading and discussing literature, more often wrote whole sentences and stories, and more often were able to use a variety of reading and writing strategies. They also scored slightly higher on most of the standardized tests and subtests employed in the studies, though the differences weren't often significant statistically.

Tentatively, we might hypothesize that the patterns for these students would hold for young learners considered educationally at-risk for various reasons, including alleged learning disabilities. That is, there is good reason to think that whole language classrooms can be close to ideal for helping learners achieve their potential (as we shall see in the next chapter). On the other hand, no classroom teacher can meet the needs of all students equally well, especially if the teacher has many students and no classroom aide or other assistant. Thus, Chapter 12 also deals with special programs, classes, and tutorial situations that foster the learning of special students by reflecting key whole language principles, including those listed above.

FOR FURTHER REFLECTION AND EXPLORATION

1. To begin further exploration, you might read one or more of the following books, each of which depicts real learners in detail, under circumstances favorable or unfavorable for the development of literacy:

   • Taylor, D. (1991). *Learning denied*. Portsmouth, NH: Heinemann. This is the story of Patrick, and of his parents, as they first tried to help Patrick in school and then increasingly found they had to protect him from the school, as it sought with increasing fervor to document and prove him learning disabled. It shows how Patrick was diagnosed as learning disabled on the basis of standardized tests administered by "experts" who had rarely worked with or tried to teach him—and in contrast, how Patrick, at home, was reading increasingly more difficult books and writing more complex stories. In order to preserve the myth of its own infallibility, the school system blinded itself to the fact that Patrick was becoming a literate and competent learner. This poignant—and infuriating—story acquires significance because, unfortunately, other children are all too often treated in a similar manner.

   • Lee, C., & Jackson, R. (1992). *Faking it: A look into the mind of a creative learner*. Portsmouth, NH: Boynton/Cook–Heinemann. This is Christopher Lee's story of how he came to acknowledge his learning difficulties but also to develop and recognize his learning strengths. Those who completely deny the existence of neurologically based learning difficulties should especially profit from this book.

   • Five, C. L. (1991). *Special voices*. Portsmouth, NH: Heinemann. This book documents how eight special learners ("learning disabled," ESL, "at-risk," etc.) became part of, and flourished within, the classroom community of this fifth-grade teacher. (Cora Five has written sketches of two more children for the next chapter of this book and a case study of another child for Weaver, 1994.)

   • Stires, S. (Ed.). (1991). *With promise: Redefining reading and writing for "special" students*. Portsmouth, NH: Heinemann. This collection of teacher stories and essays demonstrates the success of children taught through reading and writing process approaches that reflect a whole language philosophy.

2. You may find it useful to read some of the articles summarizing research on the progress of children consigned to resource room instruction that focuses on skills and subskills, with little or no opportunity for reading and writing whole texts:

   • Anderson, L. W., & Pellicer, L. O. (1990). Synthesis of research on compensatory and remedial education. *Educational Leadership, 48,* 10–16. (See also other articles in the same issue.)

- McGill-Franzen, A., & Allington, R. (1991). The gridlock of low reading achievement: Perspectives on practice and policy. *Remedial and Special Education, 12,* 20–30.
- Allington, R., & McGill-Franzen, A. (1989). Different programs, indifferent instruction. In D. Lipsky & A. Gartner (Eds.), *Beyond separate education: Quality education for all* (pp. 75–98). Baltimore: Paul Brookes Publishing Co.

12 | Whole Language for Special Learners

"I believe there are very few true learning disabled students. We have made them learning disabled by focusing on their deficits, instead of their strengths."

— Regie Routman

These students' stories consistently reveal that they can learn and flourish together with their peers in a language-rich classroom, in an environment that allows ownership, provides time, and values response.

— Cora Lee Five

Nowadays, students diagnosed as dyslexic or learning disabled are often referred to as students with special needs. I like to think of them simply as "special learners"—and I hope that someday the educational bureaucracy will recognize that *all* learners are unique, *all* are special, and *all* need to be treated and taught accordingly.

Instruction based on whole language principles is highly effective both in preventing potential reading/learning difficulties and in alleviating difficulties that have developed. This chapter deals with both prevention and alleviation. Chapter 11 outlined some of the research demonstrating the success of whole language teaching with special learners. In this chapter, a section by Linda Erdmann clarifies some of the ways whole language teaching in the primary grades helps prevent the development of reading and learning difficulties. We also consider Reading Recovery, an early intervention program that, despite its name, is designed more for prevention than for remediation. Then we examine ways of alleviating reading difficulties and to some extent other learning difficulties, in four different kinds of settings: tutorial situations, small-group programs, special classes, and regular whole language classrooms. Essentially the same kinds of instructional strategies that work with young children also work with older children, teenagers, and adults. In effect, teachers with a whole language orientation modify the environment—their assumptions, expectations, methods, and materials—in order to build upon the strengths of the individual learners, whatever their alleged or actual handicaps or needs.

TEACHING "LEARNERS WITH A DIFFERENCE" IN A WHOLE LANGUAGE CLASSROOM
LINDA ERDMANN

Until six years ago I was a special needs teacher. My environment was a resource room. My children were first and second graders who were labeled learning disabled, mildly retarded, hyperactive, attention deficit disordered, visually/perceptually/motor handicapped, developmentally delayed. My room and others like it were overflowing with kids who were there because they were unable to learn to read the way they were being taught in their classrooms, from the basal reader that exposed them to isolated phonics rules and then, right away, to the exceptions to the rule. They were unsuccessful with so-called linguistic-patterned, "a pig can jig" kind of reading. They weren't even successful with basals that used somewhat more natural language, such as "Frits can lift a log." They didn't read for pleasure or meaning. They didn't read real literature. They read exercises intended to teach them "about" reading. These kids needed to have their learning whole and meaningful, not chopped into tiny, abstract bits and pieces. They must have wondered whether the pieces of this reading puzzle would ever fall into place. They must have wondered what the puzzle would look like once it was assembled.

Having moved away from this skills-based instruction, I patterned my special needs resource room environment on the natural learning model (Holdaway, 1986, p. 62). The children were becoming readers and writers. There was joy and laughter, both in the teaching and in the children's learning in the resource room. But each day the children left the resource room to return to the skill-and-drill worksheets; to the "spit and sputter" kind of reading as they were encouraged to sound out words; to the admonition "Don't guess" as they tried to predict an unfamiliar word; to the reminder "Don't keep going back" as they reread to pick up language and meaning cues. I encouraged classroom teachers to try shared reading and guided reading, to allow children to have time to actually read and write and to select some of their own books and writing topics.

My efforts were met with varying degrees of resistance. Some colleagues recognized the success and enthusiasm that their children were experiencing in the resource room as they read real literature and wrote for real reasons. However, these teachers were convinced that what was happening could only happen in a special needs setting, with small groups of children.

So, day after day, the children returned to their own classrooms in which they held limited membership. They wanted to be full members. Not only had they missed parts of what had happened in the regular classroom, but they were not given credit for being members of the "literacy club" (F. Smith, 1988b). These children needed to belong to a community of learners. The sense of belonging was clearly missing.

Try as I might, I could not create this community within the resource room environment. The children weren't with me long enough. Each child knew that the reason for his or her being there was an alleged academic, social-emotional, or behavioral deficit. Jimmy expressed it well: "I'm not even good enough for the low group." But I wanted to make literacy happen naturally for all kids. They would all learn to use reading, writing, listening, and speaking to discover and learn through language. The children would learn and grow together. Together. Belonging. Even those we've called learning disabled. Each of us is a "learner with a difference."

But I had some knots that had to be untangled. My confusion resulted from conflicts between my assumptions about learning and the expectations associated with my role as a special needs teacher. Should I continue to give the battery of psycho-educational tests that ask children to read nonsense words, read words in isolation, and complete other tasks that have little to do with making meaning and would further convince children that they knew little? Should I continue to stigmatize them with a pathological diagnosis, remove them from their peers, and stamp them as being different from the rest? No. The deficiencies, in most instances, do not belong to the children but to the instructional program. I call them *educational disabilities*.

Educational Disabilities

The instructional programs in our schools have created educational disabilities by:

- Teaching children in ways they can't learn.
- Marching them through prescribed sets of curriculum objectives as though the sequence were sacred.
- Putting kids into ability groups, forcing those in low groups to see themselves as non-readers and nonwriters.
- Denying kids access to real books until they can "read."
- Putting six-year-old children into a position to fail.
- Expecting kids to learn language from sitting all day without talking.
- Asking questions that call for only one right answer.
- Reprimanding children for wrong answers so that they don't dare to respond again.

and then:

- Referring children to resource rooms.
- Subjecting them to testing that would further convince them they know little.
- Stigmatizing them with a pathological diagnosis.

I needed to know whether I could create the kind of learning community I believed in. I needed to demonstrate, first to myself and then, perhaps, in a subtle way to others, that the natural learning model would work. I knew I had to find a better way to reach these children. I needed a classroom.

A new principal, Paul Koulouris, listened to my plan. He listened to my belief that a whole language classroom can work for most kids. He listened when I explained that a whole learning curriculum is the most supportive curriculum, and a whole language classroom the most supportive classroom. He listened when I explained that children learn from each other, that they would learn to read and write as naturally as they had learned to speak. He listened when I asked to keep all kids in the classroom for the entire day. (I believe that by sending kids out to first one specialist and then another, we are fragmenting the very children who have the greatest difficulty coping with fragmentation.) He listened and he gave me the transfer from the special needs resource room to a first-grade classroom.

During the three years I taught first grade, I became convinced that a whole language classroom works for all children, and is essential for kids in danger of being severely mislabeled. Each year, the percentage of learners with a difference was significantly higher than in other classrooms, since those who made class lists knew I was committed to helping all children learn and be successful within the regular classroom program. The first year, for example, there were nineteen children in the classroom. Nine of those children had been identified as having special needs. Another five were considered "at risk" by classroom teachers and specialists who had worked with them previously. The other four first-grade classrooms had significantly fewer labeled children, usually no more than two or three students with identified special needs. In my first-grade classroom, there were no pull-out support services. There were no special needs groups at a table in the back of the room. Because of what I've learned about kids and their learning, I asked the speech/language specialist, Mae Timmons, and the motor development specialist, Mary Belle Small, to work within the room to support children on IEPs. While they were in my classroom, these colleagues supported the children in a naturalistic way. They joined the child in the current setting and worked with the group of children on whatever experience they were engaged in at the time.

In this setting, I watched Alex, an emergent reader, beam as I read Byrd Baylor's, *The Other Way to Listen* (1978). Alex was the first to notice the poetic language. "That's poetry," he said. "Them sounds come from deep down inside." The expressions on the faces of the other children acknowledged that Alex had noticed something they hadn't. They learned about poetry from Alex. But in reading, Alex was slower than the rest. His private kindergarten had recommended a substantially separate placement for him— that is, an all-day special education class. Alex would have spent much of his day out of the classroom. He would have missed the opportunity to grow from the rich literary experiences his classmates enjoyed. His classmates would have missed the opportunity to have their appreciation of Alex deepen because of his recognition of the beauty of language.

Also in this setting, I watched Brian, labeled attention deficit disordered, hyperactive (or ADHD, in today's terminology), and learning disabled, learn to control his body so that everything close to him didn't go flying, to follow an organizational plan for keeping track of his materials, to focus his eyes and finger on the print, to become a reader and writer.

In this setting, all the children learned and grew. Did all the children master the first-grade curriculum? Some did, and some went far beyond what is considered to be first-grade curriculum. Some did not. My view of learning is not bound by what is first-grade stuff. Only in schools do we attempt to put knowledge of the world into little boxes, to label each box with a grade level, and so limit some children's experiences and condemn others to failure. Instead, we need to value each child's growth over time. I document the growth with anecdotal records, running records, and tapes of the children's reading, writing samples, drawings, and interviews with the children and their parents.

The reason my whole language classroom worked for all kids is not because of my special needs background. The program worked because of the practice that evolved as

I applied what I learned from educators like Don Holdaway (1979) and Brian Cambourne (1988) about the way children learn (see Chapter 3). Children respond to high expectations, to immersion in an environment rich with the sights and sounds of literacy, to authentic demonstrations of skills and strategies being used efficiently, to the opportunities to try out their new understanding away from the watchful eye of the observer, to responsive teaching that accepts successive approximations, and to the love, joy, and laughter of the community in which they are full-fledged members.

Learners With a Difference: Helping them Learn in a Whole Language Classroom

I believe that *all children can learn* and flourish in a whole language classroom. Children can best learn from being together. Through being together they learn the skills needed for growing together. By labeling children and removing them from the classroom, by relegating them to a special needs table in the corner of the room, by isolating them, we have deprived the very children who most need to learn to work together of opportunities to do so.

The children in my first-grade classroom were together all day. Some children came with labels that reflected a medical model: moderately retarded with fine and gross motor involvement, language disorders, speech production difficulties, attention deficit disorder, emotionally disturbed, visual/perceptual/motor deficits. I tried to make sure that these labels remained attached to the paper in someone's file and not to the children. I was firm in communicating my expectation to special needs staff that these children were expected to be in the classroom for all academic and social development. Language support would also take place within the classroom in consultation with the speech/language specialist. The child who needed occupational therapy received help outside the classroom. This help was usually scheduled before the official start of the school day. We were together as a class the entire day. We learned from the needs that grew out of being together.

I was committed to immersing the children in the environment the entire day. I needed to convince the specialists assigned to support the children that the children's needs were being met. The specialists and I negotiated in order to arrive at the kind of data they would be willing to accept as evidence of growth. I showed them the kind of longitudinal records I would collect to document each child's development. I invited them to monitor the children's growth by visiting the classroom to observe their performance. I knew that the kind of growth I expected in young learners would probably not be demonstrated on tests of isolated skills, nonsense words, and so forth. I knew that trying to measure a year's growth with one standardized test is like trying to capture a trip around the world with one snapshot. Fortunately, these professionals agreed to leaving the children in the classroom setting as long as they were growing in the ways we agreed upon.

Throughout every moment of the day it was important to demonstrate to the children that I believed all children could learn and that I expected them to learn. Procedures for beginning each day were written on the board. During the first days of school, the procedures were simple ones: move your attendance button (on a magnetic board) to indicate whether buying lunch, milk, or nothing; Put your things in the closet neatly; Read in your *I Can Read* book (a collection of familiar songs, chants and poems which grew weekly as we learned more selections). I read the procedures to the children those first days, but soon expected them to learn to read and follow them with the help of a friend, if needed.

The expectation that all children can learn was soon internalized by the children. Denny entered our classroom in October. He had been in a self-contained special needs program. About a week after he joined us I noticed the children at his table were reading songs and chants from their *I Can Read* collections. I knelt by Denny's table and asked if he'd like to read one of the familiar chants to me. "I don't read, you know," Denny drawled in his slow, drawn-out speech. Brian, himself an early emergent reader, replied, "Sure you do. Everybody in this class is a reader and a writer!" With that comment, Brian took Denny's finger, saying, "Here, we'll do it together." And together they did it, using their memory to support their use of text as they moved their fingers together across the page. Expectations. Brian expected that Denny was a reader. He expected to help someone who needed it. He expected the experience to be joyful. And it was. This was a lesson to me to continue to act on my belief that all children can learn. The following additional principles have helped me do so.

Children learn when they are comfortable and confident. Don Holdaway taught me the importance of being an adult whom children want to emulate. I know that the way I talk and interact becomes a part of me and determines how I think and learn. I need to help children know that I like them. There is no room for grumpiness, sarcasm, belittling or uncaring comments, and put-downs. Some children are harder to bond with than others. It helps in particularly frustrating situations to remind myself that the child is using the best coping strategies available to him or her at the time and that it is my job as an educator to help that child develop more effective strategies. Some days I have to work harder to achieve these standards than others. But I know that in order for children to engage with my demonstrations, they need to see me as a person they want to be like.

Children need to know that they are trusted and respected, and that their ideas are valued. I trust them to solve problems that arise. When there was friction in the first-grade class, I asked, "What things are working well for us now? What things aren't working so well? How do you feel about what's happening? What can we do to make things better?" I listed their responses and we decided on a plan of action. "How can we help each other to carry out our plan?" was an important concluding step. Sometimes, we used puppets to make talking about difficult issues easier. At other times, role-playing was effective.

I demonstrated problem-solving strategies and trusted the children to use them. "What could you do about it?" was a frequent comment when there wasn't a chair at a place, or there was no room in the circle for a latecomer, or when the paint spilled. I also modeled a procedure we used instead of tattling. First, the child who felt offended described to the classmate what was happening, and how he or she felt about it ("I felt furious when you pushed me"). Next, the child would say what he or she wanted to happen ("I don't want you to push me anymore"). If necessary, the two could have a discussion. If the problem couldn't be solved at that level the children would add the item to the class meeting agenda. During class meeting, classmates could offer their ideas for a solution to the problem (Nelson, 1987).

The children knew that they were trusted to help each other and to solve problems. They knew that their ideas were valued when their classmates asked for help and listened to the suggestions. During a class meeting when we were discussing what things were working well and what things were not, Alex said, "Journal writing and writing workshop aren't going good for me."

Rosie asked, "What isn't working about it for you?"

Alex responded, "I don't know my letters and sounds and it takes me too long to look them up on the alphabet sheet [a sheet with letters and a picture associated with the letter sounds]. By the time I find them I forget what I want to say."

Denny commented, "You could tell your story in pictures. That's what I do."

Rosie offered, "I can tell that you have a lot to say, Alex. I'll help you read the alphabet books during workshop time so you'll learn your letters real quick."

Ben contributed, "Just don't write so much. That way you won't need so many letters."

Alex thus received the help of his peers, all trusted problem solvers.

Feeling comfortable and confident in an environment means that we recognize and accept likenesses and differences, as well as strengths and weaknesses. In the first-grade class, the children and I celebrated ways we were alike and ways we were different. Some favorite books facilitated discussion, acceptance and celebration: *Ira Sleeps Over* (Weber, 1972); *Leo, the Late Bloomer* (Kraus, 1971); *When Will I Read?* (Cohen, 1977); *Crow Boy* (Yashima, 1955) and *Molly's Pilgrim* (Cohen, 1990). I demonstrated my own strengths in reading, playing the piano, and drawing. I shared the story of how I finally learned to swim at the age of twenty-five (in spite of years and years of lessons) when a perceptive swimming instructor taught me to relax and trust in the water to support my relaxed body. I demonstrated weaknesses by trying unsuccessfully to get the basketball into the hoop and by bringing in my guitar to play for the class. As they had to hold the note until I found the new chord, the children learned that guitar playing was by no means a strength of mine.

In order for children to be comfortable and confident, the environment needs to support risk-taking. My guitar playing modeled a willingness to take risks by my having a go at something I couldn't do expertly. The class accepted and rewarded my attempt, and we discussed the importance of recognizing and acknowledging someone's best efforts.

Children learn in environments that accept and value approximations. Acceptance of approximations is especially important for learners who are struggling in one area or another, whether in social-emotional development or academic areas. As children learn, their actions are frequently crude approximations of what's expected. In class, I found it necessary to be alert to these attempts and to reinforce them so that the children got the feedback they needed as they tried to refine their behavior.

Lucas worked hard to learn social skills. He was a very large first grader. His gangly body towered over the other children. He moved awkwardly. He spoke rarely; when he did speak, he did not establish eye contact. He turned his part of a group circle into a corner as he pushed himself as far away as possible. I used a comment to reinforce the times he joined hands to form the circle, before he edged himself away ("Lucas, I noticed that you joined hands with your neighbors just now. That helped us make our circle. Thank you."). I reinforced the times he sat close to another person during choice time because, even though he wasn't ready to initiate conversation, Lucas had made an approximation of social interaction.

In the academic areas, most of the information I used in teaching the first-grade class came from watching the kids' approximations. These approximations of the conventionally correct forms were cues that guided my responses. Combined with my knowledge of the child, child development, and the curriculum, such approximations helped me create just the right conditions to nudge the child a step further. These approximations informed me as to the strategies the child was using. They provided cause for celebration, as the child grew closer and closer to conventional behavior. Noticing and valuing approximations helped me describe children in terms of what they could do.

As I used approximations in reading to guide my response, I also let approximations guide my response to children's learning the social skills necessary for building the community. Matthew's slaps on the back may have indicated that he was ready to become a member of the group, rather than the antagonistic new kid in the class. I needed to check out my observation of Matthew's rather unskilled attempt to become part of the group. To check it out, I found a moment to ask Matthew about it. Together (this could also have been done with another child) we planned his next step.

Thinking of approximations as rough drafts of social behavior helped me guide children in revising and refining their behavior. As the children and I accepted rough drafts in their reading and their written expression, we learned to accept and revise rough drafts in behavior when appropriate. Discussing actions as rough drafts helped me to guide the child's revision in ways that were nonjudgmental and nonpunitive.

Children learn from our responses. I planned and worked hard on my own teacher language, so that my responses would demonstrate acceptance and not evaluation. During shared reading, and during writing conferences, I used comments such as "Uh-huh," "I see what you mean," "Could be," "I hadn't thought about that," "That reminds me of. . . ." I modeled how to describe helpful behavior. Instead of simply saying, "That's good!" I might say, "I noticed that you moved the chair so that Lucas could get through." Frequently during the day, I commented on what someone had achieved through practice. "Lauren listened to that tape again and again. She even decided to stop the recorder at the end of each page, so that she could practice that page. Now she's ready to share." I often asked children to describe their own processs for learning something or for solving a problem.

I demonstrated that everyone's answer is valued. I tried to use comments that acknowledged a response, or comments that would teach. The positive, but judgmental comments I had previously made do not teach and may inhibit children's responses. To have met one child's response with, "Wow! That's great!" could prevent other children from sharing by making them feel that their ideas may be judged less then great.

Young children learn best in noncompetitive environments. I encouraged collaboration in the classroom, because what we can do cooperatively today, we know we'll be able to do independently tomorrow. The children helped each other work, play, and learn. Evidence of their collaboration was everywhere. Around the room were notices: "I cn hep you lern to reed *Midnight Farm*"; "Who will help me lern to read *Charlotte's Web*?" Within an hour-long workshop period, various groups would read, cast, costume, and rehearse a play. Children would invite others to serve as guest illustrators for books they were publishing. They would work in groups to do innovations of poems, to copy their new poems onto charts, and to do the illustrations together. When the children learned that Matthew was getting into trouble on the playground during recess, they came up with a plan to present to Matthew. They arranged for Matthew to have two special friends during recess to help him find activities that would be fun and appropriate. The children made a schedule and assigned two children per recess to play with Matthew (who had been slotted for a residential placement for emotionally disturbed children before he transferred to our school).

In the classroom there were no high, middle, and low groups. Neither were artificial attempts made to disguise the fact that some children were more competent in reading, just as others excelled at running, making friends, or solving problems.

Frequently I called together groups to work on reading, spelling, or writing strategies, problem solving, or guided reading. These groups were flexible and temporary.

Children at all stages of reading competence met together for literature studies. Prior to meeting, they read with partners, listened to tapes, or listened to another student read the book aloud. That way, children who may not have been able to read the text independently were able to make valuable contributions to the literature discussions.

The children supported each other. Brian had struggled to learn to read all year. Just keeping his eyes on the page was a major challenge, but eventually he mastered it. I was doing a running record as he read an unfamiliar selection, *Sing to the Moon* (Cowley, 1982). Several children noticed the difficulty of the passage and the way Brian had concentrated on the print and the pictures. A little later, I saw a line of children standing, paper and pencil in hand, in front of a beaming Brian. When I asked what was up, the responses were, "We're getting his autograph." "Did you notice how he kept his eyes on the page?" "Did you notice how he figured out 'hot water bottle' from using the picture?" "He really kept his eyes on the words!"

Children are responsible. The children were responsible for developing acceptable standards for group living in our classroom. They were responsible for the atmosphere and the conditions of the classroom. These responsibilities did not develop overnight. They developed through hard work, approximations, and many revisions. The stage for the development of this responsibility was a predictable environment, clearly communicated expectations, and class meetings to help work out the kinks.

One of the most important lessons I learned for making my classroom work for all learners is one I learned from Brian Cambourne: *Learners take responsibility for their own learning.* Once I understood this principle, I knew that I did not need ability grouping, a hierarchy of skills, a program to insure that a child mastered one skill before moving on to the next level of skill. I found that the learner determines what parts of the many demonstrations to engage with, and decides what (if anything) he or she will take from the experience. Children in the home are accustomed to assuming this responsibility as they make decisions each day about their own oral language learning. No one in that setting establishes an exact sequence of what word and what syntactical structure is to be learned. Adults in the home continue giving whole, meaningful demonstrations and trust that the child will engage with and learn what he or she needs (Cambourne, 1988, pp. 61–63).

Alex convinced me that what I learned from Brian Cambourne really worked in the classroom. In September, during shared reading, we noticed the *ow* as the hungry giant ran away from the bees, shouting, "Ow!!" (*The Hungry Giant*; Cowley, 1984a). We made lists of words with the sound. In January, when we read *The Mitten* (Tresselt, 1964), we noticed another sound of *ow*, in *snow*. Alex, a child labeled attention-deficit-disordered, hyperactive, and learning disabled, had participated in shared reading times. But he didn't understand the sound/symbol relationship of *ow*. In September, Alex was noticing the spaces between words. He was learning that words that look alike are usually the same word, that "STOP" on a traffic sign and "STOP" in a book are the same. In May, when we read *The Sunflower that Went Flop,* (Cowley, 1984c), I heard a joyous shout. "Oh, glory," Alex exclaimed. "There's that *ow!* Here it's /ow/ in flower. But look at it there! There it's /o/ in grow." Alex had connected. I learned to relax, to continue to touch lightly on the skills, and to provide lots of demonstrations of the skills and strategies readers and writers use to help them. I learned from Alex to trust children to take from the demonstrations what they need at the time.

Children learn when they make their own choices. A goal for my classroom was for my students to become self-motivated, self-directed, and self-regulated. Providing choices is an important step towards helping children become self-motivated and self-directed. We educators have limited children with special needs by making choices for them. In my classroom was a large collection of trade books for them to read. The books were in bins according to categories. Predictable books, books with lots of rhyme, rhythm, and repetition, books with minimal text and lots of supportive illustrations were mixed in with more challenging books, but marked with a self-adhesive signal dot. The dots helped emerging readers choose appropriate books. Other collections of readers such as Literacy 2000 (Rigby), Story Box and Sunshine Books (Wright Group) and Bookshelf Books (Scholastic) were in separate bins, clustered roughly by the amount of support provided by the text and illustrations. (I have learned, however, that motivation, repeated listening, and prior knowledge can support a child as he or she reads a self-selected book that I may have assumed was too difficult.)

The children sat in assigned seats at tables. However, for large parts of the day they chose their own seating arrangements. There were times when I assigned learning partners, but for many experiences children chose their own partners. I learned that in most cases they chose appropriately. Children who had difficulty reading, for example, chose competent readers for jobs that called for efficient reading. Capable readers often rushed to choose children whose strength was in drawing when the experience involved drawing or painting.

Children chose their own writing topics during writing workshop. It was important to me that children with special needs realize that their lives hold important stories for them to write about and share. Writing workshop was a favorite time for the speech/language specialist to be in the room. As she knelt beside the children she engaged them in rich dialogue about their lives. She usually repeated their stories and ended with the question, "And what are you going to do now?" She made sure to spend time with children who were on IEPs for language as well as the general population in the classroom. As she observed the rich language exchanges going on within the classroom setting, she became convinced that fewer children needed to be on special needs plans for language; they just needed to be in classrooms where they could use the language they already had.

Children chose their own learning experiences during parts of the day. Their responses to books could be in the form of making puppets and putting on a puppet show, acting out drama, creating posters, writing letters to recommend the book to friends, talking about the book, and so forth. Given choices, every child had a chance to be successful.

Who are Learners with a Difference?

In the preceding section I've outlined the beliefs and practices that helped me create a classroom that worked for all the students. For most children, these practices worked. Others needed more support. The following are strategies that helped these children. The strategies are grouped according to the characteristics of the children. I've chosen some humorous phrases, not in any way to ridicule or to attach another label to the children, but so that readers will recognize the kind of child I'm concerned with. All teachers have them!

The Little Itch is just that. Little Itches' bodies wiggle, their hands are into everything, and they can be distracting to others. For these children, it helps to:

- Clearly and specifically communicate expectations for the particular experience.
- Pick up the pace of the demonstration. During shared reading, these students are my gauge to my timing. They also let me know, by their actions and lack of engagement, whether I am back into the transmission mode, determined to teach for instant mastery rather than to touch lightly, to just demonstrate what efficient readers do, and move on.
- Issue invitations to choose their own seating location, which will help them to meet behavioral expectations.
- Involve them in the demonstration. Give them the pointer to point to the text; invite

them to put a Post-It note or a Stikki-Wikki as a frame around some part of the text or illustration.

- Establish a secret signal as a reminder to meet an agreed-upon expectation so that you don't have to disrupt the class to give these reminders.

The Firecracker is prone to temper tantrums; he or she may explode easily. I've found it helps to:

1. Try to anticipate the outburst and defuse it by giving such students a job or responsibility. (Clues are body language, or redness that begins in the neck and creeps up to the face.)
2. Help the child recognize the signals of an impending outburst and establish a place where he or she can voluntarily go to cool down.
3. Enlist the support of the group in recognizing the signals and in helping the child. Often, role playing or play with puppets, in which the puppet asks the child how friends can help, is an effective way of finding out ways to help. Sometimes children have been able to share during class meeting things that may trigger the angry outburst.
4. Read Norma Simon's book *I Was So Mad!*

Mr. or Ms. Center Stage needs to be in the spotlight continually. It helps to:

- Involve the child in changing roles. Plan group activities with role assignments written on cards the children can hang around their necks. Occasionally, assign roles such as listener, recorder, encourager, and so forth.
- Group the child with verbal peers for an activity.
- Try "My Turn, Your Turn" activities in which the children pass an object such as a beanbag or an old tennis ball back and forth. Holding the object is a tactile reminder that it's a given child's turn.
- Assign both leadership and supportive roles, keeping in mind that the goal is not to squelch leadership but to help the child to develop appropriate leadership skills.
- Use feedback from class meetings. The children share their feelings and frustrations with Center Stage and enlist his or her help in making a plan, and give feedback on how the plan is working.

The Three Sillies seem to locate each other visually, even when they aren't seated together, and engage in giggling, antics and other behavior that is probably attention-getting but is also annoying and silly. I've found it helps to:

- Laugh with them, at appropriate times.
- Avoid buying into their behavior by scolding.
- Ask, "What is the appropriate behavior right now?"
- Videotape the group. Later, in private, play the tape for the children who were involved in the behavior. Ask them to identify behaviors that are working and not working. Ask them to set goals for their behaviors that will help the group.
- Challenge them, again in private, to participate in a group activity that would take a great deal of self-control (such as passing a friendship hand-squeeze silently around

the group). I've been amazed at how well children rise to the challenge. This also provides an opportunity for positive feedback.

The Picker of Rug-fluff seems to be avoiding the demonstrations and is more involved with the fluff than with shared reading or other class activities. I've observed this behavior in children who have had previous failures with letters, sounds, and symbols. They seem to want to avoid anything having to do with print. It helps to:

- Involve the child in choosing a favorite selection.
- Let the child know that you will call on him or her next. Knowing this, the child usually tunes in. This strategy results in success when the question calls for a something the child can do.
- Mask words or letters that the children predict as they read aloud. The children become engaged with the predictions.
- Ask the child, "What do you notice?" about the text. Everyone can experience success at this nonthreatening request for a response.
- Make descriptive comments when the child notices print. "I noticed that you read with your finger and made a match between the word and what you said." "I noticed that you read 'lady' here. 'Woman' would have made sense, too. What helped you to decide?"
- Draw the child into the text by asking him or her to look for visual patterns, repetitions, and so forth.
- Ask the child to be the one to hold the pointer.
- Trust in the learner's responsibility to take from the demonstrations what he or she is ready to use at the time. (This is the hardest for me to do; but I know that children are learning, even when it may not be my agenda.)

The Whirling Dervish is constantly in motion and may have difficulty maneuvering his or her body without upsetting materials, supplies, even furniture in a crowded classroom. It helps to:

- Meet the child at the door in the morning to help him or her get set up successfully for the day. Getting off to a good start is especially important. For these children, one misstep seems to precipitate many more.
- Assign a place for group lessons. [A beanbag chair seems to have a calming effect. Sitting on the floor is usually impossible and a chair can too readily be transformed into a locomotive or the child in constant motion is likely to fall off a chair, when there is no table to help by providing an anchor. The children know that this child needs the beanbag chair to help him or her attend. They know that special accommodations of extra time or materials are often provided because it's my job to make the best possible match between each child and the classroom environment.]
- Set aside time to play "Statues," a game in which children assume various positions and hold them until a signal is given. Talk about how the bodies look and feel in the various positions. Encourage the child to assume the "Listener" position during part of a lesson.

- Teach about each person's space and practice respecting that space during lively activities.
- Provide periods of movement that end with an agreed-upon signal and the words, "See how fast I stop."
- Demonstrate taking a deep breath by inhaling silently and slowly, then silently releasing the breath between pursed lips. This helps to relax.
- Use guided visualization based on a calm, relaxed part of the book being read.
- Involve the children in quick pantomimes while reading a story. (A favorite of my students is to turn themselves into Caroline being "a paragon of virtue" as we read *Boss for a Week* (Handy, 1982).

The child who is *Slower than the Rest* is the child who is struggling to learn to read. It helps to:

- Read, read, and read some more to the child. Enlist the help of other students, older students, and volunteers from the community.
- Make sure to include many caption books, predictable books, books that are songs written down. Keep these books in a location so that the child can select some of them.
- Provide a book box to store books the child has read. Provide opportunities for him or her to reread these many times. When the box is full, the child can choose which ones to remove in order to make room for new ones.
- Help those who read with the child to understand the reading process. (I meet with volunteers and provide a booklet explaining the procedures for them to use while reading with the children. My colleague, Kathy Johnson, posts the procedures on the wall in front of the table where volunteers read with children.)
- Look at the child's miscue. Relax and give the child a chance to self-correct. We want self-regulated readers who monitor their own reading. If the child doesn't self-correct and the miscue doesn't make sense, ask, "Does that make sense?" or "Does it sound right?" If the miscue makes sense, consider not drawing attention to it.
- Notice and comment on all attempts at self-correction and use of strategies such as rereading, reading on, and so forth.
- Use guided reading to build a bridge for the child who is ready to move toward reading unfamiliar material.
- Look at progress as development over time, not as getting the child ready for next year's teacher.

This framework and these strategies have helped me create a classroom in which all children learn and flourish, a classroom that avoids creating special needs, a classroom in which children who have special needs can learn and be successful alongside their peers, a classroom in which children recognize that we all have a place and valuable contributions to make.

Jared's end-of-the-year card reflected his recognition of the philosophy I hold for myself as a professional—the philosophy I model for the children in my classroom. Jared wrote on his card, "Your rily growing in teching."

Creating the classroom I've described isn't easy. Sometimes too many needy children were placed in my room, so that it began to resemble one large resource room. Sometimes, because of budget considerations, there wasn't enough support in terms of material or personnel. Sometimes I needed another pair of hands (I turned to parent volunteers, volunteers from the retired community, and older students). There were times when I didn't have the answers and needed to turn to colleagues, but had only one or two who understood. That's changing now as the teachers in my school are becoming learners who are willing to have a go at making their classrooms work for all kids. Now, we learn from each other as we read, attend conferences, take courses, and share with each other. It's all about "rily growing in teching."

READING RECOVERY: PREVENTION THROUGH EARLY INTERVENTION

Among a growing number of educators, the Reading Recovery program is viewed as a safety net to catch and help children become effective readers and writers before they've actually "failed" at reading or writing. Marie Clay, who developed the program, considers it not a remedial program, but a way to prevent reading failure through early intervention. More particularly, Reading Recovery is a program for first graders who, after a year of schooling, may have made progress but still are not engaging sufficiently with the school's or classroom's instruction, regardless of the underlying philosophy or instructional approach (Clay, 1991b, p. 61).

Reading Recovery began in New Zealand in the early 1960s, when Marie Clay started investigating emergent reading behavior. She concluded that after only a year of instruction—typically by the age of six in New Zealand schools—children could be identified as progressing normally or as being "at risk" with respect to reading. That is, after a year or so of instruction, typically about 10 percent or so of the children with whom she worked seemed to have developed inappropriate reading strategies, or not to have developed important ones, or simply not yet to have developed the ability to coordinate different strategies in order to read effectively. This prompted Clay to develop what has come to be known as the Reading Recovery program. First brought to the United States in 1984 through the efforts of faculty at the Ohio State University, the Reading Recovery program has spread to sites in more than forty states within the United States, as well as to Australia, Canada, and Great Britain (DeFord, Lyons, & Pinnell, 1991).

The following description of the program owes much to Irene Fountas, a whole language teacher educator currently involved in Reading Recovery teacher education at Lesley College in Cambridge, Massachusetts. She has corrected some of my earlier misconceptions and contributed significantly to shaping the "Concerns and Responses" section below.

Success of Children in the Reading Recovery Program

Of course, what is most important to teachers implementing the Reading Recovery program is children's success at reading (and writing) actual texts. Children are considered to have succeeded in the program if they reach the "average" reading levels for their grade, as measured in two major ways: according to the classroom teacher's expectations, and according to re-examination on some of the tasks originally used to determine placement in the program. What the classroom and Reading Recovery teachers look for in particular is evidence of the child's ability to use reading and writing strategies effectively, fluently, and independently.

How well has the program succeeded? Clay's early research in New Zealand demonstrated encouraging results, not only at the end of the year when the children had special tutoring, but also three years later. She points out the degree of challenge inherent in the program: the children chosen for the Reading Recovery program were those with the poorest performance in reading and writing at the age of six, regardless of any other factors. Thus, the group included bicultural Maori children, bilingual Pacific Island children, children with handicaps, and children awaiting Special Class placements. Despite the fact that major gains with such a group could scarcely be expected in both reading and writing with even daily tutoring over only a thirteen-to-fourteen-week period, the children typically left the program with average levels of performance in just three to six months, and most still retained those average levels of performance three years later (Clay, 1985, p. 105).

In a more recent paper on Reading Recovery, Clay has reported that since the program was first introduced in New Zealand, hundreds of teachers in New Zealand, in Victoria, Australia, and in Columbus, Ohio, have brought thousands of low-achieving children up to average levels of reading. The Ohio project, begun in the 1984–85 school year by teacher-educators at Ohio State University, was quickly extended to the entire state of Ohio (see Pinnell, 1985; Pinnell, 1989; and various documents available from Ohio State University's Department of Educational Theory and Practice). As Clay explains it, the children are "taught to discover things about reading and writing for themselves. They were [are] trained to be independent and were [are] able to survive as learners back in their classrooms" (Clay, 1986). This has been accomplished with daily lessons like those described below: thirty-minute individual lessons that supplement regular classroom instruction for only twelve to twenty weeks. Children who have not made accelerated progress within the program after four to six months maximum are transferred to a reading specialist. In New Zealand, however, these have typically constituted only 1 percent of the total number of students of that age (Clay, 1986; 1987a; 1991b).

More recent research indicates that, of the children in the bottom 20 percent of the class who are selected for Reading Recovery in the United States, most reach the average level of their class and are discontinued from the program, usually within an average of twelve to fifteen weeks of daily instruction, for thirty minutes a day. Dunkeld (1991, p. 37) notes, for example, that the Reading Recovery program "has enabled 86 percent of the 13,000 at-risk first-grade readers receiving a full program in the United States to reach average reading levels in their first grade classrooms" (see also Pinnell, Fried, and Estice, 1991, pp. 24–26). This means that only about 3 students out of 100 remain below "average" and may need further individualized assistance. This success rate is greater than that for another compensatory program with which it has been compared (Pinnell, DeFord, & Lyons, 1988), despite the fact that children in the other compensatory program received additional instruction all year, unlike the Reading Recovery children.

The following sections describe procedures for selecting children to be included in the program, the tutorial procedure, the teacher education component, and finally some concerns about Reading Recovery that have been raised by whole language educators.

Selection for Reading Recovery

Within a school that has one or more teachers participating as Reading Recovery teachers, kindergarten teachers are asked at the end of the kindergarten year and first-grade teachers at the beginning of the first-grade year to identify their lowest-achieving children, or the ones they're most concerned about. Clay's Observation Survey (described below) is then administered to the lowest third of the class, as identified by the teachers. The children who score the lowest are included in the Reading Recovery program—typically 15 to 20 percent of the class.

The measures used in Clay's Observation Survey include the following (as described in Pinnell, Fried, & Estice, 1991; Fountas, 1992; and Clay, 1985):

1. *A letter identification task*. For fifty-four characters, this involves identifying the accurate name or sound, or a word that begins with that letter. (The fifty-four characters include 26 uppercase letters, 26 lowercase letters, and a typeset *a* and *g*.)
2. *A word test*. This includes recognition of isolated words in a list drawn from a standard list of words.
3. *Clay's Concepts About Print task*. This involves giving appropriate responses to questions about the conventions of print, in the context of a book. In order to determine young children's understanding of the nature of books and how books are read, Clay developed a Concepts About Print test and two small books to use with it, *Sand* (Clay, 1972) and *Stones* (Clay, 1979). The books are abnormal in that some pages are printed upside down and in other unusual ways, to determine children's understanding of print and their attention to it (Clay, 1985, pp. 27–30; compare Clay's Concepts About Print test with the more naturalistic procedures of Y. M. Goodman and Altwerger [n.d.] in their "Bookhandling Knowledge Task" to be used with normal books; see Y. M. Goodman, 1992a, p. 140). The Concepts About Print test helps determine the nature and extent of children's book-handling knowledge, concepts about how print works, and concepts about letters, words, and punctuation. Children's responses are analyzed to determine whether they have developed such concepts as what and where the front of a book is; where you begin reading a book and a page; that you read from left to right and return down and left for the next line; what a word is and what a letter is; where to find the first letter in a word, and the last letter; what question marks, periods, commas, and quotation marks are for.
4. *A measure of students' writing vocabulary*. This is the number of words the child can write correctly in ten minutes. The child writes his or her name and is told to write

all the words he or she knows. When the child stops writing, the investigator begins prompting for other kinds of words the child might know, until the time limit of ten minutes is reached.

5. *A dictation test*. This measures the child's accurate representation of phonemes ("separate" sounds) in a dictated sentence.

6. *Text reading*. This involves determining the level of text (in a series of increasingly longer and more challenging stories) that the child can read with 90 percent accuracy. Also, the child's miscues are analyzed to determine cues and strategies the child uses, including evidence of self-correction behavior.

Fountas points out that "Although each measure yields a numerical score, the real value of the tasks is in the insight the teacher gains from the child's attempts" (1992, p. 8). See also Clay's *An Observation Survey of Early Literacy Achievement* (1993a).

Assessment of both reading and writing is important, for together they provide a much more complete picture of the extent to which a child has acquired appropriate concepts about the written word. In fact, Clay cautions against using any of the tasks alone. Given such observational assessments, one might find such needs as the following, among many possibilities:

1. Some children may benefit from help in understanding how books are read and/or in understanding the terminology used in reading instruction (terms such as *word, letter, sound).*

2. Some children may benefit from help in using the most salient graphic cues, such as the first letter(s) and the last letter(s).

3. Some children may benefit from help in hearing the separate sounds in words and/ or in blending sounds together, when they try to make use of grapho/phonemic cues.

4. Some children may benefit from help in using semantic and syntactic cues to predict and to confirm/correct, particularly if they haven't had many experiences "reading" a book virtually from memory, and then reading by using more and more of the cues and words within the text.

5. Some children may be ready for and benefit from help with integrating all of the language cues into a workable system.

Of course, each child's strengths and needs will be unique. However, children's particular needs may derive partly from the instructional experiences they have and haven't had. Some children from whole language classrooms may especially benefit from individualized help with grapho/phonemic cues, while some children from phonics-oriented programs may especially benefit from help with syntactic and semantic cues. But not necessarily. Children from whole language classrooms may be proficient in using grapho/phonemic cues, and children from phonics-oriented classrooms may be proficient in using syntactic and semantic cues (see Chapter 7, pp. 324–325). Such observations that are contrary to what might have been predicted serve as powerful reminders that it would not be appropriate to make assumptions about what a child needs on the basis of the regular classroom instruction. Each child's strengths and needs will be different from everyone else's.

Instructional Procedures

In the Reading Recovery program, the tutor focuses on the child's particular strengths and strategy needs within the context of an individually tailored program that involves both reading and writing. The typical session includes the following (Clay, 1985, p. 56; Pinnell, Fried, & Estice, 1991, pp. 18–20; Fountas, 1992, pp. 8–9):

1. *Rereading familiar books.* Usually the lesson begins with the child rereading several familiar stories, often self-selected from those in the child's book box. This opportunity for self-selection helps give the child ownership over his or her reading.

2. *Rereading the previous day's new book.* The child reads independently the book that was introduced at the end of the previous day's lesson, while the teacher makes a running record of the child's miscues, records the child's behavior, and draws inferences regarding the child's use of language cues and reading strategies. This information helps the teacher decide how to interact with the child after the child has finished reading, and what book to introduce at the end of the lesson. During this part of the lesson, the teacher calls the child's attention to his or her most effective reading strategies—the child's reading strengths. The teacher may also help the child focus on needed strategies, within the context of the reading.

3. *Working with letters or words.* This short segment is not a lesson component per se but an optional addition, depending upon the child's needs. If a child is just beginning to learn about letters and the features of print, the teacher may work with the child, using plastic letters and a magnetic board. This activity might occur at various points in the lesson, following the running record or during the other reading components. The focus is on helping the child develop a strategy for learning how to learn letters or learning how words work.

4. *Composing and writing a message.* The child composes a brief message, usually one or two sentences long; sometimes these messages extend over several days and become stories. The message is written word by word. The child writes known words from memory, and attempts unknown words with the teacher's help (though sometimes the teacher may decide to write the word for the child). During this part of the lesson, the teacher typically focuses the child's attention on hearing the sounds in words, and on representing these sounds with letters. The child contributes the letters he or she can hear and write, with the teacher contributing the rest. Thus, all the words are spelled "correctly," according to conventional adult spelling, in order to facilitate rereading. After the message is written, the teacher writes it on a sentence strip and then cuts it apart for the child to reassemble. This written message is always read as a whole text.

5. *Reading a new book.* Each day the teacher introduces a new book, chosen to support the reader but also to offer a slightly more difficult challenge. The teacher may read the title and talk about the author, after which the teacher and child together talk about and make predictions from the pictures. This helps the child understand the plot, the important ideas, and some of the language of the story, before attempting to read it. The child then reads the book independently, but with assistance from the teacher as necessary. Teaching occurs as the teacher decides how

and when to intervene during the reading—especially what strategies to emphasize in response to the reader's strengths and needs.

Clay's latest description of such procedures is found in *Reading Recovery: A Guidebook for Teachers in Training* (1993b).

While the program looks rigid, Clay asserts that "Each child's program is determined by the child's strengths and the teacher works with what the child does well and independently" (Clay, 1991b, p. 63). The program provides a lesson framework that includes reading and writing stories, but within the lesson components there is a great deal of flexibility for the teacher to follow the strengths of the child and the child's responses, minute by minute. Thus, the program is designed to be flexible enough to work with almost any child, in an "unhurried yet accelerative way" (Clay, 1991b, p. 71).

Clearly, the work on particular skills or strategies is only a part of the total tutoring session. Skills are attended to only if they are genuinely needed in order to read or to write text, and, having received attention, such details are then embedded back into the reading or writing situation (Clay, 1991b, pp. 64, 68). As Clay points out, too much focus on detail seriously threatens the child's progress (1985, p. 53). Clay also reminds us that only a small proportion of children will need such focused lessons: "Most children (80 to 90 percent) do NOT require these detailed, meticulous and special reading recovery procedures or *any modification of them.* They will learn to read more pleasurably without them" (1985, p. 47). Most children selected for Reading Recovery, however, clearly benefit from the early intervention provided in the program.

The Teacher Education Component

The success of the Reading Recovery program depends crucially upon the knowledge and skill of the teachers. Each Reading Recovery teacher engages in a year-long program of staff development, during which time the teacher tutors four students daily, for half of the school day, and participates in weekly seminars. These seminars involve not only studying the procedures in Clay's *Reading Recovery: A Guidebook for Teachers in Training* (1993b), but also taking turns teaching a child "behind the glass," with other Reading Recovery teachers observing, describing, and analyzing the child's behavior and the instructional decisions the teacher makes; this discussion is later shared with the demonstration teacher. In addition, the Reading Recovery teachers in training read and discuss other resources to learn more about the reading process, and they receive on-site visits from specially trained teacher-leaders. (Reading recovery involves a tiered system of expertise, with Reading Recovery teachers in training, teacher leaders who supervise them, and teacher educators who train the teacher leaders. See, for example, Pinnell, 1989; Clay, 1991b; and Dunkeld, 1991.)

Over the course of the year, the teachers in training learn to question their own assumptions about reading and learning to read, to reconsider these assumptions in light of the behavior they observe in children, and to change or modify their own theoretical framework in light of both observation and the theory and research to which they are exposed. This in turn affects not only their tutoring, but their classroom teaching. As

Pinnell, Fried, and Estice put it, "In the long run, perhaps the most important benefit of Reading Recovery for teachers is the insight they acquire in the process of analyzing and articulating their own teaching decisions. They look more closely at the students they are teaching and find it easier to see strengths; further, they begin to change their views of the reading process and to develop a more refined theory of how children learn to read" (1991, p. 22).

Furthermore, the education of Reading Recovery teachers does not end with their first year of training. Following this initial year, the teachers meet four to six times each year, continuing to teach behind the glass, in order to deepen and refine their observations of children and their understanding of their own teaching.

To the extent that they extend these insights to the classrooms in which they spend their other half day, these teachers in training offer more support to the Reading Recovery children than just the half hour they spend together in a tutoring situation. But what of the children who return to classrooms where they have little opportunity to read, and little recognition of, or support for, their developing reading and writing strategies? These children may have learned to read through Reading Recovery, but unfortunately they cannot be expected to progress as well as those children who receive similar classroom support. Reading Recovery teachers are among the first to insist that Reading Recovery is not a cure, or a substitute, for poor teaching. The program is merely "something extra" for those children who most obviously need it.

It may be only as Reading Recovery teachers influence their colleagues' teaching that the program reaches its full potential. Indeed, the apparently greater success rate for Reading Recovery in New Zealand, compared with the United States, might stem not from the program itself but from the fact that children receive greater support for whole learning in New Zealand classrooms.

Reading Recovery from a Whole Language Perspective: Concerns and Responses

Reading Recovery reflects a whole language philosophy in several ways. It deals with needs of the individual; instruction in skills and strategies derives from real reading and writing situations; instruction deals with the child's needs in the context of the child's strengths, and builds on those strengths; the child is encouraged and helped to become an independent problem solver; and the child maintains ownership over the situation and the learning process by choosing many of the books that are reread, and by deciding what to write.

However, some whole language educators have raised concerns about various other aspects of Reading Recovery. Some of these concerns seem to reflect misinformation or misunderstanding, while others reflect more deep-seated philosophical differences among educators. The following is a list of concerns I have seen or heard raised, or raised myself, along with actual or hypothetical responses by committed educators actively involved in Reading Recovery—including an increasing number of whole language educators. The point is to present a balanced picture, in order to encourage other educators to weigh the pluses and minuses as judiciously as possible. (Sources for the concerns include R. K. Moss, 1991, and Y. M. Goodman, 1992b; sources for the responses include Clay, 1985, 1991a, 1991b; Dunkeld, 1991; Holdaway, 1992; and Fountas, 1992, as well as personal communication with Fountas on November 21, 1992.)

Concerns	*Responses*
1. Selection of children for the program is based partly upon tests of isolated items—e.g., letter identification, recognition of isolated words, number of words spelled correctly.	1. Yes, but these measures are only part of the total assessment, evaluated in conjunction with the child's reading of actual texts. None can be considered without all of the others; indeed, Clay particularly cautions that one must look at the whole profile, including the reading of authentic text. And we look not so much at accuracy as at *how the child attempts* these tasks, and what these attempts tell us about the child's reading and writing strategies.
2. The program involves the early identification of problems that may disappear with more time, maturation, and/or literary experiences. Given enough "comprehensible input" (pp. 65–66), children will develop productive reading strategies by themselves.	2. Meanwhile, the child knows that he or she is not learning to read and write as readily as most classmates. Why allow children to feel like failures, when we could help them?
	Also, it is easier to provide input that is comprehensible to the individual child within a tutorial setting.
	Besides, ineffective reading strategies often do *not* disappear, at least not by the end of first grade, by which time the children may be well on their way to being classified as learning disabled and/or dyslexic, or to being considered for retention.
	Furthermore, it is easier and more cost effective to replace ineffective strategies with more effective ones before the ineffective strategies have become habitual and the child has lost confidence in him- or herself as a reader.
3. A related concern is the push for accelerated progress, and the consequent pressure on both the teacher and the student to accomplish certain tasks within the thirty-minute lesson, as well as to progress to an "average"	3. Accelerated progress is necessary if the child is to catch up with peers, and it may also be necessary if the child is to avoid being retained, labeled as learning disabled or dyslexic, or sent to a long-term remedial program. The

Concerns

degree of proficiency within a few weeks or months.

4. During tutorial lessons as well as during the process of selecting children for the program, teachers emphasize accurate word identification. It appears that accuracy is what's important, rather than the development of effective reading strategies.

5. But teachers select stories that they think children can read with 90 percent accuracy, and they expect the child to achieve 95 percent accuracy on the selection. Thus, it looks as if it's the sheer number of miscues that's important, not the child's use or development of reading strategies.

6. Still, Marie Clay apparently believes that accurate word identification is important and that the meaning is *in* the text—views contrary to what has been learned from miscue research in reading and from reader-response research in literary studies.

Responses

thirty-minute lesson is steadily but comfortably paced, and the total weeks that the child spends in the program can be extended somewhat, if the child seems to be progressing adequately but to need just a little more time. Accelerated progress is possible once the children become independent in their use of reading and writing strategies.

4. It may appear that way. But all teaching is directed toward the child's development of flexible reading strategies, with a focus on using syntactic and semantic cues first, then confirming or correcting with the visual information. The teacher does not attend to all miscues, but uses judgment to select teaching points that will foster the child's effective use of strategies. However, when a child "misses" a word, this frequently offers the teacher an opportunity to support the child's more effective strategies and to demonstrate other strategies that may be less developed. Thus, accuracy may *appear* to be the goal, but it really isn't.

5. Again, it may appear this way. Each day, teachers take a running record of the child's miscues, partly to analyze miscues but also to determine the suitability of the book that the teacher introduced the previous day. The idea is to select a book that the child can read easily, so that the text will support the reader while providing some opportunities for problem solving and the development of reading strategies.

6. In constructing meaning from text, it *is* important to come as close as possible to the meaning intended by the author. Fairly accurate word identification (Clay suggests within the 90 to 94 percent range) facilitates this goal, particularly (or at least) with the simplest texts.

Concerns	*Responses*
7. Writing, also, is expected to be accurate—with the teacher's help. Invented or "constructive" spelling is not acceptable or encouraged within the Reading Recovery lesson. This suggests a a behavioral concept of learning.	7. Actually, the writing part of the lesson helps children hear the sounds in words, enabling them to use invented spelling in the regular classroom. (Typically, a beginning Reading Recovery child is not yet writing with invented spelling—and often is not even producing letterlike symbols at the outset of involvement in the program.) Also, writing is easier when the child can write some high-frequency words without having to reinvent them each time, and learning to read is easier when words are spelled the same each time they are encountered in print.
8. What the emphasis on accuracy and on habituation of ineffective reading strategies seems to amount to is a behavioral concept of reading and of learning to read and write, not the constructive concept that underlies whole language—or, for that matter, the constructive concept that permeates much of Marie Clay's own work, including the last chapters of her recent book, *Becoming Literate: The Construction of Inner Control* (1991a).	8. It's not a matter of either/or. Children do develop reading habits, both productive and unproductive, but they do so as a result of having constructed their own hypotheses about the reading process.
9. In line with the apparent behavioral orientation of the program is the emphasis on what appears to be direct instruction, rather than the learner's constructing meaning and strategies for him- or herself.	9. Again, the contradiction is more apparent than real. In the context of the teachable moment—the reader's obvious need—direct instruction, demonstration, and scaffolding are offered as means of providing "comprehensible input," from which the reader can constuct his or her own knowledge.
10. Whole language teachers with a strong background in the reading process could provide tutoring that is just as successful.	10. Maybe so—at least if they had ongoing opportunities to observe, confer with, and learn from one another, as well as the opportunity to work daily and consistently with the strengths of an individual child.

But how many whole language teachers have such a strong background in |

Concerns	*Responses*
	the reading process as that offered by the Reading Recovery program? And how many have learned to work powerfully and individually with less proficient readers to achieve the accelerated learning that is necessary if they are to catch up?
	In fact, whole language teachers may become even more effective classroom teachers from engaging in the Reading Recovery training and teaching.
11. The money spent on Reading Recovery training might better be spent educating all teachers about the reading process, reading strategies, and how to help children develop effective reading strategies.	11. Certainly Reading Recovery is not a substitute for effective classroom teaching, and it is important that all teachers be better educated in these matters. Thus, it's not a matter of either/or, but *both*. Reading Recovery teachers learn to view assessment, materials, and especially the reading process and readers themselves in new ways. Thus, they are well equipped to be change agents among their colleagues. It should be possible to take money for such inservice education from Chapter 1 funds (Slavin, 1991), since improved reading instruction reduces the number of at-risk students in need of more traditional kinds of Chapter 1 (or Special Education) services.
12. The Reading Recovery program creates a hierarchy among teachers: regular Reading Recovery teachers, teacher-leaders, and those at the top, who train the teacher-leaders.	12. It's more a network than a hierarchy. Within this network, different people play different roles for which they are particularly qualified, but all share the common experience of teaching children themselves, daily.

While the litany of concerns and responses could continue, this list captures the concerns most frequently expressed.

In a recent article, Don Holdaway emphasizes the commonalities between Reading Recovery and whole language. Among the common principles he articulates are the concern for developing theory from the careful observation of learners and the concern for helping learners become self-reliant, independent problem solvers. While whole language emphasizes supportive classroom instruction, Reading Recovery emphasizes supportive and early intervention when the individual learner has not sufficiently engaged with this instruction. Holdaway sees these as two sides of the same coin (Holdaway, 1992, p. 2).

TUTORIAL STITUATIONS BEYOND THE PRIMARY YEARS

For children beyond the primary grades who have not yet developed effective reading strategies or the ability to coordinate them efficiently, we need to think not of prevention, but of re-education. Many semisuccessful readers can develop effective reading and writing strategies by being immersed in whole language classrooms or in reading classes with a whole language orientation. Others may need, or at least benefit from, smaller group or tutorial instruction, again based on a whole language philosophy.

In this section, we consider the success of special learners in whole language tutorial situations. Then we consider small-group programs, reading and remedial classes, and finally regular whole language classrooms beyond the primary grades. (Because of space limitations, we do not include pull-in whole language instruction, in which a Special Education teacher works with individual children and small groups within the regular classroom.) Figure 12.1 includes books and articles that demonstrate the success of whole language with special learners.

Writing Individual Educational Plans (IEPs)

More than a decade ago, Peter Hasselriis wrote a landmark article in which he argued that while Public Law 94–142, the Education of All Handicapped Children Act, requires the writing of Individual Educational Plans for all students labeled as handicapped, it does not require that these plans specify narrow behavioral goals or objectives. Though the achievement of intermediate objectives is supposed to be "measurable," this does not mean that standardized tests or so-called objective measures must be used. In short, IEPs can be written with the kinds of goals and objectives that teachers have for learners in whole language classrooms, and that learners have for themselves.

Progress can be measured by many of the same means used in whole language research studies (see Chapter 6): interviews and questionnaires, miscue analysis, writing samples, lists of books read, dialogue journals and literature logs, and so forth. In addition, records of daily and periodic observations can become an important part of assessment.

Given the diversity of assessment means and measures that can be used, almost any worthwhile goal can be set for, and with, students, giving rise to more concrete objectives that can be both specified and measured. One of three examples Hasselriis offers is the following, for a ten-and-a-half-year-old student (1982, p. 19):

- *Present level of educational performance*: Interviews, observations, and the Reading Miscue Inventory indicate that he is a reader but that he is word bound. When he reads aloud he tends to focus on letters and syllables. He does not sample from print but, rather, insists on making phonic matches with all graphic cues. He is proficient at retelling literal information but does not distinguish significant from insignificant details.
- *Annual goal:* Will read complete texts aloud in a way that shows he is making sense of what he is reading. His miscues will be characterized by meaningful

Allen, J. B., & Mason, J. M. (Eds.). (1989). *Risk makers, risk takers, risk breakers: Reducing the risks for young literacy learners.* Portsmouth, NH: Heinemann.

Allen, J. B., Shockley, B., & West, M. (1991). "I'm really worried about Joseph": Reducing the risks of literacy learning. *The Reading Teacher, 44,* 458–468.

Brill, Rhonda. (1985). The remedial reader. In G. Winch & V. Hoogstad (Eds.), *Teaching reading: A language experience* (pp. 142–159). South Melbourne, Australia: Macmillan.

Dudley-Marling, C. (1990). *When school is a struggle.* New York: Scholastic.

Five, C. L. (1992). *Special voices.* Portsmouth, NH: Heinemann.

Meek, M. (1983). *Achieving literacy.* Boston: Routledge & Kegan Paul.

Phinney, M. (1988). *Reading with the troubled reader.* Portsmouth, NH: Heinemann.

Rhodes, L. K., & Dudley-Marling, C. (1988). *Readers and writers with a difference: A holistic approach to teaching learning disabled and remedial students.* Portsmouth, NH: Heinemann.

Rigg, P., & Taylor, L. (1979). A twenty-one-year-old begins to read. *English Journal, 68,* 52–56.

Routman, R. (1991). *Invitations: Changing as teachers and learners K–12.* Chapter 14, "The learning disabled student: A part of the at-risk population." Portsmouth, NH: Heinemann.

Stires, S. (Ed.). (1991). *With promise: Redefining reading and writing for "special" students.* Portsmouth, NH: Heinemann.

Weaver, C. (Ed.). (1994). *Success at last! Helping students with Attention Deficit (Hyperactivity) Disorders achieve their potential.* Portsmouth, NH: Heinemann.

FIGURE 12.1   *References on whole language with special learners*

substitutions, deletions, and insertions that indicate attention to language units as large as or larger than the sentence.

• *Short-term objectives*: Develop language experience stories on topics of interest. Dictate them to the teacher; write own stories. Read text with selected words deleted, filling in the blanks with appropriate words. Work on assisted reading with the teacher. Read text substituting appropriate words when necessary for unknown or unfamiliar language units.

Another useful article dealing with assessment and evaluation in the field of special education is Hilary Sumner's "Whole Langue Assessment and Evaluation: A Special Education Perspective" (1991). One particularly useful aspect of Sumner's article is her discussion of classroom-based assessment rather than standardized tests as a means of determining which children have learning differences and difficulties that hamper them in actual reading and writing situations. Such measures are described in detail in Max Kemp's *Watching Children Read and Write: Observational Records for Children with Special Needs* (1989).

Matching Tutorial Instruction to Readers' Needs

Assessment is important in determining what kind of tutorial help to offer a student, but of course there is no magic formula for translating the perceived characteristics, strengths, and needs of a reader into instructional strategies. What may be valuable, though, is ideas developed through years of experience in working with individual readers in ways that reflect a whole language philosophy.

Some useful resources include those in Figure 12.2. Figure 12.3 presents the "Remedial Reading Reference Chart" from an article by Rhondda Brill (1985). As Brill remarks, however, these are only some of the many techniques and activities that might be used. Using Phinney's *Reading with the Troubled Reader* (1988), one might compile a reference chart that complements Brill's, or make a single comprehensive chart from these and perhaps other sources.

Eight-year-olds in a Tutorial Book/tape Program

In an early article titled "After Decoding: What?" Carol Chomsky reported on her work with five eight-year-olds. She described the children at the outset of the tutoring program as follows (1976, p. 288):

> These children were not nonreaders. They had received a great deal of phonics training and had acquired many phonetic skills. They met regularly with the remedial reading teacher with whom they had worked intensively since first grade. After much effort, they could "decode," albeit slowly and painfully. What was so frustrating was their inability to put any of this training to use, their failure to progress to even the beginnings of fluent reading. . . . In spite of their hard-won "decoding skills," they couldn't so much as read a page of simple material to me. The attempt to do so was almost painful, a word-by-word struggle, long silences, eyes eventually drifting around the room in an attempt to escape the humiliation and frustration of the all too familiar, hated situation.

What Chomsky succeeded in using with these children was essentially a whole language tutorial program, with skills and strategies taught in context as needed. She

Goodman, Y. M., & Burke, C. L. (1980). *Reading strategies: Focus on comprehension.* Katonah, NY: Richard C. Owen.

Marek, A. M. (1989). Using evaluation as an instructional strategy for adult readers. In K. S. Goodman, Y. M. Goodman, & W. J. Hood (Eds.), *The whole language evaluation book* (pp. 157–164). Portsmouth, NH: Heinemann.

Phinney, M. Y. (1988). *Reading with the troubled reader.* Portsmouth, NH: Heinemann.

Tierney, R. J., Readence, J. E., & Dishner, E. K. (1985). *Reading strategies and practices: A compendium* (2nd ed.). Boston: Allyn & Bacon.

Figure 12.2 References with ideas for helping readers with special needs

Problem Behavior	*Remedial Techniques*
Lack of interest in reading	• Select materials that deal with topics in which the child has indicated an interest (e.g., sports page of newspaper, racing car news magazine, electronics journal, instructions for assembly of model car). These materials need not be books. Read the material to the child if he or she is not able to read it or record it on tape. (Enlist the help of able readers.) • Provide time for child to talk/write about what he or she found out from these materials. • Allow time for sustained silent reading of self-selected materials. • Share your enthusiasm for books and reading by reading aloud your favorite poems and stories and by reading silently with the children at sustained silent reading time. • Use known poems as cloze activities to create new, fun poems. Type up these new poems or write them in a Big Book so they can be shared.
Word-by-word reading	• Select materials in which the language has a natural flow. Check this by reading the text aloud yourself to find out how predictable the language is. Elements of rhyme, rhythm, and repetition make texts easy to predict. • Model proficient reading by reading aloud to the child as much as possible. • Use plays to encourage reading in a natural speaking style. • Use shared-book experience (with Big Books or teacher-made Big Books of child's own writing) so child can join in as much or as little as he or she feels confident to do. • Do lots of choral reading of poems, songs, chants, rhymes using the overhead projector. • Use a cassette tape recorder: children may record themselves reading, listen to tape, and rerecord if necessary; children may read along with prepared tape; or children may listen to taped text until confident to read text by themselves.

Figure 12.3　*Remedial reading reference chart (adapted from Brill, 1985)*

Problem Behavior	Remedial Techniques
Word-by-word reading (continued)	• Encourage child to substitute the word "something" for any unknown word when reading orally so the natural language pattern is not broken by stopping and working out words. Discuss these problem words after the text has been read. • Devise oral and written cloze activities that will encourage prediction. Poems are excellent for this activity.
Reading without understanding	• Choose material that is of personal interest to the child and not too difficult for his or her level of reading ability. • Prior to reading the text: (1) Discuss the title ("What is the story/passage about?"). (2) Talk about the illustrations ("What do the pictures tell us?"). (3) Relate content to child's own experience ("Tell me about when you went camping"). (4) Ask questions ("Do you like camping?"). (5) Encourage prediction ("What do you think might happen?"). • Read small segments of the text, one or two paragraphs, then stop and talk about what has happened thus far. Again, encourage prediction by asking "What do you think will happen next?" • Draw, map, or build up a graph of the plot over a flannel board as the story unfolds. • Use stories the child has written or dictated as reading material. Publish these stories attractively by having them typed and letting the child illustrate them. • Use children's writing and other materials for cooperative cloze and for silent, written cloze activities. • Do lots of oral retelling of silently read texts. Use both fiction and nonfiction.

FIGURE 12.3   Continued

obtained for the children two dozen picture books, recorded on tape, from which the children were to make their own selections. The task was to listen to the tape while following along in the text, until the children had become familiar enough with the book to read it fluently. In effect, they would be first memorizing the book and then learning to read it: attending to the whole and then to parts as necessary.

Chomsky explained her rationale (1976, p. 289):

> When it comes to memorizing a book, these 8 year olds are in a very different position from the pre-reader. They have already had two years of drill in word analysis, long and short vowels, word endings, blending, and so on. They can sound out words and have a fair sight vocabulary. They are beyond needing introduction to the alphabetic nature of the English writing system. What they need is to shift their focus from the individual word to connected discourse and to integrate their fragmented knowledge. It is the larger picture that they need help with, in learning to attend to the semantics and syntax of a written passage, and in developing reliance on using contextual clues from the sentence or even longer passages as they read.

Using pages that the children could already "read" fluently in semi-rote fashion, Chomsky and her graduate assistant supplemented the reading with gamelike activities involving mostly word recognition and analysis. In addition, the children did substantial writing connected with their reading: for example, they wrote stories, question-and-answer sequences, and sentences using words from the stories.

Progress at first was slow: it took four of the five children about a month to learn to read their first book fluently. After that slow beginning the pace increased, and subsequent books took less and less time, so that when the children were on their fourth or fifth book they were able to finish it in a week. Soon there seemed less and less need for the analytical work; after a while, the tutoring sessions became times for simply reading the books and discussing the story, doing some writing, or discussing some stories the children had written. Those children who progressed the most improved in both reading and writing—not a surprising outcome, given the holistic nature of the approach. In general, the children improved dramatically, not only in fluency but also in their attitude toward reading. They began reading TV commercials, cereal boxes, and magazines at home. They began picking up books to read instead of avoiding reading at all costs. In short, they began to feel and act like readers.

Repeated rereading of familiar, self-chosen texts seems to be critical in helping older readers develop proficiency, as the next section also demonstrates.

Sergio and Rudy: A Preservice Teacher and a Fifth Grader Learning Together
Suki Stone

The following example indicates how an allegedly learning disabled fifth-grade Hispanic youngster, Rudy, learned to read with the help of Sergio Cordova, a preservice teacher and instructional aide who worked with him.

Doubtless Rudy's reading difficulties were caused, at least in part, by his educational history. Migrant workers, his family moved between Texas and California every year. Because his family speaks only Spanish, the only place Rudy uses English is in school. Results from his achievment tests in fourth grade showed him to be still functioning at a preprimer level: that is, his language arts/reading level was at a readiness stage, as measured on standardized tests. Before working with Sergio, he had never learned (or retained knowledge of) the alphabet. Although he had received special education services since fourth grade, Rudy was still, as a fifth grader, having difficulty reading. As an eleven-year-old nonreader, Rudy was easily frustrated and unsuccessful while learning to read using traditional basal materials and methods. He had also developed low self-esteem as a result of his academic difficulties.

As a student at the University of Texas at Brownsville, Sergio had been introduced to the idea of using whole language principles and practices with special education students like Rudy (Weaver, 1988; 1991a; Rhodes & Dudley-Marling, 1988; Flores, Cousin, & Diaz, 1991). The whole language framework encompases the basic assumptions of holism/constructivism, as articulated by Poplin (1988a) and refined by Poplin and Stone (1992). One of these principles is that the learner learns best when he or she is passionately involved (Freire, 1970). Freire discussed the importance of passion as the impetus of transformational change, generating a love for learning whatever the learner is passionate about. So Sergio became acquainted with Rudy's greatest interests, his passions.

The first step was to interview Rudy about his interests outside the classroom. One of many things Sergio learned about Rudy was his willingness to help with cutting, pasting, and building projects in the classroom. Rudy also talked about his love for animals. Then Sergio approached him with a group of magazines containing pictures of things Rudy had talked about. Sergio told Rudy to cut out anything that interested him. Rudy chose animal pictures and wanted to write animal stories.

Sergio wrote the first couple of stories Rudy dictated. The first story was about a shark, and Rudy read it about 90 percent correctly. He reread the story three or four times, practicing until he could read it perfectly. After reading the shark story to the other resource room aide, he received much praise and encouragement from both that aide and Sergio. Then he read the shark story to a substitute teacher who had developed rapport with Rudy while teaching in his class.

After the initial story, Rudy wrote a different story every three days. He chose to put his stories into a photograph album. He began to build self-confidence as the teachers and aides complimented his ability to read. He was so proud of his book of stories that he brought a picture of himself as a three-year-old and put it in the beginning of the photograph album. Then he wrote an autiobiographical piece for the front of the book, naming it his story book. As he became more self-confident, Rudy began to be comfortable with oral reading. While Rudy read his second story aloud to Sergio, students in the classroom stopped their work and listened attentively. He looked forward to reading the stories he created and shared with Sergio. At the end of six stories, Rudy remarked that he had to write only ninety-four more stories to complete his book!

During the time Sergio worked with him, Rudy was continuing in the class basal. In the fourth grade he hadn't gone past the third story in the basal, but through writing and reading his own stories he soon accumulated enough sight words and vocabulary to read fifteen of the stories in the basal reader. His progress and interest in reading helped him develop in other academic areas as well.

Sergio used another principle of whole language in having Rudy himself choose what words he wanted to learn to spell. Rudy chose ten words from each story, filing them in alphabetical order in a box. He had found a need and a reason for learning school-related skills, such as spelling and alphabetization. His interest in animals and his newfound reading ability have become the impetus for an excitement about learning. Having learned firsthand the power of teaching from whole language principles, Sergio hopes that by the end of the school year, Rudy will be reading library books in their entirety and will have written the remaining ninety-four stories for his book.

Secondary Students Learning Through Language Experience

Fortunately, many children just naturally read for meaning and predicting and confirm/correct from context without being told to do so. Unfortunately, some do not; they read more to identify words than to construct meaning, because this is what their classroom instruction has emphasized. Such older readers benefit from the same kinds of assistance as young emergent readers. This conclusion is supported by observations from a three-year program in which British secondary-school English teachers worked intensively one-on-one, with secondary-level readers in difficulty. Margaret Meek explains (1983, p. 214):

> We confirmed our conviction that reading has to be taught as the thing that it is, holistically. To break it down into piecemeal activities for pseudosystematic instruction is to block the individual, idiosyncratic moves that pupils of this age make to interact with a text and to teach themselves how to *make it mean.* When we began, our pupils had one reading strategy. They held it in common because they had all been taught it when they first had reading lessons in school. They were efficient sounders and blenders and decipherers of initial consonants; so efficient, indeed, that words they could have recognized "at sight" were subjected to the same decoding as those they had never seen or heard before.

What they could not do effectively was use their grapho/phonemic knowledge and sampling skills effectively in a coherent approach to constructing meaning from a text.

The teachers working with these students tried focusing on the students' apparent needs, based in part on an analysis of their miscues. What proved most effective, however, was adopting a language experience approach. The teachers became scribes for each student, writing to the student's dictation, inviting the student to reread the evolving text to see if he or she had said what was wanted, then writing and discussing some more, and finally providing opportunities for the student to read the finished text to an appreciative audience. That approach did more than anything else to affect the students' view of themselves as readers and to increase their competence.

Assisting students in actually writing down parts of stories they themselves are composing may also be one of the best ways to help those who need to gain greater mastery of letter/sound correspondences. Just as one might help a beginning writer in the phonemic stage, so one might help an older writer/reader sound out words, teaching basic letter/sound patterns in the process. The older writer/reader need not write out the entire story this way, for that might become a laborious process that would inhibit composition and the sense of satisfaction that would otherwise come from having created a longer and more adult story. However, guided assistance in hearing and writing the sounds in words could greatly facilitate acquisition of the basic grapho/phonemic knowledge needed for reading, just as it does for beginning readers. In both cases, though, one must remember that a reasonable phonetic spelling is the aim for a first or rough draft—not "correct" spelling. Emphasis on perfect spelling would defeat the purpose for having the writer sound out and write words for him- or herself.

Renée: A Twenty-One-Year-Old Begins to Read with Whole Language

Perhaps an even more remarkable success story is reported in Rigg and Taylor's "A Twenty-One-Year-Old Begins to Read" (1979). The authors worked with a young woman named Renée, who was diagnosed as mentally retarded at the age of six due to the effects of cerebral palsy, and who had been placed in a program for retarded children for the next fourteen years. She had then been retested and was rediagnosed as having a normal IQ, after which she was placed in another program where the teacher taught her the alphabet and fifteen sight words. Little wonder that at the age of twenty-one she considered herself a nonreader—and not merely someone who did not read, but someone who could not learn to read.

Rigg and Taylor devised a whole language program designed to give Renée confidence in her ability to read. Into each hour of tutoring they tried to incorporate at least three of the following components, and ideally all five:

1. Sustained silent reading, with both Renée and the tutor silently reading materials of their own choice.
2. Language experience, with Renée dictating or writing stories and then reading and discussing them.
3. Retelling what was read, to focus on comprehension rather than on "wordcalling."
4. Rereading, to develop fluency and confidence.
5. Assisted reading, with the tutor reading and pointing at the words and Renée chiming in, which enabled and encouraged Renée to attempt stories that she might not have had the confidence to try on her own.

During the semester, Renée created twelve language experience stories, and read three short novels and eight stories—all in about twenty hours of instructional time. Like John's instructor (pp. 543–544), Renée's tutors didn't work at all on reading or writing "skills." Believing that she could and would read if given materials that interested her and that used "whole natural language," they structured their tutoring program accordingly. From the very first meeting, Renée was immediately able to read whole, connected text because she was reading stories that she herself had created. Because her attention was focused on getting meaning rather than on identifying words, she began to think of herself as a reader rather than a nonreader.

Rigg and Taylor sum up the results of their whole language tutoring program (1979, p. 56):

> After fifteen years of formal instruction, Renée was convinced that she could not read, and she did not read. In twenty hours of tutoring, she became convinced that she could read, and she did read. We asked Renée to do what evidently she had seldom or never been asked to do in school: We asked her to read, and then we got out of her way and let her do it.

Such reports of success should again make us suspect that much of our skills instruction with beginning readers as well as "remedial" readers is not only unnecessary but actually detrimental to the goal of literacy.

SMALL GROUPS: LEARNERS IN A LITERACY RECOVERY PROGRAM

In Nova Scotia, David Doake developed an exemplary literacy recovery program (he called it "reading recovery") for thirteen students aged eleven to twelve. Ten of the children had been retained a grade at some stage of their schooling, all were in the lowest reading group in their classroom, and most had had some "specialist," individually based tutoring. Though they had been classified on a variety of tests as being of average ability, they were making little or no progress in learning to read and write. On the Gates-McGinitie reading test, for example, their scores ranged from a grade level of 2.1 to 3.2. Doake characterizes their previous reading and writing instruction as follows (Doake, 1985, Appendix D; the program is explained more fully in Doake, 1992):

Highly structured:
- teacher controlled
- teacher the evaluating agent

Reading program (Basal type):
- controlled vocabulary
- heavy emphasis on learning word "attack" skills: phonics, little words in big words, syllabication
- more time spent on workbook exercises than on reading
- daily oral circle reading
- word accuracy emphasis rather than meaning emphasis
- seldom read to in school or at home

Writing program:
• accuracy oriented: spelling, grammar, punctuation
• little or no choice on what to write
• teacher the only audience

Handwriting
• daily
• standard script drill aimed at perfection

In contrast, Doake's literacy program included the following activities, undertaken in the spirit of whole language (Doake, 1985, Appendix H):

• Shared reading (Big Books)
• Read-along with a listening post
• Story reading to students (extensive)
• Sustained silent reading
• Reading at home to and with parents
• Individualized reading (conferences and sharing books)
• Reading in the content areas related particularly to thematic studies
• Creating plays and dramatizing them
• Learning songs, rhymes, and poems from enlarged print
• Reading to younger children from predictable books
• Thematic reading and writing resulting from initial brainstorming sessions on a topic (began with whole class projects and moved to individual studies)
• Environmental written language (used initially)
• Language experience charts and individual books
• Board News composed daily and used
• Dialogue journals
• Story writing (initially modeled after stories read)
• Story writing, using wordless picture story books
• Writing directions
• Regular reading and writing conferences
• Books made from stories written (given library cards)
• Follow-up activities from reading (writing own ending to a story, constructing a game, rewriting the story as a play and acting it out, etc.)

During the two years they were enrolled in this literacy recovery program, the students' progress was dramatic. In the year prior to their enrolling in the program, the students' average (mean) scores on the Gates-McGinitie went from approximately grade 2.2 to 2.4, an increase of only two months. In the first year of the program, the scores rose from an average of 2.4 to 3.8, an increase of one year, four months. In the third year, the scores on the Gates-McGinitie rose from an average of 3.8 to over 5.2, again an average increase of approximately one year, four months. Yet convincing as such standardized scores must be to those who hold conventional notions of educational accountability, these scores tell only part of the story. The most significant gains were in the students' attitude toward reading and writing. As Doake says, "These students received no formal instruction in reading and writing, nor did they experience any correction in their efforts to learn to read and write—and yet they have become readers and writers. They now enjoy these activities and engage in them frequently of their own volition" (Doake, 1985, pp. 5–6).

"REMEDIAL READING" AND "LEARNING DISABLED" CLASSROOMS

In the first section below, sixth-grade remedial reading teacher Marie Dionisio describes some of the reading strategies she promotes with students. This is followed by a vignette in which she describes the reading progress of one student, Teri. After that is Paul Crowley's description of John, a junior high student in a class of the "unlabeled gifted"—the term Crowley chose for learners that the school had labeled LD.

Teaching Reading Strategies in a "Remedial" Reading Class
Marie Dionisio

The reading strategies that follow grew out of my study of the work of Frank Smith (*Understanding Reading* and *Reading Without Nonsense*) and Nancie Atwell, and out of my reflections on my own reading strategies. Nancie Atwell introduced me to Frank Smith in 1987, during a workshop on reading and writing at Northeastern University's Institute on Writing and Teaching. Her interpretation and application of Smith's work prodded my continued study of pyscholinguistic theory and language development. Atwell also encouraged me to share with my students my own process for making sense of text. Being a daily, visible model of an adult who values and enjoys reading and writing is the most important of my teaching strategies.

Reading Books Students Like

In order to be good readers, students must have positive and pleasurable experiences with books. This is especially important for students who associate reading with failure. Such readers must find books and characters they can enjoy before they can take the risk of trying new strategies. For this reason, it is essential that students choose their own books and be able to abandon books they do not like. To help my students, I do a great many "book talks," but only on books I have read. Many times the books were originally recommended to me by students from previous remedial reading classes; if that is the case, I always mention it. I give a brief description of the story, share my personal response to it, and read a short excerpt. I also provide opportunities for students to share with one another the books that they like.

Using Language Expertise

Poor readers do not trust themselves with written language. They have learned to think that they are not capable of making sense of text. To dispel this myth, I demonstrate to these children that they are language experts. The years of experience they have as language users has made them experts on how language works. On an overhead transparency I present a short expanded cloze technique, one in which only a few words are given. As a class, they guess the words in order, using only their knowledge of the way sentences are put together and the growing context of the text. We discuss how they made their guesses, why synonyms and correct parts of speech are good guesses, and where they found it easiest and most difficult to make a guess. We end our discussion with a reminder to trust our knowledge of language to help us make the same kinds of guesses when we read.

Reading Fast

Most remedial readers read too slowly to make sense of text. They focus on individual words or even syllables. I demonstrate how reading too slowly can interfere with meaning construction by slowing my speech down to an imitation of word-by-word reading and sounding out. Speaking this way of course makes my message hard to comprehend. All students agree that my normal speech is much easier to understand. I draw a parallel with reading too slowly. To help them read faster I demonstrate the way peripheral vision aids readers. I discuss the idea of stopping one's eyes only on the words that carry the meaning and grouping other words around those words. We discuss the idea that increasing reading speed happens slowly.

Skipping Words Not Known

To break sixth graders of the habit of constantly sounding out words, I demonstrate how skipping an unknown word both increases speed and aids construction of meaning. I present short paragraphs that contain a word that the students do not know. I read the paragraph, skipping over the word. The students suggest meanings for the word as well as their reasons for suggesting it. We list possible meanings and identify synonyms in the list. We note how many of the suggested meanings are similar and why we think that happened. I end with a challenge for the day: in your reading today, skip over any word you do not know and see if you still understand what you read. Then, after reading time, we discuss our experiences.

Avoiding Bad Habits

Habits that slow readers down are the ones I want to eliminate. Such habits focus concentration at the word level instead of the meaning level. I discuss the following habits with students as well as the reason why they interfere with good reading:

• Moving your lips while you read slows you down.

- Pointing to the words or using a marker blocks your peripheral vision and slows you down.
- Constant rereading (which I demonstrate) confuses meaning and slows you down.
- Trying to remember all the details of what you read directs your focus from the global meaning of the text and from personal involvement in it.

Reading for Chunks of Uninterrupted Time

Comprehension hinges on exposure to chunks of text large enough to make meaning. Poor readers often take too many breaks while reading. These breaks seriously curtail meaning construction. I demonstrate how such breaks interfere with the ability to make sense of anything. I use a video or I tell a story about watching a video and being interrupted four or five times. Then we discuss why I did not like the video. I ask students to suggest ways in which readers interrupt themselves, and I list them on the board. I challenge students to read without interruptions of any kind for the entire twenty-five minutes of class reading time. At the end of that time, we discuss our experiences.

Identifying with a Character

Involvement in reading begins with a reader's identification with a character. To promote this, I talk about how putting myself in a character's place has helped me as a reader. I use specific examples of book characters with whom I have identified, why I was able to do so, and how that helped me as a reader. I challenge students to try to put themselves in the character's place and to think about what they would do in the same situation. I share my discovery that I can identify with a character even if that character is not like me in every way.

Thinking Ahead, or Predicting

Prediction is at the core of good reading. To promote prediction among remedial readers, I suggest commonplace scenarios to the class and ask them to predict what will happen next. Sometimes I read a picture book and stop for predictions. In both cases, we discuss how we arrived at our prediction. As a follow-up on another day, I use examples of how prediction helped me while reading a particular book. I challenge students to predict as they are reading and end the class with a sharing of the predictions made that day and the reasons for them.

Visualizing

Movies and video games occupy a great deal of my students' time. I use that fact to suggest that they visualize what they are reading as a way of getting involved in a story. I tell them that I see a movie in my head when I read. I ask them to close their eyes, listen to me read, and try to see what they hear. I read a passage that is both easy to visualize and interesting to the age group. I ask students to share with the class what they saw in their minds. I challenge students to see a movie in their heads as they read.

Teri: A Sixth Grader in a "Remedial" Reading Class
Marie Dionisio

Because of her second-grade standardized test scores, Teri had been labeled a remedial reader in third grade. Beginning in fifth grade, she also attended the resource room for assistance with her diagnosed learning disability. Now in sixth grade, she was still in the remedial reading class and still in the resource room. She hated reading and school. (Wouldn't you?) Four years of special reading class with another year ahead of her was proof to Teri that reading was something she would never be able to do. Furthermore, she saw absolutely no reason why she should want to read.

Remedial reading has traditionally been a sentence, like a jail term. Instruction has focused on a reader's weaknesses. Encounters with text are brief, and controlled by the teacher. The meaning of such text is minimal (if there is any meaning at all). Reading is reduced to an endless parade of skill-drill exercises. To paraphrase Frank Smith (1985), remedial reading instruction made nonsense out of what should be sense.

At the beginning of sixth grade, Teri's primary reading strategy was to sound out words. She was a word-by-word reader. To her, reading was the correct oral pronunciation of words. It had nothing to do with meaning. Even the questions at the end of everything she read were meaningless. She told me that she answered the questions by finding a word or phrase in the paragraph and copying that part as her answer. It was a matter of word matching, not meaning construction. Reading was truly meaningless for her.

Teri was like most of the remedial readers I had seen in the previous twenty years. I knew I had to change her view of reading to one of meaning construction. In order to do that, I would have to help her discover that reading could be enjoyable.

I started with allowing Teri to choose her own books. During the first ten weeks of school, mini-lessons focused on reading for meaning. I discussed the strategies that I thought would enable my students to abandon word-by-word reading and focus on meaning. During this time, Teri started ten books but finished only one: *When the Boys Ran the House* by Joan Carris. One of her classmates had read it and recommended it to her. The humor took hold of her. As a result, Teri had her first successful and enjoyable reading experience.

The concept of abandoning a book you do not like was new to Teri. Up to this point she had been told what to read. She had no choices and no ownership. Given her attitude toward reading and its lack of meaning for her, I expected her to abandon several books. I didn't expect her to abandon nine books, but it reminded me of how important it is to allow readers to abandon books they do not like. If I had interfered in Teri's decisions about books and made choices for her, she may never have come to that first enjoyable and meaning-centered reading experience.

After finishing *When the Boys Ran the House*, Teri wrote this letter to me in her reading dialogue journal:

> I liked *When the Boys Ran the House* because the author made me feel like I was a character and if it was a movie it would be a comedy movie so when I read the book it felt like a comedy to me.

This letter is evidence that Teri had adopted some new reading strategies. She was making sense out of text instead of reading purely as oral performance. She was beginning to imagine herself as the character and to visualize as she read. This novel was a clear turning point for Teri. Following it, she finished four more books and enjoyed them all. Each of them was recommended by Annie, the same classmate who had recommended *When the Boys Ran the House*. She also abandoned two books during this time.

During this same period, Teri and Annie began exchanging literary letters. In them they discussed the books both of them had read. After Teri finished the fourth of Annie's recommendations, she wrote in a journal letter, "Most of the time Annie and me compare our reactions to the same book. I like that." In their literary dialogue, Teri and Annie discussed characters, favorite scenes, and personal responses to the stories. They were discussing the very things I discussed with them, but they were doing it because they wanted to, because they saw value in it, because it was fun. Did Teri understand and enjoy what she was reading? Without a doubt!

During the third quarter, Teri began to choose books on her own and recommend them to Annie, to other classmates, and to me. After reading *Chocolate Fever* by Robert Kimmel Smith, Teri wrote to me, "I thought *Chocolate Fever* was good because I liked how the author put the characters into the story. It pulled me in." By this time Teri regularly verbalized her involvement in what she was reading. In this instance, she specified how the author had invited her into the story. I could see that she no longer saw reading as something she'd never be able to do.

During the third quarter I reviewed the reading strategies we had discussed earlier in the year by asking the class, "If a friend came to you, said he or she was having trouble with reading, and asked you for help, what would you tell that friend to do?" The students generated a list of suggestions, most of which came from the mini-lessons I had done in the fall. I listed them on chart paper, pinned them to the wall, and invited the students to try one they hadn't tried before or one they would like to do better. I also asked them to write a letter and let me know how it worked out. Here's Teri's letter:

> Today I tried to read faster and it worked really good. I read about 25 pages today. I didn't talk or take any commercial breaks during reading time, and I didn't move my lips. It all worked because I read more and I remember everything and I like the story better too.

My response was deliberately short and simple: "You really took a risk trying three things today. Terrific. So, you are saying that you were able to understand more and enjoy reading because you read faster and didn't talk. That sounds logical to me." I was sure encouragement and reinforcement of the idea that she was continuing to improve as a reader were the most valuable teaching strategies I could use.

A week later Teri again wrote about her efforts to try new strategies as a reader. "I tried to put myself in the main character's place and it worked out pretty good. I just finished *Sadako and the Thousand Paper Cranes*. It was sad. I cried." Teri's willingness to take risks as a reader is obvious. She no longer saw such attempts as opportunities for failure. Rather, she saw these risks as voyages into unchartered areas that might yield new discoveries for her.

Toward the end of the third quarter, Teri's involvement in reading went even deeper. She wrote,

> I'm reading *Ace Hits the Big Time* by Murphy and Wolkoff. So far its good. I could actually hear and feel the action. It's got a lot of action. And it pulled me right in. I love it.

Clearly, Teri was no longer the passive and disinterested caller of words she had been in September. She had become an active reader, one who is involved with character and conflict, one who sees value in reading. Furthermore, she was reading a book that was considered appropriate for sixth graders!

During the fourth quarter, Teri took more risks as a reader, read more books than any of the previous ten-week periods, and continued to grow as a reader and learner. She began to spend time at home reading books, and she told her friends and me that she did. For a child like Teri to admit that she read at home was an enormous change. On one occasion she wrote, "I started reading a book at home. It's called *Just As Long As We're Together* by Judy Blume. The book is about friends." A month later she began her letter with, "Over the vacation I read *Jelly Belly* by Robert Kimmel Smith. It was a really good book. Funny and serious too." Reading had become part of Teri's life.

At the same time, she began to hone and vary her reading strategies. We had been discussing the strategy of putting yourself in the character's place as you read. Our share session raised a good question: could a reader put herself in the character's place with equal success in every book? We debated this issue and decided it was true. The next day, Teri wrote this letter:

> I just started *Blubber* by Judy Blume. Well I tried to put myself in the main character and it wasn't me. Because it's about this girl who's fat. But in *Class Clown* by Johanna Hurwitz I put myself in the main character's place and it was me sometimes.

Teri and I discussed the idea of pretending to be with the character instead of being the character. She thought that would work for her in books like *Blubber*.

By the end of the year, Teri had changed dramatically. She enjoyed reading, saw value in being a reader, spent time reading outside of school, owned a collection of books she loved, learned from the characters and conflicts in books and, best of all, recognized the ways in which she had changed. Since September she had read nineteen novels. This was quite an accomplishment and was indicative of the reader she had grown to be. Her final evaluation delineates the changes she saw in herself.

> I changed my reading a couple of ways this year. I don't move my lips anymore and that helps me read a lot faster. I focus on the book and don't take commercial breaks while I'm reading. I try to be the main character. I also like to read on my own now. I never knew how much fun reading can be. We got to pick our own books and if we didn't like the book, we could just drop the book and start a new one. I think if you want to be a good reader, you have to read books that you like, not books that other people like. We don't have to do any comprehension sheets or work in the workbooks. Instead we write in our journals to the

other classmates or we write to Ms. Dionisio and tell her all about our book. I share my ideas with Ms. Dionisio and she shares hers with me. I really think I changed a lot this year and I'm glad I did.

Perhaps the most powerful statement in this letter is "I never knew how much fun reading can be." After all, if something is fun to do, we all tend to do it well. Certainly, Teri did not have another year of special reading class ahead of her. For the first time in her life, she saw herself as a reader.

John: A Junior High Student in a Class for the Unlabeled Gifted

Teacher Paul Crowley describes John as follows (Crowley, 1988, pp. 15–16):

> As a seventh-grader, John was enrolled in the typical junior high curriculum, with one exception: He was not in an English class but rather in a special education class for students labeled "learning disabled." This label was not new to John. He had been singled out early in his educational career, particularly for his lack of success in writing and reading. Descriptions such as "perceptual motor difficulties" and "processing deficit" were used to describe John's school problems.
>
> Like most junior high students John did not want to be thought of as different. From the first day he made this clear to his L.D. teacher. John frequently said that he didn't need the class. He came in late each day so that no one would see him enter "that room." He made sure that the door was closed for the duration of his stay, and he skipped out quickly when the bell rang.
>
> John's teacher [Paul Crowley] hated the label as much as John did, but for different reasons. As a whole language teacher he was comfortable concentrating on students' linguistic strengths, not their difficulties. Instead of lumping kids into ill-defined categories, he accepted the abilities of language users as a starting point. Instead of describing the class of four boys as "learning disabled" the teacher gave them the name "unlabeled gifted."

Instead of giving the students workbook pages to complete or drilling the students on specific reading skills, the teacher gave them whole texts. Instead of giving them fine motor exercises, he gave them a pen and paper to write with. "Reading, writing, speaking, and listening were the curriculum, whether John was studying fighter planes, working on a social studies assignment, reading about motorcycles or learning about the circulatory system" (p. 16).

By ninth grade, John had enough confidence in his reading and writing to take a regular English class, but he took the "unlabeled gifted" class as well, using it as a workshop to pursue new interests. He began reading an adventure series, typically reading two to five books a week. Then he decided to read George Orwell's *1984*. He kept a response log while reading the book: after reaching a logical stopping point, he would write what he was thinking about. Instead of writing a book report, he raised questions, explored ambiguous ideas, offered interpretations, and recorded his feelings and attitudes. He noticed intriguing parallels between *1984* and *Romeo and Juliet,* which he was reading in his regular English class. On the last day of ninth grade, writes Crowley, "John gave his teacher a beautifully written expository essay discussing the themes that John gleaned from *1984*. He thought his teacher 'might like it.' " Crowley closes his sketch of John by saying, "John has not decided where he wants to go for college, but he is sure that he wants to go to the University of Michigan for his master's degree" (p. 18). What a transformation wrought by Crowley's whole-language approach to "remedial" instruction for "learning disabled" students!

WHOLE LANGUAGE CLASSROOMS: SPECIAL LEARNERS IN A FIFTH-GRADE CLASS

The legally mandated "least restrictive environment" for students diagnosed as learning disabled is, of course, the regular classroom. In many instances, students who have not succeeded in traditional classrooms flourish in whole language classrooms, though such success requires faith in the learner, time, patience, and perseverance on the part of the teacher.

The two following vignettes of individual students are written by Cora Five, a fifth-grade teacher who, in *Special Voices* (1992), tells stories of children with special needs in her classroom community. From these vignettes of special learners, we get a sense of how Cora promotes the learning of *all* students: by creating a supportive classroom community, giving students time (the whole school year) in which to grow, offering choices and ownership, providing response and structure, and gradually expecting and allowing students to take more responsibility for their work (Hansen, 1987). These are some of the same characteristics of whole language classrooms that help prevent learning difficulties in the first place.

Alex: A Journey Toward Greater Maturity and Increased Self-esteem
Cora Lee Five

Alex, who had been placed in my fifth-grade self-contained classroom, had been classified by our district's Committee on Special Education as learning disabled in fourth grade. He had a history of learning problems and had received skills help since first grade. His Individual Educational Program (IEP) stated that he had difficulty with reading and that he tested at a beginning third-grade level at the end of fourth grade. He could not decode well, and his written and oral language were very limited. He had problems with spelling and seemed unable to express his ideas in any form. It was noted that Alex needed much time to process information and often asked for directions and questions to be repeated.

In the classroom it was suggested that Alex be taught in one-to-one situations. In previous grades Alex apparently did not participate in class discussions and was lost in a whole class or group setting. It was recommended that he receive help initiating and completing assignments. Alex's IEP specified that he was scheduled to leave the classroom to work with skills teachers four times a week.

I looked forward to having Alex in my class. I was interested to see how a workshop approach, one that insured time, ownership, and response (Giacobbe, 1986), would affect his reading and his ability to express himself.

At the beginning of the year, Alex displayed behavior problems. He shouted out, usually comments that seemed to be irrelevant. He did little work and spent a lot of time crawling around on the floor, under desks, and in the coat closet. He spoke in a babyish voice and walked like a toddler. All the children laughed at his antics. They liked him because he pretended to be, or perhaps he thought he was, dumb. His behavior got him in trouble in every class and, at least at the beginning of the year, my students thought Alex was funny. He seemed to enjoy being the class clown and was easily distracted by his peers and the events in the classroom.

I hoped Alex's image of himself would change and that he would become part of the class community of learners. I knew from past experience that it was important to establish a positive, supportive environment, one that valued ideas. This is necessary for all students, but it is especially important for children with special learning needs. In this type of environment they can take risks and gradually develop greater self-esteem. This environment usually comes first through the development of a community of writers. I spend much time at the beginning of the year modeling conferences and responses that are positive and constructive. Students learn to respond to each other in a similar way through conferences at my round conference table. I hoped Alex would become part of our community of writers. Perhaps in this way, he would be able to take himself seriously and develop self-respect.

During the first month of school, Alex was not involved in writing. I was not surprised because I knew he had done little writing in fourth-grade. When he had written, he wrote with the help of skills teachers. At the beginning of fifth grade Alex did not write, and when I tried to brainstorm topics with him, he remained silent. Sometimes he answered "I don't know" in a high-pitched voice and rolled his eyes, causing the other children to laugh at him. He seemed to enjoy acting this way. Often he crawled on the floor, examining something he found on the carpet.

Early in the year Alex would not come to the conference table by himself. I encouraged him, but he seemed to have little interest. I noticed, however, that Alex listened to the conversations as children shared drafts and explained problems they were having in writing. Eventually I coaxed him to come to the table to listen to the other children's topics. I wanted him to become part of the writing community and I hoped the experience might inspire him. He sat and said little. Sometimes he made faces and returned to his desk. When I looked at him he told me, "I'm thinking," which was a response I heard throughout the year as he sat for long periods of time doing what I assumed to be nothing. I was never sure what his words meant, but I respected his response and let him think.

Alex would sit at his desk drawing little figures instead of writing. I noticed these detailed figures and asked him to explain them to me. He was reluctant at first but then began to explain that they were pictures of a trip he had taken to the Grand Canyon. As he told me about the drawings, he told me about his trip. I suggested that perhaps his trip might be a topic for writing, and I repeated all he had told me, using the figures to help with the sequence. Alex looked surprised, then shrugged and continued to draw.

The next day he started a draft about his trip to the Grand Canyon. He wrote slowly, but he did not stop. He had a lot to tell and finished his three-page draft at the end of the week. He read it to me and decided that he liked it and didn't want to change it. I realized that he needed my help to proofread his piece. He expressed confidence about his knowledge of periods and capital letters but was very concerned about spelling.

Alex spent the next week alternating between copying his story and drawing an elaborate cover. Again I acknowledged his ability in art and gave him time to work on his cover, which he did very carefully, drawing every detail and explaining the figures to a friend who sat next to him.

When Alex completed his story, he didn't know if he wanted to share it with the class. I encouraged him, but let him make the decision. Finally, days later, he decided to read it and seemed very embarrassed. He rolled his eyes, behaved in a silly way, and waved his cover around for the class to see. At first he read in his babyish voice; but then he switched to what I described to him as his "fifth-grade" voice, but he read very fast. Despite his behavior, the class did not laugh at him (due to rules we had established); instead, they responded with many positive comments. He seemed surprised and confused at first. He was used to their laughter, not their positive response. By the time he finished calling on various classmates and listening to them, he seemed pleased, although he tried to hide his pleasure.

The next piece was somewhat easier for Alex to write. He thought about topics for a week and finally listed a few on a piece of paper. I discussed each one with him because he did not seem able to discuss topics with a peer without resorting to immature behavior. He spoke briefly about each and finally decided to write about his birthday party. Because I was teaching about the use of dialogue in my writing and reading mini lessons, I encouraged him to try to use dialogue in his draft, but he insisted that "nobody said anything," and refused. I respected his decision, realizing he was not ready.

During the next few months of school Alex began to come to the conference table to read parts of his draft. When he was not distracted by the other children, he seemed to listen to the comments of the group at the table. Sometimes he made minor revisions based on the feedback he received, but he did not respond to classmates' writing. Sometimes he came to the table to listen for a short time and then would wander back to his desk. I felt Alex was slowly becoming part of the writing community. I think that as he listened to other children responding to each other's writing, he began to realize that writing was not easy for everyone, that all writers were vulnerable, and that perhaps this environment provided a safe place for him to express his ideas.

By December Alex was showing progress. He was better able to select a topic and write a draft. For his third piece he decided to write about a bad day he had when I was absent and the class had a substitute. In this piece he wanted to include conversation and came to me to learn where to put quotation marks and when to indent. He realized the need to use the correct skills for his writing. I was pleased that he took a risk with dialogue and as a result wanted to learn. And it happened when he was ready, at his timing. I noticed his changed attitude when he wanted to learn for a meaningful purpose. He was interested, he talked, he asked questions, and after we worked on the beginning of his piece, he experimented with his draft to see if he could put quotation marks around conversation at the end. He was beginning to take charge of his writing.

I also began to notice that Alex adopted a different pattern of behavior when he felt he was being forced to do something he did not want to do or that made him feel uncomfortable or humiliated. For example, when the skills teacher came into the room to teach him writing skills, he became stubborn and would not do as she asked. He sat in silence or answered with "I don't know." The angrier and more frustrated she became, the more he refused to do. He would not perform. After she left, he reverted to his babyish behavior and crawled on the floor or disrupted the class with his "class clown" antics. He seemed to find comfort in acting dumb, or perhaps the fact that she worked with him on his writing made him feel inadequate. Perhaps he became angry when she took away his authority or control over his writing.

The situation was very different when it came to reading. Alex was present without the skills teacher for all of reading workshop and for the stories I read aloud to the class. At first he had difficulty selecting books. In the past he had been given paragraphs to read by the skills teachers, and sometimes aides or his teachers had selected books for him. In my room Alex could choose his own books, but since he had little experience with making choices, he didn't know how.

In the beginning I picked out three or four books that I knew to be favorites from years past. They were short, high-interest trade books. Alex could not choose from among the books I selected. At first I gave him short book talks and encouraged him to read a book I knew and liked. This worked and he selected one of the books. He read it slowly and attempted to sound out every word. He said a few words about the book in our daily conference and wrote a letter to me about the book in his reading journal. He wrote about a particular part in the book that he liked and included a sentence about a favorite character. After he finished his book, he came to me for another. This time he chose two books, looked at both of them carefully, and selected one that was similar to his first book. He read slowly and continued to read short books for many weeks.

From the mini-lessons I taught to the class and from my individual conferences with him, Alex gradually began to realize that he didn't have to sound out every word to make meaning. In fact, at the beginning he spent so much time trying to sound out words that he almost lost interest in the story and gave up. I explained to him that good readers skipped words they didn't know and read to the end of the sentence or the paragraph. It was only when he realized that he could skip some words that he began to read faster and became involved in the story. At times he skipped words he didn't know and returned to them after he had made sense of the context. Often he substituted words that did not change the meaning. When he explained this strategy to me, I praised him and told him the importance of what he was doing. Frequently he would check the word with me to confirm the meaning. It was in this way that I first realized the extent of his vocabulary. He became interested in using synonyms for the words he couldn't sound out. As reading became more meaningful for him he gradually began to apply his years of phonics skills to unknown words.

At the end of reading workshop he listened to his classmates' ideas during group shares and drew mazes on pieces of paper, but said very little about his own reading.

During my first reading and writing evaluation conference with Alex, he had difficulty evaluating his progress. We looked through his reading folder and reread his journal letters. We also looked through his writing folder and tried to determine his best piece. I gave him lots of time to think and respond to my questions. I wanted to hear his ideas. Alex told me that he had trouble thinking of topics in writing. He was concerned about his spelling and set a goal for himself to improve in this area. His second goal was to write more pieces. He was able to select his best story, the one about the Grand Canyon. This was the first piece he had written where he selected the topic. Alex felt he had improved in reading because, as he wrote in his journal, "I anderstand books moor. and I read moor books."

By the end of December, Alex was involved in the stories I read to the class. Even though he drew as I read, I knew he was listening because he began to enter into discussions about the book with a word or two, sometimes in his babyish voice, sometimes in his fifth-grade voice. At this time, he made two discoveries in reading. First, from the mini-lessons I taught, he began to practice reading groups of words together, taking in chunks of meaning instead of reading one word at a time. He also discovered *The Boxcar Children* (Warner, 1942) and all its sequels. From then on he was hooked on reading. He no longer had trouble selecting books. The letters in his reading journal became longer as he began to connect the experiences in the books to his own experiences. He often ended his letters with questions or predictions, and he enjoyed reading my responses. By January, Alex had finished all the books in the series. By February, he was involved in *Tales of a Fourth Grade Nothing* (Blume, 1972) and the other books that described Fudge and his adventures.

Also in February, Alex was reading books on colonial America. The class was immersed in this topic through reading, writing, simulations, films, discussions, music, and class trips. Alex was particularly interested in colonial schools and school punishments and read many trade books on this topic. He was expressing more of his ideas in his journals and in discussions. During conversations about colonial schools, the other children began to listen to him, question him, and learn from his brief answers. He seemed surprised by their interest.

Perhaps the response from his peers, his increasing self-esteem as a reader and learner, and the class environment prompted Alex to volunteer to read from the history text when the whole class read it together. Perhaps these factors, too, helped him become better able to participate in all class activities. He began to do well in math and discovered that he could help other children. He enjoyed solving problems with his peers and would run back and forth to me to see if he had come up with the correct answer. I noticed that he used his fifth-grade voice more often and that he had stopped crawling on the floor. It seemed as though he was becoming part of the greater community of learners.

During this time, Alex decided he wanted to write a report on colonial schools. He wrote a long draft, and through the response he received in conferences, he decided to divide his draft into two chapters. When his chapters were finished, he drew a colonial school for his cover and many detailed illustrations throughout the report. He even made a replica of a hornbook. Again I realized that art was an important means of communication for him. I also realized that when Alex was interested and involved, when the work was meaningful for him, when he felt he could make decisions and had some control, he stopped his babyish voice and silly behavior and put forth greater effort. He was able to write on his own and even took risks writing in another genre. He read his report to the class in his normal voice and seemed proud of his final product. He listened carefully as the students told him what they liked and what they had learned. Again he seemed surprised at their response.

Alex was becoming more involved in the stories I read to the class. He often asked when he arrived in the morning when I would read aloud and would make a comment about a character or would predict the next event or speculate on the meaning of the title (all topics of mini-lessons taught earlier). He seemed to be thinking about the stories all the time. Once after I read a chapter from *Tuck Everlasting* (Babbitt, 1975) where the spring in the Fosters' wood was explained, he said later in the day while he was copying his homework, "Oh, that's why they call it Tuck Everlasting." "Why?" I asked. "Because they can't change, they're everlasting," he explained. He was the first one in the class to express his ideas about the meaning of the title. The rest of the class thought about his remark; many agreed with him. His comment launched the class into a discussion of that particular title and titles in general. Alex was involved in the discussion.

I had my second reading/writing evaluation conference with Alex at the end of March. I was interested in the changes he expressed. He described his progress in reading by telling me, "I like books much, much more." His parents confirmed that he was reading independently at home for longer periods of time, and they were pleased with his progress. I was surprised when he told me that writing letters to me in his reading journal helped him as a reader. He explained, "You hear more words. The letters help you understand the book more." Perhaps, even though he wrote brief letters, time set aside for the letter writing gave him time to think and reflect in his own way on the books he read.

Alex set goals for himself at this second conference: to read more books, to read different kinds of books, and to read faster. When he talked to me about his writing, he told me he liked his colonial report the best because he learned a lot about colonial schools and he liked his illustrations. His writing goals for the remainder of the year were to add details to his pieces, and to work faster in drafting and copying. It was interesting that spelling had ceased to be a major concern for him.

As April turned into May, Alex discovered a series of books he decided to read with two other boys. He also encouraged me to read them and was proud and somewhat perplexed that he was finishing them faster than I was. Each morning he'd check to see where I was in a book he'd recommended and was reading at the same time. He'd discuss the parts he liked, and I'd tell him my honest feelings about some of the characters. I was delighted when he told me one day that he had read for an hour and a half one night because "I wanted to know what would happen so I couldn't stop reading." Alex had become a reader. He was now so involved in his books that instead of drawing in class, he would often take out his book, open it in his desk, and read while we were involved in another subject.

Alex continued to grow as a writer, too. He experimented with similes and began to express his feelings. In his favorite piece about his part in a team sport, he wrote:

> The ball hit me and I went flying across the field like an arrow hitting the target. . . . I kicked the ball. It went into the goal and we won by 1 point. I felt great about winning the game.

At the end of the year, Alex was able to evaluate his writing and reading with greater confidence. He knew he liked his piece that described scoring the winning point. "I put a simile in it and I told more about how I felt." He knew he had improved a lot in reading: "I read more books during the year than I can ever remember reading." He planned to read over the summer and write about some of his trips. Indeed, postcards to me from Alex arrived at various times during the summer, describing a particular vacation event. Alex had begun his journey as a reader and a writer.

Jennifer: Emerging as an Active Learner
Cora Lee Five

At the beginning of the year in my fifth-grade class, Jennifer was almost invisible. A quiet, withdrawn child, Jennifer never looked at me or her peers but kept her eyes on her desk. She barely spoke and came and went each day showing little affect. Years ago I would never have noticed her because of her "good" behavior and the actions of others who would have taken my time and attention. Now, however, it was her passivity that concerned me and focused my attention on her.

I learned from a child study meeting that Jennifer had had many learning problems since the first grade. Her limited written and oral language, plus her difficulties with reading, had required extra help from the skills teachers. There were gaps in her learning, and she needed help in initiating her work and following directions. In third and fourth grade she left her classroom several times a week for extra help in math. She had little understanding of math concepts and knew few number facts. Discussions had been held periodically as to whether to have her classified as learning disabled, but the decision had always been postponed. It was felt that part of Jennifer's problem had been her attendance. She had been absent often throughout her school experience and had missed much of the work in each grade. Because her attendance was so sporadic, she was always behind in her work and overwhelmed with assignments she had to make up. Her feelings of inadequacy increased when she returned to school, and she was soon absent again. This cycle had continued through fourth grade. She had missed much of fourth grade, and it was felt that fifth grade might be the time to have her classified as a child with special learning needs. In fifth grade she was scheduled to leave the class for skills help in math three times a week and reading twice a week.

The first day of fifth grade, Jennifer wrote a short letter to me in response to my request that the students tell me something about themselves that would help me make their fifth-grade experience more comfortable for them. She told me she did not like school, that she especially hated math, and that she preferred that I not call on her unless she raised her hand. She came to school for the next two days and was absent for half of the following week. I realized that before I could help her with anything, I had to do something to keep her in school. I needed to develop a personal connection with her. Perhaps a positive, supportive relationship with me would eventually lead to greater involvement in school activities.

I usually share my hobbies and interests with my class. I tell them about life in New York City and the unusual events that occur there, which are very different from events that happen in my students' suburban community. Sooner or later, I always tell them about my cats. This year, however, in my attempt to capture Jennifer's attention, I began by telling stories about my cats, stories in which the cats talked and acted like little humans. I made sure to tell these stories on the days Jennifer was present. After a while I noticed she was looking at me instead of at her desk when I told my stories. Whenever I passed her desk, I said a few words to her. Within a few weeks I realized that Jennifer was coming to school more regularly. Whenever she was there, I made sure I told her I was happy to see her. When she was absent, I made sure she knew what we had done in class, and I helped her complete what she had missed so she would not fall behind. One day she left a small note on a torn piece of paper on the Message Board that said, "I love the storys about your cats."

Jennifer's presence in class was the first step and remained my primary goal. As we began to work in science, history, math, and other subjects, her passivity became more apparent. Her immediate response to her work was, "I don't know." She said it quietly, without attempting to try. Often she would hand in papers with her name on them, the date, and the words "I don't know how to do this" or "I can't do this." I responded to these papers by telling her that I would help her and that she would be able to learn. When I took her aside or worked with her at her desk, she looked at me without expression and said yes to everything I tried to explain to her. I did not know if she really understood or not. Her blank look always unnerved me and left me feeling uncomfortable and helpless.

Her response to writing workshop was fortunately somewhat different. For the first few sessions of writing workshop, I model the writing process by using my own writing. I make copies of my drafts for the overhead projector and share my writing with the class. I show them how I select a topic and how I write and revise a draft. Because of Jennifer, I decided to write about my cats. She listened and watched as I talked about my ideas and then wrote them on the overhead.

When I came to her desk for a short conference, I noticed that she sat with a few blank sheets of paper. I asked her what she'd like to write about and she answered with her usual "I don't know." I explained to her where I got my ideas for my piece. "I don't have any ideas," she said flatly. She seemed very afraid to write anything on the expanse of white paper, even her name. We talked about my cats for a few minutes, and I asked her if she had any pets. After a long silence, she told me she had a dog. In response to my many questions she began to tell me about her dog. I encouraged her to write about her dog and a fight he had had with a friend's dog. When I left her desk, she was still sitting looking at her paper, but soon I noticed she began to write. Her short story began with the dog fight:

When I took my dog, Mini, to Maggie's house, Maggie's dog started to growl. My dog tried to run away. Maggie pulled her dog away. Then Mickey and Mini started to get mad. Mini started to cry. Maggie's dog started to growl and bark and get really mean.

Jennifer finished her draft but would not share it with the other children. She read it to me and made a few minor changes. She copied it and made a cover. Again she would not share it and was reluctant to have me put it on the bulletin board. Eventually, she agreed. I was very pleased she was able to complete a writing piece because I believed that through writing, she would develop confidence that would spread to other areas.

Her next writing topics were somewhat easier for her to select. Her second piece was a long, rambling, disorganized account of a trip she had taken. I used this piece to show her the many different topics she had in her piece. She was able to count the possible topics although she did not want to focus on any one of them. By her third piece, however, as a result of mini-lessons I taught to the whole class and my working with her individually, she was able to focus on one topic: getting stuck in an elevator for a few minutes. As she discussed this topic, she showed some emotion, which attracted the attention of the girl who sat next to her. I suggested that Jennifer read her draft to her new friend, which she did. She did not risk coming to the conference table to share her piece, although she listened to other children discussing their writing.

Reading workshop started in a similar way. Jennifer sat with a book she had taken from the class library. Her eyes barely moved, and she did not turn any pages. When I stopped at her desk for a conference, she told me the book was "okay." However, when she wrote her first letter to me in her reading journal, she wrote:

The book I am reading is very confuesing and I don't like it. it is hard

I wrote back, suggesting she look for another book since she did not like the one she had selected. I wanted to let her select her own book. Obediently, she followed my suggestion and took another book. However, there was little thought involved in her choice. She put one book back and picked up another. The following week, her journal letter read:

I don't like the book I'm reading and I want a new one.

"I want a new one" was the first request Jennifer made for herself. I felt hopeful and decided to suggest two or three books I thought she might like. I hoped if I could find one book that she liked she might not give up on reading. I encouraged her to read shorter books so she would not feel so overwhelmed, and gradually she began to read them. She completed these thinner books quickly and was pleased to add them to her reading log. When she read them aloud to me, I realized she made quick attempts at words she didn't know, which did not interfere with her comprehension. She was able to retell these stories, and completing many of these short books seemed to give her a sense of accomplishment that I think she needed.

Even though she was reading, for a few weeks Jennifer did not write to me because she told me she had no ideas. We discussed her books in short conferences each day. I would tell her my feelings about books I was reading, make predictions, and tell her what confused me. I modeled the kinds of responses she might make. Eventually, at the end of October, Jennifer wrote a long letter about a book I had read aloud to the class. Her letter included much of what we had discussed in whole-class mini-lessons related to the book. I was glad she was listening and thinking about what had been said. She still did not express any ideas orally and I was careful not to call on her. I wondered when she'd take a risk and raise her hand.

In November, Jennifer told me she liked ghost stories, so I recommended *Wait Till Helen Comes* (Hahn, 1986). Jennifer read this book slowly. It was longer and on a more difficult level than her other books had been. I hoped her interest in ghost stories would sustain her interest in a more challenging book. Fortunately, I was right. For the first time, her letter expressed joy in reading:

> I love the book Wait till Helen Comes the reason why I love the book is I understand it. It doesn't have a lot of big words in it and it is scary! I like books written by Mary Downing Hahn.

When Jennifer discovered Mary Downing Hahn, she became interested in reading and began to read. She spent most of the year reading Hahn's books. She read slowly and usually only read in school, despite a homework assignment to read for thirty minutes each night. She often told me she wanted to read at home, but her parents liked the whole family to watch television together so she had no time to read. I realized how important the forty-five minutes a day I had scheduled for reading was for Jennifer. It was the only opportunity she had to read on a consistent basis.

In her first reading/writing evaluation conference, Jennifer told me that the most important thing she had learned as a reader was that "I wasn't nuts about reading, but now I like it." She wanted to learn how to read faster. She was also more excited about her writing. She liked all the pieces she had written but felt the hardest part of writing for her was thinking about a topic and finding an idea. As she left the conference, she told me, "I hate going to skills." Jennifer was beginning to express her emotions.

The next day I discussed the situation with the skills teachers and it was agreed that she would leave the room for skills in math only, not for reading. Jennifer seemed pleased about the change. I began to work with her and show her how she could read faster by reading more than one word at a time. I tried a technique I had learned from Atwell and Giacobbe (1985). I used a mirror and had Jennifer watch my eye movements as I read. I explained to her that when my eyes moved they were reading groups of words at a time. Then I exchanged places with her and I described her eye movements through the use of the mirror. I showed her how her eyes could take in groups of words at once and how those groups of words were chunks of meaning. She began to practice reading more than one word at a time.

By the end of autumn, I noticed that Jennifer seemed more animated at times. She smiled and had made friends with the girl who sat next to her in class. They often whispered together and I noticed, too, that they recommended books to each other and often discussed them when we were not involved in reading. They also shared their writing drafts with each other. More important was the fact that Jennifer had been coming to school regularly. At times she arrived late, but she was not absent very often. Her mother stopped by a few times to tell me that Jennifer loved school this year and that she was surprised at the change.

Although Jennifer was not actively involved in history or science activities or discussions, she did write some of her observations and thoughts in her journals. She selected a topic for a report about colonial times. She wanted to write about colonial schools and read many short books about this topic. As she wrote her report, she began to add her thoughts and feelings. At the end of her chapter on school punishments, she wrote:

> The boy who didn't behave wore a branch on his nose for an hour or more. That must have been embarrassing! I am happy I live in 1992!

Again more of her feelings were expressed, but Jennifer was still reluctant to share her ideas and writing pieces with the class. However, she was participating in small-group conferences to a greater extent. I think she began to realize that the classroom environment was one where ideas were accepted and where her peers would not laugh at mistakes. She began to take risks.

Jennifer's interest in writing and then reading had spread to history, where she was able to use reading and writing to learn. Gradually she began to become interested in science. When we started a unit on acid rain, she showed interest by listing in her science journal all the things she wanted to learn:

> Why do we have acid rain?
> What is acid?
> how does it affect you?
> do we eat acid?
> do we drink acid rain?

Jennifer continued to work with her friend on science activities and projects. However, she needed the relationship, the talking, with her friend and with me, in order to keep herself actively involved. This interaction did not work with math. She remained passive throughout the year and made no attempt to try any work on her own. Despite my individual work with her, she reverted to her withdrawn self. Seeming resigned to the fact that she could not do math, she would not try, and relied on the skills teachers for help.

By the spring, Jennifer enjoyed and looked forward to writing. By listening to the other students read their pieces, she discovered she had many topics to write about. She began to share her completed pieces with the class, reading them in a soft voice and smiling in response to their comments. She began to experiment with dialogue and similes and was especially pleased when she wrote a good lead. She appeared to be a much happier, more confident child. She even began to raise her hand to contribute to discussions.

Jennifer's reading/writing evaluation conference at the end of the year showed her increasing involvement in reading and writing. She talked about her interest in the characters in the books she read. Her journal letters were now filled with her questions and her feelings:

I feel bad for Tallahassee because her aunt doesn't really like her and Jane isn't her friend anymore. . .

Why doesn't Liz call her and come back for her? I don't understand that. I was so mad at Liz for leaving Tallahassee. I loved that book! . . .

Mary Downing Hahn is my favorite author. I like how some of the chapters in Stepping on the Cracks [Hahn, 1992] end in a question mark. I really want to turn the page and see what the rest of the book is about.

When Jennifer discussed her writing, she said she felt she had improved in many ways. She could put in punctuation and paragraphs, which she could not do at the beginning of fifth grade. She could select her best pieces; she especially liked her story of how she learned to ride a bike. She liked it because "it has description in it." In this piece her choice of words showed her increasing interest in vocabulary:

"Let's go!" I screamed with excitement and I started pedaling. I went faster and faster until I was out of breath but I saw a bush coming up and I realized I didn't know how to coast. So before I knew it, guess who was in the bush crying and in her mother's arms with dad comforting. . . me!

When I asked Jennifer why she liked writing so much, she said, "Because I like my ideas."

As I listened to Jennifer, I realized how much progress she had made since the beginning of the year. The withdrawn, obedient little girl with "no ideas" had blossomed into a more self-confident, animated person who discovered she had ideas and was able to express her ideas and her feelings both orally and in writing. Jennifer had discovered the world of reading, too, and had experienced some of the joys of learning and the pleasure of school. In fact, at the end of June, it was difficult for Jennifer to leave. She wrote many letters to me during the summer, telling me how much she missed me and fifth grade.

In our child study meetings during the year, it was decided that Jennifer's case would not be brought before the Committee on Special Education. In sixth grade, however, despite the fact that she had made extensive progress with me in fifth grade, Jennifer was declared learning disabled. The reasons were not exactly clear to me. Perhaps the classification was the result of standardized testing at the beginning of middle school. Perhaps in a different environment in a departmentalized setting, she lost the confidence she had developed and reverted back to her shy, withdrawn self. Or perhaps Jennifer needed one more year in a self-contained classroom with an environment that valued her ideas and gave her time to grow at her own pace and to feel secure about her own abilities.

WHOLE LANGUAGE FOR ALL LEARNERS: THE FINAL WORD?

Of course, whole language is not the only classroom practice geared to honoring the strengths and meeting the needs of each learner as an individual. For example, a substantial amount of research has demonstrated that students learn to read most easily when their learning style needs and preferences are met, and that underachieving readers can make substantial and even surprising gains when they receive instruction that better meets those needs (Carbo, 1983; 1987b; LaShell, 1986). As whole language educators, we may have a lot to learn from learning/reading styles research, even while we insist—rightly, I think—that students not be viewed as having one and only one learning style.

As theory makers, perhaps all of us should attend more to what we have in common than we have done in the recent past. What is crucial is the underlying belief system: the conviction that learners primarily construct knowledge, and that whatever facilitates such knowledge construction will enhance learning. We need to recognize that this basic tenet is shared by many other educators who do not necessarily (or consciously) have a whole language orientation.

If we whole language educators remain open to re-examining and revising our theory, based upon what does and doesn't help students become active and independent readers and writers and learners, then—and only then—can we expect that whole language practices will be the best for virtually all learners, whether in regular classrooms, special classes or programs, or tutorial situations.

FOR FURTHER REFLECTION AND EXPLORATION

1. If you did activity 1 in Chapter 6, you should be well prepared to do the following activity now. Make a list of twelve easy ways to produce poor readers and another list of twelve (possibly difficult) ways to produce good readers. For the latter, consider how you would like to have been taught or how you would like someone to teach any children you may have, now or later. Be prepared to discuss. You may find it valuable to read the following two articles first, if you have not already done so:

   • Smith, Frank. (1973). Twelve easy ways to make learning to read difficult, and one difficult way to make it easy. In Frank Smith (Ed.), *Psycholinguistics and reading* (pp. 183–196). New York: Holt, Rinehart and Winston.
   • Estes, Thomas H., and Julie P. Johnstone. (1977). Twelve easy ways to make readers hate reading (and one difficult way to make them love it). *Language Arts, 54,* (pp. 891–897).

2. Develop a reference chart like Brill's, but using Margaret Phinney's *Reading with the Troubled Reader* (1988). Or make a single chart, drawing upon both sources and perhaps others.
3. Below is a selection from the reading material given to an eleven-year-old boy in a special education classroom, with his miscues marked. Examine the miscues to determine his apparent reading strengths and needs. Then discuss what kind of reading program you might design for this boy. Be as specific as possible.

light   *2 bake*
                                           1 mim
Gail and Ben can not get home. The lake is wide. "I can make

      You   *Gail*   *Gail*
a boat," said Ben. "Use the pail," said Gail. "The pail is big,"

  .   *2 not*
 is   *1 Pete boat*   *pail*   *Ben they said boat boat*
said Ben. "A nut can make a fine boat." "Nail the sail to the pole,"

                  sailed   *I we*
said Gail. Gail and Ben set sail in the boat. "It is wet in the

                         is   *to*   *is*
boat," said Gail. "The boat has a hole in it." "Take the cap," said

  and eat   *Gail*   *pail*   *said*
Ben. "Use it to bail." Gail did bail, but the hole is big. "I see
   ^

                  sail mad   *pail*   *is*
rain," said Gail. The rain came. "The sail is in the lake," said

    Tom   *Pete*
Gail. Tim is in the lake. ("Wait,") said Ben. "Save us," (said) Gail.

  Tom   *lake*   *Tim   Nut is*
Tim came up to the boat. "Tim can save us," said Ben. "Take his

          Nut is   *ride   Tim*
tail," said Gail. "Get on top," said Tim. Gail and Ben rode on top

           is   *is*
of Tim. "Tim got us home," said Gail. "Tim is a fine boat," said

Tim
Ben.

(The reader made some corrections, but most were prompted by the teacher. Since she did not indicate which were prompted and which were not, I have not marked any of the miscues as corrected.)

4. If appropriate, design a whole language literacy recovery program for students with whom you are working.

13 Whole Language Learning and Teaching for Second Language Learners
Yvonne Freeman
David Freeman

> *Before I came to America I had dreams of life here. I thought about tall Anglos, big buildings, and houses with lawns. I was surprised when I arrived to see so many kinds of people—Black people, Asians. I found people from Korea and Cambodia and Mexico. In California I found not just America, I found the world.*
>
> — (Mexican immigrant student, quoted in L. Olsen, 1988)

The faces of our students have changed dramatically. The first page of a school newsletter, sent to over four thousand parents in Fresno, California, shows the rich linguistic diversity of the public our schools now serve (see Figure 13.1). Announcements must communicate with the caretakers of these students, and to do that in Fresno, it is necessary to hold meetings in six different languages. And six is barely enough. Over sixty-eight different languages were identified on the district's 1992 home language survey.

Fresno is representative of the demographic changes taking place across the state and around the country. Figures in California project a continued increase in the number of second language students in the rest of the United States. In the 1989–90 school year, 861,531 California students were identified as LEP (limited English proficient); in 1990–91 the number rose to 986,462; and by 1992 there were 1,078,705 (California State Department of Education, 1992). In fact, while the second language school population of the United States was 1.5 million in 1985, conservative estimates predict that California alone will have 1.4 million second language learners by 1995 (R. Olsen, 1989). Between the 1985–86 school year and the 1989–90 school year the second language population in the United States increased from 1.5 million to 2.1 million.

Classrooms are filled with students who come from many different countries and speak a wide variety of languages. In California in 1990–91 the second language students represented 125 countries from around the world. Of these students, 77 percent are Spanish speaking, but there have been increasing numbers of students speaking

Roosevelt and Sequoia Merger Update:

IN PROGRESS

▲ ▲ ▲ ▲ ▲ ▲ ▲ ▲ ▲ ▲

INFORMATIONAL MEETING TO BE HELD ON TUESDAY, JULY 14

Dear Parents:

This is the second newsletter devoted to the closing of Sequoia Freshman School and the merging of the Sequoia students into Roosevelt High School. A lot of planning and work has been done by the members of the Roosevelt staff to ensure that all students receive an instructional program that allows them to graduate from high school and continue their education.

The Roosevelt High School Site Council recommended that a follow-up newsletter be mailed to parents describing the key components of the program using a question and answer format. These questions have been asked by the different audiences, but the majority of them came from students. Additionally, we are inviting you to a meeting in order to provide more information regarding these questions.

The meeting will be held on **Tuesday, July 14, 1992, at Roosevelt High School.** Please plan to attend the meeting in the language in which you feel comfortable. Each session will be conducted in accordance with the below listed schedule and only in the language designated.

Place	Time	Language
Library	2:00-2:45 p.m.	Hmong only
Library	3:00-3:45 p.m.	Lao only
Library	4:00-4:45 p.m.	Khmer only
Library	5:00-5:45 p.m.	Vietnamese only
Library	6:30-7:15 p.m.	Spanish only
Cafeteria	6:30-7:15 p.m.	English only

This newsletter has the questions and answers in English only. However, written copies of the questions and answers in other languages will be distributed at the meeting.

It has been my privilege to serve as the Area Superintendent for the Roosevelt Pyramid for two years. Mr. Carlos Garcia, who currently serves as the Area Superintendent for the Hoover Pyramid, will also become the Area Superintendent for the Roosevelt area. He is outstanding and will serve as a strong advocate. Mr. Jon Adams will continue in the position of Area Assistant Administrator.

Please mark your calendar now for the meeting of your choice on July 14th

Sincerely,
Gloria Watts

Venga a la junta el 14 de julio a las 6:30-7:15 en la Escuela Roosevelt.

จา: ຊ່ວງ ມາ ຮ່ວມ ການ ປ:ຊຸມ ທີ່ ?:ກດ ກຶ ກໍ່ ໃນ ໝູ ຜຶ 14 ເດືອນ ກໍ ຊ:ຈາ:ຄຸ, 1992 ທີ່ ໄຊ ຽູ Roosevelt High School ເວລາ 3:00 — 3:45.

Ua tiag tuaj koom nrog lub rooj sab laj uas yuav maub tso rau hnub tim 14 lub xya hli, 1992 nyob tom lub tsev qhia ntawv Roosevelt High School thaum sij hawm 2:00-2:45.

[Khmer text] "ROOSEVELT HIGH SCHOOL" [Khmer text]

....

FIGURE 13.1   School newsletter in different languages

Southeast Asian languages, Russian, Indonesian, Armenian, and Urdu. This rich diversity is not confined to California, but is a reflection of the changes across North America.

RESPONSES TO SCHOOL DIVERSITY

> Change in itself is extremely stressful, and teaching now immerses you in change. Changes in the student population and cultures and races who enroll. New kids coming in and out all the time. And because traditional methods don't work, you always have to be experimenting with different approaches so there are changes in what you're doing as a teacher. (L. Olsen & Mullen, 1990, p. 9)

The above quote from Kate, a middle school teacher, shows how seriously teachers are taking their responsibilities. One could look at linguistic and cultural diversity as a problem, but, like Kate, we prefer to see it as a unique opportunity for learning that has not been possible before. The LEP label, given to bilingual students whose English is not considered adequate, projects an attitude that these students are "limited" and have a deficit simply because they do not speak English fluently. Such labels, based on criteria established by narrowly designed, standardized tests, suggest that there is something basically wrong with those labeled. They deny the notion that diversity is a major quality of American society and suggest that diversity is something to be expunged from American classrooms (Y. S. Freeman & Y. M. Goodman, in press).

Suggestions have been made for changing the LEP label for second language learners to something more positive. Hamayan (1989) has suggested PEP, Potentially English Proficient, which emphasizes students' potential. Rigg and Allen (1989) have suggested REAL, Readers and writers of English as Another Language. Of course, those who use these terms are not simply suggesting that the new labels be substituted for the old and that the same tests be used to determine who gets labeled. If that were to happen, the attempts to make the labels positive would fail. The point is that PEP and REAL students have potential, the potential to be proficient *in two languages*. In this chapter we emphasize this potential; rather than use any labels, we refer to students in our schools who speak English as another language as *second language learners* or *bilingual learners*. Rather than being a problem, these students offer our nation the potential for an enriching diversity (D. E. Freeman & Y. S. Freeman, 1992b).

Whole language teachers are meeting this challenge of diversity because they understand students, and they understand basic principles of literacy learning. However, whole language looks different in classes that are culturally diverse. Whole language is a learner-centered approach, so when their students come from a variety of linguistic and cultural backgrounds, whole language teachers benefit from an understanding of the theories and supporting research in second language acquisition, methods of teaching a second language, and bilingual education as well as the related social, political, and cultural issues involved in teaching ESL students.

Unfortunately, many second language learners are not in classrooms with such knowledgeable teachers, and these students often get shortchanged. All teachers want to help their students, but when students enter school unable to speak English, both the students and the teachers may feel uncomfortable. When attempts at communication fail, both sides are embarrassed. As a result, students who cannot speak English are often ignored, given alternative, silent assignments to do at the back of the classroom, drilled on the bits and pieces of language (so as not to "overwhelm" them), or pulled out of the regular classroom and given over to the ESL teacher (D. E. Freeman & Y. S. Freeman, 1990).

Students in our graduate classes verify that these nonproductive practices are still common. Linda writes:

> Three years ago I had a combination 4th/5th grade class. I received two brothers from Mexico. They spoke no English. I shudder when I think about the "rinky-dink" materials and lessons I gave them. Later I discovered that our math book was at least two years behind what the boys had been doing in Mexico. The migrant aide assured me that they were in the correct class. The mother had specifically given the grade level.
>
> Toward the end of the year, the two brothers started getting in playground fights. They acted sad, angry and depressed. I'm sure they were also extremely bored. In meeting with their father, I discovered their ages. With some quick figuring, I realized that the older brother would be old enough to drive a car to his first day of 8th grade. I was allowed that June to promote one boy from 5th to 8th grade and the other into 7th grade. What a miserable first year to have in America!

Debbie, a middle school teacher, recounts a conversation with a former colleague:

> I remember a master teacher of mine when I was a student teacher. She told me she didn't have them [second language learners] write because the "gross syntactical errors" in their writing didn't make it worth the trouble. Her class was full of big, hairy-legged Lao boys coloring maps of the United States the colors she told them to use. She told me they weren't ready for reading either.

Pat, an experienced teacher who has graduate classes in both reading and second language development, has had the opportunity in the last year to visit many different classrooms with second language learners. Recently, she wrote about two separate incidents that disturbed her. In the first classroom, students were working on a very controlled phonics program.

> I saw 29 second graders respond to flash cards by reciting the sounds, key words, and the rule it exemplified. Two Hmong girls, three very limited-English speaking Hispanics, 10 ESL Hispanics, and almost 14 "at-risk" children knew the rules forward and backward, but could not apply them when they were given any text to read. The frustration level of this class was very high and this instruction is not empowering them to become creative or resourceful.

The teacher undoubtedly had good intentions. However, even though the students appeared to be actively involved in the lesson, this activity was not helping them become more proficient readers. In another classroom that Pat observed, the teacher was using basal readers with traditional ability groups. Pat described the scene:

> The students read in a round robin fashion. The students aggressively monitored each other, allowing no slips to pass unreported. One girl read very well, and I proceeded to ask her what she thought would happen next. When she did not respond another child in the group said, "She doesn't know. She only understands Spanish." She had apparently become quite adept at word calling, but since discussion does not seem to be encouraged she had no idea what she was reading.

None of these ways of teaching seem to help second language students. Because these students are denied the chance to become active participants in classroom learning communities, they learn neither the content nor the language that they need (D. E. Freeman & Y. S. Freeman, 1992a).

Whole language teachers who know about second language acquisition are able to evaluate common second language practices critically and apply strategies that best support all their students, including their bilingual students. These teachers can adapt their holistic practices, use all the resources in their classroom communities, and include second language students as both experts and fellow learners. Such teachers draw upon the rich cultural diversity of their students, support their students' first languages, and help all their students appreciate living in a multicultural society.

SECOND LANGUAGE TEACHING: A BRIEF HISTORY

In this chapter we provide some of the important concepts that whole language teachers working with second language students need. We begin with a brief history of second language teaching. We describe several of the most widely used methods for teaching a second language and the theories that support those methods. We evaluate each method in the light of whole language principles. Drawing on classroom examples, as well as research and theory, we argue that bilingual students succeed best in classrooms where teachers promote social interaction, use a variety of modes, support students' first languages, and demonstrate a firm belief in the unlimited potential of all their students. Figure 13.2 lists books and articles that provide additional information about ESL methods.

The Grammar Translation Method

From the end of the 1800s to the middle of the 1900s, foreign languages were taught almost universally by the grammar translation method. Some adults who studied a foreign language in high school or college might remember this kind of teaching. The textbooks included a series of lessons that featured a short reading, usually about a place to

Overview of Methods

Blair, R. (1982). *Innovative approaches to language teaching*. Rowley, MA: Newbury House.

Chastain, K. (1976). *Developing second language skills: Theory to practice* (2nd ed.). Boston: Houghton Mifflin.

Diller, K. (1978). *The language teaching controversy*. Rowley, MA: Newbury House.

Freeman, D. E., & Freeman, Y. S. (1992). *Whole language for second language learners*. Portsmouth, NH: Heinemann.

Richards, J., & Rodgers, T. (1986). *Approaches and methods in language teaching: A description and analysis*. New York: Cambridge University Press.

Stevick, E. (1976). *Memory, meaning and method*. Rowley, MA: Newbury House.

Stevick, E. (1980). *Teaching languages: A way and ways*. Rowley, MA: Newbury House.

Specific Methods

Total Physical Response

Asher, J. (1977). *Learning another language through actions: The complete teacher's guide*. Los Gatos, CA: Sky Oaks Publications.

Romijn, E., & Seely, C. (1979). *Live action English*. San Francisco: Alemany Press.

Segal, B. (1983). *Teaching English through action*. Brea, CA: Berty Segal.

Communicative Language Teaching

Brumfit, C. J., & Johnson, K. (Eds.). (1979). *The communicative approach to language teaching*. Oxford: Oxford University Press.

Enright, D. S., & McCloskey, M. L. (1985). Yes, talking!: Organizing the classroom to promote second language acquisition. *TESOL Quarterly, 19*(3), 431–453.

Enright, D. S., & McClosky, M. L. (1988). *Integrating English: Developing English language and literacy in the multilingual classroom*. Reading, MA: Addison-Wesley.

Rivers, W. (1983). *Communicating naturally in a second language: Theory and practice in language teaching*. New York: Cambridge University Press.

Rivers, W. (1987). *Interactive language teaching*. New York: Cambridge University Press.

Widdowson, H. (1978). *Teaching language as communication*. Oxford: Oxford University Press.

Wilkins, D. A. (1976). *Notional syllabuses*. Oxford: Oxford University Press.

The Natural Approach

Krashen, S., & Terrell, T. (1983). *The natural approach: Language acquisition in the classroom*. Hayward, CA: Alemany Press.

Suggestopedia

Lozanov, G. (1982). Suggestology and suggestopedy. In R. Blair (Ed.), *Innovative approaches to language teaching* (pp. 146–159). Rowley, MA: Newbury House.

Figure 13.2 References on methods of second language teaching

Community Language Learning

Curran, C. (1982). Community language learning. In R. Blair (Ed.), *Innovative approaches to language teaching* (pp. 118-133). Rowley, MA: Newbury House.

Sheltered English

Freeman, D. & Freeman, Y. (1988). Sheltered English instruction. *ERIC Digest.* (October). Washington, D.C.: Center for Applied Linguistics.

Freeman, Y. S. & Freeman, D. E. (1991). Using sheltered English to teach second language learners. *California English, 27*(1), 6-7, 26.

Cognitive Academic Language Learning Approach

Chamot, A., & O'Malley, M. (1987). The cognitive academic language learning approach: A bridge to the mainstream. *TESOL Quarterly, 21*(2), 227-249.

Chamot, A., & O'Malley, M. (1989). The cognitive academic language learning approach. In P. Rigg & V. Allen (Eds.). *When they don't all speak English: Integrating the ESL student into the regular classroom* (pp. 108-125). Urbana, Illinois: National Council of Teachers of English.

Problem Posing

Freeman, Y. S., & Freeman, D. E. (1991). Doing social studies: Whole language lessons to promote social action. *Social Education*, *55*(1), 29-32, 66.

Wallerstein, N. (1987). Problem posing education: Freire's method for transformation. In I. Shor (Ed.), *Freire for the classroom* (pp. 33-44). Portsmouth, NH: Boynton/ Cook-Heinemann.

Figure 13.2 Continued

visit in the country where the language being studied was spoken; a vocabulary list with the English translation given; a page or so of discussion of the grammar point or points for the lesson; and practice exercises.

In the grammar translation method students studied the verb *to be* one week and the regular verbs the next week (in the present tense only, of course). They memorized lists of words and translated sentences from English to the target language and from the target language to English. And after some time spent studying French or Spanish or German, they could ask a few questions in the new language, but they seldom could understand the answers. In fact, no one really expected them to be able to actually speak the foreign language at the end of the course. The goal was to expand the intellect by doing the exercises and to translate and read works of literature from the foreign language (Larsen-Freeman, 1986).

The Empiricist Approach

The grammar translation method of teaching a second language had many limitations, and with the advent of World War II, one of these in particular stood out. Students who had studied a foreign language through a grammar translation method could read and translate the written language, but they could not comprehend or speak the language they had studied. Since the U.S. Department of Defense needed espionage agents who could function behind enemy lines, the government became interested in effective ways of teaching people to communicate orally in foreign languages, not just read and write them.

It seemed logical for members of the Defense Department to go to linguists, people who study language, for advice about language teaching. The approach to linguistics at that time was structural. Structural linguists sought to describe observable features of languages. They believed that language study should be based on descriptions of what people using the language really said rather than prescriptive rules mandating what they should say. This approach to analyzing languages seemed ideal for developing materials for language teaching (see Chapter 3, on a linguistic approach to reading).

Most structural linguists, however, were not really interested in how language was learned. Their primary interest was in identifying the salient sounds, the vocabulary, and the structural patterns of languages. They divided language into subsystems (phonology, morphology, syntax, and semantics) and described the structures within each system. Using this information, they wrote dictionaries and grammars of the languages they were studying. They were especially interested in remote, exotic languages that had never been written down.

To apply insights from structural linguistics to teaching, it was necessary to look to theories of psychology. At that time, beliefs about learning were strongly influenced by behavioristic psychology. Like structural linguists, behavioral psychologists were also interested in observable behavior. Experiments such as those with Pavlov's dogs and Skinner's boxes led to the belief that learning takes place by operant conditioning, by repetition and practice (H. D. Brown, 1980).

Under the influence of structural linguistics and behavioral psychology, an empiricist approach to teaching language emerged. Empiricists felt that the scientific way to teach a language involved using behavioral techniques to practice and form habits with the structural patterns of the language that had been identified by linguists. Empiricists held certain premises about language learning (Diller, 1978):

1. Language is speech, not writing.
2. A language is a set of habits.
3. Teach the language, not about the language.
4. A language is what its native speakers say, not what someone thinks they ought to say.
5. Languages are different.

These premises clearly represented a reaction against the grammar translation method, which emphasized grammatically correct written language. In addition, the empiricists added the idea that learning was habit formation and that, since all languages are different, it is important to contrast the student's first language with the language being learned. This comparison, called *contrastive analysis,* was designed to determine which areas of the language to be learned would cause difficulties. Then drills could be devised to avoid errors and create good language habits.

For example, since the Spanish word *en* can be translated into English as "in," "on," or "at," the prediction would be that Spanish speakers would have trouble with these English terms, so exercises would be devised to practice them. However, further research showed that many of the predicted problem areas did not turn out to be actual problem areas. As a result, the methods based on contrastive analysis lost their theoretical support. In the meantime, many students practiced and drilled on bits and pieces of language that they found both difficult and meaningless.

The audiolingual method (ALM) is the best-known result of the empiricist approach. ALM stresses oral language, memorization of dialogues, and pattern drills while de-emphasizing grammar. Second language learners in an audiolingual classroom are treated as passive recipients of the language. Structures are presented one at a time, and students are drilled on those structures until they have mastered them. Classrooms are teacher centered, as students are led through the many repetitious drills and exercises to help them form correct habits of pronunciation and sentence word order. Since the learners don't already speak the target language, it is assumed that they have nothing to contribute to the curriculum. Students respond to directions from the teacher and text and have no input in what they learn or how they learn it.

Methods such as ALM are not consistent with principles of whole language. They are part-to-whole and teacher-centered. Furthermore, in such methods students do not use language for authentic purposes during meaningful social interaction. In addition, most instruction is limited to developing oral language.

At the time ALM methods were developed, ALM was based on the latest scientific findings; however, few students became proficient language users as a result of ALM instruction. This is one reason that many adults who studied a foreign language in high school or college cannot speak the language now. Unfortunately, the influence of the empiricist approach is evident even today in materials and practices for second language learners. Despite the emergence of new insights on language acquisition from linguistics and psychology, ALM is still the most widely used method for teaching a second language.

The Rationalist Approach

Just as structural linguistics and behavioral psychology provided the theoretical base for an empiricist approach to language teaching, generative linguistics and cognitive psychology gave rise to the rationalist approach. Influenced by the work of Chomsky, the generative-transformational school brought about a revolution in linguistics as they sought a "distinction between the observable surface level of language and the deep structure of language, that hidden level of meaning and thought which gives birth to and generates observable surface linguistic performance" (H. D. Brown, 1980, p. 11). In the same way that generative linguists posited abstract levels of meaning, cognitive psychologists considered the effect on behavior of factors, such as motivation, that could not be directly observed. Cognitive psychologists viewed learners as creative, and they saw learning as being influenced by meaning and motivation. From a cognitive perspective, the learner is not passive, but active.

For second language teaching, this new understanding led to a set of premises that differ radically from the empiricists' approach to language (Diller, 1978):

1. A living language is characterized by rule-governed creativity.
2. The rules of grammar are psychologically real.
3. People are specially equipped to learn languages.
4. A living language is a language in which we can think.

The rationalist approach received theoretical support from studies in first-language acquisition. These studies suggest that learners are capable of generating their own rules if they receive sufficient comprehensible input, messages they can understand (Krashen, 1982). Further, it was hypothesized that learning a second language is like learning the first. When exposed to a second language, students construct their own internal grammars without direct, explicit teaching of grammar or repetitious drills on forms. For example, by listening to a narrative of past events, students develop their own subconscious rule for forming past-tense verbs. Even though they probably would not be able to state the rule, they begin to use past-tense forms correctly in conversation.

Second Language Acquisition Theory: Krashen

One of the most influential writers in second language acquisition theory is Stephen Krashen (1982) (see also Chapter 3). His theory is based on Chomsky's linguistics and on studies in cognitive psychology. While Krashen's theory has been attacked by a number of researchers, his hypotheses form the basis for a number of current ESL methods. The hypotheses include:

1. The Acquisition/Learning Hypothesis.
2. The Natural Order Hypothesis.
3. The Monitor Hypothesis.
4. The Input Hypothesis.
5. The Affective Filter Hypothesis.

In the Acquisition/Learning Hypothesis, Krashen distinguishes between learning and acquisition. We *learn* a language when we receive direct instruction in rules. The rules are presented in a certain order, we practice them, and we get feedback on our efforts. On the other hand, we *acquire* a language when we pick it up naturally in situations where we use language for communicative purposes.

Another of Krashen's hypotheses is that language is acquired in a certain *natural order.* For example, the plural "s" morpheme we attach to "girl" to form "girls" comes to us earlier than the "s" we add to verbs in sentences such as "He runs."

Acquisition provides us with the language we need to communicate. Learning gives us rules we can use to *monitor* our language output. In his Monitor Hypothesis, Krashen suggests that in order to use the monitor effectively, we need a knowledge of the rules and time to apply them. Students might monitor their written language as they reach the editing stage of a story. However, monitoring requires a focus on form, not content, so monitoring is not helpful during earlier stages of writing or during speaking.

Krashen's Input Hypothesis states that we acquire language when we receive comprehensible input (messages we understand) just beyond our current level of competence. However, even though the student may be exposed to comprehensible input, the Affective Filter Hypothesis proposes that affective factors such as fear, nervousness, an unwillingness to learn, or worry can keep the input from reaching the part of the brain where language proficiency is developed. In Krashen's terms, acquisition occurs when input becomes intake, but the affective filter can block this process.

Krashen's theory of second language acquisition is consistent in many respects with the theory of first language acquisition that forms the basis for instruction in many whole language classes. Whole language teachers immerse students in meaningful reading, writing, and talk so that their students can acquire literacy. They find a number of techniques to make the input comprehensible. For example, they may have students predict what will be in a story, read the story dramatically using gestures and props to support the meaning, and then have students role-play the story. Mini-lessons or strategy lessons are designed to help students monitor their output by checking their reading and writing processes. Whole language teachers create communities of learners where students are free to risk; and, because their affective filters are down, students learn as they engage in meaningful social interactions.

The Natural Approach

Methods for teaching ESL consistent with a rationalist approach are gradually replacing older methods such as ALM. Several of the newer methods are based on Krashen's theory of second language acquisition. Krashen himself teamed with Tracy Terrel to develop what they have called The Natural Approach (Krashen & Terrell, 1983). This method is widely used. In many ways The Natural Approach is consistent with whole language learning and principles. However, it is necessary to take a close look at the Natural Approach in order to see where it differs from whole language and a sociopsycholinguistic view of learning.

In The Natural Approach of Krashen and Terrell, students move through four stages, which the authors explain are consistent with the stages children go through as they learn a first language. Lessons are designed to provide large quantities of comprehensible language input and to keep the anxiety level low. A description of sample lessons from a promotional booklet for The Rainbow Collection, a Natural Approach series for elementary school, gives an idea of how the method looks in the classroom.

In the first stage, preproduction, lessons focus on listening comprehension and building a receptive vocabulary. Students do not have to talk and usually don't, except to give the names of other students or answer yes and no questions. They are encouraged to communicate with gestures and actions. Total Physical Response (TPR), a method of learning language by responding to commands such as "sit down," "stand up," and "walk to the door" is often used as a technique during the preproduction stage. In the sample lesson for The Rainbow Collection, the teacher talks about body parts. She points to her eyes and asks the students to point to their eyes. Then they point to the ears of another student and their noses. The teacher also asks questions such as "Who is pointing to her nose?" With this type of interaction students can participate with minimal risk.

In the second stage, early production, students use one or two words or short phrases. The lessons expand the learners' receptive vocabulary, and activities are designed to motivate students to produce vocabulary they already understand. For example, in a sample discussion about plants, the teacher might have students touch and smell different plants and ask them questions such as "Do you like to smell the flowers?" and "Are the leaves brown or green?"

Once students reach the third stage, speech emergence, they speak in longer phrases and complete sentences. The lessons continue to expand students' receptive vocabulary. Activities are designed to develop higher levels of language use. In the promotional material, the lesson for this stage has a teacher holding a picture of a boy smelling a flower. The teacher asks, "What is the boy doing?" and students answer, "He smelling flower" or "Smell flower." As the lesson continues, the teacher explores the students' understanding of their senses by asking, "What do our eyes and hands tell us about the flower in the picture?" Students answer, "It's white and yellow," "Leaves are green," and "It feel smooth."

In the intermediate fluency stage students engage in conversation and produce connected narrative. They also continue to expand their receptive vocabulary, and reading and writing activities are incorporated into the lessons. The activities are designed to develop higher levels of language proficiency in content areas. In the sample lesson for this stage, the teacher is shown discussing several pictures that are related to the senses. When the teacher asks, "How do our senses help us?" one student answers, "We can know if something is hot or cold." When asked how their senses could tell them about the orange in a picture she is holding, students explain, "I smell it," "I can see it—it's round and orange," and "You could taste it." At the end of the discussion, the students and teacher write a story together about their senses.

The Natural Approach was developed to counter the emphasis that traditional methods, such as ALM, put on early production. In many second language classes, students were expected to produce the target language (by repeating words or phrases) from the very beginning. By delaying production, The Natural Approach lowers the affective filter and allows students to relax and understand what they are hearing rather than being forced to produce the new language. The Natural Approach also includes more authentic and meaningful language than the audiolingual method; however, the Natural Approach stresses building vocabulary and de-emphasizes reading and writing.

Whole Language and The Natural Approach

There is a difference between the goals of a whole language teacher who involves students in theme cycles (Edelsky, Altwerger, & Flores, 1991) and a teacher employing the Natural Approach using the Rainbow Collection series. Whole language teachers involve students in answering their own questions, solving problems, locating and reading resource materials, and sharing what they learn with others. In this way, students learn to read, write, speak, and understand. In whole language classes, bilingual students develop both their languages during these activities.

The Natural Approach materials may involve students in discussions on content area topics such as plants or the senses, but the topics are chosen by the teacher or the textbook. The students do not explore the content, but instead talk about the content to practice vocabulary. Although it is true that students using Natural Approach materials do learn both content and language, the emphasis is always on the language that is being acquired. In other words, in the Natural Approach the content is used to help students learn vocabulary. On the other hand, in a whole language class, the focus is on the content, and language develops as students need it to carry out their inquiries.

Another difference between The Natural Approach and whole language is the emphasis in The Natural Approach on oral language development. Students do some reading and writing in later stages, but the focus is not on reading from a wide variety of literature and content texts nor on writing for a variety of purposes. For the most part, the four stages of The Natural Approach follow the traditional sequence of listen, speak, read, and write. In their text on The Natural Approach, Krashen and Terrell (1983) comment that adults can begin writing sooner: "With adults both reading and writing can be profitably begun during the prespeaking and early production stages" (p. 88). However, this writing consists of copying commands into a notebook, and the reading is limited to recognizing key words written on the board. The authors warn of the danger of "supplying written input too soon" (p. 88).

Beyond the Natural Approach

Researchers in second language acquisition, including Krashen himself in work he did after developing The Natural Approach, have found that many second language learners of all ages benefit from both writing and reading before they are proficient English speakers. Hudelson (1984, 1986), Urzúa (1987), Peyton (1990), Edelsky (1986, 1989), and D. E. Freeman and Y. S. Freeman (1992b) have all documented the importance of encouraging authentic reading and writing activities with second language students. Their research shows that second language learners with only a limited control over the oral system of English can read not only print in the environment, but also texts of special interest to them. Early on in their exposure to English, bilingual students write English for a variety of purposes and may, when encouraged, even write before they speak or read.

Krashen (1985, 1993) reviewed research that showed that reading is a powerful language acquisition resource. His review included programs with sustained silent reading, self-selected reading, environmental print, and pleasure reading. This review led him to conclude, "Genuine reading for comprehension may be the only way to develop the literacy skills necessary for school success" (1985, p. 107). Not only does reading help develop literacy skills, it also provides large amounts of comprehensible input that aid oral language development. In fact, if we compare ten minutes of reading with ten minutes of listening, the reader gets much more comprehensible input than the listener.

Other researchers, using miscue analysis, have documented the progress of second language students in reading (Barrera, 1983; de Silva, 1981; K. S. Goodman, Goodman, & Flores, 1979; Hudelson, 1981a, 1981b, 1981–82; Rigg, 1986). The miscue research shows that, like native English speakers, second language learners need lots of opportunities to read a variety of texts and write for a wide range of audiences, and this exposure need not be delayed until oral language is fully developed.

Elley (1991) has conducted and summarized large-scale studies with second language students that show the positive effects of reading on language acquisition (see also Chapter 7). In all of Elley's studies children were immersed in meaningful texts, oral and written language was integrated, the focus was on meaning rather than form, and the books provided high motivation. For example, in the REAP (Reading and English Acquisition Program) study in Singapore, over five hundred students from some thirty schools were studied for three years. The program is described as "an integrated whole-language approach based upon three concepts: the shared book approach, a modified language experience approach, and a book flood of high interest illustrated story books" (Elley, 1991, p. 418).

Elley's review of nine programs showed remarkable gains in language proficiency for the students who were involved in the reading programs. In the Singapore program, students in the whole language classes made significant gains compared with students who received ALM instruction. These gains came in the areas of reading comprehension, vocabulary, grammar, listening comprehension, written composition, and ability to take down dictation. Elley concludes that the results of the nine studies "show that rapid improvements occur in reading and listening comprehension, and that these gains transfer readily to all aspects of the pupil's target language. The effects are stable and occur in pleasant non-threatening contexts, with associated gains in attitudes toward reading and books" (p. 436). Elley comments further that these studies "provide some confirmation for whole-language approaches which stress natural acquisition of literacy, without systematic instruction in particular linguistic features. They appear to provide support, too, for Krashen's Input Hypothesis because the increase in the amount of comprehensible language was a distinctive feature of all the studies cited" (p. 436).

MacGowan-Gilhooly (1991) reports on a college-level ESL program that improved students' writing by increasing their reading. Students in this whole language program read one thousand pages of popular fiction in their first writing course. "They had to read about 70 pages a week for homework, copy passages that struck them, and write responses to these passages" (p. 80). Traditional grammar instruction was dropped. The researcher concludes:

> Although, at the beginning, many students complained about the amount of work required and the lack of grammar lessons, after a few weeks both students and teachers expressed amazement at how much the students had progressed in such a short time. . . . By semester's end, most were reading and writing fluently and even more correctly than in the beginning, without having received any corrections or grammar instruction. (p. 80)

The new approach was started with the lowest level students, and its success led to adoption at all the higher levels. To date, more than three thousand students have completed the program. The results are impressive. Reading scores have almost doubled, and the writing test pass rate has risen from 35 to 56 percent.

These current second language studies by Krashen, Elley, MacGowan-Gilhooly, and others show that when second language students are involved in extensive reading, all other aspects of their language proficiency improve. The incorporation of reading as well as increased writing in second language classes signals a shift in second language teaching toward an approach consistent with whole language. For further reading on second language acquisition, see Figure 13.3.

WHOLE LANGUAGE AND SECOND LANGUAGE TEACHING: A CONVERGENCE

This brief review of the history of second language instruction shows a gradual evolution. Second language teachers have begun to adopt practices more consistent with whole language. They incorporate more authentic reading and writing activities. At the same time, many mainstream teachers who have one or several second language students in their classes are beginning to use insights from second language research and methodology to improve instruction for all their students, and especially for their second language students. In the following sections, we suggest ways these insights can influence curriculum and then provide examples of teachers who are putting these concepts into practice.

Make the Input Comprehensible by Enriching the Context

One of Krashen's best known concepts is "comprehensible input." Krashen has pointed out that second language students cannot learn something that they do not understand. The challenge for teachers, then, is to make their messages understandable, even when some of their students are not fully proficient in English. Krashen suggests that teachers can make the English instruction comprehensible by giving language contextual support. D. E. Freeman and Y. S. Freeman (1992b) have described two kinds of contextual support teachers can provide: extralinguistic and linguistic.

When students are still developing their English proficiency, they can understand messages in English more easily if those messages are embedded in a rich extralinguistic context. Whole language teachers know that the greater the contextual support provided by objects and actions, the lower the necessity for second language students to rely solely on their new language itself. When class discussions are about things or people that are not present, teachers can provide an external context by bringing in pictures. Gestures, such as holding a hand to the ear to mimic talking on the telephone,

Books

Acquisition of Second Language

Brown, H. D. (1980). *Principles of language learning and teaching*. Englewood Cliffs, NJ: Prentice Hall.

Holt, D. (1986). *Beyond language: Social and cultural factors in schooling language minority students*. Los Angeles: Evaluation, Dissemination, and Assessment Center, California State University, Los Angeles.

Krashen, S. D. (1982). *Principles and practice in second language acquisition*. New York: Pergamon Press.

Krashen, S. D. (1985). *Inquiries and insights*. Haywood, CA: Alemany Press.

Olsen, L. (1988). *Crossing the schoolhouse border: Immigrant students and the California public schools*. San Francisco: California Tomorrow.

Olsen, L., & Mullen, N. (1990). *Embracing diversity: Teachers' voices from California classrooms*. San Francisco: California Tomorrow.

Scarcella, R. (1990). *Teaching language minority students in the multicultural classroom*. Englewood Cliffs, NJ: Prentice-Hall Regents.

Acquisition of Second Language Literacy

Goodman, K. S., Goodman, Y. M., & Flores, B. (1979). *Reading in the bilingual classroom: Literacy and biliteracy*. Rosslyn, VA: National Clearinghouse for Bilingual Education.

Hudelson, S. (1989). *Write on: Children writing in ESL*. Englewood Cliffs, NJ: Prentice Hall.

Johnson, D., & Roen, D. (Eds.). (1989). *Richness in writing: Empowering ESL students*. New York: Longman.

Rigg, P., & Enright, D. S. (Eds.). (1986). *Children and ESL: Integrating perspectives*. Washington, D.C.: Teachers of English to Speakers of Other Languages.

Rigg, P., & Allen, V. (Eds.). (1989). *When they don't all speak English*. Urbana, IL: National Council of Teachers of English.

Wallace, C. (1988). *Learning to read in a multicultural society: The social context of second language literacy*. New York: Prentice-Hall.

Articles

Acquisition of Second Language

Collier, V. (1989). How long? A synthesis of research on academic achievement in a second language. *TESOL Quarterly, 23*(3), 509–532.

Lucas, T., Henze, R., & Donato, R. (1990). Promoting the success of Latino language-minority students: An exploratory study of six high schools. *Harvard Educational Review, 60*(3), 315–340.

Figure 13.3   References on second language acquisition

Phillips, S. (1972). Participant structures and communicative competence: Warm Spring children in community and classroom. In C. Cazden, V. John, & D. Hymes (Eds.). *Functions of language in the classroom* (pp. 370–394). New York: Teachers College Press.

Acquisition of Second Language Literacy

Au, K. (1980). Participation structures in a reading lesson with Hawaiian children: Analysis of a culturally appropriate instructional event. *Anthropology and Education Quarterly, 11*, 91–115.

Au, K., & Jordan, C. (1981). Hawaiian Americans: Teaching reading to Hawaiian children: Finding a culturally appropriate solution. In H. Trueba, G. Guthrie, & K. Au (Eds.), *Culture and the bilingual classroom: Studies in classroom ethnography*. Rowley, MA: Newbury House, 139–152.

Bird, L., & Alvarez, L. (1987). Beyond comprehension: The power of literature study for language minority students. *Elementary ESOL Education News, 10*(1), 1–3.

Elley, W. (1991). Acquiring literacy in a second language: The effect of book-based programs. *Language Learning, 41*(3), 375–411.

Freeman, Y. S. (1985). What preschoolers already know about print. *Educational Horizons, 64*, 22–25.

Freeman, Y. S., & Freeman, D. E. (1991). Ten tips for monolingual teachers of bilingual students. In K. Goodman, L. Bird, & Y. Goodman (Eds.), *The whole language catalog* (p. 90). Chicago, IL: American School Publishers.

Hudelson, S. (1984). Kan yu ret an rayt en ingles: Children become literate in English as a second language. *TESOL Quarterly, 18*(2), 221–237.

MacGowan-Gilhooly, A. (1991). Fluency first: Reversing the traditional ESL sequence. *Journal of Basic Writing, 10*(1), 73–87.

Peyton, J. K. (1990). *Students and teachers writing together: Perspectives on journal writing*. Washington, D.C.: Teachers of English to Speakers of Other Languages.

Rigg, P., & Hudelson, S. (1986). One child doesn't speak English. *Australian Journal of Reading, 9*(3), 116–125.

Swain, M., Lapkin, S., Rowen, S., & Hart, D. (1990). The role of mother tongue literacy in third language learning. *Language, Culture, and Curriculum, 3*, 65–81.

Urzúa, C. (1987). You stopped too soon: Second language children composing and revising. *TESOL Quarterly, 21*(2), 279–297.

Figure 13.3 Continued

enrich the context. Reading illustrated Big Books and engaging students in role-plays also provide contextual support because communication is not solely dependent on the words that are spoken.

Whole language teachers realize that language itself offers a range of clues to meaning. The more cohesive (i.e., tying ideas together) and coherent (i.e., making sense) the language is, the easier it is to understand. An expository text or a lecture is easier to follow if there is an introduction that outlines the main points. Unadapted stories are usually easier to understand than simplified texts because the natural language provides rich clues to meaning that simplified texts lack. Stories are easier to comprehend if they follow a familiar pattern. Children's stories often begin with "Once upon a time," and include a problem and a resolution. Once students internalize a pattern, each subsequent story that follows the pattern is more predictable. For second language learners, folktales often are understandable because students connect them with folktales from their own traditions. Both the format and the content are familiar.

Probably the best source of contextual support for second language learners is the use of students' first languages. Bilingual teachers often use an effective method called preview, view, and review. In the first phase of this method, the teacher *previews* the lesson in the students' first language. This helps insure that the students understand the big picture. It helps them follow the *view,* the actual lesson conducted in their second language. Finally, the teacher may provide additional context for the lesson by *reviewing* the main concepts again and/or allowing for questions in the first language.

The following list provides a summary of the different kinds of possible contextual support teachers can provide:

Extralinguistic cues are provided by situation objects or actions.	Linguistic cues are provided by use of cohesive, coherent language.
The teacher uses role-play, realia or pictures, and gestures.	The teacher uses stories with predictable patterns, outlines, and story maps.

The teacher supports students' first language.

Whole language teaching tends to provide comprehensible input for students naturally. When learners are engaged in theme cycles, answering their own questions, reading and writing about topics of interest, and drawing and dramatizing what they are learning, the language is rich in context. When students do science explorations, take surveys, read Big Books, engage in literature studies, go on field trips and make collages, the language they use is made much more comprehensible than the language of the classroom where students are seated silently in rows working individually on worksheets or on exercises from books that are rarely discussed.

When teachers provide comprehensible input by embedding language in rich context, they help all their students, not just their second language learners, develop both academic content and language proficiency. These context-embedded activities differ sharply from the context-reduced texts and practices that characterize traditional instruction.

Develop Language Proficiency in Authentic Social Interaction

Whole language teachers make the input more comprehensible by involving students in social interaction. Second language teachers have also moved toward social interaction, particularly in classes where the goal is to develop students' communicative competence.

Enright and McCloskey (1985) point out how second language research has shifted its primary focus "from the syntactic dimensions of linguistic performance to the semantic and social/contextual dimensions of language comprehension and performance" (p. 433). Their article "Yes, talking! Organizing the classroom to promote second language acquisition" explains how teachers can organize their classrooms to encourage second language learners to use language. They point out that the silent, straight-row classroom is the worst place for second language acquisition and suggest seven criteria, all consistent with whole language principles, for organizing instruction:

1. Organize for collaboration.
2. Organize for purpose.
3. Organize for student interest.
4. Organize for previous experience.
5. Organize for holism.
6. Organize for support.
7. Organize for variety.

Widdowson (1978) has captured the difference between grammatical and communicative teaching methodologies with his terms "usage" and "use." For example, a student in a traditional ESL class might develop the grammatical competence needed to produce sentences such as "I like meatballs." This sentence shows the student's mastery of usage. We would judge such a sentence in isolation as being formed correctly. On the other hand, if a speaker produced a sentence such as "I likes meatball," we would judge this usage to be incorrect.

A mastery of usage, as Widdowson argues, is not the same as a mastery of use. If I ask you "Do you like school?" it doesn't really matter whether you answer with, "I like meatballs" or "I likes meatball." Although the first response contains grammatically correct usage, neither answer shows correct use of the language. Widdowson and others have argued that in classes for second language students, too much time is spent on usage and not enough time is devoted to helping students use the language to accomplish social purposes. Yet that should be the goal of any language class.

A similar shift from a focus on usage to a focus on use can be seen in whole language classes where students write frequently. In traditional classes, writing instruction might involve practicing handwriting, spelling, or correct punctuation. This is practice in usage. In whole language classes, while teachers do discuss spelling and punctuation, the emphasis is on having students use written language to serve a variety of functions. Whole language teachers want students to use language for communication, not merely to practice usage of conventional language forms.

The movement in second language learning away from the concern with usage has been gradual. Willis (1983) classified second language classroom activities into three types: citation, simulation, and replication. Citation activities involve repeating and transforming sentences. For example, a student might change a statement into a question. Simulations are closer to true communication and include such things as discussion and role play. In replication activities, the teacher creates situations that require communication to solve a problem or play a game. However, Wilkins (1976) has pointed out that even when teachers use activities that are closer to real communication, such as role playing, their purpose often is to practice some grammatical structure in context.

Teachers who have students engage in simulations and replications have shifted from a focus on developing grammatical competence to the goal of building communicative competence. These teachers often organize their course around different language functions, such as greeting people or asking for information, rather than around grammatical forms, such as verb tenses. However, although the focus has shifted from grammar to communication, in many classes, real social interaction is still absent.

Larsen-Freeman (1986) points to the need for students to engage in real communication:

> Since communication is a process, it is insufficient for students to simply have knowledge of target language forms, meanings, and functions. Students must be able to apply this knowledge in negotiating meaning. It is through the interaction between speaker and listener (or reader and writer) that meaning becomes clear. The listener gives the speaker feedback as to whether or not he understands what the speaker has said. In this way, the speaker can revise what he has said and try to communicate his intended meaning again, if necessary. (p. 123)

It is important to clarify the difference between communicative activities and real social interaction in classrooms. When students practice verb forms or ways to introduce one another, they are not engaging in authentic language use. As Willis (1983) explains, in a role-play a store clerk can be downright rude with no risk of losing a customer. In real life, rude clerks can lose both their customers and their jobs.

Another difference between the kinds of interactions in life outside and inside many classrooms is that in the classroom the language forms or functions that are practiced are determined by the teacher or the text, not by the situation and the people interacting in it. In traditional classrooms, students use language to get better at using language. They practice certain functions so that they will be able to use those functions later. Students do not use language to accomplish social or academic purposes, such as establishing and maintaining relationships with other people or developing their knowledge of some content area. The problems and games in the classroom are not actually part of students' lives outside the classroom.

Widdowson and others have argued that students learning a second language should have a real purpose for the language they are learning. Rigg and Allen (1989) suggest that "learning a language means learning to do the things you want to do with people who speak that language" (p. viii). They emphasize the importance of working with others to give purpose to learning language. Two of Rigg and Hudelson's (1986) four principles of language development focus on conditions that promote second language acquisition (p. 117):

1. People develop a second language when they feel good about themselves and about their relationships with those around them in the second language setting.
2. Language develops when the language learner focuses on accomplishing something together with others rather than focusing on the language itself. Thus, group activities are ideal.

Many second language teachers have found they can promote social interaction by teaching language through a content area, such as science or social studies. Classes in which language is taught through content involve students in real communication because the focus is no longer on language forms or functions. Instead, students use language to accomplish academic purposes. The students in these classes collaborate on research projects, discuss class readings, edit one another's written reports, and critique each other's oral presentations. Their communication during social interaction promotes both content learning and language acquisition.

Second language teachers use social interaction to develop students' communicative competence. However, just being able to communicate in English is not enough. Students also need to develop academic competence. By teaching language through content, second language teachers facilitate the development of both communicative and academic competence for their second language students. In the same way, whole language teachers involve students in meaningful activities in which the students develop both language and content area concepts as they pursue areas of inquiry (Watson, Burke, & Harste, 1989). Both whole language and second language teachers organize their classrooms for social interaction because they recognize that all students can best develop linguistic and academic proficiency during authentic social interaction.

Use All Four Modes and More

Traditional approaches to teaching a second language follow a strict sequence: listen, speak, read, and write. This sequence parallels observations of young children acquiring their first language. Babies listen before they speak, and reading and writing are delayed for some time. Many materials for teaching ESL provide separate lessons or even books for listening, speaking, reading, and writing. Often, for older students, there are even separate classes for each of the four areas. Separating and sequencing the four modes for second language students is similar to what happens to some native speakers of English in classes where reading instruction is delayed until the students have developed their oral language and where writing is not introduced until students can already read.

Whole language teachers understand that it is unnatural to teach the four modes separately. For babies, written language does not serve a purpose, but school-age students need to develop both oral and written language. If they wait until they develop oral proficiency before beginning to read and write, they fall behind academically. In fact, students may write before they read, and for many second language students, written language develops before oral language (Hudelson, 1984). When students are involved in meaningful, authentic activities, they naturally have opportunities to speak, listen, read, and write.

From a whole language perspective, not only are students involved in the four modes of listening, speaking, reading, and writing as they learn, but all the senses are considered important. Gardner (1983) suggests that there are seven kinds of intelligence that should be valued: not only the traditional linguistic and logical-mathematical, but also spatial, musical, bodily-kinesthetic, interpersonal, and intrapersonal. Harste and Mikulecky (1984) relate the idea of multiple intelligences to literacy by referring to the semiotic systems beyond oral and written language that have communication potential. They suggest that art, math, music, and language all have their own kind of syntax, or ways of organizing information and showing relationships, as well as their own signs.

Changing from one sign system to another is called *transmediation*. For example, when students draw pictures to represent part of a story they have read or heard, they are crossing media, or transmediating. In the process of transmediation, students also transform language to re-present their knowledge using another sign system. Accessing a variety of sign systems in this way expands students' communication potential. Harste and Mikulecky believe it is critical that schools recognize all the ways that learners communicate:

> The sum of what is known across communication systems constitutes a "communication potential." By this view, society, and the school curricula which that society creates to further its ends, ought to be concerned with expanding communication potential rather than systematically shutting off certain forms of expression through overemphasizing some, and neglecting others of the humanities. (p. 49)

In some ESL classes the meaning potential is limited because students are restricted to oral language. Even in classes where reading and writing are introduced, other modes of expression are not considered. However, whole language teachers with second language students encourage students to use a variety of means to communicate their ideas.

In short, providing comprehensible input, organizing for social interaction, and facilitating the use of all modes of communication are all important in second language learning. The following examples show how teachers have put these concepts into action in classes that include second language students. The results have been exciting.

Evelyn

Two years ago the school in the farming community where Evelyn was teaching decided to discontinue the exchange of Christmas gifts because there were so many children at the school who could not afford to buy presents. Evelyn explained how she and her students created a much more meaningful Christmas sharing event than material gifts had ever produced:

> After a lengthy, rich class discussion with my second graders, it was decided we would exchange gifts which were not purchased; we would give "Gifts From the Heart." The procedure was to express written gratitude, admiration or appreciation to each person for some trait or behavior which made that person special. The students took their task very seriously and for two days they wrote

carefully and thoughtfully. Small paper bags were decorated and each name was written in calligraphy across individual bags. When all the messages were dropped into the bags, the bags were folded over and stapled, then placed under the Christmas tree. For three long days anticipation increased as the students impatiently waited to open their Gifts.

At last the exciting day arrived and after bags were distributed they were opened with more excitement than any group I have ever been with. The students read their Gifts silently alone, aloud to peers, to adults in the room and finally—to my complete astonishment—someone asked if they could share a Gift with the whole class.

Each child stood, read, grinned broadly and sat down. They listened so attentively to each other, I was amazed. The Gifts were beautiful tributes of friendship and love which were never spoken in class, and by the time everyone had shared I literally could not speak. Every single child had received twenty-nine affirmations of value and worth. (Crews, 1992, p. 4)

Many of Evelyn's second graders were still developing their reading and writing abilities. A large number of her students speak English as a second language. During this activity, all of Evelyn's students wrote and read, spoke and listened. In the process of using both oral and written language, as well as art, during meaningful social interaction, Evelyn's students developed their language proficiency and built up their classroom community.

Genaro

Genaro's fifth-grade bilingual classroom in a small farming town with a high Hispanic population provides another example of a teacher making the input comprehensible, including all four modes of language, and promoting social interaction in order to involve all his students in learning together. Genaro's class was reading *The Sign of the Beaver* (Speare, 1983), but he was not satisfied with their involvement in and understanding of the book, so he borrowed some posters for the book he had seen in the library and put them up in his room. Then he told the whole class he was going to read to them during Sustained Silent Reading (SSR), and that all of them, even those who spoke very little English, should pay special attention because they were all going to participate in a discussion after he finished.

As Genaro read, he pointed to the posters. He used a great deal of expression to make the input more comprehensible and interesting to his students. He also paused at several places and had the students talk together in groups, which included both fluent English speakers and second language students. In these groups students summarized what was happening and clarified what they did not understand. He stopped reading for the day at a place that left the main character, Matt, in a rather difficult position. He then invited his students to create a skit in groups predicting how the main character might solve his problem. Genaro was pleased and excited as he watched his students:

What I saw was a bunch of busy kids all trying to come up with a good ending for Matt. They were all so motivated that it was hard to believe. Each group came up one by one and performed their skit. I didn't know I had little actors in my class. Most made masks. Some of the skits involved creating new characters; others involved fight scenes, etc. I was also surprised by the vocabulary that was used in their skits; it went right along with the book, which showed me that they really did pay attention (even the Spanish speaking kids). I was really pleased at their effort.

If Genaro had limited his lesson to silent reading, his students would not have transacted with the literature in the way they did. By adding art and drama to reading, writing, speaking, and listening, Genaro was able to involve all his students in a meaningful language experience.

Kathy

A third example comes from a large inner-city middle school where the student body is approximately 75 percent Hispanic, 10 percent Asian and the rest is African American and Caucasian. At this school, teachers struggle to meet district and state objectives and to engage all the students in relevant curriculum. Kathy, a language arts teacher, combines a natural ability to "kid-watch" (Y. M. Goodman, 1985) with a desire to meet her students' needs as she continually revises her plans. She recalls the agony of moving away from the traditional straight rows and individual seatwork. She has struggled to find a flexible system of partner work based on mixed academic ability, ethnic balance, social factors, and student choice that works for her and her students. What has been most exciting for her is seeing her seventh and eighth graders collaborate. She is now the first to tell fellow teachers, "I'll never go back to straight rows."

While Kathy always had her students write essays and keep journals, she has made some changes in how she responds to and interacts with them. Now when students write in her class, Kathy tries to write with them and often shares what she has written. She also responds as often as possible to their writing as if she were having a personal conversation with them. She has found that her students are eager to write now that she writes back because they know that she will "talk" to them in writing about what they are thinking.

In a recent graduate class in second language acquisition, Kathy explained how the interdisciplinary (language arts, math, science, and geography) team of teachers at her school begin the year with the theme "One World/One Family" to promote cooperation and harmony among their students. Kathy explained the rationale for this unit:

Adolescence is an emotionally vulnerable time. Middle school students are beginning to see themselves as individuals separate from a family unit but unsure about where they really belong. We strive for them to see themselves as part of one human family with cultural, language, and ethnic diversity as positive and beneficial to the well-being and fulfillment of all people.

Kathy began the unit in language arts by showing the students the twelve-minute film *A Day in the Life of Bonnie Consolo* (Barr Films, 1975), about a woman born without arms. The film begins with a scene of Bonnie kneading bread with her feet and includes an incident where Bonnie is told by a store manager that other customers don't want her shopping in the store because it bothers them to watch her. Students in Kathy's class did quick-writes in their journals in response to the film and discussed their responses to the difficulties Bonnie faced.

The text for the unit is *The Acorn People* by Ron Jones (1976), a true story about his work as a counselor with severely handicapped children at a summer camp. The teens in Kathy's class were initially repulsed by the handicaps of the children, especially Spider, who has stumps for arms and legs, and Arid, who must carry his waste in a plastic bag because he has no bladder. The readers were sympathetic to Ron Jones, who initially wanted to go home. Ron didn't want to be stuck as a camp counselor whose duties include changing diapers. But soon he and the students reading his book began to realize that these physically deformed children are like themselves: people with feelings.

In the process of reading, discussing, and writing about the book, Kathy's students did different kinds of activities and talked about topics relevant to their own lives. In pairs they made labels that represented different characters in the book. They guessed which characters those labels represented and then discussed how people get labeled and how labels can be both positive and negative. Figure 13.4 shows several of the labels Kathy's students drew. The students explained why they chose those symbols: the carrot represents the "vegetable" label given the severely disabled kids in the book, who are considered worthless and incapable of human feelings; the light bulb represents Martin, who, though blind, has brightness and ideas about the world and life; the crown represents Arid, who is crowned King at the dance in the story and is, in fact, as noble as a king; and the envelope is the envelope given Ron Jones, the counselor and book author, at the funeral of one of his former campers. In the envelope was a note from the boy's mother explaining how he had never forgotten his experience at camp.

During the time that students discussed the labels, Kathy asked them to write in their literature logs about a time they experienced something similar to what happened to the characters in the book. These journal entries served as the beginnings of individual "autobiographical incidents" papers that are required by the district curriculum guides.

The students' final project, done with a partner, also fulfilled district mandates. Students designed and presented a graphic that represented plot, setting, theme, and character. Figure 13.5 shows one such drawing. The two students drew the camp in the foreground on the right for the setting, the symbolic acorn necklaces in the upper left, and a dolphin in the middle to represent Spider, the boy with no arms or legs who, once in the water, was able to do anything. They titled their work "Never Quit, Try Try Again," the theme of their piece. Another pair chose the theme "Don't judge a book by its cover" (Figure 13.6). Their drawing shows the camp and the acorn necklace with a crown, as a symbol of victory. The character Martin, the blind boy, is described in an acrostic.

At the end of the unit, students wrote about what they learned. Several explained that they had discovered that all people are the same inside and that you should not judge people by the way they look. Other students told Kathy that reading about how

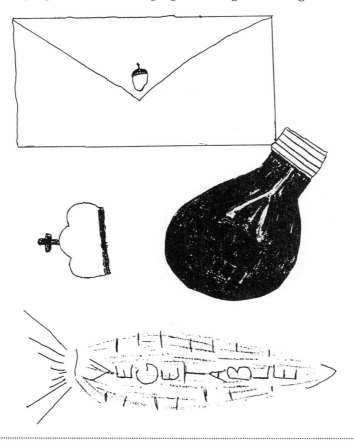

Figure 13.4   Labels from Kathy's lesson

these boys overcame their disabilities to live and enjoy life the best way they could gave them hope to keep trying always and never give up on the goals they set for themselves. As they read, wrote, discussed, and completed their graphics, the second language students in Kathy's class interacted socially and also learned important lessons about life.

Lonna

Many teachers have found that pen-pal letters provide comprehensible input and promote social interaction. The letters not only help students develop writing proficiency, but also provide many chances for students to talk and read. One year, Lonna, who teaches content reading classes to second language learners, worked in two separate inner-city high schools. Often, at one school she would talk about things the students at the other school were doing—their games, their assemblies, their clubs and dances, and their problems with English. Soon, the students in each school developed an interest in

Spider
very intelagent
swims climbs races
He was a great talker
Spider

never Quit try try Again

Figure 13.5   *"Never Quit"*

the students in the other. As Lonna talked, both classes felt they knew the other students. It was a natural extension, then, for the students to begin to write to one another. They wanted to ask questions and get to know these other second language students.

Lonna's students talked a lot as they considered possible topics for letters to be sent to their peers. They worried over how to express their ideas in standard English, and they worked together to make their letters clear to their audience. The students put more energy into these letters than they had into any previous writing assignments. When Lonna delivered the letters, the students were very excited, and if letters were delayed they were extremely disappointed. Students helped each other read the letters they received, and they carefully considered and discussed their responses. Eventually, the two classes had a get-together, which the students planned. The pen-pal letters between Lonna's two classes provided comprehensible input and a form of social interaction during which all her students developed their English proficiency in listening, speaking, reading, and writing (D. E. Freeman & Y. S. Freeman, 1992b).

Motion was perpetual
Able bodied
Red hair
Triped over a tree
Is amazing
Never gave up

LOOK OUT MOUN

DINING HALL

CAMP WIGGIN

DON'T JUDGE A ☐☐ BY IT'S COVER

FIGURE 13.6   "Don't Judge a Book by Its Cover"

Blanca

Blanca, a bilingual kindergarten teacher in a rural farming community, had her kindergartners exchange letters with students in a third-grade class. She noticed how motivated her emerging readers and writers were to write when they had a real audience. Blanca commented on how the writing led to other kinds of social interaction and promoted learning:

> My third grade partner teacher and I added a couple of science projects towards the end of the year with our kids and we were amazed at how involved they got helping each other and talking about things they were doing. This next

year we definitely are going to do more of it. They really learned a lot and I enjoyed watching them interact.

Blanca and her teaching partner helped their students develop both their language and their content knowledge through the pen-pal letters. The letters provided comprehensible input and meaningful social interaction.

Problem Posing: A Second Language Method Consistent with Whole Language

In classes where teachers with second language students follow whole language principles, lessons are designed to make the input comprehensible, to promote social interaction, and to encourage the use of different modes of communication. One second language teaching method incorporates these three principles and moves toward helping teachers and students see how learning has application in the world outside of school.

Problem Posing, developed by Freire (Wallerstein, 1987), was originally designed to help teach literacy to adults (see Chapter 9, the section on critical literacy). However, whole language teachers have adapted Problem Posing for younger students as well. In this method, the teacher first listens to the students and assesses their situation to help them determine the things that truly concern them. The teacher then chooses a "code" (a picture, a story, a song, etc.) to present to the students to help them take an objective look at their personal experiences and concerns. The code is chosen to help students focus on a particular problem area. For example, the teacher might show students a snapshot that depicts a crime being committed in the inner-city area where the students live, or a picture of a polluted neighborhood environment. The students meet in small groups (Freire calls them "culture circles") to discuss the picture. In the process, they identify or pose what they perceive as a problem. Through their collective dialogue in the culture circles, they plan for social action to improve their situation.

In discussing their situation and planning social action, students learning a second language can use the language to solve a real problem. Younger students might deal with a problem such as lack of playground space. Somewhat older students might tackle the problems presented by drug dealers on campus. Adult students could consider the effects welfare programs have on members of their community.

The key to Problem Posing is social interaction that leads to social action. There are many similarities between Problem Posing and whole language (Y. S. Freeman & D. E. Freeman, 1991a). In fact, of all the methods that have been developed to teach a second language, Problem Posing is the most consistent with the principles of whole language. The following shows how certain aspects of Problem Posing correspond to basic whole language principles:

Whole Language Principles	*Problem Posing*
1. The input is comprehensible.	1. The code is a whole story, picture, or film based on the learners' lives.

Whole Language Principles	*Problem Posing*
2. Learning takes place in social interaction.	2. Learners work collaboratively to solve community problems.
3. Learners use all four modes during authentic communication.	3. Learners talk, listen, read, and write about meaningful topics.

Several teachers with whom we have worked have used Problem Posing with their students and found that much language learning takes place. Steve, an ESL teacher in a large city, was intrigued by the possibilities that Problem Posing offered for his adult Southeast Asian students. He had been previously frustrated with workbooks and grammar-based curriculum because he knew that his students' real-world needs were not being met. Since many of his students had never learned to read or write in their first languages, he wanted to involve them in English that was meaningful but would also not be overwhelming. His opportunity to try Problem Posing came during a time when the adult school was not able to provide textbooks. Administrators told teachers to "make do."

He began with a discussion about what kinds of problems his students were having daily. In a discussion much like Freire's culture circles, Steve's class brainstormed a list of problems and concerns. The most frequent problems brought up involved substandard housing apartment complexes the students were forced to live in because of their low incomes. He asked the students to create their own codes by first drawing and labeling the problem. Figure 13.7 shows some of the codes that the students themselves created.

The following day, students shared their codes in class and together the class decided in writing to explore their general group problems as well as individual problems by answering four basic questions: What is the problem? Why is this a problem? What causes the problem? What can we do about the problem? Figure 13.8 is an example of how K. Vang and T. Moua together explored their personal problems in writing and came to a possible solution: "I go new november."

After students had written and shared the ideas from their writing, they brainstormed solutions. Some decided to try to move, but many did not have that option; so Steve and his students talked about how to file complaints with the owner if the managers did not respond. They practiced writing letters requesting service and also worked on the English they needed in order to ask for repairs. What was most exciting about these classes was the amount of interaction and enthusiasm that was generated as language was being learned. Unfortunately, when new textbooks became available, the administrators insisted that Steve use them, which left little time for Problem Posing.

Pam teaches fourth grade in a farming community where the school population is about 85 percent Hispanic. After she had read and talked about Problem Posing in our graduate classes, she had an opportunity to apply it in her own classroom. Her story shows how Problem Posing can be adapted to empower students to have faith in themselves as they develop literacy and interact socially:

> I remember one time this year, I heard a group of students complaining that the cafeteria only offered chocolate milk once a month. I told them instead of complaining about the matter they should try to do something about it. So a

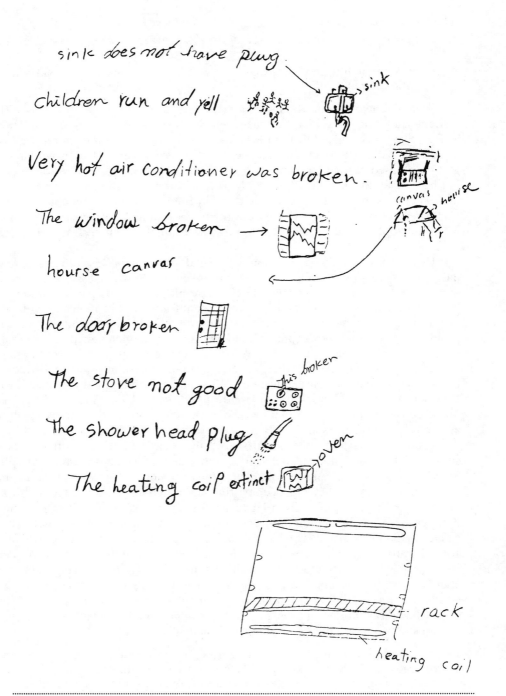

FIGURE 13.7   *Steve's students' codes*

Draw a picture of the problem.

Sink does not have a plug.

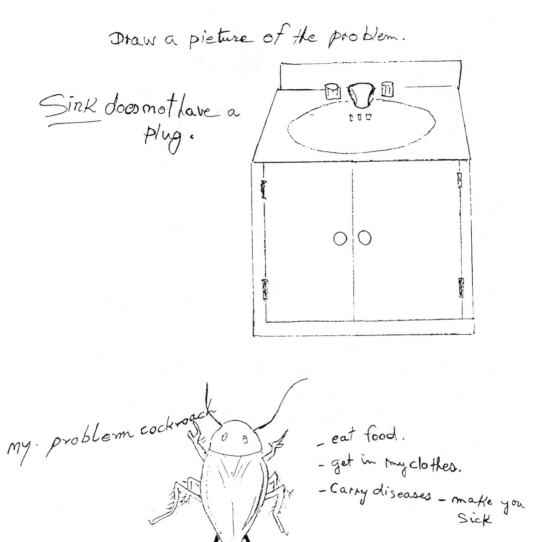

my problem cockroach

- eat food.
- get in my clothes.
- Carry diseases — make you sick

Spray poison — in a can
— hurts people

FIGURE 13.7   Continued

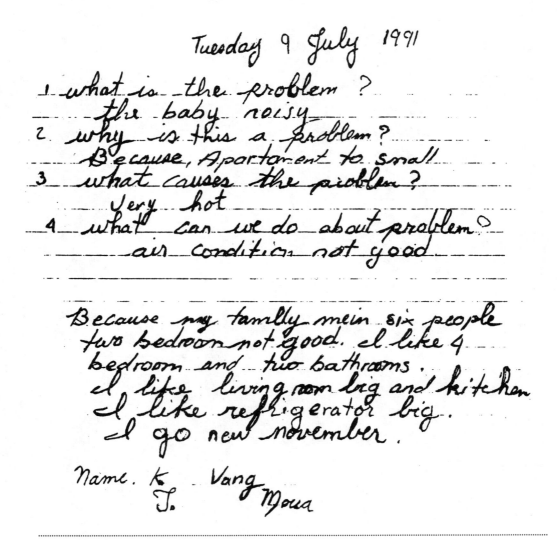

Tuesday 9 July 1991

1 what is the problem ?
    the baby noisy
2 why is this a problem?
    Because, Apartament to small
3 what causes the problem?
    very hot
4 what can we do about problem?
    air condition not good

Because my family mein six people
two bedroom not good. I like 4
bedroom and two bathrooms.
I like living room big and kitchen
I like refrigerator big.
I go new november.

Name. K   Vang
        J.   Moua

FIGURE 13.8   Problem posing and solving

group of about seven students got together and brainstormed how they could change the matter. They investigated the cost of both regular and chocolate milk and found the cost difference to be very small. They then surveyed other students to see if they agreed that chocolate milk should be served more often. They then presented their information to the head of the cafeteria who, by the way, found it very delightful that the students would do so much work to change the serving of milk. She agreed to serve it more often. (She did not realize that the students even wanted chocolate milk!)

The students in Pam's classroom solved a real problem. The code, chocolate milk, came up in a natural way. The students, with a little encouragement from their teacher, saw that there was a problem that they could try to solve themselves. In the process of investigating milk prices, surveying other fourth as well as fifth graders, and organizing their argument to present to the head of the cafeteria, they talked and listened to one another, read information about milk, made lists, and wrote survey forms. During these activities the second language learners in Pam's class learned lots of language and also learned how their involvement could make a difference in their everyday lives (D. E. Freeman & Y. S. Freeman, in press).

Problem Posing is an ESL method that illustrates the growing convergence between second language methods and a whole language approach to teaching, learning, and curriculum. Stories from classrooms like Steve's and Pam's show how both whole language and second language teachers can learn from one another. This becomes especially important as more second language students are mainstreamed into classes with native English speakers. Whole language teachers who understand second language acquisition and ESL methods can work very effectively with such classes.

We have found, however, that in some cases whole language teachers do not fully appreciate the value of supporting the development of students' primary languages. In the following sections, we review the evidence for bilingual education and then suggest ways to support a student's first language even when a teacher does not speak that language.

THEORETICAL AND RESEARCH BASIS FOR BILINGUAL EDUCATION

Whole language teachers who work with second language students recognize the importance of helping them develop competence in English. It seems logical that the best way to help students develop English proficiency is to immerse them in classrooms where they hear, speak, read, and write English all day. However, although the idea that "more English leads to more English" may be logical, it is not psychological. If students enter our schools speaking languages other than English, and if English is the only language of instruction, then students may simply not understand enough to either acquire English or learn any of the content.

We can draw on Smith's idea of demonstrations, engagement, and sensitivity to clarify the importance of first language support. Frank Smith (1981a, 1981b) tells us that learning involves demonstrations (we see people doing things), engagement (we decide we want to do those things), and sensitivity (nothing is done or said that convinces us we can't do those things). When the demonstrations are given in English to nonnative speakers, they may not understand what they are seeing or hearing. If they don't understand the demonstrations, they probably won't choose to engage in an activity. And if they don't engage in classroom activities, they may become convinced that they can't learn. At all three stages, instruction in English simply may not be comprehensible enough for learning to take place. Some students lose interest and are either directly or indirectly isolated from the classroom community. Smith argues that students who do not learn to read and write fluently do not feel they are members of the "literacy club" (1983). Similarly, second language learners who do not participate in classroom activities may never see themselves as members of the "English users' club."

Skutnabb-Kangas (1983), whose work on second language acquisition in Sweden has received international recognition, provides further reasons that instruction in a second language may not result in learning. She asks educators what happens when "the child sits in a submersion classroom [where many of the students have the language of instruction as their mother tongue], listening to the teacher explaining something that the child is then supposed to use for problem solving" (p. 116). In this situation "the child gets less information than a child listening to her mother tongue" (p. 116). If a child fails to understand even a few words, she may lose the meaning of an explanation. In addition, Skutnabb-Kangas points out that listening to a second language is more tiring than listening to one's native language. There are times that second language learners in classrooms may appear to have shorter attention spans than native speakers, but in reality, those students may simply be tired and may give up trying to make sense out of their new language.

Research in second language acquisition has shown that the most effective way for bilingual students to develop both academic concepts and English language proficiency is through their first language (Collier, 1989; Crawford, 1989; Cummins, 1981, 1989a; D. E. Freeman & Y. S. Freeman, 1992b; Hudelson, 1987; Krashen, 1985c; Krashen & Biber, 1988; L. Olsen & Mullen, 1990; Ramírez, 1991; Skutnabb-Kangas, 1983; Berman et al., 1992). For additional information on research in bilingual education, see the references in Figure 13.9.

There are many different models of bilingual education (Crawford, 1989, 1992; Berman et al., 1992), but any bilingual program includes some primary language instruction. In bilingual programs students learn English, and, at the same time, they continue to develop content knowledge through first language instruction. Krashen suggests that the best comprehensible input that teachers can give their students is messages in their primary language (Krashen, 1985; Krashen & Biber, 1988).

First language instruction provides the comprehensible input students need to develop academic concepts. Cummins (1989a) argues that a concept learned in one language transfers to a second language because there is a common underlying proficiency. For example, students learn to read only once. Students who have been taught to read in their first language don't have to relearn the whole process of reading in order to be able to read in English. In the same way, a student who learns about the water cycle in Punjabi needs English to talk and write about how the water cycle works, but the student does not have to learn the concept again in English.

Cummins' idea of a common underlying proficiency helps to explain why students with previous education in their own country often do better academically than students who have been in English-speaking schools longer but never received any schooling in their native language. Those newer students have had instruction from the beginning in a language they could understand. They developed concepts, negotiated meaning, and learned to read in their mother tongue. When they began studying in an English-

Books and Reports: Pro

Berman, et al. (1992). Meeting the challenge of language diversity: An evaluation of programs for pupils with limited proficiency in English. Project R–119/1. Berkeley, CA: BW Associates.

California State Department of Education. (1984). *Studies on immersion education: A collection for United States Educators*. Sacramento: California State Department of Education.

Cazden, C. B., & C. Snow. (Eds.). (1990). English plus: Issues in bilingual education. In *Annals of the American Academy of Political Science*, vol. 508. Newbury Park: Sage Publications.

Crawford, J. (1989). *Bilingual education: History, politics, theory and practice.* Trenton, NJ: Crane.

Crawford, J. (Ed.). (1992). *Language loyalties.* Chicago: The University of Chicago Press. (Provides an overview of the history and politics of this issue.)

Cummins, J. (1984). *Bilingualism and special education: Issues in assessment and pedagogy.* Clevedon, England: Multilingual Matters.

Cummins, J. (1989). *Empowering minority students.* Sacramento, CA: California Association on Bilingual Education.

Edelsky, C. (1986). *Writing in a bilingual program: Había una vez.* Norwood, NJ: Ablex.

Genesee, F. (1987). *Learning through two languages: Studies of immersion and bilingual education.* Cambridge, MA: Newbury House.

Hakuta, K. (1986). *Mirror of language: The debate on bilingualism.* New York: Basic Books.

Krashen, S. (1991). *Bilingual education: A focus on current research.* Occasional Papers in Bilingual Education (Report No. 3.). Washington, DC: National Clearinghouse for Bilingual Education.

Krashen, S., & Biber, D. (1988). *On course: Bilingual education's success in California.* Sacramento, CA: California Association of Bilingual Education.

Lessow-Hurley, J. (1990). *The foundations of dual language instruction.* New York: Longman.

Ovando, C., & Collier, V. (1985). *Bilingual and ESL classrooms: Teaching in multicultural contexts.* New York: McGraw Hill.

Ramírez, J. D. (1991). *Final Report: Longitudinal study of structured English immersion strategy, early-exit and late-exit bilingual education programs.* (300–87–0156). Washington, DC: U.S. Department of Education.

Skutnabb-Kangas, T. (1983). *Bilingualism or not: The education of minorities.* Clevedon, England: Multilingual Matters.

Figure 13.9 References on bilingual education

Articles and Chapters in Books: Pro

Cummins, J. (1981). The role of primary language development in promoting educational success for language minority students. In *Schooling and language minority students: A theoretical framework* (pp. 3–49). Los Angeles: Evaluation, Dissemination and Assessment Center, California State University, Los Angeles.

Cummins, J. (1989). The sanitized curriculum: Educational disempowerment in a nation at risk. In D. Johnson & D. Roen (Eds.), *Richness in writing: Empowering ESL students* (pp. 19–38). New York: Longman.

Edelsky, C. (1989). Bilingual children's writing: Fact and fiction. In D. Johnson & D. Roen (Eds.), *Richness in writing: Empowering ESL students* (pp. 165–176). New York: Longman.

Freeman, Y. S., & Freeman, D. E. (1989). Bilingual learners: How our assumptions limit their world. *Holistic Education Review* (Winter), 33–39.

Gonzalez, J. (1979). Coming of age in bilingual/bicultural education: A historical perspective. In H. Trueba & C. Barnett-Mizrahi (Eds.), *Bilingual multicultural education and the professional: From theory to practice* (pp. 1–10). Rowley, MA: Newbury House.

Hernández-Chávez, E. (1984). The inadequacy of English immersion educaton as an educational approach for language minority students in the United States. In D. Dolson (Ed.), *Studies on immersion education* (pp. 144–183). Sacramento, CA: California State Department of Education.

Krashen, S. D. (1985). Does bilingual education delay the acquisition of English? In *Inquiries and insights* (pp. 69–88). Hayward, CA: Alemany Press.

Lucas, I. (1981). Bilingual education and the melting pot: Getting burned. *The Illinois Issues Humanities Essays: 5*. Champaign, IL: Illinois Humanities Council.

Willig, A. (1985). A meta-analysis of selected studies on the effectiveness of bilingual education. *Review of Educational Research*, 55, 269–317.

Books and Articles: Con

Baker, K. A., & de Kanter, A. A. (1981). *Effectiveness of bilingual education: A review of the literature*. Washington, DC: Office of Planning and Budget, U.S. Department of Education.

Bennett, W. (1988). In defense of our common language. In *Our children and our country: Improving America's schools and affirming the common culture*. New York: Simon & Schuster.

Imhoff, G. (1990). The position of U.S. English on bilingual education. In C. Cazden & C. Snow (Eds.), *Annals of the American Academy of Political Science*, Vol. 508 (pp. 48–61). Newbury Park, CA: Sage Publications.

Porter, R. (1990). *Forked tongue: The politics of bilingual education.* New York: Basic Books.

Figure 13.9 Continued

speaking country, they transferred those experiences to the new setting. Second language learners who receive instruction only in English may have difficulty making sense of the instruction because they lack the background knowledge that the students who were educated in their own countries received. Students in English-only classrooms are faced with learning both language and content at the same time. On the other hand, students in bilingual programs can continue to develop content knowledge though instruction in their primary language while they are learning English.

Conversational and Academic Language Proficiency

Teachers may find that some of their second language students seem to communicate well in English, but they still struggle academically. If teachers assume that English is not the problem, they may view students as somehow deficient. However, in most cases, English proficiency *is* the problem. Cummins (1981) has differentiated between two kinds of language proficiency. *Conversational proficiency* is the ability to use language in face-to-face communication. *Academic proficiency* is the ability to carry out school-related literacy tasks. Cummins' research shows that conversational proficiency generally develops much more rapidly than academic proficiency. One reason for this discrepancy may be that when students talk to one another, the topics are familiar. Students can bring their background knowledge to bear to make sense of the new language. In addition, during conversation, second language students can make use of extralinguistic cues that come from gestures and objects. For example, when two students talk about who will be first on the playground swings, the situation provides strong context cues to support the language. On the other hand, the language in many traditional classrooms is not supported by context, especially when teachers lecture or assign students to read texts and answer questions.

Cummins found that it took immigrant students about two years to develop conversational proficiency but five to seven years to reach grade-level norms in academic tasks. Cummins' findings have been confirmed by Collier (1989). Collier's work is particularly important because she looked at a large number of students whose parents expected them to attend college. These students came from middle-class backgrounds and had strong parental support for education. However, it still took them at least five years to score at the norm on standardized tests in different content areas.

The research by Cummins and Collier helps to explain why students who appear to speak English well may still have difficulty in school. Academic proficiency simply takes longer to develop than conversational proficiency. Imagine what would happen if you went to China next year. Unless you already speak Chinese, it would take you about two years to converse comfortably in social situations. Even after two years, though, you would most likely not feel prepared to attend a Chinese university, listen to lectures in Chinese, read Chinese books, and write papers and take tests in Chinese. Your conversational proficiency might allow you to interact effectively in social situations, but you would be at a distinct disadvantage in an academic setting. As adults, we might choose not to attend classes in Chinese; however, our second language students do not have any such choice in schools where all the instruction is entirely in English.

Second Language Students Become Bilingual

> Two languages are cool,
> as cool can be.
> We go to school to learn them,
> especially in grade three.
> Knowing English and Spanish is one great feat;
> when you know them both, people think you're neat.
>
> All men created equal
> should be bilingual.

The poem above, written by third grader Rey Corpuz, first-place winner (K–3) of the 1992 CABE writing contest, expresses well the value Rey puts on being bilingual. While whole language teachers want their students to become proficient in English and want them to succeed academically in English, they also want their bilingual students to maintain their first language. Otherwise, the teachers really would not be supporting the whole child; they would be excluding the child's first language and culture. Unfortunately, many bilingual students receive no primary language support at all in schools. Many of the bilingual programs that do exist are transitional programs in which students are given first language support only until schools decide they no longer need it. As a result, many students never become literate in their first language and many others even lose their ability to speak and understand their native tongue (Crawford, 1989; Cummins, 1989a; Krashen, 1990; L. Olsen, 1988; Skutnabb-Kangas, 1983). In some bilingual programs, however, students receive strong literacy support in their first language. In some programs, English-speaking students also become bilingual. These are referred to as *two-way bilingual programs* (Crawford, 1989; Krashen, 1990; Krashen & Biber, 1988; L. Olsen & Mullen, 1990; Berman et al., 1992).

Even when schools have bilingual programs, most students are mainstreamed into English-only instruction after two years. These students would benefit from primary language instruction for at least five years. In a bilingual program where the first language is maintained, students are given the chance to learn concepts in their first language at the same time that they are developing proficiency in English. Without first language support, many second language learners never attain their potential. (For additional readings on developing first language literacy in Spanish–English bilingual settings, see Figure 13.10.)

When second language students are placed in good bilingual programs with whole language teachers, many of them achieve real success. In the sections that follow we describe two such teachers.

Carolina

In Kerman, California, the school district has developed a Spanish immersion program that strongly supports Hispanic children's development of their first language literacy. For two years, in first and second grades, Carolina provides a Spanish-speaking whole language classroom for her students. Except for a short time each day when students read, sing, and interact in English, learning takes place in Spanish. Students in Carolina's

Barrera, R. (1983). Bilingual reading in the primary grades: Some questions about questionable views and practices. In T. Escobedo (Ed.), *Early childhood bilingual education: A Hispanic perspective* (pp. 164–184). New York: Columbia University Press.

de Silva, A. (1981). Oral reading behavior of Spanish speaking children taught by a meaning-based program. In S. Hudelson (Ed.), *Learning to read in different languages*. Arlington, VA: Center for Applied Linguistics.

Edelsky, C. (1986). *Writing in a bilingual program: Había una vez*. Norwood, NJ: Ablex.

Edelsky, C. (1989). Bilingual children's writing: Fact and fiction. In D. Johnson & D. Roen (Eds.), *Richness in writing: Empowering ESL students* (pp. 165–176). New York: Longman.

Ferreiro, E., & Teberosky, A. (1982). *Literacy before schooling*. Portsmouth, NH: Heinemann.

Freeman, Y. S. (1988a). The contemporary Spanish basal reader in the U.S.: How does it reflect current knowledge of the reading process? *NABE Journal, 13*, 59–74.

Freeman, Y. S. (1988b). Do Spanish methods and materials reflect current understanding of the reading process? *The Reading Teacher, 41*, 654–664.

Freeman, Y. S. (1988c). Métodos de lectura en espanol: Reflejan nuestro conocimiento actual del proceso de lectura? *Lectura y Vida, 9*, 20–28.

Freeman, Y. S., & Nofziger, S. (1991). WalkuM to RnM 33: Vien Vinidos al cualTo 33. In K. S. Goodman, Y. M. Goodman, & W. J. Hood (Eds.), *Organizing for whole language* (pp. 65–83). Portsmouth, NH: Heinemann.

Hudelson, S. (1981). *Learning to read in different languages*. Arlington, VA: Center for Applied Linguistics.

Hudelson, S. (1987). The role of native language literacy in the education of language minority children. *Language Arts, 64*(8), 827–840.

Serna, I., & Hudelson, S. (in press). Emergent Spanish literacy in whole language bilingual classrooms. In R. Donmoyer & R. Kos (Eds.), *At risk students: Portraits, policies, and programs*. Albany, NY: SUNY Press.

FIGURE 13.10   *References on bilingual English–Spanish literacy*

classroom write in journals, publish books, share their writings, keep science logs, and read with buddies using their first language. Their spelling has moved naturally toward conventionality because these children read from a large variety of good children's literature in Spanish (Y. S. Freeman & Cervantes, 1991) and write several times daily.

The most exciting part of the program for Carolina has been watching her students' self-confidence grow. Children who were reluctant even to talk, children whose parents did not even believe they would succeed in school, are now, at the end of second grade, discussing trade books, publishing books of their own, describing experiences with detail and creativity, and sharing confidently.

María, one of Carolina's students, caught Yvonne's eye during a recent visit to the classroom. María smiled shyly, but did not push herself on the visitor. During Author's Chair, when a student author sits in a special chair to share some writing, María volunteered to read her story and answered the questions of her peers quietly but confidently. Later, during free choice time, María joined a group of three others who were continuing Author's Chair on their own. Though she had not asked questions in the large-group setting, María's questions to the authors in the more intimate setting proved that she understood how to interact with the texts that her peers had written. Later, when María was working on a new story, Yvonne asked if María would read her favorite story to her. María chose her story "El arvol que no tiene amigas" (in conventional spelling, "El árbol que no tiene amigas"—The Tree that Doesn't Have Any Friends) (Figure 13.11).

When Yvonne talked to Carolina later about María, Carolina explained that early in the school year María's parents had wanted to have her tested for learning disabilities because María's writing was still not legible. Carolina insisted that María was enjoying books, and that she was progressing daily. When María published "The Tree that Doesn't Have Any Friends," everyone celebrated. Since then she has published other books, as well as a content piece on dinosaurs written for the district-mandated portfolio (Figure 13.12).

The students in Carolina's classroom spend a lot of time reading. Carolina told about having to move the book baskets away from Natalia's desk because she never wanted to do anything but read! Natalia's confidence with books was obvious. Natalia read to Yvonne from a book of traditional poems, *Cuervos* (Crows). Natalia not only read the poems but also was able to explain the abstract poetry: "Uno es desdicha [One is unfortunate]," read Natalia in Spanish, and then she explained, "Tiene mala suerte" (He has bad luck). "Dos son dicha [Two are fortunate]; tienen buena suerte [They have good luck]. Tres, casamiento [Three, marriage]." At this point Natalia wanted to make it clear to me that the poetry was about a couple meeting and getting married. She pointed to the pictures that clarified this and said, "Aquí se casan" (Here is where they get married). She turned the next page and read, "Cuatro, nacimiento [Four, birth]. ¿Ves? se conocen, se casan y después tienen un bebé. [Do you get it? They meet, they get married and then they have a baby]." Students such as Natalia are developing into proficient readers in this bilingual class where they have frequent opportunities to read in their first language.

Students write often for Carolina, and much of their writing comes out of class experiences and discussion. Since the district requires several writing samples for portfolios, such as María's dinosaur example in Figure 13.12, Carolina uses that requirement as a chance for the students to respond to what they are learning. After a class trip on Amtrak, Reina and José wrote about their first train ride, an event that these children will never forget (Figure 13.13, a and b).

Later in the year, the class talked about drugs and poisons during a district-mandated health unit. In Figure 13.14a Ramón explains about the dangers of poison and clarifies his points with diagrams, and in Figure 13.14b, Raquel provides a personal example.

Figure 13.11   Maria's story

Memoria
El arbol estaba triste

Memory
The tree was sad.

Figure 13.11 Continued

El arbol que no tiene amigos
The tree that does not have friends

el arvol estava triste
por que   no tenia
amigos y una vez

FIGURE 13.11 Continued

El arbol estaba triste
por que no tenia
amigos y una vez

The tree was sad
because it didn't have
friends and one time

llego una flor y
le dijo cieres aser
mi amigo y el arvol
le dijo si ciero aser tv

FIGURE 13.11   Continued

Ilegó una flor y
le dijo, "Quieres hacer
mi amigo?" Y el arbol
le dijo, "Sí, quiero hacer tu

a flower arrived
and said to him/her [the tree], "Do you want to be
my friend?" And the tree
said to him/her [the flower], "Yes, I want to be your

Figure 13.11   *Continued*

amigo y el arbol dijo,
"Vamos a jugar y la
flor dijo, "Sí vamos a
jugar y el arbol

friend" and the tree said,
"Let's play," and the
flower said, "Yes, let's
play." and the tree

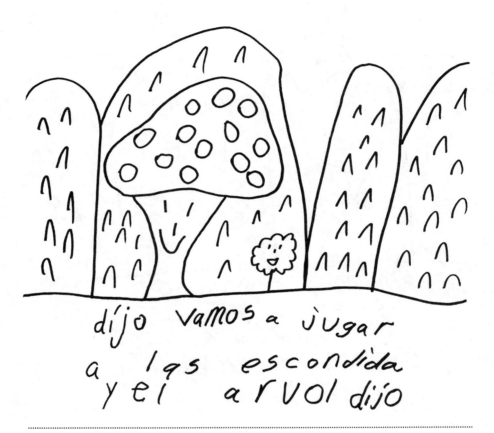

díjo Vamos a júgar
a las escondida
y el arvol dijo

Figure 13.11   Continued

dijo, "Vamos a jugar
a las escondida."
"Y el arbol dijo

said, "Let's play
hide-and-seek"
and the tree said,

tu vas a contar y
la Flor dijo sí
Hyo veinte voll a contar asta

FIGURE 3.11 Continued

"Tú vas a contar y
la Flor dijo. "Sí.
yo voy a contar hasta
veinte

"You count." And
the flower said, "Yes,
I am going to count up to
twenty."

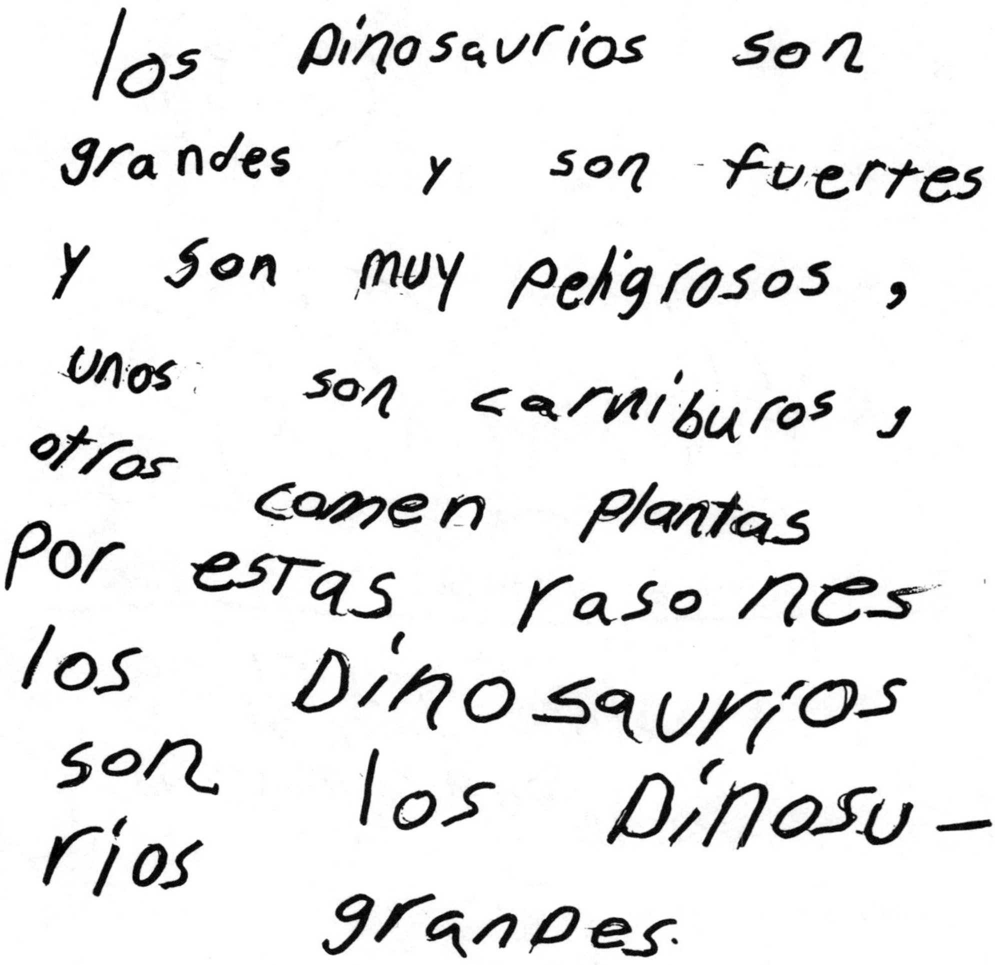

los Dinosaurios son
grandes y son fuertes
y son muy peligrosos ,
unos son carniburos ,
otros
       comen plantas
Por estas rasones
los Dinosaurios
son   los Dinosu-
rios
     grandes.

FIGURE 13.12   María's dinosaur example

los dinosaurios son grandes y son fuertes y son muy peligrosos, unos son carnivoros, otros comen plantas por estas razones los dinosaurios son los dinosaurios grandes.

Dinosaurs are big and they are strong and they are dangerous, some are carnivores, others eat plants for these reasons dinosaurs are big dinosaurs.

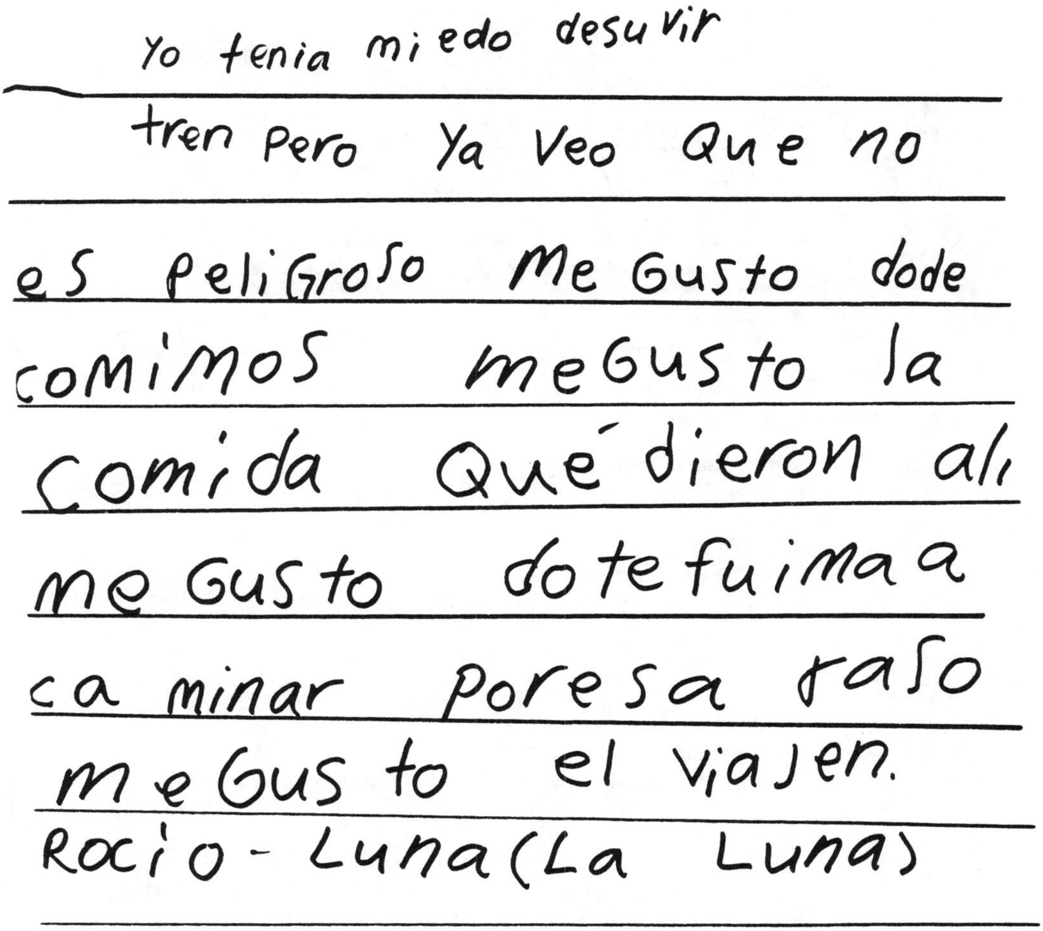

Yo tenia miedo desuvir
tren Pero Ya Veo Que no
es peliGroso Me Gusto dode
comimos meGusto la
comida Qué dieron ali
me Gusto dote fuima a
ca minar poresa raso
me Gus to el viajen.
Rocio - Luna (La Luna)

FIGURE 13.13A   Train field trip: Reina

Yo tenía miedo de subir en el tren pero ya veo que no es peligroso me gustó donde comimos me gustó la comida que dieron a mí me gustó donde fuimos a caminar. Por esta razon me (ha)gustado el viaje. Raquel—Luna (La Luna)

I was afraid to go on the train but now I see that it is not dangerous. I liked where we ate. I liked the food they gave [us]. I liked where we went to walk. For this reason I have liked the trip. Raquel—Luna "The Moon" (The nickname she chose for herself)

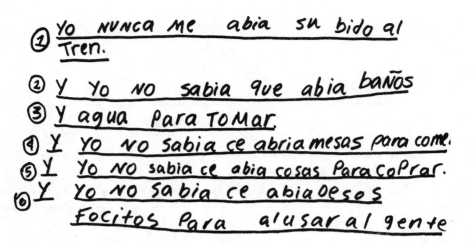

FIGURE 13.13B   *Train field trip: José*

1. Yo nunca me había subido al tren.
2. Y yo no sabía que había baños.
3. Y agua para tomar.
4. Y yo no sabía que había mesas para comer.
5. Y yo no sabía que había cosas para comprar.
6. Y yo no sabía que habia de esos foquitos para alumbrar a la gente.

1. I had never been on a train [before].
2. And I didn't know that there were bathrooms.
3. And water to drink.
4. And I didn't know that there were tables for eating.
5. And I didn't know that there were things to buy.
6. And I didn't know that there were those little light bulbs to give light for the people.

Carolina will have the opportunity to work with this class one more year as they move to third grade. She is excited about each of her students and feels confident that they all will succeed even though their days in third grade will include more English. Her students have had a good foundation of schooling in their first language. They are confident readers, writers, and learners.

Sam

Yvonne worked in Sam's Spanish/English inner-city, first- and second-grade combination bilingual classroom for a year. During that year Yvonne and Sam learned from the children that bilingual students have tremendous potential and that organizing a whole language bilingual classroom can be both challenging and exciting (Y. S. Freeman & Nofziger, 1991).

El veneno no tenemos
que dejarlo en lo bajito
solamente en el lo aj-
to y No Tenemos que
Tomar Elveneno Porque es
malo

El veneno no tenemos que dejarlo en lo bajito solamente en lo alto y no tenemos que tomar el veneno porque es malo

Poison we should not leave down low only [put it] up high and we should not take poison because it is bad [for us].

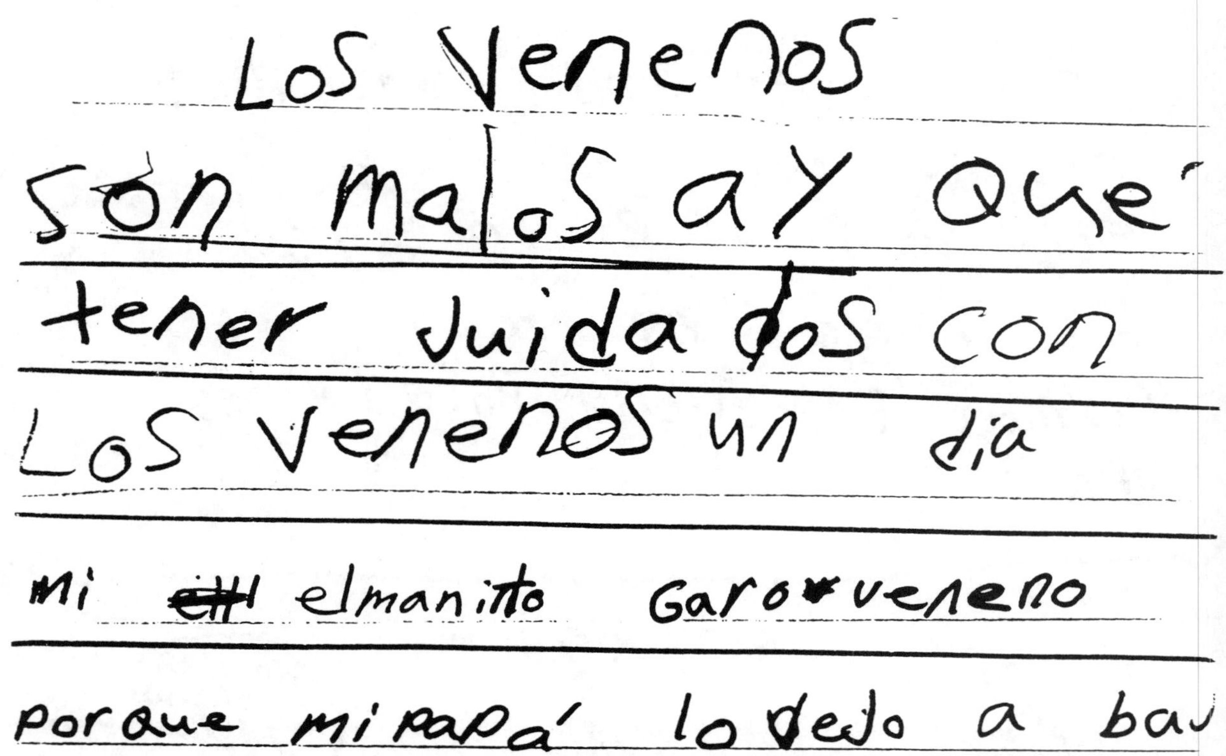

Los Venenos
son malos ay Que
tener Juidados con
Los Venenos un dia
mi ~~el~~ elmanitto Garo venero
porQue mirapá lo deso a bau
cene fer mo mucho Y lo llev
ro a la os pirta des pues
como tres dia loreGresaror
a mi casa

FIGURE 13.14B *Dangers of poison: Racquel*

Los venenos son malos hay que tener cuidado con los venenos un día mi hermanito agaró veneno porque mi papá lo dejó abajo se enfermo mucho y lo llevaron a la hospital despues como tres días lo regresaron a mi casa

Poisons are bad. It is necessary to be careful with poisons. One day my little brother got hold of some poison because my father left it down low. He got very sick and they took him to the hospital. After three days they returned him home.

One of the things that Sam wanted to try with his young bilingual students was literature studies using literature logs. He was not confident this would work, but the children proved that the logs were a powerful way to work with literature. Sam wrote about the experience:

> We have been able to give our students a good choice of books in Spanish and English. We made trips to the district resource center and several libraries to provide the children with books they would never have had access to otherwise.
>
> Because of all the discussions and the writing going on in the classroom, I decided that the next logical step was to have the children do literature response journals. I had been told by other teachers that literature journals for first and second grade would not work. However, I wanted to find out for myself. I began by asking children to write the title of the book they had just read, to write a short message about the book, and then draw a picture of their favorite part. I then responded by writing questions to encourage the students to write more. What was most exciting about doing this is that from the very beginning the children were able to respond to the literature with only a little encouragement.
>
> Now the children respond without the question probes and make very insightful observations about their readings. Through readings, written responses, and interaction, the children are able to respond very personally to what they read. The literature logs have expanded our understanding of each other as well as of what we read.

Figure 13.15 shows how Erika, a second grader, responded to the reading of "La Caperusita Roja" (Little Red Riding Hood) by drawing Red Riding Hood and the wolf and then writing, "a mi me gusta por que es bonito" (I like it because it is pretty). Sam, sitting next to her, then began to engage Erika in a written conversation: "¿Quién es bonita? [Who is pretty?]" Erika responded, "Eya" (invented spelling for *Ella,* meaning "She"). Sam continued to push by writing, "¿Cómo se llama ella? [What is her name?]" Erika wrote, "A Caperusita Roja [Little Red Riding Hood]." Next, Sam asked, "¿Qué hace la Caperua Roja? [What does Little Red Riding Hood do?]." Erika answered with a full sentence:"Fue a dejorle la comida a su abuelita [She went to leave food for her grandmother]." Through this kind of written conversation, Sam began to show his students how to write about what they read.

Josefina, another second grader, also showed how well she could write about literature. After the class had read *La calle es libre* (The Streets Are Free) (Kurusa, 1983), Josefina drew a picture of the small town on the mountains before the city took it over and wrote in invented spelling about key points in the story. She liked the parts of the story where the characters made signs to demand their rights for a place away from the streets to play, where the houses in the barrio were still among the mountains, and where the park got built. Her choices for her literature log certainly show that Josefina understood both the problem and the resolution of the story (Figure 13.16).

Students in bilingual classrooms like Sam's and Carolina's have the opportunity to read and write from the start in a language they understand. As a result, they develop both literacy and self-confidence. They have a better chance at academic success than second

Figure 13.15   Erika's literature log

FIGURE 13.16 Josefina's literature log response

La calle es libre	The street is free
A mí me gusta de este	I like from this
libro cuando estaban	book when they were
haciendo letras	making signs
y cuando había	and when there were
casas en montañas	houses in the mountains
y cuando estaban	and when they were
haciendo el parque.	building the park.

language speakers who, for the first two years of their schooling, are in classrooms where they understand little, if any, of the curriculum and fall further and further behind their English-speaking peers. Students in bilingual classes, on the other hand, develop language and academic proficiency that will later transfer into English.

HOW MONOLINGUAL TEACHERS SUPPORT BILINGUAL STUDENTS

We realize that many whole language teachers are in situations where they cannot provide bilingual instruction even though they support the concept. Classrooms like Carolina's and Sam's are not always possible for bilingual children. In many schools bilingual education is not feasible. A school may lack bilingual teachers, or students may speak a variety of different primary languages. In these circumstances teachers can still find ways to use their bilingual students' first languages and promote academic success. Many teachers with whom we have worked have involved their students in primary language reading and writing even though the teachers do not speak the first languages of all their students. We offer these teachers' creative ideas in the form of ten strategies for monolingual teachers of bilingual students (D. E. Freeman & Y. S. Freeman, 1992b; Y. S. Freeman & D. E. Freeman, 1991b):

1. Arrange for bilingual aides or parent volunteers to read literature written in the primary language to the students and then to discuss what they have read. Plan for older students who speak the first language of the children to come to the class regularly to read to or with the younger students and to act as cross-age tutors.
2. Set up a system of pen-pal letters written in the primary language between students of different classes or different schools.
3. Have students who are bilingual pair up with classmates who share the same primary language but are more proficient in English. This buddy system is particularly helpful for introducing new students to class routines.
4. Invite bilingual storytellers to come to the class and tell stories that would be familiar to all the students. Using context clues, these storytellers can convey familiar stories in languages other than English. Well-known stories such as Cinderella have counterparts (and origins) in non-English languages.
5. Build a classroom library of books in languages other than English. This is essential for primary language literacy development. At times, teachers within a school may want to pool these resources.
6. To increase the primary language resources in classrooms, publish books in languages other than English. Allow bilingual students to share their stories with classmates.
7. Encourage journal writing in the first language. A bilingual aide or parent volunteer can read and respond to journal entries. Give students a choice of language in which to read and write.
8. Look around the room at the environmental print. Include signs in the first language as well as articles and stories in English about the countries the students come from.

9. Use videotapes produced professionally or by the students to support academic learning and raise self-esteem (see Figure 13.17).
10. Have students engage in oral activities, such as show and tell, using their first language as they explain objects, games, or customs from their homelands.

Whole language teachers find ways to incorporate the first languages and cultures of their second language students. This primary language support increases bilingual students' potential for success. They feel better about themselves because they know their teachers value their first language and, thus, value them.

FAITH IN THE LEARNER

Oscar

"He's just lazy!" exclaimed Mrs. A. "Oscar is nothing but a loser."

Mrs. A's response to my question about my new fourth grade student came as quite a surprise. Oscar had been in my class for a week and refused to read or write, claiming that he didn't know how. In addition, he seemed extremely unhappy. He had been in Mexico when school began, so he was starting a month later than the rest of the class.

As a second year teacher, I had decided to seek Mrs. A's help and advice since Oscar had been in her third grade. However, believing there was much more to Oscar than laziness, I decided to observe him and figure out the real problem.

I had no previous experience with second language learners, but after watching and working with Oscar for a short time, I realized that although he seemed to speak English fluently, he really didn't know how to read and write in English.

As I earned his trust, Oscar told me that he had lived in Mexico most of his life, but had lived the last two years in Los Angeles where he attended school in a bilingual classroom. He read and wrote in Spanish as he learned to speak English. As he told me about his education in L.A., tears filled his eyes when he said, "That's why I keep telling all of you that I can't read—I can't read English."

Near tears myself, I assured Oscar that reading and writing in Spanish is just as valuable as doing so in English. I immediately obtained Spanish literature books for him. I also encouraged Oscar to do his journal writing and writer's workshop in Spanish. Oscar began to flourish! Before the year was half over, without any pressure from me, Oscar chose to read and write in English.

Oscar taught me many things that year: Don't jump to conclusions. Don't listen to cynical teachers. Students who learn to read and write in their first language make an easier transition to English. But, perhaps more importantly, Oscar taught me to have faith in my students and to empower them as learners. (Burd, 1992, p. 2.)

Through her story, Oscar's teacher, Kathy, relates a valuable lesson she learned. Children *do* want to succeed in school, and second language learners *do* have potential. Most of all, Kathy learned that what teachers do with bilingual children in their

Spanish Materials

Books

Centro para el estudio de libros infantiles y juveniles en español (Center for the Study of Books in Spanish for Children and Adolescents). California State University. San Marcos, CA 92096–0001 (6l9) 752–4070; fax (619) 752–4030. Dr. Isabel Schon, Director.

Y. S. Freeman & C. Cervantes, 1991 *Literature Books en español for Whole Language* Occasional Paper, Program in Language and Literacy, 504 Education Bldg., University of Arizona, Tucson, AZ 85721.

California Dept. of. Ed. (1991). *Recommended readings in Spanish literature: Kindergarten through grade eight.* Curriculum, Instruction and Assessment Division.

Magazines

Más
P.O. Box 1928
Marion, OH 43305–1928

La familia de hoy
Kyle, Smith,
Whittle Communications L.P.
333 Main Ave.
Knoxville, TN 37902

Hispanic
111 Massachusetts Ave. NW
Suite 200
Washington, DC 20077–2053

Comic Books
Diamond Comic
P.O. Box 1196
Costa Mesa, CA 92628

Newspapers for Classrooms
Mi Globo (available in 3 Levels)
11320 Meadow Flower Pl.
San Diego, CA 92127–9965

Scholastic News (available in English and Spanish)
Scholastic, Inc.
P.O. Box 3710
Jefferson City, MO 65102–3710

Perspectiva (upper grades)
Educational News Service
P.O. Box 177
South Hadley, MA 01075

Videos
Videoevento Productions
(content videos in Spanish)
P.O. Box 1175
Selma, CA 93662
(209) 896–6577

Madera Cinevideo
525 East Yosemite Ave.
Madera, CA 93638
1–800–828–8118 (CA)
1–800–624–2204 (outside CA)
Fax 209–661–6000

Spanish/English Videodiscs
AIMS Media
9710 De Soto Ave.
Chatsworth, CA 91311
1–800–367–2467
Fax 818–341–6700

Asian Materials

Shen's Books and Supplies
P.O. Box 20273
San José, CA 95160–0273
(408) 268–8653

Greenshower Corp.
Asia Children's Books
10937 Klingerman St.
S. El Montem, CA 91733
(818) 443–4020

Multicultural Distributing Center
Asian Indian Languages
800 N. Grand Ave.
Covina, CA 91724

Figure 13.17 Primary language resources

National Asian Center for Bilingual
   Education
Institute for Intercultural Studies
11729 Gateway Blvd.
Los Angeles, CA 90064
(213) 479–6045

Pan Asian Publications (books for children)
29564 Union City Blvd.
Union City, CA 94587
(415) 475–1185

Cheng & Tsui Co.
25 West St.
Boston, MA 02111
(617) 426–6074

A Resource Guide for Asian and Pacific
   American Students, K–12
ARC Associates, Inc.
310 Eighth St., Suite 220
Oakland, CA 94607
(510) 834–9455

Children's Books in Korean
3030 W. Olympic Blvd. #111
Los Angeles, CA 90006
(213) 387–4082

Heian International, Inc.
1260 Pacific St.
P.O. Box 1013
Union City, CA 94587
(415) 471–8440

Pacific Rim Connections, Inc.
(source for Asian Language software)
3030 Atwater Drive
Burlingame, CA 94010
(415) 697–9439

Claudia's Caravan
(multicultural multilingual materials)
P.O. Box 1582
Alameda, CA 94501
(415) 521–7871

FIGURE *13.17* Continued

classrooms makes a difference. Over the years, we have become more and more convinced that while it is important for teachers to provide comprehensible input, to promote social interaction, and to encourage the use of various modes of communication,
the most critical element for successful teaching with bilingual students is a teacher's
faith in the students' ability to learn.

It is much too common for educators to believe that non-English-speaking students
are somehow not as intelligent as students who speak English idiomatically and without
an accent. Many times this attitude is subconscious. However, this lack of belief in the
learning potential of bilingual students can have a tremendously negative effect. Many
of our graduate students have been saddened by the attitudes they have seen expressed
by other teachers or by other students toward second language students. Carolyn writes:

> Several years ago I taught first grade with a teacher who made derogatory
> remarks about her second language students right in front of the entire class.
> She complained constantly about their abilities and very seldom praised any of
> her students. It was the most depressing learning environment I have ever seen.

Roxie recalls an incident that helped her see the kinds of attitudes toward second
language students that become part of the classroom culture and are accepted by all the
students:

I have a Hispanic student in my class who is one of the so-called low achievers, and she is seated next to a student who is from the upper middle class. Last week they were given a math sheet to complete, and when they were finished they were to check their answers with their neighbor's answers. When these two students checked their answers, they reported to me that the Hispanic student had them all wrong, and in reality it was just the opposite. These two did not even question the possibility of the other student being wrong; they just assumed that the Hispanic student was.

Kathy, the middle school teacher who told the story of Oscar, bemoans the cruelty her students sometimes show toward each other even when they are all minority students:

I am continually amazed at how cruel children are to each other. They are always looking for "targets" to put down in order to feel superior. This tendency certainly reflects the power structure of society (which schools mirror) where one group proclaims its superiority over others. A favorite game of one of my Hispanic male students this year was to call out "Cat eater" to many of my Hmong male students. What of the feelings and self-esteem of the Asian victims? When schools/society continue to invalidate the cultures/languages and lives of some of its members, we are doomed to continue a power system where the rights of the elite few subvert the dignity of all.

María, a teacher and a graduate student, remembers her own schooling as a minority.

I remember hating myself because I wasn't blonde, blue-eyed and didn't have straight hair. I would set my hair in huge rollers in order to make my hair straight. I never fit in and became more of a loner. I had few friends due to the fact that it was degrading for them to have a Hispanic friend.

It is critical to create a climate where all students are validated and feel a sense of worth. This can only happen when we help students recognize their strengths.

Linda, a pull-out ESL teacher, discovered how important it is, both for the students and for their teachers, to allow students to use their first language. Several of her second language learners came from a fourth-grade classroom that was reading *Stone Soup* (e.g., McGovern, 1986). When the whole class decided to dramatize the story and videotape the results for an open house, Linda's students produced a second version in Spanish. Linda wrote about her experience of watching her ESL students perform the play in Spanish:

It was so exciting to see the video of the Spanish-speaking play. The students were confident, they spoke fluently, and their performance was superb. They were not the same students that I hear trying to speak and read haltingly in English. As I watched those students, I couldn't help but wonder how many of our very own second language learners have been labeled as learning disabled or even handicapped, or at the best, have succeeded only to an academic level of mediocrity when in their own language they would have been at the top of the class!

Darrin, a high school teacher who was discouraged by the perceived lack of interest his Hispanic students have shown over the past several years, came back to graduate school to train for a different type of teaching job. As he read about whole language, he began to try new things with his students. The results were positive:

> Today I had students pair up and talk about the 4th of July weekend, about what they usually do on the 4th, and a 4th of July weekend they'll never forget. I went around to every single student and asked what he or she had done. I learned the Spanish word for "fireworks," heard a hilarious story about a student who got run over by a boy on a bike, and found out that one student and her family had spent the night on the floor because their house was shot up last night and the night before. I felt uneasy taking a half hour of class, but when it was time to write, I couldn't believe the volume of stories that seemed to gush out of the students. Each student had two other students read and sign his paper. I've realized that for my students' language acquisition, and my own sanity, that I must begin to initiate and foster social interaction in the classroom.

Darrin's lesson succeeded because he had faith in his students. He encouraged them to use their first language and to talk about things that really mattered to them. As a result, they produced much better writing than ever before.

Individual teachers do make a difference, but teachers working together can do even more. Many schools and special programs support students and show them that they have potential as learners. We would like to share one school's writing project and a special program developed for potential high school dropouts because we believe these types of programs are the hope for the future for second language learners.

Ripperdan School in Madera, California, is a small K–8 school. About 85 percent of the students are Hispanic, many of them from families of migrant workers. Pam, an adjunct teacher of adolescent literature at our college who teaches seventh- and eighth-grade language arts at Ripperdan, shared an all-school project that is an example of how schools can help students believe in themselves. For the past five years the entire school has been involved in the writing process, an area of the curriculum strongly supported by the school administration. The principal and the fifth-grade teacher agreed to work together to collect poetry for an anthology. All the students in the school were invited to participate. Nobody's piece was rejected. Since the students all had writing folders, they picked their favorite piece of poetry to submit for the book.

Poetry was published in both Spanish and English, and students' pictures often were included. Figure 13.18 shows writing from middle school students. The first poem is a commentary on the Persian Gulf conflict; the second expresses a desire for global harmony. Figure 13.19 shows a page where younger students explored science content through poetry.

When the book was completed, an ice cream party was held. Parents and other relatives came. They heard a formal reading of the poetry, and each received a copy of the book. The dedication pages, written in both Spanish and English, show how the entire community is valued at Ripperdan School (Figure 13.20). The poetry anthology is now

Four More Days

I am waiting for the call,

To see if they're going to fight.

Four more days and I'm wondering

If I'll even see my uncle again.

I only met him once.

I hope I get to meet him again.
I wish we could have world peace!!

Latasha   Fulmer
Grade 8

In My World

In my world,

People would not be judged

By the color of their skin.

In my world,

Families would love each other

For who they are.

In my world,

People would trust each other,

And be honest with one another.

Joe Pérez
Grade 7

Figure 13.18 Ripperdan middle school poetry

El Cielo de Noche

Marte es rojo; Neptuno es azul.

Entonces ¿Cual color es nuestro planeta?

¿Sabes tu?

A mi me gusta la luna que brilla brillante.

En el cielo de noche muy gigante.

Me gustan las noches oscuras

Porque me gusta mirar las estrellas brillar,

Aunque muy lejos de mi están.

Carlos Núñez
Tercer Grado

The Night Sky

Mars is red; Neptune is blue.

Then, which color is our planet?

Do you know?

I like the moon that shines brightly
in the huge night sky.

I like dark nights
because I like to look at the stars
although they are very far from me.

Sunshine

Sunshine is bright.

Sunshine is light

That God gave us

To give us sight.

Darkness

Darkness is mean.

Darkness is lean.

I hate the darkness

Because I can't see.

Earth

Mars is red.

Saturn is big.

Earth is where I live.

Noe Alfaro
Grade 5

Rosanna Carrisosa
Grade 5

Figure 13.19 Science concepts in poetry

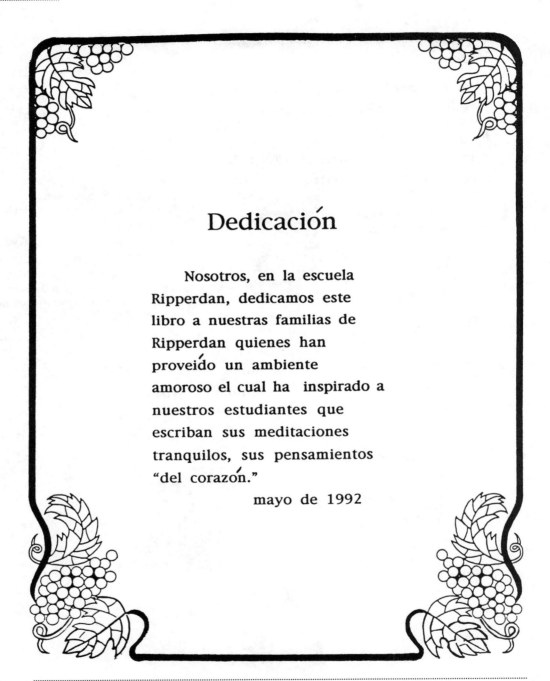

Dedicación

Nosotros, en la escuela Ripperdan, dedicamos este libro a nuestras familias de Ripperdan quienes han proveído un ambiente amoroso el cual ha inspirado a nuestros estudiantes que escriban sus meditaciones tranquilos, sus pensamientos "del corazón."

mayo de 1992

FIGURE 13.20   Dedication pages in Spanish and English

DEDICATION

We, at Ripperdan School, dedicate this book to our Ripperdan families who have provided loving surroundings and encouraged our students to write their tranquil musings, their thoughts "from the heart."

May, 1992

FIGURE 13.20 Continued

on sale at a local children's book store, and the students are excited and pleased that people are buying their book

Bobbi has been working for many years with students who are considered academically underprepared. The program she has developed, The Learning Edge, is designed to involve students in authentic and meaningful reading and writing. We began this chapter with an excerpt from a newsletter put out by a local high school that has a large second language population. This year that school sent sixty at-risk students to work with Bobbi and seven high school teachers in an intensive two-week program. In addition, three college students who had experienced The Learning Edge were included to provide minority role models, to interact with the students, and to assist the teachers with clerical tasks.

The high school students were offered ten units of credit for successfully completing the program. At parent meetings, interpreters explained the importance of the program in four different languages. The students arrived the first day somewhat reluctantly. For the most part, these students had not been successful in school, and now they were on a college campus.

Their nervousness did not last long. The first morning, the teachers gave them their "Philosophy of Learning Edge Faculty" (Figure 13.21). This statement gave the students the clear message that their teachers had a great deal of faith in their potential. Next, the teachers enthusiastically presented book talks on seven books about teens from different cultures coming of age: Cannon's *The Shadow Brothers* (1990); Crew's *Children of the River* (1989); Crutcher's *Chinese Handcuffs* (1989); Fisher-Staples' *Shabanu: Daughter of the Wind* (1989); Hazelgrove's *Ripples* (1992); Herihy's *Ludie's Song* (1988); and Yep's *Child of the Owl* (1977). Students were given binders full of interesting, relevant articles on topics such as teen violence, AIDS, teen pregnancy, gangs, abortion, gun control, corporal and capital punishment, and the use of steroids in sports. Some of the articles were serious and some were humorous, but all were chosen to stimulate discussion.

Each day began with a large-group session during which teachers read and dramatized stories and poetry. They also presented a continual soap opera that was really a mini-lesson in grammar. The teachers then divided the large group of students into different smaller groups for activities that would build a sense of community. In these small groups, students discussed their reading and wrote and shared their writing.

Although it was clear to the students that they would be doing a great deal of reading and writing, they responded positively from the very first day. The teachers' interest in them and in their opinions and their writing made a tremendous difference. Figure 13.22 shows the responses that two students, Laura and Ying, a Hispanic and a Southeast Asian, wrote in their learning logs the first week. These students had not been successful in school previously, but their logs indicate how positive they felt about doing lots of reading and writing. Bobbi's written responses to these students reveal how the teachers encouraged them to keep reading, writing and thinking.

In addition to their learning logs, the students also wrote in literature logs in response to the books they were reading. These entries served to spark lively discus-

Basic Tenets:

1. Each of you is a unique specimen of the human race. We believe your diverse cultural backgrounds make us all richer.

2. Because each of you is a unique person, you have unique stories to share with all of us. We will respect one another's stories.

3. Angels and scumbags come in all colors and both genders. We will not make generalizations about any ethnic group but see each person as an individual with diverse experience even within a culture.

4. Each of you has incredible potential to make a positive difference in the world, and the pursuit of this kind of goal brings greater personal rewards than money can buy. We want to help each of you become the *best you* possible, both personally and academically.

5. Your success in making a positive difference in the world is the cumulative result of lots of little, everyday choices, not one big decision. We will ask you to think about the implications of the everyday decisions you are making.

6. Choosing to be optimistic even when you experience the setbacks and failures that life hands all of us is the most important choice. We believe that when you have worked as hard as you can, failure becomes the fertilizer (Patino, *Success Mag.,* 1992) for future victories which are so much more rewarding.

We invite you to believe these things along with us and challenge us when you see us not living up to our beliefs.

FIGURE *13.21   Philosophy of Learning Edge faculty (By Bobbi Mason and Pam Smith, in collaboration with Louann Baker, Randy Haggard, Linda Medel, Elise Nicoletti, and Jay Pankratz, Fresno Pacific College, Summer 1992)*

sions during the literature studies. At the end of the two weeks, the students wrote about their experiences with the literature studies. Xe, a Hmong girl, wrote:

The lit-log was an great idea. This log really gave us an opportunity to express our feelings about the book. This is the first time I've really been introduce to something like this. Normally at school and other places, they only instruct you to read the book and know things about it for tests only. The lit-log really makes us understand more and more about the book and what could possibly be the author's purpose of writing the book.

Pao, a Hmong boy, wrote:

Being in reading groups has really helped because when I was reading *Child of the Owl* some parts in the story make me confused so when we got into groups I had a chance to ask my peers if they understood it and if they did for them to explain it to me.

6/24/92

So far everything is going really great for me here. Before I came to learning edge I hated to read but now I'm getting more interested in reading cause the stories in the packet are exciting, and so is the book.① Even though we do alot of work I know its for a good cause② and that its going to help me in the future.

① Terrific! Now I know it was worth all the time I spent searching for just the right articles.

② Right. Your mind is a great cause

Bobbi

FIGURE 13.22A   *Learning logs: Laura, day two*

6-24-92

The learning edge, to me
I think it's making me realize
how fun it is to read! and the
teaching, it kind of slow to me right now
but I feel am making progress
in learning the now things that's
been taught. I feel in taking this
course will be a great help to
me to understand more in improving
my reading and writing ②

① Yeah!

② I promise you that this will
make a difference.

6-25-92

Somehow I'm enjoying
Learning Edge, probably because of
the positive thinking that this
will help improved my reading +
writing + and the atmosphere
of teachers, students and people at
Pacific.

Sounds like
you are
surprised by
this.

Yeah! I'm
glad you are a
positive thinker.

Figure 13.22B   *Learning logs: Ying, days two and three*

The students also found the literature logs helped them participate more in class discussions. A reluctant Hmong boy, Mo, found his voice both figuratively and literally:

> I hope that this next coming year our english teacher would do the same what Learning Edge is doing. Ever since I came here I've learned more about reading and writing than before. Literature Study has helped me improve in speaking out loud about my feelings. It has help me see that mine and others are just the same and no ones is different.

The teachers in The Learning Edge were as excited as the students. They witnessed one small miracle after another as students not only participated enthusiastically but also showed new confidence in their reading and writing abilities. Several students who had never before read a complete book on their own proudly finished reading their books within a few days. Following their teachers' demonstrations, the students, including students who were "wannabe" gang members, put on an extemporaneous drama of Shel Silverstein poems for the whole group. At the end of the two weeks, a book of student writing was published. The group celebrated this event by sharing the stories they had written. On the last day a graduation ceremony was held, and students were encouraged as they listened to short talks by their principal and by the vice-president of the college. Then Bobbi read a Dr. Seuss book, *Oh, The Places You'll Go*, and no one doubted, including the students themselves, that they would really go places. Student evaluations at the end of the course are testimony to the newfound confidence these students gained as the result of teachers showing faith in them as learners. Such comments as "I would rather have high school be like this," "I can't wait until next year so I can try the stuff I learned here and relate it to what I am doing in my classes at Roosevelt" and "I've learned things that they would've never taught me at school, like the author's perspective, the opinions, how to skim through an article, how to write notes" show that these students found that learning is exciting and fun.

Second language learners are students with potential. Whole language practices support their learning. But whole language for second language students is not enough without an understanding of second language acquisition, ESL methods, and bilingual education. Whole language teachers who understand what best supports the needs of their bilingual students are truly able to teach the whole student.

FOR FURTHER REFLECTION AND EXPLORATION

1. Watch one second language student over a period of time. Collect writing samples, if possible, and keep a record of what the student reads. Note how the student interacts with classmates. Find out about the student's background and current home situation. Then reflect on what you have observed, analyzing the data in light of the concepts about language acquisition presented in this chapter. What factors

have contributed to this student's school success or failure? What strategies could you use to help this student? Discuss your student with others and compare your findings.

2. Consider some ways you might enrich the context in your classroom to make the input more comprehensible. Try out some of these ideas and then reflect on the results. Did the changes help students? Share your results with others.

3. Review the strategies for supporting students' primary languages. If you have second language students in your class, try some of these. Reflect on the results to see if this has made a difference. In a small group, brainstorm with others additional ways to provide primary language support.

4. During the week, conduct a language survey of your community. Keep note of all the environmental print that reflects languages other than English. In addition, note any print resources (books, magazines, newspapers, pamphlets, etc.) in other languages. Share the results with your classmates.

5. Review the ESL materials that are available in your district and evaluate them in light of the discussion presented in this chapter. What methods and what view of learning do they reflect?

6. Compare a typical ALM lesson with a reading lesson based on a basal reader skills approach. Consider the underlying theories about learning as well as the methods and materials used.

7. Write a letter to your administrator in which you present your position on the best way to work with second language students. Explain what provisions you are making to help all your students succeed. You might also want to share this letter with other teachers and with parents.

Appendix: "Petronella" by Jay Williams

In the kingdom of Skyclear Mountain, three princes were always born to the king and queen.

*   *   *   *   *

The oldest prince was always called Michael, the middle prince was always called George, and the youngest was always called Peter. When they were grown, they always went out to seek their fortunes. What happened to the oldest prince and the middle prince no one ever knew. But the youngest prince always rescued a princess, brought her home, and in time ruled over the kingdom. That was the way it had always been. And so far as anyone knew, that was the way it would always be.

*   *   *   *   *

Until now.

*   *   *   *   *

Now was the time of King Peter the twenty-sixth and Queen Blossom. An oldest prince was born, and a middle prince. But the youngest prince turned out to be a girl.

*   *   *   *   *

"Well, " said the king gloomily, "we can't call her Peter. We'll have to call her Petronella. And what's to be done about it, I'm sure I don't know."

There was nothing to be done. The years passed, and the time came for the princes to go out and seek their fortunes. Michael and George said good-bye to the king and queen and mounted their horses. Then out came Petronella. She was dressed in traveling clothes, with her bag packed and a sword by her side.

*   *   *   *   *

"If you think," she said, "that I'm going to sit at home, you are mistaken. I'm going to seek my fortune too."

"Impossible!" said the king.

Note: Asterisks are used throughout this story to suggest appropriate places to stop and predict what's coming next. Figure 9.17 provides a guided visualization based on Petronella's tasks.

"What will people say?" cried the queen.

"Look," said Prince Michael, "be reasonable, Pet. Stay home. Sooner or later a prince will turn up here."

Petronella smiled. She was a tall, handsome girl with flaming red hair, and when she smiled in that particular way it meant she was trying to keep her temper.

"I'm going with you," she said. "I'll find a prince if I have to rescue one from something myself. And that's that."

*   *   *   *   *

The grooms brought out her horse, she said good-bye to her parents, and away she went behind her two brothers.

They traveled into the flatlands below Skyclear Mountain. After many days, they entered a great dark forest. They came to a place where the road divided into three, and there at the fork sat a little, wrinkled old man covered with dust and spiderwebs.

Prince Michael said haughtily, "Where do these roads go, old man?"

"The road on the right goes to the city of Gratz," the man replied. "The road in the center goes to the castle of Blitz. The road on the left goes to the house of Albion the enchanter. And that's one."

"What do you mean by 'And that's one'?" asked Prince George.

"I mean," said the old man, "that I am forced to sit on this spot without stirring, and that I must answer one question from each person who passes by. And that's two."

*   *   *   *   *

Petronella's kind heart was touched. "Is there anything I can do to help you?" she asked.

The old man sprang to his feet. The dust fell from him in clouds.

"You have already done so," he said. "For that question is the one which releases me. I have sat here for sixty-two years waiting for someone to ask me that." He snapped his fingers with joy. "In return, I will tell you anything you wish to know."

"Where can I find a prince?" Petronella said promptly.

"There is one in the house of Albion the enchanter," the old man answered.

"Ah," said Petronella, "then that is where I am going."

"In that case I will leave you," said her oldest brother. "For I am going to the castle of Blitz to see if I can find my fortune there."

"Good luck," said Prince George. "For I am going to the city of Gratz. I have a feeling my fortune is there."

They embraced her and rode away.

Petronella looked thoughtfully at the old man, who was combing spiderwebs and dust out of his beard. "May I ask you something else?" she said.

"Of course. Anything."

"Suppose I wanted to rescue that prince from the enchanter. How would I go about it? I haven't any experience in such things, you see."

The old man chewed a piece of his beard. "I do not know everything," he said, after a moment. "I know that there are three magical secrets which, if you can get them from him, will help you."

"How can I get them?" asked Petronella.

"Offer to work for him. He will set you three tasks, and if you can do them you may demand a reward for each. You must ask him for a comb for your hair, a mirror to look into, and a ring for your finger."

"And then?"

"I do not know. I only know that when you rescue the prince, you can use these things to escape from the enchanter."

"It doesn't sound easy," sighed Petronella.

"Nothing we really want is easy," said the old man. "Look at me—I have wanted my freedom, and I've had to wait sixty-two years for it."

Petronella said good-bye to him. She mounted her horse and galloped along the third road.

*   *   *   *   *

It ended a low, rambling house with a red roof. It was a comfortable-looking house, surrounded by gardens and stables and trees heavy with fruit.

On the lawn, in an armchair, sat a handsome young man with his eyes closed and his face turned to the sky.

Petronella tied her horse to the gate and walked across the lawn.

"Is this the house of Albion the enchanter?" she said.

The young man blinked up at her in surprise.

"I think so," he said. "Yes, I'm sure it is."

"And who are you?"

The young man yawned and stretched. "I am Prince Ferdinand of Firebright," he replied. "Would you mind stepping aside? I'm trying to get a suntan and you're standing in the way."

Petronella snorted. "You don't sound like much of a prince," she said.

"That's funny," said the young man, closing his eyes. "That's what my father always says."

*   *   *   *   *

At that moment the door of the house opened. Out came a man dressed all in black and silver. He was tall and thin, and as sinister as a cloud full of thunder. His face was stern, but full of wisdom. Petronella knew at once that he must be the enchanter.

He bowed to her politely. "What can I do for you?"

"I wish to work for you," said Petronella boldly.

Albion nodded. "I cannot refuse you," he said. "But I warn you, it will be dangerous. Tonight I will give you a task. If you do it, I will reward you. If you fail, you must die."

Petronella glanced at the prince and sighed. "If I must, I must," she said. "Very well."

*   *   *   *   *

That evening they all had dinner together in the enchanter's cozy kitchen. Then Albion took Petronella out to a stone building and unbolted its door. Inside were seven huge black dogs.

"You must watch my hounds all night," said he.

Petronella went in, and Albion closed and locked the door.

*   *   *   *   *

At once the hounds began to snarl and bark. They showed their teeth at her. But Petronella was a real princess. She plucked up her courage. Instead of backing away, she went toward the dogs. She began to speak to them in a quiet voice. They stopped snarling and sniffed at her. She patted their heads.

"I see what it is," she said. "You are lonely here. I will keep you company."

And so all night long, she sat on the floor and talked to the hounds and stroked them. They lay close to her, panting.

In the morning Albion came and let her out. "Ah," said he, "I see that you are brave. If you had run from the dogs, they would have torn you to pieces. Now you may ask for what you want."

"I want a comb for my hair," said Petronella.

The enchanter gave her a comb carved from a piece of black wood.

Prince Ferdinand was sunning himself and working at a crossword puzzle. Petronella said to him in a low voice, "I am doing this for you."

"That's nice," said the prince. "What's 'selfish' in nine letters?"

"You are," snapped Petronella. She went to the enchanter. "I will work for you once more," she said.

That night Albion led her to a stable. Inside were seven huge horses.

"Tonight," he said, "you must watch my steeds."

He went out and locked the door. At once the horses began to rear and neigh. They pawed at her with their iron hoofs.

*   *   *   *   *

But Petronella was a real princess. She looked closely at them and saw that their coats were rough and their manes and tails full of burrs.

"I see what it is," she said. "You are hungry and dirty."

She brought them as much hay as they could eat, and began to brush them. All night long she fed them and groomed them, and they stood quietly in their stalls.

In the morning Albion let her out. "You are as kind as you are brave," said he. "If you had run from them, they would have trampled you under their hoofs. What will you have as a reward?"

"I want a mirror to look into," said Petronella.

The enchanter gave her a mirror made of gray silver.

She looked across the lawn at Prince Ferdinand. He was doing setting-up exercises. He was certainly handsome. She said to the enchanter, "I will work for you once more."

That night Albion led her to a loft above the stables. There, on perches, were seven great hawks.

"Tonight," said he, "you must watch my falcons."

As soon as Petronella was locked in, the hawks began to beat their wings and scream at her.

*   *   *   *   *

Petronella laughed. "That is not how birds sing," she said. "Listen."

She began to sing in a sweet voice. The hawks fell silent. All night long she sang to them, and they sat like feathered statues on their perches, listening.

In the morning, Albion said, "You are as talented as you are kind and brave. If you had run from them, they would have pecked and clawed you without mercy. What do you want now?"

"I want a ring for my finger," said Petronella.

*   *   *   *   *

The enchanter gave her a ring made from a single diamond.

All that day and all that night Petronella slept, for she was very tired. But early the next morning, she crept into Prince Ferdinand's room. He was sound asleep, wearing purple pajamas.

"Wake up," whispered Petronella. "I am going to rescue you."

*   *   *   *   *

Ferdinand awoke and stared sleepily at her. "What time is it?"

"Never mind that," said Petronella. "Come on!"

"But I'm sleepy," Ferdinand objected. "And it's so pleasant here."

Petronella shook her head. "You're not much of a prince," she said grimly. "But you're the best I can do."

She grabbed him by the wrist and dragged him out of bed. She hauled him down the stairs. His horse and hers were in a separate stable, and she saddled them quickly. She gave the prince a shove, and he mounted. She jumped on her own horse, seized the prince's reins, and away they went like the wind.

*   *   *   *   *

They had not gone far when they heard a tremendous thumping. Petronella looked back. A dark cloud rose behind them, and beneath it she saw the enchanter. He was running with great strides, faster than the horses could go.

Petronella desperately pulled out he comb. "The old man said this would help me!" she said. And because she didn't know what else to do with it, she threw the comb on the ground.

At once a forest rose up. The trees were so thick that no one could get between them.

Away went Petronella and the prince. But the enchanter turned himself into an ax and began to chop. Right and left he chopped, flashing, and the trees fell before him.

Soon he was through the wood, and once again Petronella heard his footsteps thumping behind.

She reined in the horses. She took out the mirror and threw it on the ground. At once a wide lake spread out behind them, gray and glittering.

Off they went again. But the enchanter sprang into the water, turning himself into a salmon as he did so. He swam across the lake and leaped out of the water on to the other bank. Petronella heard him coming—*thump! thump!*—behind them again.

This time she threw down the ring. It didn't turn into anything, but lay shining on the ground.

The enchanter came running up. And as he jumped over the ring, it opened wide and then snapped up around him. It held his arms tight to his body, in a magical grip from which he could not escape.

"Well," said Prince Ferdinand, "that's the end of him."

Petronella looked at him in annoyance. Then she looked at the enchanter, held fast in the ring.

*   *   *   *   *

"Bother!" she said. "I can't just leave him here. He'll starve to death."

She got off her horse and went up to him. "If I release you," she said, "will you promise to let the prince go free?"

Albion stared at her in astonishment. "Let him go free?" he said. "What are you talking about? I'm glad to get rid of him."

It was Petronella's turn to look surprised. "I don't understand," she said. "Weren't you holding him prisoner?"

"Certainly not," said Albion. "He came to visit me for a weekend. At the end of it, he said, 'It's so pleasant here, do you mind if I stay on for another day or two?' I'm very polite and I said, 'Of course.' He stayed on, and on, and on. I didn't like to be rude to a guest and I couldn't just kick him out. I don't know what I'd have done if you hadn't dragged him away."

*   *   *   *   *

"But then—" said Petronella, "but then—why did you come running after him this way?"

"I wasn't chasing him," said the enchanter. "I was chasing *you.* You are just the girl I've been looking for. You are brave and kind and talented, and beautiful as well."

"Oh," said Petronella.

"I see," she said.

"Hmm," said she. "How do I get this ring off you?"

"Give me a kiss."

She did so. The ring vanished from around Albion and reappeared on Petronella's finger.

"I don't know what my parents will say when I come home with you instead of a prince," she said.

"Let's go and find out, shall we?" said the enchanter cheerfully.

He mounted one horse and Petronella the other. And off they trotted, side by side, leaving Prince Ferdinand of Firebright to walk home as best he could.

*   *   *   *   *

Notes

1. DEFINITIONS OF READING

1. Function words are the "little words" that glue the content words together. The main types of function words are as follows: noun determiners (e.g., *the,* and *this* in the phrase *this boy);* verb auxiliaries (e.g., *will* in *will win);* prepositions (e.g., *by* in *by the lake);* and conjunctions (e.g., *because* and *and).* For a more thorough discussion of these and other parts of speech (grammatical categories), see Chapter 2.

2. In the TORP, there are eight to ten items designed to reveal each of three different teacher orientations:

> phonics: 1, 2, 3, 6, 9, 10, 12, 20, 21, 22
> skills: 4, 8, 11, 13, 14, 16, 19, 24, 25, 28
> whole language: 5, 7, 15, 17, 18, 23, 26, 27

That is, teachers who strongly agree with the phonics items have a strong phonics orientation, those who strongly agree with the skills items have a strong skills orientation, and those who strongly agree with the whole language items have a strong whole language orientation. It is possible to have more than one strong orientation. Since 1 is "strongly agree" and 5 is "strongly disagree" on the TORP, a low numerical score reflects strong agreement and a high score reflects strong disagreement.

In research validating the TORP, the teachers were preidentified as having a phonics, skills, or whole language orientation before they took the TORP. For the 90 teachers in the study (30 in each group), the average (mean) scores were as follows:

	Phonics items	Skills items	Whole language items
Phonics group	19.47	24.37	30.37
Skills group	26.87	23.87	28.23
Whole language group	48.40	47.50	9.13

The greatest and perhaps most interesting difference is between the whole language groups and the other two (see DeFord, 1985).

2. HOW LANGUAGE MEANS

1. I am grateful to my colleague Jim Burns for introducing me to a similar activity and to the book from which these "lost words" are taken: Susan Kelz Sperling's *Poplollies*

and Bellibones: A Celebration of Lost Words (1977). Given the brevity of Sperling's definitions, it is possible that some words may have been misused in my story. In any case, here are her definitions:

Bellytimber—Food, provisions
Blonke—A large, powerful horse
Blore—To cry out or bleat and bray like an animal
Crinet—A hair
Drumly—Cloudy, sluggish
Fairney cloots—Small horny substances above the hoofs of horses, sheep, and goats
Flosh—A swamp or stagnant pool overgrown with weeds
Givel—To heap up
Icchen—To move, stir
Kexy—Dry, juiceless
Lennow—Flappy, limp
Maily—Speckled
Quetch—To moan and twitch in pain, shake
Samded—Half-dead
Shawk—Smell
Sparple—To scatter, spread about
Spiss—Thick, dense
Venenate—To poison
Wam—A scar, cicatrix
Wong—Meadowlands, commons
Yerd—To beat with a rod

2. This transactional model of the reading process emphasizes the top-down processing and the irreducible complexity of the reading process more than most so-called interactive models of reading. See, for example, Rumelhart, 1977; Stanovich, 1980; and Lesgold & Perfetti, 1981.

3. For this revised version of the original figure in *Reading Process and Practice,* I thank Janet Bonifield, Sue Carter, Cheryl Chapman, Jura Hughes, Marilyn L. Peackcok, Mary Ann Savage, Jeni L. Savaria, and Linda Wybocki.

3. TEACHING READING AND DEVELOPING LITERACY

1. Here are the stories with the children's original spellings (Cramer, 1978, p. 44):

I play in the grass
And I play with my frads
And I play with Debbie.
                  —Mary

My Dad is nice
My Mom is nice
My sistrss is nice
                  —Danielle

Wane the poho   I kak My had I fel
One evng wane wt   off the bed My Mom
iut toget some hane   Tok Me tothe hsptl
he kalimd and kalimd   —Nathalie
for hanne he fnd hane.
              —John

2. During the next school year, Emily's teacher found her to be a very good speller, even in first drafts. Between the ages of nine and ten, she had caught onto spelling—without the "benefit" of having been taught to spell.

4. CONTEXT, WORD IDENTIFICATION, AND CONSTRUCTING MEANING

1. The omitted words are: (1) aren't, (2) Most, (3) three, (4) and, (5) 40, (6) of, (7) most, (8) is, (9) as, (10) Beavers, (11) dams, (12) They, (13) paws, (14) their, (15) tree, (16) pointed, (17) beaver, (18) tree, (19) about.

2. *Kalamazoo Gazette,* August 1, 1978, p. A–1. The article was a UPI tidbit originating in Chicago.

3. To see this for yourself, try a brief experiment with someone you know to be a reasonably proficient reader. First, locate a book that the person has not read, but that will not be especially difficult for him or her. Have the person begin reading a page aloud, and after a few lines stop the person's reading by suddenly turning out the light (if it is dark) or by putting your hand over the part being read. Then ask the person to tell you what words he or she saw beyond the word last focused upon. If you repeat this procedure several times, you will probably find that the person can report, on the average, about four additional words. Typically, the person will have picked up those words that complete a syntactic unit of some sort: thus, one person undertaking such an experiment reported the following, when the light was turned off five different times: *but rather because of; from the galactic rim; none completely satifactory; of the universe; but as the ship leaves.* The words perceived beyond the word focused upon consitute the person's *eye-voice span,* or *EVS*: the number of words the eye is ahead of the voice. In silent reading, of course, one has a similar *eye-memory span,* or *EMS*: the number of words the eye is ahead of the word being focused upon (Dechant, 1970, p. 18; see Anderson & Dearborn, 1952, pp. 127–136). The EVS and the EMS indicate the number of following words seen during one eye fixation, in addition to the word being identified. These additional words may be used in identifying the word being focused upon.

4. When I tried to locate "Jimmy Hayes and Muriel" through a short story index, the entry under "Frogs, horned" referred me to an entry for horned *toads.* I have since discovered that so-called horned frogs do exist, though.

5. Here is the original passage:

The crack of the rifle volley cut the suddenly still air. It appeared to go on, as a solid volley, for perhaps a full minute or a little longer.

Some of the students dived to the ground, crawling on the grass in terror. Others stood shocked or half crouched, apparently believing the troops were firing into the air. Some of the rifle barrels were pointing upward.

Near the top of the hill at the corner of Taylor Hall, a student crumpled over, spun sideways and fell to the ground, shot in the head.

When the firing stopped, a slim girl, wearing a cowboy shirt and faded jeans, was lying face down on the road at the edge of the parking lot, blood pouring out onto the macadam, about 10 feet from this reporter.

6. My opinion supported the position of the family. The definitions in some of our major dictionaries suggested that the word *passenger* at least *could* be taken to include the operator of a vehicle. Ultimately, however, the Michigan Supreme Court ruled in support of the insurance company's interpretation, arguing that the "ordinary man" would not consider the operator of a vehicle to be one of its passengers (*Kinnavy v. Traill,* 1976).

7. One important point about such "grammatical" miscues is that they are not all grammatical in nature. Their origin may be phonological, as is the apparent omission of the past tense marker by speakers of Black English Vernacular. The past tense marker is absent from Black English Vernacular primarily when the base word is a regular verb ending in a consonant other than /t/ or /d/. In such cases, addition of the past tense ending results in a consonant cluster (the examples are mostly from Fasold & Wolfram, 1970, p. 45):

stopped /pt/	rubbed /bd/
looked /kt/	hugged /gd/
laughed /ft/	loved /vd/
unearthed /θt/	seethed /ðd/
missed /st/	raised /zd/
watched /čt/	judged / ǰd/
finished /št/	
	named /md/
	rained /nd/
	hanged /ŋd/
	called /ld/
	cured /rd/

In each case, the past tense ending is represented by /t/ or /d/. Word-final consonant clusters are especially likely to be simplified when they end in a /t/ or /d/, and virtually all speakers of English show some tendancy to omit the final /t/ or /d/ when it does not represent a tense marker. Such omission is particularly common when the word in question precedes a word that begins with a consonant, as in "She *just* left" or "I'll *find* the book." Speakers of so-called standard English occasionally omit even a past tense /t/ or /d/ when the following word begins with a consonant, as in "I *missed* Mike" and "He *lived* near me." Speakers of Black English simply carry this tendancy somewhat further, with the result that they are often perceived as consistently omitting past tense markers although in reality their usage varies, as it does for all of us. The same is true of other dialect features.

8. Pearson and Johnson are in turn indebted to W. Dorsey Hammond of Oakland University in Rochester, Michigan, who is indebted to Russell Stauffer for the example.

9. I like the word *sneakers* best here, because its connotation seems to fit best with the description of the passage. Other good possibilities are *tennis shoes and gym shoes.* Check Bradbury to see which word he chose!

10. Note that in this approximation of Black English, past time is not always indicated by the verb form itself, even for verbs that express the past by some means other than the mere addition of /t/ or /d/.

11. This nonsense word comes from an article by Robert Hillerich (1977, p. 301). Hillerich explains, "To arrive at the spelling, one could consider *n* as the most likely beginning letter, although the other reasonable possibilities are *kn (know), gn (gnaw), pn (pneumonia),* and *mn (mnemonic)*. The /ē/ in medial position could be spelled *ae (aegis), e (between), ea (meat), ee (meet), ei (neither), ie (chief), eo (people), ey (keynote),* or *oe (amoeba)*; /d/ is easy—it is *d* or *dd*; /ər/ could be *ar (liar), er (term), ir (first),* or *(worm), ur (turn), ear (learn), our (journey), eur (chauffeur),* or *yr (myrtle)*; /l/ again is easy as either *l* or *ll,* but final /ē/ could be *ay (quay), i (ski), ee (see), ey (key), y (baby), e (be),* or *ois (chamois)*. In fact, we have demonstrated that the nonsense word could be spelled in 5 x 9 x 2 x 9 x 2 x 7, or 11,340 different ways. Of course, if one were unfamiliar with the influence of position, seventeen different spellings of /ē/ would have to be considered for both occurrences, increasing the possibilities to 52,020!"

5. FROM WORD PERCEPTION TO PHONICS, AND BEYOND

1. However, it is becoming evident that a significant number of children and adults have eye-based reading problems that are not diagnosed by the typical eye examination. Some researchers, particularly Mary C. Williams at the University of New Orleans and William Lovegrove of the University of Wollongong in Australia, think that visual problems in reading may stem from inefficient processing of what is called the transient subsystem—"the neural switchboard that processes information on depth, motion, and eye movements (Weiss, 1990, p. 196). Other researchers describe similar problems as a Scotopic Sensitivity Syndrome (Irlen, 1983), which includes the following apects of perception: "*photophobia* (a sensitivity to glare, brightness, and light intensity, especially fluorescent lighting), *background accommodation* (ability to accommodate the contrast of black print on white pages), *visual resolution* (seeing print without distortions), *span of focus* (perceiving groups of words clearly at the same time), and *sustained focus* (performing precise visual tasks of an extended period)" (Rickelman & Henk, 1990, p. 166). Individuals with SSS may experience some or all of these conditions, to varying degrees. Overt symptoms that may indicate Scotopic Sensitivity Syndrome include "abnormal sensitivity to light, blinking and squinting, red and watery eyes, frequent

headaches, word blurriness, print instability, slow reading, skipping and rereading lines, and difficulty reading at length due to general eye-strain and fatigue" (Richelman & Henk, 1990, p. 166). For many individuals with SSS or vision problems of a similar nature, reading is made easier by placing a sheet of translucent, colored plastic over the text being read, or by wearing tinted lenses. Different people's eyes are helped by different colors; however, some shade of blue or light gray is particularly helpful for many people (Weiss, 1990). Of course such overlays and filters (as they are commonly called) cannot help with reading problems of a non-visual origin, but for readers with some of the aforementioned eye problems, it may be worthwhile to see whether colored overlays would help. For some of the research, see Weiss, 1990; O'Connor, Sofo, Kendall, & Olsen, 1990, and Robinson & Conway, 1990; for a valuable introduction to the concept of a Scotopic Sensitivity Syndrome, see Rickelman & Henk, 1990, and/or contact the Irlen Institute for Perceptual and Learning Development, 5380 Village Road, Long Beach, CA 90808.

2. It seems to me that the terms *perception, identification,* and *recognition* are nearly synonymous; hence, I use them more or less interchangeably. My particular choice in any given instance is dictated by connotation rather than denotation: it seems to me that "percpeption" more readily includes the possibility of error, and that "identification" and "recognition" imply *accurate* perception. Note, however, that all three indicate a decision on the part of the *brain.*

3. The words, in order of occurrence, are: *could, short, about, voice, trust, scarf, drank, ghost, which, stand.* For a similar list of mutilated words, see Anderson & Dearborn, 1952, p. 189; they reproduced the words by permission from a test constructed by L. L. Thurstone.

4. One interesting example of such experiments involved the reversal of two letters at the beginning or the middle or the end of a word, as with *vaiation, avitaion,* and *aviatino* for the word *aviation.* The words were hardest to identify when the reversal occurred at the beginning, and easiest to identify when the reversal occurred in the middle: thus, the experiment suggests that beginnings are most important in word perception and middles are least important (Bruner & O'Dowd, 1958).

5. The sentence reads, "This demonstrates that text becomes relatively illegible when a comparable proportion of randomly selected letters has been removed" (Adams, 1990a, citing Miller & Friedman, 1957).

Professional Works Cited

Abrahamson, R. F. & Carter, B. (Eds.). (1988). *Books for you: A booklist for senior high students.* Urbana, IL: National Council of Teachers of English.

Adams, M. J. (1990a). *Beginning to read: Thinking and learning about print.* Cambridge: Harvard University Press.

Adams, M. J. (1990b). *Beginning to read: Thinking and learning about print: A summary.* Summarized by Steven A. Stahl, Jean Osborn, & Fran Lehr. Champaign, IL: University of Illinois, Center for the Study of Reading.

Adams, M. J., & Collins, A. (1979). A schema-theoretic view of reading. In R. O. Freedle (Ed.), *New directions in discourse processing* (pp. 1–22). Norwood, NJ: Ablex.

Adelman, H. S. (1992). LD: The next 25 years. *Journal of Learning Disabilities, 25,* 17–22.

Allen, J. (1989). Illiteracy in America: What do do about it. *The Heritage Foundation Backgrounder*, February 10. Washington, DC: Heritage Foundation.

Allen, J. B. (1985). Inferential comprehension: The effects of text source, decoding ability, and mode. *Reading Research Quarterly, 20,* 603–615.

Allen, J. B., & Mason, J. M. (Eds.). (1989). *Risk makers, risk takers, risk breakers: Reducing the risks for young literacy learners.* Portsmouth, NH: Heinemann.

Allen, J. B., Shockley, B., & West, M. (1991). "I'm really worried about Joseph": Reducing the risks of literacy learning. *The Reading Teacher, 44*, 458–468.

Allen, P. D., & Watson, D. J. (Eds.). (1976). *Findings of research in miscue analysis: Classroom implications.* Urbana, IL: ERIC Clearinghouse on Reading and Communication Skills and the National Council of Teachers of English.

Allington, R. L. (1983). The reading instruction provided readers of differing reading abilities. *The Elementary School Journal, 83*, 548–559.

Allington, R. L. (1987). Shattered hopes: Why two federal reading programs have failed to correct reading failure. *Learning 87* (16), 61–64.

Allington, R. L. (1991). The legacy of "slow it down and make it more concrete." In J. Zutell & S. McCormick (Eds.), *Learner factors/teacher factors: Issues in literacy research and instruction* (pp. 19–29). Chicago: National Reading Conference.

Allington, R. L., & McGill-Franzen, A. (1989a). Different programs, indifferent instruction. In D. Lipsky & A. Gartner (Eds.), *Beyond separate education: Quality education for all* (pp. 75–98). Baltimore: Paul Brookes.

Allington, R. L., & McGill-Franzen, A. (1989b). School response to reading failure: Instruction for Chapter 1 and special education students in grades two, four, and eight. *The Elementary School Journal, 89,* 530–542.

Allington, R., Stuetzel, H., & Shake, M. (1986). What is remedial reading: A descriptive study. *Reading Research and Instruction, 26* (1), 15–30.

Altwerger, B. (1991). Whole language teachers: Empowered professionals. In J. Hydrick (Ed.), *Whole language: Empowerment at the chalk face* (pp. 15–29). New York: Scholastic.

Altwerger, B., & Bird, L. (1982). Disabled: The learner or the curriculum? *Topics in Learning and Learning Disabilities, 1*, 69–78.

Altwerger, B., Edelsky, C., & Flores, B. M. (1987). Whole language: What's new? *Reading Teacher, 41*, 144–154.

Altwerger, B., & Resta, V. (1986). Comparing standardized test scores and miscues. Paper presented at the annual meeting of the International Reading Association, Philadelphia. May.

Altwerger, B. & Saavedra, E. (1989). Thematic units vs. theme cycles. Workshop presented at CEL conference, Winnipeg. February.

Anderson, I. H., & Dearborn, W. F. (1952). *The psychology of teaching reading.* New York: Ronald Press.

Anderson, L. W., & Pellicer, L. O. (1990). Synthesis of research on compensatory and remedial education. *Educational Leadership, 48,* 10–16.

Anderson, R. C., & Freebody, P. (1983). Reading comprehension and the assessment and acquisition of word knowledge. In B. Hutson (Ed.), *Advances in reading/language research* (pp. 231–256). Greenwich, CT: JAI Press.

Anderson, R. C., Hiebert, E. H., Scott, J. A., & Wilkinson, I. A. G. (1985). *Becoming a nation of readers: The report of the commission on reading.* Champaign, IL: Center for the Study of Reading, University of Illinois.

Anderson, R. C., Spiro, R. J., & Anderson, M. C. (1977). *Schemata as scaffolding for the representation of meaning in connected discourse.* (Tech. Rep. no. 24.) Urbana, IL: Center for the Study of Reading. (ERIC): (ED 136-236)

Andrasick, K. D. (1990). *Opening texts: Using writing to teach literature.* Portsmouth, NH: Boynton/Cook–Heinemann.

The Ann Arbor decision: Memorandum opinion and order and the educational plan. (1979). Arlington, VA: Center for Applied Linguistics.

Anthony, R. J., Johnson, T. D., Mickelson, N. I., & Preece, A. (1991). *Evaluating literacy: A perspective for change.* Portsmouth, NH: Heinemann.

Anyon, J. (1980). Social class and the hidden curriculum of work. *Journal of Education, 162,* 67–92.

Apple, M. W. (1982). *Cultural and economic reproduction in education: Essays on class, ideology and the state.* Boston: Routledge & Kegan Paul.

Applebee, A. N. (1981). *Writing in the secondary school: English and the content areas.* Urbana, IL: National Council of Teachers of English.

Applebee, A. N., Langer, J. A., & Mullis, I. V. S. (1988a). *Learning to be literate in America: Reading, writing, and reasoning.* The nation's report card. Princeton, NJ: National Assessment of Educational Progress, Educational Testing Service.

Applebee, A. N., Langer, J. A., & Mullis, I. V. S. (1988b). *Who reads best? Factors related to reading achievement in grades 3, 7, and 11.* Princeton, NJ: National Assessment of Educational Progress, Educational Testing Service.

Applebee, A. N., Langer, J. A., & Mullis, I. V. S. (1989). *Crossroads in American education.* Princeton, NJ: National Assessment of Educational Progress, Educational Testing Service.

Applebee, A. N., Langer, J. A., Mullis, I. V. S., & Jenkins, L. B. (1990). *The writing report card, 1984–88.* Princeton, NJ: National Assessment of Educational Progress, Educational Testing Service.

Arbuthnot, M. H. (1961). *The Arbuthnot anthology of children's literature.* Glenview, IL: Scott, Foresman.

Arbuthnot, M. H. (1976). *The Arbuthnot anthology of children's literature* (4th ed.). Revised by Zena Sutherland. Glenview, IL: Scott, Foresman.

Aronowitz, S., & Giroux, H. A. (1991). *Postmodern education: Politics, culture, and social criticism.* Minneapolis: University of Minnesota Press.

Asher, J. (1977). *Learning another language through actions: The complete teacher's guide.* Los Gatos, CA: Sky Oaks Publications.

Assembly Newsletter, 1 (1), 2.

Atwell, N. (1987). *In the middle: Writing, reading, and learning with adolescents.* Portsmouth, NH: Boynton/Cook–Heinemann.

Atwell, N. (Ed.). (1990). *Coming to know: Writing to learn in the intermediate grades.* Portsmouth, NH: Heinemann.

Atwell, N., & Giacobbe, M. E. (1985). Reading, writing, thinking, learning. Course at Institute on Teaching and Writing, sponsored by Northeastern University. Martha's Vineyard, MA. July.

Au, K. (1980). Participation structures in a reading lesson with Hawaiian children: Analysis of a culturally appropriate instructional event. *Anthropology and Education Quarterly, 11*, 91–115.

Au, K., & Jordan, C. (1981). Hawaiian Americans: Teaching reading to Hawaiian children: Finding a culturally appropriate solution. In H. Trueba, G. Guthrie, & K. Au (Eds.), *Culture and the bilingual classroom: Studies in classroom ethnography* (pp. 139–152). Rowley, MA: Newbury House.

Avery, C. S. (1985). Lori "figures it out": A young writer learns to read. In J. Hansen, T. Newkirk, & D. Graves (Eds.), *Breaking ground: Teachers relate reading and writing in the elementary school* (pp. 15–28). Portsmouth, NH: Heinemann.

Baddeley, A. D., & Lewis, V. (1981). Inner active processes in reading: The inner voice, the inner ear, and the inner eye. In C. A. Perfetti & A. M. Lesgold (Eds.), *Interactive processes in reading* (pp. 107–129). Hillsdale, NJ: Erlbaum.

Baghban, M. (1984). *Our daughter learns to read and write: A case study from birth to three.* Newark, DE: International Reading Association.

Bailey, M. H. (1967). The utility of phonic generalizations in grades one through six. *The Reading Teacher, 20,* 413–418.

Baker, A. & Greene, E. (1987). *Storytelling: Art and technique* (2nd ed.). New York, Bowker.

Baker, K. A., & de Kanter, A. A. (1981). *Effectiveness of bilingual education: A review of the literature.* Washington, DC: Office of Planning and Budget, U.S. Department of Education.

Baker, L., & Brown, A. L. (1984). Cognitive monitoring in reading. In J. Flood (Ed.), *Understanding reading comprehension* (pp. 21–44). Newark, DE: International Reading Association.

Banks, W. P., Oka, E., & Shugarman, S. (1981). Internal speech: Does recoding come before lexical access? In O. J. L. Tzeng & H. Singer (Eds.), *Perception of print: Reading research in experimental psychology* (pp. 137–170). Hillsdale, NJ: Erlbaum.

Baratz, J. C. (1969). Teaching reading in an urban Negro school system. In J. C. Baratz & R. W. Shuy (Eds.), *Teaching black children to read* (pp. 102–116). Arlington, VA: Center for Applied Linguistics.

Baratz, J., & Stewart, W. (1970). *Friends.* Washington, DC: Education Study Center.

Barchers, S. I. (1993). *Readers theatre for beginning readers.* Englewood, CO: Libraries Unlimited/Teacher Ideas Press.

Baren, M. (1989). The case for Ritalin: A fresh look at the controversy. *Contemporary Pediatrics, 6* (January), 16–28.

Barkley, R. A. (1990). *Attention Deficit Hyperactivity Disorder: A handbook for diagnosis and treatment.* New York: Guilford Press.

Baron, J., & Treiman, R. (1980). Use of orthography in reading and learning to read. In J. Kavanaugh & R. Venezky (Eds.), *Orthography, reading and dyslexia.* Baltimore: University Park Press.

Barr, R. (1975). Processes underlying the learning of printed words. *The Elementary School Journal, 75,* 258–268.

Barrera, R. (1983). Bilingual reading in the primary grades: Some questions about questionable views and practices. In T. Escobedo (Ed.), *Early childhood bilingual education: A Hispanic perspective* (pp. 164–184). New York: Columbia University Press.

Barrett, F. L. (1982). *A teacher's guide to shared reading.* Richmond Hill, Ontario: Scholastic.

Barrs, M. (1990). The Primary Language Record: Reflection of issues in education. *Language Arts 67,* 244–253.

Barrs, M., Ellis, S., Tester, H. & Thomas, A. (1989). [Center for Language in Primary Education]. *The Primary Language Record: A handbook for teachers.* Portsmouth, NH: Heinemann.

Bartoli, J., & Botel, M. (1988). *Reading/learning disability: An ecological approach.* New York: Teachers College Press.

Barton, B., (1986). *Tell me another: Storytelling and reading aloud at home, at school, and in the community.* Portsmouth, NH: Heinemann.

Barton, B. & Booth, D. (1990). *Stories in the classroom*. Markham, Ontario: Pembroke.

The basal reader in American reading instruction. (1987). Themed issue of *The Elementary School Journal, 87*(3).

Baskwill, J. & Whitman, P. (1988). *Evaluation: Whole language, whole child*. Richmond Hill, Ontario: Scholastic.

Bateman, B. D. (1974). Educational implications of minimal brain dysfunction. *The Reading Teacher, 27*, 662–668.

Bateson, G. (1972). *Steps to an ecology of mind*. New York: Ballantine.

Bauer, C. F. (1977). *Handbook for storytellers*. Chicago: American Library Association.

Bauer, C. F. (1985). *Celebration*. New York: H. W. Wilson.

Bauer, C. F. (1987). *Presenting reader's theater*. New York: H. W. Wilson.

Beach, R., Green, J. L., Kamil, M. L., Shanahan, T. (Eds.) (1992). *Multidisciplinary perspectives on literacy research*. Urbana, IL: National Council of Teachers of English.

Beck, I., McKeown, M. G., & McCaslin, E. S. (1983). *Vocabulary development: All contexts are not created equal*. Elementary School Journal, *83* (3), 177–181.

Becker, W. C., & Gersten, R. (1982). A follow-up of Follow Through: The later effects of the direct instruction model on children in fifth and sixth grades. *American Educational Research Journal, 19*, 75–92.

Belanoff, P., & Dickson, M. (1991). *Portfolio grading: Process and product*. Portsmouth, NH: Boynton/Cook–Heinemann.

Belt, L., & Stockley, R. (1991). *Improvisation through theatresports*. Puyallup, WA: Thespis Productions.

Benedict, S. (1991). *Beyond words: Picture books for older readers and writers*. Portsmouth, NH: Heinemann.

Bennett, W. (1988). In defense of our common language. In *Our children and our country: Improving America's schools and affirming the common culture* (pp. 180–190). New York: Simon & Schuster.

Berdiansky, B., Cronnell, B., & Koehler, J. (1969). *Spelling-sound relations and primary form-class descriptions for speech-comprehension vocabularies of 6–9 year-olds*. (Tech. Rep. no. 15.) Inglewood, CA: Southwest Regional Laboratory for Educational Research and Development.

Berko, J. (1958). The child's learning of English morphology. *Word, 14*, 150–177.

Berman, et al. (1992). Meeting the challenge of language diversity: An evaluation of California programs for pupils with limited proficiency in English. (#R–119/1) Berkeley, CA: BW Associates. (ERIC: ED 347 837)

Betts, E. A. (1946). *Foundations of reading instruction*. New York: American Book Company.

Biemiller, A. (1970). The development of the use of graphic and contextual information as children learn to read. *Reading Research Quarterly, 1*, 77–96.

Bigelow, W. (1992). Once upon a genocide: Christopher Columbus in children's literature. *Language Arts, 69*, 112–120.

Bird, L. B. (1989). *Becoming a whole language school: The Fair Oaks story*. Katonah, NY: Richard C. Owen.

Bird, L., & Alvarez, L. (1987). Beyond comprehension: The power of literature study for language minority students. *Elementary ESOL Education News, 10* (1), 1–3.

Bishop, J. E. Stroke patients yield clues to brain's ability to create language. (1933, Oct. 12). *Wall Street Journal, 74* (253) 1, 6.

Bissex, G. (1980). Gnys at wrk: A child learns to write and read. Cambridge: Harvard University Press.

Blair, R. (1982). *Innovative approaches to language teaching*. Rowley, MA: Newbury House.

Bleich, D. (1975). *Readings and feelings: An introduction to subjective criticism*. Urbana, IL: National Council of Teachers of English.

Bloom, B., Madaus, G., & Hastings, J. T. (1981). *Evaluation to improve learning*. New York: McGraw-Hill.

Bloome, D. (1985). Reading as a social process. *Language Arts, 62*, 134–142.

Bloome, D. (1987). Reading as a social process in a middle school classroom. In David Bloome (Ed.), *Literacy and schooling (*pp. 123–149). Norwood, NJ: Ablex.

Bloome, D., & Green, J. (1985). Looking at reading instruction: Sociolinguistic and ethnographic approaches. In C. N. Hedley & A. N. Baratta (Eds.), *Contexts of reading* (pp. 167–184). Norwood, NJ: Ablex.

Bloomfield, L. (1942). Linguistics and reading. *The Elementary English Review, 19,* 125–130, 183–186.

Bloomfield, L., & Barnhart, C. L. (1961). *Let's read: A linguistic approach.* Detroit: Wayne State University Press.

Blumenfeld, S. L. (1983). *Alpha-phonics: A primer for beginning readers.* Boise, ID: The Paradigm Company.

Blumenfeld, S. L. (1992). The whole language fraud. *The New American, 8,* August 10, pp. 6–8.

Blumenfeld, S. L. (1992). *The whole language fraud.* Boise, ID: The Paradigm Company.

Boatner, M. T., Gates, J. E., & Makkai, A. (1987). *A dictionary of American idioms* (2nd ed.). New York: Barrons.

Boder, E. (1973). Developmental dyslexia: A diagnostic approach based on three atypical reading-spelling patterns. *Developmental Medicine and Child Neurology 15,* 663–687.

Bogdan, D. & Straw, S. B. (1990). *Beyond communication: Reading comprehension and criticism.* Portsmouth, NH: Boynton/Cook–Heinemann.

Bond, G. L., & R. Dykstra. (1967). The cooperative research program in first-grade reading instruction. *Reading Research Quarterly, 2,* 5–142.

Bookshelf. Stage 1: Teacher's Resource Book. (1986). New York: Scholastic.

Boomer, G. (1988). Metaphors and meanings: Essays on English teaching by Garth Boomer. Ed. Bill Green. Hawthorne, Victoria: Australian Association for the Teaching of English. (Distributed in the U.S. by the National Council of Teachers of English.

Booth, D. (1986). *Games for everyone.* Markham, Ontario: Pembroke.

Booth, D. & Lundy, C. J. (1985). *Improvisation.* Toronto: Academic Press.

Booth, D., Swartz, L., & Zola, M. (1987). *Choosing children's books.* Markham, Ontario: Pembroke.

Bormuth, J. R. (1975). Literacy in the classroom. In W. D. Page (Ed.), *Help for the reading teacher: New directions in research* (pp. 60–89). Urbana, IL: National Council of Teachers of English.

Bosma, B. (1992). *Fairy tales, fables, legends, and myths: Using folk literature in your classroom.* (2nd ed.). New York: Teachers College Press.

Bradley, L., & Bryant, P. E. (1983). Categorizing sounds and learning to read—a causal connection. *Nature,* 301, 419–521.

Bradley L., & Bryant, P. E. (1985). Rhyme and reason in reading and spelling. I.A.R.L.D. Monographs No. 1. Ann Arbor: University of Michigan Press.

Brandt, R. (1992). Overview: Reconsidering our commitments. *Educational Leadership, 50,* 5.

Bransford, J. D., & McCarrell, N. S. (1974). A sketch of a cognitive approach to comprehension: Some thoughts about understanding what it means to comprehend. In W. B. Wiemer & D. S. Palermo (Eds.), *Cognition and the symbolic processes* (pp. 189–229). Hillsdale, NJ: Erlbaum.

Breneman, L., & Breneman, B. (1983). *Once upon a time: A storytelling handbook.* Chicago, IL: Nelson-Hall.

Bridge, C. (1983). Predictable materials for beginning readers. *Language Arts, 56,* 503–507.

Bridge, C. A. (1986). Predictable books for beginning readers and writers. In M. R. Sampson (Ed.), *The pursuit of literacy: Early reading and writing* (pp. 81–96). Dubuque, IA: Kendall/Hunt.

Bridge, C., Winograd, P., & Haley, D. (1983). Using predictable materials vs. preprimers to teach beginning sight words. *The Reading Teacher, 36,* 884–896.

Brill, R. (1985). The remedial reader. In G. Winch & V. Hoogstad (Eds.), *Teaching reading: A language experience* (pp. 142–159). South Melbourne, Australia: Macmillan.

Brinkley, E. (1991). Whole language and the religious Right. Paper presented at the International Reading Association, Atlanta. May.

Britton, J. (1970). *Language and learning.* London: Alen Lane, Penguin Press.

Bromley, K. D. (1991). *Webbing with literature.* Boston: Allyn & Bacon.

Brophy, J. E., & Good, T. L. (1986). Teacher behavior and student achievement. In M. C. Wittrock (Ed.), *Handbook of Research on Teaching* (3rd ed.) (pp. 328–375). New York: Macmillan.

Brown, C. S., & Lytle, S. L. (1988). Merging assessment and instruction: Protocols in the classroom. In S. M. Glazer, L. W. Searfoss, and L. M. Gentile (Eds.), *Reexamining reading diagnosis: New trends and procedures* (pp. 67–80). Newark, DE: International Reading Association.

Brown, H. D. (1980). *Principles of language learning and teaching*. Englewood Cliffs, NJ: Prentice Hall.

Brown, R. (1970). Psychology and reading: Commentary on Chapters 5 to 10. In H. Levin & J. P. Williams (Eds.), *Basic studies on reading* (pp. 164–187). New York: Basic Books.

Brown, R. G. (1991). *Schools of thought*. San Francisco: Jossey-Bass.

Brown's directory of instructional programs: Whole language/literature K–8. (1992). Mendham, NJ: Brown Publishing Network, Infinity Impressions.

Brumfit, C. J., & Johnson, K. (Eds.). (1979). *The communicative approach to language teaching.* Oxford: Oxford University Press.

Brummet, A. J. (1989a). Policy directions: A response to the Sullivan Royal Commission on Education by the Government of British Columbia. Vanouver, British Columbia. January 27.

Brummet, A. J. (1989b). Presentation to the British Columbia School Trustees Association. Vancouver, British Columbia. January 27.

Bruner, J. S. (1983a). *Child's talk: Learning to use language*. Oxford: Oxford University Press.

Bruner, J. S. (1983b). Development of a transactional self. In *New directions in studying children: Speeches from the conference of the Erickson Institute*. Chicago. April 29–30. (ERIC: ED 265 953)

Bruner, J. S. (1986). *Actual minds, possible worlds*. Cambridge: Harvard University Press.

Bruner, J. S., & O'Dowd, D. (1958). A note on the informativeness of parts of words. *Language and Speech, 1*, 98–101.

Bryant, P. E. & Impey, L. (1986). The similarities between normal children and dyslexic adults and children. *Cognition, 24*, 121–137.

Buchanan, E. (1989). *Spelling for whole language classrooms*. Katonah, NY: Richard C. Owen.

Buncombe, F., & Peetoom, A. (1988). *Literature-based learning: One school's journey*. Richmond Hill, Ontario: Scholastic.

Burd, K. (1992). Oscar. *T. I. P. S. Teacher-Inspired Practical Strategies: NCTE/ESL Assembly Newsletter, 1* (1), 2.

Burke, C. (1980). The reading interview: 1977. In B. P. Farr & D. J. Strickler (Eds.), *Reading comprehension: Resource guide*. Bloomington: School of Education, Indiana University.

Burling, R. (1973). *English in black and white*. New York: Holt, Rinehart.

Burmeister, L. E. (1968). Usefulness of phonic generalizations. *The Reading Teacher, 21*, 349–356, 360.

Buscaglia, L. (1972). *Love.* New York: Ballantine.

Busching, B.A. (1981). Readers theatre: An education for language and life. *Language Arts, 58*, 330–338.

Bussis, A. M., & Chittenden, E. A. (1987). Research currents: What the reading tests neglect. *Language Arts* 64, (March), 302–308.

Butler, A. (1984). *The Story Box in the classroom, stage 1*. Melbourne, Australia: Rigby.

Butler, A. (n.d.). Shared Book Experience. (Booklet accompanying instructional video.) Crystal Lake, IL: Rigby.

Butler, A., & Turbill, J. (1984.) *Towards a reading-writing classroom*. Rozelle, New South Wales: Primary English Teaching Association. (Available in the U.S. from Heinemann.)

Butler, K. A. (1988). Learning styles. *Learning 88*, (November–December), 30–34.

Byrne, B., & Fielding-Barnsley, R. F. (1991). Evaluation of a program to teach phonemic awareness to young children. *Journal of Educational Psychology, 83*, 451–455.

California State Department of Education. (1984). *Studies on immersion education: A collection for United States educators.* Sacramento: California State Department of Education.

California State Department of Education. (1986). *Recommended readings in literature: Kindergarten through grade eight.* Sacramento: California State Department of Education.

California State Department of Education. (1987). *English-language arts framework.* Sacramento: California State Department of Education.

California State Department of Education. (1992). Language census report for California public schools. Sacramento, CA: California State Department of Education.

Calkins, L. M. (1980). When children want to punctuate: Basic skills belong in context. *Language Arts, 57,* 567–573.

Calkins, L. M. (1983). *Lessons from a child.* Portsmouth, NH: Heinemann.

Calkins, L. M. (1986). *The art of teaching writing.* Portsmouth, NH: Heinemann.

Calkins, L. M. (1990). *Living between the lines.* Portsmouth, NH: Heinemann.

Cambourne, B. (1988). *The whole story: Natural learning and the acquisition of literacy in the classroom.* Auckland, New Zealand: Scholastic.

Carbo, M. (1978). Teaching reading with talking books. *The Reading Teacher, 32,* 267–273.

Carbo, M. (1981a). Case study of Jimmy. Roslyn Heights, NY: National Reading Styles Institute.

Carbo, M. (1981b). *Reading style inventory manual.* Roslyn Heights, NY: National Reading Styles Institute.

Carbo, M. (1983). *Reading style research supplement.* Roslyn Heights, NY: National Reading Styles Institute.

Carbo, M. (1984a). Five schools try reading style programs . . . And see how their kids have grown! *Early Years K/8, 52,* 57–61.

Carbo, M. (1984b). Why most reading tests aren't fair. *Early Years K–8* (May), 73–75.

Carbo, M. (1987a). Deprogramming reading failure: Giving unequal learners an equal chance. *Phi Delta Kappan, 69,* 197–202.

Carbo, M. (1987b). Reading style research: "What works" isn't always phonics. *Phi Delta Kappan, 68,* 431–435.

Carbo, M. (1987c). Ten myths about teaching reading. *Teaching K–8, 17,* 77–80.

Carbo, M. (1988a). Debunking the great phonics myth. *Phi Delta Kappan, 70,* 226–240.

Carbo, M. (1988b). *What reading achievement tests should measure to increase literacy in the U.S.* Research Bulletin no. 7. Bloomington, IN: Phi Delta Kappan.

Carbo, M. (1989). *How to record books for maximum reading gains.* Roslyn Heights, NY: National Reading Styles Institute.

Carbo, M. (1992). Structuring whole language for students at risk. *Teaching K–8, 22,* 88–89.

Carbo, M., Dunn, R., & Dunn, K. (1986). *Teaching students to read through their individual learning styles.* Englewood Cliffs, NJ: Prentice Hall.

Carey, R. F., Harste, J. C., & Smith, S. L. (1981). Contextual constraints and discourse processes: A replication study. *Reading Research Quarterly, 16,* 201–212.

Carrier, J. G. (1983). Explaining educability: An investigation of political support for the Children with Learning Disabilities Act of 1969. *British Journal of Sociology of Education, 4* (2), 125–140.

Carroll, J. B. (1970). The nature of the reading process. In H. Singer & R. B. Ruddell (Eds.), *Theoretical models and processes of reading* (pp. 292–303). Newark, DE: International Reading Association.

Case, A. D. (1992). The special education rescue: A case for systems thinking. *Educational Leadership, 50,* 32–34.

Cazden, C. B. (1972). *Child language and education.* New York: Holt, Rinehart and Winston.

Cazden, C. B. (1983). Adult assistance to language development: Scaffolds, models, and direct instruction. In R. Parker and F. Davis (Eds.), *Developing literacy.* Newark, DE: International Reading Association.

Cazden, C. B. (1985). Social context of learning to read. In H. Singer & R. B. Ruddell (Eds.), *Theoretical models and processes of reading* (3rd ed.), pp. 595–610. Newark, DE: International Reading Association.

Cazden, C. B. (1992). *Whole language plus: Essays on literacy in the United States and New Zealand.* New York: Teachers College Press.

Cazden, C. B., & Snow, C. (Eds.). (1990). English plus: Issues in bilingual education. In *Annals of the American Academy of Political Science* (Vol. 508). Newbury Park: Sage Publications.

Center for the Expansion of Learning and Teaching. (1992). Packet of informational sheets on whole language, phonics, and various other issues. Tempe, AZ: Center for Establishing Dialogue.

Chall, J. (1967/1983). *Learning to read: The great debate*. New York: McGraw-Hill.

Chall, J. (1983). *Stages of reading development.* New York: McGraw-Hill.

Chall, J. (1989). Learning to read: The great debate 20 years later—A response to "Debunking the great phonics myth." *Phi Delta Kappan, 70*, 521–538.

Chamot, A., & O'Malley, M. (1987). The cognitive academic language learning approach: A bridge to the mainstream. *TESOL Quarterly, 21* (2), 227–249.

Chamot, A., & O'Malley, M. (1989). The cognitive academic language learning approach. In P. Rigg & V. Allen (Eds.), *When they don't all speak English: Integrating the ESL student into the regular classroom* (pp. 108–125). Urbana, IL: National Council of Teachers of English.

Chapman, G. (1991). *Teaching young playwrights*. Portsmouth, NH: Heinemann.

Chapman, J. A. (1986). *Why not teach intensive phonics?* Pensacola, FL: Beka Books.

Chastain, K. (1976). *Developing second language skills: Theory to practice* (2nd ed.). Boston: Houghton Mifflin.

Chittenden, E., & Courtney, R. (1989). Assessment of young children's reading: Documentation as an alternative to testing. In D. S. Strickland and L. M. Morrow (Eds.), *Emerging literacy: Young children learn to read and write* (pp. 107–120). Newark, DE: International Reading Association.

Chomsky, C. (1971). Invented spelling in the open classroom. *Word, 27*, 499–518.

Chomsky, C. (1976). After decoding: What? *Language Arts, 53*, 288–296, 314.

Chomsky, C. (1979). Approaching reading through invented spelling. In L. B. Resnick & P. A. Weaver (Eds.), *Theory and practice of early reading, Vol. 2* (pp. 43–65). Hillsdale, NJ: Erlbaum.

Chomsky, N. (1965). *Aspects of the theory of syntax*. Cambridge: MIT Press.

Civil rights. (1989). *Education Reporter, 42*(July), 1, 3–4.

Clark, E. T. (1988). The search for a new educational paradigm: The implications of new assumptions about thinking and learning. *Holistic Education* 1, (Spring), 18–30.

Clarke, L. K. (1988). Invented versus traditional spelling in first graders' writings: Effects on learning to spell and read. *Research in the Teaching of English, 22*, 281–309.

Clay, M. (1972). *Sand: The Concepts About Print test*. Portsmouth, NH: Heinemann.

Clay, M. (1975). *What did I write?* Portsmouth, NH: Heinemann.

Clay, M. (1979). *Stones: The Concepts About Print test*. Portsmouth, NH: Heinemann.

Clay, M. (1985). *The early detection of reading difficulties* (3rd ed.). Portsmouth, NH: Heinemann.

Clay, M. (1986). Why reading recovery is the way it is. Paper presented at the Reading Recovery Conference, Ohio Department of Eduation, Columbus, Ohio. February 4–5.

Clay, M. M. (1987a). Implementing Reading Recovery: Systemic adaptations to an educational innovation. *New Zealand Journal of Educational Studies, 22* (1), 35–58.

Clay, M. M. (1987b). *Writing begins at home*. Portsmouth, NH: Heinemann.

Clay, M. M. (1991a). *Becoming literate: The construction of inner control*. Portsmouth, NH: Heinemann.

Clay, M. M. (1991b). Reading Recovery surprises. In D. E. DeFord, C. A. Lyons, & G. S. Pinnell (Eds.), *Bridges to literacy: Learning from Reading Recovery* (pp. 55–74). Portsmouth, NH: Heinemann.

Clay, M. M. (1993). *An observation survey of early literacy achievement*. Portsmouth, NH: Heinemann.

Clay, M. M. (1993). Reading recovery: A guidebook for teachers in training. Portsmouth, NH: Heinemann.

Clymer, T. L. (1963). The utility of phonic generalizations in the primary grades. *The Reading Teacher, 16*, 252–258.

Cochrane, O., Cochrane, D., Scalena, S., & Buchanan, E. (1984). *Reading, writing and caring*. Winnipeg: Whole Language Consultants. (Distributed by Richard C. Owen.)

Coger, L. I. & White, M. R. (1982). *Readers theatre handbook: A dramatic approach to literature* (3rd ed.). Glenview, IL: Scott, Foresman.

Coles, G. 1987. *The learning mystique: A critical look at "learning disabilities."* New York: Fawcett Columbine.

Collier, V. (1989). How long? A synthesis of research on academic achievement in a second language. *TESOL Quarterly, 23* (3), 509–532.

Coltheart, M., Masterson, J., Byng, S., Prior, M., & Riddoch, J. (1983). Surface dyslexia. *Quarterly Journal of Experimental Psychology, 35*, 469–595.

Coltheart, M., Patterson, K., & Marshall, J. C. (Eds.) (1980). *Deep dyslexia.* Boston: Routledge & Kegan Paul.

Commission on Reading. (1988). *Basal readers and the state of American reading instruction: A call for action.* Position statement. Urbana, IL: National Council of Teachers of English.

Comprehending Comprehension. (1989). *Home School Helper* 3(2), 1–2. Greenville, SC: Bob Jones University Press.

Cook, E. (1969). *The ordinary and the fabulous: An introduction to myths, legends, and fairy tales for teachers and storytellers.* New York: Cambridge University Press.

Cooper, P. J., & Collins, R. B. (1992). *Look what happened to frog: Storytelling in education.* Scottsdale, AZ: Gorsuch Scarisbrick.

Corbett, M. (1989). *The testing dilemma.* SLATE Starter Sheet. Urbana, IL: National Council of Teachers of English. June.

Cordeiro, P. (1992). *Whole learning: Whole language and content in the upper elementary grades.* Katonah, NY: Richard C. Owen.

Cordiero, P. (1992–1993). Becoming a learner who teaches. *Teachers Networking: The Whole Language Newsletter*, 12(1), 1, 3–5.

Corder, R. (1971). *An information base of reading: A critical review of the information base for current assumptions regarding the status of instruction and reading achievement in the United States.* Berkeley, CA: Educational Testing Service, Berkeley Office, U.S. Office of Education Project 0–9031. (ERIC: ED 054 922)

Corpi, L. (1992). Student writing contest. *CABE Newsletter, 14* (4), 18.

Cottrell, J. (1987b). *Creative drama in the classroom: Grades 4–6.* Lincolnwood, IL: National Textbook Company.

Council of Chief State School Officers. (1988). *Early childhood and family education: Foundations for success.* Position statement. Washington, DC: Council of Chief State School Officers.

Courtney, R. (1974). *Play, drama, and thought.* New York: Drama Book Specialists.

Cousin, P. T., & Weekley, T. (1992). Teaching students with severe language and learning problems: Constructing new views of their understanding of print. Unpublished manuscript, California State University, San Bernadino.

Crafton, L. K. (1991). *Whole language: Getting started . . . moving forward.* Katonah, NY: Richard C. Owen.

Cramer, R. L. (1978). *Children's writing and language growth.* Columbus, OH: Charles Merrill.

Cranston, J. W. (1991). *Transformations through drama.* Lanham, MD: University Press of America.

Crawford, J. (1989). *Bilingual education: History, politics, theory, and practice.* Trenton, NJ: Crane.

Crawford, J. (1992). *Language loyalties.* Chicago: University of Chicago Press.

Crenshaw, S., Pierce, K. M., Reikes, L., Slane, S. & Stopsky, F. (1989). Teaching history across the elementary curriculum: Pull-out feature, *Social studies and the young learner, 2.*

Crews, E. (1992). Gifts from the heart. *T. I. P. S. Teacher-Inspired Practical Strategies: NCTE/ESL Assembly Newsletter, 1* (1), 4.

Critchley, M. (1970). *The dyslexic child* (2nd ed.). Springfield, IL: Charles C. Thomas.

Cronnell, B. A. (1970). *Spelling-to-sound correspondences for reading vs. sound-to-spelling correspondences.* Technical Note TN2-70-15. Los Alamitos, CA: Southwest Regional Laboratory.

Crowley, P. (1988). John. In C. Gilles, M. Bixby, P. Crowley, S. R. Crenshaw, M. Henrichs, F. E. Reynolds, & D. Pyle (Eds.), *Whole language strategies for secondary students* (pp. 15–18). Katonah, NY: Richard C. Owen.

Crowley, P. (1989). "They'll grow into 'em": Evaluation, self-evaluation, and self-esteem in special education. In K. S. Goodman, Y. M. Goodman, & W. J. Hood (Eds.), *The whole language evaluation book* (pp. 237–247). Portsmouth, NH: Heinemann.

The "Culture Fair" WISC-R I.Q. Test. (1981). *The Testing Digest* (Spring), 21.

Cummins, J. (1981). The role of primary language development in promoting educational success for language minority students. In *Schooling and language minority students: A theoretical framework* (pp. 3–49). Los Angeles: Evaluation, Dissemination, and Assessment Center, California State University, Los Angeles.

Cummins, J. (1984). *Bilingualism and special education: Issues in assessment and pedagogy.* Clevedon, England: Multilingual Matters.

Cummins, J. (1989a). *Empowering minority students.* Sacramento: California Association on Bilingual Education.

Cummins, J. (1989b). The sanitized curriculum: Educational disempowerment in a nation at risk. In D. Johnson & D. Roen (Eds.), *Richness in writing: Empowering ESL students* (pp. 19–38). New York: Longman.

Cunningham, A. E. (1990). Explicit versus implicit instruction in phonemic awareness. *Journal of Experimental Child Psychology, 50*, 429–444.

Cunningham, P. M. (1977). Teachers' correction responses to black dialect miscues which are non-meaning changing. *Reading Research Quarterly, 12*, 637–653.

Curran, C. (1982). Community language learning. In R. Blair (Ed.), *Innovative approaches to language teaching.* Rowley, MA: Newbury House.

Cutler, C., & Stone, E. (1988). A whole language approach: Teaching reading and writing to behaviorally disordered children. In M. K. Zabel (Ed.), *Teaching: Behaviorally disordered youth* (pp. 31–39). Reston, VA: Council for Children with Behavioral Disorders.

Dahl, K. L., & Freppon, P. A. (1991). Literacy learning in whole-language classrooms: An analysis of low socioeconomic urban children learning to read and write in kindergarten. In J. Zutell & S. McCormick (Eds.), *Learner factors/teacher factors: Issues in literacy research and instruction* (pp. 149–158). Chicago: National Reading Conference.

Dahl, K. L., & Freppon, P. A. (1992). *Learning to read and write in inner-city schools: A comparison of children's sense-making in skills-based and whole language classrooms.* Final Report to the Office of Educational Research and Improvement. Washington, DC: U.S. Department of Education. (Grant No. R117E00134)

Dahl, K. L., Purcell-Gates, V., & McIntyre, E. (1989). Ways that inner-city children make sense of traditional reading and writing instruction in the early grades. Final report to Office of Educational Research and Improvement. Washington, DC: U.S. Department of Education. (Grant No. G008720229)

Dale, P. S. (1972). *Language development: Structure and function.* Hindsdale, IL: Dryden Press.

Dalrymple, K. S. (1989). "Well, what about his skills?" Evaluation of whole langue in the middle school. In K. S. Goodman, Y. M. Goodman, & W. J. Hood (Eds.), *The Whole language evaluation book* (pp. 110–130). Portsmouth, NH: Heinemann.

Daly, E. (1990). *Monitoring children's language development: Holistic assessment in classrooms.* Portsmouth, NH: Heinemann.

Danielson, L. C., & Bellamy, G. T. (1988). *State variation in placement of children with handicaps in segregated environments.* Washington, DC: U.S. Office of Special Education and Rehabilitative Services.

Dank, M. (1977). What effect do reading programs have on the oral reading behavior of children? *Reading Improvement, 14*, 66–69.

Danner, Horace G. (1980). *Words from the Romance languages.* Manassas, VA: Imprimis Press.

Davies, G. (1983). *Practical primary drama.* Portsmouth, NH: Heinemann.

Davis, J. H. & Behm, T. (1977). Terminology of drama/theatre with and for children: A redefinition. *Children's Theatre Review, 27*, 10–11.

Dechant, E. V. (1970). *Improving the teaching of reading* (2nd ed.). Englewood Cliffs, NJ: Prentice Hall.

DeFord, D. E. (1981). Literacy: Reading, writing, and other essentials. *Language Arts, 58,* 652–658.

DeFord, D. E. (1985). Validating the construct of theoretical orientation in reading instruction. *Reading Research Quarterly, 20*, 351–367.

DeFord, D. E., & Harste, J. C. (1982). Child language research and curriculum. *Language Arts, 59,* 590–600.

DeFord, D. E., Lyons, C. A., & Pinnell, G. S. (1991). *Bridges to literacy: Learning from Reading Recovery.* Portsmouth, NH: Heinemann.

DeLawter, J. A. (1975). The relationship of beginning reading instruction and miscue patterns. In W. D. Page (Ed.), *Help for the reading teacher: New directions in research* (pp. 42–51). Urbana, IL: National Conference on Research in English and the ERIC Clearinghouse on Reading and Communication Skills. (Available from the National Council of Teachers of English.)

Dennis, M. (1982). The developmentally dyslexic brain and the written language skills of children with one hemisphere. In U. Kirk (Ed.), *The neuropsychology of language, reading, and spelling* (pp. 185–208). New York: Academic Press.

Desberg, P., Elliott, D. E., & Marsh, G. (1980). American Black English and spelling. In V. Frith (Ed.), *Cognitive processes in spelling* (pp. 69–84). New York: Academic Press.

de Silva, A. (1981). Oral reading behavior of Spanish speaking children taught by a meaning-based program. In S. Hudelson (Ed.), *Learning to read in different languages.* Alexandria, VA: Center for Applied Linguistics.

Dewey, J., & Bentley, A. F. (1949). *Knowing and the known.* Boston: Beacon.

DeWitt, D. (1978). *Children's faces looking up.* Chicago: American Library Association.

Diller, K. (1978). *The language teaching controversy.* Rowley, MA: Newbury House.

DiStefano, P., & Killion, J. (1984). Assessing writing skills through a process approach. *English Education, 16* (4), 203–207.

Doake, D. (1985). *Whole language principles and practices in reading development with special emphasis on reading recovery.* Viewing guide accompanying videotape filmed at the 1985 "Reading for the Love of It" conference in Toronto. Richmond Hill, Ontario: Scholastic.

Doake, D. (1988). *Reading begins at birth.* Richmond Hill, Ontario: Scholastic.

Doake, D. (1992). Literacy recovery, second language learing, and learning science through holistic practices. Chapter of unpublished book manuscript. Wolfville, Nova Scotia: Acadia University.

Dobson, L. (1986a). Emergent writers in a grade one classroom. Paper presented at the Fourth International Conference on the Teaching of English, Ottawa, Ontario. May 15.

Dobson, L. (1986b). Emergent writers in a grade one classroom. *Reading-Canada-Lecture, 4* (Fall), 149–156.

Donaldson, M. (1978). *Children's minds.* New York: Norton.

Doyle, K. M. (1990). Listening to the sounds of our hearts. *Lanaguage Arts, 67,* 254–261.

Dreyer, S. (1977–89). *The bookfinder: A guide to children's literature about the needs and problems of youth ages 2–15.* 4 vols. Circle Pines, MN: American Guidance Service.

Dudley-Marling, C. (1990). *When school is a struggle.* Richmond Hill, Ontario: Scholastic.

Duffy, F. H., Denckla, M. B., Bartels, P. H., Sandini, G., & Keissling, L. S. (1980). Dyslexia: Automated diagnosis by computerized classification of brain electrical activity. *Annals of Neurology, 7,* 421–428.

Duffy, F. H., McAnulty, G. B., & Schachter, S. C. (1984). Brain electrical activity mapping. In N. Geschwind & A. M. Galaburda (Eds.), *Cerebral dominance: The biological foundations* (pp. 53–74). Cambridge: Harvard University Press.

Dunkeld, C. (1991). Maintaining the integrity of a promising program: The case of reading recovery. In D. E. DeFord, C. A. Lyons, & G. S. Pinnell (Eds.), *Bridges to literacy: Learning from Reading Recovery* (pp. 37–53). Portsmouth, NH: Heinemann.

Dunn, R., & Dunn, K. (1978). *Teaching students through their individual learning styles: A practical approach.* Reston, VA: Reston Publishing Company.

Dunn, R., & Dunn, K. (Eds.) (1990). *A review of articles and books: Learning styles model (rev. ed.).* Jamaica, NY: Center for the Study of Learning and Teaching Styles, St. John's University.

Dunn, R., & Dunn, K. (Eds.). (n.d.). *A review of articles and books: Diagnosing learning styles.* Jamaica, NY: Center for the Study of Learning and Teaching Styles, St. John's University.

DuPaul, G. J., & Barkley, R. A. (1990). Medication therapy. In R. A. Barkley, *Attention-Deficit Hyperactivity Disorder: A handbook for diagnosis and treatment* (pp. 573–612). New York: Guilford Press.

Durkin, D. (1978–1979). What classroom observations reveal about reading comprehension instruction. *Reading Research Quarterly, 14* (4), 481–553.

Durkin, D. (1990). Are the new basals any better? Presentation at the International Reading Association convention, Atlanta. May.

Dykstra, R. (1974). Phonics and beginning reading instruction. In C. C. Walcutt, J. Lamport, & G. McCracken, *Teaching reading: A phonic/linguistic approach to developmental reading* (pp. 373–397). New York: Macmillan.

Eckhoff, B. (1984). How reading affects children's writing. In J. M. Jensen (Ed.), *Composing and comprehending* (pp. 105–114). Urbana, IL: ERIC Clearinghouse on Reading and Communication Skills and the National Council of Teachers of English.

Edelsky, C. (1986). *Writing in a bilingual program: Había una vez.* Norwood, NJ: Ablex.

Edelsky, C. (1989). Bilingual children's writing: Fact and fiction. In D. Johnson & D. Roen (Eds.), *Richness in writing: Empowering ESL students* (pp. 165–176). New York: Longman.

Edelsky, C. (1990). Whose agenda is this anyway? A response to McKenna, Robinson, and Miller. *Educational Researcher, 19,* 7–11.

Edelsky, C. (1991). *With literacy and justice for all.* London: Falmer Press.

Edelsky, C. (Ed.). (1993). *Language arts topics and educational issues: Information sheets.* (ERIC: ED 359 486)

Edelsky, C., Altwerger, B., & Flores, B. (1991). *Whole language: What's the difference?* Portsmouth, NH: Heinemann.

Edelsky, C., & Draper, K. (1989). Reading/"Reading"; Writing/"writing"; text/"text." *Reading-Canada-Lecture, 7,* 201–216.

Edelsky, C., & Harman, S. (1988). One more critique of reading tests—with two differences. *English Education, 20,* 157–171.

Edelsky, C., & Smith, K. (1984). "Is that writing—or are those marks just a figment of your curriculum?" *Language Arts, 61,* 24–32.

Eeds, M., & Wells, D. (1989). Grand conversations: An exploration of meaning construction in literature study groups. *Research in the Teaching of English, 23,* 4–29.

Eggleton, J. (1990). *Whole language evaluation: Reading, writing, and spelling.* San Diego: The Wright Group.

Ekwall, E. E. (1986). *Ekwall reading inventory* (2nd ed.). Boston: Allyn & Bacon.

Elbro, C. (1990). *Differences in dyslexia: A study of reading strategies and deficits in a linguistic perspective.* Copenhagen: Munksgaard International Publishers.

Elbro, C. (1991). Differences in reading strategies reflect differences in linguistic abilities. *International Journal of Applied Linguistics, 1*(2), 228–244.

Elbro, C. (1991). Dyslexics and normal beginning readers read by different strategies: A comparison of strategy distributions in dyslexic and normal readers. *International Journal of Applied Linguistics, 1*(1), 19–37.

Elder, R. D. (1971). Oral reading achievement of Scottish and American children. *Elementary School Journal, 71,* 216–229.

Elfant, P. (In progress). *Cognitive and metacognitive strategies of first graders during a shared book experience.* New York: Unpublished doctoral dissertation, Fordham University.

Elley, W. B. (1989). Vocabulary acquisition from listening to stories. *Reading Research Quarterly, 24,* 174–187.

Elley, W. B. (1991). Acquiring literacy in a second language: The effect of book-based programs. *Language Learning, 41* (3), 375–411.

Elley, W. B., & Mangubhai, F. (1983). The impact of reading on second language learning. *Reading Research Quarterly, 19,* 53–67.

Emans, R. (1967). The usefulness of phonic generalizations above the primary grades. *The Reading Teacher, 20,* 419–425.

Engelmann, S., Haddox, P., & Bruner, E. (1983). *Teach your child to read in 100 easy lessons.* New York: Simon & Schuster.

Enright, D. S., & McCloskey, M. L. (1985). Yes, talking! Organizing the classroom to promote second language acquisition. *TESOL Quarterly, 19* (3), 431–453.

Enright, D. S., & McCloskey, M. L. (1988). *Integrating English: Developing English language and literacy in the multilingual classroom.* Reading, MA: Addison-Wesley.

Erdmann, B., & Dodge, R. (1898). Psychologische untersuchungen uber das lesen, auf experimenteller grundlage. As cited in E. B. Huey (1968).

Errington, E. P. (1993). Teachers as researchers: Pursuing qualitative enquiry in drama classrooms. *Youth Theatre Journal, 7* (4), 31–36.

Estes, T. H., & Johnstone, J. P. (1977). Twelve easy ways to make readers hate reading (and one difficult way to make them love it). *Language Arts, 54,* 891–897.

Fagan, W. T., Cooper, C. R., & Jensen, J. M. (1975). *Measures for research and evaluation in the English language arts.* Urbana, IL: National Council of Teachers of English.

Fasold, R. W., & Wolfram, W. (1970). Some linguistic features of Negro dialect. In R. W. Fasold & R. W. Shuy (Eds.), *Teaching standard English in the inner city* (pp. 41–86). Arlington, VA: Center for Applied Linguistics.

Ferreiro, E., & Teberosky, A. (1982). *Literacy before schooling* (K. G. Castro, Trans.). Portsmouth, NH: Heinemann.

Fields, M. V. (1988). Talking and writing: Explaining the whole language approach to parents. *The Reading Teacher, 41,* (May), 898–903.

Fish, S. (1980). *Is there a text in this class? The authority of interpretive communities.* Cambridge: Harvard University Press.

Fisher, B. (1991). *Joyful learning: A whole language kindergarten.* Portsmouth, NH: Heinemann.

Fitzgerald, S. (1984). Beginning reading and writing through singing: A natural approach. *Highway One, 7* (2), 6–12.

Five, C. L. (1991). *Special voices.* Portsmouth, NH: Heinemann.

Fleisher, B. M. (1988). Oral reading cue strategies of better and poorer readers. *Reading Research and Instruction, 27* (3), 35–50.

Flesch, R. (1955). *Why Johnny can't read.* New York: Harper & Row.

Flesch, R. (1981). *Why Johnny still can't read.* New York: Harper & Row.

Flores, B., Cousin, P. T., & Diaz, E. (1991). Transforming deficit myths about learning, language, and culture. *Language Arts, 68,* 370–379.

Flowers, D. L., Wood, F. B., & Naylor, C. E. (1989). Regional cerebral blood flow in adults diagnosed as reading disabled in childhood. Unpublished manuscript. Cited in Vellutino and Denckla (1991).

Flynn, J. M., Deering, W., Goldstein, M., & Rahbar, M. H. (1992). Electrophysiological correlates of dyslexic subtypes. *Journal of Learning Disabilities, 25,* 133–141.

Forester, A. D., & Reinhard, M. (1989). *The learner's way.* Winnipeg, Manitoba: Pequis Publishers.

Forness, S. R., Swanson, J. M., Cantwell, D. P., Youpa, D., & Hanna, G. L. (1992). Stimulant medication and reading performance: Follow-up on sustained dose in ADHD boys with and without conduct disorders. *Journal of Learning Disabilities, 25,* 115–123.

Fountas, I. (1992). The promise of Reading Recovery. *Whole Language Teachers Association Newsletter, 7* (2), 6–13.

Fox, M. (1987). *Teaching drama to young children.* Portsmouth, NH: Heinemann.

Freeman, D. E., & Freeman, Y. S. (1988). Sheltered English instruction. *ERIC Digest,* October. Alexandria, VA: Center for Applied Linguistics.

Freeman, D. E., & Freeman, Y. S. (1990). Learning goes from whole to part. *CABE Newsletter, 13* (3), 7.

Freeman, D. E., & Freeman, Y. S. (1992a). Enriching the context: How to and how not to. *CABE Newsletter, 14* (5), 12–13.

Freeman, D. E., & Freeman, Y. S. (1992b). *Whole language for second language learners.* Portsmouth, NH: Heinemann.

Freeman, D. E., & Freeman, Y. S. (In press). Celebrating diversity. *Whole language: Practice and research.* New York: Garland Publishing.

Freeman, E. B., & Person, D. G. (1992). *Using nonfiction trade books in the elementary classroom: From ants to zepplins.* Urbana, IL: National Council of Teachers of English.

Freeman, J. (1990). *Books kids will sit still for.* (2nd ed.). New Providence, NJ: Bowker.

Freeman, Y. S. (1985). What preschoolers already know about print. *Educational Horizons, 64*, 22–25.

Freeman, Y. S. (1988a). The contemporary Spanish basal reader in the U.S.: How does it reflect current knowledge of the reading process? *NABE Journal, 13*, 59–74.

Freeman, Y. S. (1988b). Do Spanish methods and materials reflect current understanding of the reading process? *The Reading Teacher, 41*, 654–664.

Freeman, Y. S. (1988c). Métodos de lectura en español: Reflejan nuestro conocimiento actual del proceso de lectura? *Lectura y Vida, 9*, 20–28.

Freeman, Y. S. (1989). Literature-based or literature: Where do we stand? *Teachers Networking*, 9 (Summer),13–15.

Freeman, Y. S., & Cervantes, C. (1991). Literature books en español for whole language classrooms. In K. Goodman, L. Bird, & Y. Goodman (Eds.), *The whole language catalog* (p. 184). Chicago, IL: American School Publishers.

Freeman, Y. S., & Freeman, D. E. (1989). Bilingual learners: How our assumptions limit their world. *Holistic Education Review*, Winter, 33–39.

Freeman, Y. S., & Freeman, D. E. (1991a). Doing social studies: Whole language lessons to promote social action. *Social Education, 55* (1), 29–32, 66.

Freeman, Y. S., & Freeman, D. E. (1991b). Ten tips for monolingual teachers of bilingual students. In K. Goodman, L. Bird, & Y. Goodman (Eds.), *The whole language catalog* (p. 90). Santa Rosa, CA: American School Publishers.

Freeman, Y. S., & Freeman, D. E. (1991c). Using sheltered English to teach second language learners. *California English, 27* (1), 6–7, 26.

Freeman, Y. S., & Nofziger, S. (1991). WalkuM to RnM 33: Vien Vinidos al cualTo 33. In K. S. Goodman, Y. M. Goodman, & W. H. Hood (Eds.), *Organizing for whole language* (pp. 65–83). Portsmouth, NH: Heinemann.

Freeman, Y. S., & Goodman, Y. M. (In press). Revaluing the bilingual learner through a literature reading program. *Journal of Reading and Writing, International.*

Freire, P. (1970). *Pedagogy of the oppressed.* M. B. Ramos, Trans. New York: Herder and Herder.

Freire, P. (1985). *The politics of education: Culture, power, and liberation.* South Hadley, MA: Bergin & Garvey.

Freire, P., & Macedo, D. (1987). *Literacy: Reading the word and the world.* South Hadley, MA: Bergin & Garvey.

Freppon, P. A. (1988). An investigation of children's concepts of the purpose and nature of reading in different instructional settings. Unpublished doctoral dissertation, University of Cincinnati, Ohio.

Freppon, P. A. (1991). Children's concepts of the nature and purpose of reading in different instructional settings. *Journal of Reading Behavior, 23*, 139–163.

Freppon, P. A., & Dahl, K. L. (1991). Learning about phonics in a whole language classroom. *Language Arts*, 68, 190–197.

Fulwiler, R., & Young, A. (Eds.). (1982). *Language connections: Writing and reading across the curriculum.* Urbana, IL: National Council of Teachers of English.

Gagnon, A., & Gagnon, A. (Eds.). (1988). *Canadian books for young people/Livres Canadiens pour la jeunesse* (4th ed.). Toronto: University of Toronto Press.

Gamberg, R., Kwak, W., Hutchings, M., Altheim, J., with Edwards, G. (1988). *Learning and loving it: Theme studies in the classroom.* Portsmouth, NH: Heinemann.

Gardner, H. (1983). *Frames of mind: The theory of multiple intelligences.* New York: Basic.

Gardner, H. (1987). *The theory of multiple intelligences. Annals of Dyslexia, 37*, 19–35.

Gaskins, R. W., Gaskins, J. C., & Gaskins, I. W. (1991). A decoding program for poor readers—and the rest of the class, too! *Language Arts, 68*, 213–225.

Geertz, C. (1983). *Local knowledge.* New York: Seabury.

Genesee, F. (1987). *Learning through two languages: Studies of immersion and bilingual education.* Rowley, MA: Newbury House.

Genishi, C., & Dyson, A. (1984). *Language assessment in the early years.* Norwood, NJ: Ablex.

Gentry, J. R. (1982). An analysis of the developmental spelling in *Gnys at wrk. The Reading Teacher, 36,* 192–200.

Gentry, J. R. (1987). *Spel . . . is a four-letter word.* Richmond Hill, Ontario: Scholastic. (Distributed in the U.S. by Heinemann.)

Gentry, J. R., & Gillet, J. W. (1993). *Teaching kids to spell.* Portsmouth, NH: Heinemann.

Gersten, R. (1990). Letter to the editor. *Education Week,* June 13, p. 24.

Gersten, R., and Keating, T. (1987). Long-term benefits from direct instruction. *Educational Leadership, 45,* 28–31.

Giacobbe, M. E. (1984). Helping children become more responsible for their own writing. *LiveWire, 1* (1), 7–9. (National Council of Teachers of English publication.)

Giacobbe, M. E. (1986). Learning to write and writing to learn in the elementary school. In A. R. Petrosky & D. Bartholomae (Eds.), *The teaching of writing: 85th yearbook of the National Society for the Study of Education* (pp. 131–147). Chicago: University of Chicago Press.

Gibson, E. J. (1972). Reading for some purpose. In J. F. Kavanagh & I. G. Mattingly (Eds.), *Language by ear and by eye* (pp. 3–19). Cambridge: MIT Press.

Gibson, E. J., & Levin, H. (1975). *The psychology of reading.* Cambridge: MIT Press.

Gibson, E. J., Shurcliff, A., & Yonas, A. (1970). Utilization of spelling patterns by deaf and hearing subjects. In H. Levin & J. P. Williams (Eds.), *Basic studies on reading* (pp. 57–73). New York: Basic.

Gilles, C., Bixby, M., Crowley, P., Crenshaw, S., Henrichs, M., Reynolds, F. E., Pyle, D. (Eds.). (1988). *Whole language strategies for secondary students.* Katonah, NY: Richard C. Owen.

Gilles, C. (1994). We make an idea: Cycles of meaning in literature discussion groups. In K. M. Pierce & C. J. Gilles (Eds.), *Cycles of meaning: Exploring the potential of talk in learning communities.* Portsmouth, NH: Heinemann.

Gillespie, J. T., & Naden, C. J. (Eds.). (1990). *Best books for children: Preschool through grade 6* (4th ed.). New Providence, NJ: Bowker.

Giroux, H. A. (1983). *Theory and resistance in education: A pedagogy for the opposition.* Granby, MA: Bergin & Garvey.

Glushko, R. J. (1979). The organization and activation of orthographic knowledge in reading aloud. *Journal of Experimental Psychology: Human Perception and Performance, 5,* 674–691.

Goldenberg, C. (1991). Learning to read in New Zealand: The balance of skills and meaning. *Language Arts,* 68, 555–562.

Gonzales, J. (1979). Coming of age in bilingual/bicultural education: A historical perspective. In H. Trueba & C. Barnett-Mizrahi (Eds.), *Bilingual multicultural education and the professional: From theory to practice* (pp. 1–10). Rowley, MA: Newbury House.

Goodlad, J. (1984). *A place called school: Prospects for the future.* New York: McGraw-Hill.

Goodman, K. S. (1965). A linguistic study of cues and miscues in reading. *Elementary English, 42,* 639–643.

Goodman, K. S. (1967). Reading: a psycholinguistic guessing game. *Journal of the Reading Specialist, 6,* 126–135.

Goodman, K. S. (1973). *Theoretically based studies of patterns of miscues in oral reading performance.* Detroit: Wayne State University. (ERIC: ED 079 708)

Goodman, K. S. (1982a). *Language and literacy: The selected writings of Kenneth S. Goodman.* (Frederick V. Gollasch, Ed.) 2 vols. Boston: Routledge and Kegan Paul.

Goodman, K. S. (1982b). Revaluing readers and reading. *Topics in Learning and Learning Disabilities, 1* (4), 87–93.

Goodman, K. S. (1986). *What's whole in whole language?* Richmond Hill, Ontario: Scholastic. (Distributed in the U.S. by Heinemann.)

Goodman, K. S. (1989). Whole-language research: Foundations and development. *The Elementary School Journal* 90 (November), 208–221.

Goodman, K. S. (1994). *Phonics Phacts*. Richmond Hill, Ontario: Scholastic. (Distributed in the U.S. by Heinemann.)

Goodman, K. S., Bridges, L. B., & Goodman, Y. M. (1990). *The whole language catalog*. Chicago, IL: American School Publishers.

Goodman, K. S., Bridges, L. B., & Goodman, Y. M. (1992). *The whole language catalog: Supplement on authentic assessment*. Chicago, IL: American School Publishers.

Goodman, K. S., & Buck, C. (1973). Dialect barriers to reading comprehension revisited. *The Reading Teacher, 27*, 6–12.

Goodman, K. S., & Goodman, Y. M. (1978). *Reading of American children whose language is a stable rural dialect of English or a language other than English*. Final Report, Project NIE–C–00–3–0087. Washington, DC: U.S. Department of Health, Education, and Welfare.

Goodman, K. S., & Goodman, Y. M. (1979). Learning to read is natural. In L. B. Resnick & P. A. Weaver (Eds.), *Theory and practice of early reading*, Vol. 1 (pp. 137–154). Hillsdale, NJ: Erlbaum.

Goodman, K. S., & Goodman, Y. M. (n. d.). *Annotated miscue bibliography*. Tucson: Program in Language and Literacy, University of Arizona.

Goodman, K. S., Goodman, Y. M., & Flores, B. (1979). *Reading in the bilingual classroom: Literacy and biliteracy*. Rosslyn, VA: National Clearinghouse for Bilingual Education.

Goodman, K. S., Goodman, Y. M., & Hood, W. J. (1989). *The whole language evaluation book*. Portsmouth, NH: Heinemann.

Goodman, K. S., Shannon, P., Freeman, Y., & Murphy, S. (1988). *Report card on basal readers*. Katonah, N.Y: Richard C. Owen.

Goodman, K. S. & Shannon, P. (Forthcoming). *Basal readers: A second look* (tentative title). Katonah, NY: Richard C. Owen.

Goodman, Y. M. (1976). Strategies for comprehension. In P. D. Allen and D. Watson (Eds.), *Findings of research in miscue* analysis: Classroom implications (pp. 94–102). Urbana, IL: ERIC Clearinghouse on Reading and Communication Skills and the National Council of Teachers of English.

Goodman, Y. M. (1978). Kid watching: An alternative to testing. *National Elementary Principal, 57* (June), 41–45.

Goodman, Y. M. (1985). Kidwatching: Observing children in the classroom. In A. Jaggar & M. T. Smith-Burke (Eds.), *Observing the language learner* (pp. 9–18). Newark, DE: International Reading Association.

Goodman, Y. M. (1989). Roots of the whole-language movement. *The Elementary School Journal, 90* (November), 113–127.

Goodman, Y. M. (1992a). Bookhandling knowledge task. In K. S. Goodman, L. B. Bird, & Y. M. Goodman (Eds.), *The whole language catalog supplement on authentic assessment* (p. 140). Chicago: SRA.

Goodman, Y. M. (1992b). Review of Marie M. Clay, *Becoming literate: The construction of inner control*. In K. S. Goodman, L. B. Bird, & Y. M. Goodman (Eds.), *The whole language catalog: Supplement on authentic assessment* (p. 55). Chicago: SRA.

Goodman, Y. M. (Ed.). (1990). *How children construct literacy: Piagetian perspectives*. Newark, DE.: International Reading Association.

Goodman, Y. M., & Altwerger, B. & Marek, A. (1989). *Print awareness in preschool children: The development of literacy in preschool children, research and review*. Tucson: Program in Language and Literacy, University of Arizona.

Goodman, Y. M., & Burke, C. L. (1972a). *Reading miscue inventory manual: Procedure for diagnosis and evaluation*. New York: Macmillan.

Goodman, Y. M., & Burke, C. L. (1972b). *Reading miscue inventory practice analysis manual*. New York: Macmillan.

Goodman, Y. M., & Burke, C. L. (1980). *Reading strategies: Focus on comprehension.* Katonah, NY: Richard C. Owen.

Goodman, Y. M., & Marek, A. (1989). *Retrospective miscue analysis: Two papers.* Program in Language and Literacy, Occasional Papers No. 19. Tucson: University of Arizona.

Goodman, Y. M., Watson, D. J., & Burke, C. L. (1987). *Reading miscue inventory: Alternative procedures.* Katonah, NY: Richard C. Owen.

Gordon, M. (1991). *ADHD/Hyperactivity: A consumer's guide for parents and teachers.* DeWitt, NY: GSI Publications.

Goswami, D., & Stillman, P. R. (Eds.). (1987). *Reclaiming the classroom: Teacher research as an agency for change.* Portsmouth, NH: Boynton/Cook–Heinemann.

Goswami, U. (1986). Children's use of analogy in learning to read: A developmental study. *Journal of Experimental Psychology, 42,* 73–83.

Goswami, U. (1988). Orthographic analogies and reading development. *Quarterly Journal of Experimental Psychology, 40,* 239–268.

Goswami U., & Bryant, P. (1990). *Phonological skills and learning to read.* Hove, East Sussex: Lawrence Erlbaum.

Gough, P. (1972). One second of reading. In J. F. Kavanagh & I. G. Mattingly (Eds.), *Language by ear and by eye* (pp. 331–358). Cambridge: MIT Press.

Gough, P. B., Alford, J. A., & Holley-Wilcox, P. (1981). Words and contexts. In O. J. L. Tzeng & H. Singer (Eds.), *Perception of print: Reading research in experimental psychology* (pp. 85–102). Hillsdale, NJ: Erlbaum.

Graves, D. H. (1983). Writing: *Teachers and children at work.* Portsmouth, NH: Heinemann.

Graves, D. H. (1989a). *Experiment with fiction.* Portsmouth, NH: Heinemann.

Graves, D. H. (1989b). *Investigate nonfiction.* Portsmouth, NH: Heinemann.

Graves, D. H. (1992). *Explore poetry.* Portsmouth, NH: Heinemann.

Graves, D. H., & Sunstein, B. S. (Eds.). (1992). *Portfolio portraits.* Portsmouth, NH: Heinemann.

Gray, B. (1987). How natural is "natural" language teaching—employing wholistic methodology in the classroom. *Australian Journal of Early Childhood 12*(4), 3–19.

Gray, W. S. (1948). *On their own in reading: How to give children independence in attacking new words.* Glenview, IL: Scott, Foresman.

Gray, W. S. (1960). *On their own in reading: How to give children independence in analyzing new words* (rev. ed.). Glenview, IL: Scott, Foresman.

Groff, P. (1989). An attack on basal readers for the wrong reasons. In *Two reactions to the* Report Card on Basal Readers. Bloomington, IN: Clearinghouse on Reading and Communication Skills.

Groothuis, D. (1988). *Confronting the New Age: How to resist a growing religious movement.* Downers Grove, IL: InterVarsity Press.

Grundin, H. U. (1985). A commission of selective readers: A critique of *Becoming a nation of readers. The Reading Teacher, 39,* 262–266.

Guffin, J. A. (1977). Winifred Ward: A critical biography. In R. B. Heinig (Ed.), *Go adventuring! A celebration of Winifred Ward.* New Orleans: Anchorage.

Gunderson, L., & Shapiro, J. (1987). Some findings on whole language instruction. *Reading–Canada–Lecture, 5*(1), 22–26.

Gunderson, L., & Shapiro, J. (1988). Whole language instruction: Writing in 1st grade. *The Reading Teacher, 41,* 430–437.

Gursky, D. (1991). After the reign of Dick and Jane. *Teacher Magazine* (August), 22–29.

Hakuta, K. (1986). *Mirror of language: The debate on bilingualism.* New York: Basic.

Hall, M. (1976). *Teaching reading as a language experience* (2nd ed.). Columbus, OH: Charles Merrill.

Hall, M. (1981). *The language experience approach for teaching reading: A research perspective* (3rd ed.). Newark, DE: ERIC Clearinghouse on Reading and Communication Skills and the International Reading Association.

Hall, N. (1987). *The emergence of literacy*. Portsmouth, NH: Heinemann.

Halliday, M. A. K. (1975). *Learning how to mean: Explorations in the development of language*. London: Elsevier.

Halliday, M. A. K. (1984). Three aspects of children's language development: Learning language, learning through language, and learning about language. In Y. M. Goodman, M. Haussler, & D. Strickland (Eds.), *Oral and written language development research: Impact on the schools.* (pp. 165–192). Urbana, IL: National Council of Teachers of English.

Hamayan, E. (1989). *Teach your children well*. Oak Brook, IL: Proteus Enterprises.

Hamilton, S. F. (1983). The social side of schooling: Ecological studies of classrooms and schools. *Elementary School Journal, 83*, 313–334.

Hancock, J., & Hill, S. (Eds.). (1987). *Literature-based reading programs at work*. Portsmouth, NH: Heinemann.

Hanna, P. R., et al. (1966). *Phoneme-grapheme correspondences as cues to spelling improvement*. USOE Publication No. 32008. Washington, DC: Government Printing Office.

Hansen, J. (1987). *When writers read*. Portsmouth, NH: Heinemann.

Hansen, J., Newkirk, T., & Graves, D. H. (Eds.). (1985). *Breaking ground: Teachers relate reading and writing in the elementary school*. Portsmouth, NH: Heinemann.

Harman, S., & Edelsky, C. 1989. The risks of whole language literacy: Alienation and connection. *Language Arts, 66*, 392–406.

Harp, B. (Ed.). (1991). *Assessment and evaluation in whole language programs*. Norwood, MA: Christopher-Gordon.

Harper, R. J., & Kilarr, G. (1977). The law and reading instruction. *Language Arts, 54,* 913–919.

Harris, L. A., and Niles, J. A. (1982). An analysis of published informal reading inventories. *Reading Horizons, 22,* 159–174.

Harris, T. L., & Hodges, R. W. (1981). *A dictionary of reading and related terms*. Newark, DE: International Reading Association.

Harris, V. J. (Ed.). *Teaching multicultural literature in grades K–8*. Norwood, MA: Christopher-Gordon.

Harste, J. C. (1978). Understanding the hypothesis, it's the teacher that makes the difference: Part II. *Reading Horizons, 18,* 89–98.

Harste, J. C. (1985). Becoming a nation of language learners: Beyond risk. In J. C. Harste & D. Stephens (Eds.), *Toward practical theory: A state of practice assessment of reading comprehension instruction* (Section 8, 1–122). USDE-C-300-83-0130. Bloomington, IN: Indiana University.

Harste, J. C. (1989a). Commentary: The future of whole language. *The Elementary School Journal, 90,* 243–249.

Harste, J. C. (1989b). *New policy guidelines for reading: Connecting research and practice*. Urbana, IL: National Council of Teachers of English and ERIC Clearinghouse on Reading and Communication Skills.

Harste, J., & Mikulecky, L. (1984). The context of literacy in our society. In A. Purves & O. Niles (Eds.), *Becoming readers in a complex society*. Eighty-third Yearbook of the Society for the Study of Education (pp. 47–78). Chicago, IL: University of Chicago Press.

Harste, J. C., & Short, K. G., with Burke, C. (1988). *Creating classrooms for authors: The reading–writing connection*. Portsmouth, NH: Heinemann.

Harste, J. C., Woodward, V. A., & Burke, C. L. (1984). *Language stories and literacy lessons*. Portsmouth, NH: Heinemann.

Hartwell, P. (1985). Grammar, grammars, and the teaching of grammar. *College English 47* (February), 105–127.

Harwayne, S. (1992). *Lasting impressions: Weaving literature into the writing workshop*. Portsmouth, NH: Heinemann.

Haskell, D. W., et al. (1992). Effects of three orthographic/phonological units on first-grade reading. *Remedial and Special Education, 13,* 40–49.

Hasselriis, P. (1982). IEPs and a whole-language model of language arts. *Topics in Learning and Learning Disabilities, 1* (4), 17–21.

Heald-Taylor, G. (1989). *The administrator's guide to whole language.* Katonah, NY: Richard C. Owen.

Heath, S. B. (1983). *Ways with words: Language, life, and work in communities and classrooms.* New York: Cambridge University Press.

Heimlich, J. E., & Pittelman, S. D. (1986). *Semantic mapping: Classroom applications.* Newark, DE: International Reading Association.

Heinig, R. B. (1992). *Improvisation with favorite tales: Integrating drama into the reading/writing classroom.* Portsmouth, NH: Heinemann.

Heinig, R. B. (1993) *Creative drama for the classroom teacher* (4th ed.). Englewood Cliffs, NJ: Prentice Hall.

Henderson, E. H., & Beers, J. W. (1980). *Developmental and cognitive aspects of learning to spell.* Newark, DE: International Reading Association.

Hernandez-Chavez, E. (1984). The inadequacy of English immersion education as an educational approach for language minority students in the United States. In D. Dolson (Ed.), *Studies on immersion education* (pp. 144–183). Sacramento: California State Department of Education.

Heshusius, L. (1989). The Newtonian mechanistic paradigm, special education, and contours of alternatives: An overview. *Journal of Learning Disabilities, 22,* 403–415.

Hill, M. W. (1989). *Home: Where reading and writing begin.* Portsmouth, NH: Heinemann.

Hillerich, R. L. (1977). Let's teach spelling—not phonetic misspelling. *Language Arts, 54,* 301–307.

Hillerich, R. L. (1985). Let's pretend. *Michigan Journal of Reading, 18*(Summer), 15–18, 20.

Hirsch, E. D. (1987). *Cultural literacy: What every American needs to know.* Boston: Houghton Mifflin.

Hochberg, J. (1970). Components of literacy: Speculations and exploratory research. In H. Levin & J. P. Williams (Eds.), *Basic studies on reading* (pp. 74–89). New York: Basic.

Holdaway, D. (1979). *The foundations of literacy.* Sydney: Ashton Scholastic. (Distributed in the U.S. by Heinemann.)

Holdaway, D. (1984). *Stability and change in literacy learning.* London, Ontario: University of Western Ontario. (Distributed in the U.S. by Heinemann.)

Holdaway, D. (1986). The structure of natural learning as a basis for literacy instruction. In M. R. Sampson (Ed.), *The pursuit of literacy: Early reading and writing* (pp. 56–72). Dubuque, IA: Kendall Hunt.

Holdaway, D. (1992). Reading Recovery in a context of whole language. *The Whole Language Teachers Association Newsletter, 7* (2), 1–4.

Holt, D. (1986). *Beyond language: Social and cultural factors in schooling language minority students.* Los Angeles: Evaluation, Dissemination, and Assessment Center, California State University, Los Angeles.

Huck, C. (1990). The power of children's literature in the classroom. In K. Short & K. Pierce (Eds.), *Talking about books: Creating literate communities.* Portsmouth, NH: Heinemann.

Huck, C. (1992). *Children's literature in the elementary school.* (5th ed.). Orlando: Harcourt, Brace Jovanovich College Publishers.

Huck, C., Hepler, S., & Hickman, J. (1987). *Children's literature in the elementary school.* New York: Holt, Rinehart and Winston.

Hudelson, S. (1981a). An investigation of the oral reading behaviors of native Spanish speakers reading in Spanish. In S. Hudelson (Ed.), *Learning to read in different languages.* Arlington, VA: Center for Applied Linguistics.

Hudelson, S. (1981b). *Learning to read in different languages.* Arlington, VA: Center for Applied Linguistics.

Hudelson, S. (1981–1982). An examination of children's invented spelling in Spanish. *National Association for Bilingual Education Journal, 6,* 53–68.

Hudelson, S. (1984). Kan yu ret an rayt en ingles: Children become literate in English as a second language. *TESOL Quarterly, 18* (2), 221–237.

Hudelson, S. (1986). ESL children's writing: What we've learned, what we're learning. In P. Rigg & D. S. Enright (Ed.), *Children and ESL: Integrating perspectives* (pp. 23–54). Washington, DC: Teachers of English to Speakers of Other Languages.

Hudelson, S. (1987). The role of native language literacy in the education of language minority children. *Language Arts, 64* (8), 827–840.

Hudelson, S. (1989). *Write on: Children writing in ESL*. Englewood Cliffs, NJ: Prentice Hall.

Huey, E. B. (1968). *The psychology and pedagogy of reading*. Cambridge: MIT Press. (Original work published in 1908).

Hughes, M. H., & Searle, D. (1991). A longitudinal study of the growth of spelling abilities within the context of the development of literacy. In J. Zutell, S. McCormick, L. L. A. Caton, & P. O'Keefe (Eds.), *Learner factors/teacher factors: Issues in literacy research and instruction* (pp. 159–168). Chicago: National Reading Conference.

Hunt, B. C. (1974–1975). Black dialect and third and fourth graders' performance on the Gray Oral Reading Test. *Reading Research Quarterly, 10* (1), 103–123.

Hunt, K. W. (1970). *Syntactic maturity in schoolchildren and adults*. Monographs of the Society for Research in Child Development, no. 134. Chicago: University of Chicago Press.

Hunter, Madeline. (1982). *Mastery teaching*. El Sequndo, CA: TIP Publications.

Hynd, G. W., & Hynd, C. R. (1984). Dyslexia: Neuroanatomical/neurolinguistic perspectives. *Reading Research Quarterly, 19*, 482–498.

Illiteracy: An incurable disease or education malpractice? (1989). Washington, DC: U.S. Senate Republican Policy Committee.

Imhoff, G. (1990). The position of U.S. English on bilingual education. In C. Cazden & C. Snow (Eds.), *Annals of the American Academy of Political Science* (vol. 508, pp. 48–61). Newbury Park, CA: Sage Publications.

Iran-Nejad, A. (1980). *The schema: A structural or a functional pattern*. Technical Report No. 159. Urbana, IL: University of Illinois, Center for the Study of Reading.

Iran-Nejad, A., & Ortony, A. (1984). A biofunctional model of distributed mental content, mental structures, awareness, and attention. *The Journal of Mind and Behavior, 5,* 171–210.

Irlen, H. (1983). Successful treatment of learning disabilities. Paper presented at the 91st annual convention of the American Psychological Association, Anaheim, CA. (Cited by Rickleman & Henk, 1990).

Jensen, J., & Roser, N. (1993). *Adventuring with books: A booklist for pre-K–grade 6.* (10th ed.). Urbana, IL: National Council of Teachers of English. (Earlier editions annotate earlier books.)

Jett-Simpson, M. (1989b). Creative drama and story comprehension. In J. W. Stewig & S. L. Sebasta (Eds.), *Using literature in the elementary classroom*. Urbana, IL: National Council of Teachers of English.

Johns, J. L. (1986). Students' perceptions of reading: Thirty years of inquiry. In D. B. Yaden, Jr., & S. Templeton (Eds.), *Metalinguistic awareness and beginning literacy* (pp. 31–40). Portsmouth, NH: Heinemann.

Johns, J. L., & Ellis, D. W. (1976). Reading: Children tell it like it is. *Reading World, 16,* 115–128.

Johnson, D., & Roen, D. (Eds.). (1989). *Richness in writing: Empowering ESL students*. New York: Longman.

Johnson, L., & O'Neill, C. (Eds.). (1984). *Dorothy Heathcote: Collected writings on education and drama*. Evanston, IL: Northwestern University Press.

Johnson, T., Anthony, R., Field, J., Mickelson, N., & Preece, A. (1988). *Evaluation: A perspective for change*. Crystal Lake, IL: Rigby.

Johnston, P. H. (1985). Understanding reading disability: A case study approach. *Harvard Educational Review, 55,* 153–177.

Johnson, T. D., & Louis, D. R. (1990). *Bringing it all together: A program for literacy*. Portsmouth, NH: Heinemann.

Johnston, P., & Allington, R. (1991). Remediation. In R. Barr, M. L. Kamil, P. B. Mosenthal, & P. D. Pearson (Eds.), *Handbook of reading research,* (Vol. 2, pp. 984–1012). New York: Longman.

Jones, J. L. (1990). *What's left after the Right? A resource manual for educators*. Portland, OR: Education Consulting Service. [10871 S. E. Stevens Way, Portland, OR 97266; (503) 654–0874.]

Jones, J. L. (1993). *No right turn: Assuring the forward progress of public education*. Federal Way, WA: Washington Education Association and Washington, D.C.: National Education Association.

Jones, R. (1976). *The acorn people*. New York: Bantam.

Jongsma, E. (1980). *Cloze Instruction Research: A second look.* Newark, DE: International Reading Association.

Just, M. A., & Carpenter, P. A. (1987). *The psychology of reading and language comprehension.* Needham Heights, MA: Allyn & Bacon.

Kale, J., & Luke, A. (1991). Doing things with words: Early language socialisation. In E. Furniss & P. Green (Eds.), *The literacy agenda: Issues for the nineties* (pp. 1–16). Portsmouth, NH: Heinemann.

Kami, C., Manning, M. & Manning, G. (Eds.). (1991). *Early literacy: A constructivist foundation for whole language.* Washington, D.C.: National Association.

Kantrowitz, B. (1991). The profits of reading. *Newsweek,* May 20, p. 67.

Kardash, C. A. M., & Wright, L. (1987). Does creative drama benefit elementary school students: A meta-analysis. *Youth Theatre Journal, 1,* (3) 11–18.

Karlin, R. (1980). Learning disability and reading: Theory or fact? In C. McCullough (Ed.), *Inchworm, inchworm: Persistent problems in reading education* (pp. 102–110). Newark, DE: International Reading Association.

Karolides, N. J. (1992). *Reader response in the classroom.* New York: Longman.

Kase-Polisini, J. (1988) *The creative drama book: Three approaches.* New Orleans: Anchorage.

Kasten, W. C., & Clarke, B. K. (1989). *Reading/writing readiness for preschool and kindergarten children: A whole language approach.* Sanibel: Florida Educational Research and Development Council. (ERIC: ED 312 041)

Kelly, E., Rogers, C., Maslow, A., & Combs, A. (1962). *Perceiving, behaving, becoming.* New York: Association for Supervision and Curriculum Development.

Kemp, M. (1989). *Watching children read and write: Observational records for children with special needs.* Portsmouth, NH: Heinemann.

Kennedy, D. M., Spangler, S. S., & Vanderwerf, M. A. (1990). *Science and technology in fact and fiction: A guide to children's books.* New Providence, NJ: Bowker.

King, D. R., & Watson, D. J. (1983). Reading as meaning construction. In B. A. Busching & J. I. Schwartz (Eds.), *Integrating the language arts in the elementary school* (pp. 70–77). Urbana, IL: National Council of Teachers of English.

King, M. L. (1975). Language: Insights from acquisition. *Theory into Practice, 14* (December), 293–298.

Kirtley, C., Bryant, P., MacLean, M., & Bradley, L. (1989). Rhyme, rime and the onset of reading. *Journal of Experimental Psychology, 48,* 224–245.

Klesius, J. P., Griffith, P. L., & Zielonka, P. (1991). A whole language and traditional instruction comparison: Overall effectiveness and developmnent of the alphabetic principle. *Reading Research and Instruction, 30* (2), 47–61.

Klima, E. S., & Bellugi-Klima, U. (1966). Syntactic regularities in the speech of children. In J. Lyons & R. J. Wales (Eds.), *Psycholinguistic papers* (pp. 183–208). Edinburgh: Edinburgh University Press.

Kobrin, B. (1988). *Eyeopeners! How to choose and use children's books about real people, places, and things.* New York: Penguin.

Koch, K. (1973). *Rose, where did you get that red? Teaching great poetry to children.* New York: Random House.

Koestler, A. (1969). Beyond atomism and holism—the concept of the holon. In A. Koestler & J. R. Smythies (Eds.), *Beyond reductionism* (pp. 192–227). New York: Macmillan.

Kohl, H. R. (1988) *Making theater.* New York: Teachers and Writers Collaborative.

Kohler, I. (1962). Experiments with goggles. *Scientific American, 206,* 62–72.

Kolers, P. A. (1969). Reading is only incidentally visual. In K. S. Goodman & J. T. Fleming (Eds.), *Psycholinguistics and the teaching of reading* (pp. 8–16). Newark, DE: International Reading Association.

Korty, C. (1986). *Writing your own plays.* New York: Scribner's.

Krashen, S. D. (1981). *Second language acquisition and second language learning.* Oxford: Pergamon Press.

Krashen, S. D. (1982). *Principles and practice in second language acquisition.* New York: Pergamon Press.

Krashen, S. D. (1985a). Does bilingual education delay the acquisition of English? In S. D. Krashen, *Inquiries and insights* (pp. 69–88). Hayward, CA: Alemany Press.

Krashen, S. D. (1985b). *The input hypothesis: Issues and implications*. New York: Longman.

Krashen, S. D. (1985c). *Inquiries and insights*. Haywood, CA: Alemany Press.

Krashen, S. D. (1990). *The case against bilingual education*. Tucson.

Krashen, S. D. (1991). *Bilingual education: A focus on current research*. Occasional Papers in Bilingual Education, Report no. 3. Washington, DC: National Clearinghouse for Bilingual Education.

Krashen S. D. (1993). *The power of reading: Insights from the research*. Englewood, CO: Libraries Unlimited.

Krashen, S. D., & Biber, D. (1988). *On course: Bilingual education's success in California*. Sacramento: California Association of Bilingual Education.

Krashen, S. D., & Terrell, T. (1983). *The natural approach: Language acquisition in the classroom*. Hayward, CA: Alemany Press.

Kucer, S. B. (1992). Six bilingual Mexican-American students' and their teachers' interpretations of cloze literacy lessons. *The Elementary School Journal, 92*, 555–570.

Kurusa. (1983). *La Calle es libre*. Caracas, Venezuela: Ediciones Ekaré-Banco del Libro.

Lakoff, G. (1968). Instrumental adverbs and the concept of deep structure. *Foundations of Language, 4*, 4–29.

Lambert, J. (1992). *LEP enrollment in California continues to increase. BEOutreach, 3* (1), 17.

Laminack, L. (1991). *Learning with Zachary*. Richmond Hill, Ontario: Scholastic.

Laminack, L. (1992). Learning to spell: Who's in control? Unpublished manuscript. Cullowhee, NC: Western Carolina University.

Landsberg, M. (1986). *Michele Landsberg's guide to children's book*. Toronto: Penguin.

Larsen-Freeman, D. (1986). *Techniques and principles in language teaching*. Oxford: Oxford University Press.

LaShell, Lois. (1986). Matching reading styles triples reading achievement of learning disabled students. *The Clearinghouse Bulletin on Learning/Teaching Styles and Brain Behavior, 1* (1), 4.

Lassen, N. A., Ingvar, D. H., & Skinhoj, E. (1978). Brain function and blood flow. *Scientific American, 239* (4), 62–71.

Laughlin, M. K., & Latrobe, K. H. (1990). *Readers theatre for children: Scripts and script development*. Englewood, CO: Libraries Unlimited.

Laughlin, M. K., Black, P. T., & Loberg, M. K. (1991). *Social studies readers theatre for children: Scripts and script development*. Englewood, CO: Libraries Unlimited/Teacher Ideas Press.

Lee, C., & Jackson, R. (1992). *Faking it: A look into the mind of a creative learner*. Portsmouth, NH: Boynton/Cook–Heinemann.

Lenel, J. C., & Cantor, J. H. (1981). Rhyme recognition and phonemic perception in young children, *Journal of Psycholinguistic Research, 10*, 57–68.

Lesgold, A. M., & Perfetti, C. C. (Eds.). (1981). *Interactive processes in reading*. Hillsdale, NJ: Erlbaum.

Lessow-Hurley, J. (1990). *The foundations of dual language instruction*. New York: Longman.

Lester, N. B., & Onore, C. S. (1990). *Learning change*. Portsmouth, NH: Boynton/Cook–Heinemann.

Levande, D. I. (1989). Theoretical orientation to reading and classroom practice. *Reading Improvement, 26*, 274–280.

Levy, J. (1985). Right brain, left brain: Fact and fiction. *Psychology Today* (May), 38–44.

Liberman, I. Y., & Liberman, A. M. (1990). Whole language vs. code emphasis: Underlying assumptions and their implications for reading instruction. *Annals of Dyslexia, 40*, 51–76.

Lima, C. W., & Lima, J. A. (Eds.). (1989). *A to zoo: Subject access to children's picture books* (3rd ed.). New Providence, NJ: Bowker.

Lindfors, J. W. (1987). *Children's language and learning* (2nd ed.). Englewood Cliffs, NJ: Prentice Hall.

Lipson, G. B., & Morrison, B. (1977). *Fact, fantasy, and folklore: Expanding language arts and critical thinking skills*. Carthage, IL: Good Apple.

Lloyd. (1992). Thanks for the opportunity. In B. Prete & G. E. Strong (Eds.), *Literate America emerging: Seventeen new readers speak out* (pp. 39–45). Sacramento: California State Library Foundation.

Lozanov, G. (1982). Suggestology and suggestopedy. In R. Blair (Ed.), *Innovative approaches to language teaching* (pp. 146–159). Rowley, MA: Newbury House.

Lucas, I. (1981). Bilingual education and the melting pot: Getting burned. *The Illinois Issues Humanities Essays: 5.* Champaign, IL: Illinois Humanities Council.

Lucas, T., Henze, R., & Donato, R. (1990). Promoting the success of Latino language-minority students: An exploratory study of six high schools. *Harvard Educational Review, 60* (3), 315–340.

Luke, A., Baty, A., & Stehbens, C. (1989). "Natural" conditions for language learning: A critique. *English in Australia, 89* (September), 36–49.

MacDonald, M. R. (1986). *Twenty tellable tales.* New York: H. W. Wilson.

MacDonald, M. R. (1988). *Booksharing: 101 programs to use with preschoolers.* Hamden, CN: Library of Professional Publications.

MacDonald, M. R. (1993). *The storyteller's start-up book.* Little Rock, AR: August House.

MacGowan-Gilhooly, A. (1991). Fluency first: Reversing the traditional ESL sequence. *Journal of Basic Writing, 10* (1), 73–87.

MacKenzie, T. (Ed.). (1992). *Reader's workshops: Bridging literature and literacy.* Toronto: Irwin.

Madaus, G. F. (1985). Test scores as administrative mechanisms in educational policy. *Phi Delta Kappan, 66,* 611–617.

Maguire, J. (1985). *Creative storytelling: Choosing, inventing, and sharing tales for children.* NY: McGraw-Hill.

Maguire, M. (1993). *Evaluation of the CECM bilingual program.* Research report to the Montreal Catholic School Commission. Montreal: McGill University.

Manning, G., & Manning, D. (Eds.). (1989). *Whole language: Beliefs and practices, K–8.* Washington, DC: National Education Association.

Marek, A. M. (1989). Using evaluation as an instructional strategy for adult readers. In K. S. Goodman, Y. M. Goodman, & W. J. Hood (Eds.), *The whole language evaluation book* (pp. 157–164). Portsmouth, NH: Heinemann.

Marek, A. M. (1992). Retrospective miscue analysis lesson plan. Distributed at a session on miscue analysis at the International Reading Association annual convention, Orlando, May 1992.

Marks, L. E., & Miller, G. A. (1964). The role of semantic and syntactic constraints in the memorization of English sentences. *Journal of Verbal Learning and Verbal Behavior, 3,* 1–5.

Marrs, T. (1987). *Dark secrets of the New Age: Satan's plan for a one world religion.* Westchester, IL: Crossway Books.

Martin, W. (1989). *The New Age cult.* Minneapolis, MN: Bethany House.

Matchmaker CD-Rom. (n. d.). Topeka, KS: American Econo-Clad Services.

Mathews, M. (1966). *Teaching to read, historically considered.* Chicago: University of Chicago Press.

Mayher, J. S. (1990). *Uncommon sense: Theoretical practice in language education.* Portsmouth, NH: Boynton/Cook–Heinemann.

McCarthy, B. (1980). *The 4MAT system: Teaching to learning styles with right/left mode techniques.* Napa, CA: Excel.

McCaslin, N. (1987a). *Creative drama in the intermediate grades.* Studio City, CA: Players Press.

McCaslin, N. (1987b). *Creative drama in the primary grades.* Studio City, CA: Players Press.

McCaslin, N. (1990). *Creative drama in the classroom* (5th ed.). Studio City, CA: Players Press.

McCawley, J. D. (1968). The role of semantics in grammar. In E. Bach & R. T. Harms (Eds.), *Universals in linguistic theory* (pp. 124–169). New York: Holt, Rinehart.

McConaghy, J. (1990). *Children learning through literature: A teacher researcher study.* Portsmouth, NH: Heinemann.

McConkie, G. W., & Zola, D. (1981). Language constraints and the functional stimulus in reading. In A. M. Lesgold & C. A. Perfetti (Eds.), *Interactive processes in reading* (pp. 155–175). Hillsdale, NJ: Erlbaum.

McDermott, R. P. (1974). Achieving school failure: An anthropological approach to illiteracy and social stratification. In G. D. Spindler (Ed.), *Education and cultural process* (pp. 82–118). New York: Holt, Rinehart.

McGee, L. M., & Lomax, R. G. (1990). On combining apples and oranges: A response to Stahl and Miller. *Review of Educational Research, 60*, 133–140.

McGill-Franzen, A., & Allington, R. (1991). The gridlock of low reading achievement: Perspectives on practice and policy. *Remedial and Special Education, 12* (3), 20–30.

McInnes, J. (1985). The drama of reading. In J. Kase-Polisini (Ed.), *Creative drama in a developmental context*. Lanham, MD: University Press of America.

McKean, K. (1981). Beaming new light on the brain. *Discover, 2* (December), 30–33.

McKean, K. (1985). In search of the unconscious mind. *Discover, 6* (February), 12–14, 16, 18.

McKenna, M. C., Robinson, R. D., & Miller, J. W. (1990). Whole language: A research agenda for the nineties. *Educational Researcher, 19*, 3–6.

McNamara, T. P., Miller, D. L., & Bransford, J. D. (1991). Mental models and reading comprehension. In R. Barr, M. L. Kamil, P. B. Mosenthal, & P. D. Pearson (Eds.), *Handbook of reading research* (Vol. 2, pp. 490–511). New York: Longman.

McNeill, D. (1966). Developmental psycholinguistics. In F. Smith & G. A. Miller (Eds.), *The genesis of language: A psycholinguistic approach* (pp. 15–84). Cambridge: MIT Press.

Meek, M. (1983). *Achieving literacy*. London: Routledge & Kegan Paul.

Meek, M. (1992). *On being literate*. Portsmouth, NH: Heinemann.

Menosky, D. M. (1971). A psycholinguistic description of oral reading miscues generated during the reading of varying portions of text by selected readers from grades two, four, six and eight. Doctoral dissertation, Wayne State University, Detroit.

MERIT. (1986). *Developing metacognitive skills: The key to success in reading and learning.* MERIT, Chapter 2 Project, the School District of Philadelphia, Hilda K. Carr, MERIT Supervisor.

Mewhort, D. J. K., & Campbell, A. J. (1981). Toward a model of skilled reading: An analysis of performance in tachistoscopic tasks. In G. E. MacKinnon & T. G. Waller (Eds.), *Reading research: Advances in theory and practice* (Vol. 3, pp. 39–118). New York: Academic Press.

Miller, G. A., Bruner, J. S., & Postman, L. (1954). Familiarity of letter sequences and tachistoscopic identification. *Journal of General Psychology, 50*, 129–139.

Miller, G. A., & Friedman, E. A. (1957). The reconstruction of mutilated English texts. *Information and Control, 1*, 38–55.

Miller, G. A., & Gildea, P. M. (1987). How children learn words. *Scientific American, 257* (3), 94–99.

Mills, H., & Clyde, J. A. (Eds.). (1990). *Portraits of whole language classrooms*. Portsmouth, NH: Heinemann.

Mills, H., O'Keefe, T., & Stephens, D. (1992). *Looking closely: Exploring the role of phonics in one whole language classroom*. Urbana, IL: National Council of Teachers of English.

Moffett, J. (1988). *Storm in the mountains: A case study of censorship, conflict, and consciousness*. Carbondale, IL: University of Illinois Press.

Moir, H., Cain, M., & Prosak-Beres, L. (Eds.). (1990). *Collected perspectives: Choosing and using books for the classroom*. Norwood, MA: Christopher-Gordon.

Monaghan, E. J. (1980). A history of the syndrome of dyslexia with implications for its treatment. In C. McCullough (Ed.), *Inchworm, inchworm: Persistent problems in reading education* (pp. 87–101). Newark DE: International Reading Association.

Monson, R. J., & Pahl, M. M. (1991). Charting a new course with whole language. *Educational Leadership, 48*, 51–53.

Morgan, N. & Saxton, J. (1987). *Teaching drama: A mind of many wonders*. Portsmouth, NH: Heinemann.

Moss, J. F. (1984). *Focus units in literature: A handbook for elementary school teachers*. Urbana, IL: National Council of Teachers of English.

Moss, R. K. (1991). A review of Reading Recovery from a psycholinguistic perspective. Phoenix, AZ: Paper presented at the Whole Language Umbrella Conference, August.

Murphy, S. (1986). Children's comprehension of deictic categories in oral and written language. *Reading Research Quarterly, 21*, 118–131.

Murphy, S. (1991). Authorship and discourse types in Canadian English-language basal reading programs. *Reflections on Canadian Literacy, 3* (4), 133–138.

Nagy, W. E., & Anderson, R. C. (1984). How many words are there in printed school English? *Reading Research Quarterly, 19*, 304–330.

Nagy, W. E., Anderson, R. C., & Herman, P. A. (1987). Learning word meanings from context during normal reading. *American Educational Research Journal, 24*, 237–270.

Nagy, W. E., & Herman, P. A. (1987). Breadth and depth of vocabulary knowledge: Implications for acquisition and instruction. In M. McKeown & M. Curtis (Eds.), *The nature of vocabulary acquisition* (pp. 19–35). Hillsdale, NJ: Erlbaum.

National Assessment of Educational Progress. (1991). The Integrated Reading Performance Record (IRPR). Unpublished paper. Princeton, NJ: Educational Testing Service. May.

National Center for Educational Statistics. (1993). *Digest of education statistics 1993*. U.S. Department of Education, Office of Educational Research and Improvement.

National Commission on Testing and Public Policy. (1990). *From gatekeeper to gateway: Transforming testing in America.* Chestnut Hill, MA: Boston College.

Neill, D. M., and Medina, N. J. (1989). Standardized testing: Harmful to educational health. *Phi Delta Kappan, 70*, 688–697.

Neisser, U. (1986). New answers to an old question. In U. Neisser (Ed.), *The school achievement of minority children: New perspectives.* Hillsdale, NJ: Erlbaum.

Nelms, B. F. (1988). *Literature in the classroom: Readers, texts, and contexts.* Urbana, IL: National Council of Teachers of English.

Nelson, J. (1987). *Positive discipline.* New York: Ballantine.

Newkirk, T. (1989). *More than stories: The range of children's writing.* Portsmouth, NH: Heinemann.

Newkirk, T., & Atwell, N. (Eds.). (1988). *Understanding writing: Ways of observing, learning, and teaching* (2nd ed.). Portsmouth, NH: Heinemann.

Newman, J. M. (1984). *The craft of children's writing.* Richmond Hill, Ontario: Scholastic. (Distributed in the U.S. by Heinemann.)

Newman, J. M. (1985a). Insights from recent reading and writing research and their implications for developing whole language curriculum. In J. Newman (Ed.), *Whole language: Theory in use* (pp. 7–36). Portsmouth, NH: Heinemann.

Newman, J. M. (1985b). *Whole language: Theory in use.* Portsmouth, NH: Heinemann.

Newman, J. M. (1990). *Finding our own way: Teachers exploring their assumptions.* Portsmouth, NH: Heinemann.

Newman, J. M., & Church, S. M. (1990). Myths of whole language. *The Reading Teacher, 44*, 20–26.

Nicholson, T. (1989). A comment on Reading Recovery. *New Zealand Journal of Education Studies, 24*, 95–97.

Nicholson, T. (1991). Do children read words better in context or in lists? A classic study revisited. *Journal of Educational Psychology, 83*, 444–450.

Ninio, A., & Bruner, J. (1978). The achievement and antecedents of labeling. *Journal of Child Language, 5*, 1–15.

Nix, D., & Schwarz, M. (1979). Toward a phenomenology of reading comprehension. In R. Freedle (Ed.), *New directions in discourse processing* (pp. 183–196). Norwood, NJ: Ablex.

Norton, D. (1987). *Through the eyes of a child: An introduction to children's literature* (3rd ed.). New York: Macmillan.

Novelly, M. C. (1985). *Theatre games for young performers.* Colorado Springs: Meriwether.

Oakes, J. (1985). *Keeping track: How schools structure inequality.* New Haven: Yale University Press.

O'Connor, P.D., Sofo, F., Kendall, L., & Olsen, G. (1988). Reading disabilities and the effects of colored filters. *Journal of Learning Disabilities, (23)*, 597–603.

O'Donnell, R. C., Griffin, W. J., & Norris, R. C. (1967). *Syntax of kindergarten and elementary school children: A transformational analysis.* Research Report no. 8. Urbana, IL: National Council of Teachers of English.

O'Farrell, L. (1993). Enhancing the practice of drama in education through research. *Youth Theatre Journal, 7* (4), 25–30.

Olsen, L. (1988). *Crossing the schoolhouse border: Immigrant students and the California public schools.* San Francisco: California Tomorrow.

Olsen, L., & Mullen, N. (1990). *Embracing diversity: Teachers' voices from California classrooms.* San Francisco: California Tomorrow.

Olsen, R. (1989). A survey of limited English proficient enrollments and identification procedures. *TESOL Quarterly, 23,* 469–488.

O'Neill, C., & Lambert, A. (1982). *Drama structures.* Portsmouth, NH: Heinemann.

O'Neill, C., Lambert, A., Linell, R., & Warr-Wood, J. (1977). *Drama guidelines.* Portsmouth, NH: Heinemann.

Oppenheim, J., Brenner, B., & Boeghold, B. D. (1986). *Choosing books for kids: How to choose the right book for the right child at the right time.* New York: Ballantine.

Osborn, S. (1987). *Free (and almost free) things for teachers.* New York: Perigree Books.

Ovando, C., & Collier, V. (1985). *Bilingual and ESL classrooms: Teaching in multicultural contexts.* New York: McGraw-Hill.

Pace, G. (1991). When teachers use literature for literacy instruction: Ways that constrain, ways that free. *Language Arts, 68,* 12–25.

Page, W. D. (Ed.). (1975). *Help for the reading teacher: New directions in research.* Urbana, IL: National Conference on Research in English and the National Council of Teachers of English.

Palermo, D. S. (1978). *Psychology of language.* Glenview, IL: Scott, Foresman.

Paterson, K. (1981). *Gates of excellence: On reading and writing books for children.* New York: Dutton.

Patterson, K. E., & Coltheart, V. (1987). Phonological processes in reading: A tutorial review. In M. Coltheart (Ed.), *Attention and performance XII: The psychology of reading* (pp. 421–447). London: Erlbaum Associates.

Pearson, P. D. (1978). On bridging gaps and spanning chasms. *Curriculum Inquiry, 8,* 353–362.

Pearson, P. D., & Fielding, L. (1991). Comprehension instruction. In R. Barr, M. L. Kamil, P. B. Mosenthal, & P. D. Pearson (Eds.), *Handbook of reading research* (Vol. 2, pp. 815–860). New York: Longman.

Pearson, P. D., & Johnson, D. D. (1978). *Teaching reading comprehension.* New York: Holt, Rinehart.

Peetoom, A. (1986). *Shared reading: Safe risks with big books.* Richmond Hill, Ontario: Scholastic.

Peetoom, A. (1992). *RefleXions: Professional reflections and connections.* Richmond Hill, Ontario: Scholastic.

Peetoom, A. (1993). *ConneXions: Inviting engagement with books.* Richmond Hill, Ontario: Scholastic.

Pellowski, A. (1984). *The story vine: A source book of unusual and easy-to-tell stories from around the world.* New York: Macmillan.

Perera, K. (1986). Language acquisition as a continuing process: The role of the English teacher. Paper presented at the Fourth International Conference on the Teaching of English, Ottawa, Ontario, May 13.

Perfetti, C. A. (1985). *Reading ability.* New York: Oxford University Press.

Perfetti, C. A., Bell, L. C., & Delaney, S. M. (1988). Automatic (prelexical) phonetic activation in silent word reading: Evidence from backward masking. *Journal of Memory and Language, 27,* 59–70.

Perfetti, C. A., & Hogaboam, T. (1975). Relationship between single word decoding and reading comprehension skill. *Journal of Educational Psychology, 67,* 461–469.

Perfetti, C. A., & McCutcheon, D. (1982). Speech processes in reading. In N. Lass (Ed.), *Speech and language: Advances in basic research,* Vol. 7 (pp. 237–269). New York: Academic Press.

Perspectives on basal readers. (1989). Themed issue of *Theory into Practice, 28* (4) (Autumn).

Peterson, B. (1991). Selecting books for beginning readers. In D. E. DeFord, C. A. Lyons, & G. S. Pinnell (Eds.), *Bridges to literacy: Learning from Reading Recovery.* Portsmouth, NH: Heinemann.

Peterson, R. (1992). *Life in a crowded place: Making a learning community*. Portsmouth, NH: Heinemann.

Peterson, R. & Eeds, M. (1990). *Grand converstaions: Literature groups in action*. Richmond Hill, Ontario: Scholastic.

Peterson, R. E. (1987). Books to empower young people. *Rethinking Schools, 1* (3), 8–9.

Peterson, R. E. (1991). Teaching how to read the world and change it: Critical pedagogy in the intermediate grades. In C. E. Walsh (Ed.), *Literacy as praxis: Culture, language and pedagogy* (pp. 156–182). Norwood, NJ: Ablex.

Peyton, J. K. (1990). *Students and teachers writing together: Perspectives on journal writing*. Alexandria, VA: Teachers of English to Speakers of Other Languages.

Phillips, S. (1972). Participant structures and communicative competence: Warm Spring children in community and classroom. In C. Cazden, V. John, & D. Hymes (Eds.), *Functions of language in the classroom* (pp. 370–394). New York: Teachers College Press.

Phinney, M. Y. (1988). *Reading with the troubled reader*. Portsmouth, NH: Heinemann.

Pierce, K. M. (1990). Initiating literature discussion groups: Teaching like learners. In K. G. Short & K. M. Pierce (Eds.), *Talking about books: Creating literate communities* (pp. 177–197). Portsmouth, NH: Heinemann.

Pierce, K. M. and Gilles, C. (Eds.). (1994). *Cycles of meaning: Exploring the potential of talk in learning communities*. Portsmouth, NH: Heinemann.

Pinnell, G. S. (1985). Helping teachers help children at risk: Insights from the Reading Recovery program. *Peabody Journal of Education, 62*, 70–85.

Pinnell, G. S. (1989). Reading Recovery: Helping at-risk children learn to read. *The Elementary School Journal, 90*, 161–183.

Pinnell, G. S., Deford, D., & Lyons, C. (1988). *Reading Recovery: Early intervention for at-risk first graders*. Arlington, VA: Educational Research Service.

Pinnell, G. S., Fried, M. D., & Estice, R. M. (1990). Reading Recovery: Learning how to make a difference. *The Reading Teacher, 43*, 282–295.

Polsky, M. (1989). *Let's improvise!* Lanham, MD: University Press of America.

Poplin, M. S. (1988a). Holistic/constructivist principles of the teaching/learning process: Implications for the field of learning disabilities. *Journal of Learning Disabilities, 21*, 401–416.

Poplin, M. S. (1988b). The reductionist fallacy in learning disabilities: Replicating the past by reducing the present. *Journal of Learning Disabilities, 21*, 389–400.

Poplin, M. S., & Stone, S. (1992). Paradigm shifts in instructional strategies: From reductionism to holistic/constructivism. In W. Stainback & S. Stainback (Eds.), *Controversial issues confronting special education: Divergent perspectives* (pp. 153–179). Boston: Allyn & Bacon.

Porter, R. (1990). *Forked tongue: The politics of bilingual education*. New York: Basic Books.

Powell, D., & Hornsby, D. (1993). *Learning phonics and spelling in a whole language classroom*. New York: Scholastic.

Prete, B., & Strong, G. E. (Eds.). (1991). *Literate America emerging: Seventeen new readers speak out*. Sacramento: California State Library Foundation.

Prigogine, I., & Stengers, I. (1984). *Order out of chaos: Man's new dialogue with nature*. New York: Bantam.

Probst, R. E. (1988). *Response and analysis: Teaching literature in junior and senior high school*. Portsmouth, NH: Boynton/Cook–Heinemann.

Purcell-Gates, V. (1988). Lexical and syntactic knowledge of written narrative held by well-read-to kindergarteners and second graders. *Research in the Teaching of English, 22*, 128–160.

Purcell-Gates, V., & Dahl, K. L. (1991). Low-SES children's success and failure at early learning in skills-based classrooms. *Journal of Reading Behavior, 23*, 1–34.

Raines, S. C., & Canady, R. J. (1989). *Story s-t-r-e-t-c-h-e-r-s: Activities to expand children's favorite books*. Mt. Ranier, MD: Gryphon House.

Raines, S. C., & Canady, R. J. (1991). *More story s-t-r-e-t-c-h-e-r-s*. Mt. Ranier, MD: Gryphon House.

Ramírez, J. D. (1991). *Final report: Longitudinal study of structured English immersion strategy, early-exit and late-exit bilingual education programs* (300-87-0156). Washington, DC: U.S. Department of Education.

Rasinsky, T. V., & DeFord, D. E. (1988). First graders' conceptions of literacy: A matter of schooling. *Theory into Practice*, 27 (1), 53-61.

Rayner, K., & Pollatsek, A. (1989). *The psychology of reading*. Englewood Cliffs, NJ: Prentice Hall.

Read, C. (1975). *Children's categorizations of speech sounds in English*. Research report no. 17. Urbana, IL: National Council of Teachers of English.

Read, C. (1986). *Children's Creative Spelling*. New York: Routledge.

Reading educators question advertising of "Hooked on Phonics" reading program. (1991). *Reading Today, 8*, 1, 22.

Reid, J. F. (1958). An investigation of thirteen beginners in reading. *Acta psychologica, 14* (4), 295-313.

Rethinking Schools. [Rethinking Schools Ltd., 1001 E. Keefe Ave., Milwaukee, WI 53212; (414) 964-9646]

Reynolds, R. E., Taylor, M. A., Steffensen, M. S., Shirey, L. L., & Anderson, R. C. (1982). Cultural schemata and reading comprehension. *Reading Research Quarterly, 17*, 353-366.

Rhodes, L. K. (1981). I can read! Predictable books as resources for reading and writing instruction. *The Reading Teacher, 34*, 511-518.

Rhodes, L. K. (Ed.). (1992). *Literacy assessment: A handbook of instruments*. Portsmouth, NH: Heinemann.

Rhodes, L. K., & Dudley-Marling, C. (1988). *Readers and writers with a difference: A holistic approach to teaching learning disabled and remedial students*. Portsmouth, NH: Heinemann.

Rhodes, L. K., & Shanklin, N. L. (1989). A research base for whole language. Denver, CO: LINK.

Rhodes, L. K., & Shanklin, N. L. (1992). *Windows into literacy: Assessing learners K-8*. Portsmouth, NH: Heinemann.

Ribowsky, H. (1985). *The effects of a code emphasis approach and a whole language approach upon emergent literacy of kindergarten children*. Alexandria, VA: (ERIC: ED 269 720)

Rich, S. J. (1985). Restoring power to teachers: The impact of "Whole Language." *Language Arts, 62 November*, 717-724.

Richards, J., & Rodgers, T. (1986). *Approaches and methods in language teaching: A description and analysis*. New York: Cambridge University Press.

Richards, T. S. (1989). Testmania: The school under siege. *Learning 89*, 17, 64-66.

Rickelman, R., & Henk, W. A. (1990). Colored overlays and tinted lens filters. *The Reading Teacher, 44*, 166-167.

Rief, L. (1991). *Seeking diversity: Language arts with adolescents*. Portsmouth, NH: Heinemann.

Rigg, P. (1978). Dialect and /in/ for reading. *Language Arts, 55*, 285-290.

Rigg, P. (1986). Reading in ESL: Learning from kids. In P. Rigg & D. S. Enright (Eds.), *Children and ESL: Integrating perspectives* (pp. 55-92). Washington, DC: Teachers of English to Speakers of Other Languages.

Rigg, P. (1989). Language experience approach: Reading naturally. In P. Rigg & V. G. Allen (Eds.), *When they don't all speak English: Integrating the ESL student into the regular classroom* (pp. 65-76). Urbana, IL: National Council of Teachers of English.

Rigg, P. (1990). Using the language experience approach with ESL adults. *TESL Talk, 29* (1), 188-200.

Rigg, P., & Allen, V. (Eds.). (1989). *When they don't all speak English*. Urbana, IL: National Council of Teachers of English.

Rigg, P., & Enright, D. S. (Eds.). (1986). *Children and ESL: Integrating perspectives*. Washington, D.C.: Teachers of English to Speakers of Other Languages.

Rigg, P., & Hudelson, S. (1986). One child doesn't speak English. *Australian Journal of Reading, 9* (3), 116-125.

Rigg, P., & Taylor, L. (1979). A twenty-one-year-old begins to read. *English Journal, 68*, 52-56.

Rist, R. C. (1970). Student social class and teacher expectations: The self-fulfilling prophecy in ghetto education. *Harvard Educational Review, 40*, 411-451.

Rivers, W. (1983). *Communicating naturally in a second language: Theory and practice in language teaching.* New York: Cambridge University Press.

Rivers, W. (1987). *Interactive language teaching.* New York: Cambridge University Press.

Robinson, A., Crawford, L., & Hall, N. (1990). *"Some day you will no all about me": Young children's explorations in the world of letters.* Portsmouth, NH: Heinemann.

Robinson, G. L. W., & Conway, R. N. F. (1990). Effects of Irlen colored lenses on students' specific reading skills and their perception of ability: A 12-month validity study. *Journal of Learning Disabilities, 23,* 589–596.

Romijn, E., & Seely, C. (1979). *Live action English.* San Francisco: Alemany Press.

Rosen, B. (1988). *And none of it was nonsense: The power of storytelling in school.* Portsmouth, NH: Heinemann.

Rosenblatt, L. (1964). The poem as event. *College English, 26,* 123–128.

Rosenblatt, L. (1978). *The reader, the text, the poem: The transactional theory of the literary work.* Carbondale, IL.: Southern Illinois University Press.

Rosenblatt, L. (1983). *Literature as exploration* (4th ed.). New York: Modern Language Association. (Originally published 1938.)

Ross, J. R. (1967). Constraints on variables in syntax. Unpublished doctoral dissertation, Massachusetts Institute of Technology.

Ross, J. R. (1974). Three batons for cognitive psychology. In W. B. Werner & D. S. Palermo (Eds.), *Cognition and the symbolic processes* (pp. 63–124). New York: Lawrence Erlbaum.

Routman, R. (1988). *Transitions: From literature to literacy.* Portsmouth, NH: Heinemann.

Routman, R. (1991). *Invitations: Changing as teachers and learners K–12.* Portsmouth, NH: Heinemann.

Rudman, M. K. (Ed.). *Children's literature: Resource for the classroom* (2nd ed.). Norwood, MA: Christopher-Gordon.

Rumelhart, D. E. (1977). Toward an interactive model of reading. In S. Dornic (Ed.), *Attention and performance VI* (pp. 573–603). Hillsdale, NJ: Erlbaum.

Rumelhart, D. E. (1980). Schemata: The building blocks of cognition. In R. J. Spiro, B. C. Bruce, & W. F. Brewer (Eds.), *Theoretical issues in reading comprehension* (pp. 33–58). Hillsdale, NJ: Erlbaum.

Rumsey, J. M., Berman, K. F., Denckla, M. B., Hamburger, S. D., Kruesi, M. J., & Weinberger, D. R. (1987). Regional cerebral blood flow in severe developmental dyslexia. *Archives of Neurology, 44,* 1144–1150.

Salisbury, B. T. (1986). *Theatre arts in the elementary classroom: Grade four through grade six.* New Orleans: Anchorage Press.

Salisbury, B. T. (1986). *Theatre arts in the elementary classroom: Kindergarten through grade three.* New Orleans: Anchorage Press.

Sampson, M. R. (Ed.). (1986). *The pursuit of literacy: Early reading and writing.* Dubuque, IA: Kendall Hunt.

Santa, C. M. (1981). Children's reading comprehension: A final word. In C. M. Santa & B. L. Hayes (Eds.), *Children's prose comprehension: Research and practice* (pp. 157–170). Newark, DE: International Reading Association.

Sawyer, R. (1962). *The way of the storyteller.* New York: Viking.

Scarcella, R. (1990). *Teaching language minority students in the multicultural classroom.* Englewood Cliffs, NJ: Prentice Hall Regents.

Schatz, E. K., & Baldwin, R. S. (1986). Context clues are unreliable predictors of word meanings. *Reading Research Quarterly, 21,* 439–453.

Scher, A., & Verrall, C. (1992). *200 + ideas for drama.* Portsmouth, NH: Heinemann.

Schwartz, D., & Aldrich, D. (Eds.). (1985). *Give them roots . . . and wings!* (2nd ed.). New Orleans: Anchorage Press.

Schickendanz, J. A. (1990). The jury is still out on the effects of whole language and language experience approaches for beginning reading: A critique of Stahl and Miller's study. *Review of Educational Research, 60,* 127–131.

Schimmel, N. (1982). *Just enough to make a story: A source book for storytelling*. Berkeley, CA: Sister's Choice Press.

Schott, J. C. (1989). Holy Wars in education. *Educational Leadership, 47*, 61–66.

Sebasta, S. (1981). Why Ruldolph can't read. *Language Arts, 58*, 545–548.

Segal, B. (1983). *Teaching English through action*. Brea, CA: Berty Segal.

Seidenberg, M. S., & McClelland, J. L. (1989). A distributed, developmental model of word recognition and naming. *Psychological Review, 96*, 523–568.

Serna, I., & Hudelson, S. (In press.) Emergent Spanish literacy in whole language bilingual classrooms. In R. Donmoyer & R. Kos (Eds.), *At risk students: Portraits, policies, and programs*. Albany, NY: SUNY Press.

Seymour, P. K., & Elder, L. (1986). Beginning reading without phonology. *Cognitive Neuropsychology, 3*, 1–36.

Shannon, C. E. (1948). A mathematical theory of information. *Bell System Technical Journal, 27*, 379–423, 623–656.

Shannon, P. (1985). Reading instruction and social class. *Language Arts, 62*, 604–613.

Shannon, P. (1989a). *Broken promises: Reading instruction in twentieth century America*. Granloy, MA: Bergin & Garvey.

Shannon, P. (1989b). The struggle for control of literacy lessons. *Language Arts, 66*, 625–633.

Shannon, P. (1990). *The struggle to continue: Progressive reading instruction in the United States*. Portsmouth, NH: Heinemann.

Shannon, P. (Ed.). (1992). *Becoming political: Readings and writings in the politics of literacy education*. Portsmouth, NH: Heinemann.

Shapiro, J. (1990). Research perspectives on whole-language. In V. Froese (Ed.), *Whole-language: Practice and theory*. Boston: Allyn & Bacon.

Sharp, Q. Q. (1989). *Evaluation: Whole language checklists for evaluating your children: For grades K to 6*. New York: Scholastic.

Shaywitz, S. E., Escobar, M. D., Shaywitz, B. A., Fletcher, J. M., & Makuch, R. (1992). Evidence that dyslexia may represent the lower tail of a normal distribution of reading ability. *The New England Journal of Medicine, 326* (3), 145–150.

Shor, I. (1986). *Culture wars: School and society in the conservative restoration, 1969–1984*. New York: Routledge & Kegan Paul.

Shor, I. (1987). *Freire for the classroom: A sourcebook for liberatory teaching*. Portsmouth, NH: Boynton/Cook–Heinemann.

Shor, I. (1992). *Empowering education: Critical teaching for social change*. Chicago: University of Chicago Press.

Short, K., & Armstrong, J. (1993). "More than facts": Exploring the role of talk in classroom inquiry. In K. M. Pierce & C. J. Gilles (Eds.), *Cycles of meaning: Exploring the potential of talk in learning communities*, pp. 119–138. Portsmouth NH: Heinemann.

Short, K. G., & Burke, C. L. (1991). *Creating curriculum: Teachers and students as a community of learners*. Portsmouth, NH: Heinemann.

Short, K. G., & Pierce, K. M. (Eds.). (1990). *Talking about books: Creating literate communities*. Portsmouth, NH: Heinemann.

Shuy, R. W. (1967). *Discovering American dialects*. Urbana, IL: National Council of Teachers of English.

Sierra, J. (1987). *The flannel board storytelling book*. New York: H. W. Wilson.

Siks, G. B. (1958). *Creative dramatics: An art for children*. New York: Harper & Row.

Siks, G. B. (1964). *Children's literature for dramatization*. New York: Harper & Row.

Siks, G. B. (1983). Drama with children (2nd ed.). New York: Harper & Row.

Simmons, D. C. (1992). Perspectives on dyslexia: Commentary on educational concerns. *Journal of Learning Disabilities, 25*, 66–70.

Simon, D. P., & Simon, H. A. (1973). Alternative uses of phonemic information in spelling. *Review of Educational Research, 43*, 115–137.

Simons, H. D., & Ammon, P. (1989). Child knowledge and primerese text: Mismatches and miscues. *Research in the Teaching of English, 23*, 380–398.

Sinatra, R., & Stahl-Gemake, J. (1983). *Using the right brain in the language arts.* Springfield, IL: Charles C. Thomas.

Sinclair, P. (1992). *E for environment: An annotated bibliography of children's books with environmental themes.* New Providence, NJ: Bowker.

Sklar, D. J. (1990). *Playmaking: Children writing and performing their own plays.* New York: Teachers and Writers Collaborative.

Skutnabb-Kangas, T. (1983). *Bilingualism or not: The education of minorities.* Clevedon, England: Multilingual Matters.

Slavin, R. E. (1987). Making Chapter 1 make a difference. *Phi Delta Kappan, 69*, 110–119.

Slavin, R. E. (1991). Chapter 1: A vision for the next quarter century. *Phi Delta Kappan, 72*, 586–592.

Sleeter, C. E. (1986). Learning disabilities: The social construction of a special education category. *Exceptional Children, 53*, 46–54.

Slobin, D. I. (1971). *Psycholinguistics.* Glenview, IL: Scott, Foresman.

Slobin, D. I. (1972). They learn the same way all around the world. *Psychology Today, 6* (July), 72–74, 82.

Sloyer, S. (1982). *Readers theatre: Story dramatization in the classroom.* Urbana, IL: National Council of Teachers of English.

Smith, B. K. (1966). *Dictionary of English word-roots.* Savage, MD: Rowman & Littlefield.

Smith, E. B., Goodman, K. S., & Meredith, R. (1970). *Language and thinking in the elementary school.* New York: Holt, Rinehart.

Smith, F. (1971). *Understanding reading.* Hillsdale, NJ: Erlbaum.

Smith, F. (1975). *Comprehension and learning: A conceptual framework for teachers.* Katonah, NY: Richard C. Owen.

Smith, F. (1979). *Reading without nonsense.* New York: Teachers College Press.

Smith, F. (1981a). Demonstrations, engagement, and sensitivity: The choice between people and programs. *Language Arts, 58*, 634–642.

Smith, F. (1981b). Demonstrations, engagement, and sensitivity: A revised approach to language learning. *Language Arts, 58*, 103–112.

Smith, F. (1983). *Essays into literacy: Selected papers and some afterthoughts.* Portsmouth, NH: Heinemann.

Smith, F. (1985). *Reading without nonsense* (2nd ed.). New York: Teachers College Press.

Smith, F. (1988a). *Insult to intelligence: The bureaucratic invasion of our classrooms.* Portsmouth, NH: Heinemann.

Smith, F. (1988b). *Joining the literacy club: Further essays into education.* Portsmouth, NH: Heinemann.

Smith, F. (1988c). *Understanding reading* (4th ed.). Hillsdale, NJ: Erlbaum.

Smith, F. (1990). *To think.* New York: Teachers College Press.

Smith, F. (1992). Learning to read: The never-ending debate. *Phi Delta Kappan, 73*, 432–441.

Smith, F. (Ed.). (1973). *Psycholinguistics and reading.* New York: Holt, Rinehart.

Smith, K. (1990). Entertaining a text: A reciprocal process. In K. Short & K. Pierce (Eds.), *Talking about books: Creating literate communities.* Portsmouth, NH: Heinemann.

Smith, N. B. (1965). *American reading instruction: Its development and its significance in gaining a perspective on current practices in reading.* Newark, DE: International Reading Association.

Smith, R. J., & Barrett, T. C. (1974). *Teaching reading in the middle grades.* Reading, MA: Addison-Wesley.

Sorensen, N. A. (1983). A study of the reliability of phonic generalizations in five primary-level basal reading programs. Doctoral dissertation, Arizona State University, Tempe.

Spann, S., & Culp, M. B. (Eds.). (1975). *Thematic units in teaching English and the humanities.* Urbana, IL: National Council of Teachers of English.

Spann, S., & Culp, M. B. (Eds.). (1977). *Thematic units in teaching English and the humanities: First supplement.* Urbana, IL: National Council of Teachers of English.

Sperling, S. K. (1977). *Poplollies and bellibones: A celebration of lost words*. New York: Clarkson N. Potter.

Spoehr, K. T. (1981). Word recognition in speech and reading: Toward a theory of language processing. In P. D. Eimas & J. L. Miller (Eds.), *Perspectives on the study of speech* (pp. 239–282). Hillsdale, NJ: Erlbaum.

Spolin, V. (1963/1983). *Improvisation for the theater*. Evanston, IL: Northwestern University Press.

Spolin, V. (1975/1989). *The theater game file*. St. Louis: CEMREL. (Reissued in 1989 by Northwestern University Press, Evanston, IL.)

Spolin, V. (1986). *Theater games for the classroom: A teacher's handbook*. Evanston, IL: Northwestern University Press.

Stahl, S. A. (1992). Saying the "p" word: Nine guidelines for exemplary phonics instruction. *The Reading Teacher, 45* (8), 618–625.

Stahl, S. A., & Miller, P. D. (1989). Whole language and language experience approaches for beginning reading: A quantitative research synthesis. *Review of Educational Research, 59*, 87–116.

Stanovich, K. E. (1980). Toward an interactive-compensatory model of individual differences in the development of reading fluency. *Reading Research Quarterly, 16*, 32–71.

Stanovich, K. E. (1981). Attentional and automatic context effects in reading. In A. M. Lesgold & C. A. Perfetti (Eds.), *Interactive processes in reading* (pp. 241–267). Hillsdale, NJ: Erlbaum.

Stanovich, K. E. (1984). The interactive-compensatory model of reading: A confluence of developmental, experimental, and educational psychology. *Remedial and Special Education, 5*, 11–19.

Stanovich, K. E. (1991). Word recognition: Changing perspectives. In R. Barr, M. L. Kamil, P. B. Mosenthal, & P. D. Pearson (Eds.), *Handbook of reading research* (Vol. 2, pp. 418–452). New York: Longman.

Stauffer, R. G. (1960). Productive reading-thinking at the first grade level. *The Reading Teacher, 13*, 183–187.

Stauffer, R. G. (1969). *Directing reading maturity as a cognitive process*. New York: Harper & Row.

Stauffer, R. G., & Cramer, R. (1968). *Teaching critical reading at the primary level*. Newark, DE: International Reading Association.

Stephens, D. (1991). *Research on whole language: Support for a new curriculum*. Katonah, NY: Richard C. Owen.

Sternberg, R. J. (1989). The tyranny of testing. *Learning 89* (17), 60–63.

Stevick, E. (1976). *Memory, meaning and method*. Rowley, MA: Newbury House.

Stevick, E. (1980). *Teaching languages: A way and ways*. Rowley, MA: Newbury House.

Stewig, J. W. (1983). *Informal drama in the elementary language arts program*. New York: Teachers College Press.

Stice, C. F., & Bertrand, N. P. (1989). The texts and textures of literacy learning in whole language versus traditional/skills classrooms. Unpublished manuscript, Tennessee State University, Nashville (Stice) and Middle Tennessee State University, Murfreesboro (Bertrand).

Stice, C. F., & Bertrand, N. P. (1990). *Whole language and the emergent literacy of at-risk children: A two-year comparative study*. Nashville: Center for Excellence, Basic Skills, Tennessee State University. (ERIC ED 324 636)

Stires, S. (Ed.). (1991). *With promise: Redefining reading and writing needs for special students*. Portsmouth, NH: Heinemann.

Strickland, D., & Cullinan, B. (1990). Afterword. In M. Adams, *Beginning to read: Thinking and learning about print* (pp. 425–434). Cambridge: Harvard University Press.

Strickland, R. G. (1964). The contribution of structural linguistics to the teaching of reading, writing, and grammar in the elementary school. *Bulletin of the School of Education, 40* (1). Bloomington, IN: Indiana University.

Stuckey, J. E. (1991). *The violence of literacy*. Portsmouth, NH: Heinemann.

Subject guide to children's books in print. New Providence, NJ: Bowker. (Annual).

Sudzina, M. (1986). *An investigation of the relationships between the reading styles of second graders and their achievement in three different basal reader programs*. Doctoral dissertation, Temple University.

Sulzby, E., & Teale, W. (1991). Emergent literacy. In R. Barr, M. L. Kamil, P. B. Mosenthal, & P. D. Pearson (Eds.), *Handbook of reading research* (Vol. 2, pp. 727–758). New York: Longman.

Sumner, H. (1991). Whole language assessment and evaluation in special education classrooms. In B. Harp (Ed.), *Assessment and evaluation in whole language programs* (pp. 137–157). Norwood, MA: Christopher-Gordon.

Sutherland, Z. (1986). *The best in children's picture books: The University of Chicago guide to children's literature, 1979–1984.* Chicago: University of Chicago Press.

Sutherland, Z., & Arbuthnot, M. H. (1991). *Children and books* (8th ed.). New York: HarperCollins.

Swain, M., Lapkin, S., Rowen, S., & Hart, D. (1990). The role of mother tongue literacy in third language learning. *Language, Culture, and Curriculum, 3,* 65–81.

Swartz, L. (1988). *Dramathemes: A practical guide for teaching drama.* Markham, Ontario: Pembroke. (Available in the U.S. from Heinemann.)

Tanenhaus, M. K., Flanigan, H., & Seidenberg, M. S. (1980). Orthographic and phonological activation in auditory and visual word recognition. *Memory and Cognition, 8,* 513–520.

Tanner, F. A. (1987). *Readers theatre fundamentals.* Topeka, KS: Clark Publishing.

Tarlington, C., & Verriour, P. (1991). *Role drama.* Portsmouth NH: Heinemann.

Taylor, D. (1989). Toward a unified theory of literacy learning and instructional practices. *Phi Delta Kappan, 71,* 184–193.

Taylor, D. (1990). Teaching without testing: Assessing the complexity of children's literacy learning. *English Education, 22,* 4–74.

Taylor, D. (1991a). Early literacy development and the mental health of young children. Paper presented at the International Reading Association, Atlanta, May.

Taylor, D. (1991b). *Learning denied.* Portsmouth, NH: Heinemann.

Taylor, D., & Dorsey-Gaines, C. (1988). *Growing up literate: Learning from inner-city families.* Portsmouth, NH: Heinemann.

Taylor, W. L. (1953). Cloze procedure: A new tool for measuring readability. *Journalism Quarterly, 30,* 415–433.

Tchudi, S. (1987). *The young learner's handbook.* New York: Charles Scribner's Sons.

Teaching Tolerance. [Southern Poverty Law Center, 400 Washington Avenue, Montgomery, AL 36195].

Teale, W. H. (1982). Toward a theory of how children learn to read and write naturally. *Language Arts, 59,* 550–570.

Temple, C., & Marshall, J. C. (1983). A case study of developmental phonological dyslexia. *British Journal of Psychology, 74,* 517–533.

Temple, C. A., & Burns, J. (1986). The meaning of a basal reader story. Presentation at the Fourth International Conference on the Teaching of English, Ottawa, May 12.

Temple, C., & Gillet, J. W. (1984). *Language Arts.* Boston, MA: Little, Brown.

Temple, C., Nathan, R., Temple, F., & Burris, N. (1993). *The beginnings of writing* (3rd ed.). Boston: Allyn & Bacon.

Thompson, G. (1991). *Teaching through themes.* New York: Scholastic.

Tierney, R. J., Carter, M. A., & Desai, L. E. (1991). *Portfolio assessment in the reading-writing classroom.* Norwood, MA: Christopher-Gordon.

Tierney, R. J., Readence, J. E., & Dishner, E. K. (1990). *Reading strategies and practices: A compendium* (3rd ed.). Boston: Allyn & Bacon.

Tovey, D. R. (1979). Teachers' perceptions of children's reading miscues. *Reading Horizons, 19,* 302–307.

Tovey, D. R. (1980). Children's grasp of phonics terms vs. sound-symbol relationships. *The Reading Teacher, 33,* 431–437.

Treiman, R. (1985). Phonemic analysis, spelling, and reading. In T. H. Carr (Ed.), *The development of reading skills* (pp. 5–18). San Francisco: Jossey-Bass.

Treiman, R. (1986). The division between onsets and rimes in English syllables. *Journal of Memory and Language, 25,* 476–491.

Treiman, R. (1988). The role of intrasyllabic units in learning to read and spell. In P. Gough (Ed.), *Learning to read* (pp. 65–106). Hillsdale, NJ: Erlbaum.

Treiman, R. (1993). *Beginning to spell: A study of first-grade children.* New York: Oxford University Press.

Treiman, R., & Baron, J. (1981). Segmental analysis ability: Development and relation to reading ability. In G. E. MacKinnon and T. G. Waller (Eds.), *Reading research: Advances in theory and practice* (Vol. 3, pp. 159–198). New York: Academic Press.

Treiman, R., & Chafetz, J. (1987). Are there onset- and rime-like units in printed words? In M. Coltheart (Ed.), *Attention and performance XII: The psychology of reading* (pp. 281–298). Hillsdale, NJ: Erlbaum.

Trelease, J. (1985). *The read-aloud handbook* (Rev. ed.). New York: Viking.

Trelease, J. (1989). *The new read-aloud handbook.* New York: Penguin.

Tunnell, M. O., & Jacobs, J. S. (1989). Using "real" books: Research findings on literature based reading instruction. *The Reading Teacher, 42,* 470–477.

Turner, R. L. (1989). The "great" debate: Can both Carbo and Chall be right? *Phi Delta Kappan, 71,* 276–283.

Unsworth, L. (1988). Whole language or procedural display? The social context of popular whole language activities. *Australian Journal of Reading, 11* (June), 127–137.

Urzúa, C. (1987). You stopped too soon: Second language children composing and revising. *TESOL Quarterly, 21* (2), 279–297.

Van Allen, R. (1976). *Language experiences in education.* Boston: Houghton Mifflin.

VanMeter, V. (1990). *American history for children and young adults: An annotated bibliographic index.* Englewood, CO: Libraries Unlimited.

Vellutino, F. R. (1991). Introduction to three studies on reading acquisition: Convergent findings on theoretical foundations of code-oriented versus whole-language approaches to reading instruction. *Journal of Educational Psychology, 83,* 437–443.

Vellutino, F. R., & Denckla, M. B. (1991). Cognitive and neuropsychological foundations of word identification in poor and normally developing readers. In R. Barr, M. L. Kamil, P. B. Mosenthal, & P. D. Pearson (Eds.), *Handbook of reading research* (Vol. 2, pp. 571–608). New York: Longman.

Venezky, R. L. (1967). English orthography: Its graphical structure and its relation to sound. *Reading Research Quarterly, 2,* 75–106.

Venezky, R. L. (1970a). Regularity in reading and spelling. In H. Levin & J. P. Williams (Eds.), *Basic studies on reading* (pp. 30–42). New York: Basic.

Venezky, R. L. (1970b). *The structure of English orthography.* The Hague: Mouton.

Verriour, P. (1989). "This is drama": The play beyond the play. *Language Arts, 66,* 276–286.

Villiers, U. (1989). *Luk mume dade I kan rite.* New York: Scholastic. (Also available in a Spanish edition.)

Von Bertalanffy, L. (1968). *General systems theory.* New York: George Braziller.

Von Dras, J. (1990). Transitions toward an integrated curriculum. In K. G. Short and K. M. Pierce (Eds.), *Talking about books: Creating literate communities (pp. 121–133).* Portsmouth, NH: Heinemann.

Vygotsky, L. S. (1978). *Mind in society: The development of higher psychological processes.* (M. Cole, V. John-Steiner, S. Scribner, & E. Souberman, Eds.). Cambridge: Harvard University Press.

Vygotsky, L. S. (1962/1986). *Thought and language.* (A. Kozulin, Trans.). Cambridge: MIT Press.

Wadsworth, B. J. (1989). *Piaget's theory of cognitive and affective development.* New York: Longman.

Wagner, B. J. (1976). *Dorothy Heathcote: Drama as a learning medium.* Washington, DC: National Education Association.

Wagner, B. J. (1978). Educational drama and language development. In R. Baird Shuman (Ed.), *Educational drama for today's schools* (pp. 87–96). Metuchen, NJ: Scarecrow Press.

Wagner, B. J. (1988). Research currents: Does classroom drama affect the arts of language? *Language Arts, 65,* 46–55.

Wallace, C. (1988). *Learning to read in a multicultural society: The social context of second language literacy.* Englewood Cliffs, NJ: Prentice Hall.

Wallerstein, N. (1987). Problem posing education: Freire's method for transformation. In I. Shor (Ed.), *Freire for the classroom* (pp. 33–44). Portsmouth, NH: Boynton/Cook–Heinemann.

Walsh, C. E. (Ed.). (1991). *Literacy as praxis: Culture, language, and pedagogy.* Norwood, NJ: Ablex.

Wang, M. C., Walberg, H., & Reynolds, M. C. (1992). A scenario for better—not separate—special education. *Educational Leadership, 50*, 35–38.

Ward, W. (1957). *Playmaking with children* (2nd ed.). New York: Appleton-Century-Crofts.

Ward, W. (1952). *Stories to dramatize.* New Orleans: Anchorage Press. Reissued 1983.

Watson, D. J. (Ed.). (1987). *Ideas and insights: Language arts in the elementary school.* Urbana, IL: National Council of Teachers of English.

Watson, D. J. (1989). Defining and describing whole language. *The Elementary School Journal, 90* (November), 130–141.

Watson, D. J., Burke, C., & Harste, J. (1989). *Whole language: Inquiring voices.* Richmond Hill, Ontario: Scholastic.

Watson, D. J., & Crowley, P. (1988). How can we implement a whole-language approach? In C. Weaver, *Reading process and practice: From socio-psycholinguistics to whole language* (pp. 232–279). Portsmouth, NH: Heinemann.

Way, B. (1967). *Development through drama.* Atlantic Highlands, NJ: Humanities Press.

Wayman, J. (1980). *The other side of reading.* Carthage, IL: Good Apple.

Weaver, C. (1980). *Psycholinguistics and reading: From process to practice.* Cambridge, MA: Winthrop.

Weaver, C. (1985). Parallels between new paradigms in science and in reading and literary theories: An essay review. *Research in the Teaching of English, 19*, 298–316.

Weaver, C. (1986). Reading as a whole-brain process: Both reality and metaphor. Paper presented at the Fourth International Conference on the Teaching of English, Ottawa, Ontario, May 11. (ERIC: ED 273 926)

Weaver, C. (1988). *Reading process and practice: From socio-psycholinguistics to whole language.* Portsmouth, NH: Heinemann.

Weaver, C. (1989). The basalization of America: A cause for concern. In *Two reactions to* The Report Card on Basal Readers. Bloomington, IN: ERIC Clearinghouse on Reading and Communication Skills.

Weaver, C. (1990a). *Understanding whole language: From principles to practice.* Portsmouth, NH: Heinemann.

Weaver, C. (1990b). Weighing claims of "phonics first" advocates. *Education Week*, March 28, 1990. (ERIC: ED 334 557)

Weaver, C. (1991a). *Alternatives in understanding and educating Attention-Deficit students: A systems-based whole language perspective.* Concept paper no. 3. Urbana, IL: National Council of Teachers of English. (ERIC: ED 337 755)

Weaver, C. (1991b). The hidden agenda of intensive, systematic and extensive phonics. Paper presented at the annual meeting of the International Reading Association, Las Vegas, May. (ERIC: ED 334 558)

Weaver, C. (1992a). The politics of phonics and whole language: From reflection to action. In M. Bixby, D. King, S. Ohanian, S. Crenshaw, & P. Jenkins (Eds.), *Selected proceedings from the first annual Whole Language Umbrella conference—Perspectives on whole language: Past, present, potential* (pp. 170–185). Columbia, MO: Whole Language Umbrella.

Weaver, C. (1992b). The promise of whole language education for students with ADHD. *The CH.A.D.D.ER Box*, a newsletter for members of CH.A.D.D (Children with Attention Deficit Disorders: A national support group for information on Attention Deficit Disorders.), *5* (4), 1, 7–8.

Weaver, C. (1993). Understanding and educating students with Attention Deficit Hyperactivity Disorder: Toward a system theory and whole language perspective. *American Journal of Speech-Language Pathology: A Journal of Clinical Practice, 2*, 79–89.

Weaver, C. (Ed.). (1981). *Using junior novels to develop language and thought: Five integrative teaching guides.* Urbana, IL: National Council of Teachers of English.

Weaver, C. (Ed.). (1994). *Success at last!: Helping students with Attention Deficit (Hyperactivity) Disorders achieve their potential.* Portsmouth, NH: Heinemann.

Weaver, C., Chaston, J., & Peterson, S. (1993). *Theme exploration: A voyage of discovery.* Richmond Hill, Ontario: Scholastic. (Distributed in the U.S. by Heinemann.)

Weaver, C., & Groff, P. (1989). *Two reactions to The Report Card on Basal Readers.* Bloomington, IN: ERIC Clearinghouse on Reading and Communication Skills.

Weaver, C., & Henke, L. (Eds.). (1992). *Supporting whole language: Stories of teacher and institutional change.* Portsmouth, NH: Heinemann.

Weaver, C., & Stephens, D. (1990). What does the research say? Research in support of whole-to-part. In C. Weaver, *Understanding whole language: From principles to practice* (pp. 109–141). Portsmouth, NH: Heinemann.

Weaver, C. A. III, & Kintsch, W. (1991). Expository text. In R. Barr, M. L. Kamil, P. B. Mosenthal, & P. D. Pearson (Eds.), *Handbook of reading research,* Vol. 2 (pp. 230–245). New York: Longman.

Webb, C. A. (Ed.). (1991). *Your reading: A booklist for junior high and middle school students* (8th ed.). Urbana, IL: National Council of Teachers of English. (Earlier editions annotate earlier books.)

Weber, R. (1970). First-graders' use of grammatical context in reading. In H. Levin & J. P. Williams (Eds.), *Basic studies on reading* (pp. 147–163). New York: Basic Books.

Weiss, R. (1990). Dyslexics read better with the blues. *Science News, 138,* Sept, 29, p. 196.

Wells, G. (1986). *The meaning makers: Children learning language and using language to learn.* Portsmouth, NH: Heinemann.

White, C. (1990). *Jevon doesn't sit at the back anymore.* Richmond Hill, Ontario: Scholastic.

Whitin, D. J., Mills, H., & O'Keefe, T. (1990). *Living and learning mathematics: Stories and strategies for supporting mathematical literacy.* Portsmouth, NH: Heinemann.

Widdowson, H. (1978). *Teaching language as communication.* Oxford: Oxford University Press.

Wiggins, G. (1989). A true test: Toward more authentic and equitable assessment. *Phi Delta Kappan, 70,* 703–713.

Wilde, S. (1989). Understanding spelling strategies: A kidwatcher's guide to spelling, Part 2. In K. S. Goodman, Y. M. Goodman, & W. J. Hood (Eds.), *The whole language evaluation book* (pp. 227–236). Portsmouth, NH: Heinemann.

Wilde, S. (1992). *You kan red this! Spelling and punctuation for whole language classrooms, K–6.* Portsmouth, NH: Heinemann.

Wilde, S. (Forthcoming). *What's a schwa sound anyway (and why should I care?).* Portsmouth, NH: Heinemann.

Wilkins, D. A. (1976). *Notional syllabuses.* Oxford: Oxford University Press.

Willig, A. (1985). A meta-analysis of selected studies on the effectiveness of bilingual education. *Review of Educational Research, 55,* 269–317.

Willis, J. D. (1983). *The implications of discourse analysis for teaching oral communication.* Unpublished master's thesis, University of Birmingham, Birmingham, England.

Wilms, D. M. (Ed.). (1985). *Science books for children: Selections from Booklist, 1976–1983.* Chicago: American Library Association.

Wilson, G. & Moss, J. (1991). *Tried and true: 500 nonfiction books children want to read.* New Providence, NJ: Bowker.

Wilson, M. (1988). How can we teach reading in the content areas? In C. Weaver, *Reading process and practice: From socio-psycholinguistics to whole language* (pp. 280–320). Portsmouth, NH: Heinemann.

Winkel, L. (1988). *The elementary school library collection: A guide to books and other media* (16th ed.). Williamsburg, PA: Brodart.

Winograd, P. N., Wixson, K. K., & Lipson, M. Y. (Eds.). (1989). *Improving basal reading instruction.* New York: Teachers College Press.

Wise, B. W., Olson, R. K., & Treiman, R. (1990). Subsyllabic units as aids in beginning readers' word learning: Onset-rime versus post-vowel segmentation. *Journal of Experimental Child Psychology, 49,* 1–19.

Witelson, S. F. (1977). Neural and cognitive correlates of developmental dyslexia: Age and sex differences. In C. Shagass, S. Gershon, & A. J. Friedhoff (Eds.), *Psychopathology and brain dysfunction* (pp. 15–49). New York: Raven Press.

Wittig, A. J. (1989). *U.S. government publications for the school media center.* Englewood, CO: Libraries Unlimited.

Wixon, K. K., & Lipson, M. Y. (1986). Reading dis(ability): An interactionist perspective. In T. E. Raphael (Ed.), *The contexts of school-based literacy* (pp. 131–148). New York: Random House.

Worthy, M., & Bloodgood, J. Enhancing reading instruction through Cinderella tales. *The Reading Teacher, 46,* 290–301.

Wylie, R. E., & Durrell, D. D. (1970). Teaching vowels through phonograms. *Elementary English, 47,* 787–791.

Ysseldyke, J. E., & Algozzine, B. (1982). *Critical issues in special and remedial education.* Boston: Houghton Mifflin.

Ysseldyke, J. E., Algozzine, B., Shinn, M. R., & McGue, M. (1982). Similarities and differences between low achievers and students classified as learning disabled. *Journal of Special Education, 16,* 73–85.

Ysseldyke, J. E., Thurlow, M. L., Graden, J., Wesson, C., Deno, S., & Algozzine, B. (1983). Generalizations from five years of research on assessment and decision making. *Exceptional Education Quarterly, 4* (1), 75–93.

Ysseldyke, J. E., Thurlow, M. L., Mecklenburg, C., & Graden, J. (1984). Opportunity to learn for regular and special education students during reading instruction. *Remedial and Special Education, 5,* 29–37.

Zaidel, E. (1979). The split and half brains as models of congenital language disability. In C. L. Ludlow & M. E. Doran-Quine (Eds.), *The neurological bases of language disorders in children: Methods and directions for research* (pp. 55–89). NINCDS Monograph no. 22. Bethesda, MD: U.S. Department of Health, Education, and Welfare.

Zarillo, J. (1989). Teachers' interpretations of literature-based reading. *The Reading Teacher, 43,* 23–28.

Literature Cited

Aardema, Verna. (1981). *Bringing the rain to Kapiti plain*. Illus. Beatriz Vidal. New York: Dial.

Adoff, Arnold. (1979). *Eats Poems*. New York: Lothrup, Lee & Shepard.

Aliki. (1983). *A Medieval Feast*. New York: Thomas Y. Crowell.

Allen, Roach Van. (1986). *Three Dogs at the Door*. Allen, TX: DLM Teaching Resources.

Allen, Thomas B. (1989). *On Grandaddy's Farm*. New York: Alfred A. Knopf.

Anno, Mitsumasa. (1975). *Anno's Alphabet: An Adventure in Imagination*. New York: Harper.

Arbuthnot, May Hill. (1961). *The Arbuthnot Anthology of Children's Literature*. Glenview, IL: Scott, Foresman.

Arbuthnot, May Hill. (1976). *The Arbuthnot Anthology of Children's Literature*. (4th ed.). Glenview, IL: Scott, Foresman.

Asch, Frank. (1985). *Bear Shadow*. New York: Simon & Schuster.

Asimov, Janet, & Asimov, Isaac. (1983). *The Norby Chronicles*. New York: Berkley.

Babbitt, Natalie. (1975). *Tuck Everlasting*. New York: Farrar, Straus & Giroux.

Ball, Zachary. (1962). *Bristle Face*. New York: Holiday House.

Barr, Jene. (1949). *Little Circus Dog*. Chicago: Albert Whitman.

Barrett, Judi. (1978). *Cloudy with a Chance of Meatballs*. Illus. Ron Barrett. New York: Atheneum.

Baylor, Byrd. (1978). *The Other Way to Listen*. Illus. Peter Parnall. New York: Macmillan.

Bennett, Jill (Ed.). (1987). *Noisy Poems*. Illus. Nick Sharratt. New York: Oxford University Press.

Berenstain, Stan, & Berenstain, Jan. (1971). *Bears in the Night*. New York: Random House.

Berenzy, Alix. (1989). *A Frog Prince*. New York: Henry Holt.

Blume, Judy. (1972). *Tales of a Fourth Grade Nothing*. New York: Dutton.

Blume, Judy. (1978). *Blubber*. New York: Dell.

Blume, Judy. (1988). *Just as Long as We're Together*. New York: Dell.

Boynton, Sandra. (1987). *A is for Angry: An Animal and Adjective Alphabet* (2nd ed.). New York: Workman Publishing.

Bradbury, Ray. (1957). *Dandelion Wine*. Garden City, NY: Doubleday.

Briggs, Raymond. (1970). *Jim and the Beanstalk*. New York: Puffin.

Brown, Claude. (1965). *Manchild in the Promised Land*. New York: Macmillan.

Brown, Marc. (1985). *Hand Rhymes*. New York: Puffin.

Brown, Margaret W. (1972). *The Runaway Bunny*. New York: Harper & Row. (First published in 1942.)

Browne, Anthony. (1986). *Piggybook*. New York: Alfred A. Knopf.

Burgess, Anthony. (1963). *A Clockwork Orange*. New York: Norton.

Burnett, Frances Hodgson. (1987). *The Secret Garden*. New York: Bantam. (First published in 1911.)

Cameron, Polly. (1961). *"I Can't" Said the Ant*. New York: Scholastic.

Cannon, A. E. (1992). *The Shadow Brothers*. New York: Dell.

Capote, Truman. (1989). *A Christmas Memory*. New York: David McKey. (Originally published in 1956.)

Carle, Eric. (1981). *The Very Hungry Caterpillar*. New York: Philomel.

Carris, Joan. (1983). *When the Boys Ran the House*. New York: Dell.

Chase, Richard. (1948). "Ashpet." In *Grandfather Tales* (pp. 115–123). Boston: Houghton Mifflin.

Ciardi, John. (1989). *The Hopeful Trout and Other Limericks*. Illus. Susan Meddaugh. Boston: Houghton Mifflin.

Climo, Shirley. (1989). *The Egyptian Cinderella*. Illus. Ruth Hellar. New York: Harper Collins.

Climo, Shirley. (1993). *The Korean Cinderella*. Illus. Ruth Hellar. New York: Harper Collins.

Cochrane, Orin. (1988). *Cinderella Chant*. Winnipeg: Whole Language Consultants. (Distributed in the U. S. by Richard C. Owen.)

Coerr, Eleanor. (1979). *Sadako and the Thousand Paper Cranes*. New York: Dell.

Cohen, Barbara. (1990). *Molly's Pilgrim*. New York: Bantam.

Cohen, Miriam. (1977). *When Will I Read?* New York: Dell.

Cole, Babette. (1988). *Prince Cinders*. New York: Putnam.

Cole, William (Ed.). (1981). *Poem Stew*. New York: Lippincott.

Cowley, Joy. (1982). "Meow." In *Sing to the Moon*. In Storybox in the Classroom series, Stage 1. San Diego: The Wright Group.

Cowley, Joy. (1984a). *The Hungry Giant*. In Story Box in the Classroom series, Stage 1. San Diego: The Wright Group.

Cowley, Joy. (1984b). *I'm the King of the Mountain*. Katonah, NY: Richard C. Owen.

Cowley, Joy. (1984c). *The Sunflower That Went Flop*. San Diego: The Wright Group.

Cowley, Joy. (1988). *Greedy Cat*. Illus. Robyn Belton. Wellington, New Zealand: Department of Education. (Distributed in the U.S. by Richard C. Owen.)

Crew, Linda. (1989). *Children of the River*. New York: Dell.

Crow Dog, Mary. (1991). *Lakota Woman*. New York: Zebra Books.

Crutcher, Chris. (1989). *Chinese Handcuffs*. New York: Dell.

Dahl, Roald. (1950). "Poison." In *Someone Like You*. New York: Knopf.

Dahl, Roald. (1982). *Revolting Rhymes*. Illus. Quentin Blake. New York: Knopf.

Dunrea, Oliver. (1988). *Deep Down Underground*. New York: Macmillan.

Ehlert, Lois. (1989). *Eating the Alphabet: Fruits and Vegetables from A to Z*. San Diego: Harcourt Brace Jovanovich.

Ehlert, Lois. (1990). *Growing Vegetable Soup*. San Diego: Harcourt Brace Jovanovich.

Fisher-Staples, Suzanne. (1989). *Shabanu: Daughter of the Wind*. New York: Alfred A. Knopf.

Fleischman, Paul. (1985). *I Am Phoenix: Poems for Two Voices*. New York: Harper & Row.

Fleischman, Paul. (1988). *Joyful Noise: Poems for Two Voices*. New York: Harper & Row.

Forbes, Esther. (1943). *Johnny Tremain*. New York: Dell.

French, Fiona. (1986). *Snow White in New York*. New York: Oxford.

Friedman, Ina R. (1987). *How My Parents Learned to Eat*. Illus. Allen Say. Boston: Houghton Mifflin.

Gelman, Rita Golden. (1977). *More Spaghetti, I Say!* New York: Scholastic.

George, Jean Craighead. (1972). *Julie of the Wolves*. New York: Harper & Row.

George, Jean Craighead. (1986). *One Day in the Prairie*. Illus. Bob Marstall. New York: Thomas Y. Crowell.

Giblin, James Cross. (1982). *Chimney Sweeps*. New York: Thomas Y. Crowell.

Goetz, Lee Garrett. (1966). *A Camel in the Sea*. New York: McGraw-Hill.

Greene, Graham. (1940). *The Power and the Glory*. New York: Viking Press.

Gwynne, Fred. (1987). *The Sixteen Hand Horse*. New York: Simon & Schuster.

Gwynne, Fred. (1988a). *A Chocolate Moose for Dinner*. New York: Simon & Schuster.

Gwynne, Fred. (1988b). *The King Who Rained*. New York: Simon & Schuster.

Gwynne, Fred. (1990). *Little Pigeon Toad*. New York: Simon & Schuster.

Hahn, Mary Downing. (1986). *Wait Till Helen Comes: A Ghost Story*. New York: Clarion.

Hahn, Mary Downing. (1992). *Stepping on the Cracks*. Boston: Houghton Mifflin.

Handy, Libby. (1982). *Boss for a Week.* New York: Scholastic.

Hay, Sara Henderson. (1963). *Story Hour*. Illus. Jim McMollan. New York: Doubleday.

Hazelgrove, William Elliott. (1992). *Ripples*. Chicago: Pantonne Press.

Hendershot, Judith. (1987). *In Coal Country*. Illus. Thomas B. Allen. New York: Alfred A. Knopf.

Herihy, Dirlie. (1988). *Ludie's Song*. New York: Puffin Books.

Hoban, Russell. (1964). *Bread and Jam for Frances*. New York: Harper & Row.

Hoban, Russell. (1966). *The Little Brute Family.* New York: Macmillan.

Hodges, Margaret. (1990). *The Kitchen Knight: A Tale of King Arthur*. Illus. Trina Schart Hyman. New York: Holiday House.

Hooks, William. (1987). *Moss Gown*. Illus. Donald Carrick. New York: Clarion.

Huck, Charlotte. (1989). *Princess Furball*. Illus. Anita Lobel. New York: William Morrow.

Hundal, Nancy, (1990). *I Heard My Mother Call My Name*. Illus. Laura Fernandez. Toronto: Harper Collins.

Hunter, Mollie. (1975). *A Stranger Came Ashore*. New York: Harper & Row.

Hurwitz, Johanna. (1988). *Class Clown*. New York: Scholastic.

Johnson, Crockett. (1955). *Harold and the Purple Crayon*. New York: Harper & Row.

Jones, R. (1976). *The Acorn People*. New York: Bantam.

Keats, Ezra Jack. (1962). *The Snowy Day*. New York: Viking.

Kellogg, Steven. (1984). *Paul Bunyan.* New York: William Morrow.

Koningsburg, E. L. (1967). *From the Mixed-Up Files of Mrs. Basil E. Frankweiler*. New York: Atheneum.

Kraus, Robert. (1971). *Leo, the Late Bloomer*. New York: Crowell.

Leaf, Monro. (1936). *The Story of Ferdinand*. New York: Viking Penguin.

Lear, Edward. (1986). *Edward Lear's ABC: Alphabet Rhymes for Children*. Illus. Carol Pike. Topsfield, MA: Salem House.

Lee, Dennis. (1983). *Jelly Belly: Original Nursery Rhymes*. Illus. Juan Wijngaard. New York: Bedrick/Blackie.

Levinson, Riki. (1985). *Watch the Stars Come Out*. Illus. Diane Goode. New York: Dutton.

Lindbergh, Reeve. (1987). *Midnight Farm.* New York: Dial.

Lobel, Arnold. (1981). *On Market Street*. Illus. Anita Lobel. New York: Mulberry Books (William Morrow).

Louie, Ai-Ling. (1982). *Yeh Shen: A Cinderella Story from China*. Illus. Ed Young. New York: Philomel.

Ludski, Trevor, & Martin, Greg. (1989). *Little Red*. Markham, Ontario: Markon Press.

Macauley, David. *Castle*. (1977). Boston: Houghton Mifflin.

Marshall, Edward. (1981). *Three by the Sea*. Illus. James Marshall. New York: Dial.

Marshall, James. (1972). *What's the Matter with Carruthers?* Boston: Houghton Mifflin.

Martin, Rafe, & Shannon, David. (1992). *The Rough-Face Girl.* New York: G. P. Putnam's Sons.

McCloskey, Robert. (1968). *Lentil*. New York: Viking Penguin. (First published in 1940.)

McCloskey, Robert. (1943). *Homer Price*. New York: Viking Penguin.

McCormick, Dell J. (1936). *Paul Bunyan Swings His Axe*. Caldwell, ID: Caxton.

McDermott, Gerald. (1974). *Arrow to the Sun: A Pueblo Indian Tale*. New York: Puffin.

McGovern, Ann. (1968). *Stone Soup*. Illus. Winslow Pinney Pels. New York: Scholastic.

McKissack, Patricia C. (1986). *Flossie and the Fox*. Illus. Rachael Isadora. New York: Dial.

McMillan, Bruce. (1990). *One Sun: A Book of Terse Verse*. New York: Holiday House.

Milne, A. A. (1924). *When We Were Very Young*. New York: E. P. Dutton.

Muller, R. (1984). *Tatterhood.* New York: Scholastic.

Munsch, Robert N. (1980). *The Paper Bag Princess*. Illus. Michael Martchenko. Buffalo, NY: Firefly.

Murphy, Barbara B., & Wolkoff, Judie. (1982). *Ace Hits the Big Time*. New York: Dell.

Nicoll, Helen. (Ed.). (1983). *Poems for 7-Year-Olds and Under*. New York: Puffin.

Nikly, Michelle. (1981). *The Princess on the Nut, Or the Curious Courtship of the Son of the Princess on the Pea*. Illus. Jean Claverie. Trans. Lucy Meredith. Boston: Faber and Faber.

Numeroff, Laura Joffe. (1985). *If You Give a Mouse a Cookie*. Illus. Felicia Bond. New York: Harper.

Obligado, Lillian. (1983). *Faint Frogs Feeling Feverish, and Other Terrifically Tantalizing Tongue Twisters*. New York: Puffin.

Orwell, George. (1949). *1984*. New York: Harcourt Brace Jovanovich.

Parish, Peggy. (1963). *Amelia Bedelia*. New York: Harper-Collins.

Parry, Caroline. (Ed.). (1991). *Zoomerang a Boomerang: Poems to Make Your Belly Laugh*. Illus. Michael Martchenko. New York: Puffin.

Paterson, Katherine. (1978). *The Great Gilly Hopkins*. New York: Harper & Row.

Paulsen, Gary. (1987). *Hatchet*. New York: Bradbury.

Perkins, Al. (1969). *Hand, Hand, Fingers, Thumb*. New York: Random House.

Perrault, Charles. (1985). *Cinderella*. Retold by Amy Ehrlich. Illus. Susan Jeffers. New York: Dial.

Porter, William S. (1936). *The Complete Works of O. Henry*. Garden City, NY: Doubleday, Doran.

Prelusky, Jack. (1986). *Ride a Purple Pelican*. Illus. Garth Williams. New York: Greenwillow.

Prelutsky, Jack (Ed.). (1983). *The Random House Book of Poetry for Children*. Illus. Arnold Lobel. New York: Random House.

Rawls, Wilson. (1977). *Summer of the Monkeys*. New York: Dell.

Roberts, Tom. (1990). *The Three Little Pigs*. Illus. David Jorgensen. Westport, CT: Rabbit Ears.

Rockwell, Anne. (1977). *Albert B. Cub & Zebra: An Alphabet Storybook*. NY: Harper.

Rounds, Glen. (1936). *Ol' Paul the Mighty Logger*. New York: Holiday House.

Ryan, Cheli Duran. (1971). *Hildilid's Night*. New York: Macmillan.

Ryder, Joanne. (1982). *The Snail's Spell*. Illus. Lynne Cherry. New York: Frederick Warne.

Rylant, Cynthia. (1982). *When I Was Young in the Mountains*. Illus. Diane Goode. New York: Dutton.

Rylant, Cynthia. (1983). *Miss Maggie*. New York: Dutton.

Rylant, Cynthia. (1984). *Waiting to Waltz: A Childhood*. New York: Bradbury.

Rylant, Cynthia. (1985). *The Relatives Came*. New York: Bradbury.

Saint-Exupéry, Antoine de. (1971). *The Little Prince*. San Diego: Harcourt Brace Jovanovich. (First published 1943.)

Saltman, Judith. (Ed.). (1985). *The Riverside Anthology of Children's Literature* (6th ed.). Boston: Houghton Mifflin.

Sanders, Scott Russell. (1989). *Aurora Means Dawn*. Illus. Jill Kastner. New York: Bradbury.

Sans Souci, Robert D. (1989). *The Talking Eggs*. Illus. Jerry Pinkney. New York: Dial.

Scieszka, Jon. (1989). *The True Story of the Three Little Pigs! by A. Wolf*. New York: Viking Penguin.

Scieszka, Jon. (1991). *The Frog Prince, Continued*. Illus. Steve Johnson. New York: Viking Penguin.

Sendak, Maurice. (1962). *Chicken Soup with Rice*. New York: Harper & Row.

Seton, Anya. (1954). *Katherine*. Boston: Houghton Mifflin.

Seuss, Dr. [Theodore Seuss Geisel]. (1960). *Green Eggs and Ham*. New York: Random House.

Seuss, Dr. [Theodore Seuss Geisel]. (1972). *In a People House*. New York: Random House.

Seuss, Dr. [Theodore Seuss Geisel]. (1990). *Oh, the Places You'll Go*. New York: Random House.

Sewell, Anna. (1877). *Black Beauty*. New York: Penguin.

Sharmat, Mitchell. (1980). *Gregory, the Terrible Eater*. New York: Four Winds.

Silverstein, Shel. (1974). *Where the Sidewalk Ends*. New York: Harper.

Simon, Norma. (1974). *I Was So Mad!* Toronto: General Publishers.

Smith, Doris Buchanan. (1973). *A Taste of Blackberries*. New York: Scholastic.

Smith, Robert Kimmel. (1978). *Chocolate Fever*. New York: Dell.

Smith, Robert Kimmel. (1982). *Jelly Belly*. New York: Dell.

Smucker, Anna Egan. (1969). *No Star Night*. Illus. Steve Johnson. New York: Alfred A. Knopf.

Soto, Gary. (1991). *Baseball in April*. San Diego: Harcourt Brace Jovanovich.

Speare, Elizabeth G. (1983). *The Sign of the Beaver*. New York: Dell.

Steptoe, John. (1987). *Mufaro's Beautiful Daughters: An African Tale*. New York: Lothrop, Lee, & Shepard.

Stewart, Sarah. (1991). *The Money Tree*. Illus. David Small. New York: Farrar, Straus & Giroux.

Taylor, Mildred D. (1976). *Roll of Thunder, Hear My Cry*. New York: Bantam.

Thayer, Ernest Lawrence. (1988). *Casey at the Bat*. Illus. Barry Moser. Boston: David R. Godine.

Tresselt, Alvin. (1964). *The Mitten*. New York: Scholastic.

Turkle, Brinton. (1976). *Deep in the Forest*. Boston: Houghton Mifflin.

Turkle, Brinton. (1981). *Do Not Open*. New York: Dutton.

Van Allsburg, Chris. (1987). *The Z Was Zapped: A Play in Twenty-Six Acts*. Boston: Houghton Mifflin.

Van Allsburg, Chris. (1988). *Two Bad Ants*. Boston: Houghton Mifflin.

Viorst, Judith. (1981). *If I Were in Charge of the World, and Other Worries*. New York: Aladdin.

Vozar, David. (1993). *Yo, Hungry Wolf! A Nursery Rap*. Illus. Betsy Lewin. New York: Doubleday.

Vuong, Lynnette Dyer. (1982). *The Brocaded Slipper and Other Vietnamese Tales*. Illus. Vo-Dinh Mai. Reading, MA: Addison-Wesley.

Warner, Gertrude C. (1942). *The Boxcar Children*. Niles, IL: Albert Whitman & Co.

Watson, Joy. (1989). *Grandpa's Slippers*. Illus. Wendy Hodder. New York: Scholastic.

Weber, Bernard. (1972). *Ira Sleeps Over*. Boston: Houghton Mifflin.

White, E. B. (1952). *Charlotte's Web*. New York: Dell.

Williams, Jay. (1973). *Petronella*. Illus. Friso Henstra. New York: Parents' Magazine Press.

Williams, Jay. (1978). *The Practical Princess and Other Liberating Fairy Tales*. New York: Scholastic.

Williamson, Joanne. (1961). *The Glorious Conspiracy*. New York: Knopf.

Wiseman, Bernard. (1978). *Morris Has a Cold*. New York: Dodd, Mead.

Yagawa, Sumiko. (1981). *The Crane Wife*. New York: Morrow.

Yashima, Taro. (1955). *Crow Boy*. New York: Viking Press.

Yep, Laurence. (1977). *Child of the Owl*. New York: Harper & Row.

Yolen, Jane. (1981). *Sleeping Ugly*. Illus. Diane Stanley. New York: Coward-McCann.

Yorinks, Arthur. (1988). *Company's Coming*. Illus. David Small. New York: Crown.

Zion, Gene. (1964). *The Sugar Mouse Cake*. New York: Scribner.

Audio-visual and Instructional Materials Cited

Alpha-phonics: A Primer for beginning readers, by Samuel L. Blumenfeld. (1983). Boise, ID: The Paradigm Company.

Building Belief, Parts I and II. (1974). Evanston, IL: Northwestern University Film Library.

A Day in the Life of Bonnie Consolo. (1975). Barr Films.

Explode the Code, by Nancy Hall & Rena Price. (1976-1991). Cambridge: Educators Publishing Service.

Fiesta, in the Houghton Mifflin reading program. (1971). (Includes "Camel in the Sea.") Boston: Houghton Mifflin.

Hooked on Phonics. Orange, CA: Gateway Educational Products.

Impressions, by Jack Booth, David Booth, & Jo Phenix. (1989; there are alternate editions). Toronto and New York: Harcourt Brace Jovanovich / Holt, Rinehart and Winston.

Journeys in Reading and the Language Arts, by Jaap Tuinman. (1989). Toronto: Ginn & Co.

LINK Packs. (dates vary). Denver, CO: LINK.

Lippincott Basic Reading, by Charles C. Walcutt & Glenn McCracken. (1975). New York: Macmillan.

Lippincott's Beginning to Read, Write, and Listen, by Pleasant Rowland. (1988). Macmillan McGraw Hill School Publishing Co.

Literacy 2000. Crystal Lake, IL: Rigby.

Literature First: Phonics with a Purpose. (1989). Cleveland, OH: Modern Curriculum Press.

Literature Study: Karen Smith's Classroom. (1990). Videotape. Tucson: Center for Establishing Dialogue.

Opening Doors, in The Macmillan Reading Program, by Albert J. Harris & Mae Knight Clark, Senior Authors. (1965). New York: Macmillan.

Primary Phonics, and *More Primary Phonics*, by Barbara W. Makar. Cambridge: Educators Publishing Service.

Reading House Series: Comprehension and Vocabulary. (1980). New York: Random House.

Reading Mastery: DISTAR (1988). Chicago: SRA.

RefleXions, by Linda Cameron & Adrian Peetoom. (1991-1994). Richmond Hill, Ontario: Scholastic Canada.

Three Looms Waiting. (1971). London: BBC Production. (Distributed in the U.S. by Time-Life Films.)

Teach Your Child to Read in 100 Easy Lessons, by Siegfried Engelmann, Phyllis Haddox, & Elaine Bruner. (1983). New York: Simon & Schuster.

Weavers, in the Houghton Mifflin reading program. (1983). (Includes "Petronella.") Boston: Houghton Mifflin.

Whole Language Sourcebooks. Grades 1–2 (1986) and Grades 3–4 (1988) by Jane Baskwill & Paulette Whitman. Grades 5–6 (1991) by Jane Baskwill & Steve Baskwill. (Title varies slightly from volume to volume.) Richmond Hill, Ontario: Scholastic.

Windchimes, in the Houghton Mifflin reading series by W. K. Durr, J. M. LePere, & R. H. Brown. (1976). (Includes "What's the Matter with Carruthers?"). Boston: Houghton Mifflin.

You Can Read! (n. d.). Videotape program. Indianapolis, IN: You Can Read!

Literature Collections and Programs

The following publishers are among those particularly well known to whole language educators as offering one or more excellent collections of literature. Information on most of these current programs is taken from *Brown's Directory of Instructional Programs: Whole Language/Literature K–8*, by Brown Publishing Network (Mendham, NJ: Infinity Impressions, 1992). For more information, one can consult this reference. Be warned, however, that there really is no such thing as a whole language *instructional* program, though some of the collections of literature below are accompanied by teaching suggestions that can support whole language teaching. Some of these collections are more whole language than others, with respect to the accompanying teaching suggestions. In many instances, books for the primary grades can be purchased as Big Books, or as Big Book/small book sets, often with an accompanying audio cassette.

DLM; P.O. Box 4000, One DLM Park, Allen, TX 75002; 1-800-527-4747

> Bill Martin's Sounds of Language books, Grades 1–4.
> Bill Martin and John Archambault's Bobber Books, Pre-K to Grade 2.
> Bill Martin's Treasure Chest of Poetry (with John Archambault and Peggy Brogan), Grades Pre-K to 3.
> And other collections of literature, including poetry and literature relevant to themes

Harcourt Brace Jovanovich/Holt, Rinehart and Winston; School Department, National Customer Service Center, Dowden Road, Orlando, FL 32887; 1-800-225-5425

> Bill Martin Big Books (1982), for the primary grades.

LINK, the Language Company; 1675 Carr Street, Suite 209–N, Lakewood, CO 80215; 1-800-637-7993

> LINK PAKS include a set of activities designed to extend children's experiences with literature. Each PAK includes the book itself, plus these activities. Suggested level of books ranges from Pre-K to Grade 7.

Modern Curriculum Press; 13900 Prospect Road, Cleveland, OH 44136; 1-800-321-3106

> MCP Big Books (presumably for the primary grades).
> Language Works (apparently for Grades 1–4).

Recorded Books, Inc.; 270 Skipjack Road, Prince Frederick, MD 20678; 1-800-638-1304

> Catalogue lists hundreds of audio recordings of books on cassette tape, for a wide range of ages, children through adult.

Richard C. Owen; P. O. Box 585, Katonah, NY 10536; 1-800-336-5588

> Ready to Read Class Sets and Packages, with accompanying materials (text cards, Big Books, audiotapes, video books, professional supports). Grades K–2. Developed in New Zealand.
> Joy Cowley author package. For emergent readers.
> Whole Language Consultants reading materials (especially for upper grades).

Rigby; P. O. Box 797, Crystal Lake, IL 60014; 1-800-822-8661

> Informational Books, Grades K–6.
> Poetry, Rhymes, and Stories for Shared Reading, Grades Pre-K–4.

Stories and Rhymes for Guided and Independent Reading, Grades K–3.
Traditional Tales, Rhymes and Contemporary Stories.
More Traditional Tales and Contemporary Stories, Grades Pre-K–4.

Scholastic; P. O. Box 7502, Jefferson City, MO 65102; 1-800-325-6149

Book Center, Grades 2–6.
Pleasure Reading, Grades K–9.
Read by Reading Collection, Grades K–1.
Scholastic Banners: Teaching with Themes (1991), Grades K–2.
Bookshelf (1989), Grades K–2.
Big Books and Big Book Libraries (collections), Grades K–3.
Sprint Libraries (1989; organized into theme-based units), Grades 3–6.
Bridges: Moving from the Basal into Literature (1990), Grades K–6.
Text Extenders: Basal Correlated Libraries (1987, 1984), Grades 1–6.

(Scholastic tries to provide something for everyone. The collections and programs above include everything from basal-correlated collections of trade books, programs with fairly traditional teaching suggestions, theme-based programs, text sets with teacher-direction, to simply collections of books for pleasure reading.)

Scholastic Canada; 123 Newkirk Road, Richmond Hill, Ontario, L4C 3G5.

RefleXions (1991–1994), by Linda Cameron & Adrian Peetoom, Grades K–8. This is almost an "unprogram," for the teacher's manual describes how the text sets were used by the authors in specific classrooms, just to indicate one direction that discussion might take. The teacher's role is not strictly prescribed, yet the example scenarios will help teachers see how the books might be discussed in the classroom. This is an excellent resource for teachers needing support for moving into whole language teaching.

(Some of the programs above listed under Scholastic-U.S. were produced originally by Scholastic Canada, but are now also distributed by Scholastic in the U.S. As of this writing, the *RefleXions* program was not yet available through the U.S. distributor.)

Troll Associates; 100 Corporate Drive, Mahwah, NJ 07430; 1-800-526-5289

First-Start Easy Readers Read-Alongs; Collections 1, 2, 3, 4, 5, Grades K–2.
First-Start Easy Readers Big Book Reading Units, Grades K–2.
Giant First-Start Readers Big Book Reading Units, Grades K–2.
Troll Classics Big Book Reading Units, Grades K–4.
Read-Along Fairy Tales, Grades K–4.
Illustrated Classics Read-Along Units, Grades K–6.
Scary Mysteries Read-Along Units, Grades 2–4.
Wonder Tales Read-Along Units, Grades K–6.
Favorite Tales Reading Stations, Grades K–3.
American Folk Heroes (read-alongs), Grades 4–6.
Several other read-along collections and units as well.

The Wright Group; 19201 120th Avenue, Bothell, WA 98011; 1-800-523-2371

The Sunshine Series:
Sunshine Emergent Level (Level 1), Ages 5–6, Grades K–2.
Sunshine Early Fluency Level (Levels 2–5), Ages 6–7, Grades 1–2.
Sunshine Fluency Level (Levels 6–11), Ages 7–8, Grades 2–3.

The Story Box:

Emergent Level (Level 1), Ages 5–7, Grades K–2.

Early Fluency Level (Levels 2–7), Ages 6–7, Grades 1–2.

TWiG Books: Emergent Level (Level 1), Ages 5–6, Grades K–1 (these nonfiction books correlate with the emergent levels in the Sunshine Series and the Story Box series).

The Song Box: Emergent/Early Fluency, Ages 5–10, Grades K–5 (singing and chanting).

The Book Bank: Emergent Level (Level 1), Ages 5–6, Grades K–1 (collection of literature)

The Book Bank: Early Fluency/Fluency, Ages 6–8, Grades 1–3 (collection of literature).

Index